D1349001

2,000
FAVOURITE
FRENCH RECIPES

2,000

FAVOURITE

FRENCH RECIPES

AUGUSTE ESCOFFIER

Translated from the French by Vyvyan Holland
Edited by Marion Howells
Foreword by André L. Simon

TREASURE PRESS

Jacket photography © Reed International Books Limited/Clive Streeter

First published as *Ma Cuisine* in 1965 by
The Hamlyn Publishing Group Limited,
part of Reed International Books,
by arrangement with Flammarion & Cie
Revised edition 1984
Reprinted 1989

This edition published in 1991 by
Treasure Press
Michelin House
81 Fulham Road
London SW3 6RB

Reprinted 1992

ISBN 1 85051 694 4

Printed in Czechoslovakia
50856/02

Contents

Foreword

André L. Simon

Escoffier is hailed today by all the best chefs, in all civilised countries, as The Master, and by all men and women who are blessed with a sensitive, cultured taste as the finest chef of the past one hundred years. Such unanimity is exceedingly rare, not to say unique: there cannot be more patent proof of Escoffier's right to the unchallenged position which he occupies in the realm of Gastronomy.

We all know that Escoffier was a great chef, but what sort of man was he? To judge our fellow-men must always be a matter of personal approach, and the two outstanding qualities which endeared him to me more than any other were his crystal-clear sincerity and his simplicity: there was nothing that he hated more than humbug and affectation. You could not say that he was humble any more than proud, but he was always plainly, simply, naturally himself, not shy, not flurried, but at ease, ready to listen and ready to talk, as and when the occasion demanded, whether greeted by Kaiser Wilhelm, on board the latest liner of the Hamburg-Amerika Line, as *Empereur des Chefs*, or turning down categorically one of the Marquis d'Hautpoil's suggestions, at the Carlton.

Another outstanding feature of Escoffier's personality was his love of work: he was a born worker, and never happier than when he had a lot to do or to see to: to get something done and done well, cost what it might in time or trouble, was an aim in itself, his ambition, his hobby and his love: the reward he prized was the satisfaction of achievement and success, much more than any money.

Escoffier was born in 1847, at Villeneuve-Loubet, in the Alpes Maritimes, the Cannes hinterland, and he was twelve years old when he started work in a kitchen where there was no electricity, no gas, no running hot and cold water, and none of the many labour-saving gadgets of today: a mayonnaise had to be made by hand — it was easy — and a *Brandade de morue* had to be pounded by hand, which was not so easy.

From 1859 until 1921, when he resigned from the London Carlton, Escoffier was not only at work for sixty-two years, but most of the time at work in the heat and din of some big kitchen, to say nothing of the strain of constant concentration of mind, aware, as every responsible chef is, that there is always the risk of a culinary disaster.

Escoffier must have been tough indeed, to work as he did almost to the end. He died in 1935, but for fully ten years after his 'retirement' Escoffier was still not merely active but quite busy: the last time I met him, at the Carlton, in Herbodeau's office, he was 79, but by no means an 'old man'. Escoffier was as near a proud man as he could ever be, on the day when, in 1920, President Raymond Poincaré, on a visit to London, gave the veteran and dearly beloved Escoffier the *Croix de la Legion d'Honneur*. Many of his French friends and admirers — and they were indeed many — were understandably disappointed that it should have happened in London, but they had their chance later: they gave him a magnificent banquet at the Palais d'Orsay, in Paris in 1928, when Escoffier was raised to *Officier de la Legion d'Honneur*.

Although Escoffier was always a doer, and no dreamer, he had the soul of a poet: he was highly sensitive but never neurotic, and he had a vivid yet disciplined imagination. He was always ready to look for and to welcome anything new, so long as it was truly good, better or best, not because it was new. Although he did not enjoy the privilege of a classical education, he had the born orator's gift of expression; his prose always is good grammar, and it is often good prose. It has the only too rare qualities of directness and precision which are invaluable when one writes about the preparation and presentation of food. They say that practice makes perfect, and Escoffier had certainly considerable practice as a writer and teacher. During a great number of years he wrote regularly in *L'Art culinaire* of Paris, and other culinary magazines and journals, about the *Cuisine classique* and the *Cuisine régionaliste*, as well as a number of books. The first in date of his books, I think, was his *Mémoires d'un cuisinier de l'armée du Rhin*, an account of his wartime service at Headquarters of the *Armée du Rhin* in 1870. One of his earlier books, one in which he gave expression to his passionate love of flowers, was *Les Fleurs de Cire*. It was first published in 1885 and there were a number of later editions; it is, as far as I know, the only book with Escoffier's verse as well as prose, nor can there be many other books in praise of artificial flowers made of wax, for the decoration of the dining-room table, with directions how to make them stand safely in *socles* of mutton fat. My own copy of this little book once belonged to a Miss Marguerite Kennell, to whom it was given by Escoffier with an inscription worth reproducing, as it shows that, at 72, the Master was not only *amiable* but *galant*:

À Mademoiselle Marguerite Kennell. Permettez-moi de venir vous offrir ce petit recueil et de lui ajouter le nom d'une fleur oubliée, la Mignonne Marguerite, Fleurette au coeur d'Or, aux blanches corolles que la jeunesse aime si tendrement effeuiller.

Escoffier's great chance may well have been his coming to London with César Ritz in 1890, the year after the opening of the Savoy, for it made it possible for Ritz to show the great and the rich how luxury could be free from vulgarity: it also made it possible for Escoffier to show how a gracious way of living was inseparable from the presence of the ladies, and how the pleasures of the table could be exquisite without being extravagant.

The 25 years which preceded World War I were the greatest years of Escoffier's career, and they may well be called the Golden Age of Western Civilisation, when there was real money, golden sovereigns and louis-d'or, and when taxation was so reasonable one could inherit the wealth and taste of one's forebears, and hand over both to one's children. There were no cinemas then, and no 'TV personalities', but there were great artistes like Melba and Sarah Bernhardt, Mary Garden and Adelina Patti, and others, who have become immortal, thanks to Escoffier, who gave their names to some of the children of his culinary genius — Pêches Melba, Fraises Sarah Bernhardt, Poires Mary Garden, and so on.

Escoffier was a good man and a great chef, who has now gone to his rest as all good men and others have done before. Escoffier was also a great teacher, and, happily, that great teacher is still with us and always will be, thanks to his books. The most practical of all, *2,000 Favourite French Recipes*, has at long last become available to the great many men and women who love all that is best to eat, but did not until now have the chance to read Escoffier in English.

Preface to the English edition

Marion Howells

Auguste Escoffier was unquestionably one of the greatest chefs the world has known and deservedly called the 'King of Chefs and the Chef of Kings'. In *2,000 Favourite French Recipes*, however, he looks at everyday cooking and in his introduction claims that 'the ordinary housewife will find delicious recipes within the limits of her purse'.

He was, of course, referring to the French housewife of perhaps fifty years ago, although this book was first published in 1934, a year before his death. His words, though, apply just as much to the British and American housewife of today, for, with a little imagination and discrimination on her part, the majority of the recipes in this book is within the scope of all who enjoy the pleasures of eating.

No attempt has been made to anglicise the recipes — that was not the object of the translation — but obviously in a few cases it would be impossible to achieve the same exquisite result without the ingredients listed by Monsieur Escoffier. Nothing, for instance, can replace the aroma of the fresh black truffles of Périgord or the white truffles of Piedmont, though the preserved ones are excellent for garnish. And, except for very special occasions, today's housewife would find poached foie gras beyond her means. Again, in several recipes a garnish of cocks' combs and cocks' kidneys is used, but these are almost unobtainable outside France. While they undoubtedly enhance the dish, they are not the essential part of the garnish.

Because they can be adapted for young lamb, recipes with baby Pauillac lamb (lamb under one year old) have been included.

Escoffier says he compiled the recipes with the chef and restaurateur in mind as well as the housewife. The professional cook with stocks and fumets, ample time and a battery of equipment at his disposal, will have no problem. The housewife, however, may be a little overwhelmed by the recipe that needs only a few spoonfuls of demi-glace sauce or meat jelly which needs lengthy preparation, but alternatives have been given.

Throughout this book I have used English and American liquid proportions. The American proportions are given in brackets after the English measures.

The editing of *2,000 Favourite French Recipes* has been a most pleasurable task and I hope all who use it will capture some of the delights we owe to the man who was the *doyen* of *haute cuisine*.

Introduction

Auguste Escoffier

Before explaining the methods of preparing the dishes in this guide to everyday cooking, I think it will be helpful to make a few observations on the foods which form the basis of our diet.

The extremely active existence we lead does not leave us leisure to devote the necessary care to the upkeep of our bodies. We are apt to forget that, like a clock, the body will stop if it is not oiled or wound up from time to time. Nature supplies the raw materials in their simplest forms, so we must know how to make the best use of them, otherwise we invite a mass of minor ailments.

Basic foods, solid or liquid, are derived from either the animal or vegetable kingdoms. Each has a particular flavour — sweet, salty, sour, bitter, acid and so on. The most flavoursome and nourishing foods are ox, sheep and calf's flesh, poultry, game and well fermented and well cooked wheat bread. Meat should be chosen from animals that are neither too young nor too old.

Meats are more nourishing than vegetables, but to make the best of them both they should be eaten together.

Salt or dried meats suit people with strong digestions; others should avoid them.

Fish is less nourishing than meat but is indispensable to our existence, both from the nutritive and the economic standpoint.

Milk is a simple and natural food, and the new-laid egg, lightly cooked in its shell, is easily digested and nourishing, while fresh or dried vegetables are very wholesome.

A good and fine dinner should preferably end with fruit which, apart from cleansing the mouth, is the apotheosis of the dinner, especially when accompanied by a delicious *marquise*.

Coffee, carefully prepared and taken some time after the meal, in the drawing-room, helps the digestion. Its delicate aroma rises to the head, revives the mind — and then conversation sparkles.

Food can be boiled in water, braised in its own juice, roasted, grilled or fried. Boiling has its advantages if it is not prolonged when the meat is to be eaten. Broth is the result of this method of cooking meat.

Braised meat absorbs the flavour of the other ingredients, becomes tender and the goodness is preserved in the juice.

Roast or grilled meat retains nearly all its soluble ingredients and has an appetising flavour, as the direct action of the heat seals the outside and drives all the juice towards the centre.

Frying is the best method of cooking certain fish, but some people find it indigestible, because of the fat absorbed during the cooking. So, for them, grilling or poaching is better.

Seasoning assists the gastric juices but must not be overdone, as an immoderate use of it is ruinous to health. As a general principle it is advisable to leave the table without having satisfied one's appetite to repletion. Neglect of this is often the cause of indigestion.

It is best to vary the diet, for monotony jades the appetite and this reacts on the digestion.

This book is not just an *aide-mémoire* for the experienced cook but a kitchen book of recipes which are put as clearly as possible, so as to make them practical. Although the book is intended for everyday cooking, it is none the less valuable to the restaurateur, the head waiter and the chef. The ordinary housewife will find here delicious recipes within the limits of her purse. One must not forget that good sound cooking, even the very simplest, makes a contented home.

Useful facts and figures

Notes on metrication

Metric conversions have not been included in the individual recipes in this book but in future we shall all be working in metric units. To guide the reader the following chart may be found helpful. Exact conversion from Imperial to metric measures does not usually give very convenient working quantities so it has been found acceptable to round off into units of 25 grams. The table shows the recommended equivalents.

Ounces	Approx. g to nearest whole figure	Recommended conversion to nearest unit of 25
1	28	25
2	57	50
3	85	75
4	113	100
5	142	150
6	170	175
7	198	200
8	227	225
9	255	250
10	283	275
11	312	300
12	340	350
13	368	375
14	397	400
15	425	425
16 (1 lb)	454	450
17	482	475
18	510	500
19	539	550
20	567	575

Note: When converting quantities over 20 oz first add the appropriate figures in the centre column, then adjust to the nearest unit of 25. As a general guide, 1 kg (1000 g) equals 2.2 lb or about 2 lb 3 oz. This method of conversion gives good results in most cases but in certain cake and pastry recipes a more accurate conversion is necessary to produce a balanced recipe. On the other hand, quantities of such ingredients as vegetables, fruit, meat and fish which are not critical are rounded off to the nearest quarter of a kg as this is how they are likely to be purchased.

Liquid measures: The millilitre is normally used for liquid measures up to and including 1 pint (600 ml). For amounts over 1 pint, litres and fractions of litres are used.

Imperial	Approx. ml to nearest whole figure	Recommended ml
¼ pint	142	150 ml
½ pint	283	300 ml
¾ pint	425	450 ml
1 pint	567	600 ml
1½ pints	851	900 ml
1¾ pints	992	1000 ml (1 litre)

Notes for American and Australian users

All liquid measures in the recipes have been given in Imperial and American units of measurements. The Imperial pint is 20 fl oz and the American pint is 16 fl oz. In Australia the American 8-oz measuring cup is used in conjunction with the Imperial pint of 20 fl oz.

It is important to remember that the Australian tablespoon differs from both the British and American tablespoons; the table below gives a comparison. The British standard tablespoon, which has been used throughout this book, holds 17.7 ml, the American 14.2 ml, and the Australian 20 ml. A teaspoon holds approximately 5 ml in all three countries.

British	American	Australian
1 teaspoon	1 teaspoon	1 teaspoon
1 tablespoon	1 tablespoon	1 tablespoon
2 tablespoons	3 tablespoons	2 tablespoons
3½ tablespoons	4 tablespoons	3 tablespoons
4 tablespoons	5 tablespoons	3½ tablespoons

An Imperial/American guide to solid measures

Imperial	American
1 lb butter or margarine	2 cups
1 lb flour	4 cups
1 lb granulated or castor sugar	2 cups
1 lb icing sugar	3 cups
1 lb minced meat	2 cups
2 oz fresh breadcrumbs	1 cup
4 oz chopped nuts	1 cup
5 oz dried fruit	1 cup
7 oz rice	1 cup

Oven temperatures

The table below gives recommended equivalents.

	°F	°C	Gas Mark
Very cool	225	110	$\frac{1}{4}$
	250	120	$\frac{1}{2}$
Cool	275	140	1
	300	150	2
Moderate	325	160	3
	350	180	4
Moderately hot	375	190	5
	400	200	6
Hot	425	220	7
	450	230	8
Very hot	475	240	9

Les Sauces

SAUCES

The preparation of sauces requires a great deal of care. One must not forget, in fact, that it is through the subtlety by which our sauces are constructed that the French cuisine enjoys such a world-wide supremacy.

I will not enter here into the details which the preparation of sauces requires in the large kitchens of restaurants and hotels. This would be superfluous.

On the contrary, the object of this work is to simplify formulae, to make them as clear as possible, to bring them within the grasp of everyone and to make the housewives' task an easy one.

In our cuisine we have three fundamental sauces, which are:

The so-called 'sauce espagnole', which is in fact just a brown roux bound with a brown stock.

The thick white sauce, or 'velouté', which only differs from the espagnole by being made with white stock, bound with a roux kept as white as possible.

Sauces prepared with these brown and white juices or stocks are used in various preparations of fish, meat, poultry, game, etc. Being added to these, they heighten their flavour.

Béchamel sauce. This sauce, from the economic point of view, may be considered the queen of sauces. It lends itself to many delicious preparations and harmonises as well with eggs, fish and meat as with poultry and different kinds of game and vegetables. An additional advantage is that its preparation takes little time.

Following this, we have tomato sauce, which also plays an important part in modern cookery.

Then there is meat glaze, which is not always appreciated at its true value and which, nevertheless, when it is carefully treated can occasionally be of the greatest use.

In the large kitchens of hotels and restaurants, these basic sauces are prepared every morning, and it is only in this way that a rapid service, in the best conditions, can be secured.

These 'mother sauces' allow, at a moment's notice, the preparation of all the small compound sauces, recipes for which will be found farther on.

SAUCES DE BASE
BASIC SAUCES

Les roux

THE ROUX

The roux are the bases of most sauces.

Roux brun

BROWN ROUX

——————— Roux to bind 2½–3 pints (U.S. 6¼–7½ cups) brown stock: 1½ oz. clarified butter, slightly more sieved flour

Place the butter in a saucepan of convenient size, blend with the flour and cook slowly. Once cooked, the brown roux should be nut-brown in colour and very smooth.

Roux blond

LIGHT BROWN ROUX

The ingredients are the same as for brown roux, but cooking must be done very slowly, and discontinued as soon as the roux begins to turn colour.

Préparation des jus ou fonds bruns

PREPARATION OF BROWN SAUCE OR STOCK

To make 9 — 10 pints (U.S. 11 — 12½ pints) brown stock: 6½ lb. shin of beef, 4½ lb. shin of veal, some bacon rind boiled for 10 minutes, 8 oz. onions, 8 oz. carrots, 1 bouquet (tied in a piece of muslin) composed of 1 sprig parsley, 1 bay leaf, 1 sprig thyme and 1 small clove garlic, 13 pints (U.S. 16¼ pints) boiling water, salt and pepper, butter

Bone the meat, cut it into two small pieces and lay on one side. Break the bones up as small as possible; remove the marrow from the beef bones. Put the bacon rind and the chopped onions and carrots into a large stewpan, arrange the bones on this bed of vegetables. Add 1 pint (U.S. 2½ cups) of water, place the stewpan over a low heat, cover it and reduce the water completely. Add the rest of the boiling water. Throw in the bouquet, 1 good pinch of salt for each pint of water and 1 pinch of pepper. Bring to the boil, and simmer gently for at least 5 hours, maintaining the level of the stock with boiling water as it reduces.

When the stock is ready, brown the pieces of meat which have been laid aside, gently in butter in a saucepan, add ½ pint (U.S. 1¼ cups) of the stock, cover the saucepan, reduce stock completely over a moderate fire and repeat the operation twice, then add the remainder of the stock. Bring to the boil, skim if necessary, then partly cover the saucepan, and continue to cook slowly for 3 hours, strain through a fine sieve and leave to get quite cold. Remove the fat and use as required.

Meat which has been used to make the second stock can be boiled again in water for 2 hours, or can be used to form an excellent hash.

The stock obtained from this second boiling may be added to various braises.

The bones from the first stock may be boiled again very slowly for 4 — 5 hours, to extract all the gelatinous matter contained in them. The stock thus obtained, mixed with the foregoing stock, reduced to a thick brown sauce, constitutes meat jelly *(glace de viande)*.

Fonds blanc simple

SIMPLE WHITE STOCK

To make 9—10 pints (U.S. 11—12½ pints) white stock: 10 lb. shin and shoulder of veal, 10—12 pints (U.S. 12½—15 pints) water, 1 oz. salt, 1 sprig parsley, 1 bay leaf, 1 sprig thyme, 2 cloves, 8 oz. carrots, 8 oz. onions, 2 oz. leeks, ½ small head celery

Bone the meat, tie it up with string, put it into a saucepan with the broken-up bones, water and salt. Bring to the boil, skim carefully, add the herbs and vegetables. The time necessary for cooking over a low heat is about 2½ hours. Strain through a fine strainer into a bowl and keep until needed.

Fonds de volaille

CHICKEN STOCK

The ingredients are the same as for the simple white stock, adding a few giblets and the carcase of a chicken.

Fonds ou jus de veau brun

VEAL STOCK

To make 7 pints (U.S. 8¾ pints) stock: 8 oz. onions cut in fairly thick rings, 4 oz. carrots, some bacon rind boiled for 8 minutes, 6½ lb. boned shin and shoulder of veal, 10—11 pints (U.S. 12½—13¾ pints) simple white stock (see above), 1 bouquet tied in muslin composed of 1 sprig parsley, 1 bay leaf and 1 sprig thyme

Put the onions, carrots and bacon rind in a large thick-bottomed saucepan and on this spread the meat cut up small and the bones. Moisten with 1 pint (U.S. 2½ cups) of white stock, let it reduce completely, then add the remainder of the stock and the bouquet.

Remove the saucepan from the fire and place it on a corner of the stove, partly covered. Bring to the boil, skim and keep simmering for 3 hours.

Strain through muslin and keep until needed.

The meat and the bones which have been used in making this stock may be boiled again in water for 2 hours and then strained through a fine sieve. This can be used to make the sauce for various braises or further reduced to make meat jelly.

Jus de veau lié à l'arrow-root

VEAL STOCK THICKENED WITH ARROWROOT

> To make 2 pints (U.S. 5 cups): 4 pints (U.S. 10 cups) veal stock (see page 20), 2 oz. arrowroot

Reduce the veal stock by half. Add the arrowroot mixed smoothly with a little cold stock. Cook for 1 minute and strain through a fine sieve.

Glace de viande

MEAT JELLY

Good meat jelly is made by reducing brown and white stock.

As the reducing progresses and the stock becomes more concentrated, it is passed through muslin and placed into smaller saucepans. The clearness of the jelly depends upon the careful skimming carried out in the course of the reducing. Reducing can be carried out fairly quickly to start with, but towards the end it must be done very gently over a very moderate heat. The jelly is ready when it has acquired a syrupy consistency, and coats the back of a spoon with a shiny and clinging layer.

In large kitchens, after taking out the first stock, the meat is reboiled for several hours. Meat jelly is specially used to finish off certain sauces, by giving them lightness, flavour and refinement; but it should be used carefully.

Sauce brune, dite 'sauce espagnole'

BROWN SAUCE, CALLED 'ESPAGNOLE SAUCE'

> To make 2 pints (U.S. 5 cups) brown sauce: 3½ oz. brown roux (see page 18), 2 pints (U.S. 5 cups) brown stock, 1 oz. diced bacon fat, 1 oz. chopped onion, 1½ oz. diced carrot, 1 sprig thyme, 1 small bay leaf, few sprigs parsley, 1 oz. butter

Make the roux and allow to cool for a few minutes, add the brown stock and whisk until it is free from lumps. Bring to boiling point, whisking all the time. Add herbs and diced vegetables browned in bacon fat and butter. Draw to side of stove; leave to simmer for 3 hours, adding little cold stock occasionally to facilitate the clearing of sauce. Rub through a sieve; stir now and then whilst cooling,

Sauce demi-glace

DEMI-GLACE SAUCE

The sauce called demi-glace is sauce espagnole (see page 21) to which, at the last moment, is added some rather strong brown veal stock or fine meat jelly.

Demi-glace tomatée

DEMI-GLACE WITH TOMATO

Add to the above recipe the third of its volume of tomato sauce.

Velouté simple

PLAIN WHITE SAUCE

To make a good white sauce, proceed as for sauce espagnole replacing brown stock by white stock, keeping to the same proportions as for sauce espagnole (see page 21).

Simmer very gently for about 1½ hours in order to facilitate clearing and to obtain a transparent sauce.

Into a bowl strain the sauce through a fine sieve, and stir occasionally whilst cooking. Keep until required.

Note While the cooking and the clearing are proceeding for the sauce espagnole and the velouté sauce, the scum that rises to the surface should be removed from time to time.

For the velouté sauce, the bouquet for sauce espagnole is optional.

To facilitate the clearing of the sauces, the saucepans used should be fairly tall compared with their width.

The bottom of the saucepan should not rest on the stove, it should be slightly raised on one side with a little iron wedge.

Sauce blonde ou sauce parisienne *(sauce allemande)*

VELOUTÉ SAUCE BOUND WITH EGG YOLKS

Few tablespoons freshly made mushroom sauce (never use preserved mushrooms for this purpose), 1 pint (U.S. 2½ cups) white stock, 5 egg yolks, pinch coarsely ground pepper, little ground nutmeg, 2 pints (U.S. 5 cups) velouté sauce, little melted butter

In a thick-bottomed saucepan place together the mushroom sauce, white stock, egg yolks, pepper and nutmeg. Mix with an egg whisk, add the velouté sauce, bring to the boil and cook fairly quickly continually stirring with a spatula, scraping the bottom of the saucepan. Reduce the sauce until it coats the spatula, then strain through muslin.

Stir it lightly; cover the surface with a little melted butter to prevent a film forming. Keep until required.

Sauce suprême

CHICKEN VELOUTÉ SAUCE WITH CREAM

To make 2 pints (U.S. 5 cups): 2 pints (U.S. 5 cups) white chicken velouté sauce (see page 22), ⅜ pint (U.S. approx. 1 cup) very fresh cream, 3−4 tablespoons meat jelly made from veal or chicken stock (see page 20)

Reduce the chicken sauce by about ⅜ pint (U.S. approx. 1 cup) then add the cream and meat jelly. Cook for a few minutes and strain through muslin.

Sauce béchamel

BÉCHAMEL SAUCE

To make 2 pints (U.S. 5 cups) : 3½ oz. light brown roux (see page 18), 2 pints (U.S. 5 cups) boiling milk, 1 good pinch salt, 1 pinch coarse pepper, little ground nutmeg, ½ medium-sized onion stuck with 1 clove, bouquet composed of 1 sprig parsley, ½ bay leaf, 1 sprig thyme, melted butter

Make the roux and leave to cool a little. Add the milk, whisking all the time, and bring to boiling point again. Add seasoning, onion and bouquet. Simmer for 25−30 minutes, taking care to lift one side of the pan off the heat as described for plain white sauce (see page 22). Strain the sauce through muslin and cover the surface with a little melted butter. Keep until required.

Sauce tomate

TOMATO SAUCE

To make 2 pints (U.S. 5 cups): 7 lb. fresh tomatoes, 6 tablespoons oil or 3 oz. butter, pinch salt, pinch pepper, 1 sprig parsley, ½ clove garlic

Halve the tomatoes and remove the seeds. Put into a pan with the oil or butter, seasonings and flavourings. Cover and simmer 30—35 minutes. Strain through a fine strainer. Cover the surface with a little melted butter and keep till required.

This method of preparing tomato sauce has the advantage of being quick and of preserving all the freshness and the flavour of the fruit.

If you cannot get fresh tomatoes, you can replace them by canned tomatoes which you can buy from any grocer.

PETITES SAUCES BRUNES COMPOSÉES

COMPOUND BROWN SAUCES

Sauce bigarade ou orange pour caneton rôti

ORANGE SAUCE FOR ROAST DUCK

Rind and juice 1 orange, rind and juice ½ lemon, 1 wine glass old Frontignan (Muscatel), 1 liqueur glass dry Curaçao, 9 tablespoons demi-glace sauce (see page 22)

Thinly peel the orange and lemon and cut into fine julienne. Blanch for 5—6 minutes, then drain, and put into a small pan with the orange and lemon juice; keep hot. Heat the Frontignan in a small pan and reduce to half its volume. Add the Curaçao and sauce, boil for a few seconds then add the orange and lemon peel. Serve separately in a sauceboat and, at the same time, oranges, peeled and cut into quarters and arranged in a salad bowl.

Sauce bordelaise

BORDELAISE SAUCE

To make ½ pint (U.S. 1¼ cups): 6 tablespoons red or white wine, 1 teaspoon chopped shallot, pinch coarse pepper. 9 tablespoons demi-glace sauce (see page 22), little tomato sauce, 1½ oz. fresh beef marrow

Put the wine, shallot and pepper together in a pan and boil until reduced to half its volume. Add the demi-glace and tomato sauce. Boil for a few minutes, then strain through a fine sieve. To finish add the beef marrow cut into rings and poached for a few seconds in meat stock or salted water.

This is specially recommended to serve with beef.

Sauce bourguignonne

BURGUNDY SAUCE

To make ½−¾ pint (U.S. 1¼−2 cups): 1 oz. butter, 2 oz. streaky bacon, 2 tablespoons finely chopped onion, 2 tablespoons finely chopped carrot, 1 bay leaf, 1 sprig thyme, parsley, 1½ pints (U.S. 3¾ cups) good red wine, 4 oz. butter, 1½ tablespoons flour

Heat the butter, add the chopped bacon, onion and carrot and brown lightly. Add the herbs and the wine. Boil until reduced to half its volume. Strain through a fine sieve. Mix 2 oz. butter with the flour and add to the sauce to bind it. Finally add the remaining 2 oz. butter.

This is specially recommended for various egg dishes and for some kinds of fish.

Sauce bretonne

BRETON SAUCE

To make about 1 pint (U.S. 2½ cups) sauce: 2 tablespoons finely chopped onion, 1 oz. butter, ½ pint (U.S. 1¼ cups) white wine, ½ pint (U.S. 1¼ cups) espagnole sauce (see page 21), ½ pint (U.S. 1¼ cups) tomato sauce (see page 132), 1 clove garlic, few sprigs parsley

Brown the onion in the butter. Add the wine and boil till reduced to half the quantity. Add the sauces, crushed garlic and parsley. Boil for 8−10 minutes, then strain through a fine sieve.

Note This sauce is used almost exclusively for *haricots à la bretonne*.

Sauce aux cerises

CHERRY SAUCE

——————— To make about ½ pint (U.S. 1¼ cups): 6 tablespoons white wine, 6 tablespoons cherry juice, pinch mixed spice, grated rind 1 orange, 4—5 tablespoons gooseberry jelly, 4—5 tablespoons stoned cherries

Put the wine, cherry juice, spice and orange rind into a pan and boil until reduced to half the quantity. Add the jelly and cherries and boil for a few minutes. Serve in a sauce-boat with venison, roast or braised duck or goose.

Sauce chasseur

HUNTSMAN SAUCE

——————— 5 oz. raw chopped mushrooms, 1 tablespoon butter, 1 tablespoon oil, 1 teaspoon chopped shallot, 3 tablespoons brandy, 6 tablespoons white wine, ½ pint (U.S. 1¼ cups) demi-glace sauce (see page 22), 2—3 tablespoons tomato sauce, 1 tablespoon meat jelly (see page 21), little chopped parsley

Fry the mushrooms in butter and oil, browning them lightly. Add shallot and brandy. Reduce the white wine to half its volume and add. Complete with demi-glace sauce, tomato sauce and meat jelly. Boil for a few minutes, then add a little chopped parsley.

This sauce is served with tournedos, lamb stew, fillet of beef, fillet of chicken, etc.

Sauce chaudfroid brune

BROWN CHAUDFROID SAUCE

——————— To make 2 pints (U.S. 5 cups): 1¼ pints (U.S. 3 cups) reduced demi-glace sauce (see page 22), 1 pint (U.S. 2½ cups) calf's foot jelly, 3—4 tablespoons Madeira

Put the demi-glace in a pan with the calf's foot jelly and boil till reduced to about three-quarters of its volume. Add the Madeira and strain through muslin. Stir until the sauce thickens sufficiently to coat the food for which it is intended.

For a brown chaudfroid sauce for duck or game add ¼ pint (U.S. ⅝ cup) gravy from the duck or game to the reduced demi-glace.

When truffles are available a few slices may be added to the sauce.

Sauce chevreuil

VENISON SAUCE

To make 2 pints (U.S. 5 cups): ½ pint (U.S. 1¼ cups) good red wine, 2 pints (U.S. 5 cups) demi-glace sauce, 3—4 peppercorns

Boil the wine until reduced to half its quantity. Add the demi-glace and boil for 10—12 minutes. Add crushed peppercorns and cook a further 5—6 minutes. Strain through a fine sieve and keep hot in a bain-marie or a double saucepan.

This sauce is used to accompany venison.

Sauce diable

DEVIL SAUCE

To make about ½ pint (U.S. 1¼ cups): ½ pint (U.S. 1¼ cups) white wine, 2 finely chopped shallots, ½ pint (U.S. 1¼ cups) demi-glace sauce (see page 22), pinch cayenne pepper or little finely chopped red pepper

Put the wine and shallots in a pan and boil till reduced by two-thirds. Add the demi-glace sauce and boil a few minutes longer. Add cayenne or chopped red pepper.

Specially recommended for chicken, pigeon, pig's trotters.

As a variation, either 1 tablespoon English mustard, 1 dessertspoon Worcestershire sauce, or 1 tablespoon anchovy butter may be added.

Excellent for grilled fish.

This sauce is usually prepared in small quantities as required.

Sauce grand veneur

ROYAL HUNTSMAN SAUCE

To make about 2 pints (U.S. 5 cups) sauce: 3 tablespoons redcurrant jelly, ¼ pint (U.S. 1¼ cups) fresh cream, 1¾ pints (U.S. generous 4¼ cups) venison sauce (see above)

Melt the jelly in a pan and gradually whip in the cream. Add the venison sauce and boil for a few minutes.

Sauce italienne

ITALIAN SAUCE

To make 1½ pints (U.S. 3¾ cups): 1½ pints (U.S. 3¾ cups) demi-glace sauce with tomato (see page 22), 4 tablespoons finely shredded mushrooms, 4 oz. cooked streaky shredded bacon, pinch chopped parsley

Put all ingredients, except parsley, together and boil for 5–6 minutes, then add the parsley.

Sauce moelle

MARROW SAUCE

Reduce a demi-glace sauce (see page 22) right down. Add some butter and just before serving add 3½ oz. very fresh beef marrow, cut into dice and poached for a few minutes. Finally add a pinch of chopped parsley.

Sauce périgueux

DEMI-GLACE SAUCE WITH TRUFFLES

To 1 pint (U.S. 2½ cups) demi-glace sauce (see page 22) reduced right down, add 3 tablespoons truffles, carefully peeled and chopped. Finally add a few tablespoons Madeira. This sauce is for small entrées.

Sauce piquante

PIQUANTE SAUCE

To make about 1 pint (U.S. 2½ cups) sauce: 6 tablespoons vinegar, 2 tablespoons finely chopped shallot, 1 pint (U.S. 2½ cups) demi-glace sauce (see page 22), 2 tablespoons chopped gherkins, 1 teaspoon chopped parsley, 1 teaspoon tarragon

Put the vinegar and shallot together in a pan and boil till reduced to half the quantity. Add the sauce and simmer for 8–10 minutes. Remove from the heat and add gherkins, parsley and tarragon.

This sauce is specially recommended for boiled or roast pork. It is also good with boiled beef.

Sauce poivrade ordinaire

ORDINARY PEPPER SAUCE

To make about 1½ pints (U.S. 3¾ cups) sauce: 2½ oz. butter, 1½ oz. chopped onion, 1½ oz. diced carrot, 1 bay leaf, 1 sprig thyme, 1 sprig parsley, 1¾ pints (U.S. 4 cups) wine vinegar, 1 pint (U.S. 2½ cups) demi-glace sauce (see page 22)

Heat 1 oz. butter in a pan and brown the onion and carrot. Add herbs and vinegar and boil until the quantity is reduced to half. Add the sauce and reduce a little further. Strain through a fine sieve and add the remaining butter.

This sauce is approximately for 8 – 10 persons.

Note When the poivrade sauce is used as an accompaniment to venison, or certain game which has been marinaded, a few tablespoons of the marinade may be added.

PETITES SAUCES BLANCHES COMPOSÉES

LIGHT COMPOUND SAUCES

Sauce aurore

VELOUTÉ SAUCE WITH TOMATO PURÉE

This is a velouté sauce (see page 22) to which a very red tomato purée has been added. The proportions are 3 of the velouté sauce to 1 of tomato purée. To finish the sauce 4 oz. butter should be incorporated to every 2 pints (U.S. 5 cups) of sauce.

ANOTHER METHOD

Melt 2 tablespoons butter in a small saucepan, mix with 1 dessertspoon paprika; warm it for a few seconds and add it to 1¾ pints (U.S. 4 cups) of béchamel sauce (see page 23) with cream.

Note Do not confuse paprika, which is a sweet pepper, with cayenne pepper.

Sauce béarnaise
BÉARNAISE SAUCE

———————— To make ½ pint (U.S. 1¼ cups) sauce: 6 tablespoons white wine, 6 tablespoons tarragon vinegar, 2 teaspoons chopped shallot, pinch chopped tarragon, small pinch coarse pepper, pinch salt, 1 oz. butter, 3 egg yolks, 8 oz. softened butter, cayenne pepper, chopped tarragon, chopped chervil

Put the wine, vinegar, shallot, herbs, seasoning and 1 oz. butter into a pan and boil until reduced by two-thirds. Remove from the heat and leave to cool for a few minutes. Add egg yolks and return to a very low heat. Gradually add the softened butter as described for mayonnaise (see page 40) and stir with a wooden spoon.

The binding of the sauce is produced by the gradual cooking of the egg yolks, so it is very important to make béarnaise sauce over a very low heat.

When the butter has been incorporated, strain the sauce through muslin; season by putting in a little cayenne pepper and complete with a little chopped tarragon and a small pinch chopped chervil.

This sauce need not be served very hot.

Sauce béarnaise tomatée, dite 'sauce Choron'
BÉARNAISE SAUCE WITH TOMATO, CALLED 'CHORON SAUCE'

Make a béarnaise sauce as above but without the final addition of chopped tarragon and chervil. Add a quarter of its volume of very reduced tomato purée.

Sauce béarnaise à la glace de viande, dite 'sauce Valois'
BÉARNAISE SAUCE WITH MEAT JELLY, CALLED 'VALOIS SAUCE'

Make a béarnaise sauce. Complete it by adding 2 tablespoons melted meat jelly (see page 21).

Sauce au beurre
BUTTER SAUCE

———————— To make 1 pint (U.S. 2½ cups) sauce: 1½ oz. flour, 1½ oz. melted butter, 1 pint (U.S. 2½ cups) boiling salted water, 4—5 egg yolks, 2 tablespoons hot milk or cream, 8 oz. softened butter

Smoothly mix the flour and melted butter. Add the water all at once, whisking rapidly. Mix together the egg yolks and milk or cream and stir into the sauce. Remove from the heat. Strain through muslin and gradually add the softened butter.

Sauce aux câpres
CAPER SAUCE

This is butter sauce (see page 30) with, at the last moment, the addition of 2−3 tablespoons small capers to each 1¾ pints (U.S. 3¾ cups) sauce. This sauce is recommended for poached fish.

Sauce cardinal
CARDINAL SAUCE

Béchamel sauce (see page 23) with cream to which has been added 2−3 oz. lobster butter to each pint (U.S. 2½ cups) of sauce. Season with a little cayenne pepper.

Sauce chaudfroid blanche ordinaire
ORDINARY WHITE CHAUDFROID SAUCE

To make 2 pints (U.S. 5 cups) sauce: 1½ pints (U.S. 3¾ cups) velouté sauce (see page 22), 1¼ pints (U.S. 3⅛ cups) calf's foot jelly, ½ pint (U.S. 1¼ cups) cream, seasoning

Put the velouté sauce in a thick-bottomed shallow pan. Place over quick heat and stir in the calf's foot jelly. Use a wooden spoon and stir from the bottom of the pan mixing the jelly well with the sauce. Add a third of the cream and cook quickly until the whole is reduced one-third. Season and correct the consistency of the sauce. Strain through muslin. Add the rest of the cream slowly and stir while the sauce is cooling to a coating consistency.

Sauce chaudfroid blonde
LIGHT CHAUDFROID SAUCE

Proceed as for the ordinary chaudfroid sauce replacing the white sauce with *sauce parisienne* (see page 22) and using only half the amount of cream.

Sauce chaudfroid aurore

CHAUDFROID SAUCE WITH TOMATO PURÉE

Prepare the chaudfroid sauce according to the first recipe, add 6 tablespoons tomato purée much reduced or 1 teaspoon paprika warmed gently in butter.

Sauce crevettes

SHRIMP SAUCE

To 1 pint (U.S. 2½ cups) béchamel sauce with cream (see page 23) or to 1 pint (U.S. 2½ cups) *sauce parisienne* (see page 22) add 3½ oz. shrimp butter (see page 51), and 2 teaspoons paprika.

Sauce curry à la crème

CREAM CURRY SAUCE

1½ oz. butter, 1 tablespoon finely chopped onion, 1 teaspoon curry powder, ½ pint (U.S. 1¼ cups) béchamel sauce, 3—4 tablespoons fresh cream

Melt the butter in a small saucepan and add the onion. As soon as it begins to brown, add the curry powder, cook for a few seconds, stirring the mixture with a spoon. Add the sauce and simmer over low heat for a few minutes. Strain the sauce through muslin or a fine sieve, and finally add the cream.

The béchamel sauce may be replaced by velouté sauce (see page 22) or *sauce parisienne* (see page 22) but a little extra cream must be added.

Sauce au paprika rose

PAPRIKA SAUCE

The same ingredients as for curry sauce, except that the curry powder is replaced by the same quantity of paprika. Finish the sauce with a few tablespoons of fresh cream.

Note It is difficult to give the correct proportions for the use of curry powder and of paprika, because of the varying amounts of cayenne pepper that these two products contain.

Sauce diplomate ou sauce riche

DIPLOMATIC SAUCE OR RICH SAUCE

To 1 pint (U.S. 2½ cups) *sauce parisienne* (see page 22) add 6 table-spoons fish sauce, few tablespoons freshly cooked mushroom sauce, few pieces butter, 2 tablespoons lobster butter, 2–3 tablespoons lobster flesh and 1 tablespoon diced truffles.

Sauce groseilles, dite 'groseilles à maquereau'

GOOSEBERRY SAUCE

———————— To make about ¾ pint (U.S. 1⅞ cups): 8 oz. green unripe gooseberries, 2 tablespoons white wine, ½ pint (U.S. 1¼ cups) butter sauce (see page 30)

Cook the gooseberries for a few minutes in boiling water. Drain, and finish cooking with the wine. Rub through a fine sieve. Add the purée obtained to the butter sauce.

This sauce is particularly suitable for grilled or boiled mackerel.

Sauce hollandaise

HOLLANDAISE SAUCE

———————— 4 egg yolks, 4 tablespoons cold water, 1 lb. fresh butter, few teaspoons water, pinch salt, pinch coarse pepper, lemon juice, few teaspoons water

Put the egg yolks and water in a casserole and place it on the corner of the stove over very low heat. Add the butter as for mayonnaise (see page 40), stirring with a small whisk. While the sauce is being made add the extra water.

This sauce should be fairly thick, though at the same time it should be light. The sauce will thicken as the butter is added and as the eggs cook.

Complete the seasoning with the necessary salt, pepper and a few drops of lemon juice, then strain the sauce through muslin or through a fine sieve.

Sauce aux huîtres

OYSTER SAUCE

For this sauce 3—4 oysters per person are usually required.

The oysters are warmed in their juice, then drained and coated with a cream béchamel or a *sauce parisienne* (see page 22) with fish flavouring.

Sauce ivoire

IVORY SAUCE

This is *sauce parisienne* (see page 22) with the addition of a quarter of its volume of meat jelly made from shin of veal and chicken stock (see page 21).

Sauce Joinville

JOINVILLE SAUCE

To 1 pint (U.S. 2½ cups) of *sauce parisienne* (see page 22) add 4 oz. shrimp butter (see page 51). Garnish with little shrimps and 2 tablespoons truffles cut into julienne.

Sauce Mornay

MORNAY SAUCE

To 1 pint (U.S. 2½ cups) of cream béchamel sauce (see page 23) add, at the last moment, 3½ oz. fresh butter and 3 tablespoons grated Parmesan cheese.

This sauce is for fish, fowl and vegetables.

Sauce mousseline

MOUSSELINE SAUCE

This is a hollandaise sauce (see page 33) to which is added just before serving 2 tablespoons whipped cream for every 1 pint (U.S. 2½ cups) of sauce.

This sauce is served as an accompaniment to poached fish and to vegetables such as asparagus, salsify, artichokes, etc.

Sauce moutarde
MUSTARD SAUCE

——————— Add 1 tablespoon Dijon or English mustard to ½ pint (U.S. 1¼ cups) butter or hollandaise sauce (see pages 30 and 33)

This sauce is prepared just before it is due to be served. Maître d'hôtel butter can also be served. Mix 2 teaspoons mustard with 3½ oz. butter, before adding seasoning and lemon juice. This butter is a good accompaniment to all grilled fish.

Sauce normande
NORMANDY SAUCE

In Parisian restaurants this sauce was formerly made as follows: To 1 pint (U.S. 2½ cups) *sauce parisienne* (see page 22), reduced as required, add 5−7 oz. good butter just before serving. Nowadays a white wine sauce with a fish flavouring replaces this recipe.

Sauce smitane (crème aigre)
SOUR CREAM SAUCE

——————— To make about 1½ pints (U.S. 3¾ cups) sauce: 2 tablespoons finely chopped onion, 1 oz. butter, ½ pint (U.S. 1¼ cups) dry white wine, 1 pint (U.S. 2½ cups) sour cream, juice ½ lemon

Lightly brown the onion in the heated butter. Add the wine and almost completely reduce. Add the sour cream and allow to boil for a few moments. Strain through a fine sieve and finally add the lemon juice.

Sauce ou purée soubise
SOUBISE OR ONION SAUCE

——————— 1 lb. white onions, 5 oz. Carolina rice, 1¼ pints (U.S. 3 cups) white stock, pinch salt, pinch white pepper, good pinch sugar, 2 tablespoons butter, 6 tablespoons fresh cream

Chop the onions and cook in boiling salted water for 5−6 minutes. Drain, and put into a well buttered pan. Add rice, stock, salt, pepper and sugar. Bring to boiling point and simmer until done. Pound the rice and onions in a mortar, then put all through a fine sieve. Return the resultant purée to the pan, heat up quickly and finally add butter and cream.

Sauce soubise tomatée
SOUBISE SAUCE WITH TOMATO

To ½ pint (U.S. 1¼ cups) soubise sauce add 6 tablespoons concentrated tomato purée.

Sauce vénitienne
VENETIAN SAUCE

To make about 1 pint (U.S. 2½ cups) sauce: ½ pint (U.S. 1¼ cups) tarragon vinegar, 2 chopped shallots, pinch chervil, pinch coarse pepper, 5 oz. butter, ½−¾ pint (U.S. 1¼−scant 2 cups) *sauce parisienne* (see page 22), 2 tablespoons sieved green spinach, 1 tablespoon finely chopped tarragon and chervil mixed

Put the vinegar, shallots, chervil, pepper and 1 oz. of the butter in a pan. Boil quickly until reduced by two-thirds. Add the *sauce parisienne*, boil for a few seconds, then strain through a fine strainer. Add the rest of the butter, spinach and tarragon and chervil.

Sauce Villeroy
VILLEROY SAUCE

This is simply *sauce parisienne* (see page 22) reduced to a thick consistency. It is used to coat certain kinds of food before dipping in breadcrumbs. When reducing the sauce, use a wooden spoon and be sure to stir the bottom of the pan.

Sauce Villeroy tomatée
VILLEROY SAUCE WITH TOMATOES

The ordinary Villeroy sauce (see page 36) to which a third of its volume of tomato purée is added.

Sauce vin blanc
WHITE WINE SAUCE

This sauce can be made in two ways.

First method To 1 pint (U.S. 2½ cups) boiling velouté sauce (see page 22) with fish essence and very reduced, add 3 egg yolks mixed with a few tablespoons fish essence. Complete the sauce by very slowly adding 10 oz. butter.

Second method Reduce to half its volume 9 tablespoons good fish essence. Add 4—5 egg yolks and finish the sauce with 1 lb. butter, proceeding as for hollandaise sauce (see page 33).

SAUCES ANGLAISES CHAUDES
HOT ENGLISH SAUCES

Sauce aux airelles

CRANBERRY SAUCE

8 oz. cranberries, 1 pint (U.S. 2½ cups) water, sugar

Put the cranberries and water into a pan, cover and cook till tender. Strain all through a sieve and add sugar to taste.

This sauce is a speciality for roast turkey.

Cranberries can also be cooked as a compote and served lightly sugared.

Sauce au beurre à l'anglaise

BUTTER SAUCE

This sauce is almost the same as the French butter sauce (see page 30). The only difference is that it is not bound with egg yolks.

Sauce aux câpres

CAPER SAUCE

This is butter sauce (see above) to which is added 2 tablespoons small capers to every 1 pint (U.S. 2½ cups) sauce.

This sauce is served with poached fish and is the indispensable accompaniment to boiled mutton.

Sauce au céleri

CELERY SAUCE

———————— 3 heads celery, 1 onion finely chopped, béchamel sauce (see page 23)

Use the hearts and tender sticks of the celery, wash and chop finely. Put into a pan with the onion and just cover with white stock. Cover and cook gently until tender.

Drain the celery, pound it, and strain through a fine sieve. Place the purée obtained in a saucepan and add the same quantity of béchamel sauce.

This sauce accompanies boiled or braised poultry.

Sauce crème à l'anglaise

CREAM SAUCE

This is none other than the French *sauce diable* (see page 27) to which is added 2 tablespoons Worcestershire sauce, and 2−3 tablespoons cream for each ½ pint (U.S. 1¼ cups) sauce.

Sauce aux oeufs à l'anglaise

EGG SAUCE

A béchamel sauce (see page 23) to which is added 2 chopped hard-boiled eggs for every ½ pint (U.S. 1¼ cups) sauce.

This is used to accompany haddock and cod.

Sauce au pain

BREAD SAUCE

———————— 4 oz. fresh white breadcrumbs, pinch salt, 1 small onion stuck with 1 clove, 1 tablespoon butter, 1 pint (U.S. 2½ cups) boiling milk, 6 tablespoons cream

Mix together the breadcrumbs, salt, onion and butter. Add the boiling milk and simmer for 15 minutes. Remove the onion, then whisk the sauce until smooth. Finally add the cream.

This sauce is served with poultry and game.

Note With game, fried breadcrumbs and fine potato straws are also served.

Sauce persil

PARSLEY SAUCE

———— To ½ pint (U.S. 1¼ cups) English butter sauce (see page 37) add 3 tablespoons scalded and chopped parsley

This sauce is served with calf's head, calf's feet, brains, fish, etc.

Sauce aux pommes

APPLE SAUCE

This is a compote of apples sweetened with the addition of a little powdered cinnamon.

This compote is served warm and accompanies goose, duck, pork, roast meat, etc.

Note This accompaniment to certain roasts is not peculiar to England, it is also used in Germany, Belgium and Holland. In these countries roast game is always accompanied by a compote of apples or cranberries, or a compote of hot or cold fruit.

Sauce réforme

REFORM SAUCE

———— To 1 pint (U.S. 2½ cups) devil sauce (see page 27) add 2 gherkins, 1 hard-boiled egg white, 2 mushrooms, ½ oz. truffle and 1 oz. tongue, all cut into julienne

This is specially used for reform cutlets.

Sauce sauge et oignons

SAGE AND ONION STUFFING

———— 2 large white onions, 5 oz. breadcrumbs, milk, 1 tablespoon chopped sage, salt and pepper

Bake the onions till tender. When cold chop them finely. Add the breadcrumbs, soaked in milk and well drained, sage and seasoning.

This is used as stuffing for roast duck.

It can also be served separately in a sauce-boat, in which case add a few tablespoons good gravy.

Sauce Yorkshire

YORKSHIRE SAUCE

1 tablespoon thinly shredded orange peel, ¼ pint (U.S. 1¼ cups) port wine, 2 tablespoons demi-glace sauce (see page 22), 2 tablespoons redcurrant jelly, pinch cinnamon, pinch cayenne pepper, juice 1 orange

Cook the orange peel for a few minutes in the wine, then strain and retain the shreds. Return the wine to a pan, add the sauce, jelly, cinnamon and cayenne pepper. Boil for a few seconds, then strain. Add the orange juice and shredded orange peel.

This is served with roast or braised duck and with braised ham.

SAUCES FROIDES
COLD SAUCES

Sauce mayonnaise

MAYONNAISE SAUCE

Most of the compound cold sauces start with mayonnaise which, for that reason, is considered a 'mother-sauce' in the same way as espagnole and velouté sauces.

The making of mayonnaise is very simple but one must pay attention to certain rules as shown in the following method:

3—4 egg yolks, with the thread removed, ¼ oz. fine salt, pinch white pepper, 1 teaspoon tarragon vinegar or 1 teaspoon lemon juice, 2 teaspoons Dijon mustard (optional), 1 pint (U.S. 2½ cups) oil, 2 tablespoons boiling water

Put the egg yolks into a basin, add the salt, pepper, a little of the vinegar or a few drops of the lemon juice and the mustard if used. Stir the eggs with a whisk, add the oil drop by drop to begin with, and then let it pour slowly into the sauce, as it begins to bind. Add a few drops of vinegar or lemon juice from time to time. Finally add the boiling water, the object of which is to ensure cohesion and to prevent it disintegrating, if it has to be kept.

Note The idea that the addition of the seasoning at the beginning is a cause of curdling is wrong. On the contrary, it is shown scientifically that the liquefying salt increases the power of assimilation of the egg yolks.

It is an error to think that the making of mayonnaise should be carried out on ice, since cold is the most frequent cause of curdling. During cold weather the oil should be kept at the temperature of the kitchen.

The causes of curdling are as follows:

1 Too rapid addition of oil at the beginning.
2 Employing oil which is too cold.
3 Too much oil for the number of eggs used.

Sauces mayonnaises diverses
VARIOUS MAYONNAISE SAUCES

For hors-d'oeuvre and even for cold entrées one can obtain a great variety of mayonnaise, with the creamy part of lobster and other crustaceans, crayfish, shrimps, prawns, anchovies, hard-boiled eggs, paprika, curry, tomatoes, etc.

It is only necessary to pound one of these foods and mix the purée with a little mayonnaise, then strain through a fine sieve and add, to the purée obtained, equal parts or two-thirds of mayonnaise. It is all a matter of taste and imagination.

Sauce Chantilly
CHANTILLY SAUCE

This is a mayonnaise with the addition of whipped cream. Just before serving add 2 tablespoons whipped cream to each ½ pint (U.S. 1¼ cups) mayonnaise.

Sauce raifort aux noix fraîches
HORSERADISH SAUCE WITH FRESH WALNUTS

5 oz. grated horseradish, 5 oz. walnuts, peeled and finely chopped, pinch salt, 1 dessertspoon castor sugar, 2 tablespoons white breadcrumbs, ½ pint (U.S. 1¼ cups) fresh cream, 1 dessertspoon vinegar or lemon juice

Mix together all ingredients, adding vinegar or lemon juice to taste at the end.

This sauce is best served with trout, salmon or char.

Sauce ravigote ou vinaigrette

RAVIGOTE OR VINAIGRETTE SAUCE

————— ½ pint (U.S. 1¼ cups) oil, 3 tablespoons vinegar, 1 tablespoon small capers, pinch parsley, pinch tarragon, chervil, chopped chives, pepper and salt

Mix well together. If desired, one may add to this sauce 1 tablespoon finely chopped onion, 1 tablespoon mustard, 1 tablespoon Worcestershire sauce and 1 chopped hard-boiled egg.

This is served with calf's head, calf's feet, sheep's trotters and for cold fish.

Sauce rémoulade

RÉMOULADE SAUCE

————— ½ pint (U.S. 1¼ cups) mayonnaise, 2 tablespoons Dijon mustard, 1 tablespoon chopped gherkins, ½ tablespoon chopped capers, pinch chopped parsley, chopped chervil, chopped tarragon, ½ tablespoon anchovy essence

Mix all the ingredients together.

Sauce suédoise

SWEDISH SAUCE

————— 1 pint (U.S. 2½ cups) thick apple compote, 1 dessertspoon made mustard, 1 tablespoon grated horseradish, ½ pint (U.S. 1¼ cups) mayonnaise sauce (see page 40)

Mix all ingredients together well. If preferred an equal amount of fresh cream and the juice of 1 lemon can be substituted for the mayonnaise.

This sauce is an accompaniment to hot or cold roast pork or goose.

Sauce tartare

TARTARE SAUCE

————— 4—5 hard-boiled egg yolks, salt, freshly ground pepper, ½ pint (U.S. 1¼ cups) oil, 1 teaspoon vinegar, 2 tablespoons mayonnaise, 1 tablespoon chopped chives

Sieve the egg yolks and pound into a paste with the salt and pepper. Gradually work in the oil, add vinegar, and lastly the mayonnaise and chives.

Sauce verte

GREEN SAUCE

1½ oz. spinach leaves, 1½ oz. watercress, 1 oz. parsley, 1 oz. tarragon, 1 oz. chervil, ½ pint (U.S. 1¼ cups) mayonnaise, pinch cayenne pepper

Put the spinach, watercress, parsley, tarragon and chervil into boiling water for 3−4 minutes. Drain, rinse in cold water and press to remove as much water as possible. Pound the leaves well and twist in a cloth to extract the juice. Add this to the mayonnaise and finally add the cayenne pepper.

SAUCES ANGLAISES FROIDES
COLD ENGLISH SAUCES

Sauce Cumberland

CUMBERLAND SAUCE

4 tablespoons redcurrant jelly, 6 tablespoons port wine, ½ tablespoon shallot,* finely chopped, 1 tablespoon grated orange rind, 1 tablespoon grated lemon rind,** juice 1 orange, juice ½ lemon, 1 dessertspoon dry mustard, 1 dash cayenne pepper, ½ teaspoon powdered ginger (optional)

Melt the jelly and add all the other ingredients.

* The shallot should be plunged for a moment in boiling water and squeezed in a cloth, before adding to the other ingredients.

** The orange and lemon peel can be cut into julienne if preferred, in which case they should be put into boiling water for a few minutes and well drained before adding.

The sauce is especially good with cold venison.

Sauce menthe

MINT SAUCE

1½ oz. mint leaves, 2 tablespoons powdered sugar, 5—6 tablespoons vinegar, pinch salt

Chop the mint and add the other ingredients.
This is to accompany hot or cold lamb.

Sauce raifort

HORSERADISH SAUCE

4 oz. grated horseradish, 2 oz. powdered sugar, pinch salt, 4 oz. freshly prepared breadcrumbs, ½ pint (U.S. 1¼ cups) fresh cream, 1 dessertspoon vinegar

Mix the horseradish, sugar, salt and breadcrumbs together. Add the cream and mix well. Just before serving, stir in the vinegar.
This sauce accompanies boiled or roast beef and should be served cold.

Garnitures

GARNISHES

GARNITURES POUR PETITES ENTRÉES
GARNISHES FOR LIGHT ENTRÉES

These garnishes are usually self-explanatory, but it is important to remember that care must be taken with the gravies and sauces which should accompany light entrées, such as: noisettes, cutlets, scallops, tournedos, chicken fillets, chicken suprême, game, etc., especially if these entrées are garnished with vegetables served with butter, such as: peas, asparagus tips, French beans, flageolets and mixed vegetables. In this case, a light meat jelly (see page 21) mixed with butter in the proportions of 4 oz. butter to 6 tablespoons meat jelly should be added to the sauce.

The meat jelly, instead of breaking up the butter, as happens when one uses a simple demi-glace sauce, helps to bind it more firmly and gives it a delicious taste.

I will limit myself to giving recipes, with a few modifications, for the garnishes which I believe to be the most interesting.

Garniture à l'alsacienne

ALSATIAN GARNISH

(for poultry, fillet of beef, tournedos, fillets of chicken, partridges, quails, etc.)

Fresh noodles prepared à l'alsacienne (see page 677), scallops of foie gras sautéed in butter, truffles cut in thin slices, all coated with demi-glace sauce (see page 22) with Madeira.

Garniture andalouse

ANDALUSIAN GARNISH

(for fillet of beef, veal, saddle of lamb, poultry)

Medium-sized halved red sweet peppers, grilled and stuffed with pilaf rice,* halved aubergines au gratin (see page 595), and demi-glace sauce with tomato (see page 22)

* 8 oz. Carolina rice, ½ finely chopped onion fried in 2 oz. butter till well browned; 2 pints (U.S. 5 cups) white stock (see page 20) added and cooked, covered, for about 20 minutes in a moderate oven.

Garniture arlésienne

STUFFED TOMATOES WITH AUBERGINES AND RICE

Tomates farcies à la provençal (see page 659).

Aubergines fried in oil. Pilaf rice as above but with a pinch of saffron added to the rice while frying.

Garniture à la boulangère

ONION AND POTATO GARNISH

Onion and potatoes sliced and braised in butter for 12–15 minutes, seasoned and added to the meat after it has been cooking for 30 minutes.

A good sauce should accompany this very bourgeois dish.

Garniture à la bourgeoise

CARROT AND ONION GARNISH

———— 1 lb. small carrots, 10 oz. small onions, 4 oz. diced bacon, all browned in butter

This garnish is added to the dish when it is nearly ready, and finishes its cooking in the pan.

Garniture à la bourguignonne

ONION AND MUSHROOM GARNISH
(for braised beef)

———————— 10 oz. small onions, 10 oz. mushrooms, cut into quarters, 4 oz. diced bacon, all cooked in butter

These ingredients are arranged round the dish at the end of the cooking. A good red wine should be added to the sauce.

Garniture châtelaine

ARTICHOKE, MUSHROOM AND TRUFFLE GARNISH

Medium-sized, freshly cooked artichoke bottoms garnished with a salpicon of ox-tongue, mushrooms, truffles, foie gras, all cut up small and coated with béchamel sauce (see page 23) sprinkled with grated cheese and butter and slightly browned.

Small patties with asparagus tips, potatoes cut into small pieces the size of walnuts, cooked in butter and rolled in meat jelly (see page 21).

The joint is served on a dish of the appropriate size, surrounded with the artichoke bottoms, alternating with the patties. Potatoes are served separately.

Accompaniment The gravy from the pan, to which a light demi-glace sauce (see page 22) has been added.

Garniture chipolata

CHIPOLATA GARNISH
(for meat and poultry)

———————— 10 cooked chipolata sausages, 20 small browned onions, 20 chestnuts cooked in consommé, 5 oz. streaky bacon diced and browned, 20 small carrots peeled and cooked in butter (optional)

Place the joint on a dish of the required size, surround it with the garnish or serve it separately.

At the same time, serve a demi-glace sauce (see page 22) added to the gravy of the joint.

Garniture Choisi

BRAISED LETTUCE GARNISH
(for large joints of meat)

Halve and braise 6 lettuce (see page 632). Put into a buttered dish, sprinkle with grated cheese and cover with marrow sauce (see page 28) to which a little tomato has been added. Add some new potatoes cooked in butter and rolled in meat jelly (see page 21) 5−6 minutes before serving.

Accompaniment The gravy from the pan, to which a little demi-glace sauce (see page 22) has been added.

Garniture favorite

FOIE GRAS GARNISH
(for fillets of chicken and sautéed noisette of lamb)

This is made of scallops of foie gras, floured and sautéed in butter. Thin slices of truffle and very green asparagus tips.

Accompaniment The gravy from the saucepan in which the noisettes have been sautéed (see page 349) with a few tablespoons white stock (see page 20), meat jelly (see page 21) and fresh butter.

Note It is very important, in the making of this sauce, to keep the butter in which the meat has been cooked. The butter is often drained off before the sauce is made; this is a great mistake, because the butter, having acquired the delicate flavour of the lamb, will convey its delicacy to the sauce.

Garniture financière

VEAL QUENELLES GARNISH

18 veal or poultry quenelles (see pages 57, 467) moulded in a dessertspoon and poached in salted water, 15 small mushrooms cooked in butter and lemon juice, 12 cock's combs, 12 chicken livers, 3 oz. truffles cut into thin slices, 20 stoned olives

Place all the ingredients into a saucepan and cover with a demi-glace sauce with Madeira (see page 22).

In this case it is better to serve the garnish separately, and to serve the dish simply with a little of the gravy from the pan.

Garniture flamande

VEGETABLE GARNISH
(for a joint of roast meat)

Carrots and turnips cut into small pieces and cooked in white stock (see page 20), then tossed in butter, braised cabbage (see page 614) made into balls the size of an egg, streaky bacon cooked with the cabbage and cut into strips, and rings of cooked saveloy. Boiled potatoes are served separately.

Accompaniment The gravy from the pan in which the joint has been cooked.

Garniture forestière

MUSHROOM AND POTATO GARNISH
(for meat and poultry)

Mushrooms sautéed in a frying pan in equal quantities of butter and oil and sprinkled with parsley. Potatoes cut into small cubes, cooked in butter and sprinkled with a few tablespoons meat jelly (see page 21).

Accompaniment Sliced truffles, seasoned with salt and freshly ground pepper, coated with demi-glace sauce (see page 22) to which has been added the well reduced gravy from the roasting tin.

Garniture Godard

GODARD GARNISH
(for large joints and poultry)

Godard garnish is only *garniture financière* to which is added calf's or lamb's sweetbreads.

This garnish, as well as many others, rarely figures on menus today.

Garniture jardinière

MIXED VEGETABLE GARNISH
(for joints)

Carrots and turnips cut into balls or diced and cooked in consommé and tossed in butter, and peas, flageolets and French beans cut into thin small lozenges before being cooked in the usual way then tossed in butter, and small flowerets of cooked cauliflower. This garnish should be arranged on the serving dish in small heaps of alternating colour.

Accompaniment A rather thick gravy.

Garniture macédoine, ou macédoine de légumes

MACEDOINE OF VEGETABLES
(for joints)

This garnish contains the same ingredients as the jardinière (see above), but the vegetables are mixed together with butter. They are arranged in a vegetable dish, and served separately or in artichoke bottoms freshly cooked. In the latter case the garnish may be arranged round the dish.

Accompaniment Rather thick gravy or a light demi-glace sauce (see page 22).

Garniture ménagère

PEA AND POTATO GARNISH
(for roast fillet of beef)

Peas cooked *à la française* (in butter with onions), braised lettuce (see page 632), Macaire potatoes (see page 651) or potatoes au gratin.

Accompaniment Gravy from the dish in which the fillet has been cooked. The potatoes and the peas are served separately.

Garniture Marie-Louise

ARTICHOKES WITH MUSHROOM PURÉE GARNISH
(for fillet of beef, saddle of lamb, poultry)

Artichoke bottoms, freshly cooked and filled with mushroom purée, sprinkled with grated cheese and butter and lightly browned, thin slices of truffles heated in butter and meat jelly (see page 21), green asparagus tips with butter

1 slice of truffle is placed on each artichoke bottom. The asparagus tips are served in a vegetable dish.

Accompaniment Gravy from the dish in which the meat has been cooked.

Garniture marquise

MACARONI AND SHRIMP GARNISH
(for poultry)

Macaroni cooked in boiling salted water, then bound with butter and Parmesan cheese to which thin slices of truffle have been added; a few shrimps coated with béchamel sauce (see page 23) to which a little cream has been added and finished with shrimp butter.* The garnish is served separately in a silver dish and the poultry lightly covered with *sauce suprême* (see page 23).

* Some shrimps and any available trimmings finely pounded with an equal quantity of butter added and rubbed through a sieve.

Garniture piémontaise

MUSHROOM AND TOMATO GARNISH
(for joints and poultry)

Mushrooms and tomatoes peeled, sliced and seeded, and fried together in oil for 10—12 minutes. Sprinkled with grated cheese, and salt and pepper, 1 small clove of garlic and a little chopped parsley added. Covered and reheated before serving.

At the same time a *riz à la piémontaise* (see page 668) is served.

Accompaniment Gravy from the dish.

Garniture portugaise

STUFFED TOMATO AND COURGETTE GARNISH
(for joints and poultry)

Stuffed tomatoes, sliced courgettes or baby marrows, fried in butter and- seasoned with salt and pepper, 1 clove of garlic and a little chopped parsley, pilaf of rice (see page 669)

The rice and the baby marrow are served separately.

Accompaniment The gravy from the pan in which the joint or poultry was cooked. A little demi-glace sauce (see page 22) can be added if preferred.

Garniture provençal

STUFFED TOMATOES WITH CÈPES GARNISH
(for joints)

———————— Stuffed tomatoes provençal (see page 658) and cèpes or mushrooms browned in oil, and a generous sprinkling of parsley

Accompaniment Tomato sauce *à la provençal* with the gravy from the pan.

Note If liked French beans and potatoes cooked in boiling salted water can be served at the same time.

Garniture renaissance

SPRING VEGETABLE GARNISH
(for roast and braised meat)

This garnish is used in April and May when spring vegetables are available.

It is composed of as many spring vegetables as possible, each one being cooked according to its kind. The garnish is arranged in piles around the dish.

Accompaniment The gravy from the pan slightly thickened with flour.

Garniture Richelieu

STUFFED TOMATO, MUSHROOM AND LETTUCE GARNISH
(for beef)

———————— Stuffed tomatoes (see page 658), grilled mushrooms, braised lettuce, new potatoes cooked in butter and rolled gently in meat jelly (see page 21)

Accompaniment Gravy from the pan, slightly thickened with flour, or demi-glace sauce (see page 22).

Note In the Richelieu garnish, the tomato is essential. It is the symbol of the Cardinal's hat.

Garniture Rossini

NOODLES AND FOIE GRAS GARNISH
(for meat and poultry)

Noodles with Parmesan cheese in the Italian manner (see page 673),
scallops of foie gras seasoned with salt and pepper, sautéed in butter,
thin slices of truffle coated with a fine demi-glace sauce (see page 22)
to which a little Marsala has been added.

Garniture sicilienne

SEMOLINA AND SWEETBREAD GARNISH
(for braised chicken)

——————— 10 little cakes of semolina, as in *Gnocchi à la romaine* (see page 672)
sprinkled with flour and browned on both sides in butter, 10 little
scallops cut from a braised calf's sweetbread

Arrange the cakes on a round dish, place a scallop of sweetbread on
each of them, and top with a slice of truffle. Cover completely with
béchamel sauce (see page 23), sprinkle lightly with grated cheese and
brown. In the centre of the dish arrange some peas cooked in the usual
way.

The chicken is served on a separate dish, with the gravy from the pan
which must be reduced and then thickened with butter.

Garniture Talleyrand

MACARONI, TRUFFLE AND FOIE GRAS GARNISH
(for braised poultry)

——————— 8 oz. macaroni cooked in salted water and drained well, 5 oz. butter,
3½ oz. grated cheese, half Gruyère and half Parmesan, 3½ oz. truffles
cut into julienne or in thin slices, and 3½ oz. pâté de foie gras cut
into large dice, all mixed with the macaroni

This garnish is served separately to accompany a large chicken.

Accompaniment The gravy from the pan in which the chicken was
cooked, reduced, and then 6 tablespoons tomato demi-glace sauce added
(see page 22).

Garniture toulousaine

KIDNEY AND SWEETBREAD GARNISH
(for boiled stuffed chicken)

10 cock's combs, 12 chicken's kidneys, 7 oz. mushrooms, 3½ oz. truffles, 3½ oz. lamb's sweetbreads, all placed in a saucepan with a few spoonfuls of Madeira. These should be quickly warmed and coated with *sauce parisienne* (see page 22). The fowl should be covered with the same sauce

The garnish should be served separately as an accompaniment to a good-sized fowl.

Note For the vegetables mentioned in the foregoing garnishes, see the methods of preparing them in the section on Vegetables.

It should be remembered that from the nutritional point of view vegetables are in general the best accompaniment to meat.

By using vegetables in season the garnishes can be varied endlessly.

For family cooking, it is usual to serve only one garnish with a joint, in addition to the vegetables.

PANADAS

Panade au pain

BREAD PANADA

8 oz. stale breadcrumbs, ½ pint (U.S. 1¼ cups) boiling milk, pinch salt

Soak the breadcrumbs thoroughly in the milk and leave until the milk is absorbed. Add the salt.

Put into a pan and stir over fairly quick heat until the panada is dry and leaves the sides of the pan clean.

Turn on to a buttered dish and leave to cool.

This is generally used for forcemeat for fish.

Panade à la farine

FLOUR PANADA

½ pint (U.S. 1¼ cups) water, pinch salt, 2 oz. butter, 5 oz. sifted flour

Put the water, salt and butter into a saucepan and bring to the boil. Remove from heat and add the flour.

Return to the heat and stir over fairly quick heat as for the bread panada above.

This panada is useful for all forcemeat.

Panade à la frangipane

FRANGIPANI PANADA
(generally used for stuffing poultry and fish)

4 egg yolks, 3 oz. melted butter, pinch salt, pinch pepper, little grated nutmeg, ¼ pint (U.S. 1¼ cups) boiling milk

Stir the eggs and the flour in a saucepan, add the melted butter, salt, pepper and nutmeg; add the boiling milk very slowly, stirring all the time.

Place on the stove over gentle heat and cook for 5 − 6 minutes, beating with an egg whisk. When it is thick, place on a wetted plate to cool.

FARCES
STUFFINGS AND FORCEMEATS

Préparation des quenelles

PREPARATION OF QUENELLES

They are shaped in a spoon or in a ladle, in various sizes, put into a buttered fireproof dish and carefully covered with boiling white stock (see page 20) or simply with salted boiling water. Cover the dish and allow the quenelles to poach for 10 − 12 minutes on the corner of the stove. Above all, do not let the liquid boil; the quenelles should poach very gently.

By following these instructions carefully you will get a quenelle which is firm and light.

Quenelles can also be put into small buttered dariole moulds, placed in a deep pan and covered with salted water. They should be covered in the pan and poached slowly with care taken that the water does not boil. This last method is the most practical, for as soon as the quenelle is cooked it will leave the mould and rise to the surface.

Farce fine de volaille à la crème

FINE FORCEMEAT OF CHICKEN WITH CREAM

————————— 1 lb. boned young chicken, 1 level teaspoon salt, very small pinch white pepper, 2 egg whites, 1–1¼ pints (U.S. 2½–3 cups) fresh thick cream

Pound the chicken in a mortar with the seasoning. Add the egg whites slowly and then rub through a fine sieve. Put into a flat dish and leave on ice for at least 1 hour.

Then stir in the cream very gently and keep on ice until required for use.

Note Using the same method one can prepare fine quenelles with the flesh of partridge, pheasant, grouse, hare, rabbit, duck and even with fillet of veal and of beef. These quenelles are suitable for soups, mousses and mousselines.

Farce à la panade et au beurre

FORCEMEAT FOR ORDINARY QUENELLES

————————— 1 lb. well boned fillet or leg of veal without gristle, 1 level teaspoon salt, small pinch pepper, very small pinch nutmeg, 8 oz. flour panada (see page 54), 8 oz. butter, 2 whole eggs and 4 egg yolks

Cut the meat into dice and pound it in a mortar with seasoning. Take out the pounded meat, then pound the panada; add the butter, put back the veal and pound well to ensure the thorough mixture of the ingredients. Then add the eggs and the egg yolks, one by one; rub through a sieve, and keep on ice until required for use.

Farce de volaille à la panade et à la crème

CHICKEN FORCEMEAT WITH PANADA AND CREAM

————————— 1 lb. young chicken meat, well boned, 1 level teaspoon salt, pinch white pepper, very small pinch nutmeg, 3 egg whites, 7 oz. frangipani panada (see page 55), 1–1¼ pints (U.S. 2½–3 cups) very fresh cream

Pound the chicken with the seasoning, and one by one add the egg whites. Add the panada and stir vigorously to ensure that the ingredients are well mixed. Strain through a fine sieve; place the mixture in a shallow dish, smooth it with a spatula, and leave it on ice for 45 minutes. Add the cream a little at a time and keep on ice until required.

For game and fish, the same procedure.

Note It is always advisable to test the forcemeat by poaching a little of it before proceeding to make the quenelles.

Farce de perdreau à la panade

PARTRIDGE PANADA FORCEMEAT

8 oz. raw partridge meat, salt, pepper, nutmeg, 7 oz. panada, 7 oz. butter, 5 egg yolks

For pheasant or young rabbit forcemeat use the same proportions, and proceed as described in the preceding recipes.

Godiveau à la crème

VEAL FORCEMEAT FOR QUENELLES TO SERVE WITH VOL-AU-VENT

1 lb. fillet veal from which all gristle, etc., has been removed, 1 lb. beef kidney fat, 1 level teaspoon salt, generous pinch pepper, generous pinch ground nutmeg, 2 whole eggs and 2 egg yolks, $\frac{1}{2}$ pint (U.S. $1\frac{1}{4}$ cups) cream

Chop the veal and the fat separately, put them together in a mortar and pound them until they are completely mixed together, adding the seasoning, the eggs and the yolks, one by one, pounding briskly all the time.

Rub through a fine sieve, arrange on a dish and let it remain on ice until the next day.

The next day, cool the mortar by putting ice into it, pound the forcemeat again and add the cream to it little by little. Before making it into quenelles poach a little of this mixture to test it for flavour and consistency.

Note The cream can be replaced by the same quantity of iced water.

The quenelles made from this forcemeat are used as garnish for vol-au-vent or for hot beef or chicken pies. They are usually rolled by hand on a floured table and are the size of an ordinary cork. They are poached in salted water.

Farce à gratin pour pâtés chauds ordinaires

GRATIN FORCEMEAT FOR ORDINARY PIES

To make 1 lb. forcemeat: 2½ oz. butter, 4½ oz. fat bacon, 4½ oz. fairly thick veal, 4½ oz. calf's liver (these last 3 ingredients cut into pieces size of a small walnut), truffle parings, 1 sprig thyme, ½ bay leaf, 2 chopped shallots, 1 teaspoon salt, pinch pepper, 6 tablespoons Madeira, 4 tablespoons very reduced and cold demi-glace sauce (see page 22), 3 egg yolks

Heat half the butter in a sauté pan, add the bacon and brown it quickly, then add the veal; as soon as this has taken on a slightly brown colour, add the calf's liver, truffle parings, thyme, bay leaf, shallots, salt and pepper. Brown the liver quickly then turn everything out on to a dish. Add the Madeira to the sediment left in the pan and mix well.

Pound the meat in a mortar, add the rest of the butter, the egg yolks, the Madeira and the demi-glace sauce. Rub through a fine sieve; put the forcemeat into a bowl and smooth it with a spatula. Leave on ice until required.

Note In the preparation of this forcemeat, the calf's liver can be replaced by pig's liver, chicken liver, or duck, goose or turkey liver after carefully removing the gall bladder or any parts that may have been contaminated by it.

Farce à gratin pour pâtés de gibier

GRATIN FORCEMEAT FOR GAME PIES

The same ingredients and method for forcemeat as for ordinary pies except that the veal can be replaced, as required, by the flesh of wild rabbit, hare, pheasant, etc. At the end may be added 2 oz. truffled pâté de foie gras passed through a sieve.

Farce de porc, dite 'chair à saucisses'

PORK FORCEMEAT (SAUSAGE MEAT)

This is made of equal parts of lean pork and fat bacon seasoned with salt, pepper and spices.

Pork forcemeat is used for ordinary pies and terrines and numerous dishes which will be dealt with in the specific sections.

Farce de veau et porc

VEAL AND PORK FORCEMEAT

To make 2 lb. forcemeat: 8 oz. fillet veal, 8 oz. lean pork, 1 lb. fat bacon, 2 whole eggs, ¼ oz. spiced salt,* 2 tablespoons brandy
  * Spiced salt is made by mixing 4 oz. fine dry salt with ½ oz. pepper and ⅓ oz. mixed spice. This should be kept in a dry air-tight jar

Cut up the veal, pork and bacon. Place in a mortar and pound well. Gradually add the eggs, then seasoning, and lastly the brandy. Rub through a sieve.

Though this forcemeat is used principally for galantines, it is also used for pâtés and terrines.

Farce de volaille, veau et porc

CHICKEN, VEAL AND PORK FORCEMEAT

8 oz. chicken meat, 3½ oz. veal without gristle, 3½ oz. lean pork, 14 oz. fresh bacon, ½. oz. spiced salt (see above), 2 whole eggs, 6 tablespoons brandy

Cut up the meat and the bacon separately, put them together in a mortar with the seasoning. Pound them finely, add the eggs one by one, finally add the brandy and rub through a sieve.

Farce de gibier, veau et porc

GAME, VEAL AND PORK FORCEMEAT

This is prepared in the same way as the preceding recipe but substitute 8 oz. game for the chicken meat.

Potages

SOUPS

THOUGHTS ABOUT SOUPS IN GENERAL

From the earliest times France has always been the country where soup has been the prelude to good meals.

The preparation of soup requires the most strict attention because the success of the meal depends very largely on the impression it makes on the guests.

It is very important that soup should be served almost boiling.

On this subject I will relate an amusing story which is true and is to the point here.

'My Lord,' said the Prince Bishop of Passau one day to the last Prince of Condé, 'I have ordered that during the whole of the time you do me the honour of being my guest, the greatest care shall be paid to the preparation of the soup, because the French are a nation of soup eaters.' 'And boiling, too!' the old émigré replied.

Soups may be divided into two classes — thick and clear. They are prepared with or without meat.

It is with beef that the excellent pot-au-feu is made, a very French dish which, in spite of its simplicity, provides a complete meal for the soldier and the working classes. It is also a favourite with the rich.

The pot-au-feu is the basis of the bourgeois croûte-au-pot and of most of the meat soups. And it is through the care with which it is prepared that fine consommés are obtained.

Today we see it taking place of honour on the most opulent tables under the guise of 'Petite marmite'.

It is also the basis of the famous poule-au-pot of King Henri IV and of the poule-au-riz of King Louis Philippe.

Pot-au-feu

In France the pot-au-feu is the symbol of family life. In order to get this dish in perfect condition and have all the required qualities, it is of the utmost importance that the meat and vegetables should be perfectly fresh.

The pieces of beef which are chosen for preference come from the shoulder (U.S. chuck), the silverside (U.S. bottom round), the flank, the top ribs and the rump.

If the meat is to be served at table then the top ribs and the rump are the two parts which are most suitable.

You will need for 8 – 10 persons: 3 lb. rump steak, 1¼ lb. top ribs, 1 lb. chopped bones, 4½ quarts (U.S. 5½ quarts) cold water, 1 oz. salt, 4 peppercorns, 4 medium-sized carrots, 2 turnips, 2 leeks, 1 parsnip, 1 onion stuck with 2 cloves, 1 lettuce, 1 stick celery, 1 small piece chervil, 1 bay leaf, 1 clove garlic, ½ small cabbage which has been boiled for 8 – 10 minutes, cooled and tied up.

The cabbage and the garlic may be left out. All the vegetables must be carefully peeled and well washed.

Tie up the meat and put it with the bones, water and salt into a large earthenware pot or, if not available, a large saucepan. Place over the heat; when it comes to the boil, skim carefully, add ½ pint (U.S. 1¼ cups) cold water, bring to the boil again and skim a second time.

As soon as it is boiling well, remove to the side of the stove, cover it three-quarters over with its lid and let it simmer gently. At the end of 45 minutes simmering, add all the vegetables and spices, and continue to simmer for 3 – 3½ hours.

The time of cooking cannot be fixed very exactly, as this depends very much upon the quality of the meat.

To serve Carefully lift the meat followed by the vegetables from the pot. Slice up some of the vegetables and put them in a soup tureen with little slices of bread dried in the oven or toasted.

Arrange the remainder of the vegetables round the beef. Skim the grease from the broth, strain through a fine sieve and pour it into the tureen. This broth will be all the better with the addition of a few chicken's giblets.

In addition to the vegetables, the following are often served as an accompaniment: gherkins, vinegar pickles, mustard, coarse salt, or even tomato sauce, piquante sauce, or horseradish sauce (see pages 132, 28, 44).

PETITE MARMITE

This is the same as pot-au-feu to which is added a young chicken or the carcase of a chicken and a few giblets.

The cabbage, after being blanched for 8–10 minutes in boiling water and allowed to cool, is cooked separately for a short time in broth; the carrots and the turnips are cut into small pieces and the leeks into 1½-inch pieces.

The broth is served in soup plates with the vegetables and chicken, if they are used, cut into small pieces.

Petite marmite is accompanied by marrow bones and small slices of bread cut from a long French loaf *(flute)*.

The beef, cut into small cubes, is served with the cabbage on a separate plate, at the same time as the soup is placed before the guest.

It is customary to pass freshly grated Parmesan cheese round at the same time.

Le pot-au-feu en Provence

PROVENÇAL POT-AU-FEU

At one time, in Provence, pot-au-feu was made with mutton as beef was very rare there, especially in most of the villages. The reason was the difficulty of transport. This old custom has not disappeared and many people still prefer mutton to beef; it is all a question of taste.

Mutton, when it is of good quality, makes an excellent broth and the flesh is very good to eat. The meat should be chosen from the shoulder, the neck and the breast.

This pot-au-feu is usually reserved for the family luncheon at midday on Sundays. Here is the recipe:

> 1 medium-sized cabbage, 4 tablespoons olive oil, 2 tablespoons finely chopped onion, 6 oz. chopped streaky bacon, 7 oz. rice, pinch chopped parsley, 1 clove garlic (optional), salt and pepper, 2 eggs, 3–4 tablespoons grated cheese (optional)

Remove the coarse outer leaves from the cabbage, remove some of the larger remaining ones and plunge them into boiling water for 8–10 minutes to soften. Drain well and put them on to a piece of muslin.

Divide the rest of the cabbage into four, boil for 10 minutes in salted water, then drain and chop it up. Heat the oil, add the onion and bacon and sauté for a few minutes without browning. Add the chopped cabbage and continue cooking for a few minutes. Remove from the heat, add the rice, boiled for a few seconds and drained well, parsley, garlic, seasoning, beaten eggs and cheese. Mix all well together.

Place some of this mixture in the centre of each cabbage leaf, draw the edges together to form little cabbage shapes and tie securely so that they retain their shape while cooking.

These little stuffed cabbages are cooked with the meat. They should be added after the broth has been skimmed and left until the meat has cooked. When ready to serve, move the cabbage on to a hot dish and remove the string and the muslin. The meat is served on another dish surrounded by the vegetables.

Remove as much fat as possible from the broth and strain it into a soup tureen into which some slices of toast have been put. This is served at the same time as the meat and cabbage.

La poule-au-pot du roi Henri IV

THE POULE-AU-POT OF KING HENRI IV

This poule-au-pot is nothing more than pot-au-feu to which is added a young stuffed chicken, a piece of smoked bacon and some rice.

———————— To make the stuffing you will need: 8 oz. streaky bacon finely chopped, 3½ oz. breadcrumbs, 1 pinch chopped parsley and tarragon, 2 new-laid eggs, salt, pepper, grated nutmeg

Mix all these ingredients well together, stuff the chicken with them and truss it.

To serve The chicken is removed from the saucepan, untrussed, placed on an oval dish and surrounded by the beef, the bacon and some of the vegetables. Pour the soup into the soup tureen and serve immediately.

Henri IV soup or poule-au-pot which is actually served in restaurants is only petite marmite accompanied by rice cooked in the broth and served separately.

La poule-au-riz du roi Louis-Philippe

CHICKEN LOUIS PHILIPPE WITH RICE

The poule-au-riz of Louis Philippe is, I am afraid, only a legend. The chicken, which one often hears mentioned, is probably only the King's promise, made to his people, assuring them that thenceforward his faithful subjects would be able to add a chicken, surrounded by a large dish of rice, to their humble pot-au-feu on Sundays. Lucky were those who got it; history does not tell us much about them.

The ingredients for poule-au-riz are almost identical with Henri IV's poule-au-pot except that double the quantity of rice is added in order to make the soup thicker.

Consommés pour potages clairs

CONSOMMÉ FOR CLEAR SOUPS

The word 'consommé' means broth after it has been clarified.

For broths which are to be clarified, cabbage must be omitted.

Although, for a family meal, I am not in favour of clarification, because it makes the soup lose its delicate aroma, nevertheless here is the recipe:

> To make 5 pints (U.S. 6¼ pints) consommé: 1¾ lb. lean beef, few chicken giblets, 1–2 carcases from roast chicken, 2–3 egg whites, ¼ pint (U.S. ⅝ cup) cold water, 7 pints (U.S. 8¾ pints) cold stock, 1 small sprig chervil, 1 stick celery

Chop the meat and giblets into small pieces and put into a large pan with all the other ingredients. Put over moderate heat and stir till boiling. Cover and simmer for 35–40 minutes, then strain through muslin. Keep hot in a bain-marie or double saucepan. When ready to serve, add the garnish as required.

Consommé de gibier

GAME SOUP

In family meals, game soup is not much appreciated, but if necessary one can add to the meats of the petite marmite 1 or 2 partridges, or a hen pheasant, both half roasted.

If necessary, also clarify the broth in the ordinary way with half lean meat and half hare's flesh.

Consommé rapide

QUICK CONSOMMÉ

———————— 2 lb. lean beef, few chicken giblets, 1 leek (white part only), 1 carrot, 1 stick celery, 1 lettuce, 1 sprig chervil, 7 pints (U.S. 8¾ pints) cold water, 1 onion stuck with 2 cloves, 1 teaspoon salt, 5—6 peppercorns

Chop the meat and giblets into small pieces and put into a pan with the leek, carrot, celery and lettuce, all finely chopped, and chervil. Add water and stir till boiling. Move to the side of the stove, add onion, salt and peppercorns. Cover and simmer very gently for 50 minutes. Strain through muslin, remove the fat and, if necessary, add a few drops of browning to give it a nice colour.

Bouillon rafraîchissant

REFRESHING BROTH

———————— 1¾ lb. lean veal, 3½ pints (U.S. 4½ pints) water, pinch salt, 1 tablespoon cucumber seeds, 1 lettuce, 2—3 sprigs chervil

Chop the meat and put into a pan with the water and salt. Bring to boiling point and skim. Add the cucumber seeds and simmer very gently for 45 minutes. Add the chopped lettuce and chervil and continue to simmer a further 20 minutes.

Strain through muslin or a fine sieve and remove as much fat as possible before serving.

Autre bouillon rafraîchissant

ANOTHER REFRESHING BROTH

———————— 10 oz. shin of veal, legs and giblets of medium-sized chicken, 3½ pints (U.S. 4½ pints) water, 4—5 tablespoons pearl barley, 1 lettuce, 1 carrot, 1 onion, few crushed vegetable marrow seeds, 1 sprig chervil

Chop up the meat and put into a pan with the giblets and water. Bring slowly to boiling point, then skim carefully. Add all the other ingredients, cover and simmer over a low heat for 1½ hours.

Strain through a fine sieve.

Bouillon d'herbes

HERB BROTH

———————— 1 small onion, 1 leek, 4 tablespoons pearl barley, ½ small lettuce, few sprigs chervil, 2 oz. watercress, 2 oz. sorrel, 2 oz. purslane, 3 pints (U.S. 3¾ pints) water, pinch salt

Chop the onion and leek, wash the barley and chop the lettuce and herbs. Put all together into a pan with the water and salt and boil for 30 minutes.

Editor's note Purslane is an old-fashioned herb and if it is not available add parsley in its place.

Eau de riz

RICE WATER

———————— 8 oz. rice, 2½ pints (U.S. 3 pints) water, few slices lemon or orange, few lumps sugar

Wash the rice, add the water and boil for 30 minutes. Put the lemon slices and sugar into a jug and strain the water on top.

Eau d'orge

BARLEY WATER

This is made in precisely the same way as rice water, substituting barley for rice and boiling for 1 hour instead of ½ hour.

Eau de réglisse et chicorée sauvage

LIQUORICE AND WILD CHICORY WATER

———————— 2 oz. liquorice root, 1 handful leaves wild chicory, few slices lemon

Put the liquorice root and chicory into a saucepan with water and boil for 30 minutes. Pour into a jug into which a few slices of lemon have been placed.

Beef-tea (ou suc de viande de boeuf) et gelée de viande pour malades

BEEF TEA AND MEAT JELLY FOR INVALIDS

BEEF TEA

————— You will need for 1 cup: 1 lb. very lean stewing beef, 4 tablespoons water, pinch salt

Very finely shred or chop the meat. Put into a jar or basin (or use a double boiler) and gradually add the water and salt. Cover and leave to stand for ½ hour, pressing the meat occasionally with a wooden spoon. Place the jar in a saucepan of cold water and bring slowly to boiling point, then simmer for 3 hours, taking care to add extra boiling water from time to time to replace what is lost by evaporation.

Remove the jar and strain the contents through muslin.

MEAT JELLY

The same ingredients, adding an extra 4 oz. chopped shin of beef and 1½ oz. meat from a calf's foot, cut into strips, boiled for a few minutes and allowed to cool. After straining through muslin, pour into little cups.

Note For the jelly, use 8 tablespoons water on the meat instead of 4.

The beef tea and the jelly may be improved by adding to the meat indicated the flesh of 1 or 2 chicken's legs.

Pâtes diverses pour potages clairs (Pâtes dites d'Italie)

ITALIAN PASTA FOR CLEAR SOUPS

————— These pastas are used in the proportion of 2 oz. per 1¾ pints (U.S. 4¼ cups) of pot-au-feu or broth

10 or 12 minutes are required for cooking, according to the quality of the pasta.

The same quantity and method for fine vermicelli.

Note It is always advisable to throw the pasta into salted boiling water for 2 seconds before cooking it in the broth.

Perles du Japon

JAPANESE PEARLS

――――――― 2½ oz. Japanese pearls are needed for every 1¾ pints (U.S. 4¼ cups) of consommé

Time required for cooking: 20–25 minutes.

Editor's note Japanese pearls are a kind of rice, and ordinary rice can be used if the pearls are not available.

Le sagou, le tapioca

SAGO AND TAPIOCA

――――――― 2–3 oz. are needed for every 1¾ pints (U.S. 4¼ cups) of consommé

Time required for cooking: 15–18 minutes.

Le riz

RICE

――――――― 1½–2 oz. rice required for every 1¾ pints (U.S. 4¼ cups) of consommé

Time required for cooking: 20–25 minutes.

Note The rice should be placed in a saucepan and covered with boiling water. Boil for 2 minutes, then drain before putting it in the broth to finish cooking it.

When the rice is a garnish to the consommé, it should be cooked in sufficient ordinary broth and be thoroughly drained before being added to the consommé.

La semoule

SEMOLINA

――――――― 3 tablespoons semolina required for every 1¾ pints (U.S. 4¼ cups) of consommé

Time required for cooking: 18–20 minutes.

ROYALES DIVERSES POUR CONSOMMÉS
VARIOUS ROYALES FOR CONSOMMÉS

Royale ordinaire pour consommés
ORDINARY ROYALE FOR CONSOMMÉ

———————— 1 whole egg, 3 egg yolks, ⅜ pint (U.S. approx. 1 cup) boiling consommé or stock

Lightly beat the eggs and gradually add the consommé. Strain through muslin or a fine sieve. Put into small greased moulds or dariole tins. Place in a covered bain-marie and poach for 12–15 minutes.

Note The water in the bain-marie should be just below boiling point.

When the royale is firm, remove the moulds and leave them to get quite cold. Then cut into small cubes or other shapes and put in a pan with enough consommé to cover them. Keep warm and add to the soup just before serving.

Royale à la crème
CREAM ROYALE

———————— 1 whole egg, 3 egg yolks, ⅜ pint (U.S. approx. 1 cup) cream, pinch salt, pinch grated nutmeg

Lightly beat the eggs, add cream and seasoning. Strain through muslin and poach in a bain-marie (see above).

Royale de crème de riz
CREAM OF RICE ROYALE

———————— 3½ oz. rice flour, 4 tablespoons milk, pinch salt, 4 egg yolks

Mix the rice smoothly with the milk, add salt and lightly beaten egg yolks. Strain through muslin and poach as for ordinary royale (see above).

Royale de tomate
ROYALE OF TOMATO PURÉE

———————— 6 tablespoons well seasoned tomato purée, 4 tablespoons cream, pinch sugar, 1 whole egg, 3 egg yolks

Mix together the tomato purée, cream and sugar. Add the lightly beaten eggs.

Put into buttered dariole moulds and poach in a bain-marie.

Royale de volaille
ROYALE OF CHICKEN PURÉE

———————— 2 oz. cooked white chicken meat, 2 tablespoons béchamel sauce (see page 23), 2 tablespoons fresh cream, pinch grated nutmeg, 1 small egg, 2 egg yolks

Pound the meat in a mortar, add the sauce, cream and nutmeg. Add the lightly beaten eggs. Rub through a fine sieve and poach as for other royales.

A royale can also be made with a pheasant, partridge or young hare base, by proceeding as for royale of chicken except that the béchamel sauce is replaced by 4 tablespoons demi-glace sauce (see page 22) much reduced. Poach in the same way in little dariole moulds.

Note These royales can be used as light meals for children and invalids, in which case they should be turned out of the moulds and lightly coated with a little brown or white sauce and accompanied by a purée of fresh vegetables: peas, asparagus tips, chicory, French beans, etc.

PROFITEROLES POUR POTAGES
PROFITEROLES FOR SOUPS

Profiteroles, little balls of choux paste the size of a small walnut, are cooked like small cream buns.

Pâte à choux ordinaire
ORDINARY CHOUX PASTE

———————— 1 pint water (U.S. 2½ cups), 3½ oz. butter, good pinch salt, 10 oz. flour, 6 eggs

Put the water, butter and salt into a pan and bring to boiling point. Remove from the heat, add the flour and mix well with a wooden spoon.

Return to the heat and cook, beating all the time until the paste leaves the sides of the pan. Cool, then gradually beat in the eggs.

CONSOMMÉS ET POTAGES CLAIRS
CONSOMMÉS AND CLEAR SOUPS

Consommé aux ailerons de volaille
CONSOMMÉ WITH CHICKEN WING TIPS

Petite marmite (see page 62) in which wing tips have been cooked. Bone and stuff these with finely chopped chicken. Sew up the opening in the wing tips.

To serve Take the wing tips out of the marmite and remove the sewing thread, place the wing tips in the tureen, and add 2 tablespoons cooked rice for each wing tip used in the consommé.

Strain the consommé through muslin and pour it into the tureen.

Note For a large party, the wing tips are cooked separately, either braised or simply cooked in broth.

The garnish may be completed by adding a few tablespoons of plainly boiled peas and a few pieces of carrot, the size of peas, cooked in broth.

Consommé à l'ancienne
OLD-FASHIONED CONSOMMÉ

Consommé petite marmite

For the garnish Cut the required number of slices from a long French loaf and arrange in a circle in a fairly deep dish. Put some of the vegetables from the petite marmite in the centre of each slice. Sprinkle the bread and the vegetables with a little of the consommé and leave for 6–8 minutes, then brown lightly.

Serve this garnish separately.

Consommé aurore

CONSOMMÉ WITH TOMATO PURÉE

A little tapioca put into petite marmïite, with the addition of a quarter of its volume of sieved tomato purée

For the garnish Put the yolks of 2−3 hard-boiled eggs through a sieve and add to the soup just before serving.

Consommé dit 'à la bonne femme'

CONSOMMÉ WITH VEGETABLES

———— You will need for 6 persons: 2 lb. neck of mutton, 7 oz. pearl barley, 1 level teaspoon salt, 4 oz. carrots, 4 oz. onions, 1 stick celery, 1 bouquet of 1 bay leaf and 1 sprig parsley, pinch freshly ground pepper

Bone the meat and tie into shape. Put it with the bones into a large pan and add 5 pints (U.S. 6¼ pints) cold water. Bring to boiling point and skim. Add the well washed barley and salt. Simmer gently as for pot-au-feu (see page 61). Half-way through the cooking add the chopped vegetables and bouquet.

When ready to serve, put the meat into a tureen and remove the string. Remove the bones and bouquet from the soup, add the freshly ground pepper and pour it over the meat.

Consommé brunoise

CONSOMMÉ WITH VEGETABLES AND CHERVIL

———— 10 oz. carrots, 7 oz. turnips, 3 leeks (white part only), 1 stick celery, 1 small onion, 2 oz. butter, pinch salt, 1 teaspoon sugar, 1 pint (U.S. 2½ cups) water, little chervil, 3−4 tablespoons cooked garden peas (optional)

Dice the vegetables, put into a pan with the butter, salt and sugar. Cover and sauté gently for about 20 minutes. Add water and continue cooking over low heat.

When required for use add the vegetables to the consommé with the chervil and peas if liked.

Consommé brunoise au riz

CONSOMMÉ WITH VEGETABLES, CHERVIL AND RICE

Just before serving add 4 tablespoons cooked rice to every 1¾ pints (U.S. 4¼ cups) soup. The rice can be cooked separately or in the consommé. Pearl barley, tapioca or pasta can be used instead of rice.

Consommé brunoise can also be thickened with egg yolks and cream or with a third of its volume of dried vegetable purée, beans, split peas, lentils, etc., or with *sauce suprême* (see page 23).

Consommé Carmen

CONSOMMÉ WITH TOMATO PURÉE AND SWEET RED PEPPER

Make a petite marmite (see page 62) and prepare the garnish half an hour before serving.

———————— You will need for 5—6 persons: 1 tablespoon finely chopped onion, 1 oz. butter, 3½ oz. rice, 4 tablespoons tomato purée, 1 sweet red pepper, ½ pint (U.S. 1¼ cups) consommé.

Brown the onion in the butter, add the rice and stir for a few seconds. Add the tomato purée, red pepper — peeled, grilled (broiled) and diced — and the consommé. Cover and cook for 20 minutes.

To serve Cut the white meat from the chicken used to make the petite marmite into cubes and put into a tureen with the rice mixture. Boil up the consommé and strain through muslin into the tureen.

Consommé Cendrillon

CHICKEN CONSOMMÉ WITH TRUFFLES AND KIDNEYS

———————— You will need for 6 persons: 3½ pints (U.S. 8¾ cups) *consommé Madrilène* (see page 77)

Garnish 2 oz. truffles cooked in old Frontignan (Muscatel) wine, and then cut into julienne, 6 tablespoons rice cooked in the consommé, 12 chicken's kidneys skinned and poached in the consommé

Consommé chasseur

GAME CONSOMMÉ FLAVOURED WITH PORT

The base for this consommé is petite marmite to which has been added a partridge or a hen pheasant.

Garnish for 1¾ pints (U.S. 4¼ cups): 3 tablespoons celery cut into julienne, 6 tablespoons pearl barley cooked in consommé

To serve Cut the breast of the partridge or pheasant into strips and put into a tureen with the celery and barley.

Boil up the petite marmite and pour into the tureen.

Consommé Colbert

CONSOMMÉ WITH SPRING VEGETABLES

This is a clarified consommé, or simply a petite marmite strained through muslin, with a garnish of 1 poached egg per person, diced cooked spring vegetables, garden peas and a few leaves of chervil.

Consommé croûte-au-pot

PETITE MARMITE

Cut the vegetables from the marmite — carrots, turnips, leeks — into small pieces and arrange in a vegetable dish. Cut some slices from a long French loaf, remove some of the crumb, sprinkle with a little fat from the pan and grill. Arrange with the vegetables.

Consommé aux diablotins

PETITE MARMITE WITH 'DIABLOTINS'

'Diablotins' are slices from a *flûte* (a *flûte* is a long French loaf) ⅛-inch thick, covered with thick béchamel sauce (see page 23) flavoured with grated cheese and cayenne pepper. They should be lightly browned and served separately on a paper doily.

The consommé may be completed with small discs of very fresh beef marrow, poached in broth, and a pinch of chopped chervil.

Consommé dominicaine

CONSOMMÉ WITH PASTA AND PEAS

———————— Petite marmite with Italian pasta and fresh peas cooked in salted water, grated cheese served separately

This consommé may be thickened with egg yolks, or with a purée of fresh or dried vegetables, or with chicken velouté sauce (see page 23).

Consommé à l'écossaise

SCOTCH BROTH

Make a pot-au-feu with neck of mutton instead of beef. When the meat is cooked, bone it, cut the meat up into small pieces about the size of a walnut, put them into a saucepan with 4 tablespoons well cooked pearl barley, 2 tablespoons brunoise of vegetables prepared and cooked as indicated for *consommé brunoise* (see page 72). This quantity of barley and vegetables is sufficient for 2 pints (U.S. 5 cups) broth.

Just before serving, pour the meat and the vegetables into the soup tureen and add the necessary broth.

Consommé Francillon

CONSOMMÉ WITH BEEF MARROW

———————— Petite marmite strained through muslin

Garnish Halve a small lettuce and braise, arrange in a deep dish with a nice slice of beef marrow lightly poached in broth placed on each half. Sprinkle with freshly grated cheese and coat with a few tablespoons tomato sauce mixed with a third of its volume of meat jelly.

To serve Put the lettuce on an individual serving plate with 3 – 4 thin slices of French bread which have been dried in the oven. Pour the boiling consommé on top.

Consommé Hélène

CHICKEN CONSOMMÉ WITH TOMATO JUICE

Garnish Ordinary royale (see page 69) poached in small buttered dariole tins and cut into small dice, and small cheese profiteroles

For the profiteroles, follow the instructions on page 70 but use only half the quantity of ingredients given and add 2 oz. grated cheese.

Put the paste into a forcing bag with a plain nozzle and pipe little balls, the size of a small nut, on to a baking sheet. Bake for 20—25 minutes in a moderate oven.

Consommé Flammarion

CONSOMMÉ WITH STAR-SHAPED PASTA

This is a consommé to which is added Italian pasta in the form of stars cooked in boiling salted water.

Serve with freshly grated cheese.

Consommé Isabella

CHICKEN CONSOMMÉ WITH QUENELLES OF CREAMED CHICKEN

——————— Chicken consommé

Garnish Quenelles of creamed chicken (see page 467) moulded in a small teaspoon, garden peas and a little truffle cut into fine julienne

Consommé Jeannette

CONSOMMÉ WITH POACHED EGGS

——————— Petite marmite

Garnish Small poached eggs, peas, and Italian pasta cooked in boiling salted water

Consommé julienne

CONSOMMÉ WITH ROOT VEGETABLES

——————— 3½ pints (U.S. 8¾ cups) consommé
Garnish 4 oz. carrots, 4 oz. turnips, 1 leek (white part only), 1 stick celery, ½ onion, 2 tablespoons butter, pinch salt, pinch sugar, small piece cabbage (2—3 oz.), 1 tablespoon each sorrel, lettuce and chervil cut into julienne

The vegetables should all be cut to the same size so that they cook evenly. Cut the carrots, turnips, leek and celery into julienne, slice the onion finely. Put all into a pan with the butter, salt and sugar. Cover and sauté for 10–15 minutes. Add 1 pint (U.S. 2½ cups) of the consommé and the cabbage which should be pre-cooked for 10 minutes in boiling salted water, drained and cut into strips. Simmer till the vegetables are tender. When ready to serve, add the rest (2½ pints (U.S. 6¼ cups)) of the boiling consommé, and the julienne of sorrel, lettuce and chervil.

Consommé Lorette
CONSOMMÉ WITH PARTRIDGE PURÉE

—————— Petite marmite

Garnish Ordinary royale or one made with partridge purée (see page 112) and a small julienne of truffles and raw mushrooms warmed for a few seconds in a small glass of Frontignan (Muscatel)

Consommé Madrilène
CHICKEN CONSOMMÉ WITH TOMATOES

This is a chicken consommé to which is added, at the time of clearing, 3 or 4 very ripe chopped tomatoes to each 1 lb. meat. It is important that the tomatoes are not peeled as the skin gives this consommé its pretty pink colour. It can be served hot or cold, and preferably in cups.

Served hot, it is accompanied by cheese straws, lightly sprinkled with paprika.

Cold, and slightly jellied, this is one of the most pleasant consommés to serve in hot weather.

Consommé Mireille
CONSOMMÉ WITH EGG YOLKS AND CREAM

This is petite marmite, thickened with egg yolks and cream and served with small slices of French bread, dried in the oven, and grated cheese.

—————— Allow 3 egg yolks and 2 tablespoons fresh cream for every 2 pints (U.S. 5 cups) consommé

Note If preferred, the bread can be replaced by fine vermicelli cooked in the consommé.

Consommé Nana

POT-AU-FEU WITH BREAD AND CHEESE

This is pot-au-feu with the following garnish:

Cut some slices from a long French loaf and dry them in the oven. Put them into a tureen in layers alternately with grated Gruyère and Parmesan cheese.

Place poached eggs on top, allowing 1 for each person, and pour the hot broth on top. If liked, 2 – 3 tablespoons tomato purée can be added to the pot-au-feu.

Note If more than 4 eggs are required, it is better to serve them separately.

Consommé ou potage à la queue de boeuf (à ma façon)

OXTAIL SOUP (MY OWN RECIPE)

2 lb. oxtail, 1¼ lb. boned shin of veal, 1 boned calf's foot, 4 oz. onion, 4 oz. carrots, ¼ bottle dry Frontignan (Muscatel), water, ⅜ pint (U.S. 1 scant cup) tomato purée, 1 bouquet composed of parsley, 1 piece celery, 1 clove garlic and 1 bay leaf, few crushed peppercorns, 1 teaspoon salt

Cut the oxtail into 8 pieces, and the veal into pieces the size of a walnut. Blanch the calf's foot for a few minutes.

Put all the meat and crushed bones into a large pan with the chopped onion and carrot, wine and an equal quantity of water. Cover and put over low heat until the liquid has reduced to three-quarters of its volume. Add 1 pint (U.S. 2½ cups) water and continue cooking until the liquid is almost entirely reduced. Add 6 pints (U.S. 7½ pints) warm water, tomato purée, bouquet, salt and peppercorns. Bring to boiling point and simmer for 4 hours.

Remove the pieces of oxtail and place them in the soup tureen. Add the calf's foot cut into small cubes, and keep warm. Remove the crushed bones and the bouquet, rub the remaining veal and vegetables through a fine sieve, keeping it for a few moments on the corner of the stove to give the fat time to rise to the top. Skim off the fat, bring to boiling point again and pour into the tureen with the beef and the calf's foot. If liked a few tablespoons of barley cooked in broth can be added.

Consommé printanier
CHICKEN CONSOMMÉ WITH CARROTS AND TURNIPS

———————— Chicken consommé
Garnish New carrots and turnips cut into little strips about ½ inch long and cooked in the consommé, fresh peas, and French beans diced small and cooked in boiling salted water, braised lettuce cut into small squares, chervil leaves

Put all these into the tureen and pour the boiling consommé over them.

Note As a variation, *consommé printanier* may contain, as a supplementary garnish: chicken quenelles; various royales (see pages 69 – 70); poached eggs, etc., in which case the chosen garnish should be mentioned and the soup should be called *printanier aux quenelles* or *printanier à la royale*.

Formerly, when the *printanier* was garnished with chicken quenelles, it was called *printanier impératrice*.

The consommé may also be thickened with egg yolks and cream, or with a chicken velouté with cream, using equal parts of consommé and velouté sauce (see page 22), or with a purée of haricot beans or dried peas, etc.

Consommé aux quenelles de volaille et moelle
CONSOMMÉ WITH CHICKEN QUENELLES AND BEEF MARROW

———————— Petite marmite
Garnish Chicken quenelles (see page 56) poached in broth, diced beef marrow, very fresh and poached in broth and a few small chervil leaves

Note As a variation the quenelles may be replaced by a royale of chicken purée (see page 70) poached in dariole moulds and cut into rounds.

Asparagus tips or peas cooked in boiling salted water may be added to the garnish.

Consommé Renaissance

CONSOMMÉ WITH FRESH VEGETABLES AND COCK'S KIDNEYS

———————— *Garnish for 3½ pints (U.S. 4½ pints) consommé:* 4 oz. carrots, 4 oz. turnips cut small and cooked in consommé, 18 cock's kidneys poached in consommé and peeled,* 2 sieved yolks of hard-boiled eggs, few chervil leaves

* The cock's kidneys may be replaced by chicken quenelles (see page 56) in the shape of the cock's kidneys.

Put all these into a tureen and pour the boiling consommé over them.

Consommé favori de Sarah Bernhardt

SARAH BERNHARDT'S FAVOURITE CONSOMMÉ

———————— 2 pints (U.S. 5 cups) chicken consommé
Garnish 3—4 slices fat bacon, 1 small carrot, 1 medium onion, 10 oz. shin of veal, 2 tablespoons melted butter, 1 pint (U.S. 2½ cups) consommé, bouquet composed of parsley, ½ bay leaf and 1 sprig thyme, velouté sauce (see page 22) to which a little tomato purée has been added

Put the bacon in boiling water for 10 minutes, then drain and when cool put it into a saucepan. Add the carrot and onion, thinly sliced, the veal cut into small pieces and the butter. Add ½ pint (U.S. 1¼ cups) consommé. Put over low heat and cook until it is reduced by two-thirds.

Add the other ½ pint consommé and the bouquet. Cover and continue cooking over moderate heat.

The meat must be thoroughly cooked so that it can be puréed.

Remove the bouquet, then rub all the ingredients through a fine sieve: mix the resulting purée with an equal quantity of tomato velouté sauce.

In addition, serve some vermicelli cooked in consommé, then drained and finished with butter and grated Parmesan cheese.

Consommé Solange

CONSOMMÉ WITH PEARL BARLEY AND CHICKEN MEAT

———————— Petite marmite
Garnish Pearl barley cooked in the consommé, braised lettuce cut into small squares, julienne of breast of chicken cooked in the marmite

Put all together in the tureen and pour over the boiling consommé.

Consommé à la Talleyrand
CONSOMMÉ WITH QUENELLES OF PHEASANT

——————— Petite marmite to which a semi-cooked pheasant has been added
Garnish Cream quenelles of pheasant (see page 56) moulded in
a dessertspoon (2 quenelles per person), fine julienne of truffle cooked
in Frontignan wine (Muscatel)

Put the quenelles and the truffle in the soup tureen and pour over the
boiling consommé. With the consommé serve Parmesan cheese straws.

Consommé Wladimir
CHICKEN CONSOMMÉ WITH CHEESE QUENELLES

——————— Chicken consommé
Cheese quenelles: 4½ oz. fresh white cheese, pinch salt, 4½ oz. softened
butter, 2 eggs, 4½ oz. flour, 2 tablespoons fresh cream, grated Parmesan
cheese, little butter

Mash the cheese in a basin, add salt, butter, egg yolks, flour and cream.
Thoroughly mix together. Add stiffly beaten egg whites.

Mould the quenelles with a dessertspoon and poach them lightly
without letting the water boil. Drain and arrange in a dish. Sprinkle
with grated cheese and moisten with a little melted butter. Put into the
oven for a few minutes.

Note The cheese quenelles can be replaced by cream of chicken
quenelles (see page 56).

LES POTAGES LIÉS
THICK SOUPS

Eggs, cream and butter provide the best thickening for soups.

The veloutés may have a base of flour, barley, ground rice, oatmeal,
cornflour (cornstarch) or panadas (see pages 54–55), but they can also
be thickened with eggs, butter and cream, or simply with cream.

Purées of dried vegetables, such as peas, lentils, white haricot beans,
can be finished with 1½ oz. butter and 6 tablespoons cream to every
1¾ pints (U.S. 4¼ cups) soup.

Soup made with dried vegetables is very economical but the nutritive
value is improved with the addition of fresh vegetables, e.g. lettuce,
leek, carrot or celery. Fresh cream can be added if liked.

PURÉES, CRÈMES ET VELOUTÉS
PURÉES, CREAMS AND WHITE SOUPS

Bisque ou coulis d'écrevisses

CRAYFISH SOUP

20–25 medium-sized craynsh, butter, mirepoix of 1½ oz. carrot, 1½ oz. onion, ¼ bay leaf, sprig thyme and parsley, seasoning, 2 tablespoons brandy, ⅜ pint (U.S. approx. 1 cup) white wine, 3 pints (U.S. 7½ cups) white stock, 4 oz. ground rice, pinch cayenne pepper

Wash each crayfish and remove the intestine by gently twisting the shell of the middle of the tail.

Melt 2 tablespoons butter in a pan, add the diced vegetables and herbs and cook till the vegetables are brown. Add the crayfish, a little salt and freshly ground pepper, and sauté for a few minutes. Add brandy and white wine, and cook till reduced a little. Add ½ pint (U.S. 1¼ cups) white stock and cook for 10 minutes.

Take out the crayfish, remove the fish from the shells and retain the tails and 6–8 heads.

Pound the remainder with 2 oz. butter.

Add remaining white stock to the contents of the pan, bring to boiling point. Add the rice, mixed smoothly with a little cold stock, and continue the cooking for 15 minutes. Add the pounded shells and a pinch of cayenne pepper and boil for a further 1 minute. Put through a fine sieve and keep hot in a bain-marie until required.

Note A little butter put on top of the soup will prevent a skin forming. Just before serving add 3½–4 oz. fresh butter.

Garnish Divide the crayfish tails and heads in half lengthwise and fill with a little fish stuffing poached in boiling salted water.

Crayfish cream soup Finish with fresh cream instead of butter, and garnish with small quenelles instead of the heads and tails of the crayfish.

Crayfish velouté Just before serving gradually add a mixture of 2 egg yolks and ⅜ pint (U.S. approx. 1 cup) boiling cream.

Bisque de crabes

CRAB SOUP

Proceed as for crayfish soup, replacing the crayfish with small crabs which should be put into fresh water for one or two hours, before being cooked.

Bisque de crevettes roses

SHRIMP SOUP

Use 1½ lb. live shrimps and proceed in the same way as for crayfish soup

Note To thicken the soup, the cream may be replaced by 10 oz. rice cooked in boiling white stock for 20 minutes.

Bisque de homard

LOBSTER SOUP

Replace the shrimps by 1½ lb. small fresh lobsters. Cut them up, cook them in a mirepoix and proceed as for shrimp soup.

Garnish A few tablespoons of lobster meat kept back from the soup and cut into dice

Bisque de langoustines

DUBLIN BAY PRAWN SOUP

This is prepared exactly the same as the shrimp soup.

Purée de céleri-rave

CELERIAC PURÉE

1 lb. celeriac, 3 tablespoons butter, 2 pints (U.S. 5 cups) white stock or water, 8 oz. potatoes, milk, fresh cream (optional)

Cut the celeriac into thin slices and cook for a few minutes in boiling salted water. Drain well and put into a pan with 1 good tablespoon butter. Cover and cook over low heat for about 10 minutes. Add stock or water, and a little salt if water is used. Add potatoes, sliced thinly. Cover and cook slowly till the vegetable is soft.

Rub through a sieve and return the purée to the pan. Add sufficient milk to bring to the desired consistency and bring to boiling point. Finish with 2 tablespoons of butter or fresh cream.

Garnish with fried croûtons and, if liked, a little chopped chervil.

Note Cauliflower, turnip or Jerusalem artichoke purée is made in the same way.

Purée Crécy

CARROT PURÉE

————— 4 tablespoons butter, 1 lb. carrots, 1 onion, pinch salt, pinch sugar, 2 pints (U.S. 5 cups) white stock, 4½ oz. rice

Melt 2 tablespoons butter in a pan, add thinly sliced carrots and onion. Add the salt and sugar and sauté for a few minutes. Add stock and well washed rice, cover and simmer till the carrots and rice are soft. Pass through a sieve and return the purée to the pan. Add sufficient extra stock to bring to the right consistency, then reheat. Finish with 2 tablespoons butter.

Garnish with fried croûtons.

Cream of carrot soup Add ⅜ pint (U.S. approx. 1 cup) boiling cream just before serving.

Velours soup This consists of ⅝ cream of carrot soup and ⅜ tapioca consommé.

Purée de gibier

GAME PURÉE

————— 2 partridges or 1 hen pheasant, 8 oz. lentils which should be almost cooked, 2 pints (U.S. 5 cups) stock or water, bouquet of 1 sprig parsley, 1 sprig thyme and ½ bay leaf, 1 medium-sized onion stuck with 1 clove, salt and pepper, 3—4 oz. butter

Half roast the game, then put into a pan with the lentils, stock, bouquet and onion. Cover and simmer gently.

Take out the game and remove the bones, then pound the flesh in a mortar with the lentils.

Put the purée back into the pan with the soup and rub through a sieve. Return to the pan, add seasoning and extra stock if required to give the right consistency. Reheat and before serving add the butter.

Garnish if liked with fried croûtons, or with some rice or pearl barley cooked in consommé.

Cream of game soup Add ⅜ pint (U.S. approx. 1 cup) boiling cream before serving and this can be garnished with small quenelles of game (see page 56) or with a julienne of mushrooms, truffles and partridge or pheasant.

Purée parmentier

POTATO PURÉE

——————— 3 oz. butter, 2 leeks (white part only), 1¼ lb. potatoes, 2½ pints (U.S. 3 pints) stock or water, seasoning, milk, ¼ pint (U.S. ⅝ cup) cream

Melt 1 oz. butter in a pan, add the leeks sliced thinly and sauté for a few minutes without browning. Add the potatoes cut into quarters and the stock and cook until the potatoes are soft, then mash them and rub all through a sieve. Return to the pan and add sufficient milk or stock to give the right consistency. Season and reheat and add the cream and remaining butter just before serving.

Garnish with fried croûtons or with Italian pasta or vermicelli cooked separately.

The addition of a little tomato purée makes an excellent soup.

Purée de pois frais

FRESH PEA PURÉE

This can be made in two ways:

——————— 2 lb. garden peas, white stock

Cook the peas quickly in boiling salted water, strain and rub the peas through a fine sieve. Return the purée to the pan and add some white stock.

In this way the purée has a good colour.

——————— 2 lb. garden peas, 3 oz. butter, 1 small lettuce, pinch sugar, 2 spring onions, ½ teaspoon salt, ½ pint (U.S. 1¼ cups) water

Put all the ingredients together and cook till the peas are tender. Rub through a fine sieve. Return the purée to the pan, add some white stock and bring to boiling point.

In this way, the purée is less bright in colour but has a more delicate flavour.

In both cases add 2–3 oz. butter before serving and garnish with some cooked peas and a little chopped chervil or mint.

Cream of pea soup Add about ½ pint (U.S. 1¼ cups) fresh cream at the last moment.

Purée de potiron à la bourgeoise
PUMPKIN PURÉE WITH VERMICELLI

—————— 1 lb. pumpkin, 1 pint (U.S. 2½ cups) water, ¼ teaspoon salt, 1 teaspoon
sugar, milk, 3 oz. vermicelli, 1½ oz. butter or 6 tablespoons cream

Peel and dice the pumpkin and cook in the water with salt and sugar.
Rub through a fine sieve. Return to the pan and add sufficient boiling
milk to give the right consistency.

Add the vermicelli or, if preferred, an equal quantity of Italian pasta.
Continue cooking until the vermicelli is done. Finally add butter or
cream.

Purée de potiron à la ménagère
PUMPKIN PURÉE WITH HARICOT BEANS

Add to the previous recipe a third of the quantity of purée of white
haricot beans.

At home the housewife makes this soup when beans are left over from
the previous day's dinner; this is a way of using them up and of making
an excellent soup.

Purée de potiron au riz
PUMPKIN PURÉE WITH RICE

Prepare a pumpkin purée according to the first recipe above, replacing
the vermicelli with rice cooked in broth.

An excellent soup can also be made by adding an equal quantity of
potato purée to the pumpkin.

Purée portugaise
TOMATO PURÉE WITH HERBS

—————— 1 oz. butter, 2 oz. streaky bacon, 1 medium-sized onion, 1 medium-
sized carrot, ½ bay leaf, 1 sprig thyme, 1 sprig parsley, 1½ lb. tomatoes,
1 clove garlic, 8 oz. rice, 3 pints (U.S. 7½ cups) water

Heat the butter, add the diced bacon, chopped onion and carrot and brown lightly. Add herbs, peeled and seeded tomatoes and garlic. Simmer until the tomatoes are tender, then rub all through a fine sieve. Return the purée to the pan, add the rice and water and cook over low heat for 20 – 25 minutes.

Purée ou coulis de poulet à la reine

CHICKEN PURÉE

1 plump chicken (about 2½ lb.), 2½ pints (U.S. 5⅞ cups) white stock, 8 oz. cooked rice, 3 egg yolks, ⅜ pint (U.S. approx. 1 cup) cream, 3 – 4 oz. fresh butter

Prepare the chicken and cook it in the stock. When ready, remove from the pan, bone it and reserve some of the white meat for garnish.

Pound up the rest of the chicken, add the rice and some of the stock in which the chicken was cooked. Rub through a sieve and put the purée into a pan with the rest of the stock. Heat to boiling point.

Just before serving, thicken with the egg yolks and cream and finally add the butter.

Garnish with the pieces of chicken retained – cut into dice.

Note The rice can be replaced by rice flour or cream of rice. Use 3 tablespoons, mixed smoothly with a little stock or water, for each 1½ pints (U.S. 3¾ cups) liquid.

Potage Bagration

CHICKEN PURÉE WITH VEAL

Cook a chicken as for chicken purée adding to it 1 lb. lean veal cut into pieces. Add 2 egg yolks mixed with 3 tablespoons freshly grated Parmesan cheese.

Garnish Small macaroni sticks ¾ inch long, cooked in ordinary broth

Potage Saint-Germain

PEA SOUP

This is none other than purée of fresh peas and is prepared as on page 85.

LES CRÈMES
CREAM SOUPS

(Quantities for 4 – 5 persons)

Ground rice, barley and oatmeal, cooked with milk and seasonings, can be used in the preparation of cream soups.

Crème de riz

CREAM OF RICE

———— 1¾ pints (U.S. 4¼ cups) milk, 1 small onion stuck with 2 cloves, few peppercorns, pinch salt, bouquet of 2 sprigs parsley, 1 sprig thyme and ½ bay leaf, 4 tablespoons ground rice, cold milk

Put the milk into a pan with the flavourings and seasonings and bring slowly to boiling point. Add the rice mixed smoothly with a little cold milk and stir well. Simmer for 20 minutes over very low heat, then strain through a fine strainer.

This will form the basis of some of the soups to follow, but with the addition of 6 tablespoons fresh cream it makes an excellent soup as it is.

Cream of barley and cream of oatmeal are prepared in the same way.

Pour obtenir une crème d'asperges

TO MAKE CREAM OF ASPARAGUS

———— 1 lb. small green asparagus, 1 tablespoon butter, 1¾ pints (U.S. 4¼ cups) cream of rice (as above), 6 tablespoons fresh cream

Prepare the asparagus and cook in boiling salted water. Put aside about a quarter of the heads for garnish. Put the rest into a pan with the butter,

toss for a few seconds, then add the cream of rice. Strain through a fine
strainer and when ready to serve reheat with the cream but do not boil.
   Garnish with the asparagus tips kept in reserve.

Pour obtenir une crème de céleri
TO MAKE CREAM OF CELERY

> 12 oz. celeriac, 2 tablespoons butter, salt, freshly ground pepper,
> pinch sugar, 1¾ pints (U.S. 4¼ cups) cream of rice (see page 88)

Cook the celeriac in boiling salted water, drain and put into a pan with
the butter. Cover and sauté for 8—10 minutes, add seasoning. Rub
through a fine sieve and add this purée to the cream of rice.
   Garnish with fried croûtons and a few tablespoons cooked rice.

Crème de topinambours
CREAM OF JERUSALEM ARTICHOKE

This is prepared exactly as cream of celery.

Pour obtenir une crème de champignons
TO MAKE CREAM OF MUSHROOMS

> 8 oz. cultivated mushrooms, as fresh and as white as possible, 1¾ pints
> (U.S. 4¼ cups) cream of rice (see page 88), ¾ pint (U.S. scant 2 cups)
> fresh cream

Wash the mushrooms and rub quickly through a wire sieve. Add at
once to the cream of rice.
   Just before serving add the cream.
   Garnish Croûtons fried in butter, julienne of mushrooms stewed
in butter, julienne of truffles, Italian pasta poached in white consommé,
and so on

Pour obtenir une crème d'écrevisses
TO MAKE CREAM OF CRAYFISH

See crayfish soup (page 82).

Pour obtenir une crème au curry
TO MAKE CREAM OF CURRY

────────── 1 small teaspoon curry powder, 1 teaspoon butter, ½ pint (U.S.
1¼ cups) fresh cream, little white stock, 1¾ pints (U.S. 4¼ cups)
cream of rice (see page 88)

Heat the curry powder in the butter for a few seconds. Add 3–4 tablespoons cream and a little stock. Strain into the cream of rice. Heat before
serving and finally add the rest of the cream.

Garnish Indian rice (see page 668), fine vermicelli, Italian pasta, etc.

Crème écossaise
SCOTCH CREAM

Prepare as for cream of curry but replace the cream of rice with the same
amount of cream of barley.

Garnish A fine brunoise of vegetables cooked in butter and broth

Pour obtenir une crème de laitue
TO MAKE CREAM OF LETTUCE

────────── 10 oz. lettuce, 2 tablespoons butter, 1¾ pints (U.S. 4¼ cups) cream
of rice, 3–4 tablespoons fresh cream

Cook the lettuce in boiling salted water, drain and chop well. Put into
a pan with the butter and sauté for a few minutes. Add the cream of rice
and simmer for 12–15 minutes. Strain through a fine sieve. Just before
serving, reheat and add the cream.

Garnish Japanese pearls, tapioca, chicken quenelles, ordinary royale
(see page 69)

Pour obtenir une crème au paprika rose
TO MAKE CREAM OF PAPRIKA

This cream is prepared exactly the same as the curry cream (see above)

but the curry is simply replaced by powdered paprika. The garnish is also the same.

Note It is very difficult to give the exact quantity of curry and paprika because of the amount of cayenne pepper that they contain. They should not be used unless they are sweet. This particularly applies to paprika.

These two soups are excellent if they are carefully made.

Pour obtenir une crème de volaille

TO MAKE CREAM OF CHICKEN

————————— 10 oz. boiled chicken meat, 1¾ pints (U.S. 4¼ cups) cream of rice, 3—4 tablespoons fresh cream

Pound the chicken meat with a little of the cream of rice. Strain through a fine sieve and add to the rest of the cream of rice. Reheat and add the fresh cream just before serving.

Crème de volaille

CREAM OF CHICKEN

————————— Proceed as indicated for chicken purée (see page 87) and replace the thickening of egg yolks and butter by ⅜ pint (U.S. approx. 1 cup) very fresh cream for every 1¾ pints (U.S. 4¼ cups) soup

Garnish Asparagus tips, plain boiled peas, vegetable brunoise, truffle julienne, breast of chicken cut into small cubes, mushroom quenelles, etc. The name of the ingredient added to the cream should be mentioned when used. For instance:

Cream of chicken with asparagus tips

Cream of chicken with petits pois

Cream of chicken with quenelles

Japanese pearls and small Italian pasta are also excellent garnishes for chicken creams.

VELOUTÉS

(Recipes for 4–5 persons)

Note Speaking generally, veloutés require a thickening of 2–3 egg yolks and 2 oz. very fresh butter. Alternatively, one can mix the egg yolks with a few tablespoons cream or boiling milk.

> ———————— To make a velouté for 4 or 5 persons: pot-au-feu (see page 61) using chicken giblets, 1¾ lb. shin of veal, 1¾ lb. lean beef, 7 oz. butter, 4½ oz. flour, 2 egg yolks, 3–4 tablespoons cream

When the pot-au-feu is ready, heat 4 oz. butter and add flour. Cook for 5–6 minutes over very low heat, stirring with a wooden spoon so as to obtain a white roux. Mix with 2½ pints (U.S. 6¼ cups) of the prepared broth, using a small egg whisk so as to avoid lumps. Bring to the boil, then simmer for 25–30 minutes.

Strain the velouté through a conical strainer into a saucepan, and spread a little butter over the surface to avoid the formation of skin; keep warm. Just before serving the soup, add the egg yolks mixed with the cream and 3 tablespoons of the velouté. Stir and reheat until just below boiling point. Finally, add the rest of the butter and strain again through a conical strainer. Serve as hot as possible.

The garnishes for veloutés can be varied — they may be small croûtons fried in butter, rice, pearl barley, seed tapioca cooked in consommé, small diced chicken breasts, chicken quenelles, asparagus tips, truffle julienne, mushrooms, etc.

For chicken veloutés, add to the pot-au-feu a spring chicken and proceed in the same way as the above velouté.

ANOTHER METHOD OF PREPARING AN EXCELLENT VELOUTÉ WITHOUT USING BROTH

> ———————— 4 oz. butter, 1 medium-sized onion, 1¼ lb. veal, bouquet of ½ bay leaf, 1 sprig thyme, 1 sprig parsley, 2½ pints (U.S. 6¼ cups) hot water, 4 tablespoons barley flour or rice flour, 2–3 egg yolks, 3–4 tablespoons cream

Melt 2 oz. butter in a saucepan, add the thinly sliced onion and veal cut into small pieces. Sauté for 10–12 minutes over low heat. Add the bouquet and hot water and bring to boiling point.

Mix the barley flour smoothly with a little cold water and whisk into the soup. Simmer for 40−50 minutes.

Strain and keep hot in a bain-marie. Just before serving add egg yolks, cream and the remaining butter as described above.

TO MAKE AN ORDINARY VELOUTÉ

────────── 2 pints (U.S. 5 cups) white stock, 4 tablespoons barley flour, rice flour or cornflour (cornstarch), little cold water, 2− 3 egg yolks, 2 oz. butter, 3−4 tablespoons cream

Bring the stock to boiling point. Mix the barley flour smoothly with a little cold water and add to the stock, whisking all the time. Simmer for 20−25 minutes. Strain and put a little butter on top to prevent a skin forming. Keep warm in a bain-marie.

Just before serving add the egg yolks, cream and butter as described in the preceding recipes.

Serve very hot.

Velouté au curry et au paprika

CURRY AND PAPRIKA VELOUTÉ

Proceed as for cream of curry or cream of paprika (see page 90), substituting milk for broth.

At the last moment thicken with 2 egg yolks mixed with 6 tablespoons of cream.

In the curry and paprika veloutés, cream is indispensable and the butter is omitted.

Garnish Rice or pearl barley, cooked in the broth, are recommended.

Velouté de tomates

TOMATO VELOUTÉ

Mix together equal parts of cream of rice velouté (see page 88) and tomato purée. At the last moment add 2½ oz. fresh butter or few tablespoons fresh cream.

Egg yolks are not used for tomato velouté.

Garnish Rice, pearl barley, seed tapioca, Italian pasta, vermicelli all go well with tomato velouté.

Velouté de poisson au curry

CURRY-FLAVOURED FISH VELOUTÉ

——————— 4—5 whiting (about 1 lb.), 1½ oz. butter, 1 medium-sized onion, 2 teaspoons curry powder, bouquet of 1 sprig parsley, 1 bay leaf, 1 sprig thyme, 1 teaspoon salt, freshly ground pepper, pinch saffron, 1¾ pints (U.S. 4¼ cups) hot water, 1¼ pints (U.S. approx. 3¼ cups) cream of rice velouté (see page 88)

Prepare the fish and cut into small pieces.

Melt the butter, add the finely chopped onion and sauté for a few minutes without browning. Add the curry powder, fish, bouquet and seasonings. Add the hot water. Bring to boiling point and boil for 10 minutes. Add the cream of rice velouté and bring to boiling point again. Strain through a hair sieve.

Before serving reheat without boiling and add a little fresh butter.

Garnish Cooked rice or vermicelli or small slices of French bread dried in the oven

Soupe de poisson au court-bouillon

FISH SOUP MADE WITH COURT-BOUILLON

——————— 1 whiting (about 8 oz.), 1 onion, 1 carrot, 1 bay leaf, 1 sprig parsley, 1 sprig thyme, freshly ground pepper, ½ teaspoon salt, 3 tablespoons butter, 2¼ pints (U.S. 5⅝ cups) hot water, 3 tablespoons rice flour, little cold water, 2 egg yolks

Prepare the fish, cut into pieces and put it into a pan with the finely sliced onion and carrot, herbs and seasoning. Add 1 tablespoon butter and the hot water. Boil briskly for 8—10 minutes.

Mix the rice flour smoothly with a little cold water. Add to the soup, stirring well and continue to cook for another 20 minutes. Strain through a fine sieve.

Finish by thickening with the egg yolks mixed with a little of the soup and finally add the remaining butter.

Shrimps, poached oysters or rice could be used for garnish.

Sole, because of its strong flavour, should not be used in court-bouillon meant for soup.

POTAGES LIÉS SPÉCIAUX
SPECIAL THICK SOUPS

Potées, soupes et potages aux legumes carbures
VEGETABLE SOUPS

Soupe à l'albigeoise
ALBIGEOISE SOUP

Recipe for about 10 persons: For this soup follow the recipe for petite marmite (see page 62) but instead of the meats given in that recipe use silverside of beef (U.S. bottom round), shin of veal, 1 slice and 1 knuckle smoked ham, country sausage and preserved goose (*confit d'oie*)

Add a garnish of carrots, turnips, leeks and cabbage, all sliced, and young dried broad or kidney beans in double the quantity of the other vegetables. Let them cook gently. Pour the broth and the vegetables into the tureen on slices of household bread and thin slices of preserved goose.

Note Seasoning should be added carefully, bearing in mind the saltiness of the ham.

Soupe à l'auvergnate
AUVERGNAT SOUP

Prepare a *potée* (pork and vegetable soup) with salted boar's head in cold water. Garnish with carrots, turnips, leeks and potatoes, all sliced, and the heart of a medium-sized cabbage. Add 9 tablespoons of well picked-over lentils and simmer gently.

Pour the broth and the vegetables into the soup tureen on thin slices of brown bread and a little of the boar's head cut into large dice.

Note These soups or *potées* differ very little from one district to another and are all based on the same principle. They are, in fact, only a kind of rustic pot-au-feu.

In certain parts of the country haricot beans are added, in others broad beans, lentils or peas.

Soupe à la bonne femme

LEEK SOUP

——————— You will need for 5–6 persons: 3–4 leeks (white part only), 4½ oz. butter, 3 pints (U.S. 7½ cups) hot water, 1 lb. potatoes, 1 teaspoon salt, thin slices French bread

Thinly slice the leeks and sauté in 2 oz. butter until they begin to soften. Add the water, sliced potatoes and salt. Cook over a moderate heat.

Just before serving, add the rest of the butter and pour into a tureen in which has been put some thin slices of French bread dried in the oven.

Soupe dauphinoise

TURNIP AND PUMPKIN SOUP

——————— You will need for 5–6 persons: 5 oz. turnips, 5 oz. pumpkin, 5 oz. potatoes, 2 heaped tablespoons butter, 1¾ pints (U.S. 4¼ cups) water, 1 pint (U.S. 2½ cups) boiling milk, 1 teaspoon salt, 2½ oz. vermicelli, pinch chervil

Slice the vegetables and sauté for a few minutes in the butter. Add the water, boiling milk and salt, cover and cook over moderate heat.

About 20 minutes before the end of the cooking add the vermicelli.

Just before serving add the chervil.

Garbure à la béarnaise

VEGETABLE AND PRESERVED GOOSE SOUP

Prepare a *potée* with bacon fat, preserved goose, turnips, potatoes, half heart white-hearted cabbage and white haricot beans, either fresh or dried. Add water and a little salt and simmer gently for 2½–3 hours.

To serve Arrange the vegetables in a fireproof dish, alternating them with little pieces of fat and preserved goose.

Cover with thin slices of long French bread, sprinkle with grated cheese and brown.

Sprinkle with few tablespoons of the broth and leave for 15 minutes.

Pour the broth of the *potée* into the tureen and serve the vegetables at the same time.

Garbure à l'oignon

ONION SOUP

8 oz. onions, 2 oz. butter, 2 tablespoons flour, 3½ pints (U.S. approx. 8¾ cups) white stock, little béchamel sauce (see page 23), few slices French bread dried in the oven, grated cheese, 2—3 tablespoons melted butter

Cut the onion into thin slices and brown lightly in the butter. Add the flour and continue cooking until it is a light brown colour. Add the stock and cook for 10—12 minutes.

Strain and keep hot.

Remove the onion left in the pan and mix it with a little béchamel sauce. Rub through a sieve and spread the purée on the slices of bread. Sprinkle them with cheese, put into a dish and brown.

Pour a little of the broth and some melted butter on top and leave them for a few minutes before serving.

The soup is served in the tureen and the bread separately.

Note In restaurants, onion soup is sometimes gratinated or browned in the tureen, in which case the slices of bread are spread over the surface either with or without the strained onion, according to the taste of the customer. The surface is sprinkled with grated cheese and melted butter and then quickly browned.

Soupe paysanne

PEASANT SOUP

> You will need for 8—10 persons: 10 oz. carrots, 7 oz. turnips, 2 leeks (white part only), 1 stick celery, 3½ oz. butter, 3½ pints (U.S. 8¾ cups) white stock, pea soup (see page 88)

Slice all the vegetables finely and sauté for a few minutes in the butter. Add the stock, cover and leave to simmer.

Just before serving, add one-third its volume of pea soup.

Serve with slices of French bread dried in the oven.

Potage Thourin

THOURIN SOUP

This is onion soup (see page 97) made entirely with milk and thickened, at the last moment, with 2—3 egg yolks mixed with 6 tablespoons very fresh cream and a little butter.

Serve with grated cheese and small slices of long French bread dried in the oven.

Note This soup can be served with the onion, or strained.

Soupe provençale, dite 'aigo bouido' (soupe à l'eau bouillie)

PROVENÇAL SOUP, CALLED 'BOILED WATER SOUP'

> 3½ pints (U.S. 8¾ cups) water, ⅜ pint (U.S. approx. 1 cup) olive oil, 1 teaspoon salt, pinch pepper, 8 cloves garlic, 1 bay leaf, 1 sprig each thyme, sage, parsley

Boil all the ingredients together, then strain the soup through a sieve and pour on to slices of bread placed in the tureen and sprinkle with chopped parsley.

Note Sometimes poached eggs on slices of bread are added to this soup.

SÉRIE DES POTAGES ET SOUPES ÉTRANGÈRES
FOREIGN SOUPS

Potage coky-lecky
COCKY LEEKIE SOUP

1 plump chicken, 3½ pints (U.S. approx. 8¾ cups) clear veal stock or broth, 4—5 leeks (white part only), 1 oz. butter, 1 pint (U.S. 2½ cups) chicken stock

Cook the chicken in the veal stock.

Cut the leeks into julienne and sauté for a few minutes in the butter. Add the chicken stock and continue the cooking.

To serve Strain the chicken broth, add the chicken meat, chopped small, and the leek julienne.

Note One can serve a prune compote at the same time, but this is optional.

This is a very popular soup in England where it is served at shooting luncheons.

Potage minestra (soupe italienne)
MINESTRONE SOUP (ITALIAN SOUP)

2 oz. streaky bacon, 1½ oz. grated salt pork fat, 2 pints (U.S. 5 cups) water, 1 teaspoon salt, 1 medium-sized carrot, 1 turnip, 1 stick celery, 2 medium-sized potatoes, 3—4 oz. piece cabbage, 2—3 tomatoes, 8 oz. garden peas, 4 oz. green beans (haricot verts), 3½ oz. rice or spaghetti, 1 clove garlic, 1 pinch basil, 1 pinch chopped chervil

Chop the bacon and pork fat and heat for a few minutes in a large saucepan. Add the water and salt and bring to boiling point. Add the carrot, turnip, celery and potatoes, all sliced, the cabbage cut into strips and tomatoes peeled and seeded.

Cover and simmer for about 30 minutes. Add peas, beans, broken into small pieces, and rice and continue the cooking over low heat for 35—40 minutes.

Finally, add the crushed garlic, basil and chervil.

Note Any vegetables in season may be used for minestrone.

Potage mock-turtle, ou 'fausse tortue' (cuisine anglaise)
MOCK TURTLE SOUP (ENGLISH RECIPE)

This is Windsor soup (see page 106) made with calf's head instead of calf's feet.

Potage mulligatawny (cuisine anglaise)
MULLIGATAWNY SOUP (ENGLISH RECIPE)

1 medium-sized chicken, 2 oz. butter, 1 large onion, 1 teaspoon curry powder, 3½ pints (U.S. 8¾ cups) stock, 1 sprig parsley, 1 stick celery, 1 tablespoon rice flour, 6 tablespoons fresh cream

Cut the chicken into small joints. Heat the butter in a large pan, add the finely chopped onion and brown lightly, add the chicken and curry powder and sauté all for 8–10 minutes. Add the stock, parsley and chopped celery and bring to boiling point. Mix the rice flour smoothly with a little cold stock and stir into soup. Cover and cook over low heat for 35–40 minutes. Remove the pieces of chicken from the saucepan, trim them and keep them warm in a little of the broth. Strain the soup through a fine sieve, replace the resulting purée in the saucepan, bring quickly to the boil and finally add the cream.

Place the pieces of chicken in the tureen and pour the boiling soup over them.

Serve with Patna rice cooked Indian fashion (see page 668).

A young rabbit can be used for this soup instead of chicken.

Potage stschy (potage russe)
SHTCHY SOUP (RUSSIAN SOUP)

This Russian soup is simply a sauerkraut soup, which is much to be recommended and which housewives might well adopt.

1 tablespoon butter, 4 tablespoons finely chopped onion, 1 tablespoon flour, 7 oz. sauerkraut, 3½ pints (U.S. 8¾ cups) white stock, 12 oz. brisket or flank of beef, 1 sprig parsley, ½ bay leaf, pinch freshly ground pepper

Heat the butter and lightly brown the onion. Add the flour and cook for 1 minute. Add the sauerkraut, washed in warm water, well drained and chopped, and the stock. Blanch the beef for 5–6 minutes then cool before adding to the other ingredients. Add herbs and pepper. Cover and simmer for 2½–3 hours.

Just before serving, remove the meat from the saucepan, cut it into large dice and put into the tureen. Remove the grease from the soup and pour it over the meat. Remove the parsley and the bay leaf.

Serve with a little sour cream.

Note If sauerkraut is not available, it may be replaced by a medium-sized cabbage heart boiled for 5–6 minutes and allowed to cool.

Potage à la tortue

TURTLE SOUP

Turtle soup is seldom appreciated in France and therefore rarely figures on the menu.

In England, where turtle soup is often served, an excellent one can be bought in cans.

It is also available in America.

PURÉES DE LÉGUMES SECS

SOUPS MADE WITH DRIED VEGETABLES

Purée de lentilles

LENTIL SOUP

1 lb. lentils, 3½ pints (U.S. 8¾ cups) cold water, 2 oz. streaky bacon, 1 medium-sized carrot, 1 medium-sized onion, few sprigs parsley, ¼ bay leaf, 1 teaspoon salt, 2½ oz. fresh butter

Wash the lentils, add the water and bring slowly to boiling point. Add the mirepoix, made by browning the diced bacon, carrot and onion in a little butter, parsley, bay leaf and salt.

Cover the pan and simmer until the lentils are cooked. Strain the soup, pound the lentils and rub through a sieve. Return the resultant purée to a pan and add sufficient of the liquor to give the required consistency. Finally, add the butter.

Garnish Croûtons fried in butter

The garnish may be varied by adding a few tablespoons of rice, Italian pasta, vermicelli or vegetable brunoise. Whichever garnish is used, it should be cooked separately in brown stock.

Purée de haricots blancs

WHITE HARICOT BEAN SOUP

1 lb. white haricot beans, 3½ pints (U.S. 8¾ cups) warm water, 1 medium-sized carrot, cut into quarters, 1 medium-sized onion stuck with 2 cloves garlic, 1 sprig parsley, ½ bay leaf, 1 teaspoon salt, 3½ oz. butter or ¼ pint (U.S. ⅝ cup) cream

Soak the beans for some hours (or overnight) in tepid water. Drain and put into a pan with the warm water. Bring slowly to boiling point, add the vegetables and herbs, cover and leave to simmer.

Half-way through the cooking add the salt.

When the beans are tender, drain and retain the broth.

Pound the beans in a mortar, add the resultant purée to the broth, then rub all through a fine sieve. Add a little extra stock if necessary to give the required consistency.

Just before serving, add the butter or cream.

White haricot bean soup with the addition of one-third its quantity of tomato purée makes an exquisite soup.

Garnish Italian pasta or vermicelli, both cooked in stock

Purée de pois cassés

SPLIT PEA SOUP

1 lb. split peas, 2¼ pints (U.S. 5⅝ cups) water, 1 teaspoon salt, small mirepoix as for the lentil soup (see page 101), 2 leeks (green part only), 3—4 tablespoons fresh butter

Wash the peas and put into a pan with the water, salt, mirepoix and shredded leeks. Cover and cook gently until the peas are done. Pass all through a sieve and return the purée to the pan. Add sufficient boiling stock to give the required consistency.

Just before serving add the butter.

Garnish Small croûtons cut from the inside of a loaf and fried in butter, rice, tapioca, Italian pasta or vermicelli cooked in broth

The addition of one-third tomato purée makes an excellent soup.

MISCELLANEOUS SOUPS

Potage ambassadeur

AMBASSADOR SOUP

Croûte-au-pot to which is added one-third quantity of pea soup

Potage Derby

OXTAIL AND TOMATO SOUP

—————— You will need for 5—6 persons: 1¼ lb. braised oxtail, 3½ oz. rice cooked in broth, 3½ pints (U.S. 8¾ cups) tomato soup with little butter (see page 93)

Remove the meat from the oxtail and cut it into small pieces. Remove the fat from the braise and put it through a fine strainer. Add it to the meat.

Put the meat and rice into a tureen and pour the boiling tomato soup over.

Potage Faubonne

WHITE HARICOT BEAN SOUP WITH VEGETABLES

To 1¾ pints (U.S. 4¼ cups) white haricot bean soup, add 4 tablespoons julienne of vegetables cooked in consommé.

Potage fémina

CHICKEN SOUP THICKENED WITH EGG AND CREAM

Prepare 1¾ pints (U.S. 4¼ cups) chicken purée (see page 87) thickened with 3 egg yolks and 6 tablespoons cream.

Just before serving, add to the purée a spring garnish, composed of fresh vegetables cooked in consommé.

Potage Germiny

CHICKEN CONSOMMÉ WITH SORREL

7 oz. fresh sorrel leaves, 1 oz. butter, 1¾ pints (U.S. 4¼ cups) chicken consomme, 6 egg yolks, ¼ pint (U.S. ½ cup) fresh cream, 2½ oz. fresh butter

Cook the sorrel for a few minutes in the butter, then rub through a sieve and add to the chicken consommé. Just before serving, add a thickening of eggs and cream, as for custard cream. Finally add the butter. Do not let the soup boil at any time during the preparation. Serve with thin slices of French bread dried in the oven.

Potage Georgette

CHICKEN CONSOMMÉ WITH ASPARAGUS PURÉE

Exactly the same preparation as for Germiny soup, except that the sorrel is replaced by an asparagus purée.

Garnish Chicken quenelles

Invalid-soupe

INVALID SOUP

1 lb. chicken breast cooked in stock, 1¼ pints (U.S. approx. 3¼ cups) milk, 3—4 egg yolks, 6 tablespoons Frontignan wine (Muscatel)

Pound the chicken in a mortar. Add ½ pint (U.S. 1¼ cups) boiled milk and strain through a fine sieve. Put the resultant purée into a clean pan and add ¾ pint (U.S. scant 2 cups) boiling milk. Thicken with the egg yolks and Frontignan wine.

Potage Jubilé

JUBILEE SOUP

Pea soup (see page 88) with quenelles of chicken (see page 56).

Potage champenois

ROOT VEGETABLES AND POTATO SOUP

Consommé with root vegetables (see page 76) added to equal parts of potato soup (see page 85).

Potage Lamballe

GREEN PEA SOUP WITH TAPIOCA

Add to 1¾ pints (U.S. 4¼ cups) of pea soup (see page 88) 1 pint (U.S. 2½ cups) rather thick consommé of tapioca (see page 68).

Potage Madelon

MADELON SOUP

Tomato soup (see page 93) with vermicelli

Potage Colette

COLETTE SOUP

Sweet paprika soup completed by adding a few tablespoons rice cooked in broth

Potage Delisia

DELYSIA SOUP

Lobster cream (see page 83) with tapioca

Potage Réjane

SPRING CHICKEN AND LEEK SOUP

————— 1 spring chicken, 3½ pints (U.S. 8¾ cups) stock, 2 leeks (white part only), 2 oz. butter, 7 oz. potatoes

Cook the chicken in the stock.

Cut the leeks in half and put into boiling water for 1 minute, drain, then put into a pan with the butter and sauté for a few minutes without browning.

Add the potatoes cut into thin slices and the water in which the chicken was cooked and simmer until the vegetables are cooked.

Cut the breast of chicken into fine julienne and add to the soup with a little butter.

Serve with thin slices of French bread dried in the oven.

The rest of the chicken can be used for other dishes.

Potage de santé

HEALTH SOUP

———————— Add to 2½ pints (U.S. 6¼ cups) of parmentier soup (see page 85) 2 oz. sorrel leaves melted in butter. Just before serving add 2 oz. very fresh butter and a pinch chervil.

Serve with thin slices of French bread, dried in the oven.

Potage Windsor

WINDSOR SOUP

———————— You will need for 6—8 persons: 2 calf's feet, 4½ oz. carrots, 4½ oz. onions, 2½ oz. butter, few sprigs parsley, 1 bay leaf, sprig thyme, 1 lb. shin of veal, ½ pint (U.S. 1¼ cups) white wine, 3½ pints (U.S. 8¾ cups) consommé, ¼ pint (U.S. ⅝ cup) tomato purée, 4 tablespoons rice flour, 6 tablespoons Madeira, pinch freshly ground pepper, pinch cayenne pepper

Bone the calf's feet, put into a pan and cover with cold water. Bring slowly to boiling point, then drain and plunge the feet into cold water.

Dice the carrots and onions and put into a pan with the butter, cook until lightly browned, then add herbs and the meat from the calf's feet and the veal cut into small pieces. Cover and sauté all together for a few minutes. Add the wine and boil until it has completely reduced.

Add the consommé and tomato purée. Partly cover the pan and simmer until the meat is cooked. Remove the calf's feet, cut the meat into small pieces and keep hot in a little of the broth.

Mix the rice flour smoothly with a little of the broth and stir into the soup. Simmer for a further 15—20 minutes.

Rub the soup through a sieve, then return to the pan and keep hot.

Just before serving, skim the fat from the soup and add the Madeira, freshly ground pepper and cayenne.

If liked, garnish with small quenelles.

Note This soup can be varied by adding 2 small teaspoons curry powder to the vegetables, after browning. In this case the quenelles are replaced by a few tablespoons rice cooked Indian fashion.

This soup can be made in the same way, by replacing the calf's feet by calf's head.

Hors-d'oeuvre

In a dinner, the hors-d'oeuvre are defined as a side dish and as such are a contradiction in terms. They should, if they are represented by oysters, be served only at meals which do not include soup.

Hors-d'oeuvre which include fish, either in oil or smoked, or heavily seasoned salads, cling to the palate and make the soup that follows tasteless and insipid, unless it is served extremely hot. Hence the importance of soup being served absolutely boiling.

HORS-D'OEUVRE CHAUDS
ET HORS D'OEUVRE FROIDS
HOT AND COLD HORS-D'OEUVRE

Hot hors-d'oeuvre which formerly took their place in all dinner menus before or after the soup are now almost completely abandoned.

Their disappearance is due, in principle, to the appearance on the tables of fashionable restaurants of various foreign products, such as Russian caviar.

Fresh caviar is certainly the finest and the most luxurious hors-d'oeuvre, provided that it really is fresh and of the best quality. But many people do not appreciate its true value.

Smoked salmon, when it is prepared with freshly caught salmon, deserves to be classed among the more delicate hors-d'oeuvre. Plovers' eggs, pretty little shrimps, fresh oysters, nutritious and full of flavour, are pleasant prefaces which, instead of spoiling a dinner, bring a rich note into the composition of the menu. But it is of paramount importance that these hors-d'oeuvre should be accompanied by exquisite white wines, in order to prepare the palates of the guests for the arrival of the soup.

Unfortunately, for some years now, the use of cold hors-d'oeuvre for dinner has been abused, hence the great number of heavy and heavily seasoned dishes that have found their way on to the menu, and it is against these abuses, in the name of good French cooking, that we feel it necessary to protest; because undoubtedly these overspiced dishes detract from the taste of the soup that follows them.

But, if cold hors-d'oeuvre are not always in harmony with dinners, they become indispensable for luncheons; their varied and numberless combinations, enhanced by elegant presentation, can only whet the appetite and favourably impress the guests.

Hot hors-d'oeuvre have this to be said for them, that in certain circumstances they can be served as small entrées and thus economically complete a menu that might appear to be rather slight. They are sometimes served at luncheon after cold hors-d'oeuvre.

Anchois aux poivrons

ANCHOVIES WITH SWEET RED PEPPERS

2 large red peppers, salt and pepper, 1 tablespoon vinegar, 2 tablespoons olive oil, little chopped parsley, rolled anchovy fillets, chopped hard-boiled egg, extra parsley

Grill (U.S. broil) red peppers; remove thin outer skin and divide in half, remove the seeds and cut them lengthwise into ¼-inch slices. Season with salt, pepper, vinegar, olive oil and a little chopped parsley. Arrange on an hors-d'oeuvre dish. Surround the peppers with rolled fillets of anchovies and surround these with a ring of chopped hard-boiled egg and parsley.

The peppers can be replaced with potatoes cooked and puréed, well dried and rubbed through a metal strainer so as to form small vermicelli, then sprinkled with a light vinaigrette sauce (see page 42).

Anguille au vin blanc et paprika

EELS WITH WHITE WINE AND PAPRIKA

3 lb. skinned eels, cut into slices 2 inches long, 2 thinly sliced onions, 1 *bouquet garni* composed of 1 bay leaf, sprig parsley and sprig thyme, 2 cloves garlic, ½ teaspoon salt, pinch freshly ground pepper, 1 tablespoon sweet paprika, 1¾ pints (U.S. 4¼ cups) white wine

Put all ingredients together in a sauté pan. The fish should be just covered by the wine. Cover and bring to the boil. Simmer for 20—25 minutes, according to the size of the fish.

Note If liked, ½ pint (U.S. 1¼ cups) calf's foot jelly may be added to the wine.

When the fish is ready, arrange the pieces in an earthenware dish. Strain the liquor through a fine sieve and pour over the fish.

Keep on ice and serve on small hors-d'oeuvre dishes.

Curried eels are served in exactly the same way, with the paprika replaced by curry powder.

Anguille à la provençale

EELS IN THE PROVENCE FASHION

3 lb. skinned eels, 4 tablespoons olive oil, 2 tablespoons chopped onion, pinch salt, pinch pepper, ½ pint (U.S. 1¼ cups) white wine, 6 tomatoes, 1 tablespoon chopped parsley, ½ clove garlic, 1 bay leaf, 1—2 sweet peppers (optional)

Cut up the eels as in the preceding recipe. Heat the olive oil in a saucepan and add the chopped onion. When it begins to brown lightly, add the pieces of eel, salt, pepper, white wine, peeled and finely chopped tomatoes, parsley, crushed garlic and bay leaf. Cover the saucepan and cook over a moderate heat for 20—25 minutes.

If liked, 1—2 sweet peppers, seeded and cut into julienne, may be added.

When the cooking is complete, arrange the pieces of eel in a dish with the liquor and allow to cool.

Note A pinch powdered saffron or saffron leaves may be added to the pieces of eel just before they have finished cooking.

Artichauts à la grecque
GREEK STYLE ARTICHOKES

3–4 dozen very small globe artichokes
For the marinade: 2¼ pints (U.S. 5⅜ cups) water, ½ pint (U.S. 1¼ ---,
olive oil, 1 teaspoon salt, juice 3 lemons, pinch pepper, pinch coriander
seed, bouquet of 1 sprig each parsley, fennel, thyme, celery leaf and
1 bay leaf

Put all ingredients together and bring to boiling point.

Choose for preference very small globe artichokes the size of a small
walnut; trim them and shorten the leaves and place immediately in the
boiling marinade.

Boil for about 20 minutes then turn the artichokes out on to an earthenware dish and allow to cool in the marinade.

If the artichokes are the size of eggs, it will be necessary, after trimming
them, to divide them into quarters. The main point is that the artichokes,
whether large or small, should be tender.

Small onions are prepared in the same way as artichokes. Larger ones
need to be boiled in salted water before being put into the marinade.

Celery and fennel divided into quarters, leeks cut into 2½-inch lengths,
hearts of endive or chicory are prepared in the same way, but they must
all have 8–10 minutes in boiling salted water before being put into the
marinade. Finish cooking as for the artichokes. Hearts of cabbage,
cauliflower and cos lettuce, etc., may also be cooked in the Greek way.

Barquettes diverses
VARIOUS BOAT-SHAPED PUFF PASTRY MOULDS

Barquettes are used very largely in the preparation of hors-d'oeuvre.
These oval tartlet shells can be used for a variety of fillings.

Tartlets are prepared in the same way but are usually round in shape.

Pâte pour tartelettes et barquettes
PASTRY FOR TARTLETS AND BARQUETTES

1 lb. flour, 8 oz. butter, 2 egg yolks, ¼ teaspoon salt, pinch sugar,
about ¼ pint (U.S. ⅝ cup) cold water

Sift the flour on to a pastry board. Make a well in the centre and add the butter, egg yolks, salt and sugar. Add water gradually. Mix all well together, kneading lightly. Shape into a ball, cover with a cloth and leave for at least 2 hours.

Roll out and line tartlet or oval tartlet moulds with the dough and fill them before cooking with either rice or small haricot beans, etc. Cook in the ordinary way. When done, remove the filling and let them cool. The rice, etc., is used to ensure the tartlets will keep their shape.

Mousse de foie gras pour barquettes et tartelettes
FOIE GRAS MOUSSE FOR TARTLETS AND BARQUETTES

1 lb. truffled foie gras, 6 oz. fresh butter, ½ pint (U.S. 1¼ cups) fresh cream

Rub the foie gras through a fine sieve and put the resulting purée in a basin; add the softened butter, stirring briskly with a wooden spoon to get a smooth mixture, then gradually add the half-whipped cream. Use to fill the barquettes.

Note—this is very important This mixture must never be made on ice. The same applies to all mousses having butter as their solid ingredient.

Mixtures containing jelly are not to be recommended for barquettes or tartlets.

Taking as a basis the foie gras mousse, before adding the cream one can mix with it, either half-and-half or one-third of the following: purée of chicken, partridge, pheasant, woodcock, ham, tongue, etc.

Note It is important that mousses which contain cream should not be kept more than 2—3 hours before use.

Purée de volaille
CHICKEN PURÉE

8 oz. breast of cooked chicken, 4—5 tablespoons chicken velouté or béchamel sauce (see page 23)

Pound the chicken in a mortar, add the sauce and rub through a fine sieve.

Add to the foie gras mousse as above.

Purées de jambon et de langue

HAM AND TONGUE PURÉES

As for the chicken purée, simply replacing the breast of chicken with
the same quantity of ham or tongue.

Purée de perdreaux

PARTRIDGE PURÉE

2 roasted partridge, 1 wine glass white wine, 1 shallot, pinch mixed
spice, pinch freshly ground black pepper, ½ bay leaf, ½ pint (U.S.
1¼ cups) thick demi-glace sauce strengthened with a little meat jelly
(see page 22)

Pound the meat from the partridge in a mortar. Chop up the carcases,
bones and livers and put into a saucepan with the white wine, finely
chopped shallot, spice, black pepper and bay leaf. Reduce the wine by
two-thirds. Add the sauce and boil for a few minutes, strain and mix
with the partridge meat. Rub through a fine sieve and mix the purée
with the mousse of foie gras (see page 111).

Pheasant, woodcock and Rouen duckling purées are prepared in the
same way.

Mousse de foies de volaille

CHICKEN LIVER MOUSSE

15 chicken livers, salt, pepper, 2—3 crushed sprigs parsley, 1 chopped
shallot, 2 oz. butter, 2 oz. bacon fat, 4 oz. softened butter, 6 tablespoons fresh cream

Remove the gall bladder from the livers, being very careful not to break
them. Add seasoning, parsley and shallot.

Make the butter and bacon fat very hot in a sauté pan, put in the livers
and sauté for 5—6 minutes.

Remove and pound in a mortar, then rub through a fine sieve.

Add the softened butter to the resultant purée, stirring it in well with
a wooden spoon. Then add the lightly whipped cream.

These mousses can not only be served as hors-d'oeuvre in barquettes
or tartlets, but also as cold entrées, in which case a jelly mould is lined

with jelly and then filled with one of the chosen mousses. Keep on ice until just before serving then turn out on to a dish.

Note The barquettes and tartlets, after being filled with mousse, may be decorated to taste with a very light layer of jelly.

Mousse d'oeufs

EGG MOUSSE

8 eggs, boiled for 8 minutes, 6 oz. softened butter, 6 tablespoons fresh cream

Remove the yolks from the eggs and rub through a fine sieve. Gradually add the butter, stirring well with a wooden spoon. Finally add the lightly whipped cream.

The flavour of this mousse can be varied by adding a little anchovy or smoked salmon butter, etc.

Note These 'butters' for hors-d'oeuvre are simply made by adding various flavouring to the butter.

Betteraves pour hors-d'oeuvre et salades

BEETROOTS FOR HORS-D'OEUVRE AND SALADS

Beetroots are either baked in the oven, steamed or simply boiled in water.

The beetroot is cut into julienne, sliced thinly or cut into small cubes; it is then seasoned with salt, pepper, vinegar, olive oil, chopped parsley and chervil. A tablespoon English mustard can also be added or, even better, a few tablespoons of grated horseradish.

A little chopped cooked onion may also be added.

Betterave en salade à la crème

BEETROOT IN A CREAM SALAD DRESSING

The beetroot is cut into julienne and mixed with a dressing consisting of thick cream to which is added a little made English mustard, lemon juice and seasoning of salt and pepper.

Betterave à la provençale
BEETROOT PROVENÇAL STYLE

10 oz. beetroot cooked in the oven, 2 medium-sized baked onions, 1 dessertspoon anchovy essence, 1 teaspoon made English mustard, 1 tablespoon vinegar, 3 tablespoons olive oil, pinch freshly ground pepper, salt

Cut the beetroot into cubes.

For the sauce Pound the onions and rub through a fine sieve. Add all the other ingredients. Be sure not to add too much salt as the anchovy essence is rather salty. Mix the beetroot with the sauce.

Canapés

Canapés are made with bread cut into $\frac{1}{4}$-inch slices and the crust removed. They can be fried in clarified butter, but preferably toasted and lightly buttered while they are hot. This keeps them soft.

The garnish most suitable for canapés is fresh butter with a purée added or finely minced meat, chicken, foie gras, fish, cheese, fillets of anchovies or herring, caviar, shrimps, lobster, crayfish, etc.

Canapé d'anchois
ANCHOVY CANAPÉS

Canapés lightly covered with anchovy butter and garnished with tails of shrimps cut into half lengthwise. Follow the same method for other canapés.

Caviare
CAVIAR

This is served in a special pot, bedded in ice, and either accompanied by *blinis* or thin slices of buttered rye bread. It is sometimes accompanied by chopped onion and lemon juice, but this should be discouraged, as fresh caviar, with its exquisite taste, needs no further seasoning.

Instead of fresh caviar, pressed and salted caviar can be used for the preparation of hors-d'oeuvre. This, while not possessing the taste of fresh caviar, is liked by many people.

Editor's note Blinis are small pancakes which originated in Russia.

Cèpes marinés

MARINATED CÈPES (MUSHROOMS)

Choose cèpes (mushrooms) that are very fresh and small. Put them into boiling water for a few seconds then shake them in a cloth to rid them of superfluous moisture and then sauté them in oil. Season with salt and pepper, and put them in an earthenware dish and cover with the following marinade.

———— *Quantities for* 2—2¼ *lb. cèpes:* ½ pint (U.S. 1¼ cups) good vinegar, ¼ pint (U.S. 1¼ cups) white wine, 9 tablespoons olive oil, 2 crushed cloves garlic, 1 sprig thyme, 2 bay leaves, pinch pepper, pinch coriander seed, 1 sprig fennel, 1 sprig parsley

Boil all the ingredients together for 10 minutes, then pour over the cèpes and leave for 10 days.

Serve the cèpes with the marinade.

Céleri-rave

CELERIAC

Cooked or raw, celeriac is cut into julienne and is seasoned with sauce vinaigrette (see page 42) with mustard.

Cerises en surprise

PURÉE OF PÂTÉ DE FOIE GRAS WITH CHAUDFROID SAUCE

With some good pâté de foie gras reduced to purée, shape small balls the size of a cherry; dip these into a chaudfroid sauce with paprika (see page 31) and place them on a cake tray; as soon as the sauce begins to harden, coat them with light aspic jelly (see page 116).

Keep in the refrigerator. To make bunches of cherries add stalks of natural cherries to them; but as there is usually a shortage of fresh ones, take dried cherries and dip them into warm water for 30 minutes, drain them and dry in a cloth, then roll them in slightly green butter.

With these surprise cherries arranged in little tartlets, which have been lined with a light layer of a mousse of either foie gras or chicken or game, one may get an illusion of eating real cherries.

One may also make small baskets with pastry which can be filled with these cherries interspersed with piped green butter.

ASPIC JELLY

——————————— 4 lb. knuckle of veal, 3 lb. knuckle of beef, 3 lb. chopped veal bones, 3 calf's feet, boned and blanched, 8 oz. fresh pork rind, blanched and with all fat removed, 1 oz. salt, 8 oz. carrots, 6 oz. onions, 2 oz leeks, 1 stick celery, *bouquet garni*, 2 lb. lean minced beef, 1 egg white, few drops lemon juice, chervil, tarragon

Put the veal, beef, veal bones, calf's feet artd pork rind into a large pan with 16 pints (U.S. 20¼ pints) cold water. Bring slowly to boiling point, then skim and add the salt. Simmer for 4 hours.

Remove the meat, leave the stock to cool a little, then remove all the fat.

Add the vegetables, cut into fairly large pieces and the *bouquet garni* and simmer a further 2 hours. Strain and leave to cool. Remove any more fat which may have settled on the surface and pour the clear liquid off carefully into a pan, without disturbing the sediment at the bottom of the basin.

When quite cold, test the consistency of the aspic, which should be quite firm, but if necessary add a little gelatine.

Pound the minced beef with the egg white and a sprig of chervil and tarragon. Add the lemon juice. Add to the aspic and bring slowly to boiling point, stirring all the time. Draw to the side of the stove and simmer for 30 minutes.

Cool, remove any fat from the surface, then pour slowly through a scalded jelly bag and leave to drip. If the aspic is not sufficiently clear, repeat the process.

When required for use, sherry, Madeira, hock, Champagne, etc., can be added to taste.

A SIMPLER METHOD USING GELATINE

——————————— 1 carrot, 1 turnip, 1 onion, 1 stick celery, 1 lemon, 2—3 tablespoons tarragon or chilli vinegar, 3—4 peppercorns, 2—3 tablespoons sherry, salt, 1½ oz. gelatine, 1½ pints (U.S. 3¾ cups) stock, 2 egg whites and shells

Prepare the vegetables, quarter the carrot, turnip and onion, chop the celery and put into a large pan with the thinly pared lemon peel, lemon juice, vinegar, peppercorns, sherry, salt, gelatine, egg whites and crushed egg shells. Whisk over low heat and bring almost to boiling point whisking all the time. Allow the froth to rise to the top of the pan, then draw to the side of the pan and leave for 5 minutes.

Strain through a scalded jelly bag as described in the previous recipe.

Cerises au vinaigre
VINEGAR CHERRIES
_____

2 lb. cherries,* 4 cloves, 1-inch stick cinnamon, little grated nutmeg, 2 sprigs tarragon, 1¾ pints (U.S. 4¼ cups) vinegar, 7 oz. brown sugar
*Use Morello cherries which are not too ripe. Shorten the stalks and pierce each cherry with the point of a needle at the end opposite the stalk.

Put the cherries into a jar with the cloves, cinnamon, nutmeg and tarragon.

Boil the vinegar and sugar and allow to get completely cold before pouring over the cherries.

Leave for 15—20 days before use.

The marinade is served with the cherries.

Cerneaux au verjus
GREEN WALNUTS IN VERJUICE

This hors-d'oeuvre can be served from the beginning of August until the middle of September, that is when the kernel of the walnut is completely formed.

Open the nuts and remove the walnut without breaking it. Remove the yellow skin and throw the nuts at once into cold water.

Serve on an hors-d'oeuvre dish, sprinkled with verjuice and a little rock salt.

Editor's note Verjuice is extracted from large unripened grapes. If it is not available, add a few drops of wine vinegar.

Cervelle ravigote
BRAINS WITH SAUCE

Well cleaned calf's, sheep's or lamb's brains, poached in a *court-bouillon*, cooled and cut into scallops.

Trim and arrange on an hors-d'oeuvre dish. Coat with a ravigote sauce with mustard (see page 42) to which has been added a little chopped hard-boiled egg and the sieved trimmings from the scallops.

Champignons de couche au vin blanc

MUSHROOMS WITH WHITE WINE

——————— 1 lb. button mushrooms, 4—5 tablespoons olive oil, salt, pepper, 1 tablespoon finely chopped onion, 1 tablespoon finely chopped parsley, juice 2 lemons, ¼ pint (U.S. ⅝ cup) white wine

Wash and dry the mushrooms carefully in a cloth.

Heat the oil in a pan, add the mushrooms and all the other ingredients. Cover and cook for 3 minutes.

Leave to cool, then serve in an hors-d'oeuvre dish with the sauce.

As a variation, 1 tablespoon English mustard may be added to the sauce.

Champignons de couche à la tomate

MUSHROOMS WITH TOMATO

——————— 1 lb. button mushrooms, 4—5 tablespoons olive oil, 1 tablespoon finely chopped onion, salt, pepper, 1 small clove garlic, pinch chopped parsley, 3—4 tablespoons vinegar, 6 tablespoons white wine, 8 tablespoons tomato purée

Choose small mushrooms and prepare as in the previous recipe.

Heat the oil in a saucepan, add the onion, and as soon as it begins to brown add the mushrooms; sauté them for 1—2 minutes. Add the salt and pepper, garlic, parsley, vinegar, white wine and tomato purée. Cover the saucepan and cook rapidly for 3—4 minutes. Leave to cool and serve on hors-d'oeuvre plates.

Note Tomatoes play an important part in hors-d'oeuvre and the method of cooking and presenting them may be varied in many ways.

Chou-fleur à la grecque

CAULIFLOWER IN THE GREEK MANNER

Divide the cauliflower into small pieces and cook for 4—5 minutes in salted water.

Drain and cook in the same manner as artichokes (see page 110). Serve in the same way.

Choux rouges

RED CABBAGE

Cut the cabbage into small julienne and marinate in good vinegar for a few hours. Drain and season as an ordinary salad, with or without mustard.

Choux verts en paupiettes

PAUPIETTES OF GREEN CABBAGE

———————— Tender cabbage leaves, little cooked rice, 3—4 chopped anchovies, 1—2 hard-boiled egg yolks, black olives, oil

Use only the tender leaves of cabbage. Cook them in boiling salted water, then drain, and when cool cut into small squares.

Mix the rice, anchovies and chopped egg yolks together and season very well.

Put a little of this mixture on each piece of cabbage and roll up.

Arrange on an hors-d'oeuvre dish, surround with black olives and sprinkle the top with a little oil.

Concombres

CUCUMBERS

———————— Peel the cucumbers, cut them in half lengthwise, remove the seeds and slice them thinly. Sprinkle with salt and leave for 25 minutes. To remove excess water, drain thoroughly and season with pepper, olive oil, vinegar and chopped chervil.

Thus prepared, cucumber in England is used as an accompaniment to boiled salmon, hot or cold. One can, however, make various salads with it, by mixing it with peeled, seeded and thinly sliced tomatoes; chopped onions, fillets of anchovies, tunny fish, lobster cut into small cubes, sliced truffles, sliced breast of chicken, hard-boiled eggs, rice cooked in salted water, etc.

Crèmes pour hors-d'oeuvre

CREAMS FOR HORS-D'OEUVRE

Excellent creams can be prepared for hors-d'oeuvre with smoked salmon, tunny fish, poached chicken, fillets of game, hard-boiled eggs, etc.

Chop 4½ oz. of one of the ingredients mentioned, mix with 2 oz. butter and gradually add 3 – 4 tablespoons very fresh cream. Rub through a fine sieve. Season according to the ingredient chosen.

These creams can be put into small dariole moulds, or they can be used to garnish small barquettes, or as a filling for little éclairs made of savoury chou paste.

Éperlans marinés

MARINATED SMELTS

24 smelts, salt, freshly ground pepper, 6 tablespoons olive oil, 6 tablespoons white wine vinegar, 6 tablespoons water, 1 bay leaf, 1 sprig parsley, 1 sprig thyme, 1 medium-sized onion

Fry the smelts in oil, then arrange in a dish, sprinkle with salt and pepper and pour the oil over.

Put the white wine vinegar in a pan with the water, bay leaf, parsley, thyme and onion. Bring to boiling point and boil for 8 – 10 minutes.

Pour over the smelts and leave for 24 hours.

Serve with the marinade.

Fenouils (pieds de)

FENNEL STEM

According to their size, the bulbous stems of fennel are divided into 4 or 6 portions and are then prepared in exactly the same way as Greek style artichokes (see page 110).

Figues

FIGS

These are only used as hors-d'oeuvre when they are ripe. They are arranged on vine leaves with crushed ice surrounding them. Smoked ham, cut very thin, is served with them.

In Italy, figs are accompanied by botargo (see page 128).

Frivolités

FRIVOLITIES

This word describes the collection of small preparations for hors-d'oeuvre, of which barquettes, tartlets, cherries with foie gras and very small sweet apples are graceful and light examples.

Fruits de mer

SEA FRUIT

Under this generic name come every kind of shellfish, except oysters

Harengs à la dieppoise

DIEPPE STYLE HERRINGS

Choose very fresh herrings, clean them, arrange them in a sauté dish, cover them with a boiling marinade prepared in advance.

To make this marinade you will need: ⅔ white wine, ⅓ vinegar, small slices carrot, sliced onion, thyme, bay leaf, sprig parsley and thinly sliced shallot.

Poach the herrings over low heat for 12 minutes and let them cool in the marinade.

These are served very cold, accompanied by the marinade, slices of carrot and onion and thin slices of lemon.

Filets de harengs

FILLETS OF HERRING

Fillets of herring cleaned and left to soak in milk for about 1 hour to remove the salt.

Place in an hors-d'oeuvre dish and sprinkle olive oil over them.

Harengs à la livonienne

HERRINGS WITH POTATOES AND APPLES

Choose large smoked herrings, fillet them and keep heads and tails.

Skin the fillets and cut into cubes. Mix with an equal quantity of cold cooked diced potato and russet apples cut into dice. Sprinkle with chopped parsley, chervil, tarragon and fennel. Season with salt and pepper and sprinkle with a little oil and vinegar.

Arrange on a dish in the shape of herrings, placing a head and tail at either end.

Harengs Lucas

SMOKED HERRINGS WITH SAUCE

Smoked herrings, 2 hard-boiled egg yolks, salt and pepper, 1 teaspoon made mustard, 2 tablespoons vinegar, 5 tablespoons oil, 1 dessertspoon chopped chervil, 1 dessertspoon chopped gherkin, little finely chopped shallot

Soak the herrings first in warm water, then leave for about 1 hour in milk to remove excess salt.

Fillet the fish, cut into strips and arrange in an hors-d'oeuvre dish.

To prepare the sauce, mix the egg yolks with salt, pepper and mustard. Add half the vinegar, then gradually add the oil as for mayonnaise (see page 40). Finally add the rest of the vinegar, chervil, gherkin and shallot.

Pour this sauce over the herrings.

Harengs roulés

ROLLED HERRINGS

Fresh herrings with soft roes, little made mustard, finely chopped onion, 1 pint (U.S. 2½ cups) vinegar, *bouquet garni*, 1 onion stuck with 1 clove, few peppercorns, 5—6 tablespoons oil

Fillet the herrings and remove the roes. Spread the fillets lightly with mustard, sprinkle with onion and roll up into paupiettes. Secure with cotton. Put into a dish with the herring roes.

Boil the vinegar with the *bouquet garni*, onion and peppercorns and strain it over the fish. Leave to get cold.

Remove the roes and rub through a fine sieve. Add the vinegar to the purée obtained, stir in the oil, and pour over the herring fillets. Leave for 2−3 days to marinate.

Serve on hors-d'oeuvre dishes.

Huîtres

OYSTERS

Oysters are one of the finest hors-d'oeuvre. They can be served at dinner and at luncheon. They should be served very cold and, this is important, properly opened.

Serve brown bread and butter, not too thinly cut, and a sauce made of vinegar, coarse-ground pepper and chopped shallot. Serve with wedges of lemon.

Never wash the oysters after they are opened.

Huîtres cocktails

OYSTER COCKTAILS

Prepare a cocktail glass for each person. Put into each glass 6 newly opened oysters. Add 2−3 drops tabasco sauce, 1 tablespoon tomato ketchup, few drops Worcestershire sauce and 6 drops lemon juice. Serve very cold.

Huîtres marinés

MARINATED OYSTERS

For 1 minute poach freshly opened oysters in a little *court-bouillon* of white wine and herbs. Allow to cool in the liquor and serve on hors-d'oeuvre dishes with a light ravigote sauce (see page 42) to which has been added a few tablespoons of the *court-bouillon*.

Maquereaux marinés

MARINATED MACKERELS

Choose small ones, and treat them in exactly the same way as Dieppe style herrings (see page 121).

Melon cantaloup

CANTALOUP MELON

Choose a perfectly ripe melon and serve on green leaves with crushed ice around it.

Melon cocktail

Cut the fruit of a ripe melon into cubes and put into a bowl. Sprinkle with sugar and keep it on ice. When ready to serve add some kirsch, maraschino, port or brandy, according to taste.

Serve in small Champagne glasses.

Note During hot weather 1 tablespoon orange ice can be added to the melon.

Melon frappé au porto

CHILLED MELON WITH PORT

Choose a cantaloup melon which is just ripe. Cut a piece off the top about 2−3 inches in diameter. Remove all the seeds with a silver spoon and then scoop out the fruit. Sprinkle it with sugar and port wine and then replace in the melon case. Surround with crushed ice and put into the refrigerator for 2 hours. To serve, arrange the melon on crushed ice and use very cold plates.

Note Brandy or Curaçao can be used instead of port wine, and if liked a few tablespoons of orange ice may be added.

Melons (petits, confits au vinaigre)

SMALL PICKLED MELONS

Choose small green melons, cut them into pieces, cover with salt and leave for 10 hours. Wash in vinegar and water ($\frac{2}{3}$ vinegar and $\frac{1}{3}$ water).

Put into jars with a few small white onions, a little tarragon and a few chillis.

Boil 1$\frac{3}{4}$ pints (U.S. 4$\frac{1}{4}$ cups) vinegar with 3$\frac{1}{2}$ oz. sugar and pour over the melon. The vinegar can be used hot or cold.

Seal the jars and the melon will be ready in 10−12 days.

Moelle de végétaux divers

VEGETABLE HEARTS

The hearts or tender parts of such vegetables as artichokes, cabbage, cos lettuce, endive, chicory and sprigs of cauliflower make an excellent hors-d'oeuvre.

They can be prepared as for Greek style artichokes (see page 110) with various seasonings.

Moules

MUSSELS

Cook the mussels as usual and remove from their shells. Serve on hors-d'oeuvre dishes with a ravigote sauce with mustard (see page 42) to which a little of the water in which they were cooked has been added. One can also make a delicious broth by adding a little saffron to the water before cooking.

Remove the mussels when they are cooked and boil the water rapidly to reduce it a little. Then while still boiling pour it over the mussels.

Leave to get cold before serving.

Note The mussels can be left in the half shell if preferred.

Museau et palais de boeuf

OX MUZZLE AND PALATE

After blanching, cooling and scraping, cook in a light white stock, with bay leaf, thyme, sprigs parsley and a few peppercorns. Leave to cool.

To serve Slice thinly and serve with a ravigote sauce (see page 42) composed of chopped onion and parsley, mustard, olive oil and vinegar.

Editor's note These pieces of offal are seldom used today, although at one time they were very popular.

Before cooking, they should be soaked for 6—8 hours in cold salted water.

Oeufs farcis

STUFFED EGGS

Hard-boiled eggs are served as hors-d'oeuvre in a variety of ways. They are usually cut in half lengthwise, the yolks removed, sieved, seasoned with salt and pepper and mixed with an equal quantity of butter. The mixture is then piped back into the hollow of the egg white. Cover with a little mayonnaise sauce (see page 40) and serve on hors-d'oeuvre dishes.

Note To vary this, add a little anchovy, smoked salmon, tunny fish or sardine butter to the egg yolks.

With imagination and a little thought, a great variety of hors-d'oeuvre can be prepared.

Oeufs de pluvier

PLOVERS' EGGS

Cook the eggs for 8 minutes in boiling water and leave to cool. Remove a small part of the pointed end of the egg with a knife; this is a necessary precaution in order to ensure that the egg is in good condition, in which case the white is slightly transparent.

In England, where these eggs are considered a delicacy, they are sometimes arranged in nests made of green moss, but a nest of freshly cut watercress, carefully arranged, would strike a better note.

Oignons à l'orientale

ONIONS WITH SULTANAS

2¼ lb. small peeled onions, 1¼ pints (U.S. approx. 3 cups) water, ¼ pint (U.S. 1¼ cups) vinegar, 4 tablespoons olive oil, 6 tablespoons tomato purée, 4½ oz. sugar, 5 oz. sultanas, small teaspoon salt, pinch cayenne pepper, bouquet composed of 1 bay leaf, sprigs thyme and parsley

Place all these ingredients in a saucepan, cover and put over moderate heat. Boil for 40 – 50 minutes. At this point the onions should be cooked and the liquid should be reduced by two-thirds. It should be just thick enough to coat the onions and sultanas, and look like a dark tomato sauce.

OLIVES

Olives of all kinds make good hors-d'oeuvre and are served straight from the brine in which they are bottled.

Olives farcies

STUFFED OLIVES

Choose very large olives and remove the stones. Stuff them as you wish with tunny fish, anchovy, smoked salmon or sardine butter.

Olives noires

BLACK OLIVES

These are served on hors-d'oeuvre dishes, lightly sprinkled with olive oil and a little freshly ground pepper. They are sometimes mixed with anchovy fillets.

Poivrons rouges (doux)

SWEET RED PEPPERS

Lightly grill (U.S. broil) peppers and remove skin loosened by the heat. Cut them in halves lengthwise, remove the seeds, then cut into strips and season with oil, vinegar, salt and freshly ground pepper. Serve on hors-d'oeuvre dishes.

Note By way of variation, anchovy fillets, black olives and Provençal style tomatoes (see page 659) may be served with the peppers.

Poireaux à la grecque

GREEK STYLE LEEKS

Cut the white parts of the leeks into 3-inch pieces; cook them for 8 – 10 minutes in boiling salted water and finish the cooking in a marinade similar to that given in Greek style artichokes (see page 110).

Poitrines d'oie fumées

SMOKED GOOSE BREAST

This should be carved as thinly as possible, and served surrounded with
sprigs of parsley.

Boutargue de mulet

GREY MULLET ROE

This is much appreciated by the Italians. The roe is cut into slices as
thinly as possible and sprinkled with olive oil and lemon juice. In season,
fresh figs are served with it.

The nutritive properties of botargo are almost identical with those
of caviar.

Radis roses

PINK RADISHES

These should be very fresh and firm. Their preparation is too well known
to be mentioned, but they are often used for the decoration of hors-
d'oeuvre on account of their pretty colour.

Radis noirs

BLACK RADISHES

Peel them, slice thinly and sprinkle with fine salt. Leave for 20 minutes,
then drain them and season with pepper, oil and vinegar.

Rougets à l'orientale

RED MULLET ORIENTAL STYLE

Red mullet, salt, pepper, oil, white wine, tomatoes, peeled and
chopped, sprigs parsley, fennel, thyme, 1 bay leaf, 1 clove garlic, pinch
saffron

Choose small fish. Arrange in a sauté pan and season with salt and
pepper. Sprinkle lightly with oil and cover with the wine. Add the tomatoes, herbs, garlic and saffron. Bring to the boil and cook for 8—10
minutes, according to the size of the fish.

Royans

FRESH SARDINES

This is a fresh fish, of the same family as the sardine. It is grilled and served with butter and lemon.

SALADES
SALADS

The preparation of salads for hors-d'oeuvre can be left to the imagination of the person making them. The variety is endless, and almost everything in the kitchen can be used for them.

Rice is often the main ingredient; it is usually cooked in salted water for a maximum period of 16—18 minutes, and then well drained and cooled.

Salade Bergerette

RICE, EGG AND CHIVE SALAD

This consists of rice, sliced hard-boiled egg and chopped chives mixed lightly with a little cream to which salt and pepper has been added.

In addition, a little grated horseradish or mustard may be used.

Salade brésilienne

BRAZILIAN SALAD

This consists of rice and fresh pineapple cut into cubes, mixed with a little fresh cream and seasoned with salt and lemon juice.

Salade catalane

CATALONIAN SALAD

———————— Rice, white Spanish onions cooked in the oven and cut into cubes, grilled (U.S. broiled) sweet red peppers, peeled and cut into cubes, anchovy fillets

Mix with a little ordinary vinaigrette sauce (see page 42).

Salade des midinettes

RICE AND PEA SALAD

Equal parts of rice and very green peas mixed with vinaigrette sauce (see page 42) to which has been added chopped chervil and tarragon.

Salade monégasque

NONAT AND TOMATO SALAD

———— Rice, nonats* poached in salted water, tomatoes peeled and cut into small cubes, pepper, salt, sweet herbs, oil and vinegar
*Nonats are small Mediterranean fish.

Arrange the nonats and tomatoes on a bed of rice and pour the dressing over.

Salade niçoise

SALAD NIÇOISE

Tunny fish in oil, tomato, anchovy fillets cut into cubes, mixed with vinaigrette sauce (see page 42) with chopped tarragon, chervil and chives. A little mustard may be added.

Salade italienne

ITALIAN SALAD

———— Rice, peas cooked in boiling salted water, drained and cooled, carrots cut into small cubes and cooked in boiling salted water

Mix with a little vinaigrette sauce (see page 42).
These ingredients make a salad of the Italian national colours.

Salade Otero

SWEET RED PEPPER SALAD

———— Grilled (U.S. broiled) sweet red peppers, skinned and cut into julienne, peeled tomatoes, divided into quarters, anchovy fillets and white Spanish onion cooked in the oven and cut into cubes

Mix all the ingredients with vinaigrette sauce (see page 42) with the addition of mustard.

Salade de boeuf parisienne

BEEF AND POTATO SALAD

———————— Cold boiled beef, cut very thinly, boiled potatoes, thinly sliced

Pour over a little vinaigrette sauce (see page 42) to which may be added chopped tarragon, chives or chervil.

Note Green beans, tomatoes, hard-boiled eggs, watercress, etc., may also be added to the meat and potatoes.

Salade de paysan provençal

PROVENÇAL PEASANT SALAD

———————— Tomatoes cut in quarters, chopped onion, thinly sliced cucumber and anchovy fillets, seasoned with vinegar, olive oil, salt and pepper

Salade de pieds de mouton et de pieds de veau

SHEEP'S AND CALF'S FEET SALAD

Cook the sheep's and calf's feet in the ordinary way, bone them and cut into fillets while they are still warm.

Season with vinaigrette sauce (see page 42) with mustard.

Salade Réjane

RICE, CUCUMBER AND CHICKEN SALAD

———————— Rice, thinly sliced cucumber, cooked for a few minutes in salted water and well drained, julienne of chicken's breast and truffles

Season with vinaigrette sauce (see page 42) to which some herbs have been added.

Tartelettes de thon

TUNNY FISH TARTLETS

These are small tartlets filled with finely chopped tunny fish mixed with mayonnaise sauce (see page 40).

Garnish with chopped hard-boiled eggs and criss-cross the tops with anchovy fillets. Sprinkle a little chopped parsley on top.

Tomates à la génoise

TOMATOES WITH TUNNY FISH

Choose some medium-sized, rather firm tomatoes, slice them and remove the seeds; arrange them on an hors-d'oeuvre dish alternately with thin slices of tunny fish. Surround with a border of boiled potatoes cut to about ¾ inch and sprinkle the whole with vinaigrette sauce (see page 42) to which a little anchovy essence has been added.

Tomates fantaisies

FANCY TOMATOES

Choose firm, medium-sized tomatoes, peel them, cut a slice from the top and remove the seeds. Drain well and season with salt and pepper. Fill with a mixture of creamed hard-boiled egg yolks and butter.

Leave until the filling hardens, then cut each tomato into 6 sections, not cutting right to the bottom. Open out like a rosette and arrange on five small lettuce leaves. This will give a pretty effect of an open flower.

Tomatoes may be filled in the same way with small cooked vegetables, fish meat or poultry mixed with a little mayonnaise (see page 42), but in this case choose small tomatoes and do not cut them.

Sauce tomate pour hors-d'oeuvre

TOMATO SAUCE FOR HORS-D'OEUVRE

——————— 2¼ lb. ripe tomatoes, salt, pepper, 1 dessertspoon chopped parsley, ¼ clove garlic, 6 tablespoons olive oil

Peel the tomatoes, cut in half and remove the seeds. Chop them, and put into a pan with the other ingredients. Cover and simmer gently for 30 minutes.

ANOTHER RECIPE

————— 2¼ lb. ripe tomatoes, 6 tablespoons oil, 2 tablespoons finely chopped onion, ½ pint (U.S. 1¼ cups) vinegar, salt, pepper, 1 dessertspoon chopped parsley, ¼ clove garlic

Prepare the tomatoes as described above. Heat the oil, add the onion and as soon as it begins to brown add the vinegar. Reduce a little, then add the tomatoes and other ingredients. Cover, and simmer gently for 30 minutes.

Note Fresh tomatoes may be replaced by canned tomatoes.

In both recipes, a few tablespoons of tomato purée may be added.

Truites tyroliennes

TROUT WITH TOMATO SAUCE

Select very small river trout of an even size. Clean them, dip in flour and fry in olive oil. Sprinkle with salt, put them into a dish and cover with tomato sauce (2) (see above). Leave to marinate for 24 hours and serve on small square china plates.

Note Various kinds of fish, such as eels and mackerel, cut into pieces or filleted, can be prepared in the same way.

Sardines in oil, skinned, arranged in a shallow dish and covered with tomato sauce (2) (see above) and marinated for 24 hours, are very much better than sardines preserved in tomato sauce.

I have not included here the many hors-d'oeuvre which one finds in grocers' shops, such as smoked and fresh ham, smoked tongue, beef, sausages, salami, canned fish, sardines, herrings, salmon and a mass of other ingredients.

Oeufs

EGGS

There are many different ways of cooking eggs: they can be boiled, shirred, baked, fried, poached, soft-boiled, cooked in a mould, *en cocotte*, hard-boiled, scrambled and made into omelets.

The essential condition is that they should be perfectly fresh.

Oeufs sur le plat

SHIRRED EGGS

For 2 eggs, heat 2 teaspoons fresh butter in a fireproof dish. Slide the eggs carefully into it and baste the yolks with a little of the butter. Cook in the oven, and add seasoning after the eggs have cooked.

Oeufs à la poêle

FRIED EGGS

Take 2 eggs. Heat 2 tablespoons butter in a pan; when it begins to brown, slide the eggs in; prick and gently lift the white of the eggs with the prongs of a fork. Season after cooking.

Oeufs à l'américaine

AMERICAN STYLE EGGS

Cook 2 eggs in a pan, slide them on to a hot plate and add 2 slices of grilled bacon and 1 grilled tomato.

Oeufs à l'anglaise

ENGLISH STYLE EGGS

Cook the eggs in a pan and trim them with a round cutter. Place each egg on a piece of toast.

Oeufs au bacon

EGGS AND BACON

Fry 2 thin slices of bacon and place them on a dish with some of the fat from the bacon. Break 2 eggs over the bacon and cook in the oven.

Oeufs Bercy

EGGS WITH SAUSAGES AND TOMATO SAUCE

Cook the eggs in a fireproof china dish. Place 2 small grilled sausages between the yolks, and surround the eggs with a ring of tomato sauce.

Oeufs au beurre noir

EGGS WITH BLACK BUTTER

Take 2 eggs, cook them in ¾ oz. butter heated in a pan until it is nearly black, season and slide them on to a dish. Heat a little vinegar in the pan and pour it over the eggs.

Oeufs chasseur

FRIED EGGS WITH SAUCE CHASSEUR

These are fried eggs garnished with chicken's livers tossed in butter, with *sauce chasseur* (see page 26).

Oeufs Cluny

EGGS WITH CHICKEN CROQUETTES

The same as eggs with sausages (see above), except that the sausages are replaced by chicken croquettes (see page 454).

Oeufs à la diable

DEVILLED EGGS

The eggs must be cooked in a pan containing slightly browned butter. Season and slide on to a dish. Sprinkle the surface with breadcrumbs fried in butter with a little dry mustard added and, to finish, heat a little vinegar in the pan and pour it over the eggs.

Oeufs Jeanne Granier

EGGS WITH ASPARAGUS TIPS AND TRUFFLES

Put 1 tablespoon asparagus tips, a little cream and a few thin slices of truffle in the bottom of a fireproof dish. Break the eggs over them and cook in the oven. Place 1 tablespoon asparagus tips and 1 slice of truffle between each egg yolk.

Oeufs Isaline

EGGS WITH TOMATOES AND CHICKEN LIVERS

Prepare some fried eggs (see page 134). Cut some small tomatoes in half and cook in a little olive oil. Chop some chicken's livers, add a pinch of herbs and sauté in butter. Put on top of the tomatoes and arrange round the eggs.

Oeufs Meyerber

EGGS WITH KIDNEYS AND SAUCE PÉRIGUEUX

Fry eggs. After cooking, between the yolks place a grilled lamb's or sheep's kidney. Surround with a ring of sauce périgueux (see page 28).

Oeufs mistral

STEAMED EGGS WITH TRUFFLES

1 clove garlic, thinly sliced peeled truffles, salt, freshly ground pepper, 1 tablespoon olive oil, 1 tablespoon melted meat jelly (see page 21), 4 eggs

Rub the bottom of a dish with the garlic and cover with a layer of truffles, season and pour on the oil and meat jelly. Break the eggs carefully on

top. Put the dish into a deep pan containing about ¼ inch boiling water.
Cover completely and the eggs will cook perfectly in the steam.

Oeufs Mireille

STEAMED EGGS WITH TRUFFLES AND CREAM

———————— Butter, truffles, peeled and thinly sliced, salt, pepper, 1 tablespoon
melted meat jelly (see page 21), 4 tablespoons boiling cream, 4 eggs

Butter the bottom of a dish and cover with slices of truffle, season and
pour in the meat jelly and cream. Break the eggs carefully on top and
cook as described for steamed eggs with truffles above.

Oeufs au parmesan

EGGS WITH PARMESAN CHEESE

Butter a fireproof dish. Cover the bottom with fresh cream. Break the
eggs into the dish, sprinkle with grated Parmesan cheese and pour melted
butter on top. Cook in the oven.

Oeufs à la portugaise

BAKED EGGS WITH TOMATOES

———————— 2 ripe tomatoes, 1 tablespoon oil, salt, pepper, little chopped parsley,
1 small clove garlic chopped, 4 eggs

Peel and seed the tomatoes, then chop them. Cook for 10 minutes in the
hot oil. Add seasoning and flavouring and put into a fireproof dish.
Break the eggs carefully over the tomatoes and cook in the oven.

Oeufs provençal

PROVENÇAL STYLE EGGS

———————— 2—3 ripe tomatoes, 1 tablespoon olive oil, salt and pepper, fresh
breadcrumbs, little chopped parsley, 1 clove garlic, 4 eggs

Cut the tomatoes in half and remove the seeds. Heat the oil in a pan,
put in the tomatoes, cut side down, cook for a few minutes, then turn
them over, add seasoning, sprinkle with the breadcrumbs and parsley
and add the garlic. Continue the cooking, then put them into a fireproof
dish. Break the eggs carefully over the tomatoes and cook in the oven.

OEUFS FRITS
FRIED EGGS

Oeufs frits Cavour

FRIED EGGS WITH PIEDMONT RISOTTO

Cut some tomatoes in half, remove the seeds and cook them in oil.

Arrange on a dish and garnish with *riz à la piémontaise* (see page 668). Place a fried egg on each tomato.

Serve separately a little veal stock (see page 20) to which a little tomato purée has been added.

Oeufs frits à la française

FRENCH FRIED EGGS

Heat 6 tablespoons oil in a small pan. Break an egg on to a plate, add seasoning and slide the egg into the oil. Incline the pan forward and with a wooden spoon fold the white over the yolk. This, solidified by contact with the hot oil, should envelop it completely. Drain the egg and continue in the same way.

Note Only 1 egg should be done at a time.

Fried eggs are usually served with sauce or garnishes served separately. Eggs themselves serve as garnishes to various fish and poultry dishes.

The following sauces are good accompaniments to fried eggs: tomato (see page 132), curry (see page 32), paprika (see page 32), bordelaise (see page 25), béarnaise (see page 30). Spinach and rice in various forms also go well with fried eggs.

Oeufs frits à la serbe

EGGS FRIED IN THE SERBIAN MANNER

Prepare a pilaf of rice (see page 669) to which has been added some aubergine, cubed and tossed in oil. Arrange some fried eggs on the rice and intersperse with small strips of grilled ham.

Separately serve a paprika sauce (see page 32).

OEUFS POCHÉS ET MOLLETS
POACHED AND SOFT-BOILED EGGS

Oeufs pochés
POACHED EGGS

Have ready 2 pints (U.S. 5 cups) boiling water to which has been added ⅛ oz. salt and 1 tablespoon vinegar. Break the eggs in the water, when just boiling. Reduce the heat and poach for 2−3 minutes without boiling. Remove the eggs carefully and put into cold water. Trim off the edges and keep them in warm salted water or in ordinary broth until required.

Oeufs mollets
SOFT-BOILED EGGS

Put the eggs into boiling water and cook for 3−4 minutes. Cool, remove the shells and keep the eggs warm in warm salted water.
All the following recipes using poached eggs can apply to soft-boiled eggs.

Oeufs pochés à l'aurore
POACHED EGGS WITH AURORE SAUCE

Put the poached eggs on croûtons fried in butter and serve with *sauce aurore* (see page 29).

Oeufs pochés bénédictine
POACHED EGGS WITH COD AND CREAM SAUCE

Pound some cod with a little garlic, oil and cream and add some chopped truffles. Arrange the poached eggs on this, and cover with a cream sauce (see page 38).

Oeufs pochés bourguignonne

POACHED EGGS WITH WINE SAUCE

──────────── ½ pint (U.S. 1¼ cups) red wine, *bouquet garni* of ½ bay leaf, 1 sprig each parsley and thyme, ¼ clove garlic, 2 slices onion, 3 eggs, croûtons fried in butter, 1 tablespoon butter, 1 teaspoon flour

Put the wine into a pan with the *bouquet garni*, garlic and onion and boil for 5–6 minutes. Strain, return to the pan and poach the eggs in the wine. Drain and put them in a dish on top of the croûtons. Reduce the wine by half, remove from the heat, and thicken with the butter and flour mixed together.

Pour this sauce over the eggs.

Oeufs pochés cardinal

POACHED EGGS WITH DICED LOBSTER IN BÉCHAMEL SAUCE

Mix some small cubes of lobster with quarter quantity chopped truffle. Bind with a little béchamel sauce (see page 23). Use this to line some tartlet cases and put a poached egg into each tartlet. Coat with béchamel sauce.

Oeufs châtelaine

POACHED EGGS ON CHESTNUT PURÉE

Poached or soft-boiled eggs, arranged on a light chestnut purée and lightly covered with a well reduced veal stock (see page 20) to which a little butter has been added.

Oeufs Colette

POACHED EGGS WITH ASPARAGUS TIPS

Poached or soft-boiled eggs, arranged on a bed of asparagus tips mixed lightly with cream, and coated with light buttered meat jelly (see page 21).

Oeufs pochés florentine

POACHED EGGS WITH SPINACH

──────────── 8 oz. spinach, butter, 6–8 poached eggs, béchamel sauce (see page 23), cream, grated cheese

Cook the spinach and drain thoroughly. Chop and return to the pan
with a little butter. Cook for a few minutes, then turn into a fireproof
dish. Arrange the eggs on top and coat with the sauce to which a little
cream has been added. Sprinkle with grated cheese, add a little melted
butter and brown lightly before serving.

Oeufs aux crevettes roses à la danoise

POACHED EGGS WITH SHRIMPS

Arrange some poached eggs in a serving dish. Cover with béchamel
sauce (see page 23) to which a generous quantity of freshly cooked
shrimps has been added.

Garnish with leaves of flaky pastry.

Oeufs pochés grand-duc

POACHED EGGS WITH TRUFFLES AND SHRIMPS

Croûtons fried in butter, poached eggs, 1 thin slice truffle for each egg,
few shrimps, béchamel sauce (see page 23), cream, grated cheese,
butter, green asparagus tips

Put the croûtons into a fireproof dish and arrange the eggs in a circle
on top. Put a slice of truffle on each egg and a few shrimps in between.
Coat with béchamel sauce to which a little cream has been added. Sprinkle
with grated cheese and a little melted butter and brown before serving.

Garnish the centre of the dish with asparagus tips sautéed for a few
minutes in butter.

Oeufs pochés Maintenon

POACHED EGGS WITH SEMOLINA AND SOUBISE SAUCE

Arrange some poached eggs on semolina cooked as for gnocchi (see
page 671) and fried in butter. Coat with soubise sauce (see page 35)
to which a small julienne of chicken breast, truffle and mushrooms has
been added. Sprinkle with grated cheese, pour a little melted butter
over, and brown before serving.

Oeufs pochés Manon

POACHED EGGS WITH WHITEBAIT

2 tablespoons chopped onion, 1 chopped leek (white part only), 2 tablespoons olive oil, 1 dessertspoon curry powder, 2 medium-sized tomatoes, ⅛ clove garlic, *bouquet garni* of 1 sprig each parsley and thyme and 1 bay leaf, 1¾ pints (U.S. 4¼ cups) boiling water, ¼ oz. salt, few crushed peppercorns, 1 lb. whitebait, few leaves saffron, 6—8 poached eggs, croûtons fried in oil

Brown the onion and leek in the hot oil. Add the curry powder, sliced tomatoes, garlic and *bouquet garni*. Cover and sauté for about 10 minutes, then add the boiling water. Add salt and peppercorns. Boil for a few minutes then add the whitebait and saffron.

Continue boiling for 10—12 minutes. Rub all through a sieve into a clean pan and keep hot.

Arrange the poached eggs on the croûtons in a deep serving dish and pour some of the liquor over.

Oeufs pochés à la Mornay au gratin

POACHED EGGS WITH CHEESE SAUCE

Butter a pan and cover the bottom with a thin layer of béchamel sauce (see page 23). Arrange some poached eggs on the sauce and sprinkle them with grated cheese, cover with more béchamel sauce, sprinkle with cheese and add a little melted butter. Brown before serving.

Oeufs pochés à la moelle

POACHED EGGS WITH BEEF MARROW

Place some poached eggs in a deep buttered dish. Cover them with a demi-glace sauce (see page 22) to which a little tomato purée has been added, with thin rounds of beef marrow, poached in stock.

Serve with hot toast.

Oeufs pochés niçoise

POACHED EGGS WITH PARMESAN CHEESE AND DEMI-GLACE
SAUCE

Arrange some poached eggs in a deep dish which has been buttered and
sprinkled with grated Parmesan cheese and a few tablespoons of
glace sauce with tomato purée added (see page 22).
Cover the eggs with more grated Parmesan.
Reduce the remaining sauce and pour over the eggs.
Cover and keep warm for 2−3 minutes before serving.

Oeufs pochés à la d'Orléans

POACHED EGGS WITH CHICKEN BREASTS AND SAUCE SUPRÊME

Line some tartlets with breast of chicken cut into small cubes and cover
with a few tablespoons *sauce suprême* (see page 23), then arrange on
a serving dish. Put a poached egg into each tartlet and coat with more
sauce. Put a slice of truffle dipped into meat jelly on each egg and serve
as hot as possible.

Oeufs pochés à la reine

POACHED EGGS WITH MACARONI AND CHEESE

———————— Macaroni, truffle cut into julienne, butter, grated Parmesan cheese,
cream, poached eggs, béchamel sauce (see page 23)

Break the macaroni into short pieces and cook in the ordinary way.
Drain and add a little julienne of truffle, butter, grated cheese and
cream.
Put the macaroni into a serving dish and arrange the eggs on top.
Cover with béchamel sauce, sprinkle with cheese, add a little melted
butter and brown before serving.

Oeufs Stanley
SOFT-BOILED EGGS WITH SOUBISE SAUCE

Put some soft-boiled eggs (see page 139) into a deep dish. Add 1 tablespoon curry powder to 1 pint (U.S. 2½ cups) *sauce ou purée soubise* (see page 35) and pour over the eggs.

A small quantity of truffle cut into julienne can be added in place of the curry powder.

Serve with Indian style rice (see page 668).

Oeufs à la Villeroy
FRIED COLD POACHED EGGS

Poach some eggs, dry them carefully and coat with Villeroy sauce (see page 36). Leave to cool, then flour them, brush with beaten egg, and roll in finely sifted breadcrumbs. A few minutes before serving, fry in hot butter till golden brown.

Serve tomato sauce (see page 132) separately.

Note The Villeroy sauce can be omitted and the poached eggs fried as described above.

These fried eggs, together with poached and soft-boiled eggs, can be served with a variety of sauces and purées of meat and vegetables such as – curry sauce (see page 32), paprika sauce (see page 32), *sauce suprême* with truffles (see page 23), soubise purée (see page 35), mushroom purée (see page 606) and puréed or minced game, poultry or meat.

OEUFS COCOTTE
EGGS IN COCOTTE

A *cocotte* is a small fireproof china or earthenware dish in which eggs are cooked.

Eggs in cocotte are a special type of poached egg. The basic type is eggs in cocotte with cream, but often, as a variation, the cream is replaced by various sauces, red wine, thickened gravy, poultry and game purée, asparagus tips, etc.

These little cocottes are served on table napkins or lace doilies.

Oeufs cocotte à la crème

EGGS IN COCOTTE WITH CREAM

Warm the cocottes, put a piece of butter the size of a walnut in each together with 1 very fresh egg. Add a small pinch salt and 1 tablespoon boiling cream. Poach in a closed bain-marie, or put the cocottes in a shallow pan with enough boiling water to come within ½ inch of the top of the cocotte, and cook in the oven partially covered.

The eggs are cooked when the whites are almost set and the yolks are glossy.

Oeufs cocotte Mireille

EGGS IN COCOTTE WITH TRUFFLES

Warm the cocottes. Put into each a piece of butter the size of a walnut, 2 tablespoons melted meat jelly (see page 21), 1 tablespoon carefully peeled and chopped truffle, 1 new-laid egg, a very small pinch of salt and 1 tablespoon boiling cream. Poach in a bain-marie.

Oeufs cocotte Rachel

EGGS IN COCOTTE WITH ASPARAGUS TIPS

The same method as for eggs in cocotte with truffles (above). When the eggs are poached, put 1 dessertspoon asparagus tips sautéed in butter in the centre of each cocotte.

Oeufs cocotte Rosemonde

EGGS IN COCOTTE WITH BÉCHAMEL SAUCE

Butter the cocottes, put into each 1 dessertspoon béchamel sauce (see page 23) to which a little cream has been added and on this 1 new-laid egg. Add a small pinch salt and 1 small teaspoon grated Parmesan cheese. Cover with a little more béchamel sauce, sprinkle with grated cheese, add a little melted butter and place the cocottes in a tray containing a little boiling water. Cook uncovered in the oven for 4 minutes.

Note During the truffle season, a few tablespoons chopped truffle may be added to the béchamel sauce.

Oeufs cocotte à la tomate
EGGS IN COCOTTE WITH TOMATOES

3–4 ripe tomatoes, 1 tablespoon butter or oil, salt and pepper, pinch chopped parsley, 1 small clove garlic (optional), 6–8 eggs

Peel and seed the tomatoes. Chop them and put into a pan with the butter, seasoning and parsley. Cover and simmer for 12–15 minutes.

Put 1 tablespoon of this purée into each cocotte, add the egg and sprinkle with salt and pepper. Poach in a bain-marie.

When the eggs are cooked, a little melted meat jelly (see page 21) may be added if liked.

OEUFS MOULÉS
EGGS IN A MOULD

These eggs are cooked in small moulds of various shapes. The moulds are buttered and decorated according to the nature of the dish. The eggs are either broken directly into the moulds or added in the form of scrambled eggs and poached in a bain-marie.

These eggs are usually turned out on to small pieces of bread fried in butter, but this method is by no means exclusive and the eggs may be turned out directly on to the serving dish.

If liked, the fried bread may be replaced by semolina cooked as for gnocchi (see page 671), cut to the required size, floured and fried in butter.

Oeufs moulés Cécilia
MOULDED EGGS WITH SAUCE SUPRÊME

Butter thickly some small moulds such as those used for rum baba and decorate them with trimmings of truffle. Cover the sides of the moulds with fine forcemeat of creamed chicken (see page 56), break 1 egg into each mould and poach them in a bain-marie, or a covered saucepan, avoiding letting the water boil.

Turn the eggs out on rounds of flaky pastry, and cover them with *sauce suprême* (see page 23) to which a few tablespoons melted meat jelly (see page 21) have been added.

As a variation, these eggs may be prepared by giving them other names, more or less fancy, and replacing the chicken forcemeat by fish or various game forcemeats, and using either curry sauce (see page 32) or paprika sauce (see page 32) or red wine, tomato, meat jelly sauces, etc.

Oeufs moulés Polignac
MOULDED EGGS WITH CHATEAUBRIAND SAUCE

Butter thickly some small moulds such as those used for rum baba. Decorate the bottom with thin slices of truffle, break a very fresh egg into each, salt them lightly and poach them in an open bain-marie. Turn the eggs out on to a serving dish, arranging them in a circle, and cover them with chateaubriand sauce.*

As a variation and under another name, chosen to describe the sauce or the garnish, one can prepare moulded eggs with shrimp sauce (see page 32), with Chambertin, or with *sauce chasseur* (see page 26), etc.

Editor's note Chateaubriand sauce is made by heating 2 tablespoons meat glaze with 1 tablespoon white stock. Add 4 oz. fresh butter a little at a time, 1 tablespoon chopped parsley, few drops lemon juice and a pinch cayenne pepper.

OEUFS À LA COQUE
BOILED EGGS

It is no use for me to enlarge on the preparation of boiled eggs. Everyone ought to know that the first essential is that the egg should be as fresh as possible. The time of cooking in boiling water varies according to personal taste. Some people think that 1 minute is enough, while others insist on 2–3 or even 4 minutes.

To get eggs of good flavour, the hens must be fed on either rice, oats, barley or maize. It must not be forgotten that the nature of the food taken by the hen influences the egg and gives it a more or less agreeable taste.

I have made several experiments in this field; 3 boiled eggs have each had a different taste, the reason being that the hens which laid them were let loose and fed upon different foods.

OEUFS BROUILLÉS
SCRAMBLED EGGS

This can be a very delicate dish if proper care is taken in preparing it.

Scrambled eggs should be creamy and soft. They are usually served in silver dishes and sometimes in small tartlets.

Formerly it used to be the custom to surround scrambled eggs with small, rather thick croûtons fried in butter or with small triangles of freshly cooked flaky pastry.

Nowadays, because of the speed with which food is served, these little details are neglected, which is very regrettable.

In the old days, scrambled eggs were made in a bain-marie; there was more certainty of them being perfectly cooked, but the operation took longer.

With a little care the same result can be obtained by cooking the eggs over a low heat, so that the cooking may be done slowly, to give that perfect homogeneity which makes the eggs soft.

The right way to prepare scrambled eggs is as follows: Choose a saucepan with a thick bottom; melt 2 oz. butter, without heating it too much, add 6−8 very fresh eggs, beaten, salt and pepper; cook the eggs over moderate heat, stirring them continuously with a wooden spoon and scraping the bottom of the saucepan, until the eggs begin to bind and to thicken. Then add 2 oz. fresh butter, without ceasing to stir with the spoon.

I am not in favour of adding cream to scrambled eggs.

They may have various garnishes added to them such as: asparagus tips, black and white truffles, cheese, tomatoes, morels, mushrooms, veal and lamb's kidneys, cock's kidneys browned in butter, shrimps, etc.

Oeufs brouillés Catherinettes

SCRAMBLED EGGS WITH CHEESE AND TRUFFLES

Scrambled eggs, prepared and cooked as described above, with 2 tablespoons grated cheese and a small julienne of truffles added. Arrange them in a dish, surround with croûtons fried in butter, and in the centre put some cock's kidneys slightly browned in butter and rolled in meat jelly (see page 21).

Oeufs brouillés Georgette

SCRAMBLED EGGS WITH TRUFFLES AND SHRIMPS (U.S. PRAWNS)

Scrambled eggs prepared and cooked as on page 148 with 2 table-spoons grated Parmesan cheese, thin slices of truffle and some shrimps added. Arrange in a dish and sprinkle with a few tablespoons meat jelly (see page 21).

Surround with croûtons of bread fried in butter.

Oeufs brouillés grand'mère

SCRAMBLED EGGS WITH CROÛTONS AND HAM

Scrambled eggs prepared and cooked as on page 148, to which are added a few tablespoons of very small fried croûtons and small cubes of cooked ham lightly browned in butter.

Oeufs brouillés aux morilles

SCRAMBLED EGGS WITH MORELS

Scrambled eggs prepared and cooked as on page 148. Arrange them on a dish, garnish the centre with creamed morels and sprinkle them with a few tablespoons meat jelly (see page 21).

Note If desired, a few thin slices of truffle may be added to the morels and the dish is then called *oeufs brouillés périgourdine*.

Oeufs brouillés Madelon

SCRAMBLED EGGS MADELON

Prepare and cook scrambled eggs according to the original recipe, mix them with 2–3 tablespoons grated cheese, and arrange in a dish. Garnish the centre with 3–4 lamb's kidneys cut lengthwise in half and tossed in butter, the sauce thickened with 1 tablespoon melted meat jelly (see page 21), 2 tablespoons tomato purée and 1 tablespoon butter. Croûtons are optional.

Note A few thin slices of truffle may be added to the eggs, in which case they are called *oeufs bergère*.

Oeufs brouillés aux pointes d'asperges
SCRAMBLED EGGS WITH ASPARAGUS TIPS

Prepare and cook the eggs according to the original recipe, and mix with them 2−3 tablespoons asparagus tips sautéed in butter. Arrange in a dish and decorate the centre with a few specially chosen asparagus tips.

Garnish with small crescents of flaky pastry or croûtons fried in butter.

Oeufs brouillés Rachel
SCRAMBLED EGGS WITH TRUFFLES AND ASPARAGUS TIPS

Prepare and cook the eggs according to the original recipe, then add a thin julienne of truffles. Arrange in a dish. In the centre put a large bunch of asparagus tips, surround these with nice slices of truffle lightly heated in a tablespoon of melted meat jelly (see page 21).

Garnish with triangles of flaky pastry or croûtons fried in butter.

Oeufs brouillés tomates
SCRAMBLED EGGS WITH TOMATOES

Prepare and cook the eggs according to the original recipe. Add 2−3 tomatoes peeled, seeded, chopped and tossed in butter.

Put into a dish and, if liked, sprinkle the top with a generous tablespoon melted meat jelly (see page 21) to which a little butter has been added.

Oeufs brouillés aux truffes
SCRAMBLED EGGS WITH TRUFFLES

Prepare and cook the eggs according to the original recipe. Mix with them thinly sliced fresh truffles lightly tossed in butter and arrange in a dish. Surround with slices of truffle coated with meat jelly (see page 21) to which an equal amount of butter has been added.

Croûtons fried in butter and triangles of flaky pastry go well with these eggs.

Oeufs brouillés Véronique

SCRAMBLED EGGS WITH CHEESE AND NOODLES

Prepare and cook the eggs according to the original recipe. Add 2 – 3 tablespoons freshly grated cheese. Arrange in a dish and cover the top with noodles freshly sautéed in butter.

The noodles give a pleasant nutty flavour and can well replace the croûtons.

Oeufs brouillés Victor-Emmanuel

SCRAMBLED EGGS WITH WHITE PIEDMONTESE TRUFFLES

Prepare and cook the eggs according to the original recipe. Add 3 – 4 tablespoons freshly grated Parmesan cheese and arrange in a warm dish. Cover the top with finely sliced white Piedmontese truffles, season them with salt and freshly ground pepper and sprinkle with a few tablespoons melted meat jelly (see page 21). Cover the dish and, if the eggs are very hot, the heat from them will be enough to cook the truffles.

OEUFS DURS
HARD-BOILED EGGS

Little thought is usually given to the cooking of hard-boiled eggs. Yet the correct time for cooking should be strictly observed. Cooking for too long gives the egg an unpleasant taste and makes it tough.

The time for cooking an egg in boiling water is from 7 – 8 minutes according to the size of the egg. As soon as the eggs are cooked, they should be plunged into cold water. This makes them easier to shell.

Hard-boiled eggs play an important part in hors-d'oeuvre and salads.

Excellent cutlets can be made with hard-boiled eggs, and they are a great help in the planning of menus for days of abstinence.

Egg cutlets lend themselves to all the garnishes usually served with lamb cutlets, noisettes of lamb, fillets of chicken and chicken suprême, partridge, pheasant, etc.

Hard-boiled eggs can be served in various ways, e.g. with béchamel (see page 23), mushroom or onion sauce (see page 35).

They can also be served on a purée of sorrel or spinach, or with chicory.

Côtelette d'oeufs

EGG CUTLETS

▬▬▬▬▬▬ 6 hard-boiled eggs, 2 tablespoons truffle, 8—10 tablespoons well reduced béchamel sauce (see page 23), cream, 3 egg yolks, flour, egg and breadcrumbs for coating

Dice the eggs, add the truffle, peeled and diced or cut into thin slices. Add a little cream to sauce and mix with the eggs. Then add egg yolks.

Turn this mixture out on a dish and smooth the surface. When it is cold, divide into pieces the size of an egg, and shape into small cutlets. Flour them lightly and coat with beaten egg, and roll in breadcrumbs.

Fry in clarified butter till brown on both sides.

Serve the sauce of your choice separately.

Cromesquis d'oeufs

HARD-BOILED EGGS IN BATTER

Use the same mixture as for egg cutlets. When it is cold, divide it into balls the size of a small egg and flatten them slightly. A minute or two before serving, dip them into a light batter and fry in deep fat. Drain, and serve them on a table napkin, garnished with parsley.

Serve tomato sauce (see page 132) separately.

Oeufs à la tripe

HARD-BOILED EGGS WITH ONION SAUCE

Hard-boiled eggs cut into slices and coated with béchamel sauce (see page 23) to which has been added a little cream and 1 tablespoon chopped onion, lightly browned in butter.

Oeufs durs farcis

STUFFED HARD-BOILED EGGS

▬▬▬▬▬▬ 6 hard-boiled eggs, béchamel sauce (see page 23), 1 teaspoon finely chopped parsley, 1 teaspoon anchovy essence, salt, pepper, pinch ground nutmeg, 1 teaspoon finely chopped chives, butter, grated cheese

Cut the eggs in half lengthwise, take out the yolks and rub through a fine sieve. Put the resulting purée in a small basin, add 2 tablespoons béchamel sauce, parsley, anchovy essence, salt, pepper, ground nutmeg, and the chives sautéed in a little butter. Fill the eggs with this mixture, piling it up. Cover with a little more béchamel sauce, sprinkle with grated cheese, moisten with melted butter and brown under the grill (U.S. broiler).

If liked, serve with tomato sauce (see page 132) or with spinach.

Vol-au-vent d'oeufs

EGG VOL-AU-VENT

6—8 hard-boiled eggs, 2—3 truffles, 3 oz. butter, 1 pint (U.S. 2½ cups) béchamel sauce (see page 23), 1 freshly cooked vol-au-vent case

Cut the eggs into quarters, and thinly slice the truffles. Add the butter to the sauce, then stir in the eggs and truffles and fill the vol-au-vent case.

Note If liked, the truffles can be replaced with shrimps (U.S. prawns), in which case the sauce should be finished with shrimp butter (see page 51.

LES OMELETTES
OMELETS

To make an omelet is a simple matter, but in order to succeed a certain amount of practice is needed and there are certain details to be observed.

For the perfect omelet, the eggs must be well beaten so as to reach the necessary homogeneity. Do not pour the eggs into the omelet pan until the butter begins to take on a slightly brown colour; the eggs coming in contact with the hot butter will give the omelet all the required lightness and nutty flavour, and at the same time that pretty golden colour which makes it so appetising.

Generally allow 2 eggs per person, 4 eggs for two, and 5 for three. To obtain a good omelet, the number of eggs should be limited to 8 or at the most to 10.

In order not to have to repeat each time the number of eggs in the following recipes, we will adopt as a basis the omelet with 5 eggs. Seasoning required will be pinch salt, pinch pepper (optional) and 1 oz. butter to finish.

Omelette simple

PLAIN OMELET

As soon as the eggs are poured into the hot butter, shake the omelet pan to and fro so that the eggs cook evenly, or stir rapidly with a fork; tilt the pan in the direction opposite to the handle and, with the help of the fork, give the omelet an oval shape.

Place the omelet on a warm dish, being careful not to break it.

Note The omelet should be creamy inside and firm and golden on the outside.

Omelette aux artichauts

ARTICHOKE OMELET

Cut a medium-sized artichoke bottom into quarters, slice finely and cook in butter. Mix with the eggs and make an omelet as described above.

As a variation, very thin slices of potato can be cooked with the artichokes; or thinly sliced truffles can be added.

Omelette aux champignons

MUSHROOM OMELET

Peel and slice 6 medium-sized mushrooms and sauté them quickly in butter, season with salt, pepper and chopped parsley. Mix with the eggs and proceed to make the omelet.

As a variation either 1 pinch chives or 2 tablespoons tomatoes sautéed provençal style (see page 660) can be added to the mushrooms.

Omelette aux cèpes

CÈPE OMELET

The same as for mushroom omelet, except that cèpes are usually only obtainable in cans in Britain and would not need to be sautéed.

Omelette aux épinards

SPINACH OMELET

Cook some spinach, drain well, pressing it hard to extract the water, chop it coarsely, and sauté in butter to remove as much of the moisture as possible. Season with salt and pepper. Mix it with the eggs and cook the omelet in a pan which has been lightly rubbed with garlic.

Omelette à l'espagnole

SPANISH OMELET

To the eggs add 1 tablespoon finely sliced onion lightly browned in butter and seasoned with salt, pepper and chopped parsley.
Make the omelet in the form of a pancake.

Omelette aux fines herbes

OMELET AUX FINES HERBES

To the eggs add 1 tablespoon herbs consisting of chopped parsley, chives, chervil and tarragon.

Omelette aux foies de volaille

CHICKEN'S LIVER OMELET

Cut 2 chicken's livers into dice, toss in butter. Season with salt and pepper, then add a little chopped parsley and 2 tablespoons demi-glace sauce (see page 22) to which a little white wine has been added.
Make the omelet, cut through the centre and fill with the livers.

Omelette au fromage

CHEESE OMELET

Mix 1 tablespoon grated Gruyère and 1 tablespoon grated Parmesan cheese with the eggs and, if liked, 1 tablespoon fresh cream. Cook the omelet in the ordinary way.

Omelette grand'mère

OMELET WITH CROÛTONS AND CHOPPED PARSLEY

Prepare the eggs and just before cooking add 3 tablespoons finely diced bread croûtons tossed in butter, and a pinch of chopped parsley.

Omelette au jambon

HAM OMELET

For a ham omelet either cooked or smoked ham may be used. The ham should be diced, sliced or chopped very finely and tossed in butter before adding to the eggs. Then make the omelet in the ordinary way.

As a variation, one can either add potatoes sliced finely and cooked in butter, or mushrooms finely sliced and tossed in butter, or aubergines fried in oil, or chopped parsley, chives, etc.

Omelette au lard

BACON OMELET

Cut 2 oz. bacon fat into cubes or slice it finely. Brown for 1 minute in butter and add to the eggs. Make the omelet at once.

Another recommended method: Make a plain or omelet aux fines herbes and place on it 4 or 5 slices of very hot grilled bacon.

Omelette à la moelle

OMELET WITH BEEF MARROW

Make a plain omelet and partly split it lengthwise. Fill the centre with large cubes of beef marrow, poached for a few minutes in salted water, drained and rolled in meat jelly (see page 21). Garnish the top of the omelet with rounds of marrow, also poached. Sprinkle them with chopped parsley and put a little meat jelly on top.

Omelette aux morilles

OMELET WITH MORELS

Carefully wash 12 morels and cut them in half to remove any impurity that may be found inside them. Toss them quickly in butter to evaporate as much moisture as possible. Sprinkle them with 2 tablespoons melted meat jelly (see page 21) and 3 tablespoons cream. Season with salt and pepper. Shake the saucepan so that the cream and the meat jelly are thoroughly mixed. Make an omelet in the ordinary way; partly split it and fill the centre with the morels.

Omelette mousseline

MOUSSELINE OMELET

Put 3 egg yolks and 2 whole eggs into a bowl with pinch salt and 2 table-spoons thick cream; beat them together as instructed for the plain omelet. Add the 3 egg whites stiffly beaten. Pour this mixture into a pan containing 2 oz. very hot butter. Stir briskly, bringing the edges towards the centre.

This omelet may be served folded or flat.

As a variation, one may add thin slices of truffle, grated cheese, asparagus tips, etc.

Omelette Nantua

SHRIMP (U.S. PRAWN) OMELET

Prepare a plain omelet, partially cut through the centre and fill with the following mixture:

Sprinkle 2−3 tablespoons shrimps with a little melted meat jelly (see page 21). Bind with 3−4 tablespoons thick cream or creamy béchamel sauce (see page 23).

As a variation, the shrimps (U.S. prawns) may be replaced by prawns (U.S. shrimps) or by lobster cut into little cubes.

Omelette aux nonats

OMELET WITH NONATS

The nonat is a small Mediterranean fish, considered to be a great delicacy in Provence.

At the very last moment, before pouring the eggs into the omelet pan, add 4 tablespoons nonats tossed in a little clarified butter, then proceed in the usual way.

This omelet may also be made by cooking the nonats for 1 minute in salted water and draining them well before mixing with the eggs.

Omelette à l'oseille

SORREL OMELET

Cook 2−3 tablespoons chopped sorrel in a little butter and add to the beaten eggs, then cook the omelet at once.

Omelette à l'oignon à la lyonnaise

ONION OMELET

Slice 2 tablespoons onion very thinly and fry in butter until they begin to colour. Mix them with the beaten eggs, and then cook the omelet immediately.

It may be served flat or may be folded.

Omelette parmentier

POTATO OMELET

Slowly cook 4−5 tablespoons finely diced potato in a little clarified butter, until soft but hardly coloured.

Add this to the eggs with a pinch chopped parsley, immediately before making the omelet.

Omelette provençale

PROVENÇAL STYLE OMELET

Rub a clove of garlic gently over the bottom of the omelet pan, then add 2 tablespoons olive oil and make it very hot. Add 2 medium-sized peeled and seeded tomatoes either cut into thin slices or in large cubes, and a pinch chopped parsley. Cook for a few minutes and then add to the eggs. Make the omelet as usual.

Omelette aux rognons

KIDNEY OMELET

Make a plain omelet. Partially cut through the centre and fill with 2−3 veal or lamb's kidneys diced, seasoned with salt and pepper, sautéed briskly and mixed, away from the fire, with a few tablespoons boiling demi-glace sauce (see page 22) and little dabs of butter.

Omelette Rossini

TRUFFLE OMELET WITH FOIE GRAS

Make a truffle omelet and arrange on top of it small scallops of fresh foie gras, rolled in flour and tossed in butter.

Surround the omelet with a few tablespoons demi-glace sauce (see page 22) to which has been added 1 tablespoon butter.

Omelette au thon

TUNNY FISH OMELET

Add to the eggs 4 tablespoons tunny fish cut into cubes, and a pinch chopped parsley. Make the omelet in the usual way and serve a small sauce-boat of melted anchovy butter separately.

Omelette aux truffes

TRUFFLE OMELET

Add to the eggs 2—3 tablespoons truffle sliced thinly and seasoned with salt and freshly ground pepper. Make the omelet and arrange some large slices of truffle warmed in slightly buttered meat jelly (see page 21) on top.

Omelette aux pointes d'asperges

OMELET WITH ASPARAGUS TIPS

Add to the eggs 3 tablespoons asparagus tips cooked in salted water, drained and sautéed for a few minutes in butter. Cook the omelet in the ordinary way, split it down the middle and fill with a bunch of asparagus tips.

As a variation, thinly sliced pieces of truffle may be added to the asparagus tips.

Omelette à la ménagère
HOUSEWIFE'S OMELET

Choose some large macaroni or Italian pasta and cook it in boiling salted water; keep it fairly firm and as soon as it is ready drain it and let it cool.

Heat 4 tablespoons butter or lard in a fairly large pan, add the macaroni and cook until it is a good golden colour. Add 5—6 well beaten eggs and season with salt and pepper. Stir well with a fork and proceed as for an ordinary omelet. To turn the omelet, slide it out on to a dish, then reverse it back into the pan and brown on the underside. Slide the omelet again on to a large round dish.

Of all the recipes given above, this is my favourite.

Omelette crêpe
PANCAKE OMELET

Thoroughly beat 2 eggs with 1 teaspoon cream and a pinch salt. Heat $\frac{1}{2}$ oz. butter in an omelet pan. When nut-brown add eggs. Shake pan briskly and toss the omelet like a pancake for a second to colour the other side, slide on to hot plate, put on it 2 slices of bacon crisp from grill (U.S. broiler). This should be served and eaten as hot as possible.

OEUFS FROIDS
COLD EGGS

Eggs used in these dishes may be poached, soft-boiled or hard-boiled.

Their arrangement demands minute care. You must have artistic imagination and good taste, yet be restrained and correct in decoration. In my long experience I have come to the conclusion that a deep square silver or porcelain dish is the best for presenting eggs in jelly. This kind of dish can easily be put on to crushed ice, which will allow the jelly to retain the quality and freshness which make it perfect.

Type fondamental d'oeufs pochés ou mollets à la gelée
BASIC METHOD FOR POACHED OR SOFT-BOILED EGGS IN JELLY

Well dry and trim some cold poached eggs and coat them with white chaudfroid sauce (see page 31). Place a slice of truffle on the centre of each one.

Put the serving dish on ice and mask it with some chicken aspic jelly to the depth of about ¼ inch. When set, arrange the eggs on the jelly and mask them with more jelly. Leave to set. When ready to serve put the completed dish on to a larger dish and surround with crushed ice.

The preparation of cold egg dishes can be varied in many ways by using different sauces and different garnishes.

Thus white chaudfroid sauce can be varied by adding paprika, thick tomato sauce or shrimp butter.

Truffles, chervil leaves, tarragon leaves, red Spanish peppers, shrimps (U.S. prawns), etc., are all suitable garnishes.

It is not essential to coat the eggs with sauce before putting them on the jelly. Poached eggs may also be arranged on various mousses, of tomato, crayfish, ham, tongue, foie gras, chicken, paprika, Chambertin, etc.; but in this case they must always be covered with aspic jelly.

They should be described on the menu as, for instance: Tomato mousse with poached or soft-boiled eggs (see tomato mousse, page 660).

When the garnish applied to the eggs consists of several ingredients, a more or less fancy name must be invented, but it should, as far as possible, approach the truth, either by mentioning the principal ingredient, or by an appropriate description.

Oeufs à l'alsacienne

POACHED EGGS WITH PAPRIKA CHAUDFROID SAUCE

Poached eggs coated with paprika chaudfroid sauce (see page 32) decorated as liked and arranged on a mousse of foie gras, the eggs interspersed with julienne of truffles and breast of chicken

Oeufs à l'andalouse

ASPIC OF POACHED EGGS AND CHICKEN MOUSSE

Poached eggs, coated with white chaudfroid sauce (see page 31) to which has been added a light infusion of saffron to give it a pale yellow colour.

Stand the serving dish on ice, and half fill it with chicken mousse with paprika (see page 463). When this has set, arrange the eggs on it, and intersperse them with a fine julienne of truffles. Then cover completely with aspic jelly.

Oeufs à la d'Aumale

ASPIC OF POACHED EGGS AND HAM MOUSSE

The same preparation as that for aspic of poached eggs and chicken mousse, only the chicken paprika mousse is replaced by a ham mousse and the eggs are interspersed with julienne of ham.

Oeufs pochés ou mollets à la gelée

POACHED OR SOFT-BOILED EGGS IN JELLY

Carefully dry the eggs, trim them and arrange on a thin bed of aspic jelly. Decorate as liked, and cover with more jelly.

To vary the presentation and the flavour, before covering with jelly, one can intersperse the eggs with either ham, tongue, chicken's breasts, truffle, pheasant or partridge, etc., all cut into fine julienne; or with asparagus tips, peas, etc.

As an alternative, the eggs may be served with a Russian salad, vegetable salad, *salade Rachel* or just a simple salad. At the same time serve mayonnaise in a sauce-boat.

Oeufs Richelieu

POACHED EGGS WITH CRAYFISH MOUSSE

Poached eggs coated with a cream chaudfroid sauce (see page 31) with a slice of truffle on each egg, arranged on a mousse of crayfish interspersed with crayfish tails and bunches of asparagus tips and the eggs covered with jelly

Oeufs Rigolette

POACHED EGGS WITH CHICKEN MOUSSE

Poached eggs coated with *sauce chaudfroid aurore* (see page 32) arranged on a bed of chicken mousse (see page 56) interspersed with cock's kidneys poached in white stock. Arrange bunches of asparagus tips in the centre of the dish and cover with aspic jelly.

Poissons

FISH

POISSONS D'EAU DOUCE
FRESH-WATER FISH

Soupe de poissons mode provençal
PROVENÇAL STYLE FISH SOUP

—————— 2 lb. carp, perch or tench, 2 onions, 2 leeks, 2–3 tomatoes, 2 cloves garlic, pinch chopped parsley, 1 bay leaf, 1 stick celery, water, salt, pepper, pinch saffron (optional), slices white bread

Clean and cut fish into pieces. Put into a pan with chopped onion, chopped leeks (white part only), tomatoes, peeled, seeded and chopped, crushed garlic, parsley, bay leaf and chopped celery.

Cover with water, add salt, pepper and saffron and boil briskly for 15 minutes.

Put bread into a tureen. Arrange fish on a dish and pour a little of the soup over it. Pour the rest into the tureen.

The soup is served first, followed by the fish, and this is sometimes accompanied by aïoli sauce sometimes called *beurre de Provence*.

Editor's note AÏOLI SAUCE (*beurre de Provence*)

—————— 1 oz. garlic, 1 egg yolk, pinch salt, ½ pint (U.S. 1¼ cups) oil, lemon juice

Pound the garlic as finely as possible in a mortar. Add the yolk and salt.

Add oil, first drop, by drop and work it in thoroughly with the pestle. Add the rest of the oil gradually to get a complete amalgamation. As the sauce thickens add a few drops of lemon juice and cold water.

Note Should the sauce curdle, take a fresh egg yolk and gradually work the curdled mixture into it.

Soupe de perches à la menagère

PERCH SOUP

About 3 lb. perch each weighing about 8 oz., 3½ pints (U.S. 8¾ cups) water, 1 onion, 1 bay leaf, 2 cloves garlic, 1 sprig parsley, ½ oz. salt, few crushed peppercorns, 4 tablespoons olive oil, 5—6 tomatoes, 10 oz. rice, pinch saffron, 2 leeks

Clean and fillet the fish. Keep flesh in a cool place for future use (see page 165). Put the bones, heads and trimmings into a large pan with the water. Add the sliced onion, bay leaf, cloves garlic, parsley, salt and peppercorns. Boil for 20 minutes, then strain through a fine sieve. This is the *court-bouillon.*

Heat the oil in a pan, add the sliced leeks (white part only) and the tomatoes peeled, seeded and chopped. Cook for a few minutes, then add *court-bouillon.* Bring to boiling point, then add the rice and saffron. Cook for 25—30 minutes. The soup should be rather thick and the rice well cooked.

Note Rice may be replaced by vermicelli, macaroni or potatoes, or the soup can just be poured over slices of bread.

Burbot, small carp, tench, pike, etc., can be used in the same way. In the U.S.A. this would include buffalo fish, and white fish.

OTHER WAYS OF MAKING COURT-BOUILLON

COURT-BOUILLON — WITH VINEGAR

5 pints water (U.S. 6¼ pints), ¼ pint (U.S. ⅝ cup) vinegar, 1 oz. rock salt, 6 oz. chopped carrots, 8 oz. chopped onions, bouquet of 1 sprig thyme, 1 bay leaf and few parsley stalks, ¼ oz. peppercorns

Put all ingredients, except peppercorns, into a pan. Heat to boiling point and simmer for 1 hour. Add peppercorns 12 minutes before the end of the cooking. Strain through muslin. This is used for cooking trout, salmon or shellfish.

WITH WHITE WINE

2 pints (U.S. 5 cups) white wine, 2 pints water, 3 oz. chopped onions, *bouquet garni,* ½ oz. rock salt, few peppercorns

Put all ingredients except peppercorns into a pan. Heat to boiling point and simmer 30 minutes. Add peppercorns 12 minutes before the end of the cooking. Strain through muslin. Used for poaching fresh-water fish.

PLAIN COURT-BOUILLON FOR FISH
2 pints (U.S. 5 cups) cold water, ¼ oz. salt, ¼ pint (U.S. ⅝ cup) milk, thinly peeled rind 1 lemon

Immerse the fish in the cold liquid, bring slowly to boiling point. Draw to the side of the stove and leave till the fish is cooked.

Emploi des filets de perche et autres poissons indiqués

TO USE FILLETS OF PERCH AND SIMILAR FISH

Season the fillets, coat with flour and fry in oil or in butter *à la meunière* or coat with flour, then with egg and breadcrumbs and fry in butter or oil. Serve with a tomato sauce (see page 132).

Alose grillée

GRILLED (U.S. BROILED) SHAD

If it is to be served whole, choose a shad weighing 1 – 1¼ lb.

For the marinade Olive oil, lemon juice, 1 sprig parsley, small sprig thyme, 1 bay leaf, salt and pepper.

Clean fish thoroughly and make one or two deep incisions in the fleshy part of the back. Cover fish with marinade and leave for about 1 hour. Then grill (U.S. broil) gently for about 30 minutes, basting occasionally with a little oil or butter.

Serve with maître-d'hôtel butter, anchovy butter (see page 114), béarnaise sauce (see page 30) or with sorrel cooked in butter, bound with egg yolk and cream and seasoned with salt and pepper.

If the shad is rather big it can be cooked whole in the oven, in which case sprinkle lightly with breadcrumbs and baste with oil from time to time during the cooking.

If it is to be served in slices cut the slices about ¼ inch thick; season with salt and pepper, marinate as described above and then grill (U.S. broil).

Editor's note In American cookery, this fish is suitable for cooking on a plank.

Anguilles

EELS

Eels can be served in several ways: fried, *en matelote*, *à la meunière*, *à la poulette*, *à la provençal*, etc. It is important that the eels are caught in running water, so that they do not have a muddy taste.

Anguille frite

FRIED EEL

Choose small eels, skin and clean them thoroughly then cut into pieces. Season with salt and pepper, coat with flour and fry in oil.

Anguille matelote

EEL STEW

A *matelote* is the name given in French cooking to a fish stew made with red or white wine.

———————— About 2 lb. eels, 2 onions, *bouquet garni*, 2—3 cloves garlic, few peppercorns, salt, 2 pints (U.S. 5 cups) red wine, 6 tablespoons brandy, few mushrooms, browned in butter, small glazed onions, 3 oz. butter, 2 oz. flour

Choose medium-sized eels, clean and skin them and cut into pieces. Put into fairly shallow pan with the sliced onion, *bouquet garni*, garlic, peppercorns and salt. Add red wine and bring to boiling point. Add the brandy, flame it, then cover and cook till eels are tender. To serve, arrange the fish in a deep dish and surround with mushrooms and onions. Mix the butter and flour together and add gradually to the liquor. When thickened, strain over the eels and garnish with fried croûtons.

Note White wine can be used in this recipe instead of red wine.

Anguille meunière

EELS MEUNIÈRE

———————— Eels, salt, pepper, flour, butter, lemon juice, parsley

Choose medium-sized eels; cut into portions, season, coat with flour and cook in butter. Arrange on a serving dish, sprinkle with lemon juice and chopped parsley. Add a few dabs of butter to the pan and as soon as it begins to bubble pour it over the eel.

Note For variation, cèpes browned in butter may be mixed with the eels after they are cooked.

Anguille à la poulette
EELS WITH ONIONS AND MUSHROOMS

About 2 lb. eels, 2¼ oz. butter, 2 oz. flour, ½ pint (U.S. 1¼ cups) white wine, ½ pint (U.S. 1¼ cups) water, 12 small onions, *bouquet garni*, salt, pinch pepper, mushrooms, 3 egg yolks, 4–5 tablespoons cream, parsley

Skin the eels and cut into portions; put into a saucepan, cover with cold water and bring to the boil for a few seconds; drain and leave to cool. Heat the butter with the flour and cook for a few minutes without colouring. Add the eel and stir with a wooden spoon, making sure that each piece of eel is mixed with the roux. Add the wine and water, onions, *bouquet garni*, salt, and pepper. Bring to the boil and simmer for 25–30 minutes. Arrange the eel in a deep dish with the onions and a few mushrooms tossed in butter. Thicken sauce with the yolks and cream mixed together, and strain over the eels. Sprinkle lightly with parsley. Serve with plain boiled potatoes.

Anguilles à la provençale
PROVENÇAL STYLE EELS

2–3 lb. eels, salt, pepper, flour, 5 tablespoons oil, 4 tablespoons chopped onions, ½ pint (U.S. 1¼ cups) white wine, 1½ lb. tomatoes, chopped parsley, 1 clove garlic

Skin and cut eels into portions and put into boiling water for a few seconds, drain and dry, season with salt and pepper and coat with flour.

Heat the oil, add onions and when beginning to brown add the eel. Fry until starting to brown, then add wine and cook until reduced by half. Add tomatoes, peeled, seeded and chopped, salt and pepper, parsley and garlic. Cover and simmer for 25–30 minutes. Some potato can be added with the tomato and this would make an excellent luncheon dish.

Note Medium-sized eels, cut up and cooked in a *court-bouillon* with white wine and herbs left to cool in the liquor make an excellent hors-d'oeuvre.

Anguille tartare
EELS TARTARE

————————— Medium-sized eels, cleaned, skinned and cut into portions, *court-bouillon* with white wine, flour, egg and breadcrumbs

Cook the eels in the *court-bouillon* then drain and cool. Coat with flour, then with egg and breadcrumbs, and fry in butter.

Serve with *sauce tartare* (see page 42).

When peas and new potatoes are in season an excellent eel stew can be made as follows:

————————— Small eels, salt, pepper, flour, butter, few small onions, peas, new potatoes, *bouquet garni*

Cut eels into pieces, season with salt and pepper, coat with flour and brown for a few minutes in butter. Add onions, peas, and potatoes. Cover with water, add *bouquet garni* and adjust seasoning.

Cover and cook for 30—35 minutes over moderate heat.

Note The potatoes can be omitted, and the peas can be replaced by broad beans.

Barbeau et barbillon
BARBEL (U.S. CATFISH MAY BE SUBSTITUTED)

Note The hard roe of this fish should not be used as it is thought to be poisonous.

Barbeau au court-bouillon à la ménagère
BARBEL IN COURT-BOUILLON

For *court-bouillon:*

————————— 2 pints (U.S. 5 cups) white wine, 2 pints water, 1 onion, sliced thinly, 1 sprig parsley, 1 stick celery, 1 sprig thyme, 1 bay leaf, 1 clove garlic, rock salt, few peppercorns

Cook all together for 30 minutes, then strain.

Cook the barbel in the *court-bouillon*, and serve with caper sauce (see page 31) and boiled potatoes.

Barbel cooked in *court-bouillon* as above, allowed to cool and served with vinaigrette (see page 42) or mayonnaise sauce (see page 40) makes an excellent luncheon dish. It can be served with potato salad.

The *court-bouillon* in which the fish was cooked will make a good basis for soup.

FOR THE SOUP

Butter, 1 medium-sized onion, 1 leek, 3—4 tomatoes, 4 pints (U.S. 10 cups) *court-bouillon*, slices white bread, saffron (optional)

Heat butter, add chopped onion and chopped white part of the leek and brown lightly. Add tomatoes, peeled, seeded and chopped, and cook for about 10 minutes. Add a little of the *court-bouillon*, then simmer for 12—15 minutes.

Put bread into a tureen, pour tomato mixture over and then more of the boiling *court-bouillon*. A pinch of saffron may be added.

Instead of pouring the soup over slices of bread, some thick vermicelli can be cooked in the soup, in which case the saffron is essential. Grated cheese should be handed with the soup.

Note Vinegar should not be added to a *court-bouillon* if it is required for soup or rice pilaf.

Excellent soups and pilafs can be made from the *court-bouillon* in which fish, or bones and trimmings of fish have been cooked, but I would repeat, only on condition that vinegar has not been used.

Here is an example.

PEASANT STYLE VEGETABLE SOUP

2 oz. butter, 1 leek, 1 onion, 8 oz. carrots, 1¼ lb. potatoes, 1 stick celery, melted butter, 4 pints (U.S. 10 cups) *court-bouillon* of carp, perch, pike, etc., slices toast

Add the thinly sliced vegetables to melted butter. Add the *court-bouillon* and boil briskly for 30—35 minutes.

Put some slices of toast into a tureen and pour the soup over.

Barbillon

SMALL BARBEL

This is the name given to small 1 — 1¾ lb. barbel. It is usually an ingredient in a *matelote* which includes several fish.

For a *matelote* proceed according to the instructions for *anguille matelote* (see page 166).

Barbillon grillé

GRILLED (U.S. BROILED) BARBILLON

Make one or two incisions in the back of the fish and brush it with oil then grill (U.S. broil) it slowly.

Maître d'hôtel butter, anchovy butter (see page 114), mayonnaise sauce (see page 40), etc., go well with grilled barbillon.

Barbillon à la meunière

YOUNG BARBEL MEUNIÈRE

Choose small fish. Make one or two incisions in the backs, salt and pepper, coat with flour and fry in butter. Arrange on a dish, with a squeeze of lemon. Add a few dabs of fresh butter to the butter left in the frying pan, and when it begins to bubble pour over the fish.

Barbillon au four

YOUNG BARBEL BAKED IN THE OVEN

Choose fish of medium size. Make one or two incisions in the back, season and put into a fireproof dish, brush with oil or melted butter and cook in the oven.

For a more substantial dish, surround the fish with cubed potatoes and a little chopped onion. Season the vegetables and baste with a little oil or melted butter during the cooking process. Sprinkle with chopped parsley before serving.

Barbillon à la bonne femme

YOUNG BARBEL WITH SHALLOTS AND MUSHROOMS

1 — 1½ lb. barbel, butter, salt, pepper, chopped parsley, 2 shallots, few mushrooms, 3 — 4 tablespoons breadcrumbs, 1 wine glass white wine, juice ½ lemon

Make one or two incisions in the fleshy part of the back of the fish and put into a well buttered fireproof dish. Add salt, pepper, parsley, chopped shallots and finely chopped mushrooms. Cover with the breadcrumbs. Add wine and lemon juice and cook in a slow oven, basting frequently.

Brème

BREAM

Bream is a rather coarse fish, which may be used in a *matelote*. Large bream are usually grilled (U.S. broiled) or cooked in the oven.

Brochet

PIKE

As far as possible, choose fish weighing between 4 – 5 lb. But never use the roe of pike.

Pike is prepared in many different ways. I will only give the simpler ones here.

Brochet au vin rouge

PIKE WITH RED WINE

1 small pike, 1 onion, 1 sprig parsley, 1 sprig thyme, 1 bay leaf, 1 stick celery, 2 cloves garlic, few peppercorns, red wine, salt

Put pike into a fish kettle with all the flavourings. Add enough red wine to cover and a little salt. Simmer until the fish is tender.

Pilaw de brochet

PILAF OF PIKE

1 3–4 lb. pike, salt, pepper, flour, 1¼ pints (U.S. 3 cups) water, 1 sprig parsley, 1 sprig thyme, 1 bay leaf, 1 onion, salt, few crushed peppercorns, 2 oz. butter, 1 tablespoon finely chopped onion, 8 oz. rice

Fillet the pike and cut into pieces about the size of a walnut, season with salt and pepper and coat with flour.

Put the head, backbone and trimmings of the fish into a pan with the water, parsley, thyme, bay leaf, finely sliced onion, salt and peppercorns. Cook for 15 minutes, then pass the *court-bouillon* through a strainer.

Heat the butter in a casserole, add the finely chopped onion, and when lightly browned add the rice. Mix well, and add two-thirds *court-bouillon*, cover and cook for 18 minutes, preferably in the oven.

While the rice is cooking, fry the pieces of pike in butter, and when the rice is ready add the fish. Serve with tomato (see page 132), curry (see page 32), or paprika sauce (see page 32).

Brochet au court-bouillon

PIKE IN COURT-BOUILLON

Prepare a *court-bouillon* with white wine as given on page 164. No vinegar should be added so that the remaining *court-bouillon* can be used for soup. Poach the fish and serve hot with either caper sauce (see page 31), red wine sauce or hollandaise sauce (see page 33), or serve cold with mayonnaise or ravigote sauce or green sauce (see pages 40, 42, 43).

In Lyons, excellent quenelles are made with the flesh of large pike.

Carpe au vin rouge

CARP WITH RED WINE

—————————— You will need for 6 or 8 persons:
1 carp,* 5 oz. butter, 2 oz. flour, 2 teaspoons anchovy essence, some small glazed onions, cèpes or mushrooms, tossed in butter
*Choose a carp without scales, and cook as instructed for pike with red wine (see page 171), or in *court-bouillon*.

Make a roux with 2 oz. of the butter and the flour; let the flour cook for a few moments; remove from heat and gradually add some of the liquor in which the fish was cooked, to give a coating sauce.

Simmer for 15—20 minutes. Strain sauce through a fine strainer into another saucepan and add remaining butter and anchovy essence.

Arrange carp in a serving dish, surround with small glazed onions, cèpes or mushrooms tossed in butter and covered with part of the sauce. Serve the rest of the sauce separately.

Carp cooked in *court-bouillon*, with wine, can be served hot or cold.

Carp cooked in a white wine *court-bouillon* is called *saumonée* and when accompanied by a ravigote sauce (see page 42) or a cream horse-radish sauce (see page 44) makes an excellent luncheon dish.

Court-bouillons left over from these dishes may be used for poaching other fish and for various matelotes.

Matelote de carpe

CARP STEW

Choose the smaller carp for a *matelote*, and proceed in the same way as for *anguille matelote* (see page 166).

Filets de carpe à l'anglaise

ENGLISH STYLE FILLETS OF CARP

Fillet a medium-sized carp, clean and trim, and season with salt and pepper, dip in flour, then coat with egg and breadcrumbs. Fry in oil or in butter.

Serve with maître d'hôtel butter.

Laitances de carpe

CARPS' ROES

Carps' roes are a much sought after dish and can be cooked in various ways.

Poach for a few moments in salted water, drain, dry, season with salt and pepper and coat with flour. Then cook in butter. Arrange on a very hot serving dish, squeeze a little lemon juice over and sprinkle with chopped parsley.

One may also, after flouring the roes, dip them into beaten egg, then in breadcrumbs, and fry in butter.

Serve with maître d'hôtel butter or béchamel sauce (see page 23) to to which thinly sliced eggs have been added.

Laitances périgourdine

CARPS' ROES WITH TRUFFLES

Poach the roes in salted water, drain, dry them and cook for a few minutes in butter. Arrange on a dish which has been masked with béchamel sauce (see page 23). Add a few thin slices of truffle. Cover with béchamel sauce, sprinkle grated cheese on top, pour a little melted butter over and brown lightly under the grill (U.S. broiler) or in the oven.

Laitances de carpes Joinville

CARPS' ROES WITH CRAYFISH TAILS AND TRUFFLES

Prepare as in the last recipe, adding fresh-water crayfish tails, cut lengthwise, with the truffles.

The crayfish may be replaced by shrimps.

Laitances de carpes à la florentine
CARPS' ROES WITH SPINACH

Poach roes in salted water, drain and dry them and fry for a few minutes in butter. Arrange on a bed of spinach which has been blanched, well drained, pressed and coarsely chopped, then heated in butter to extract all the moisture. Cover with béchamel sauce (see page 23), sprinkle with grated cheese, place a little melted butter on top and lightly brown under the grill (U.S. broiler) or in the oven.

Lotte à la Dugléré
BURBOT WITH TOMATOES AND WINE

1 lb. burbot, salt, pepper, flour, 1 tablespoon finely chopped onion, 3—4 tomatoes, pinch chopped parsley, 3—4 tablespoons white wine, 1½ oz. butter, lemon juice

Slice filleted fish and season with salt and pepper. Coat with flour and arrange in a buttered sauté pan. Add the onion, tomatoes, peeled, seeded and chopped, parsley and wine. Cook fairly quickly for about 15—20 minutes.

Arrange fish on a serving dish. Add the butter and lemon juice to the sauce and pour over the fish.

Lotte à la provençale
PROVENÇAL STYLE BURBOT

1 lb. burbot, salt and pepper, flour, 2 tablespoons finely chopped onion, 4—5 tomatoes, pinch chopped parsley, 1 clove garlic, pinch saffron, 4—5 tablespoons olive oil, 1 wine glass white wine, 1 wine glass water, toast

Fillet and prepare the fish as described for *lotte à la Dugléré* (see above), and arrange in a sauté pan. Add onion, tomatoes, peeled, seeded and chopped, parsley, garlic, and saffron. Pour over the oil, add white wine and the water. Cover and cook fairly quickly for 15—20 minutes.

Arrange the scallops on slices of toast and pour the sauce over them.

Provençal style burbot is also served with rice pilaf; in which case omit the toast.

Lotte à la meunière

BURBOT MEUNIÈRE

———————— Burbot, salt, pepper, butter, lemon juice

Slice the filleted fish, season with salt and pepper, coat with flour and fry in butter.

Arrange on a serving dish, and sprinkle with lemon juice. Add a few dabs of butter to the butter left in the frying pan, heat briskly and pour over the fish.

Note This may be accompanied by sauté potatoes, purée of potatoes, plain boiled potatoes, spinach, sorrel, etc.

The same method is used for all fish cooked *à la meunière*. The flesh of the burbot, being rather firm, is excellent in stews, with peas, broad beans, potatoes, aubergines, baby marrows, etc.

Perche

PERCH

Small perch are usually fried.

Medium-sized perch are cooked *à la meunière*, or are one of the ingredients of a mixed *matelote*.

Large perch are poached in *court-bouillon* or baked in the oven.

Saumon

SALMON

Whole salmon are usually cooked in *court-bouillon* with vinegar flavoured with onion, chopped carrot, parsley, bay leaf, thyme, salt and peppercorns. Cover the pan and bring slowly to the boil, then simmer very gently.

Any of the following sauces can be served with salmon cooked in this way:

Caper (see page 31), shrimp (see page 32), hollandaise (see page 33), cardinal (see page 31), oyster (see page 34), mousseline (see page 34), ravigote (see page 42), Venetian (see page 36).

Darnes de saumon

SALMON STEAKS

Salmon steaks are pieces of varying thickness cut from the middle of the fish.

These are cooked in *court-bouillon*, according to instructions given for whole salmon and the same sauces accompany them.

However, from my own experience, the vinegar in the *court-bouillon* may be omitted with advantage.

Coquilles de saumon

SCALLOPED SALMON

This is usually made with cooked salmon, carefully boned and mixed with béchamel sauce (see page 23), then put into scallop shells, sprinkled with grated cheese and melted butter and browned.

Note Slices of truffle and thinly sliced mushrooms may be mixed with the salmon, and thinly sliced hard-boiled eggs.

Côtelettes de saumon

SALMON CUTLETS

12 oz. cooked salmon, 4 oz. mushrooms, 1 oz. truffles, 2 egg yolks, ½ — ¾ pint (U.S. 1¼ — 1⅞ cups) thick béchamel sauce (see page 23) egg and breadcrumbs for coating, butter, fried parsley

Flake the fish finely, add mushrooms and truffles finely chopped, egg yolks and enough béchamel sauce to give a fairly firm mixture. Divide into equal portions and form into cutlet shapes.

Coat with egg and breadcrumbs, and fry in butter just before serving. Garnish with fried parsley.

If liked *sauce curry à la crème* (see page 32) may be served with the cutlets.

Côtelettes de saumon Pojarski

SALMON CUTLETS POJARSKI

12 oz. cooked salmon, 2 oz. butter, 2 oz. breadcrumbs, 1 — 2 table-spoons cream, salt, pepper, butter for frying

Bone and skin the fish and flake coarsely. Add the butter, and bread-crumbs moistened with a little cream. Mix all very well together and season with salt and pepper.

Divide into 5 – 6 equal parts and shape into cutlets on a floured board. Just before serving, fry in clarified butter, until brown on both sides.

Arrange in a ring on the serving dish and garnish with one of the following: crayfish or shrimps, oysters, truffles, mushrooms, cèpes, cucumbers, curried or paprika rice, mixed with a little béchamel or Normandy sauce (see pages 23, 35).

Darne de saumon Chambord

SALMON STEAK WITH HERBS AND RED WINE

1 fairly thick salmon steak, little chopped onion, little chopped carrot, butter, 1 sprig parsley, 1 bay leaf, 1 sprig thyme, red wine, salt, few peppercorns

Put the fish into a sauté pan, and sprinkle with a mirepoix made by lightly browning the onion and carrot in butter. Add parsley, bay leaf and thyme, then enough red wine barely to cover the fish. Add a little salt and peppercorns.

Cover and simmer gently.

Arrange the steak on an oval dish and surround it with the following garnish: quenelles of fish, moulded in a tablespoon, mushrooms, seasoned carp's roe, floured and tossed in butter; truffles cut into quarters, crayfish, croûtons fried in butter.

Serve *sauce bourguignonne* (see page 25) separately.

Darne de saumon Daumont

SALMON STEAK WITH HERBS AND WHITE WINE

Cook the steak as explained above for the *darne de saumon Chambord*, replacing the red wine with white wine.

Drain the salmon, arrange on an oval dish, surround with quenelles of fish, mushrooms, slices of truffle, small vol-au-vent cases filled with shrimps and roes poached in butter.

Serve with Normandy sauce (see page 35).

Darne de saumon régence

SALMON STEAK WITH FISH QUENELLES

Prepare the steak as instructed for the *darne de saumon Daumont* (see page 177), and cook in the same way. Drain and place on an oval dish. Garnish with fish quenelles, roes poached in butter, truffle slices, piles of crayfish and small oyster patties.

Serve with Normandy sauce (see page 35).

Darne de saumon royale

SALMON STEAK WITH MOUSSELINE QUENELLES OF FISH

Prepare and cook as instructed for the *darne de saumon Daumont* (see page 177). Place on an oval dish, and garnish with mousseline quenelles of fish, mushrooms, slices of truffle and potatoes cut with a ball cutter and cooked in boiling salted water.

Serve with Normandy sauce (see page 35).

Saumon grillé

GRILLED (U.S. BROILED) SALMON

Cut the steaks from a medium-sized salmon, if possible about ¾–1 inch thick. Season with salt, sprinkle with oil and grill (U.S. broil) gently.

Serve with maître d'hôtel butter, anchovy butter or béarnaise sauce (see pages 114, 30 and 30).

Saumon à la meunière

SALMON MEUNIÈRE

Cut the salmon into steaks, not too thick, season with salt, coat with flour and fry in butter. Remove pan from the heat. Arrange fish on a serving dish and sprinkle with lemon juice. Add 1 tablespoon fresh butter to the butter left in the pan, heat it, and as soon as butter starts bubbling pour over the salmon.

Saumon froid

COLD SALMON

As far as possible, salmon which is to be served cold should be cooked whole, or in thick pieces or steaks, and cooled in *court-bouillon*. Small pieces cooked separately are inclined to be dry.

When serving cold salmon, the skin may be removed so that the fish can be decorated more easily, but the true gourmet will always prefer it presented to him in its silvery robe.

In any case, the decoration of a piece of cold salmon should be restrained; above all, never make use of softened butter, whether coloured or not.

Montpellier butter is the only one that suits cold salmon.

All the cold sauces go well with cold salmon, as well as vegetable salads.

MONTPELLIER BUTTER

2 oz. watercress, 1 oz. parsley, 1 oz. chervil, 1 oz. chives, 1 oz. tarragon, 1½ oz. chopped shallot, ¼ oz. spinach, 1 tablespoon chopped capers, 4 oz. gherkins, 1 clove garlic, 4 anchovy fillets, 1½ lb. butter, 3 hard-boiled egg yolks, 2 raw egg yolks, 8 tablespoons oil, salt, cayenne pepper

Put watercress, parsley, chervil, chopped chives, tarragon, shallot and spinach into a pan and cover with boiling water. Boil for 2 minutes, then drain, press in a cloth to remove all the water, and put the leaves, etc., into a mortar with the capers, gherkins, garlic and well washed anchovies.

Pound all well together.

Mix this paste with the butter, add the yolks, and finally add the oil very gradually. Pass through a tammy cloth or fine sieve. Season with salt and pepper.

Note This butter is sometimes used as a coating for fish, in which case the oil and egg yolks are omitted.

Truite au bleu

BLUE TROUT

For this dish it is essential to use live trout. Have ready a large, fairly shallow pan of boiling water to which salt and vinegar have been added. Medium-sized trout of about 5−7 oz. will take only a few minutes to cook.

About 10 minutes before they are required, take the trout from the water in which they are kept and stun them with a sharp bang on the head; clean them quickly and sprinkle with vinegar, then plunge them into the boiling water, when they will immediately curl up and the flesh will break.

Serve on a table napkin and garnish with parsley.

Serve boiled potatoes separately and melted butter or hollandaise sauce (see page 33).

Truite à la meunière

TROUT MEUNIÈRE

After cleaning make one or two incisions in the back of the fish, sprinkle with salt and coat with flour, then cook in butter till brown on both sides.

Put the fish on to a serving dish, squeeze a little lemon juice over and sprinkle with chopped parsley.

Add a little extra butter to that left in the pan, and when it begins to bubble pour on to the trout.

River trout can also be cooked in a reduced *court-bouillon* with red or white wine and may be eaten hot or cold.

Truite de rivière au vin rouge

RIVER TROUT WITH RED WINE

River trout, butter, few slices carrot, few slices onion, 2−3 sprigs parsley, 1 bay leaf, salt, freshly ground pepper, red wine, 4 oz. butter, 1 oz. flour, few drops anchovy essence, slices toast

Clean the trout and put into a buttered fireproof dish with thin slices of carrot and onion, parsley, bay leaf, salt and pepper. Cover with red wine. Put a lid on the dish and cook in the oven, basting from time to time.

Pour the liquor from the fish and put it into a small pan, boil until one-third reduced.

Mix 1 oz. butter with the flour and add to the sauce a little at a time, until at the desired thickness. Strain into a clean pan, add the remaining butter and the anchovy essence.

Put the fish on slices of toast, on to a serving dish, and pour the sauce over.

Truite de rivière à la bonne femme

RIVER TROUT WITH VEGETABLES

6 5–7-oz. trout, salt, pepper, 2 oz. butter, 2 medium-sized onions, 2 medium-sized carrots, 1 stick celery, water, white wine, 1 bay leaf, pinch chopped parsley, 3 oz. butter, ½ oz. flour

Clean the trout, season with salt and pepper and arrange in a fireproof dish.

Heat the butter in a pan, add the onions, carrot and celery cut into julienne and ½ pint (U.S. 1¼ cups) water. Cover and stew gently for 20–25 minutes. Strain and put the vegetables on top of the trout.

Add equal quantities of white wine and water to cover the fish, then add bay leaf and parsley. Cover and cook in the oven, basting from time to time.

Remove trout to a serving dish then one-third reduce the liquor.

Mix butter and flour together, and add gradually to the liquor, then pour over the fish. Serve with boiled potatoes.

Any of the following make a suitable garnish:

Small tomatoes, peeled, seeded and filled with vegetable salad, shrimps, etc. Stuffed hard-boiled eggs, barquettes filled with purée of tunny, sardine or anchovy, little aspics of shrimps or prawns, small lettuce hearts, etc.

Note Small carp, perch, tench or pieces of turbot can be prepared in the same way and make excellent luncheon dishes which cannot be too highly recommended.

Mousse de saumon et mousselines à la crème

SALMON MOUSSE AND CREAM MOUSSELINE

Mousses and mousselines have the same basic forcemeat. Mousses are made in large moulds, and mousselines, which are used in other dishes, are moulded in tablespoons.

FOR THE FORCEMEAT

———— 12 oz. fresh salmon, salt, pepper, ½ pint (U.S. 1¼ cups) fresh cream

Pound the fish thoroughly, add salt and pepper and rub through a fine sieve.

Put into a basin and keep on ice for at least one hour.

Keeping the mixture on ice, gradually add the cream, working it in well with a wooden spoon.

Keep on ice until required for use.

Moulage de la mousse

TO MOULD A MOUSSE

Butter the inside of a mould of the required size, and decorate the sides with slices of truffle. Fill about three-quarters full, then put it into a bain-marie with boiling water coming about half-way up the mould. Cover the bain-marie and let the mousse poach, keeping the water at about 203° F. — do not let it boil.

For a mould holding 2 pints (U.S. 5 cups) allow about 30–35 minutes.

Mousselines are moulded in a tablespoon, like large oval quenelles. When they are ready put into a buttered sauté pan, then cover with very hot salted water, taking care to pour the water through a pointed strainer, so as not to spoil the shape of the mousselines. Cover the pan and allow to poach for 12–15 minutes in simmering water. Avoid boiling.

These mousses should be very light, but at the same time firm.

Mousselines may also be moulded in small moulds and poached in a bain-marie.

POISSONS DE MER
SEA FISH

WHITEBAIT, BLANCHAILLE AND NONATS

Whitebait, which abound in the Thames and around the coasts of the North Sea, are much the same as the blanchaille of the Mediterranean. Nonats are similar to whitebait and blanchaille and are also found in the Mediterranean.

Whitebait is much appreciated in England and at one time was often served as the second fish course at large dinner parties and banquets.

To cook, it should be coated very liberally with flour, then put into a frying basket and shaken well to remove surplus flour.

Heat some lard or oil, and plunge the fish in for about one minute. Be careful not to fry too many at one time.

Drain well, season with salt and cayenne pepper and serve on a table napkin or dish paper garnished with fried parsley.

Blanchailles are treated in the same way.

Nonats are not so fragile as whitebait and blanchailles. They are sautéed in butter or oil and either served by themselves or with an omelet. They can also be poached for a minute or two in *court-bouillon*, cooled and then served in a salad.

Nonats aux épinards à la niçoise
NONATS AND SPINACH

4—5 tablespoons oil, 1 lb. blanched and coarsely chopped spinach, 8 oz. nonats, 2 eggs, salt, pepper, breadcrumbs, olive oil

Heat the oil in a sauté pan, add spinach and cook quickly until dry. Turn into a basin and add the nonats, poached for 1 minute in *court-bouillon*, beaten eggs, salt and pepper. Mix all well together, then put into a buttered fireproof dish. Smooth the surface, sprinkle with breadcrumbs and a little olive oil. Put into the oven for about 20 minutes to brown.

Bouillabaisse à la marseillaise

BOUILLABAISSE

Editor's note No book of this kind would be complete without a recipe for bouillabaisse, and M. Escoffier has given us here a recipe from his friend Caillat.

There are many variations of this famous dish which is traditional all along the Mediterranean coast, but unfortunately many of the fish used are only found in the Mediterranean and are virtually unknown in England and America. However, M. Escoffier gives alternatives such as gurnet, weever, cod, sole and even mussels.

HERE IS M. CAILLAT'S RECIPE:

You will need for 10 persons:

5—6 lb. fish (hog-fish, chapon, John Dory, whiting from Palangre, conger eel, boudreuil, roquier, mullet, crayfish or prawns), 4 oz. onion, 2 oz. leek (white part only), 2 tomatoes, 2 cloves garlic, 1 teaspoon chopped parsley, large pinch saffron, 6 tablespoons olive oil, 1 bay leaf, 1 sprig savory, pinch fennel leaf, water, salt, pepper, slices French loaf

Cut the large fish into slices, and leave the small ones whole.

Chop onion and leek, peel, seed and chop the tomatoes, crush garlic and put all into a large pan with the parsley, saffron, oil, bay leaf, savory and fennel. Add the fish, except any with soft flesh, like mullet and whiting.

Add enough water just to cover the fish, and season with salt and pepper. Bring to boiling point and boil for 7—8 minutes, then add remaining fish and continue cooking briskly for a further 15 minutes.

Put some slices of a long French loaf into a deep tureen (in Marseilles a special bread called Marette is used), and pour the broth over.

Serve the fish separately.

Note The bread for bouillabaisse must never be toasted or fried.

White fish like whiting must always be included in a bouillabaisse, as it helps to bind it.

Bouillabaisse de morue

BOUILLABAISSE OF SALT COD

You will need for 8−10 persons:
4 tablespoons chopped onion, 2 tablespoons chopped leek, ¼ pint (U.S. ⅝ cup) olive oil, 1 small clove garlic chopped, 3½ pints (U.S. 8¾ cups) water, pinch salt, pepper, pinch saffron, *bouquet garni*, 2½ lb. rather thick white salt cod, 5−6 potatoes, 4 tablespoons oil, 1 teaspoon coarsely chopped parsley, slices toast

Add the onion, leek and garlic to the oil and cook for a few minutes without browning. Add water, salt and pepper, saffron and *bouquet garni*. Bring to boiling point, then add thickly sliced potatoes and cook for 12−15 minutes.

Wash fish thoroughly, scrape, then cut into 2−2½ inch cubes. Add to the *court-bouillon* with the oil. Continue cooking rather briskly until fish and potatoes are well done. Just before the end of the cooking, add the parsley.

Serve with slices of toast rubbed with garlic and sprinkled with some of the *court-bouillon*.

Anchois

ANCHOVIES

Anchovies are usually served as hors-d'oeuvre, or used as flavourings in various dishes.

Fresh anchovies can be served fried.

Bar ou loup de mer

BASS

Large bass are poached in salted water and are served with a sauce suitable for salmon, trout or turbot.

Small and medium bass are cooked *à la meunière* and grilled (U.S. broiled). They may also be put on a baking dish, seasoned with salt and pepper, sprinkled with oil, coated with breadcrumbs and cooked in the oven. This method is suitable for both large and small bass.

Before cooking, make one or two incisions in the back of the fish.

Serve with maître d'hôtel or anchovy butter (see page 114) or béarnaise or rémoulade sauce (see pages 30 and 42).

BLOATERS

Bloaters, which are smoked herrings, are served for breakfast. They are simply grilled (U.S. broiled).

Cabillaud

COD

Cod is cooked in water, and all the sauces that are served with turbot are suitable with it.

Cabillaud bouilli

POACHED COD

Poached cod can be cooked whole in pieces or steaks. It is accompanied by floury potatoes cooked in boiling salted water.

Serve with melted butter to which a little chopped parsley and chopped hard-boiled egg has been added or with hollandaise sauce (see page 33).

Cabillaud grillé

GRILLED (U.S. BROILED) COD

Cut the fish into slices about 1¼ inch thick. Season with salt and pepper and coat with flour. Brush with melted butter or olive oil and grill (U.S. broil) gently.

Serve with maître d'hôtel or anchovy butter (see page 114) or with béarnaise sauce (see page 30).

Cabillaud frit

FRIED COD

Cut fish into slices about ¾ inch thick. Season, coat with flour and fry.

Place on a dish with fried parsley and lemon. Serve with tomato (see page 132) or tartare sauce (see page 42).

Cabillaud à la provençale

PROVENÇAL STYLE COD

1½—2 lb. cod, 3—4 tablespoons oil, 2 tablespoons chopped onion, salt, pepper, flour, 4—5 tomatoes, parsley, 1 clove garlic, 1 bay leaf, 1 wine glass white wine

Cut fish into ¾-inch-thick slices, then cut in half and remove the bone. Heat the oil in a sauté pan, add onion and cook for a few minutes.

Season the fish, coat with flour and put into pan. Cook for a few minutes, then turn fish and add the tomatoes, peeled, seeded and chopped, little chopped parsley, garlic, bay leaf and wine. Cover and cook for 12—15 minutes.

Serve with freshly boiled potatoes.

Cabillaud à la portugaise

COD WITH SWEET RED PEPPERS AND TOMATOES

1½ — 2 lb. cod, 2 tablespoons chopped onion, 2—3 sweet red peppers, 3—4 tablespoons oil, salt, pepper, 5—6 tomatoes, chopped parsley, 1 bay leaf

Prepare fish as described above. Cook onion and chopped peppers for a few minutes in hot oil. Add fish and season with salt and pepper. Add tomatoes, peeled, seeded and chopped, parsley and bay leaf.

Cover and cook for 12—15 minutes.

Serve with *riz à la créole* (see page 666).

Carrelet ou plie

PLAICE OR DAB

There are many ways of cooking this fish, and because of its soft and fragile flesh it is generally filleted. Season the fillets lightly, flour them, then coat with egg and breadcrumbs. Fry in butter and serve with maître d'hôtel butter. Alternatively 1—2 tablespoons melted meat jelly (see page 21) can be added to the butter.

Colin

HAKE

All the ways of cooking cod may be applied to hake.

Pilaw de colin

PILAF OF HAKE

—————— 1½ lb. hake, salt, pepper, flour, onion, 1 bay leaf, few peppercorns, 1¼ pints (U.S. 3 cups) water, 2 tablespoons butter, 8 oz. rice, butter for frying

Cut fish into ⅜-inch cubes, season with salt and pepper and roll in flour.

Put the bone and trimmings into a pan with a thinly sliced onion, bay leaf and peppercorns. Add the water and a little salt, and boil for 12—15 minutes, then strain through a fine strainer.

Heat the butter in a pan, add 1 tablespoon finely chopped onion and cook until onion begins to brown, then add rice and fish stock. Cover and cook for 18 minutes, then strain.

Fry fish in butter, then mix with the rice. Serve accompanied by tomato, curry or paprika sauce (see pages 132 and 32).

Congre ou anguille de mer

CONGER EEL OR SEA EEL

This may be prepared by cooking in a *court-bouillon* (see page 164) and serving it with caper sauce (see page 31) and boiled potatoes, or fried and served with tomato or tartare sauce (see pages 132 and 42).

Dorade

SEA BREAM

The best kind is the one with a yellow rim to its eyes.

The true way of cooking sea bream is to grill (U.S. broil) it, or to bake it in the oven brushed with oil and sprinkled with fine breadcrumbs.

Serve with either a béarnaise sauce (see page 30), maître d'hôtel butter or a tomato sauce (see page 132).

Éperlans

SMELTS

The methods of cooking smelts are limited — they are generally fried and served on a table napkin.

Éperlans à l'anglaise
SMELTS IN THE ENGLISH MANNER

See whiting in the English manner (page 192).

Éperlans à la meunière
SMELTS MEUNIÈRE

———————— Smelts, salt, flour, butter, squeeze lemon juice

Clean the fish, sprinkle with salt, then roll in flour. Fry in butter, then put on to the serving dish and add the lemon juice.

Add a little more butter to that left in the pan, heat, and when it begins to bubble pour over the fish.

Aiglefin
HADDOCK

The best way to cook this is to divide it in half lengthwise, removing the backbone and skin. Put both fillets into a frying pan with ½ tablespoon butter and 3−4 tablespoons boiling milk. Cook, covered, for 4−5 minutes.

Serve with plain boiled potatoes, or melted butter, to which a little chopped hard-boiled egg may be added.

Harengs
HERRINGS

Herrings are usually grilled (U.S. broiled) and accompanied by maître d'hôtel butter, sometimes with the addition of mustard sauce (see page 35).

Filets de harengs à l'anglaise
FILLETS OF HERRING IN THE ENGLISH MANNER

———————— Herrings, salt, pepper, butter, egg, breadcrumbs

Carefully clean and fillet the herrings, removing the roe. Season fish and roes with salt and pepper.

Brush fish with melted butter, coat with egg and breadcrumbs and fry in butter. Cook the roes at the same time.

To serve, arrange herrings on a hot dish, put some maître d'hôtel butter on each and top with the roe.

Harengs farcis

STUFFED HERRINGS

———————— Herrings with soft roes, salt, pepper, breadcrumbs, milk, little chopped
parsley, pinch grated nutmeg, 1 shallot, 2—3 mushrooms, butter,
lemon juice

Split the herrings, remove the roe, and take out the backbone. Sprinkle
fish with a little salt and pepper. Put roes into a basin, add 2 tablespoons
breadcrumbs moistened with milk, parsley and nutmeg. Chop the shallot
and mushrooms and toss lightly in butter. Add to the roes with a little
seasoning and mix all well together. Put a spoonful of the mixture on
each herring, and re-form it. Arrange the fish in a fireproof dish, brush
with melted butter and sprinkle with breadcrumbs. Bake in a moderate
oven. Before serving, sprinkle with chopped parsley and lemon juice.
Serve with tomato sauce (see page 132).

Maquereau à l'anglaise

MACKEREL IN THE ENGLISH MANNER

Slice mackerel and poach in a *court-bouillon* (see page 164) to which
some fennel leaves have been added.
Serve with a purée of green gooseberries.

Maquereau grillé

GRILLED MACKEREL

Cut off the mackerel's head; open the fish from the back cutting the
backbone in two places, without separating the halves. Put the roe aside
on a buttered plate. Season the mackerel, brush with melted butter and
grill (U.S. broil) gently. Season the roes and cook them at the last
moment. Arrange on a hot dish. Put 1 tablespoon maître d'hôtel butter
and the roe on each fish, then re-form the mackerel.

Filets de maquereau aux moules

FILLETS OF MACKEREL WITH MUSSELS

———————— Salt, pepper, 3 medium-sized mackerel, flour, butter, chopped parsley,
2½ pints (U.S. 6¼ cups) mussels, 1 onion, 1 sprig parsley, ¼ pint (U.S.
⅝ cup) water, freshly ground pepper

Season filleted fish, coat with flour and arrange in a well buttered fireproof dish. Sprinkle with chopped parsley.

Put the well washed mussels into a pan with thinly sliced onion, parsley, water and pinch pepper. Cover and cook until the mussels open. Remove from heat and strain liquid carefully over the mackerel. Cover dish and cook in a quick oven.

Remove mussels from their shells and put with the mackerel. When the fish is cooked, the liquor should have reduced considerably.

Maquereau à la provençale

PROVENÇAL STYLE MACKEREL

2 medium-sized mackerel, salt, pepper, flour, 3 tablespoons oil, 2 tablespoons chopped onion, 1 wine glass white wine, 5—6 tomatoes, pinch chopped parsley, 1 clove garlic, pinch saffron (optional)

Cut the mackerel into pieces. Season with salt and pepper and coat with flour.

Heat the oil in a shallow saucepan or in an earthenware casserole, add onion when it begins to brown, put in the mackerel. Add the wine, peeled, seeded and chopped tomatoes, parsley, and garlic. Simmer for 15 — 18 minutes. Turn the fish during the cooking so it is cooked evenly.

Serve with rice pilaf (see page 669).

Maquereau frit

FRIED MACKEREL

Cut the mackerel in pieces, sprinkle with salt, coat with flour and fry in deep fat.

Serve with tomato or tartare sauce (see pages 132, 42).

Merlan

WHITING (U.S. SOMETIMES KNOWN AS SILVER HAKE)

Whiting is one of the most delicate of fish. It is often used in invalid diets, when it is grilled (U.S. broiled) or poached, and served with butter.

Merlans à l'anglaise

WHITING IN THE ENGLISH MANNER

Split the fish down the back and remove the backbone. Season and lightly flour the fillets, dip in beaten egg, then in very fine breadcrumbs. Fry in clarified butter.

Arrange on a long hot plate and serve with maître d'hôtel butter slightly softened.

Merlans Bercy

WHITING WITH WHITE WINE

4 medium-sized whiting, 4 teaspoons finely chopped shallot, ½ wine glass white wine, ½ wine glass water, salt, pepper, juice 1 lemon, butter, chopped parsley

Split the fish, remove the backbone and open out flat.

Put into a buttered fireproof dish, sprinkle with shallot, add the wine and the water.

Season with salt and pepper and add lemon juice. Dot with butter and cook in a moderate oven, basting frequently.

When cooked, the liquid should be almost completely reduced.

Sprinkle with parsley before serving.

Merlans Colbert

WHITING WITH MAÎTRE D'HÔTEL BUTTER

Split the whiting down the back, take out the backbone and sprinkle with salt, dip in milk then coat with flour.

Coat with egg and breadcrumbs and fry.

Arrange on a long, very hot dish, and serve with maître d'hôtel butter.

Merlans diable

DEVILLED WHITING

The same method as for *merlans à l'anglaise* (see page 192) except that a little melted meat jelly (see page 21) and a pinch of red pepper should be added to the maître d'hôtel butter.

Merlans dieppoise

WHITING WITH WINE, MUSHROOMS AND MUSSELS

4 whiting, ½ wine glass white wine, *court-bouillon*, cooked mushrooms, cooked mussels, white wine sauce (see page 212)

Split the whiting along the back, put into a sauté pan with the white wine and enough *court-bouillon* barely to cover. Cook carefully, then remove to a serving dish and garnish with mushrooms and mussels.

Reduce the liquor in which the fish was cooked, strain and add to the white wine sauce, then pour over the fish.

Note This method may be simplified by cooking the mussels in advance, and using the strained liquor to cook the fish.

The whiting should be put into a well buttered fireproof dish covered with the liquor and cooked in the oven, basting frequently.

When the fish is cooked the liquor should be almost completely reduced. Garnish with the mussels removed from their shells.

Merlans aux fines herbes

WHITING AUX FINES HERBES

4 medium-sized whiting, salt, pepper, flour, butter, ½ wine glass white wine, ¼ wine glass water, juice 1 lemon, pinch chopped parsley

Split the fish down the back and remove backbone. Open out and sprinkle with salt and pepper, coat with flour and arrange in a well buttered fireproof dish. Add wine and the water and lemon juice. Cook in a moderate oven for 8 – 10 minutes, when the liquid should be almost completely reduced.

Serve with a little more butter and sprinkle with parsley.

Merlans au gratin (à la ménagère)

WHITING AU GRATIN

——————— 4 whiting, flour, salt, pepper, chopped parsley, lemon juice, butter, 2 chopped shallots, 4 oz. mushrooms, 1 wine glass white wine, fresh breadcrumbs, 4—5 tablespoons tomato sauce (see page 132)

Split the whiting down the back and remove the backbone. Coat with flour and put into a buttered fireproof dish. Sprinkle with salt and pepper, chopped parsley and lemon juice.

Heat 2 tablespoons butter, add shallots and chopped mushrooms and cook for a few minutes, stirring. Adjust seasoning and add the wine. Boil for 5—6 minutes, then add 4 tablespoons breadcrumbs and tomato sauce. Pour over the fish, sprinkle with more breadcrumbs and a little melted butter.

Cook in a moderate oven for 10—12 minutes.
Sprinkle with parsley before serving.

Merlans sur le plat

BAKED WHITING

——————— 4 whiting, salt, pepper, flour, 1 onion, 1 sprig parsley, ½ bay leaf, few peppercorns, ½ pint (U.S. 1¼ cups) water, 3—4 tablespoons white wine, lemon juice

Split the whiting down the back, remove head and backbone. Season fish with salt and pepper, coat with flour and arrange flat in a well buttered fireproof dish.

Put the heads, bones and any trimmings from the fish with the finely sliced onion, parsley, bay leaf and peppercorns. Add water, and boil for 12—15 minutes. Strain through a fine strainer and pour over the fish. Add the white wine and a squeeze of lemon juice.

Cook in a moderate oven, basting frequently. When the fish is cooked, the liquid should be reduced to the consistency of syrup.

Serve at once.

Mousse de merlan

WHITING MOUSSE

——————— 1 lb. whiting, salt, white pepper, 2 egg whites, 1 pint (U.S. 2½ cups) thick cream, truffle for decorating

Pound the flesh of the whiting finely with the seasoning; add egg whites very slowly and then pass through a fine sieve.

Put the mixture into a basin and keep it on ice for 30 minutes. Add the cream very slowly, stirring gently with a wooden spatula and keeping the mixture on ice.

At this stage it should be firm and light.

Butter a jelly mould of the size required; decorate the sides with some slices of truffle; fill mould with the prepared mixture, and put it in a saucepan with enough boiling water to come half-way up the mould; cover and simmer for 25 – 30 minutes, do not allow to boil.

Arrange on a round dish and serve with one of the following sauces: white wine (see page 212), curry (see page 32) cardinal (see page 31), paprika (see page 32).

Merlan Richelieu
WHITING WITH MAÎTRE D'HÔTEL BUTTER AND TRUFFLES

Prepare and cook the whiting as for *merlans à l'anglaise* (see page 192) and garnish with a row of truffles on maître d'hôtel butter, sprinkled with 1 tablespoon meat jelly (see page 21).

Vol-au-vent de quenelles de merlan cardinal
VOL-AU-VENT OF QUENELLES OF WHITING

Creamed quenelles of whiting, moulded in dessertspoons and poached at the last moment; an equal amount of crayfish tails, or scallops of lobster or crayfish, slices of truffle

Mix with béchamel sauce (see page 23) finished with shrimp butter (see page 51).

Serve in a vol-au-vent case with some good slices of truffle arranged on top.

Morue
SALT COD

Before it is ready for use, salt cod should soak for at least 24 hours, if possible in running water; otherwise it should be put into a large dish and the water changed frequently.

2 – 2½ lb. salt cod is sufficient for 6 or 7 persons.

Morue à l'anglaise

SALT COD IN THE ENGLISH MANNER

Cut the cod into pieces of about 6−8 oz., put into a saucepan and cover with cold water. Bring to boiling point then reduce the heat and simmer for a good 15 minutes, so that the cod may poach without boiling. Drain and garnish with parsley.

Serve with boiled potatoes or boiled parsnips, and melted butter to which a little chopped hard-boiled egg has been added, or cream sauce (see page 38) with chopped hard-boiled egg.

Morue à la bénédictine

SALT COD WITH POTATOES

———————— 2−2½ lb. salt cod, 1 lb. cooked mashed potatoes, ¼ pint (U.S. ⅝ cup) oil, ½ pint (U.S. 1¼ cups) boiling milk, breadcrumbs

When the cod is cooked, drain, remove all skin and bone and pound it. Mix thoroughly with the potatoes and gradually add the oil and milk.

The mixture should be quite soft. Place it in a buttered fireproof dish, smooth the surface, sprinkle with fine breadcrumbs, pour a little oil over and brown in the oven.

Morue au beurre noir

SALT COD WITH BLACK BUTTER

———————— 2 lb. salt cod, parsley, squeeze lemon juice, 5 oz. black butter

Cut the cod into 6−8-inch pieces, and poach. Drain and remove the skin. Put on to the serving dish, sprinkle with coarsely chopped parsley and the lemon juice, then cover with black butter.

Editor's note

To make black butter Cook the butter until it is a good brown colour and begins to smoke, then add 1 tablespoon well washed and dried parsley leaves.

Morue à la béchamel

SALT COD WITH BÉCHAMEL SAUCE

Poach the cod, drain well and remove the skin, then coat with béchamel sauce (see page 23) to which a few tablespoons cream and butter have been added. Serve with boiled potatoes.

Note If preferred, some chopped hard-boiled egg may be added to the sauce.

Morue frite

FRIED SALT COD

Cut the cod into cubes and poach for 8 — 10 minutes; drain, then coat with flour, and fry in a few tablespoons oil or butter, turning so that the fish browns on both sides.

The bottom of the frying pan may be rubbed lightly with garlic.

Arrange the cod on a serving dish, and sprinkle with a dash of vinegar and chopped parsley. Add 2 tablespoons butter to the pan in which the fish was cooked, and when it begins to colour pour over the fish.

Morue à la lyonnaise

SALT COD LYONNAISE

2—2½ lb. salt cod, 2 medium-sized onions, butter, pinch pepper, parsley, 2 tablespoons vinegar

Poach the fish, drain well and skin. Finely slice onions and cook in the butter until they begin to colour. Add fish, cut into pieces, pepper and a little chopped parsley. Sauté all together for a few minutes. Lastly add the vinegar.

Note 12 oz. — 1 lb. medium-sized potatoes, sliced thinly and tossed in butter, may be added to the cod.

Morue à la provençale

PROVENÇAL STYLE SALT COD

2—2½ lb. salt cod, 4—5 tablespoons oil, 1 onion, 5—6 tomatoes, 1 clove garlic, freshly ground pepper, 4 oz. black olives, 2 large sweet red peppers (optional)

Poach fish, drain and remove the skin. Heat the oil in a pan, add the finely chopped onion, and when it begins to brown add the tomatoes, peeled, seeded and chopped, garlic and pepper. Add the fish and olives, and if peppers are used, they should be seeded, grilled and sliced. Simmer all together for about 20 minutes. Plainly boiled potatoes or a dish of *riz à la créole* (see page 666) may be served with this dish.

Brandade de morue

BRANDADE OF SALT COD

2—2½ lb. salt cod, 1½ pints (U.S. 3¾ cups) oil, 1 clove garlic, about ¼ pint (U.S. 1¼ cups) boiling milk

Cut fish into large pieces and poach for 10 minutes only, calculating from the time the water boils (the fish must be barely cooked). Drain well, and remove any bone and skin.

Heat ½ pint (U.S. 1¼ cups) oil and when quite hot add the fish, stirring vigorously until it forms a smooth paste.

Remove from the heat, add the garlic and work in the rest of the oil drop by drop, stirring vigorously all the time.

From time to time add 2—3 tablespoons of the boiling milk until that too has been absorbed.

When the brandade is finished it should have the consistency and colour of potato purée.

Serve surrounded with triangles of fried bread.

Brandade de morue truffée

TRUFFLED BRANDADE OF SALT COD

The brandade being finished (see recipe above), incorporate into it 5—7 oz. raw truffles, either chopped or sliced.

Serve in a vegetable dish, and decorate with slices of truffle. Cover it immediately.

Note The brandade of salt cod may be served in a vol-au-vent case.

Morue aux épinards à la florentine

SALT COD WITH SPINACH

4—5 tablespoons butter, 1 lb. cooked spinach, salt, pepper, nutmeg, 2—2½ lb. salt cod, poached and skinned, béchamel sauce (see page 23), grated cheese

Heat the butter in a sauté pan, add the spinach, coarsely chopped, salt, pepper and nutmeg. Cook until spinach is dry, then turn into a fireproof dish. Smooth the surface and arrange cod on the spinach.

Cover with sauce and sprinkle with cheese. Add a little melted butter and brown in the oven or under the grill (U.S. broiler).

MUSTÈLE

This fish, which is found mainly in the Mediterranean, is somewhat similar to the turbot.

It has a very delicate flesh and should be eaten as soon as caught, as it does not travel well.

It is generally prepared in the same way as *éperlans à la meunière* (see page 189), *à l'anglaise* (see page 189), or *à la Richelieu* (see page 195).

Mulet ou lubine

GREY MULLET

This is prepared in the same way as bass (see page 185).

Raie au beurre noir

SKATE WITH BLACK BUTTER

Among the various species of skate the one called 'thornback' is the best.

In England, Belgium and Holland, skate is sold trimmed and cleaned, and there is nothing to do but proceed with the cooking.

If it has not been cleaned, brush, wash and cut it up. Cook in salted water, allowing ½ oz. salt and ¼ pint (U.S. ⅝ cup) vinegar per 2 pints (U.S. 5 cups) water.

When cooked, drain, remove the skin and place on the serving dish, cover with black butter (see page 196) to which is added a pinch of coarsely chopped parsley.

Heat 2−3 tablespoons good vinegar in the pan which was used for the black butter, and pour it over the skate.

Small skate may be cooked *à la meunière*, without being cooked in water first.

Foie de raie à l'anglaise

SKATE LIVER IN THE ENGLISH MANNER

Poach the liver in a plain *court-bouillon*, then drain and cut into slices. Coat the slices with flour and then with egg and breadcrumbs and fry in butter. Serve with mashed potatoes and tomato (see page 132) or béarnaise sauce (see page 30).

Rouget

RED MULLET

As the red mullet has no gall bladder, many people are content to remove the gills, without gutting the fish. Certain gourmets cook it without scaling it, but this is not practical.

The flesh of the red mullet has a very special taste and has the advantage of being very light and easily digestible. The most sought after are the red rock mullet of the Mediterranean.

To obtain the full flavour and delicacy of the red mullet, it is better to grill (U.S. broil) or to cook it in butter or olive oil, in a frying pan or in the oven.

Maitre d'hôtel butter goes very well with grilled red mullet.

Rougets à la bordelaise

RED MULLET WITH BORDELAISE SAUCE

Choose as far as possible red mullet weighing between 5−7 oz. each, the right size for 1 person.

Scale, score them lightly on both sides or simply make an incision in the backs along the backbone. Season with salt and pepper, brush with oil and grill (U.S. broil). Serve on a very hot plate garnished with parsley.

Serve a bordelaise sauce at the same time (see page 25).

Rougets en caisse

RED MULLET IN FOIL

Grill (U.S. broil) the red mullet which should be, as far as possible, of the same size, or cook them in oil or butter.

Cut some foil or greaseproof paper into pieces large enough to cover the fish and allow 1 for each person.

Oil the paper and place 1 red mullet on each. Cover with some *sauce italienne* (see page 28), sprinkle with chopped parsley and fold the paper over to form a 'parcel'.

Put into a moderate oven for a few minutes to heat.

Rougets au gratin

RED MULLET AU GRATIN

Allow 1 red mullet for each person, 4—5 mushrooms, 3—4 tablespoons white wine, salt, pepper, breadcrumbs, butter, lemon juice, parsley
For duxelle sauce 1 tablespoon butter, 1 tablespoon oil, 4 oz. mushrooms, little chopped onion, 1 chopped shallot, white wine, parsley

To make the sauce Heat the butter and oil, add chopped mushrooms, onion and shallot and cook until the onion begins to brown. Moisten with a little white wine and add a little chopped parsley.

Arrange the red mullet on a buttered dish, surround with slices of mushrooms, sprinkle with white wine, season lightly with salt and pepper and cover with the duxelle sauce. Sprinkle with dry breadcrumbs, brush with melted butter and cook in a moderate oven for 10—12 minutes according to the size of the fish.

Before serving, sprinkle with lemon juice and chopped parsley.

Rougets à la nantaise

RED MULLET WITH WINE AND SHALLOTS

5—6 red mullet about 5—7 oz. each, salt and pepper, 5—6 tablespoons white wine, 2 shallots. chopped finely. ½ tablespoon butter. pinch freshly ground pepper, 4 tablespoons melted meat jelly (see page 21), 4 oz. butter, few drops lemon juice, pinch chopped parsley

Score the red mullet, reserve the livers, season with salt and pepper and grill (U.S. broil).

Put the wine into a pan with the shallots. butter and freshly ground pepper. Boil rapidly until reduced to one-third. Add melted meat jelly and the butter a little at a time. Add the livers of the fish mashed with a little butter. Finally add a few drops of lemon juice and the chopped parsley and cook for a few minutes.

Arrange the fish on a very hot dish and cover with the sauce.

Rougets à la provençale

PROVENÇAL STYLE RED MULLET

Grill (U.S. broil) 5—6 red mullet, or cook in a frying pan. Arrange on a very hot dish and cover with the following sauce: 4—5 medium-sized tomatoes, 3 tablespoons oil, salt, pepper, 1 small clove garlic and a pinch chopped parsley.

Peel, seed and chop the tomatoes, and put into a saucepan with the oil, season with salt and pepper, add the garlic and parsley. Simmer for 15—20 minutes.

Note A small pinch saffron or an infusion of saffron leaves may be added to the tomato. In this case the fish may be placed on bread moistened with the sauce as in bouillabaisse (see page 184).

Rouget à la façon d'un gourmet provençal

RED MULLET COOKED IN THE WAY OF A PROVENÇAL GOURMET

4 red mullet, oil, 2—3 truffles, ½ tablespoon fresh butter, salt, pepper 4—5 tablespoons meat jelly (see page 21), 1 clove garlic, maître d'hôtel butter, cayenne pepper

Season fish with salt and pepper, brush with oil and grill (U.S. broil).

Peel and slice truffles then put into a small pan with butter, salt, pepper and meat jelly. Cover and keep hot, but do not allow to boil.

When fish is cooked, rub the bottom of the serving dish with garlic. Arrange the fish in the dish and cover generously with maître d'hôtel butter to which a little cayenne has been added.

Put the truffles on top and serve at once.

To lovers of good things, I can recommend this dish.

John-Dory ou Saint-Pierre

JOHN DORY

This rather ugly fish has a very delicate flesh, little sought after in France, but much appreciated in England.

The different ways of preparing turbot, brill and fillets of sole may be applied to fillets of John Dory.

In England, it is simply cooked in salted water, served with boiled potatoes and melted butter and garnished with parsley.

Sardines et royans

SARDINES

Sardines are used in a great number of recipes. My friend Caillat has devoted 150 excellent recipes to this fish which I recommend to my readers. Here is the title of the work: *150 manières d'accommoder les Sardines.*

The simplest way of cooking sardines and of appreciating all the delicacy of their flavour is to grill (U.S. broil) or fry them in oil or in butter. Maître d'hôtel butter is the best accompaniment to grilled sardines.

Editor's note M. Escoffier is, of course, referring to French sardines. They abound round the coast of Sardinia from whence the name is derived. They are extremely delicate and cannot travel long distances, so unfortunately the only sardines available in England are preserved in oil or brine.

In the U.S.A. young fresh herrings can be used instead of fresh sardines.

Sardines aux épinards à la provençale

SARDINES WITH PROVENÇAL STYLE SPINACH

2—2½ lb. fresh sardines, salt, pepper, breadcrumbs, 1—2 teaspoons anchovy essence, pinch mixed herbs, water, 2½ lb. spinach, 4 tablespoons oil, 1 clove garlic, 2 eggs, grated cheese

Wash sardines carefully, remove heads, split down the front and remove the backbone. Season with salt and pepper.

Mix the breadcrumbs, pinch pepper, anchovy essence and herbs together and moisten with a little water. Stuff fish sparingly with this mixture and re-form.

Wash the spinach well in running water. Heat the oil, add garlic and spinach and cook until spinach is tender and dry.

Season with salt and pepper and add the well beaten eggs.

Put the spinach into a fireproof dish and arrange the sardines on top. Sprinkle with breadcrumbs and cheese mixed together. Brush with oil, and put into a moderate oven until the sardines are cooked and browned.

Note If the spinach is not very tender, it should be pre-cooked in a little salted water.

Soles et filets de soles

SOLES AND FILLETS OF SOLE

Remove the black skin, scale the white skin and cut off the heads at a slant; trim the fish and wash thoroughly.

To facilitate cooking the soles, carefully loosen the fillets from the backbone on the skinned side, using the point of a knife.

For 2 persons a 10-oz. sole should be chosen.

Sole arlésienne

POACHED SOLE WITH ONIONS AND TOMATOES

1 tablespoon finely chopped onion, pinch parsley, 1 sole, 3 tablespoons white wine, 3 tablespoons water, juice ½ lemon, 2 tomatoes, salt, pepper, 1 tablespoon butter, aubergines for garnish, flour, oil

Butter a fireproof dish, and put the onion and parsley in the bottom. Put the sole on top and add wine, the water and the lemon juice. Add tomatoes, peeled, seeded and chopped, and seasonings. Cover and cook in a moderate oven for 12—15 minutes.

Put sole on to a serving dish, stir the butter into the liquor remaining in the dish and pour over the fish. Garnish with slices of aubergine dipped in flour and fried in oil.

Sole à la bonne femme

SOLE BONNE FEMME

1 chopped shallot, pinch parsley, 2 oz. mushrooms, 1 sole, 4 tablespoons white wine, 4 tablespoons hot water, salt, pepper, juice ½ lemon, 3 tablespoons butter, 1 tablespoon flour

Butter a fireproof dish and put the shallot, parsley and chopped mushrooms in the bottom. Put the sole on top and cover with wine, water, seasoning and lemon juice. Cover, and put into a moderate oven for 5 minutes, then add 1 tablespoon butter mixed with the flour and continue cooking for a further 10—12 minutes.

Put the sole on to a serving dish, add the remaining butter to the liquor in the dish and pour over the fish. Return to the oven or put under a grill (U.S. broiler) to brown.

Sole au Chambertin

SOLE WITH CHAMBERTIN WINE

This is prepared as for *sole à la bonne femme* (see page 204), except that the fish is cooked in red wine and no water is added.

The method for sole bonne femme and for sole with Chambertin wine can be applied equally to turbot, brill, whiting, etc.

Sauce bonne femme is also used as a basis in various other dishes. By the addition of ingredients such as tomatoes, truffles, lettuce, sorrel, etc., and by using a little imagination, it is possible to produce a great variety of dishes.

Sole Colbert

SOLE FRIED IN EGG AND BREADCRUMBS

Remove the black skin and make an incision along the backbone with the point of a knife, from ½ inch from the head to within ¼ inch of the tail. Loosen the fillets as far as the small bones; break the backbone in 2 or 3 places so it can be removed easily when the sole is cooked.

Dip the sole in milk, flour it, then dip in beaten egg and breadcrumbs and roll back the loosened fillets from the backbone.

Fry the sole, take out the backbone, fill the cavity with maître d'hôtel butter and serve on a very hot dish.

Sole Dugléré

SOLE POACHED IN WHITE WINE, BUTTER AND TOMATOES

1 12-oz.—1-lb. sole, 2 tablespoons butter, 1 dessertspoon finely chopped onion, 2 tomatoes, pinch chopped parsley, salt, pepper, 3—4 tablespoons white wine, 1 teaspoon flour, few drops lemon juice

Clean the sole thoroughly and remove the black skin. Divide sole into 4 pieces crossways and put into a shallow saucepan with half the butter, onion, peeled, seeded and chopped tomatoes, parsley, salt, pepper and wine. Cook for 10—12 minutes.

Arrange the fish on a serving dish. Mix remaining butter with flour, and add to the liquor left in the pan. Add the lemon juice and pour over the fish.

Sole à la florentine

POACHED SOLE WITH SPINACH AND CHEESE

1 sole, 1 tablespoon butter, 4 tablespoons white wine, salt, pepper, spinach, béchamel sauce (see page 23), grated cheese

Poach sole in a shallow pan with butter, wine and the same amount of water. Season with salt and pepper.

Put some spinach, cooked in boiling water, then coarsely chopped and sautéed in butter, into a serving dish.

When sole is cooked, remove fillets from the backbone, and arrange on the spinach in the original form of the fish; cover with béchamel sauce to which the liquor from the dish has been added. Sprinkle with cheese and brown in the oven or under the grill (U.S. broiler).

Sole au gratin

SOLE AU GRATIN

1 12-oz.—1-lb. sole, butter, salt, pepper, 3—4 tablespoons white wine, 2 oz. mushrooms, 1 tablespoon *duxelles* (see page 201), breadcrumbs, 6—8 tablespoons demi-glace sauce with tomato (see page 22), parsley, lemon juice

Clean fish, remove the black skin and loosen the fillets along the backbone. Put into a buttered dish, skinned side down.

Season with salt and pepper, add wine and finely chopped mushrooms.

Mix *duxelles* with the sauce and pour over the fish. Sprinkle with breadcrumbs, dot with butter and put into a moderate oven to cook.

Before serving, sprinkle with lemon juice and chopped parsley.

Sole grillé

GRILLED SOLE

Clean sole and remove the black skin. Lightly score both sides, season with salt and pepper, brush with oil and grill (U.S. broil) under moderate heat.

Serve with parsley and wedges of lemon.

Maître d'hôtel butter or béarnaise (see page 30), devil (see page 27) or tartare (see page 42) sauce are good accompaniments to grilled sole.

Sole Lutetia

BAKED SOLE WITH TRUFFLES AND MUSHROOMS

Choose a 12-oz. sole, clean carefully and put into a well buttered fireproof dish. Add salt and pepper and 3 tablespoons hot water. Cook for 10−12 minutes in a moderate oven, basting from time to time.

Serve in the dish in which it is cooked, garnished with a fine julienne of truffles and mushrooms bound with a little cream and meat jelly (see page 21).

Sole ménagère

BAKED SOLE WITH RED WINE

1 12-oz.−1-lb. sole, red wine, 1 onion, 1 bay leaf, 1−2 sprigs parsley, 6−8 peppercorns, 1 tablespoon butter, 2 teaspoons flour, salt, pepper

Put sole into a fireproof dish, just cover with wine, and add thinly sliced onion, bay leaf, parsley and peppercorns. Cook in a moderate oven.

Remove sole to a serving dish. Strain liquor into a small pan, reduce a little and then thicken with the butter and flour mixed together. Check the seasoning, and pour sauce over the fish.

Sole à la meunière

SOLE MEUNIÈRE

1 sole, salt, milk, flour, butter, lemon juice, parsley

Prepare the sole, sprinkle with salt, then dip in milk, coat with flour and fry in butter.

Arrange on a hot serving dish, add a squeeze of lemon juice and sprinkle with parsley. Add 1 tablespoon butter to that remaining in the pan. Heat quickly, and when it begins to bubble pour over the fish.

Sole Mornay

SOLE MORNAY

1 sole, salt, butter, 3–4 tablespoons water, béchamel sauce (see page 23), little grated Gruyère and Parmesan cheese

Put fish into a buttered fireproof dish, sprinkle with salt, add 1 tablespoon butter and the water. Cook in a moderate oven 10–12 minutes.

Strain liquor into a small pan, reduce a little, then add to 6–8 tablespoons béchamel sauce. Put half this sauce into the serving dish, place sole on top and cover with remaining sauce. Sprinkle with cheese, dot with butter and brown in the oven or under the grill (U.S. broiler).

Sole Murat

SOLE WITH POTATO AND ARTICHOKE BOTTOMS

1 12-oz. sole, 1 medium-sized potato, 2 small artichoke bottoms, butter, juice ½ lemon, parsley, meat jelly (see page 21)

Cook *sole à la meunière* (see page 207). Meanwhile, dice potatoes and artichoke bottoms and sauté separately in butter. When cooked, mix together. Alternatively, slices of tomato can be used. They should be seasoned with salt and pepper, dipped in flour and sautéed in oil.

To serve the sole, put on to a hot dish, garnish with the potatoes and artichokes or tomato slices. Sprinkle fish with lemon juice and chopped parsley and add a few pieces of meat jelly.

Add a little more butter to the liquor left in the pan, reheat and pour over.

Sole à la normande

SOLE WITH WINE, OYSTERS AND CRAYFISH

You will need for 2 persons:
1 12-oz. sole, onions, parsley, ½ bay leaf, juice ½ lemon, salt, freshly ground pepper, ½ wine glass white wine, 1 wine glass water, butter, 20 mussels, 4 oysters, 4 mushrooms, gudgeon, egg, breadcrumbs, 2 small crayfish, *court-bouillon*, flour, 3 egg yolks, 2 tablespoons cream, croûtons

Remove the black skin and head from the fish and loosen the fillets.

Put a sliced onion, sprigs parsley, bay leaf and lemon juice into a fireproof dish. Add sole, season with salt and pepper. Add wine, water and a few dabs butter. Cover and cook in a moderate oven for 12—15 minutes, basting from time to time.

Cook mussels, with a finely sliced onion, sprigs parsley and a pinch freshly ground pepper.

Poach oysters, sauté mushrooms in butter, coat gudgeon with egg and breadcrumbs and fry; cook crayfish in *court-bouillon*.

When sole is cooked, put on to a serving dish, surround with mussels, removed from the shell, oysters and mushrooms and keep hot.

Put liquor from the fish, and that in which the mussels were cooked, into a pan, and reduce to about ¼ pint (U.S. ⅔ cup). Add 1 dessertspoon butter, mixed with 1 dessertspoon flour and boil for a few minutes. Remove from heat, and add yolks and cream mixed together.

Strain through a fine sieve and finish with 1 tablespoon butter.

Reheat without boiling and pour over fish.

Garnish with gudgeon, crayfish and croûtons.

Sole sur le plat

BAKED SOLE WITH WINE AND LEMON JUICE

1 12-oz. sole, salt, pepper, ½ glass white wine, ½ glass water, juice ½ lemon

Remove black skin and head from fish. Wash carefully and loosen fillets on skinned side.

Put into a well buttered fireproof dish, skinned side down. Add salt and pepper, wine, the water and lemon juice.

Cook in a moderate oven, basting from time to time until sole is cooked and liquid thick enough to glaze the fish.

Note In the recipes for sole in which white wine is one of the ingredients, lemon juice is indispensable. O therwise thewine takes on a rather unattractive grey colour.

Sole sur le plat aux moules
BAKED SOLE WITH MUSSELS

—————— Mussels, 1 sole, salt, pepper, ½ wine glass white wine, 3 —4 tablespoons water, juice ½ lemon, 1 shallot, parsley, 1 tablespoon fresh bread-crumbs

Cook mussels, remove from shells and keep hot in the liquor.

Prepare the fish as described for *sole sur le plat* (see page 209), put into a buttered fireproof dish with seasoning, wine, water, lemon juice, finely chopped shallot and some of the liquor in which the mussels were cooked.

Cook in a moderate oven, basting frequently. When sole is cooked, arrange mussels around the dish, sprinkle fish with parsley and bread-crumbs and continue cooking a further 2 minutes.

Sole Richelieu
FRIED SOLE WITH MAÎTRE D'HÔTEL BUTTER AND TRUFFLES

—————— 1 12-oz. sole, milk, flour, egg, breadcrumbs, butter, maître d'hôtel butter, truffles, meat jelly (see page 21)

Remove head and black skin and loosen fillets on the skinned side.

Dip fish in milk, flour, then in egg and breadcrumbs and fry in clarified butter.

To serve Put fish on to a serving dish, remove backbone and put some maître d'hôtel butter in the cavity.

Coat some truffles with a little meat jelly and arrange on the maitre d'hôtel butter.

Sole au court-bouillon à la russe
SOLE IN COURT-BOUILLON, IN THE RUSSIAN MANNER

—————— 1 oz. butter, 2 —3 small new carrots, 1 small onion, 2 sprigs parsley, 1 12-oz. sole, squeeze lemon juice, 1 tablespoon fresh butter

Melt butter, add thinly sliced carrot, onion and parsley and sauté for a few minutes. Add 6 tablespoons water and cook gently until vegetables are tender.

Remove to a fireproof dish. Prepare sole and place on top. Cook in a moderate oven or on top of the stove, basting frequently. When fish is cooked and the liquid reduced by half, add the lemon juice and the butter. Serve in the sauce dish.

Sole Saint-Germain

GRILLED SOLE WITH BÉARNAISE SAUCE

———— 1 sole, salt, pepper, melted butter, fresh breadcrumbs, small potato balls

Prepare sole, season, dip in melted butter, then coat with breadcrumbs, pressing them on well with a palette knife.

Brush with melted butter and grill (U.S. broil) gently.

Garnish with potatoes cooked in butter.

Serve with a béarnaise sauce (see page 30).

Sole au vin blanc chez soi

SOLE IN WHITE WINE

———— 1 medium-sized onion, 2—3 sprigs parsley, 1 12-oz. sole, salt, pepper, 3 tablespoons white wine, 6 tablespoons hot water, 2 tablespoons butter, juice 1 lemon, 1 teaspoon flour, 2 egg yolks

Put sliced onion into a fireproof dish with parsley. Prepare the sole and lay on top. Add salt and pepper, wine, the hot water, 1 tablespoon butter and lemon juice. Cover and cook in a moderate oven. Remove fish to a hot serving dish.

Mix remaining butter with flour and add to liquor in which fish was cooked. Boil for a few minutes, then remove from heat and add egg yolks mixed with 1 tablespoon sauce. Strain, and pour over fish.

Sole prepared in this way may be garnished with mussels, oysters, mushrooms, soft roe.

Sole aux fines herbes

SOLE WITH PARSLEY

Prepare and cook sole as in preceding recipe, just adding chopped parsley to the white wine sauce.

Sole au vin rouge

SOLE WITH RED WINE

Proceed as for the *sole sur le plat* (see page 209) but substitute red for white wine and add 1 tablespoon meat jelly (see page 21).

FILETS DE SOLE
FILLETS OF SOLE

According to the kind of dish required, fillets of sole are usually left in their natural state, that is to say flat, but can be folded, or rolled into paupiettes.

The thin membrane which lies just beneath the skin can be removed, as it is one reason for the contraction of the fillets during cooking. But usually it is enough to score the sides of the fillets lightly. Never bear heavily on a fillet of sole; the blade of the knife should be passed lightly over, pressing gently.

Fillets of sole should be poached in a very little water, with the pan covered and not allowed to boil. Boiling hardens and also causes the fillet to contract.

'Poach' means to cook at boiling point but not allowed to boil.

Fillets of sole are often cooked in a *court-bouillon* made as follows:

—————— Bones and trimmings from 3 soles, 1 finely chopped onion, 2 sprigs parsley, 1 bay leaf, few peppercorns, pinch salt, juice 1 lemon, 6 tablespoons white wine, ¾ pint (U.S. 1⅞ cups) water.

Put all ingredients together. Boil gently for 12–15 minutes, then strain through a fine strainer. This *court-bouillon* or *fumet poisson* is also used to prepare the white wine sauce for *sole normande* (see page 208), *sole dieppoise* (see page 216), *sole à la bonne femme* (see page 204) and *sole aux fine herbes* (see page 211).

FOR WHITE WINE SAUCE

—————— 1 tablespoon butter, 1 tablespoon flour, ½ pint (U.S. 1¼ cups) *court-bouillon*, 1–2 egg yolks, 1 tablespoon fresh cream, 1 tablespoon butter

Heat butter, add flour and cook for a few seconds without browning. Add *court-bouillon* slowly, stirring or whisking well. Simmer for 12–15 minutes then strain through a fine sieve into a clean pan. Thicken with yolks and cream and finally add butter. Keep hot without boiling.

Note The cream is not essential, as the egg yolks may be mixed with 2 tablespoons cream.

ANOTHER METHOD OF PREPARING THE SAUCE

Heat *court-bouillon* to boiling point, then add 1 tablespoon butter mixed with 1 tablespoon flour. Simmer for 8 – 10 minutes, then strain and thicken with 1 – 2 yolks as described in the first method.

Filets de sole à l'américaine
FILLETS OF SOLE IN THE AMERICAN MANNER

Fold fillets and season lightly with salt and pepper. Put into a sauté pan, sprinkle with 4 or 5 tablespoons *court-bouillon* and add 1 tablespoon butter; cover and poach for 10 or 12 minutes, then dish up in the shape of a turban.

Garnish the centre with *homard américaine* (see page 240); coat the fillets and the garnish with lobster sauce (see *sauce cardinale*, page 31).

Filets de sole à l'anglaise
FILLETS OF SOLE, ENGLISH FASHION

Salt fillets lightly, dip in flour, in beaten egg, then in freshly prepared breadcrumbs, and cook in butter.

Serve in a hot dish, and cover with maître d'hôtel butter.

Filets de sole Antonelli
FILLETS OF SOLE WITH A TRUFFLE RISOTTO

Cut fillets into strips, salt lightly, dip in flour and sauté in butter.

Prepare a risotto (see page 668) with white Piedmont truffles. Put risotto in a deep dish and set up fillets of sole in the middle. If white Piedmont truffles are not available, use black Périgord truffles.

This is an excellent luncheon dish.

Filets de sole belle meunière
FILLETS OF SOLE MEUNIÈRE WITH PROVENÇAL STYLE TOMATOES

Prepare and cook fillets as for *sole à la meunière* (see page 207). Serve on a bed of thinly sliced mushrooms tossed in butter; surround with small *tomates farcies à la provençale* (see page 659), and sprinkle fillets with the butter left after cooking.

Filets de sole caprice

GRILLED FILLETS OF SOLE WITH BANANAS

Dip fillets in melted butter and then in freshly prepared breadcrumbs.
Press crumbs on well with a palette knife. Brush with melted butter and
grill (U.S. broil) gently.

Put half a banana, cooked in butter, on each fillet.

Serve with a sour-sweet tomato sauce.*

* *Editor's note* M. Escoffier does not give a specific recipe for this sauce
but a good tomato sauce (see page 132) would go well with this dish.

Filets de sole cardinal

FILLETS OF SOLE WITH FISH FORCEMEAT

Fillets of sole, *court-bouillon* (see page 164), 1—2 tablespoons butter,
croûtons, few pieces lobster tails, béchamel sauce (see page 23),
lobster butter (see page 114)

For forcemeat:

6 oz. whiting, 4 oz. breadcrumbs, soaked in milk then squeezed
thoroughly, 1 tablespoon butter, 1 dessertspoon chopped chives,
1 teaspoon chopped parsley, 1 teaspoon chopped chervil, salt, pepper,
nutmeg, 1 egg

Make the forcemeat by pounding whiting and mixing all other ingredients with it.

Spread a little forcemeat on each fillet, fold over, and poach in *court-
bouillon*, to which the butter has been added.

Serve on croûtons, place a piece of lobster tail on each fillet and cover
with béchamel sauce to which a little lobster butter has been added.

Filets de sole à la catalane

FILLETS OF SOLE WITH TOMATO SAUCE AND PILAF OF RICE

4 fillets sole, *court-bouillon*, butter, juice ½ lemon, 2 tomatoes, 1 tablespoon meat jelly (see page 21), 2 tablespoons tomato sauce (see
page 132), 1 tablespoon butter, pilaf of rice (see page 669), red peppers

Roll fillets into paupiettes, and poach in *court-bouillon* to which a little
butter and lemon juice has been added.

Halve the tomatoes, remove seeds, season with salt and pepper and cook as described for *à la provençale* (see page 659). Put fillets in tomato cases and arrange on a serving dish, in the shape of a crown.

Reduce *court-bouillon*, add meat jelly, tomato sauce and butter and pour over the fish.

Serve with rice pilaf and grilled red peppers, skinned and cut into julienne.

Filets de sole châtelaine
FILLETS OF SOLE WITH MACARONI AND CHEESE

You will need for 6 persons:
2 soles (each about 12 oz.), salt, pepper, 5—6 tablespoons hot water, juice ½ lemon, 1 sprig parsley, ¾ pint (U.S. 1⅞ cups) béchamel sauce (see page 23), 1 lb. cooked macaroni, 1 tablespoon grated Gruyère cheese, 1 tablespoon grated Parmesan cheese, 1 truffle, extra cheese for sprinkling, butter

Remove skin from both sides of the fish, remove the fillets, fold in half, and flatten slightly. Arrange in a buttered sauté pan, season with salt and pepper, add the hot water, lemon juice and parsley. Cover and cook over moderate heat for 10—12 minutes.

Drain macaroni carefully and add cheese, truffle, peeled and cut into julienne, freshly ground pepper, and 3—4 tablespoons béchamel sauce. Put macaroni on to a serving dish and arrange fillets of sole on top.

Add liquid in which sole was cooked to remaining sauce and pour over the fish. Sprinkle with a little more cheese, dot with butter and brown in the oven or under the grill (U.S. broiler).

Fillets of brill, turbot, cod, or steaks of salmon can be prepared in the same way.

Filets de sole Chauchat
POACHED FILLETS OF SOLE WITH MORNAY SAUCE

Fillets of sole, *court-bouillon*, butter, lemon juice, Mornay sauce (see page 34), small freshly cooked potatoes, cut into rounds

Fold fillets and poach in *court-bouillon* to which a little butter and lemon juice has been added.

Line the bottom of the serving dish with Mornay sauce. Arrange fillets in the centre and surround with potato. Cover fish and potato with sauce and put under a hot grill (U.S. broiler) to glaze.

Filets de sole Clarence

POACHED FILLETS OF SOLE WITH LOBSTER AND RICE PILAF

——————— Fillets of sole, *court-bouillon*, butter, lemon juice, 1 lobster cooked *américaine* (see page 240), 2 small teaspoons curry powder, rice pilaf (see page 669)

Fold fillets and cook as described above. Arrange on a serving dish in the shape of a crown and keep hot.

Add curry powder to the lobster sauce. Remove flesh from the lobster shells and add to sauce.

Reheat and pour over the fillets.

Serve with rice pilaf.

Filets de sole dieppoise

POACHED FILLETS OF SOLE WITH NORMANDY SAUCE

——————— 1 12-oz. sole, salt, pepper, 2 tablespoons *court-bouillon*, freshly cooked mussels, shrimps, Normandy sauce (see page 35)

Lay fillets in a long buttered dish, season with salt and pepper, and sprinkle with the *court-bouillon* and 2 tablespoons water in which the mussels have been cooked. Cover and cook for 10—12 minutes, basting the fillets from time to time with the liquid. Arrange fish on a serving dish, surround them with freshly cooked mussels and shrimps, and coat with Normandy sauce.

A simpler method is to cook and serve the fish in the same dish. In which case thicken the liquid in which the fish was cooked, with 1 dessertspoon butter, and 1 dessertspoon flour mixed together.

Filets de sole Doria

FRIED FILLETS OF SOLE WITH CUCUMBER

Prepare and cook the fillets *à la meunière* (see page 207). Prepare a garnish of cucumber, cut into balls with a vegetable scoop.

Cook for a few minutes in boiling salted water then drain and toss in butter.

Filets de sole en épigrammes
FILLETS OF SOLE WITH FISH FORCEMEAT

Cover one side of the fillets with fish forcemeat (see page 550), fold in half and poach in *court-bouillon*.

Leave to cool, then dip in egg and breadcrumbs and fry in clarified butter until a golden brown.

Any of the garnishes used for fillets of sole are suitable.

Filets de sole à la florentine
FILLETS OF SOLE WITH SPINACH AND CHEESE

————— Fillets of sole, *court-bouillon* (see page 164), butter, spinach, béchamel sauce (see page 23), grated cheese

Poach fillets in a little *court-bouillon* and butter. Cook spinach, drain and chop coarsely, then dry off in butter over gentle heat.

Arrange fillets on a bed of spinach, coat with sauce, sprinkle with cheese, dot with butter and brown in the oven or under the grill (U.S. broiler).

Filets de sole grand-duc
POACHED FILLETS OF SOLE WITH CRAYFISH TAILS AND TRUFFLES

————— 4 fillets of sole, *court-bouillon*, butter, 8 crayfish tails, 4 thin slices truffle, béchamel sauce (see page 23), grated cheese, asparagus tips

Fold fillets and poach in *court-bouillon* and butter.

Arrange on a serving dish in the form of a crown with the points towards the centre of the dish. Place 2 crayfish tails and a slice of truffle on each fillet.

Coat with sauce, sprinkle with cheese and dot with butter. Brown in the oven or under the grill (U.S. broiler).

Before serving, put a bunch of asparagus tips, dipped in butter, in the centre.

Filets de sole au gratin à la bonne femme
FILLETS OF SOLE AU GRATIN WITH TOMATO SAUCE

———————— 1 medium-sized or 2 small filleted soles, seasoning, flour, parsley, shallot, 3–4 tablespoons *court-bouillon* (see page 164), 2 oz. mushrooms, 1 tablespoon oil, 3 tablespoons tomato sauce (see page 132), 1 tablespoon dry breadcrumbs, butter, lemon juice, parsley

Season fillets, dust with flour and put into a buttered fireproof dish. Add a little chopped parsley and shallot. Moisten with the *court-bouillon*.

Sauté mushrooms for a few minutes in oil, add salt and pepper and tomato sauce and pour over fish. Sprinkle with breadcrumbs, dot with butter and cook in a moderate oven. Before serving, add a squeeze of lemon juice and sprinkle with chopped parsley.

Filets de sole au curry
CURRIED FILLETS OF SOLE

———————— 1 12-oz. sole, filleted, salt, pepper, butter, *court-bouillon* (see page 164), 1 dessertspoon chopped onion, 1 teaspoon curry powder, white wine sauce (see page 212), rice

Fold fillets in half, season and poach in *court-bouillon* and butter. Remove to a serving dish.

Sauté onion in 1 oz. butter until brown, add curry powder and mix well. Add this to the sauce and pour over the fish.

Serve with rice cooked *à l'indienne* (see page 668).

Filets de sole Joinville
POACHED FILLETS OF SOLE WITH SHRIMPS (U.S. PRAWNS) AND NORMANDY SAUCE

———————— Fillets of sole, salt, pepper, *court-bouillon* (see page 164), butter, crayfish, heart-shaped croûtons, truffle, Normandy sauce (see page 35), crayfish butter (see page 114), about 12 shrimps (U.S. prawns)

Fold fillets, season with salt and pepper and poach in *court-bouillon* and butter. Put a small piece of crayfish at the end of each fillet. Dish up on the croûtons. Place a good slice of truffle and a crayfish tail on each fillet. Cover with Normandy sauce to which a crayfish butter has been added.

Serve with extra Normandy sauce to which the shrimps (U.S. prawns) and 1 tablespoon truffles cut into cubes have been added.

Filets de sole Marguery

POACHED FILLETS OF SOLE WITH MUSSELS, SHRIMPS (U.S. PRAWNS) AND WHITE WINE SAUCE

————————— 1 12-oz. sole, filleted, salt, pepper, 2 tablespoons *court-bouillon* (see page 164), mussels, shrimps (U.S. prawns), white wine sauce (see page 212)

Put fillets into a buttered fireproof dish, season and add the *court-bouillon*. Cover and cook in moderate oven for 8 – 10 minutes.

Garnish with freshly cooked mussels and shrimps (U.S. prawns) and coat with sauce.

Brown in the oven or under the grill (U.S. broiler).

Filets de sole mignonette à la ménagère

FILLETS OF SOLE WITH NOODLES AND TOMATO SAUCE

————————— Fillets of sole, salt, pepper, flour, butter, noodles

Cut fillets of sole into strips; season with salt and pepper, dust with flour and sauté in butter.

Take about the same quantity of noodles and sauté them in butter. Mix the fish and noodles together.

Serve with tomato sauce (see page 132).

Filets de sole Murat

FILLETS OF SOLE WITH POTATO AND ARTICHOKE BOTTOMS

————————— 1 medium-sized potato, 2 artichoke bottoms, seasoning, butter, 1 12-oz. sole, 6 thick slices tomato, oil, pinch chopped parsley, 2 tablespoons meat jelly (see page 21), juice $\frac{1}{2}$ lemon

Cube potatoes and artichokes, season and toss separately in butter until cooked.

Cut fish into strips, season and toss in butter until cooked. Put the vegetables and fish together on a serving dish. Garnish with tomato slices, seasoned and sautéed in oil.

Sprinkle with parsley, melted meat jelly and lemon juice, and finally a little browned butter.

Filets de sole Newburg

FILLETS OF SOLE WITH LOBSTER NEWBURG

—————— 1 1¼-lb lobster, 1 12-oz. sole, filleted, butter, *court-bouillon* (see page 164)

Prepare a lobster Newburg (see page 245), taking care to divide the tail into 4 pieces. Keep hot.

Cube remaining lobster flesh, and add to the sauce.

Fold and poach the fillets of sole in butter and *court-bouillon*. Put into a shallow serving dish and place a slice of lobster on each fillet. Coat with the Newburg sauce.

Filets de sole à la normande (mode de la fermière)

NORMANDY STYLE FILLETS OF SOLE (AS COOKED BY THE FARMER'S WIFE)

—————— 1 12-oz. sole, filleted, salt, pepper, 2—3 tablespoons cider, lemon juice, 5—6 tablespoons fresh cream

Put fillets into a buttered fireproof dish, season and add cider and a few drops lemon juice. Cover and cook for 8—10 minutes. Add cream, and cook a further few minutes, basting continuously.

Serve with sauté potatoes.

Filets de sole Otero

POACHED FILLETS OF SOLE ON BAKED POTATOES

—————— 4 good-sized baked potatoes, 4 tablespoons shrimps (U.S. prawns), béchamel sauce (see page 23), 1 12-oz. sole, filleted, *court-bouillon* (see page 164), butter, grated cheese

Cut a slice lengthwise from each potato and remove as much of the inside as possible.

Mix shrimps (U.S. prawns) with a little béchamel sauce, and put 1 tablespoon into each potato case.

Fold fillets and poach in a little *court-bouillon* and butter. Then put one into each potato case. Add enough béchamel sauce to fill completely.

Sprinkle with cheese, dot with butter and brown in the oven or under the grill (U.S. broiler).

Note If preferred, fish can be rolled into paupiettes.

Potato removed from the cases should be served separately.

Filets de sole à l'orientale

FILLETS OF SOLE IN THE ORIENTAL MANNER

Prepare the fillets as for *filets de sole Newburg* (see page 220), but add a little curry powder to the sauce.

Dish the fillets, pour the sauce over and serve with rice cooked Indian fashion (see page 668).

Filets de sole Orly

FILLETS OF SOLE IN BATTER

When fillets of sole are to be coated with batter and fried, it is best to poach them first in a little *court-bouillon* and butter as described in the foregoing recipes.

Allow to cool a little, then dip in batter, and fry just before required.

Garnish with fried parsley and serve with tomato sauce (see page 132).

Filets de sole en paupiettes

FILLETS OF SOLE PAUPIETTES

Fillets should be carefully trimmed and flattened slightly to avoid any contraction during cooking, then covered with forcemeat, with or without truffles, and rolled into the shape of a cork.

So they do not lose shape during cooking, choose a pan into which they can be packed tightly. Just cover with *court-bouillon* and poach.

They can also be poached wrapped in paper. The difficulty about this is that one is never sure of the quality of the paper, some of which, when heated, emits an unpleasant smell which is absorbed by the fish.*

All garnishes used for fillets of sole suit paupiettes.

* *Editor's note* This does not apply in the same way today. Greaseproof paper and foil are generally reliable.

Filets de sole à la paysanne

FILLETS OF SOLE COOKED PEASANT FASHION

——————— Salt, pepper, 1 12-oz. sole, filleted, 2 small carrots, 2 small onions, 1 small piece celery, butter, 2—3 tablespoons hot water, pinch chopped parsley, salt, sugar, 2 tablespoons fresh peas

Season fish, fold in half and put into a buttered fireproof dish.

Slice vegetables thinly and put into a pan with some butter and the hot water. Add parsley and a pinch salt and sugar. Simmer slowly for a few minutes, then add peas and continue cooking till vegetables are tender.

Pour all over the fish and cook in a moderate oven.

Add a few dabs of butter before serving.

Filets de sole en pilaw

PILAF OF FILLETS OF SOLE

Cut fillets into pieces, season, sauté in butter and mix with a pilaf of rice (see page 669).

Serve with tomato or curry sauce (see pages 132, 32).

Note When aubergines are in season, a small one cut in cubes and sautéed in butter may be mixed with the rice, with a few tablespoons freshly cooked peas.

Filets de sole Polignac

POACHED FILLET OF SOLE WITH WHITE WINE SAUCE

——————— 1 sole, filleted, butter, *court-bouillon* (see page 164), 4—5 mushrooms, ¼ oz. butter, lemon juice, truffle, 5—6 tablespoons white wine sauce (see page 212)

Fold fillets and poach in butter with a few tablespoons *court-bouillon*.

Cut mushrooms into julienne, put into a small saucepan with the butter and few drops lemon juice. Stew for 1—2 minutes, then add liquid from fillets.

Boil till reduced then mix in a few slices of truffle cut in julienne and the sauce.

Arrange fillets on a very hot dish, coat with sauce and glaze quickly under the grill (U.S. broiler).

Filets de sole provençale

PROVENÇAL STYLE FILLETS OF SOLE

1 tablespoon finely chopped onion, butter, 2 tomatoes, peeled, seeded and chopped, salt, pepper, 1 clove garlic, chopped parsley, 1 12-oz. sole, filleted, 3—4 tablespoons white wine

Slightly brown onion in butter, add tomatoes, seasoning, crushed garlic, pinch parsley and cook gently for about 15 minutes. Lay fillets lengthwise in lightly oiled fireproof dish, season and add wine. Cover with tomato mixture.

Cook in a moderate oven for 10—12 minutes. Serve immediately, sprinkled with parsley.

Note A few black olives may be added.
Butter may be used for the dish instead of oil.

Filets de sole portugaise are prepared in the same way, but 1 large sweet pepper, peeled, grilled (U.S. broiled) and cut into julienne is added to the tomato.

Filets de sole Rachel

POACHED FILLETS OF SOLE WITH TRUFFLES AND WHITE WINE SAUCE

1 12-oz. sole, filleted, butter, few tablespoons *court-bouillon* (see page 164), truffle, white wine sauce (see page 212), small patty cases, asparagus tips

Fold fillets in half, poach in butter and sprinkle with the *court-bouillon*. Arrange on a very hot oval dish. Place a large slice of truffle on each fillet and cover with sauce. At each end of the dish place small patties filled with asparagus tips dipped in melted butter.

Alternatively the fillets may be served on croûtons.

Filets de sole Saint-Germain

FILLETS OF SOLE WITH BÉARNAISE SAUCE

Season fillets, dip in melted butter and then in fresh breadcrumbs, pressing them on well with a palette knife. Sprinkle with more butter and grill (U.S. broil) gently.

Arrange fillets on a very hot dish, and surround with small *noisette* potatoes cooked in butter and rolled in 2 tablespoons light meat jelly (see page 21). (Noisettes are cut from large potatoes with a vegetable scoop.) Serve with well seasoned béarnaise sauce (see page 30).

Filets de sole Véronique

POACHED FILLETS OF SOLE WITH GRAPES

Fold fillets, season with salt and pepper, and poach in butter with 2 tablespoons *court-bouillon* (see page 164). Arrange on a hot dish and garnish with fresh Muscat grapes, peeled and pipped. Coat with white wine sauce (see page 212) and glaze quickly under the grill (U.S. broiler).

Filets de sole Victoria

POACHED FILLETS OF SOLE WITH TRUFFLES AND CRAYFISH BUTTER

Fillets of sole, *court-bouillon* (see page 164), 2 tablespoons lobster, 2 tablespoons truffle, béchamel sauce (see page 23), crayfish butter (see page 114), grated cheese, butter

Fold fillets and poach in *court-bouillon*. Arrange on a long, buttered dish. Garnish with lobster and truffle cut into small cubes and cover with béchamel sauce to which a little crayfish butter has been added. Sprinkle with grated cheese, dot lightly with butter and brown lightly.

Filets de sole Walewska

POACHED FILLETS OF SOLE WITH PRAWNS AND MORNAY SAUCE

4 fillets of sole, 3—4 tablespoons *court-bouillon*, salt, pepper, 4 Dublin Bay prawns,* 8 thin slices truffle, seasoning, Mornay sauce (see page 34), grated cheese, butter
* If Dublin Bay prawns are not available, use 6 or 8 crayfish tails.

Put the fillets into a buttered dish, sprinkle with *court-bouillon,* season with salt and pepper, cover and cook for 8 – 10 minutes.

Arrange on a long dish. Surround with the prawns divided in two lengthwise and truffle, and cover with sauce.

Sprinkle with grated cheese, dot with butter and glaze quickly under the grill (U.S. broiler).

Timbales de filets de sole Grimaldi

TIMBALE OF FILLET OF SOLE

1 timbale pastry case, baked blind, 36 small crayfish, mirepoix, truffle, butter, 5 oz. macaroni, Parmesan cheese, béchamel sauce (see page 23), cream, fish forcemeat (see page 550), 12 fillets sole, salt, pepper

Prepare and cook the timbale case. It should be rather wide in proportion to its height and decorated according to choice.

Cook the crayfish in the mirepoix, remove the tails, cut in two lengthwise, and keep hot in a tablespoon of butter, with slices of truffle.

Pound crayfish shells finely and mix with 7 oz. butter. Place in a small saucepan, and put in a bain-marie.

When butter melts, strain through a fine sieve into a bowl containing a few pieces of ice and a little water. When the butter solidifies, take it out and place on a plate.

Cut macaroni into small pieces and cook in salted water, but do not let it get too soft. When cooked, drain and return to the pan, add 2 tablespoons fresh butter, a little grated Parmesan cheese and a few tablespoons cream béchamel sauce. Add 3 oz. truffles thinly sliced and keep hot.

Put truffled fish forcemeat on fillets, roll into paupiettes and poach in *court-bouillon.*

Add about ½ pint (U.S. 1¼ cups) cream béchamel sauce to crayfish tails and slices of truffle; heat and add crayfish butter. Season.

To serve Fill timbale half-way with the macaroni; place paupiettes on top, cover with garnish of slices of truffle and crayfish tails. Put top on timbale and serve.

Timbale de filets de sole Richelieu

TIMBALE OF FILLET OF SOLE RICHELIEU

This is the same as the *timbales de filets de sole Grimaldi*, on page 225, except that the macaroni is replaced by ravioli with spinach.

Filets de sole froids

COLD FILLETS OF SOLE

Fold fillets and poach in butter with a few drops of lemon juice. Leave to get cold then coat with a very light chaudfroid sauce (see page 31).

Decorate each fillet according to your fancy: tarragon leaves, tomatoes, truffles, hard-boiled eggs, fillets of anchovies, etc.

Place a square dish on a block of ice, line this with a light layer of aspic jelly, arrange the fillets symmetrically on it, garnish the spaces between the fish either with a macedoine of vegetables, with very green asparagus tips, or with shrimps (U.S. prawns) or crayfish tails.

Cover the fish and its garnish completely with aspic jelly.

Filets de sole sur mousse de tomate

FILLETS OF SOLE ON TOMATO MOUSSE

Prepare, poach and decorate fillets as described above. Place dish on a block of ice half filled with tomato mousse (see page 660), arrange fillets of sole on the mousse, then cover with aspic jelly.

Note Tomato mousse may be replaced, according to taste, by mousse of crayfish, curry mousse, sweet red pepper mousse, Chambertin mousse.

Paupiettes de sole à la gelée

PAUPIETTES OF SOLE IN JELLY

Garnish one side of fillets with truffled fish forcemeat (see page 550) roll into the shape of a cork, poach in a good *court-bouillon* (see page 164) and let them cool in the stock. When cold, drain, dry well, trim the edges and cut across into 4 pieces.

To serve Proceed in the same way, as described in the preceding recipes, either on aspic or a mousse.

STOCKFISH, TUNNY, TURBOT AND WEEVER

Stockfish ou morue de norvège séchée

STOCKFISH OR DRIED NORWEGIAN COD

MODE NIÇOISE

AS COOKED IN NICE

You will need for 8—10 persons:
2½ lb. stockfish, 3—4 oz. intestines, 1 large onion, 1 leek, ⅓ pint (U.S. 1¼ cups) oil, *bouquet garni* of parsley, thyme, bay leaf, fennel and basil, 1 clove garlic, 4 lb. tomatoes, salt, pepper, 2½ lb. small new potatoes, 6—8 oz. black olives

Beat fish hard with a wooden pestle or mallet, saw into 3 pieces and soak in cold water for 3—4 days, changing the water frequently.

One day before fish is to be cooked, soak intestines, preferably in running water.

After the necessary soaking, scrape fish, remove backbone and skin.

Add onion and leek sliced thinly to oil and sauté until lightly browned. Add *bouquet garni,* crushed garlic, tomatoes, peeled, seeded and chopped, fish and intestines.

Add salt and pepper, cover and simmer for 1¾ hours.

30 minutes before the end of the cooking, add potatoes and olives.

Note The tomatoes should provide enough liquid, but if not sufficient to cover the potatoes, add a little hot water. Canned tomatoes can be used if necessary.

Thon frais

FRESH TUNNY FISH

Tunny fish is sliced and cooked on a bed of herbs. It may be garnished with spinach, sorrel, tomatoes, carrots, turnips, peas, etc.

Turbot

One gauges the freshness and the quality of turbot by the brightness of the eye, the whiteness of the skin and the thickness of the fillets.

Large pieces of turbot can be cooked in *court-bouillon* and are served garnished with sprigs of parsley.

Cooking After gutting and cleaning the turbot, make an incision along the underside of the backbone to loosen the fillets; put to soak in cold salted water for about 1½ hours, to free it from any impurities. Place in a fish kettle and cover with cold water; add salt in the proportion of ¼ oz. to every 2 pints (U.S. 5 cups) water, 6 tablespoons milk and a slice of peeled and seeded lemon.

Put the fish kettle over the heat and bring gently to the boil, then move to side of stove and continue to simmer very gently, to ensure perfect cooking.

When the water comes to boiling point, allow 6−7 minutes for each 1 lb. of fish.

Turbot pour service de détail

TURBOT COOKED IN PIECES

Cut turbot along its back, following the backbone, then slice or scallop.

Cook in *court-bouillon* as for the whole fish, described above.

Accompaniment for turbot, whether whole or in pieces: plain boiled potatoes, cooked at the last moment.

Sauces Hollandaise (see page 33), caper (see page 31), cardinal (see page 31), shrimp (see page 32), Venetian (see page 36).

Cadgery de turbot

TURBOT KEDGEREE

1 lb. cooked turbot, curried béchamel sauce (see page 32), 1 lb. rice cooked as for pilaf (see page 669), 5−6 hard-boiled eggs

Remove all skin and bone from the fish. Add 3−4 tablespoons sauce to the rice, and cube the eggs. Arrange layers of fish, rice and eggs in a deep dish and coat with sauce.

Note Kedgeree can also be prepared dry, that is without the addition of sauce to the rice. Instead, add one-third quantity of plainly boiled peas, and serve sauce separately.

Turbot gratin crème
CREAMED TURBOT AU GRATIN

Duchess potatoes (see page 646), béchamel sauce (see page 23), cooked turbot, salt, pepper, milk, butter, grated cheese

Put a ring of duchess potatoes on a buttered fireproof serving dish. It should be about three-quarters inch thick at the base, tapering a little towards the top and about 1¼ inches high.

Put a little béchamel sauce in the centre of the ring. Add the turbot, seasoned and mixed with a little milk and butter. Cover fish with sauce and sprinkle with grated cheese. Brush potato ring with a little melted butter and put in a moderate oven to brown.

The duchess potatoes can be replaced by some boiled potatoes cut into rings, and arranged round the dish in overlapping slices.

Coquilles de turbot au gratin
SCALLOPS OF TURBOT AU GRATIN

Béchamel sauce (see page 23), cooked turbot, grated cheese, butter

Put some sauce into scallop shells, place some pieces of hot turbot on top and cover with more sauce. Sprinkle with grated cheese, dot with butter and brown quickly under the grill (U.S. broiler).

Turbot Richelieu
TURBOT WITH NORMANDY SAUCE

1 6—8-lb. turbot, *court-bouillon* (see page 164), white wine, melted butter, 1 lobster, cooked in *court-bouillon*, Normandy sauce (see page 35), mushrooms, truffle, crayfish butter (see page 114)

Poach turbot in a *court-bouillon* with wine and put on to a serving dish. Add a little melted butter. Remove flesh from the lobster without breaking it and arrange down the centre of the turbot.

Chop remaining lobster and add to the sauce with some slices of mushroom and truffle. Add a little crayfish butter and serve separately.

Serve also, potatoes, cut into balls with a vegetable scoop, cooked in boiling salted water, then drained and tossed in butter.

Turbot froid

COLD TURBOT

It is essential that turbot which is to be served cold should not be cooled too much. The gelatinous nature of its flesh explains the importance of this.

When it is just sufficiently cooled and accompanied by one of the cold sauces that suit fish, turbot can rival salmon or trout served in the same way.

Turbotins

CHICKEN TURBOT

Chicken turbot may be classed among the most delicate fish and are very simple to prepare.

They vary very much in size, from small ones suitable for 3 – 4 persons to large ones sufficient for 10 – 12 persons; furthermore, they are always tender and white and can be cooked in a variety of ways.

They may be cooked and served like turbot; grilled (U.S. broiled) *à la meunière* or poached in *court-bouillon* or in white wine.

Note Whichever way the chicken turbot is being cooked, whether it is poached or grilled, an incision must be made in the back to loosen the fillets. This facilitates the cooking, and helps to prevent the fish curling up.

Turbotin à l'amiral

POACHED CHICKEN TURBOT WITH WHITE WINE

Poach the turbot in *court-bouillon* (see page 164) with white wine.

To serve Arrange on a dish of appropriate size with the dark side downwards. Cover with Normandy sauce (see page 35) to which a little crayfish butter (see page 114) has been added.

Garnish with little patties of crayfish tails, oysters, carp roe or slices of truffle.

Serve the remaining sauce separately, and also a dish of potatoes, cut with a vegetable scoop, cooked in boiling salted water and tossed in butter.

Turbotin bonne femme

BAKED CHICKEN TURBOT WITH WHITE WINE

1 2½-lb. turbot, salt, pepper, ⅝ pint (U.S. approx. 1 cup) white wine, lemon juice, 6 tablespoons fish stock, 1 shallot, 4 oz. mushrooms, butter, mixed herbs, 1 dessertspoon flour, 3 tablespoons cold water, 2 egg yolks

Remove fins from the fish, loosen fillets on the dark side, and put into a well buttered fireproof dish, dark side uppermost. Add seasonings, wine, lemon juice and stock. (If no stock is available use water, a little sliced onion and 1–2 sprigs parsley.)

Cook in a moderate oven, basting frequently.

Chop shallot finely, slice mushrooms, and cook in butter with a pinch mixed herbs, salt, pepper and lemon juice.

When the turbot is cooked, put on to a serving dish, dark side downwards, and keep hot.

Strain liquor and bring to boiling point. Add flour, mixed smoothly with 2 tablespoons cold water, and cook for a few minutes.

Remove from the heat, add egg yolks mixed with 1 tablespoon water, and then 2 oz. butter, adding only a little at one time.

Finally stir in the mushrooms. Pour over fish and glaze under the grill (U.S. broiler).

Note This dish can be varied by adding 2 tomatoes peeled, seeded and chopped, to the mushrooms while they are cooking. It would then be called *turbotin d'autun* (Old French for autumn). Alternatively add 1 tablespoon truffle, cut into julienne, or add some lettuce leaves, chopped and sautéed in butter.

Turbotin Dugléré

CHICKEN TURBOT WITH TOMATOES AND ONIONS

—————— 1 2½-lb. turbot, 4–5 tomatoes, 4 oz. onion, 2 shallots, 1 clove garlic, pinch chopped parsley, 1 bay leaf, ¾ pint (U.S. 1⅞ cups), white wine, 8 tablespoons water, juice 1 lemon, seasoning, 1 dessertspoon flour, 2 tablespoons butter

Cut fish across into 5–6 pieces. Put tomatoes, peeled, seeded and chopped, chopped onion, chopped shallot, crushed garlic, parsley and bay leaf into a well buttered fireproof dish. Add wine, 6 tablespoons water and lemon juice. Arrange fish on top and season with salt and pepper. Cover, and cook in a fairly slow oven for 15–20 minutes.

When cooked, remove the fish to a serving dish, reconstructing the shape of the fish.

Strain liquor into a pan, and add flour mixed smoothly with the remaining cold water. Boil for a few minutes, then gradually add butter. Pour over the fish.

Note The flour can be omitted, and the sauce thickened with extra butter.

Turbotin fermière

CHICKEN TURBOT WITH RED WINE

The same recipe and method as for *turbotin bonne femme* (see page 231) except that the white wine is replaced by double the quantity of red wine, that is to say ¾ pint (U.S. 1⅞ cups) red wine instead of ⅜ pint (U.S. approx. 1 cup) white wine. The water or fish stock is omitted, but add 1 bay leaf, 2 sprigs parsley and some onion rings to the wine.

Turbotin à la mode de Hollande

CHICKEN TURBOT IN THE DUTCH FASHION

—————— Turbot, 1 lobster, *court-bouillon* (see page 164)

For this dish, the turbot is poached in salted water and served with a lobster.

The lobster should be freshly cooked in *court-bouillon* then opened along the top of the tail with scissors, the flesh removed, cut into slices and replaced quickly. Arrange lobster on the fish.

Serve with plainly boiled potatoes and a sauce-boat of melted butter to which has been added chopped hard-boiled egg, parsley, salt and pepper.

Turbotin régence
CHICKEN TURBOT WITH QUENELLES OF WHITING AND OYSTERS

1 3—3½-lb. turbot, white wine, fish stock, butter, Normandy sauce (see page 35)
Garnish 12 quenelles of whiting (see page 550) moulded in a tablespoon, 18 oysters, bearded and poached, 12 small button mushrooms, sautéed in butter, 12 slices truffle, crayfish tails

Poach fish in wine, stock and butter. Put on to a serving dish and surround with garnish. Coat the fish with a little Normandy sauce and serve remainder separately.

Escalopes de turbotin
SCALLOPS OF CHICKEN TURBOT

1 small turbot, salt, pepper, squeeze lemon juice, 3—4 tablespoons fish stock, butter, 12 slices truffle, 36 crayfish tails, cream béchamel sauce (see page 23), duchess potatoes (see page 646), 1 egg yolk, grated cheese, fairly firm Parmesan cheese soufflé mixture (see page 238)

Cut 12 small scallops, each about 2—3 oz., from turbot fillets, and arrange in a well buttered sauté pan. Season, add the lemon juice and the fish stock. Cover and simmer for a few minutes. Add the truffle and crayfish tails and coat with a little sauce. While fish is cooking, arrange potato in a ring on a fireproof serving dish, brush with beaten egg and brown in the oven.

Put the scallops in the centre and sprinkle with a little grated cheese. Cover the whole with the cheese soufflé mixture; cook in a quick oven.

Vive
WEEVER

Weever is a fish of inferior quality, the chief use of which is for bouillabaisse. Nevertheless it may be fried or cooked *à la meunière*, and treated very much like whiting.

SERIE DE COQUILLAGES, CRUSTACÉS, MOLLUSQUES

SHELLFISH, CRUSTACEANS, MOLLUSCS

Crabe à l'anglaise

CRAB ENGLISH STYLE

———————— 1 crab, 1 teaspoon made mustard, pinch cayenne pepper, oil, vinegar, parsley, 1—2 hard-boiled eggs, anchovy fillets.

Cook crab in salted water and leave to go cold. Break off claws and legs and remove flesh, break it up well with a fork. Remove and discard the undershell, tail flap and stomach bag. Remove flesh from inside and put the creamy part into a basin. Add mustard, pepper and a little oil and vinegar. Then add the flesh taken from the claws and legs.

Fill top shell with this mixture, smoothing it into a dome shape.

Serve on a napkin with the claws arranged on either side and decorate as liked with parsley, eggs and anchovy fillets.

Note 1—2 tablespoons mayonnaise and chopped hard-boiled egg can be added to the mixture.

Crevettes

PRAWNS OR SHRIMPS

Editor's note Crevettes are translated as prawns (U.S. shrimps) or shrimps (U.S. prawns). M. Escoffier sometimes refers to *crevettes grises* when he intends to use the small shrimp, and *crevettes roses* for prawns. With one exception, in the following recipes, prawns or shrimps may be used.

Apart from their use in hors-d'oeuvre and garnishes, prawns and shrimps are prepared in various ways, a few of which are given in the following recipes.

Coquilles de crevettes

PRAWNS (U.S. SHRIMPS) IN SCALLOP SHELLS

———————— Duchess potatoes (see page 646), prawns (U.S. shrimps), béchamel sauce (see page 23), grated cheese, butter

Line some scallop shells with potato. Fold prawns (U.S. shrimps) into some sauce and pile in the centre. Sprinkle with grated cheese, dot with butter and brown in the oven or under the grill (U.S. broiler).

Crevettes au curry

CURRIED PRAWNS (U.S. SHRIMPS)

———————— 2 oz. butter, 3 tablespoons finely chopped onion, 1 teaspoon curry powder, 1 lb. freshly cooked prawns (U.S. shrimps), béchamel (see page 23) or Normandy (see page 35) sauce

Heat butter, add onion and brown lightly. Add curry powder and mix well.

Bind prawns (U.S. shrimps) with sauce, add onion, mix well and reheat.

Serve with *riz à l'indienne* (see page 668).

Crevettes au paprika rose

PRAWNS (U.S. SHRIMPS) WITH PAPRIKA

This is the same as curried prawns (U.S. shrimps), except that the curry is replaced with paprika.

Serve with pilaf of rice (see page 669).

Crevettes frites

FRIED SHRIMPS (U.S. PRAWNS)

Choose very small shrimps (U.S. prawns) that have just been caught. Roll in flour without peeling and fry in oil. Drain, season with salt mixed with a pinch of cayenne pepper, and serve.

Mousse froide de crevettes

COLD MOUSSE OF PRAWNS (U.S. SHRIMPS)

———————— You will need for 6–8 persons:
1 lb. uncooked prawns (U.S. shrimps), mirepoix, white wine, brandy,
2 oz. butter, ¼ pint (U.S. 1¼ cups) white stock, meat jelly (see page
21), ½ pint (U.S. 1¼ cups) fresh thick cream, ½ pint (U.S. 1¼ cups)
aspic jelly (see page 116)

Cook the prawns (U.S. shrimps) in a mirepoix with wine and brandy
as described for the bisque on page 82. Peel and put prawns (U.S.
shrimps) on one side, and pound the shells in a mortar with the butter.
Add stock to liquor in which the prawns (U.S. shrimps) were cooked.
Boil for a few minutes, then add the pounded shells. Continue to boil
for a few seconds, then pass through a fine sieve.

Put the resultant purée into a basin and stand on ice. Whisk in the
aspic jelly, and, when it begins to thicken, add the half-whipped cream.

Pour into a serving dish, standing on ice. Spread the prawns (U.S.
shrimps) over the top and cover lightly with a little aspic.

Écrevisses

CRAYFISH

Crayfish should always be prepared at the last moment.

Wash, remove the intestine which is found under the middle of the
tail. This is done by holding it with the point of a small knife and drawing
it gently out.

Écrevisses à la bordelaise

CRAYFISH WITH VEGETABLES AND WINE

———————— 2 oz. carrot, 2 oz. onion, 2 sprigs parsley, ½ bay leaf, 1 sprig thyme,
2 oz. raw lean ham, 2 tablespoons butter, 24 large crayfish, salt, pepper,
cayenne pepper, 2 liqueur glasses brandy, 1 wine glass white wine,
3 tablespoons meat jelly (see page 21), 4 oz. butter, parsley

Chop carrot and onion and put into a pan with the parsley, bay leaf,
thyme, ham, finely chopped, and butter. Sauté gently together until
vegetables are tender.

Add crayfish and seasoning and toss over brisk heat for 2 minutes. Add brandy and wine, cover and cook for 10 minutes.

Arrange crayfish in a serving dish. Add meat jelly to the sauce and gradually whisk in butter, a little at a time. Add a pinch chopped parsley and pour over the fish.

Écrevisses en buisson

CRAYFISH IN A BUSH

Cook crayfish in a *court-bouillon* prepared as for *écrevisses à la nage* (see below).

The crayfish are hooked on by their tails to the special utensil made for this purpose, and garnished with sprigs of parsley.

Coquilles d'écrevisses cardinal

SCALLOPS OF CRAYFISH WITH SHRIMP (U.S. PRAWN) BUTTER

———— Shrimp (U.S. prawn) butter (see page 51), béchamel sauce (see page 23), crayfish, truffle slices, grated cheese, butter

Add a little shrimp butter to the sauce and put some into scallop shells. Put 6 crayfish in each shell with 1 or 2 slices of truffle and cover with more of the sauce. Sprinkle with cheese, dot with butter and brown lightly.

Écrevisses à la nage

CRAYFISH IN COURT-BOUILLON

———— 2 oz. carrot, 2 oz. onion, 3 shallots, 2 sprigs parsley, 1 bay leaf, 1 sprig thyme, ½ pint (U.S. 1¼ cups) white wine, ⅜ pint (U.S. approx. 1 cup) water, little rock salt, pinch cayenne, crayfish

Cut carrot and onion into rings, chop shallots and put into a pan with parsley, bay leaf, thyme, wine, water and seasoning. Boil for 10 minutes. Add crayfish and cook gently for 10 minutes, then pour all into a serving dish.

Soufflé d'écrevisses à la florentine
CRAYFISH SOUFFLÉ

Editor's note This recipe and the two which follow have a cheese soufflé base, and as the recipe is not included in this book here is the recipe M. Escoffier used in his other famous book, *Guide to Modern Cookery*.

PARMESAN SOUFFLÉ

8 oz. flour, 1¼ pints (U.S. 3 cups) milk, salt, pepper, nutmeg, 8 oz. grated Parmesan cheese, 1½ oz. butter, 5 eggs

Mix flour smoothly with a little of the cold milk and put remainder on to heat. Add mixed flour and stir till boiling. Add salt, pepper and nutmeg. Remove from the heat, add cheese, butter and egg yolks. Pass through a fine sieve, then fold in the stiffly beaten egg whites.

CRAYFISH SOUFFLÉ

Add 2 tablespoons crayfish butter (see page 114) after adding the egg yolks.

Put a layer of the mixture in a buttered soufflé dish, add thin slices of truffle and some crayfish, then another layer of the soufflé mixture. Cook in a moderate oven for 20–25 minutes.

Soufflé d'écrevisses Léopold de Rothschild
CRAYFISH SOUFFLÉ WITH ASPARAGUS TIPS AND BLACK TRUFFLES

The same procedure as in the preceding recipe but add a few tablespoons freshly cooked asparagus tips, slices of truffle and crayfish.

Soufflé d'écrevisses à la piémontaise
CRAYFISH SOUFFLÉ WITH WHITE PIEDMONT TRUFFLES

Proceed as above, but instead of black truffles use very thinly sliced white Piedmont truffles.

Timbales de queues d'écrevisses

TIMBALE OF CRAYFISH TAILS

You will need for 8 persons:
1 lb. macaroni, 2 tablespoons butter, 4 tablespoons grated Parmesan cheese, cream béchamel sauce (see page 23), 50 crayfish, 2 liqueur glasses brandy, 1 wine glass white wine, truffles, pinch salt, pepper, pinch cayenne pepper, crayfish butter (see page 114)

Cook the macaroni till just soft, then add butter, grated cheese and 3 tablespoons sauce.

Toss crayfish for a few minutes in butter, add brandy and wine and sauté for 10—12 minutes. Remove the shells and use them for the crayfish butter.

Put the crayfish into a pan with 3—4 oz. thinly sliced truffle. Add the seasoning.

Add some crayfish butter to about ⅔ pint (U.S. 1⅞ cups) sauce and put with the crayfish and truffle. Reheat carefully.

Fill the serving dish about two-thirds full with macaroni mixture, put crayfish mixture on top and cover with the rest of the macaroni.

Garnish with thin slices of truffle and crayfish and serve very hot.

Vol-au-vent de queues d'écrevisses

VOL-AU-VENT OF CRAYFISH TAILS

60 crayfish, butter, brandy, white wine, 4 oz. truffles, seasoning, 1 vol-au-vent case, cream béchamel sauce (see page 23), 18 quenelles of sole (see page 55), moulded in a dessertspoon

Cook the crayfish in butter, brandy and white wine, as instructed in the previous recipe. Shell them and put the tails in a saucepan with the truffles, carefully peeled, and cut into slices, butter, and seasoning. Keep this hot.

Put the vol-au-vent case on the serving dish; cover the bottom with a few tablespoons sauce, then put in quenelles, crayfish tails and slices of truffle.

The quenelles may be replaced by small chickens' eggs or even by pigeons' eggs.

Mousse d'écrevisses

CRAYFISH MOUSSE

——————— You will need for 6 – 8 persons:
¼ pint (U.S. ⅝ cup) aspic jelly (see page 116), 40 medium-sized crayfish, mirepoix, brandy, white wine, 3 oz. butter, ½ pint (U.S. 1¼ cups)
white chicken stock, ½ pint (U.S. 1¼ cups) fresh thick cream, chervil
or tarragon leaves

Pour a little aspic jelly into the bottom of a soufflé mould and leave
on ice. Cook the crayfish with the mirepoix, brandy and wine as described
on page 82. When they are cooked, remove shells and pound them in
a mortar with the butter.

Add the stock to the liquor left after cooking crayfish. Put pounded
shells into this and boil for 2 minutes, then pass through a fine sieve.
Put the resultant purée into a clean pan and stand on ice. Whisk in the
aspic jelly and as soon as it begins to set add the half-whipped cream.
Pour at once into the prepared soufflé mould, and keep on ice until the
whole begins to set.

Arrange crayfish on top and garnish with chervil or tarragon leaves.
Cover with a thin layer of aspic and when quite set serve on ice.

HOT LOBSTER

Homard américaine

AMERICAN STYLE LOBSTER

——————— 1 2¼-lb. lobster, 5 oz. butter, salt, pepper, 4 tablespoons oil, 4—5 tablespoons brandy, ¼ pint (U.S. ⅝ cup) white wine, 2 shallots, chopped,
6 tomatoes, pinch chopped parsley, 1 small clove garlic, pinch cayenne,
4—5 tablespoons melted meat jelly (see page 21), 4—5 tablespoons
demi-glace sauce (see page 22), 3½ oz. butter, juice ½ lemon

The first essential for this dish is to have a live lobster. Cut it lengthwise,
and remove the little bag near the head which usually contains some
grit. Remove the coral which is near this little bag and is soft and slightly
greenish in colour, and mix it with 2½ oz. butter (this is used later for
the sauce). Remove the legs, and break the claws so that the flesh can
be easily removed when the lobster is cooked. Cut each half of the
lobster into 3—4 pieces and season with salt and pepper. Heat the oil

and 1 oz. butter in a sauté pan, put in the lobster and toss until the shell has turned a bright red colour and the lobster is cooked.

Add the brandy, wine, shallots, tomatoes, peeled, seeded and finely chopped, parsley, garlic, cayenne pepper, meat jelly and sauce.

Cover and cook over brisk heat for 18—20 minutes.

Arrange the pieces of lobster in a deep dish. Add the coral to the liquid left in the pan and cook for a few seconds. Remove from the heat and add the remaining butter a little at a time, and the lemon juice. Pour this over the lobster and sprinkle with chopped parsley.

Note The half shells of the lobster should be arranged side by side on the serving dish, and the pieces of lobster, coated with the sauce, will be in the centre.

Serve with a pilaf of rice (see page 669).

Homard à l'américaine sans carapace

AMERICAN STYLE LOBSTER WITHOUT SHELL

Prepare the lobster according to the preceding recipe.

Take lobster meat from body, claws and legs and arrange on a serving dish. Coat with the sauce. The shell of the lobster can be used in the preparation of lobster butter and an excellent soup can be made with it.

Homard à la bordelaise

LOBSTER WITH RED WINE AND MUSHROOMS

Homard à la bordelaise is not much in demand. It can be prepared in various ways but, in my opinion, the best way is to prepare it as for *homard américaine* (see page 240), merely replacing the white wine with red Bordeaux and adding 4 or 5 tablespoons of finely chopped fresh mushrooms.

When the lobster is cooked, arrange pieces and claws on a serving dish.

Finish the sauce by adding the coral mixed with butter as described previously, and pour over the lobster.

Note Homard à la bordelaise is cooked exactly like *écrevisses à la bordelaise* (see page 236), except that the crayfish are cooked whole and the lobster in pieces.

Homard cardinal

LOBSTER WITH CARDINAL SAUCE

———————— 1 lobster, butter, truffle, cardinal sauce (see page 31), grated cheese, parsley

Cook the lobster in a *court-bouillon* (see page 164), then cut it lengthwise in two; take the meat from the shell and from the claws; cut it in pieces and keep hot with a little melted butter and some thin slices of truffle.

Line each half shell of the lobster with cardinal sauce, put the slices of lobster and the truffles on top. Coat the surface with a little of the lobster sauce; sprinkle with grated cheese; and add a little melted butter.

Put the half shells on a serving dish and glaze in the oven or under the grill (U.S. broiler).

Garnish with sprigs of parsley.

Homard Clarence

LOBSTER WITH WINE AND BRANDY

Prepare the lobster as described for *homard américaine* (see page 240) but, before adding the brandy and wine, add ½ dessertspoon good curry powder. Complete the sauce by adding only 2 oz. butter and 4 tablespoons fresh cream.

Serve the lobster as you wish, with or without the shell.

At the same time, serve *riz à l'indienne* (see page 668).

Homard en coquilles à la Mornay

SCALLOPS OF LOBSTER WITH CHEESE AND TRUFFLES

———————— Butter, béchamel sauce (see page 23), grated cheese, 1 cooked lobster, truffles, salt, pepper

Choose some scallop shells of medium size, butter them and place at the bottom of each one 1 tablespoon béchamel sauce and 1 tablespoon cheese.

Thinly slice the lobster flesh, put into a saucepan with quarter its volume of thin slices of truffle. Season very sparingly with salt and pepper;

warm and place lobster and truffles in the shells; cover with béchamel sauce, sprinkle with grated cheese and melted butter and glaze quickly in the oven or under the grill (U.S. broiler).

Note Homard en coquilles can be prepared in its shell.

Homard à la crème

CREAMED LOBSTER

—————— 1 live lobster, butter, olive oil, 3—4 tablespoons brandy, ½ wine glass white wine, thin cream, salt, pinch cayenne pepper, truffles, 4 table-spoons meat jelly (see page 21), few drops lemon juice

Cut up the lobster as for *homard américaine* (see page 240), and sauté in the butter and olive oil. When the flesh is cooked and the shell coloured, add the brandy and wine. Allow liquid to reduce, then just cover with cream, season with salt and cayenne pepper. Cover and finish cooking the lobster.

Now remove the flesh from the shells, arrange in a serving dish with one-third quantity of truffles just heated in butter. Reduce the cream to half its original volume and add the melted meat jelly and the lemon juice.

2 or 3 tablespoons béchamel sauce (see page 23) may be added after reducing the cream.

Strain the sauce through muslin and pour it over the pieces of lobster.

Croquettes de homard

LOBSTER CROQUETTES

—————— 1 lobster, *court-bouillon* (see page 164), mushrooms, truffles, béchamel sauce (see page 23), 1—2 egg yolks, egg, breadcrumbs, parsley

Cook the lobster in *court-bouillon* and cut into small cubes.

Cube about one-third of mushrooms and truffles. Put ingredients together, and add enough sauce to bind, then thicken with the egg yolks. Spread smoothly on to a wet plate and leave to get cold.

Divide into equal parts and form into cutlet shapes. Coat with egg and breadcrumbs and fry. Garnish with fried parsley and serve with curry or cardinal sauce (see page 31).

Homard bouilli à la hollandaise

BOILED LOBSTER WITH PARSLEY

Cook the lobster in a simple *court-bouillon* (see page 164) and, when it is ready, drain and cut in two lengthwise.

Dish up garnished with parsley.

Serve with freshly cooked very floury potatoes and a sauce-boat of melted butter to which chopped hard-boiled egg may be added.

Homard grillé

GRILLED (U.S. BROILED) LOBSTER

The lobster is usually cut lengthwise while still alive, seasoned with salt and pepper and grilled (U.S. broiled) slowly.

It is, however, better to half-cook the lobster in *court-bouillon* (see page 164), as in this way the flesh of the lobster does not harden as it does when grilled (U.S. broiled) raw. The lobster is cut in half when taken from the *court-bouillon*, brushed with melted butter and grilled (U.S. broiled) until the cooking is complete.

Before serving, break the claws, so that the meat can easily be removed, and garnish with parsley.

Serve with melted butter, to which a little cayenne has been added, or with *sauce diable* (see page 27).

Homard à la française

LOBSTER IN THE FRENCH WAY

1 2—2½-lb. lobster, butter, salt, pepper, ½ pint (U.S. 1¼ cups) white wine, 3—4 tablespoons brandy, 3 tablespoons onion and carrot, cut into julienne, pinch chopped parsley, 6 tablespoons fish stock, 4—5 tablespoons velouté (see page 22), 3 egg yolks, 3—4 tablespoons cream

Slice lobster and put into a sauté pan with 1 oz. hot butter; season with salt and pepper.

When the flesh is cooked, add the wine and brandy. Then add onion and carrot, stewed in butter, parsley, fish stock and velouté.

Cover the saucepan and cook for 18—20 minutes. Put the lobster into a deep dish, thicken the liquor with egg yolks and cream, and finally add 3½ oz. butter. Pour this sauce over the lobster.

Homard à la Newburg

LOBSTER WITH BRANDY AND MADEIRA

This can be prepared with either a live or cooked lobster.

1 WITH LIVE LOBSTER

———————— 1 2–2½-lb. lobster, 2 oz. butter, salt, pepper, 2 tablespoons brandy, ¼ pint (U.S. ⅝ cup) Madeira, ½ pint (U.S. 1¼ cups) plus 6 tablespoons cream, 3 egg yolks

Cut lobster in half lengthwise, then each half into 2 or 3 pieces. Remove and discard the little bag of grit near the head. Remove the creamy part and pound with 1 oz. butter.

Heat remaining butter in a sauté pan. Put in the pieces of lobster, with a little salt and pepper. Sauté until the shell is red and lobster cooked. Add brandy and Madeira and cook until it is reduced by two-thirds. Add ½ pint (U.S. 1¼ cups) cream, cover and cook for 15–20 minutes.

Remove pieces of lobster and keep hot in a covered pan.

Mix egg yolks with the cream and add to sauce, with creamy part from the lobster pounded with butter.

Reheat without boiling, and pour over lobster before serving.

2 WITH COOKED LOBSTER

———————— 1 2–2½-lb. lobster, *court-bouillon* (see page 164), salt, pepper, ¼ pint (U.S. ⅝ cup) Madeira, ¼ pint (U.S. ⅝ cup) cream, 3 egg yolks, 2½ oz. butter

Cook the lobster in *court-bouillon* for 20–25 minutes.

Remove the meat from the tail, discarding membrane underneath, and cut into even slices. Arrange in a well buttered sauté pan, add a little salt and pepper and heat through, turning once. Add wine and reduce by about two-thirds. Just before serving, add cream and egg yolks mixed together. Draw pan to the side of the stove and add butter, a little at a time. As yolks cook, the sauce will thicken.

Serve at once in a hot dish.

Mousse de homard

HOT LOBSTER MOUSSE

You will need for 8 persons:
1 live 2-lb. lobster, good pinch salt, 1 pinch cayenne, 3 egg whites, 1 pint (U.S. 2½ cups) fresh cream, 3 tablespoons cold velouté (see page 22) or béchamel sauce (see page 23).

Halve lobster lengthwise and carefully remove the meat, put into mortar with the salt, cayenne, and egg whites. Pound as fine as possible, add the sauce and pass through a fine sieve.

If it is a hen lobster with coral, add it to the meat.

Place the resulting purée into a bowl, and let it remain on ice for 30 minutes. Then add the cream, very slowly, a little at a time.

Poach the mousse in a jelly mould of the correct size.

This requires a great deal of care. Put a saucer at the bottom of a saucepan, place the mould on top and pour in boiling water to reach half-way up the mould. Cover the saucepan and never let the water boil. The mousse is actually cooked in the steam. Allow about 25 to 30 minutes.

Note For mousselines, poach in dariole moulds.

To serve Turn out the mould on to a round dish.

Cardinal (see page 31), curry (see page 32), paprika (see page 32) or oyster (see page 34) sauce are all suitable to serve with this mousse.

Homard thermidor

LOBSTER THERMIDOR

Halve lobster lengthwise, season flesh with salt and pepper and grill (U.S. broil) slowly. Line the half shells with a light layer of cream béchamel sauce (see page 23) to which a little English mustard has been added. Replace the pieces in the shell and cover with more sauce. Sprinkle with melted butter and glaze quickly under the grill (U.S. broiler).

Homard Victoria

LOBSTER WITH NORMANDY SAUCE

1 2–2½-lb. lobster, butter, salt, pepper, truffle, 3–4 tablespoons Madeira, ¼ pint (U.S. ⅝ cup) Normandy sauce (see page 35)

Prepare the lobster exactly as described for lobster Newburg (see page 245).

Arrange scallops in a well buttered sauté dish, season with salt and pepper and heat through, turning once. Add one-third of thinly sliced and seasoned truffle, wine and sauce, and finally the butter, a little at a time.

Note The Normandy sauce may be replaced by *sauce suprême* (see page 23).

COLD LOBSTER

Mousse de homard

LOBSTER MOUSSE

Cook the lobster in a mirepoix with white wine and brandy, as described for the crayfish mousse (see page 240).

Scallop the flesh of the lobster tail, coat with mayonnaise sauce mixed with an equal quantity of aspic jelly (see page 116) or with ordinary chaudfroid sauce (see page 31). Arrange on top of the mousse, decorate it and cover with aspic.

Aspic de homard

LOBSTER IN ASPIC

The old method was to coat and decorate a plain or fancy mould with aspic jelly (see page 116) and to fill it with alternate layers of lobster, slices of truffle and jelly.

The disadvantage of this method is that one is apt to get too much jelly which destroys the delicacy of the dish.

It is better to use a fairly deep dish instead of a mould. Set a light layer of jelly in the bottom and stand the dish on ice. Then fill with pieces of lobster, interspersed with a few slices of truffle. Place a few leaves of tarragon on top, then cover with aspic jelly. Serve in the dish, surrounded by crushed ice.

Mayonnaise (see page 40) or ravigote sauce (see page 42) and a vegetable or green salad are good accompaniments.

Aspic de homard à la russe

RUSSIAN STYLE LOBSTER IN ASPIC

Mix equal quantities of mayonnaise and aspic jelly (see page 116) together and when beginning to thicken coat some slices or scallops of lobster.

Decorate with truffle, pimento and tarragon and place on a bed of aspic as described above.

Put some Russian salad (see page 583) between the lobster and cover all over with aspic.

Serve surrounded by crushed ice.

With a little imagination, this dish can be presented in many different ways. Instead of Russian salad one can use plovers' eggs, pigeons' eggs, stuffed hard-boiled eggs, stuffed olives, anchovy fillets or tunny fish.

Homard aux sauces diverses

LOBSTER WITH VARIOUS SAUCES

Cook the lobster in *court-bouillon* (see page 164), leave to get cold, then halve lengthwise. Break the carapace of the claws to make the extraction of the meat easier; garnish with sprigs of parsley.

Serve with mayonnaise sauce (see page 40), or one of its derivatives: rémoulade, tartare, ravigote (see page 42).

Mayonnaise de homard

LOBSTER MAYONNAISE

Cook the lobster in *court-bouillon* (see page 164) and let it cool; scallop the meat, season lightly with salt and pepper, add a few drops of vinegar and a dash of oil.

Put some chopped lettuce into a salad bowl and season lightly. Lay the scalloped lobster on this. Cover with mayonnaise sauce (see page 40) and decorate with fillets of anchovy, capers, stoned olives, quarters of hard-boiled egg and small lettuce hearts.

SPINY LOBSTER, MUSSELS AND SCALLOPS

Langouste

SPINY LOBSTER, SEA CRAYFISH OR ROCK-LOBSTER

All the recipes, hot or cold, applicable to lobsters, apply equally well to the spiny lobster.

Langouste à la parisienne et à la russe

SPINY LOBSTER PARISIAN AND RUSSIAN STYLE

The preparation of *langouste à la parisienne* and *à la russe* is sometimes confused, but the distinction is that in *à la parisienne* pieces of lobster are simply coated with aspic jelly while for *langouste à la russe* they are coated with a mixture of mayonnaise and aspic. However, today they are generally coated with chaudfroid sauce.

▬▬▬ 1 3-lb. live lobster, *court-bouillon* (see page 164), truffle, aspic jelly (see page 116), artichoke bottoms, vegetable salad, mayonnaise, hard-boiled eggs, lettuce

Tie the lobster to a small board, with the tail well stretched out. Cook it in *court-bouillon* and let it cool. Cut a strip of the shell from the back of the head to the tail. It should then be possible to remove the meat without breaking it.

Cut meat into even-sized pieces, put a slice of truffle on each and coat several times with aspic so that they are completely covered.

To serve Fix the shell on a wedge-shaped piece of bread placed at one end of the serving dish — so that the lobster is half upright. Arrange the pieces of lobster on this overlapping a little, with the larger pieces at the head.

Mix trimmings from the lobster with a little vegetable salad and bind with mayonnaise. Put a little of this on each artichoke bottom and put a slice of truffle on top.

Surround the lobster alternately with the artichoke bottoms, halved hard-boiled egg and small lettuce hearts.

Cut some firm aspic jelly into fancy shapes and arrange in a border round the dish.

Langoustines

DUBLIN BAY PRAWNS

Around the Mediterranean, a small lobster not exceeding 1 lb. in weight is called a Dublin Bay prawn, so any recipe given for lobsters can be used for them.

However, real Dublin Bay prawns are quite different: they are about the size of a large crayfish and can be bought from any fishmonger.

These too can be used in the recipes given for crayfish or lobster.

Moules

MUSSELS

PRELIMINARY PREPARATION OF MUSSELS

Choose mussels of medium size and very fresh; clean carefully and put into a saucepan with thinly sliced onion, sprigs of parsley, coarse ground pepper and ½ glass water. Cover and cook for a few minutes, just until mussels open.

After cooking, take from the heat and remove 1 shell from each mussel and put the one with the mussel in it in an earthenware pot. Decant the cooking liquid and pour over the mussels.

Moules à la marinière

MUSSELS WITH WHITE WINE

2—3 pints (U.S. 5—7½ cups) mussels, ½ pint (U.S. 1¼ cups) white wine, 2 tablespoons chopped shallot, 5—6 tablespoons freshly made breadcrumbs, 3 oz. butter, large pinch chopped parsley, juice ½ lemon

Prepare the mussels as described above and leave on the half shell. Heat wine and shallot until wine is two-thirds reduced. Add ½ pint (U.S. 1¼ cups) of liquor in which the mussels were cooked and the breadcrumbs. Add the mussels and toss for a few minutes, then add butter, parsley and lemon juice.

Serve in a vegetable dish.

Note If liked, the breadcrumbs may be replaced by a good velouté (see page 22).

Moules à la poulette

MUSSELS WITH SAUCE ALLEMANDE

2—3 pints (U.S. 5—7½ cups) mussels prepared as above, ½ pint (U.S. 1¼ cups) *sauce allemande* (see page 22), juice 1 lemon, chopped parsley

Prepare the mussels as in the recipes above. Reduce liquid left in the pan to 6 tablespoons, then add the sauce. Toss the mussels in this for a few minutes, then add lemon juice. Serve in a vegetable dish and sprinkle with chopped parsley.

Moules à la toulonnaise

MUSSELS WITH SAUCE ALLEMANDE AND RICE

2—3 pints (U.S. 5—7½ cups) mussels, ½ pint (U.S. 1¼ cups) *sauce allemande* (see page 22), 2—3 egg yolks, butter, rice, fish stock, pinch powdered saffron

Cook mussels as described on page 250, and remove from the shells. Put into a pan with 1 tablespoon of the cooking liquor and the sauce. Keep hot. When required, thicken the sauce with egg yolks and a little butter.

Cook rice in part liquor from the mussels and part fish stock. Drain, add saffron and arrange in a ring on the serving dish. Place the mussels in the centre.

Coquilles Saint-Jacques

SCALLOPS

12 scallops, 1 oz. butter, 6 tablespoons white wine, juice 1 lemon, salt, pepper, 2—3 oz. mushrooms

Choose fresh scallops. Brush, wash and put on the stove until they open. Detach the scallop from the deep shell with a palette knife. Place scallops in a saucepan, cover with water, cook for 6 — 8 minutes and drain.

Divide the white part into thin slices, scallop the coral and cube the beards. Put all into a saucepan with the butter, wine, lemon juice, seasoning and sliced mushrooms. Cover and cook for 15—18 minutes.

Coquilles Saint-Jacques crème gratin

SCALLOPS WITH GRATIN SAUCE

————————— 12 scallops, cream béchamel sauce (see page 23), grated cheese, butter

Cook scallops as previously described (see page 251) then thoroughly wash and scrub the deep shells.

Reduce liquor by two-thirds and add to about ½ pint (U.S. 1¼ cups) sauce. Put a little of this sauce into each scallop shell, add the sliced white part of the scallop, the coral and beards. Cover with more sauce, sprinkle with cheese and dot with butter, then brown slightly. A few truffles may be added.

Editor's note In the U.S.A. where scallops are seldom sold in their shells, serve in small dishes.

Coquilles Saint-Jacques, after cooking, may be prepared *à l'américaine, à la Newburg, au curry, à la provençale*.

Coquilles Saint-Jacques à la provençale

PROVENÇAL STYLE SCALLOPS

————————— 12 scallops, flour, butter, 3 tablespoons oil, 2 tablespoons finely chopped onion, 1 wine glass white wine, 7—8 tomatoes, 1 clove garlic, parsley, salt, pepper

Open the scallops as described on page 251. Thickly slice white part and coat with flour. Heat 1 oz. butter and oil, put in the fish and onion and cook until the fish begins to brown. Add wine, tomatoes, peeled, seeded and chopped, garlic, little chopped parsley, seasoning and the thinly sliced coral and beards.

Cover and cook for about 20 minutes. Finally add a little butter and serve in a deep dish.

Note A dish of rice pilaf (see page 669) may be served with the scallops.

Escargots et grenouilles
SNAILS AND FROGS' LEGS

ESCARGOTS
SNAILS

COOKING SNAILS

Choose snails which are closed up. Remove the hard seal, wash them in several different waters and clean finally with rock salt and vinegar.

Wash again in running water to remove all the mucus, then cover completely with water and boil for 5–6 minutes.

Drain, and leave to get cold, then take them out of their shells and discard the black end. Put to cook in ½ white wine and ½ water, using enough to cover completely. Add some thinly sliced carrots, onions and shallots and a *bouquet garni*. Add ¼ oz. salt for each 2 pints (U.S. 5 cups) liquid and cook over a low heat for about 3 hours. Let them cool in their cooking liquid. Wash the shells and leave to drain and dry on the stove.

Escargots à la bourguignonne
BURGUNDY STYLE SNAILS

50 snails, 10 oz. butter, 1 oz. shallot, finely chopped, 1 clove garlic (crushed), 1 tablespoon chopped parsley, salt, pepper, breadcrumbs

Cook the snails as instructed above, and drain well. Meanwhile make some butter *à la bourguignonne* by mixing all remaining ingredients together. If not used at once, keep on ice.

Put a small piece of the butter, the size of a hazel-nut, into each shell, put the snail back in its shell and cover with a little more butter. Arrange the snail with a little water at the bottom, sprinkle a few breadcrumbs over the butter and heat in the oven for 7–8 minutes.

Escargots sautés aux tomates
TOSSED SNAILS WITH TOMATO

48 snails, 4—5 tablespoons oil, 2 tablespoons onion, 1 wine glass white wine, 7—8 tomatoes, 1 small clove garlic, parsley

Cook the snails as instructed on page 253, and drain them. Heat oil in a saucepan and add finely chopped onion. When onion begins to brown, put in the snails, cook for a few minutes, moisten with the wine and add a few tablespoons of the liquor in which the snails were cooked.

Reduce this by half. Add tomatoes, peeled, seeded and chopped, garlic and a large pinch chopped parsley. Cover and cook for 15—18 minutes over a low heat. Dish the snails in their shells, in a deep dish, and serve with a pilaf of rice (see page 669).

Escargots à la façon d'un gourmand
SNAILS AS THE CONNOISSEUR LIKES THEM

Snails, chopped truffle, meat jelly (see page 21), butter, freshly ground pepper, pinch red pepper, chopped parsley, garlic, water, breadcrumbs

Cook the snails, let them cool in their cooking liquid and drain them.

Mix the truffle with a little meat jelly, put a small teaspoon into each shell, replace the snail and put a little more of the mixture on top.

Season butter with the pepper, parsley and garlic and spread over the opening to seal it. Arrange the snails, on a snail dish if possible, with a little water at the bottom, and put into the oven for 10—12 minutes. Before serving, put a small teaspoon of breadcrumbs fried in butter into each snail.

GRENOUILLES
FROGS' LEGS

Grenouilles sautées aux fines herbes
FROGS' LEGS TOSSED IN PARSLEY

Trim the frogs' legs. Season with salt and pepper, and sauté them in butter.

Arrange in a dish, squeeze a little lemon juice over them and sprinkle with chopped parsley.

Note Some devotees rub the bottom of the frying pan lightly with garlic before putting in the butter.

Grenouilles frites

FRIED FROGS' LEGS

Trim the frogs' legs, marinate for 30 minutes before cooking, with lemon juice, a dash of oil, salt and pepper and chopped parsley.

Just before serving, dip in a light batter and fry in deep fat.

Drain and serve with fried parsley.

Grenouilles à la poulette

FROGS' LEGS WITH NORMANDY SAUCE

———— Legs of 36 frogs, butter, stock in which mushrooms have been cooked, salt, pepper, ¼ pint (U.S. 1⅞ cups) Normandy sauce (see page 35), parsley, crayfish or slices of truffle

Trim the frogs' legs. Put into a pan with 1½ oz. butter, enough mushroom liquor to barely cover, salt and pepper. Cover and cook for 12—15 minutes over low heat, when legs should be cooked and liquor reduced. Add the sauce and a little more butter. Arrange in a dish, and sprinkle with parsley, chopped mushrooms, crayfish, or slices of truffle.

ANOTHER RECIPE

———— Legs of 36 frogs, butter, 3 tablespoons flour, 1 wine glass white wine, 1 pint (U.S. 2¼ cups) hot water, salt, peppercorns, parsley, bay leaf, 3 egg yolks, 2 tablespoons cream

Trim frogs' legs, put into a pan with 1½ oz. butter and sauté for a few minutes. Sprinkle flour over, then add wine, water, flavourings and seasoning. Cook for 10—12 minutes over low heat. Remove from heat, strain liquor into a saucepan and keep legs hot. Thicken sauce with egg yolks and cream, finally add a few dabs butter.

Note A few mushrooms sautéed in butter, and a pinch chopped parsley could be added to the sauce.

Serve the frogs' legs covered with sauce.

Nymphes à l'aurore

FROGS' LEGS POACHED IN WHITE WINE

Trim frogs' legs, poach in a *court-bouillon* (see page 164) with white wine and allow to cool in the liquid.

When cold, drain and dry well; coat with a chaudfroid sauce (see page 31) to which a little paprika has been added. The chaudfroid should be a pinkish-gold colour like the dawn.

Line a deep silver or glass dish with a layer of aspic jelly (see page 116) to which some Moselle has been added.

Arrange legs on aspic and add a few tarragon leaves to resemble seaweed. Cover with more aspic and leave to set.

Serve with dish surrounded by crushed ice.

La Viande

MEAT

LE BOEUF
BEEF

Boeuf bouilli

BOILED BEEF

Boiled beef is not always fully appreciated, although it is true that the meat which has produced broth cannot fail to have lost some of its essential properties.

However, it is indisputable that a good pot-au-feu will always be a comforting and very homely dish.

Note Boiled beef should never be left to cool in its broth. Brisket, silverside and topside are the cuts of beef generally used for boiling. Silverside is also salted and boiled.

Boeuf au gratin

BEEF AU GRATIN

3 tablespoons chopped onion, butter or lard, 1 lb. cooked minced beef, salt, pepper, grated nutmeg, ½ pint (U.S. 1¼ cups) tomato sauce (see page 132), chopped parsley, garlic, potato purée, 1 tablespoon breadcrumbs, 1 tablespoon grated cheese

Sauté the onion in ½ oz. butter till lightly brown. Add the beef and season with salt, pepper and grated nutmeg. Add the tomato sauce, chopped parsley and a little garlic. Allow to simmer for 7–8 minutes. Turn the mince into a fireproof dish deep enough for the mince to three-quarters fill it. Cover with a purée of potatoes. Sprinkle with the breadcrumbs and grated cheese mixed together. Dot with butter and brown in oven.

Boeuf à l'arlésienne

BEEF WITH AUBERGINES AND TOMATOES

———————— Boiled beef, 2 medium-sized onions, 4—5 tablespoons oil, 3—4 aubergines, 1—1½ lb. tomatoes, 4 large red peppers, salt, pepper, parsley, garlic

Cut the beef into slices about ⅜ inch thick and arrange on a serving dish. Thinly slice the onions and put in a frying pan with the oil.

When they begin to brown, add the aubergines, peeled and sliced, and sauté for 7—8 minutes over moderate heat. Add the tomatoes, peeled, seeded and chopped, and the red peppers, grilled and cut into strips. Season with salt and pepper, chopped parsley and a suspicion of garlic. Allow to simmer for 18—20 minutes. Pour over the slices of beef and put into a moderate oven for a few minutes.

Boeuf miroton

BOILED BEEF WITH SAUCE

———————— 1 lb. cold boiled beef, 3 medium-sized onions, butter or cooking fat, 1 tablespoon flour, ½—¾ pint (U.S. 1¼—1⅞ cups) stock, 2 tablespoons vinegar, salt, pepper, *bouquet garni* (include ½ clove garlic if liked), 3—4 gherkins or capers, breadcrumbs

Cut the meat into thin slices and arrange in a fireproof dish. Sauté thinly sliced onion in 1 oz. butter until it begins to brown. Add flour and cook for a few minutes, then add stock and vinegar. Bring to boiling point, add seasoning and *bouquet garni*, cook for 10—12 minutes. The sauce should then be fairly thick. Add the thinly sliced gherkins and pour the sauce over the meat.

Sprinkle with breadcrumbs, dot with butter and brown in the oven.

Boeuf sauté lyonnaise

SAUTÉ OF BEEF WITH ONIONS

———————— 2—3 large white onions, 4 tablespoons butter or lard, 1 lb. cold boiled beef, salt, pepper, 2 tablespoons vinegar, chopped parsley

Slice the onions thinly and put into a frying pan with the butter or lard. When it begins to brown, add the meat, sliced thinly or cut into small cubes, season with salt and pepper and sauté for 7—8 minutes over a slow heat.

Just before serving, add the vinegar and sprinkle with parsley.

Boeuf sauté parmentier

SAUTÉ OF BEEF WITH SAUTÉ POTATOES

2 medium-sized onions, 1 tablespoon butter, 1 lb. cold boiled beef, salt, pepper, 1 lb. sauté potatoes, parsley

Lightly brown chopped onions in butter. Add the thinly sliced beef, season with salt and pepper and sauté for 7—8 minutes. Then add the sauté potatoes, and continue to cook for a few moments.

Sprinkle with chopped parsley and serve.

Boeuf provençal

PROVENÇAL STYLE BEEF

2 lb. ripe tomatoes, 4—5 tablespoons oil, salt, pepper, chopped parsley, 1 clove garlic, 1 lb. cold boiled beef

Peel, seed and chop the tomatoes coarsely, put into a pan with the oil and season with salt and pepper, parsley and garlic. Cover and cook over a low heat for about 12 minutes. Add the beef cut into cubes the size of a walnut and simmer for 12—15 minutes. If liked a few black or green olives, or finely chopped mushrooms sautéed in the oil, may be added.

Serve with mashed, boiled or sautéed potatoes, macaroni or noodles.

Boeuf à la tyrolienne

BEEF IN THE TYROL FASHION

───────── 1 lb. cold boiled beef, 2 large onions, 2 tablespoons oil, 4 tablespoons
vinegar, 7—8 tomatoes, salt, pepper, parsley, 1 clove garlic

Cut the beef in thin slices and arrange on a fireproof dish.

Brown the thinly sliced onions in the oil, add the vinegar and allow
to reduce a little. Add the tomatoes, peeled, seeded and thinly sliced,
season with salt and pepper, pinch of coarsely chopped parsley and
garlic. Cook over a low heat for 15—18 minutes. Pour over the meat and
put dish into a moderate oven for 7—8 minutes.

Sprinkle with chopped parsley before serving. Serve with potatoes
or macaroni as given above.

Palets de boeuf à la ménagère

BEEF WITH POTATOES AND CHIVES

───────── 1 lb. cold boiled minced beef, 1 lb. boiled potatoes, 2 eggs, salt, pepper,
grated nutmeg, 1 tablespoon chopped chives, butter or lard

Mix beef with the well mashed potatoes. Add the beaten eggs, seasoning
and flavourings. Mix all well together. Divide into pieces the size of an
egg, then flatten and pat into small rounds. Fry in butter or lard until
browned on both sides.

Salade de boeuf

BEEF SALAD

───────── 1 lb. cold boiled beef, 2 teaspoons dry mustard, salt, pepper, 3 tablespoons vinegar, 7—8 tablespoons oil, little chervil, tarragon, 2 chopped
hard-boiled eggs

Slice the beef and arrange in a salad bowl. Mix all the ingredients for
the dressing and beat lightly with a fork. Pour over the meat, and leave
for 30 minutes before serving.

The salad may be varied by adding French beans, potatoes, tomatoes, cucumber, etc.

Serve some finely chopped chives or onions separately.

DIVISION DU BOEUF
CUTS AND SECTIONS OF BEEF

Aloyau

SIRLOIN (U.S. LOIN)

This joint includes the lumbar region starting from the last rib down to the rump and includes the fillet (U.S. tenderloin).

The sirloin (U.S. loin) is usually roasted and is usually served underdone, or 'rare'.

All vegetables go well with it. Sirloin (U.S. loin) should be roasted carefully and is served with gravy made with the meat sediment left in the roasting tin, and stock or water.

The gravy should contain a certain amount of fat.

Sirloin (U.S. loin) is also served cold, accompanied by meat jelly (see page 21) and various salads.

Amourettes et cervelles

BEEF MARROW AND BRAINS

Marrow is usually sold with brains and is often served with them. However, it is sometimes cooked separately and may, in one form or another, make a special dish, or a garnish.

Because of their lightness, brains and marrow are specially recommended for children and elderly people.

Calves' brains and marrow are preferable to those of beef, but the treatment is identical.

After washing in several waters, the surrounding membranes must be removed, then washed again, to clean thoroughly.

Brains and marrow are cooked in *court-bouillon* (see page 164) lightly acidulated with vinegar and with a *bouquet garni*.

Cooking time 20 — 25 minutes, according to size.

Fritot d'amourettes

MARROW FRITTERS

———————— Marrow, lemon juice, oil, salt, pepper, parsley, batter (see page 690), tomato sauce (see page 132)

Cut the freshly cooked marrow into 3-inch slices, marinate for 20 minutes in lemon juice, a little oil, salt, pepper and chopped parsley.

Then dip in a light batter, fry quickly, drain and serve with tomato sauce.

Freshly cooked marrow cut into little cubes, chopped truffles added and coated with béchamel sauce (see page 23) make a delicious garnish for small patties.

CERVELLE
BRAINS

Cervelle au beurre noir

BRAINS WITH BLACK BUTTER

———————— Brains, beef marrow, salt, pepper, black butter (see page 196), chopped, parsley, hot vinegar

Cut cooked brains into slices and arrange in a ring on a round dish. Put some sliced beef marrow in the centre and season with salt and pepper. Cover with black butter to which a little parsley has been added, allowing 2 oz. for each brain. Sprinkle with a little hot vinegar before serving.

Cervelle à la bourguignonne

BURGUNDY STYLE BRAINS

———————— Calves' brains, mushrooms and small onions glazed in butter, *sauce bourguignonne* (see page 25), croûtons, cut into small heart shapes and fried

Cut sliced cooked brains and put into a sauté pan with the mushrooms and onions. Simmer for 7—8 minutes. Serve on a dish covered with sauce and surrounded by the croûtons.

Crépinettes de cervelle

BRAIN CRÉPINETTES

———————— Cooked calves' brains, sausage meat, chopped truffle, salt, pepper, butter, breadcrumbs

Cut the brains into small pieces and mix with an equal amount of sausage meat. Add a little chopped truffle, salt and pepper.

Divide into small pieces, flatten and form into cutlet shapes. Dip in melted butter, coat with breadcrumbs, brush with a little more butter and grill (U.S. broil).

Serve with mashed potatoes or a purée of peas or beans, etc., and *sauce diable* (see page 27).

Fritot de cervelle

BRAIN FRITTERS

When the brains are cooked, cut them up, marinate, and cook as described for *fritot d'amourettes* (see page 262).

Cervelle à la génoise

BRAINS IN THE GENOESE MANNER

———————— Calves' brains, salt, pepper, flour, butter, oil, grated Parmesan cheese, tomato sauce (see page 132), veal stock

Slice brains, season lightly and coat with flour. Heat a little butter and oil together, and brown lightly. Butter the bottom of a fireproof dish, sprinkle with cheese and cover with a thin layer of tomato sauce reduced with a little veal stock. Arrange the brains on this, and cover with more sauce. Dot with butter, cover, and heat through in the oven.

Cervelle à l'italienne

ITALIAN STYLE BRAINS

Prepare the brains as shown in *cervelle à la génoise* above. After browning, arrange in a ring on a very hot dish and pour an Italian sauce (see page 28) in the centre.

Cervelle napolitaine

BRAINS WITH MACARONI

Cooked brains, salt, pepper, flour, egg, breadcrumbs, oil, butter, macaroni

Cut the brains into large slices and season with salt and pepper. Dip in flour, then in beaten egg and breadcrumbs and in half oil, half butter.

Arrange in a ring on a very hot dish; garnish the centre with *macaroni napolitaine* (see page 676).

Pain de cervelle à la ménagère

BRAIN LOAF

12 oz. cooked calves' brains, salt, pepper, 8 oz. breadcrumb panada (see page 54), 3 oz. butter, 4 eggs

Season brains with salt and pepper and pound in a mortar with the panada, softened butter and beaten eggs. Rub through a fine sieve and put into a buttered charlotte tin.

Cook in the oven in a bain-marie, at a very low heat for about 30 – 35 minutes.

Leave for 5 – 6 minutes before turning out, and serve with tomato (see page 132) or piquant (see page 28) sauce.

Palets de cervelle

BRAIN RISSOLES

Cooked calf's brain, sausage meat, 2 tablespoons breadcrumbs, 1 dessertspoon cream, salt, pepper, pinch nutmeg, flour, egg, breadcrumbs, butter

Cut the brain into small cubes and mix with quarter of sausage meat. Add breadcrumbs moistened with cream, salt, pepper and nutmeg. Divide into small pieces, flatten and form into rounds. Coat with flour, then with egg and breadcrumbs and, fry in clarified butter.

Serve on a hot dish with a purée of chestnuts, potatoes, spinach or *oeufs à la tripe* (see page 152) and serve *sauce poivrade à la crème* (see page 29).

Cervelle à la poulette

BRAISED BRAINS WITH ALLEMANDE SAUCE

Slice the freshly cooked brains, put in a serving dish and coat with *sauce allemande* (see page 22).

Cervelle royale

BRAINS IN COCOTTE

———— 1 calf's brain, butter, 4 egg yolks, 6 tablespoons cream, salt, pepper, meat jelly (see page 21)

Stew the brain in butter, and pass through a fine sieve. Add the egg yolks and cream to this purée, season with salt and pepper and put the mixture into small buttered cocottes. Cook them in a bain-marie over very low heat. Just before serving, add a small teaspoon of melted meat jelly to each cocotte.

Subrics de cervelle

BRAIN SUBRICS

———— 8 oz. cooked calf's brains, salt, pepper, 8 oz. cooked spinach, ½ pint (U.S. 1¼ cups) fairly thick pancake batter (see page 704), fat for frying

Cut the brains into small cubes, add salt and pepper, well drained, chopped and buttered spinach and about the same quantity of pancake batter. Drop in spoonfuls into hot fat and fry till brown on both sides.

CONTREFILET
CONTREFILET (U.S. SIRLOIN)

The contrefilet is the cut situated partly above the loin and partly above the chine. It is treated the same as the fillet, and all recipes for the fillet apply to it. It is preferable roasted, whether boned or not.

ENTRECÔTE
STEAK

Although, as its name indicates, the entrecôte (U.S. steak) is the part which is found between two ribs, it is often taken from the contrefilet (U.S. sirloin) for convenience.

The entrecôte may be grilled or sautéed. The weight of an entrecôte for two persons is about 8 oz. and it should be about 1 inch thick.

The weight of a double entrecôte is between 12 oz. and 1 lb.

'Minute' steak, cut thin, weighs about 4 oz.

To be grilled or sautéed the meat should be of first quality and well hung.

When dealing with a double piece, whether it be steak or porterhouse steak, do not have it too thick. One should not need to beat the meat unmercifully to flatten it and be able to cook it. This is a great mistake. Meat, when heavily beaten, has its fibres broken and when it is cooked the blood separates from the flesh so all one gets is a piece of meat without any flavour.

In principle, all meat that is to be grilled (U.S. broiled) or sautéed should be beaten only very lightly.

Entrecôte aux champignons
STEAK WITH MUSHROOMS

Steak sufficient for 2 persons, butter, 2—3 tablespoons Madeira or white wine, 12 small cooked button mushrooms, 5—6 tablespoons demi-glace sauce (see page 22)

Sauté the steak in butter, and put on to a hot plate.

Mix the wine with the sediment left in the pan, then add mushrooms and a little of their liquor, and demi-glace sauce. Reduce for a minute or two. Arrange the mushrooms on the steak, strain the sauce through a fine strainer and pour it over the mushrooms.

The best accompaniment is a dish of mashed potatoes.

Entrecôte béarnaise
STEAK BÉARNAISE

Brush the steak with butter or oil, sprinkle with salt and grill (U.S. broil). Serve on a long dish and add 1 tablespoon light meat jelly (see page 21) adding a tablespoon butter. Serve with béarnaise sauce (see page 30).

Soufflé, straw, buttered or sauté potatoes may be served around the steak or separately.

Grilled (U.S. broiled) steak may be accompanied by Bercy butter, or *sauce bordelaise* (see page 25), or with mushrooms with *fines herbes*, or grilled or sauté tomatoes. Potatoes cooked in any way go well with it.

'Minute' steak should be grilled quickly and served immediately on a hot dish. Serve with any of the above accompaniments.

Entrecôte Mirabeau

STEAK WITH ANCHOVY FILLETS AND OLIVES

Grill (U.S. broil) the steak and place it on a round dish; criss-cross with strips of fillets of anchovy and tarragon leaves that have been put into salted boiling water for a few seconds. Surround the steak with stoned olives.

Serve anchovy butter separately and soufflé, fried or sauté potatoes.

Côtes en entrecôtes de detail

ENTRECÔTE STEAKS IN DETAIL

Entrecôte steaks cut in various sizes are usually grilled or sautéed, but they should not really be over 2 lb. if they are to be cooked evenly.

All the methods described for the cooking of steak can be applied.

CÔTE DE BOEUF
RIBS OF BEEF

Ribs of beef are usually roasted. The time of cooking naturally depends on the size and the quality of the joint. It can, however, be calculated at approximately 15 – 20 minutes per 1 lb.

This joint must only be used when it has been well hung, as this is when it is tender.

Ribs of beef may equally well be braised, but in this case cut them into pieces, each of 2 – 3 ribs.

Côte de boeuf braisé

BRAISED RIBS OF BEEF

———————— Ribs of beef, onions, carrots, few pieces bacon rind without fat, salt, pepper, few tablespoons cooking fat, 1 pint (U.S. 2½ cups) white wine, 1 calf's foot, *bouquet garni*, stock

The meat should be boned, rolled and tied with string.

Line a large casserole or braising pot with sliced onions, carrots and bacon rind. Put in the lightly seasoned meat, and the cooking fat. Add the wine, and cook over low heat until the wine is almost reduced. Add the calf's foot, boned and skinned, *bouquet garni* and enough stock to cover. Cover the pan and put into a moderate oven, basting frequently during the cooking.

Test with a skewer to ascertain when the meat is cooked. Then remove from the pan, and keep hot with the calf's foot.

Strain the stock through a fine sieve. Leave to stand until the fat settles, then remove it. If the stock is still thin at this stage, reduce it quickly to one-third its original volume. If preferred the stock can be thickened with arrowroot, using 1 tablespoon to each pint, or add 2−3 tablespoons demi-glace sauce with tomato (see page 132).

Put the meat on to a serving dish, with the calf's foot cut into small pieces, and pour some of the stock over. Return to the oven for a few minutes. The dish can be garnished with some of the following: carrots, braised lettuce, celery, turnips, glazed onions, mashed potatoes, stuffed cabbage, etc.

Italian pasta, such as macaroni, spaghetti, lasagne, etc., go well with braised beef.

FILET DE BOEUF
FILLET OF BEEF

The fillet of beef is the best part of the animal. It is usually served 'larded', and in certain preparations truffles are inserted into it, in which case it has strips of fat bacon tied to it.

Fillet of beef which is to be served as an entrée is either pot roasted or roasted.

Unless otherwise stated, it should always be slightly pink inside.
Notes on cutting up beef Formerly it was usual, in butchers' shops,
to cut beef as follows:

The top part was for beefsteaks (weight 6−8 oz. for 2 persons). The
middle part was reserved for porterhouse steaks (10−12 oz. for 3−4
persons), and for fillets (6−8 oz. for 2 persons).

From the thin end were cut tournedos (3 pieces altogether, 5−6 oz.
for 2 persons). Then the flattened part at the end, divided in two lengthwise, furnished the *filets mignons* (5−6 oz. for 2 persons).

This method of cutting the fillet of beef is excellent, and produces the
best yield.

When it is to be roasted, it should have the connective tissues and
sinews carefully removed and then be studded with lard or larded.
A precaution which deserves to be mentioned is to put flattened slices
of beef fat on the side which is not larded or studded − this may be held
in place with string.

Fillet of beef must be roasted in a fairly hot oven and kept a little rare.

Time of cooking on a spit 9 minutes per 1 lb. and 15 minutes per 1 lb.
in the oven. Baste frequently and salt the joint during the cooking.

Hampes ou onglées

THIN FLANK OR SHORT RIBS

These are very tender and juicy pieces which furnish excellent beefsteaks
and exquisite paupiettes; cut in little cubes, they are sautéed in butter
like kidneys, or may be grilled (U.S. broiled) and are garnished in the
same way.

In any case the skin and gristle must be removed.

Filet de boeuf à l'arlésienne

POT ROAST WITH AUBERGINES

———————— Pot roasted fillet surrounded by stuffed aubergines and tomatoes

Serve the cooking liquor separately, having added a little demi-glace
sauce with tomato (see page 22).

Rôtis de boeuf à l'anglaise

ENGLISH ROAST BEEF

English roast beef is always rather well cooked, and is invariably accompanied by Yorkshire pudding.

For pot roasting the fillet of beef is prepared as for roasting, except that instead of being put on the spit or in a roasting tin it is placed on a bed of onion, thinly sliced carrots, *bouquet garni,* and celery, and dotted with butter. Cover the pan and put it in a moderate oven. Baste from time to time and add salt before the cooking is complete. Above all, avoid burning the vegetables.

As soon as it is cooked, take the joint out of the pan and keep it warm.

Remove vegetables and to the cooking liquor add a glass of Madeira or white wine, and some good gravy, the quantity being determined by the size of the joint; allow to boil for a few seconds, strain through a fine sieve and skim off some of the grease.

Remove the string and any extra fat from the meat, surround it with the chosen garnish, and add a little of the cooking liquor. A little demiglace sauce (see page 22) may be added.

Filet de boeuf bouquetière

FILLET OF BEEF WITH VEGETABLES

Stud the fillet with thin strips of fat bacon and roast or pot roast it. Serve surrounded with vegetables, alternating their colour.

Strain the gravy from the roasting tin, reduce it a little, skim if necessary and serve separately.

Filet de boeuf financière

FILLET OF BEEF WITH FINANCIÈRE GARNISH

Stud the fillet with thin strips of bacon and pot roast it. Put on to a serving dish and arrange around it financière garnish (see page 48). Pour a little of the financière sauce over the garnish and serve the rest separately.

Filet de boeuf Godard

POT ROAST FILLET OF BEEF WITH GODARD GARNISH

Stud the fillet with strips of bacon and tongue, alternately, and pot roast it.

Prepare a Godard garnish (see page 49) and when the meat is cooked put on to a serving dish. Arrange the quenelles on either side, and the rest of the garnish in small piles. Cover with a little of the Godard sauce.

Strain, and reduce the gravy left. Add it to remaining Godard sauce and serve separately.

Filet de boeuf jardinière

ROAST FILLET OF BEEF WITH VEGETABLES

Stud the fillet with thin strips of bacon and roast it. Moisten simply with a few tablespoons of its own gravy, not skimmed, and serve with fresh buttered vegetables and some much reduced gravy.

Filet de boeuf Madrilène

FILLET OF BEEF WITH STUFFED TOMATOES AND RICE

Stud the fillet with thin strips of bacon and pot roast it. Serve surrounded by stuffed tomatoes (see page 659) and pilaf rice (see page 669).

Reduce the cooking liquor, add a little demi-glace sauce with tomato (see page 22) and some sweet red peppers grilled and cut into julienne, and serve separately.

Filet de boeuf nivernaise

POT ROAST FILLET OF BEEF WITH CARROTS AND ONIONS

Stud the fillet with thin strips of bacon and pot roast it. Serve surrounded by new carrots and glazed onions arranged alternately.

Strain the cooking liquor, skim and thicken slightly and serve separately.

Filet de boeuf à la Talleyrand

FILLET OF BEEF WITH TRUFFLES AND MADEIRA

————— Fillet of beef, truffles, Madeira, 5 oz. macaroni, butter, grated Gruyère and grated Parmesan cheese, 2½ oz. pâté de foie gras

Stud the fillet with truffles and marinate in Madeira for several hours. Then interlard it, tie it with string and pot roast it in Madeira. Put on a serving dish with a little of the cooking liquor.

Cook the macaroni until just tender, drain and add a little butter, the cheese, 2 oz. truffles cut in julienne and the pâté de foie gras cut into cubes.

Serve separately with a demi-glace sauce (see page 22) to which some Madeira and julienne of truffle have been added.

Fillets of beef may be accompanied by various garnishes, according to the season of the year and individual taste.

Potatoes, which I have not mentioned in the recipes above, are always and in all circumstances, and no matter how they are cooked, a valuable addition to fillet of beef.

Filet de boeuf froid

COLD FILLET OF BEEF

Fillet of beef which is to be served cold is roasted or pot roasted, slightly underdone or rare inside. When cooked, trim underneath and at the sides, then coat with aspic jelly.

Cold fillet of beef may be accompanied by either vegetables in aspic jelly, salad or Russian salad, and may be surrounded by artichoke bottoms garnished according to taste; also asparagus tips garnished with chopped truffles. Stuffed tomatoes (see page 659) and *aubergines farcies à la provençale* (see page 596) also go very well with it.

Note As far as possible, avoid using canned artichoke bottoms. Whatever garnish is decided upon for cold fillet of beef, it should always be accompanied by a dish of aspic jelly, surrounded by ice.

In England, cold meats are usually accompanied by hot potatoes, and with various kinds of pickles.

Horseradish sauce with cream is also very much appreciated as an accompaniment.

BIFTECK
BEEF STEAK

In principle, beef steak was formerly taken from the top end of the fillet, but it may also come from the contrefilet or the head of the sirloin.

Beef steak may be cooked in the same way as the recipes given for entrecôte.

Bifteck à l'américaine

BEEF STEAK WITH RAW EGG

Cut the steak from the fillet, remove the fat and the sinews, mince the meat and season with salt and pepper. Reshape the steak on a serving dish in little round flat cakes. Hollow out a small place in the centre and put a raw egg yolk into each.

Serve chopped capers, onion and parsley separately.

Bifteck à la hambourgeoise

HAMBURGER STEAK

2 small eggs, chopped onion lightly browned in butter, salt, pepper, nutmeg, 12 oz. minced beef steak, flour, clarified butter for frying

Add the eggs, 3 teaspoons chopped onion, salt, pepper and nutmeg to the beef.

Reshape the steak into 3–4 round cakes, flour them and cook in clarified butter. Serve with 1 teaspoon chopped onion browned in butter on each cake.

Bifteck à la russe

RUSSIAN STYLE BEEF STEAK

Prepare the steak as for hamburgers (see above) but replace the onion on each with 1 fried egg trimmed to shape.

Chateaubriand

PORTERHOUSE STEAK

The porterhouse steak comes from the centre of the fillet. It is difficult to fix its exact weight, because it depends so much on the thickness of the fillet, but one weighing about 12 oz. – 1 lb. is best.

Originally the porterhouse steak was always accompanied by a sauce made of meat jelly (see page 21), to which twice its weight of maître d'hôtel butter was added, and potatoes sautéed in butter.

Nowadays, the porterhouse steak is accompanied by any of the sauces and garnishes recommended for grilled (U.S. broiled) fillets and tournedos.

BITOKES
BITOKS (RUSSIAN COOKERY)

Bitokes à la russe

RUSSIAN RISSOLES

1 lb. lean beef, 4 oz. butter, 4 oz. white breadcrumbs, cream, salt, pinch pepper, pinch nutmeg, flour, clarified butter for frying, 6 tablespoons sour cream, 2–3 tablespoons demi-glace sauce (see page 22) or meat jelly (see page 21)

Mince the beef, removing any gristle, and add butter, breadcrumbs lightly moistened with cream, salt, pepper and nutmeg. Mix together thoroughly.

Divide mixture into 7–8 parts, shape each into a round, sprinkle with flour and cook in clarified butter. Arrange them in a ring on a round dish.

Drain off butter in the cooking pan and replace it with the sour cream, reduce it for some seconds, then add 2–3 tablespoons very reduced demi-glace sauce, or 2 or 3 tablespoons meat jelly.

Strain the sauce and serve separately with a dish of sauté potatoes.

Note If you have no sour cream, add the juice of ½ lemon to the sauce. Bitoks can be dipped in beaten egg and breadcrumbs before frying.

FILETS DE BOEUF SAUTÉS
OU GRILLÉS

SAUTÉED OR GRILLED FILLETS
OF BEEF

These fillets are cut to the weight of 6—7 oz. at the outside, and are cooked like entrecôtes and tournedos.

All the garnishes and sauces that accompany the entrecôtes and tournedos apply to fillets.

FILETS MIGNONS

Filets mignons of beef are usually cut from the centre fillet, then cut in half lengthwise and trimmed into flat triangles.

Season lightly with salt and pepper, dip in melted butter, then in breadcrumbs, brush over with a little more butter and grill (U.S. broil).

Serve with any vegetable garnish and with *sauce béarnaise* (see page 30), *sauce piquante* (see page 28) or *sauce Choron*.

Note Sauce Choron is *sauce béarnaise* with the addition of a little tomato purée.

Filets mignons en chevreuil

HEART-SHAPED FILETS MIGNONS

Bacon or pork fat, 6—7 filets mignons cut as described above, peppercorns, 1 carrot, 1 onion, 1 bay leaf, 1 sprig parsley, 1 sprig thyme, 2—3 tablespoons oil, 2 tablespoons vinegar, 6 tablespoons red wine, oil for frying, heart-shaped croûtons, *sauce poivrade* (see page 29) or *sauce chasseur* (see page 26)

Lard the fillets on the thickest part, put into a bowl with the peppercorns, thinly sliced carrot and onion, bay leaf, parsley, thyme, oil, vinegar and red wine. Cover, and keep on ice if possible for 24 hours. Then drain and dry the fillets and sauté in very hot oil. Serve on heart-shaped croûtons fried in oil or butter. Reduce marinade to about two-thirds its original quantity, strain, and add to *sauce poivrade* or *sauce chasseur*.

In addition to the sauce, serve with a purée of chestnuts, lentils, red haricot beans or sweet potatoes.

TOURNEDOS

Tournedos are small slices of fillet of beef, cut round and rather thick, weighing about 3½–4 oz. They are sautéed quickly in butter, or grilled (U.S. broiled).

Formerly it was customary to serve sautéed tournedos on croûtons, but this has fallen into disuse for many reasons. However, if you are going to use croûtons, they should be fried in butter and, at the last moment, covered with meat jelly (see page 21), which forms an insulation between the meat and the bread, and prevents the latter from absorbing any juice coming from the meat.

Chateaubriand sauce, otherwise meat jelly enriched with butter and completed with a few drops of lemon juice, should accompany all sautéed tournedos if garnished with buttered vegetables, asparagus tips, *jardinière*, etc.

This sauce has the advantage of binding the vegetables together, which is not the case when either the Madeira or white wine sauce is used.

Garnish with truffle, mushrooms, lettuce, celery, etc.

Tournedos andalouse

TOURNEDOS WITH AUBERGINES AND RED PEPPERS

4 oz. finely chopped onion, oil, 8 oz. aubergines, 8 oz. tomatoes, 1–2 sweet red peppers, salt, pepper, parsley, 1 clove garlic, 4–6 3½–4-oz. tournedos, butter

Sauté the onion in 2–3 tablespoons oil for a few minutes, add the aubergines sliced finely, the tomatoes, peeled, seeded and chopped, peppers, seeded and sliced thinly, seasoning, little chopped parsley and garlic.

Cook gently for 20–25 minutes, then put into a serving dish and keep hot.

Sauté the tournedos in equal quantities of oil and butter and put on the bed of vegetables.

Add a little good gravy to the liquor left in the pan in which the tournedos were cooked and pour it over them.

Serve with *riz à la créole* (see page 666).

Tournedos arlésienne

TOURNEDOS WITH AUBERGINES AND TOMATOES

Prepare in the same way as for *tournedos andalouse* above, but omit the red pepper. Serve with a dish of plain boiled potatoes.

Tournedos béarnaise

TOURNEDOS WITH BÉARNAISE SAUCE

Grill the tournedos and arrange them on a very hot dish. Surround with small *noisette* potatoes (see page 653) rolled in light meat jelly (see page 21). Cover the tournedos with Chateaubriand sauce (see page 523) and serve with beárnaise sauce (see page 30).

Tournedos bordelaise

TOURNEDOS WITH POACHED BEEF MARROW

Grill the tournedos and arrange them on a very hot dish. Place a large slice of poached beef marrow on each one, with a pinch of chopped parsley in the centre.

Serve a bordelaise sauce (see page 25) separately.

Potatoes cooked by any method make a suitable accompaniment.

Tournedos champignons

TOURNEDOS WITH MUSHROOMS

Tournedos, butter, mushrooms, Madeira, demi-glace sauce (see page 22)

Sauté the tournedos in butter and place on a round dish. Allow 3—4 mushrooms for each tournedos and sauté in butter.

Add a little Madeira and the liquor left from the mushrooms to the pan in which the tournedos were cooked. Add the mushrooms and enough demi-glace sauce to cover. Cook for a few seconds, then pour over the tournedos. Serve with mashed potatoes.

Tournedos chasseur

TOURNEDOS WITH BRANDY AND WHITE WINE

Salt, pepper, 4 tournedos, butter, brandy, white wine, 1 shallot, 12 mushrooms, 6 tablespoons demi-glace sauce with tomato (see page 22), 1 tablespoon meat jelly (see page 21), pinch chopped parsley

Season and sauté the tournedos in butter and arrange on a round dish. Add a little brandy and white wine to the pan in which the tournedos were cooked and mix well with remaining butter and sediment. Add minced shallot, and the mushrooms sliced and sautéed in butter. Add the demi-glace sauce, meat jelly and parsley. Boil for a few seconds and pour over the tournedos.

Tournedos Choron

TOURNEDOS WITH ARTICHOKE BOTTOMS

Seasoning, 4 tournedos, butter, 4 artichoke bottoms, asparagus tips or peas, *noisette* potatoes (see page 653), meat jelly (see page 21), little white wine, 2–3 tablespoons good stock

Season tournedos and sauté in butter and arrange on a serving dish.

Garnish with artichoke bottoms, topped with asparagus tips or buttered peas, alternating with *noisette* potatoes, buttered and rolled in meat jelly.

Add a little wine and stock to the pan in which the tournedos were cooked. Boil, then pour over the tournedos.

Serve with Choron sauce, i.e. béarnaise sauce with tomato (see page 30).

Tournedos à l'estragon

TOURNEDOS WITH TARRAGON

Seasoning, tournedos, butter, tarragon leaves, white wine, demi-glace sauce (see page 22), 1 tablespoon chopped tarragon leaves

Season the tournedos, sauté them in butter, and arrange on a serving dish. Put a few leaves of scalded tarragon on each tournedos. Add a little white wine and some demi-glace sauce to the pan in which the tournedos were cooked. Reduce for 2–3 seconds, add the tarragon leaves and pour over the tournedos. Serve with sauté, mashed or *pommes de terre Macaire* (see page 651).

Tournedos favorite

TOURNEDOS WITH FOIE GRAS AND TRUFFLES

Seasoning, tournedos, butter, seasoned floured foie gras, demi-glace sauce (see page 22), sliced truffles

Season the tournedos, sauté them in butter and arrange on a hot dish.

Place a small scallop of foie gras, sautéed in butter, on each tournedos and cover with demi-glace sauce. Garnish with slices of truffle.

Serve with small *noisette* potatoes (see page 653) cooked in butter and rolled in meat jelly (see page 21), and buttered asparagus tips.

Tournedos Judic

TOURNEDOS WITH TRUFFLES AND KIDNEYS

Seasoning, tournedos, butter, braised lettuces (see page 632), sliced truffles, cocks' combs and kidneys, demi-glace sauce. (see page 22), Madeira

Season and sauté the tournedos in butter. Place them on a serving dish and surround with small braised lettuces. Cover tournedos with a fine ragoût composed of slices of truffle, cocks' combs and kidneys, coated with a succulent demi-glace sauce with Madeira.

Tournedos Mistinguette

TOURNEDOS WITH HERBS AND WINE

1 oz. carrot, ¼ oz. onion, 1 oz. lean raw ham, pinch thyme, 1 bay leaf, butter, 1 liqueur glass brandy, 2—3 tablespoons white wine, 3—4 tablespoons meat jelly (see page 21), pinch chopped parsley, salt and pepper, 6 tournedos, 4 oz. truffled foie gras

Prepare the mirepoix by cooking the finely chopped carrot, onion and ham, with thyme and bay leaf, very slowly in butter, for about 30 minutes. Add the brandy, wine, meat jelly and parsley. Mix 2 oz. butter and foie gras together and rub through a sieve, then add to the sauce.

Season the tournedos and sauté them quickly in butter.

Arrange on a hot dish and pour the sauce over.

Serve with *pommes de terre Macaire* (see page 651).

Tournedos Montpensier

TOURNEDOS WITH PÂTÉ DE FOIE GRAS CROÛTONS

——————— Seasoning, tournedos, butter, croûtons, pâté de foie gras, meat jelly (see page 21), demi-glace sauce (see page 22), truffles, asparagus tips

Season the tournedos and sauté in butter. Fry the required number of croûtons in butter, and spread with pâté de foie gras to which a little meat jelly has been added.

Arrange the tournedos on the croûtons. Pour over some well reduced demi-glace sauce and garnish with slices of truffle.

Serve with asparagus tips and melted butter.

Tournedos niçoise

NIÇOISE STYLE TOURNEDOS

——————— Tournedos, butter, oil
For the tomato sauce à la provençale: 4 tablespoons oil, 5—6 ripe tomatoes, salt, pepper, pinch of chopped parsley, small piece of crushed garlic (the size of a pea)

To make the sauce Heat the oil, add the peeled, seeded and chopped tomatoes, little salt and pepper, parsley and garlic. Cover, and cook over very gentle heat for 15—18 minutes.

Season the tournedos and sauté in half butter and half oil. Arrange on a serving dish and cover with the sauce.

Serve with French beans, lightly browned in butter or oil.

Tournedos piémontaise

PIEDMONT STYLE TOURNEDOS

——————— Seasoning, tournedos, butter, 3—4 tablespoons white wine, 3—4 tablespoons tomato juice

Season the tournedos and sauté in butter, then put on to a serving dish.

Add the white wine and the tomato juice to the butter and sediment left in the pan. Reduce for a few seconds and pour over the tournedos.

Serve with risotto (see page 668) to which some chopped white truffles have been added.

Tournedos Rachel

TOURNEDOS WITH BORDELAISE SAUCE

Seasoning, 4 tournedos, butter, 4 slices beef marrow, bordelaise sauce (see page 25), 4 artichoke bottoms, asparagus tips

Season and sauté the tournedos, arrange on a serving dish. Put a slice of beef marrow on each and cover with bordelaise sauce.

Garnish with braised artichoke bottoms topped with asparagus tips. Potatoes can be served as an additional garnish.

Tournedos Rossini

TOURNEDOS WITH TRUFFLES AND NOODLES

Seasoning, 4 tournedos, butter, 4 croûtons, fried in butter, meat jelly (see page 21), 4 slices foie gras, Madeira, 12 slices truffle, demi-glace sauce (see page 22)

Season and sauté the tournedos in butter. Cover each croûton with a little meat jelly and place the tournedos on top. Arrange on a serving dish. Sauté foie gras in butter and place a slice on each tournedos. Add a little Madeira to the pan in which the tournedos were cooked, boil, add the slices of truffle and the very well reduced demi-glace sauce. Pour over the tournedos.

Serve with a dish of noodles, mixed with butter and Parmesan cheese.

Tournedos tyrolienne

TOURNEDOS WITH TYROLEAN SAUCE

4 tournedos, butter, Tyrolean sauce
For the sauce 1 medium-sized onion, flour, 1 tablespoon oil, 1 tablespoon butter, 2 tablespoons vinegar, 4—5 tomatoes, salt, pepper, 1 clove garlic, pinch chopped parsley

Thinly slice onion, dip in flour and brown lightly in oil and butter. Add vinegar and heat until it has evaporated. Add tomatoes, peeled, seeded and chopped, seasoning, garlic and parsley. Cook for 15 minutes over gentle heat.

Season and sauté the tournedos in butter, arrange on a hot dish and pour the sauce over.

I could go on for ever with the various tournedos; but I have limited myself to giving what I consider to be the most interesting recipes.

LANGUE DE BOEUF
OX TONGUE

Ox tongue can be used fresh or salted; but, even when it is to be served fresh, it is an advantage to put it into salt for 24 hours in advance.

Salt tongue is cooked in plain water; fresh tongue in water with the addition of herbs and then braised.

Langue de boeuf bouillie

BOILED OX TONGUE

Ox tongue, 2 onions, 2 cloves, *bouquet garni* of 2 sprigs parsley, 2 bay leaves and 2 sprigs thyme, 1 clove garlic, salt, 12 peppercorns

Soak the tongue in cold water for about 1 hour. Put into a saucepan and cover with fresh water. Add the onions stuck with cloves, the *bouquet garni* and the garlic. Add ½ teaspoon salt per 2 pints (U.S. 5 cups) water and the peppercorns. Cover the saucepan, bring to the boil and simmer. After 1½ hours, take the tongue from the saucepan and remove the skin, then return to the pan, and continue cooking until done.

Boiled ox tongue is served with piquante (see page 28), tomato (see page 132) or Italian sauce (see page 28).

Suitable accompaniments Spinach, chicory, mashed potatoes, or a purée of peas, lentils or chestnuts, etc.

Langue de boeuf braisée, fraîche ou demi-salée

FRESH OR HALF-SALTED BRAISED TONGUE

Ox tongue, carrots, onions, few bacon rinds, *bouquet garni*, 1 pint (U.S. 2½ cups) white wine, beef stock, 6 tablespoons demi-glace sauce (see page 22)

Prepare and cook the tongue as above, for 1½ hours. Remove the skin and place tongue in a braising pan on a bed of thinly sliced vegetables, bacon rinds and *bouquet garni*. Add the wine and cook until reduced to two-thirds. Add 1 part of the stock in which the tongue has been cooked and 2 parts of beef stock so tongue is two-thirds covered. Cover and put into the oven, continue braising until the tongue is quite cooked.

Arrange the tongue on a long dish; strain, skim, and strain again the cooking liquor, reduce to one-third of volume. Thicken with the demi-glace sauce or simply with 1 tablespoon arrowroot mixed smoothly with a little cold water. Potato flour can be used instead of arrowroot.

Cover the tongue with a thin layer of the sauce and put the dish in the oven for a few minutes. Garnish as you wish with carrots, braised onions or sauerkraut.

The accompaniments suggested above for boiled tongue are also suitable for braised tongue. Buttered noodles can also be served as accompaniments to braised tongue.

Langue de boeuf à la bourgeoise

OX TONGUE WITH ONIONS AND CARROTS

1 ox tongue, 24 small onions, butter, 36 new carrots, 1 small *bouquet garni*, few bacon rinds (without fat), stock

Prepare the tongue and cook it for 1½ hours as instructed above, remove the skin and put tongue into a braising pan, add the onions, lightly browned in butter, carrots, *bouquet garni* and the bacon rinds. Moisten with 1 part of the cooking liquor from the tongue and 2 parts stock. Cover the pan, put into the oven, basting from time to time until it is thoroughly cooked.

Serve the tongue surrounded with the vegetables.

Langue de boeuf froid

COLD OX TONGUE

In hot weather ox tongue which is to be served cold should be kept in brine for 10 days at a fairly low temperature to avoid any possibility of fermentation. When required it should be put to soak in cold water for some hours. It is then cooked in fresh water for 3½—4 hours, according to its size.

When cooked, remove from pan and skin it. Wrap in greaseproof paper and leave to get cold. When quite cold, trim and re-form into its original shape, then cover with a layer of aspic jelly (see page 116) mixed with meat extract.

Serve it on a long dish, and garnish as you wish with a macedoine of vegetables, little moulds of Russian salad, aspic jelly cut into fancy shapes, etc.

Museau de boeuf

OX MUZZLE

Ox muzzle is only used in salad, after being cooked slowly for at least 6 hours in slightly salted water with a little vinegar.

PALAIS DE BOEUF
OX PALATE

Ox palate, which was very much used in *ancienne cuisine*, is almost completely neglected in modern cooking. This, in my opinion, is a pity.

After soaking it in cold water, boil for a few minutes in fresh water, drain, let it cool and then remove the skin.

Cook gently in a very thin white sauce (see page 22) for about 4 hours.

Palais de boeuf grillé

GRILLED OX PALATE

Having cooked it, divide the ox palate into squares of 2—2½ inches across. Dip these in melted butter, sprinkle with dry breadcrumbs and grill (U.S. broil) gently.

Serve with a rémoulade (see page 42) or a tartare sauce (see page 42),

Palais de boeuf à la tyrolienne

OX PALATE WITH TYROLEAN SAUCE

After cooking the ox palate, cut it into strips, dip in flour, fry in oil and season with salt and pepper. Sprinkle with chopped parsley and serve coated with Tyrolean sauce (see page 281).

Paleron

NECK OR CHUCK

This is the fleshy part of the shoulder. It is used for broth, can be boiled or braised, or used in daubes, and for *boeuf bourguignonne*.

POINTE DE CULOTTE OU CULOTTE
TOPSIDE OF RUMP

This is the favourite part for boiled beef and more especially for braised beef.

Whether to be boiled or braised, the joint should be between 3 – 4 lb.

Boiled joints are usually accompanied by the vegetables with which they are cooked, or, if preferred, by braised cabbage, rice forcemeat, tomato sauce, horseradish sauce, etc.

Carrots, celery leaves, glazed onions, endives, braised lettuce; mashed potatoes, peas, haricot beans; various Italian pasta (macaroni, spaghetti, noodles, lasagne, etc.) go well with braised topside.

Pièce de boeuf ou culotte de boeuf à la bourguignonne

BURGUNDY STYLE TOPSIDE OF BEEF

Lard the joint, following the grain of the meat with large pieces of bacon fat dipped in Armagnac and sprinkled with spices and chopped parsley. Marinate for 2 hours with some herbs, namely, parsley, bay leaf, sprigs of thyme, red wine and a few tablespoons Armagnac.

Proceed as described for braised ribs of beef (see page 268), replacing the white wine by double the amount of red wine, and adding the wine to the marinade. Baste frequently during the cooking.

When the joint is cooked, remove from the pan, place on to a serving dish, moisten with a little of its cooking liquor, not skimmed, and keep hot in the oven.

Strain the cooking liquor into a shallow pan, and skim off the fat. Add one-third of its volume of demi-glace sauce (see page 22) and reduce the sauce to the required consistency.

If demi-glace sauce is not available, thicken the sauce with 1 tablespoon arrowroot mixed smoothly with 2 – 3 tablespoons cold water.

Put the topside on to a serving dish, surround with small glazed onions, rather large dice of streaky bacon slightly browned in butter, and some mushrooms sautéed in butter.

Put a little of the sauce over the joint and its garnish, and serve the rest separately.

Pièce de boeuf à l'écarlate

PICKLED TOPSIDE OF BEEF

A joint of topside weighing about 9 lb. should be put into brine for 8 – 10 days.

It is then cooked in water with carrots, onions stuck with cloves and a *bouquet garni*.

Sauerkraut accompanies this joint and any other of the garnishes for boiled beef.

Pièce de boeuf à la flamande

TOPSIDE OF BEEF WITH VEGETABLES

———————— Topside, cabbage, carrots, turnips, butter, stock, potatoes, sausages, bacon

Braise the topside as described for braised ribs of beef (see page 268).

Place on to a serving dish and surround with small balls of braised cabbage, little piles of carrots, turnips cut into the shape of large cloves of garlic and cooked in butter, stock, small boiled potatoes, rings of sausage not containing garlic and sliced bacon cooked with the cabbage.

Moisten the joint with the cooking liquor, and put it into the oven for a few moments.

Serve the cooking liquor separately.

Pièce de boeuf à la mode

BEEF WITH SPICES AND PARSLEY

———————— 4 – 4½ lb. topside, 1 lb. pork fat, brandy, spices, chopped parsley, seasoning, butter, ½ pint (U.S. 1¼ cups) white wine, 2 calf's feet, 1 onion, 2 cloves, *bouquet garni* of 2 sprigs parsley, 1 bay leaf and 2 sprigs thyme, stock, 1 lb. small carrots, 20 small glazed onions

Lard the joint with the pork fat cut into strips ⅛ inch wide. Dip them in brandy and sprinkle lightly with spices and chopped parsley.

Season joint lightly, tie with string, place in a braising pan and sprinkle with a little melted butter. Add the wine and 6 tablespoons brandy; cover and cook over low heat until wine is reduced to one-third its volume.

Now add the calf's feet boned and skinned, rind from the bacon used for larding, onion stuck with cloves, and the *bouquet garni*. Cover the joint with stock and simmer, covered, for 1 hour. Then add the carrots, cover the pan again and continue to simmer until the joint is cooked.

Before serving, remove the string. Put the joint in the oven for 5−6 minutes, basting constantly to glaze it; then put it on the serving dish and arrange the carrots, the calf's feet cut into pieces, and the onions around the meat.

Skim the cooking liquor, reduce it by one-third, strain, and pour it over the joint and its garnish.

Note Alternatively, the cooking liquor may be thickened by adding ¼ pint (U.S. 1¼ cups) demi-glace sauce (see page 22) or 1 dessertspoon arrowroot mixed smoothly with a little cold water.

Remember that all braised meat must be treated with care, simmered gently, and well cooked.

Boeuf à la mode froid

COLD BEEF À LA MODE

Cold beef *à la mode* is an excellent luncheon dish, especially for picnics.

Prepare the beef as described above and put into a bowl with the carrots, onions and calf's feet. Cover completely with the cooking liquor.

Note Cold beef *à la mode* should be cooked the previous day and kept in the refrigerator so that the gravy solidifies into jelly.

Plat de côte

FOREQUARTER FLANK

The forequarter flank is one of the most delicate pieces of beef.

When boiled, served with some of its cooking liquor, and accompanied by a creamed horseradish sauce, it is worthy of a royal table.

It is with pieces of flank of about 1½ oz. each that the best goulashes are made and the most succulent sautés of Bourguignonne and Provençal beef.

Poitrine de boeuf

BRISKET

This can be prepared in the same way as forequarter flank. It may be served boiled or salted, hot or cold, and makes an excellent dish.

QUEUE DE BOEUF
OX TAIL

Queue de boeuf à l'auvergnate

OX TAIL AUVERGNE STYLE

1 ox tail, seasoning, white wine, carrots, onions, *bouquet garni*, small glazed onions, chestnuts, consommé

Cut the tail into pieces 2—2½ inches long, season lightly and braise in white wine, on a bed of thinly sliced carrots and onions, and a *bouquet garni*, as instructed for braised ribs of beef (see page 268). Then put into a deep dish, with the onions and chestnuts cooked in consommé.

Strain the stock through a fine sieve, skim, reduce and pour it over the pieces of tail. As an alternative, the ox tail can be served with a purée of chestnuts (see page 637).

Queue de boeuf chipolata

OX TAIL WITH CHIPOLATAS

Braise the pieces of tail as instructed for *queue de boeuf à l'auvergnate* (see above).

When the flesh comes away from the bones, put the pieces into a deep dish and add some small carrots cooked in butter and stock, glazed onions, chestnuts cooked in consommé and chipolata sausages.

Strain the cooking liquor through a conical sieve, skim off the grease, and add ½ pint (U.S. 1¼ cups) demi-glace sauce (see page 22). Reduce and pour over the ox tail.

Queue de boeuf farcie

STUFFED OX TAIL

1 large ox tail, salt and pepper, carrots, onions, *bouquet garni*, ½ pint
(U.S. 1¼ cups) white wine, ½ pint demi-glace sauce (see page 22) or
1 tablespoon arrowroot
For the forcemeat 12 oz. lean beef, 12 oz. sausage meat, 4 oz. breadcrumbs moistened with milk, 2 eggs, 2 tablespoons chopped truffle,
pinch grated nutmeg, spices, all mixed very well

Disregard the thin part of the tail and bone the rest without breaking it.
Season inside with salt and pepper and then fill it with the forcemeat.

Tie the tail up again, wrap in a cloth as for a galantine, and cook for
about 1½ hours like boiled beef.

Now take it out of the pan, remove the cloth, untie it, and place the
ox-tail in a braising pan on a bed of thinly sliced carrots and onions.
Add the *bouquet garni*, white wine and some of the liquor in which the
ox tail was cooked.

Cover the pan and finish cooking over low heat.

Arrange the pieces of ox-tail in a dish, moisten with a few tablespoons
of the cooking liquor, and keep hot.

Strain the braising mixture through a fine sieve, skim it, and add the
demi-glace sauce or the arrowroot.

Reduce this sauce to the right consistency.

Fresh vegetables, vegetable purées or pasta can accompany stuffed
ox tail.

Queue de boeuf grillée

GRILLED OX TAIL

Cut the ox tail into pieces about 3 inches long. Cook in salted water
with a bay leaf, few peppercorns and a sprig of parsley.

When cooked, dip the pieces in melted butter and then in dry breadcrumbs and grill (U.S. broil) gently.

Serve with a puréed vegetable and one of the following sauces: diable
(see page 27), piquante (see page 28), tomato (see page 132).

Note If serving with *sauce diable*, mix a little mustard with the breadcrumbs.

Queue de boeuf à la hochepot

OX TAIL HOTCHPOTCH OR RAGOÛT OF BEEF

———————— 1 ox tail, 2 pig's feet, 1 pig's ear, water, salt, 1 small cabbage, 12 small onions, 20 small carrots, 10 small turnips, few chipolatas

Cut the ox tail into pieces and put into a pan with the pig's feet, each cut into 4 pieces and the pig's ear, whole.

Cover with water and add ½ teaspoon salt for every 2 pints (U.S. 5 cups) water. Bring to the boil and skim, then cook gently for 2 hours.

Then add the quartered cabbage, the onions, and carrots, turnips cut into large olive shapes. Continue to simmer for another 2 hours.

Arrange the ox tail around the centre of a long dish and put the vegetables in the middle. Surround with the grilled chipolatas, the pieces of pig's feet, and the ear cut in wide strips.

Serve a dish of boiled potatoes separately.

Note As a variation, the ox-tail may be braised instead of being boiled; in which case the onions and the carrots should be braised with the ox-tail, and the pig's feet and ear boiled separately.

The cabbage leaves can be stuffed and braised.

Put the ox-tail in the middle of a long dish and surround with the stuffed cabbage, interspersed with the carrots and onions. Put the pieces of pig's feet, the pig's ear cut in strips and the grilled chipolata sausages at each end.

Serve with a dish of plain boiled potatoes.

Queue de boeuf en daube à la provençale

PROVENÇAL STYLE DAUBE OF OX TAIL

Proceed exactly as instructed for *daube à la provençale* (see page 296), replacing the pieces of beef with sections of ox tail.

Serve with mashed potatoes.

Italian pasta, cooked in various ways, also goes well with this dish.

TÊTE D'ALOYAU
RUMP STEAK

In French butchery, this is the part of beef found at the end of the rump. It is the true rump steak, and may be grilled (U.S. broiled) or sautéed, but in either case the outside must be sealed.

All the recipes for steaks, beef steaks or fillets may be applied to it. In England, where rump steak originated, it is usually grilled (U.S. broiled).

Tête d'aloyau à l'anglaise

ENGLISH RUMP STEAK

When the rump steak is ready, put it on a hot dish and put a thick piece of grilled kidney fat on top.

Serve with grated horseradish.

Rognons de boeuf

BEEF KIDNEYS

Beef kidneys, however they are prepared, are not very digestible, and people with weak digestions should avoid them.

—————— Beef kidney, seasoning, flour, oil, butter, chopped parsley

Remove the fat and any sinew from the kidney and thickly slice. Plunge for a few seconds in boiling water, then drain and dry. Season with salt and pepper, flour and sauté quickly in half oil and half butter.

Drain, then sprinkle with chopped parsley. Arrange in a dish and coat with one of the following: — *sauce tomate provençale* (see page 280), *sauce tyrolienne* (see page 281), *sauce vin blanc* (see page 36), *sauce chasseur* (see page 26).

TRIPES
TRIPE

Tripe is the lining of the stomach of the ox and makes a very light and nourishing dish. It is generally bought ready cooked, in which case it will only need to be blanched.

To do this, wash the tripe, put it into a pan and cover with cold water. Bring to the boil, pour off the water, then cover again with fresh cold water. Bring slowly to boiling point, and simmer for 2−3 hours.

Note If the tripe has not been previously prepared it must first be washed in tepid water, well scraped and rinsed, and blanched several times. It must then be put into fresh cold water and simmered for 6−7 hours.

Gras-double à l'anglaise
ENGLISH STYLE TRIPE

2 lb. cooked tripe, 2 white Spanish onions, 3 oz. butter, 2 pints (U.S. 5 cups) boiling milk, ½ teaspoon salt, pinch freshly ground pepper, 1 sprig parsley, 1 bay leaf, 2 tablespoons flour

Cut the tripe into 2½-inch squares. Slice onions finely and put them into a saucepan with the butter. Cover and allow the onions to stew over a low heat without browning. After 15 minutes, add the tripe, cover and cook for 15 minutes. Add the boiling milk, salt, pepper, parsley and bay leaf. Allow to boil for 5 minutes, then thicken the milk with the flour mixed smoothly with a little cold milk. Simmer for 15−18 minutes, then remove bay leaf before serving.

Gras-double à la génoise
TRIPE WITH TOMATO SAUCE

2 lb. freshly cooked tripe, 4−5 tablespoons oil, ½ pint (U.S. 1¼ cups) stock, 1 pint (U.S. 2½ cups) tomato sauce (see page 132), grated Parmesan cheese

Cut the tripe into 2−2½-inch squares. Heat the oil in a sauté pan, add tripe and sauté for a few moments until moisture has evaporated.

Reduce the stock to half its original quantity and add it to the tomato sauce.

Arrange the pieces of tripe in dish, pour the sauce over and sprinkle with cheese.

Gras-double à la lyonnaise

TRIPE AND ONIONS

2 lb. cooked tripe, butter or lard, seasoning, 2 onions, 1 tablespoon vinegar, chopped parsley

Cut the tripe into strips, and sauté in butter or lard. Season with salt and pepper.

In another pan, sauté the finely chopped onion. Put it with the tripe and continue cooking until well browned.

Arrange the tripe and onions in a serving dish. Heat the vinegar, pour over the tripe and onions and sprinkle with parsley.

Gras-double à la provençale

PROVENÇAL STYLE TRIPE

2 lb. cooked tripe, flour, 4—5 tablespoons oil, 2 onions, seasoning, 1½ lb. tomatoes, chopped parsley, 1 clove garlic

Cut the tripe into thin slices and sprinkle lightly with flour.

Heat the oil and the minced onions. When these begin to brown, add the tripe, season with salt and pepper and sauté for a few minutes. Add the tomatoes, peeled, seeded and chopped, parsley and crushed garlic. Correct the seasoning and simmer for 15—18 minutes.

Serve with boiled or sauté potatoes.

Gras-double à la tyrolienne

TRIPE WITH ONIONS AND TOMATOES

This is prepared the same way *as gras-double à la provençale* (see above) except that 3—4 tablespoons vinegar are added to the onion before adding the tomatoes.

Serve with boiled or sauté potatoes, or a dish of macaroni.

Tripes à la mode de Caen

TRIPE IN THE CAEN MANNER

The preparation of tripe in the Caen manner calls for special treatment which it is not always easy to give. It is preferable, in the circumstances, to go to the people who specialise in its preparation.

Editor's note In Paris and many other places in France, *tripes à la mode de Caen* can be bought at any time of the year cooked, and ready to serve.

PRÉPARATIONS DIVERSES DU BOEUF
VARIOUS PREPARATIONS OF BEEF

Pâté de bifteck

BEEF STEAK PIE

2 lb. lean beef, salt, freshly ground pepper, pinch nutmeg, 1 tablespoon chopped onion, pinch chopped parsley, 8—12 oz. potatoes, water puff or short pastry (see page 682), beaten egg

Cut the beef into strips ⅛ inch thick. Season with salt, pepper and nutmeg. Add onion and parsley.

Place the meat in pie dish with the potatoes cut into the shape of olives in the centre. Turn the edges of the strips of meat over them and add water to just cover the meat. Damp the edges of the dish and place a strip of pastry round it. Damp the strip and then put on the pastry crust. Decorate as liked. Glaze with an egg, and cook in a slow oven for about 2 hours.

Pâté de biftecks et de rognons

BEEF STEAK AND KIDNEY PIE

Proceed as for beef steak pie above, replacing the p otatoes by the same weight of beef, veal, or sheep's kidney, thinly sliced, a few mushrooms sautéed in butter, a chopped onion and parsley. The cooking time is the same.

Pouding de biftecks

BEEF STEAK PUDDING

For suet pastry 2 lb. flour, 1¼ lb. beef suet very finely chopped or grated and with all skin removed, large pinch salt, enough water to make a firm dough
For filling 2 lb. lean beef, salt, pepper, pinch nutmeg, 1 tablespoon chopped onion, pinch chopped parsley, water

Line pudding basin with two-thirds of the pastry reserving one-third for the top.

Cut the meat into strips and fill the basin, adding the seasoning and flavouring. Add water to just cover the meat. Cover with the remaining pastry, pressing the edges well together. Tie a cloth over the pudding, securing it under the rim of the basin.

Put the pudding into boiling water and boil for 3−3½ hours, or the pudding may be cooked in a pressure cooker.

Remove cloth before serving and place the basin on a table napkin.

This method of cooking meat has its advantages, but calls for a certain amount of care.

On several occasions I have cooked poultry and truffled pheasants in this way, with perfect results. But my greatest success, on the occasion of a shooting dinner, was a pudding containing 24 fat woodcock with 24 medium-sized truffles, carefully cleaned and cooked for one minute in some good Madeira wine.

For this dish, the woodcock were browned for a few minutes in butter, then placed in the pudding bowl with the 24 truffles, then sprinkled with a fine demi-glace sauce with a veal base, added to the Madeira in which the truffles were cooked.

Pouding de biftecks et d'huîtres

BEEF STEAK AND OYSTER PUDDING

Proceed as for the beef steak pudding (see above), adding 36 uncooked oysters.

Carbonades à la flamande

FLEMISH CARBONADES OF BEEF

2 lb. lean beef, salt, pepper, clarified dripping, butter, 4—5 large onions, *bouquet garni*, 1 bottle beer, brown stock, 4 oz. brown roux (see page 18), 2 oz. brown sugar

Cut the meat into thin slices, season with salt and pepper, and brown quickly in a little dripping. Remove to a casserole. Add a little butter to the pan if necessary, add the chopped onions and brown lightly, then put with the meat in alternate layers, with the *bouquet garni* in the centre. Add the beer to the sediment left in the pan, bring to boiling point, and thicken with the roux. Lastly add the sugar. Pour over the meat in the casserole, cover and cook in a slow oven for $2\frac{1}{2}$—3 hours.

Note The carbonade is usually served in the casserole as it is, but if preferred the onion may be removed.

Daube à la provençale

PROVENÇAL STYLE DAUBE OF BEEF

2 lb. lean beef, strips bacon fat, chopped parsley, 4 cloves garlic, spices, 4 onions, 2—3 carrots, salt, pepper, $1\frac{3}{4}$ pints (U.S. $4\frac{1}{4}$ cups) red wine, 1 wine glass wine vinegar, 2—3 tablespoons brandy, 4—5 tablespoons oil, *bouquet garni*, skin of $\frac{1}{4}$ orange

Cut the beef into about 8 pieces. Lard each with a thick strip of bacon fat rolled in chopped parsley, mixed with 1 crushed garlic clove and spices.

Put beef into a pan with 2 onions, quartered, chopped carrots, salt, pepper and spices. Add the wine, wine vinegar, and brandy, and leave to marinate for 4—5 hours.

Put 4 oz. chopped bacon fat and the oil into a casserole. When the bacon has melted, add remaining onions, quartered, and sauté till brown. Add the meat and vegetables drained from the marinade. Cook till the meat is brown, stirring from time to time. Add *bouquet garni*, orange skin and 3 cloves garlic. Add the marinade and cook till it is reduced by half, then add 1 pint (U.S. $2\frac{1}{2}$ cups) boiling water. Cover very tightly and cook in a slow oven about 5 hours.

Mushrooms may be added.

A dish of lasagne or macaroni, sprinkled with cheese and some of the liquor from the daube, makes an excellent accompaniment.

Estouffade à la provençale
PROVENÇAL STEW

1 lb. neck or chuck of beef, 1 lb. forequarter flank, flour, 8 oz. streaky bacon, butter or oil, 3—4 onions, salt, pepper, 1 bottle red wine, 2 pints (U.S. 2½ cups) stock or water, *bouquet garni* of 2 sprigs parsley, 1 bay leaf, 2 sprigs thyme, 1 clove garlic, 1 lb. mushrooms

Cut the meat into pieces of about 3—4 oz. and sprinkle with flour.

Dice the bacon, put into boiling water for a few minutes, drain, then brown in the butter or oil. Remove to a plate.

Put the meat and quartered onions into remaining fat, add salt and pepper, and sauté for a few minutes. Add the wine and cook until reduced by half. Add the boiling stock or water, *bouquet garni* and garlic. Cover and simmer for 2½—3 hours.

Pour on to a sieve. Put the pieces of meat back into the pan with the bacon and the mushrooms quartered and sautéed in butter.

Skim the liquor, return to the pan, and simmer a further 18—20 minutes.

If liked 2—3 tablespoons tomato purée and a few black olives may be added.

Mashed potatoes, macaroni, noodles, lasagne or gnocchi make a good accompaniment.

Émincés
SLICED BEEF

This is a method of using left-over roast or braised meat. Beef, veal, mutton, lamb or venison can be used in this way.

Viandes rôties
ROAST MEAT

Cut the meat into very thin slices and arrange on a lightly buttered serving dish. Cover with boiling sauce or gravy.

Meat which has been roasted should never be allowed to boil, or it will be tough.

Viandes braisées

BRAISED MEAT

Cut the meat into thin slices, arrange on a serving dish and cover it with one of the following sauces: Italian (see page 28), poivrade (see page 29), Tyrolean (see page 281), tomato (see page 132). Cover the dish and allow to stand for a few moments.

Potatoes, cooked in various ways, vegetable purées, chicory with cream sauce, green beans, and various forms of Italian pasta, are good accompaniments for both dishes.

FRICADELLES

Fricadelles are a kind of meat ball made with either raw or cooked meat, as follows:

Fricadelle avec viande crue

FRICADELLES WITH RAW MEAT

1¼—1½ lb. lean meat, free from gristle and sinew, butter or lard, 1 lb. breadcrumbs, milk, 3 eggs, 3 tablespoons chopped onion, fried in butter, salt, pepper, nutmeg

Chop the meat and mix thoroughly with 12 oz. butter. Add the breadcrumbs moistened with milk, eggs, onions, salt, pepper and grated nutmeg. Divide the mixture into about 12 pieces, and form into round cakes on a floured board or marble slab.

Fry in butter or lard, turning from time to time to brown nicely on both sides.

Any vegetable purée, or piquante (see page 28) or tomato sauce (see page 132) are suitable accompaniments.

Fricadelle avec viande cuite

FRICADELLES WITH COOKED MEAT

2—2½ lb. cooked beef, 8 oz. cooked mashed potatoes, 3 tablespoons chopped onion, 1 tablespoon chopped parsley, 2 eggs, salt, pepper, nutmeg, butter or lard

Chop the meat and mix with all the other ingredients.

Proceed in thesame way as in the preceding recipe and fry on both sides in butter or lard.

These fricadelles may be served as they are, or accompanied by tomato sauce (see page 132), piquante sauce (see page 28), spinach, chicory, etc.

GOULASH

The success of this dish depends very much on the paprika which is used in its preparation. In the first place, one must be sure that it is of the best quality, pink in colour and sweet to the taste, because most of the paprikas which are found in the shops are too hot, and are nothing but cayenne pepper, the use of which makes this goulash quite inedible.

Goulash à la hongroise
HUNGARIAN GOULASH

2 lb. lean beef, preferably from the forequarter flank, 2 oz. butter or lard, 3—4 tablespoons chopped onion, salt, pepper, 1 dessertspoon paprika, 8—12 oz. tomatoes, 1 pint (U.S. 2½ cups) hot water, *bouquet garni*, 1—1½ lb. potatoes

Cut the meat into 3—4-oz. pieces. Heat the butter in a sauté pan, add meat and onion and sauté until lightly browned. Transfer all to a casserole.

Add seasoning, paprika, tomatoes, peeled, seeded and chopped, water and *bouquet garni*.

Cover and cook in a slow oven for 1½ hours.

Add the quartered potatoes, and extra boiling water as required. The potatoes should be just covered.

Continue cooking for another hour or until meat and potatoes are tender.

Note The potatoes may be omitted, in which case the cooking liquor should be reduced by half and the goulash should be accompanied by rice, Italian pasta or plainly boiled potatoes.

Hachis

HASH

Beef hash is prepared exactly as mutton or lamb hash, but mutton and lamb is the best meat to use in this way (see page 351).

Hash may be made with all kinds of meat, poultry, game and venison. It is an excellent way of using up cold meat.

PAUPIETTES

Thin slices beef, sausage meat, breadcrumbs, milk or broth, large pinch chopped parsley, 1 small shallot, salt, pepper, nutmeg, carrots, onions, bacon rashers, good stock, few tablespoons demi-glace sauce (see page 22) (optional)

Paupiettes are made with thin slices of meat taken from the sirloin, and should weigh from $3\frac{1}{2} - 4$ oz. They should be flattened to measure 8×4 inches. Mix some sausage meat with one-third its volume of breadcrumbs, moistened with milk or broth; add the chopped parsley, chopped shallot, salt, pepper and grated nutmeg. Spread this mixture on the pieces of meat. Roll into the shape of a cork, and secure with cotton. Then wrap each in a rasher of fat bacon.

The paupiettes are now arranged in a sauté pan just large enough to fit them, on a bed of thinly sliced carrots and onions and the scalded bacon rinds. Cover with stock and braise in the ordinary way.

Before serving, unwrap the paupiettes and place on a round dish, skim fat from cooking liquor, reduce to one-third its volume and pour over the paupiettes. Demi-glace sauce may be added.

Peas, jardinière, spinach, chicory, any vegetable purées, or risotto make a good accompaniment.

Loose-Tinken ou oiseaux sans tête

LOOSE-TINKEN, OR BIRDS WITHOUT HEADS

This is the name given in Belgium to paupiettes garnished in the middle with a large piece of seasoned bacon. These are treated in exactly the same way as *carbonades à la flamande* (see page 296).

Boeuf salé et fumé

SALT SMOKED BEEF

Salt smoked beef should be soaked for a fairly long time before being cooked; it is then boiled in plenty of water.

Smoked beef is treated in the same way.

Sauerkraut, red or ordinary cabbage, braised or stuffed, mashed potatoes, or purée of peas, are suitable accompaniments.

LE VEAU
VEAL

Amourettes et cervelle

MARROW AND BRAINS

I class these together because of their similarity and because the same recipes are applicable to both.

The preparation and cooking is exactly the same as for beef marrow and brains (see page 261).

Amourettes Tosca

VEAL MARROW WITH CRAYFISH

————————— 12 oz. poached marrow, butter, 24 crayfish, 3—4 oz. truffles, cream béchamel sauce (see page 23), 2 teaspoons crayfish butter (see page 114), 4 oz. cocchiletti (shell-shaped pasta), Parmesan cheese

Cut the marrow into pieces 1—1½ inches long and put into a pan with 1 oz. butter, crayfish and sliced truffles. Cover with béchamel sauce to which the crayfish butter has been added and keep hot.

Cook the cocchiletti, drain well, then add some butter, grated Parmesan cheese and 1 tablespoon béchamel sauce. Put half into a serving dish, add half the ragoût of marrow, cover with the rest of the cocchiletti and finish with the remaining ragoût.

Cervelle Béatrice
POACHED BRAINS WITH TRUFFLED FOIE GRAS
———————— Poached brains, truffled foie gras, béchamel sauce (see page 23), egg, breadcrumbs, butter, asparagus

Cut poached and well drained brains into small cubes. Mix with one-third their volume of truffled foie gras and enough béchamel sauce to bind.

Roll into balls the size of eggs and flatten into rounds, ½ inch thick, on a floured board. Dip in beaten egg and then in freshly prepared breadcrumbs. Fry in clarified butter until a good golden brown.

Dish in a circle, and garnish the centre with buttered asparagus.

Cervelle au beurre noir ou noisette
BRAINS WITH BLACK BUTTER OR BRAINS NOISETTE
The same procedure as for beef brains (see page 262).

Cervelle Mireille
BRAINS WITH SEMOLINA AND TRUFFLE
———————— Poached brains, flour, butter, rounds of semolina, truffle, béchamel sauce (see page 23), grated cheese, asparagus tips

Cut the brains into slices about ¾ inch thick. Flour them and fry till a golden brown in butter.

Serve them in a circle on rounds of semolina (see page 671) of the same size, browned in butter. Place a slice of truffle on each one and cover with béchamel sauce. Sprinkle with grated cheese, dot with butter and glaze in a salamander or under the grill (U.S. broiler). Garnish with buttered asparagus tips.

Vol-au-vent de cervelle aux oeufs
BRAIN VOL-AU-VENT WITH EGGS
———————— 1–2 poached brains, 1–2 tablespoons butter, 3 hard-boiled eggs for each brain, truffles, cream béchamel sauce (see page 23), 1 vol-au-vent case

Cut the poached brains into slices. Place them in a sauté pan with the hot butter, chopped eggs and some slices of truffle. Heat through, then add some cream béchamel sauce. Serve in a hot vol-au-vent case.

COEUR DE VEAU
CALF'S HEART

Coeur de veau à la hongroise

HUNGARIAN STYLE CALF'S HEART

1 calf's heart, veal dripping or butter, salt, pepper, 1 wine glass red or white wine, 12 small onions, 24 small carrots, bouquet of 2 sprigs parsley, 1 bay leaf and 2 sprigs thyme, stock

Brown the heart in veal dripping or butter, season with salt and pepper, add the wine and all the other ingredients with enough stock to cover. Cover the saucepan and simmer for 1½ hours.

CÔTES DE VEAU
VEAL CHOPS

Veal chops may be grilled, but are usually sautéed.

Côte de veau bordelaise

VEAL CHOPS WITH ARTICHOKE BOTTOMS

2 veal chops, butter, 1 wine glass white wine, 2 tablespoons white stock, 1 tablespoon meat jelly (see page 21), 6 small glazed onions, 2–3 tablespoons cubed potatoes, artichoke bottoms, fried parsley

Sauté the chops in butter and put on to a serving dish. To the butter left in the pan add white wine, stock and the meat jelly. If the butter does not combine easily with the meat jelly, add 1 or 2 tablespoons stock or water.

Surround the chops with onions, potatoes cooked in butter, and some artichoke bottoms thinly sliced and sautéed in butter. Pour the cooking liquor over the chops.

Garnish with a little fried parsley.

Côte de veau en cocotte à la paysanne

STEWED VEAL CHOPS WITH VEGETABLES

———————— 1 veal chop, butter, 1—2 tablespoons stock or water, 4 small onions, 4 new carrots, 4 small potatoes, cut into olive shapes, *bouquet garni* of 1 sprig parsley and ½ bay leaf, pinch salt, 4 tablespoons fresh young peas

Sauté the chop in butter, place it in a serving dish and keep hot. Add the stock or water to the fat left in the pan, boil up, and pour over the chop.

Into another saucepan put the onions, carrots, potatoes, *bouquet garni*, salt, peas, and ½ oz. butter; add sufficient water to cover the vegetables. Cover and cook gently. When cooked, remove *bouquet garni* and pour the vegetables over the chop.

Côte de veau froide

COLD VEAL CHOPS

Cold veal chops make an excellent luncheon dish. In this case the chops are braised like topside of veal (see page 313), served in a deep china dish, surrounded by their cooking liquor, with the fat removed and strained through a fine strainer. This liquor sets as jelly and it is the best accompaniment that one can give.

One can, however, also serve any kind of salad.

Côte de veau marquise

VEAL CUTLETS WITH MADEIRA AND TRUFFLE

———————— 1 veal chop, butter, 2 tablespoons Madeira, 1 small truffle, 1 dessert-spoon meat jelly (see page 21), 3 tablespoons fresh cream, 1 table-spoon foie gras, buttered asparagus tips

Sauté the chop in butter and put into a serving dish. To the butter left in the pan, add the Madeira, the truffle carefully peeled and cut into julienne, the meat jelly, and the cream. Boil for a few seconds and then add the foie gras; strain through a fine sieve and pour over the chop.

Serve with a garnish of buttered asparagus tips.

Côte de veau milanaise

MILANAISE STYLE VEAL CHOP

1 veal chop, egg, breadcrumbs, butter, cooked macaroni, butter, Parmesan cheese, julienne of truffle, tongue, mushroom, tomato sauce (see page 132)

Coat chop with egg and breadcrumbs and sauté in butter. Put on to a serving dish.

Mix some butter and grated Parmesan with the freshly cooked macaroni and add a little truffle, mushroom and tongue all cut into julienne. Arrange around the chop and add a little tomato sauce.

Côte de veau panée

VEAL CHOP WITH BREADCRUMBS

Salt, 1 veal chop, flour, egg, breadcrumbs, butter, 1 tablespoon meat jelly (see page 21), 2 tablespoons stock, 1 tablespoon butter

Sprinkle a little salt on the chop, coat with flour, then dip in egg and freshly made breadcrumbs, cook gently in clarified butter. Put on to a serving dish.

Melt the meat jelly in a small pan, add the stock and 1 tablespoon butter, mix well and pour over the chop.

Any of the following are suitable as accompaniments: spinach, chicory, buttered peas, mashed potatoes, carrots, noodles, spaghetti, chestnut purée.

Côte de veau sautée

SAUTÉED VEAL CHOP

1 veal chop, flour, butter, 2—3 tablespoons stock

Season chop with salt, flour and brown lightly on both sides in butter. Continue the cooking over a low heat, being very careful that the butter does not burn. On no account should the butter in which the chop is cooked be discarded. By adding the stock to it an excellent sauce can be made, and this should be poured over the chop.

Any of the following make good accompaniments: spinach, chicory, buttered peas, *petits pois à la française* (see page 642), mashed potatoes, carrots, sautéed tomatoes, noodles.

Côte de veau Pojarski

POJARSKI VEAL CHOPS

———————— 1 veal chop, butter, breadcrumbs, cream, salt, egg

Remove the meat from the bone, take away any skin and gristle. Chop the meat and add a quarter of its weight of butter and the same amount of breadcrumbs moistened with cream. Season with salt and replace the mixture along the bone, reshaping the chop in its original form. Coat with egg and breadcrumbs and cook in butter.

Note One may discard the bone, in which case the mixture can be shaped into 2 chops.

Côte de veau aux truffes

TRUFFLED VEAL CHOP

———————— 1 veal chop, butter, 2 tablespoons Madeira, 2 tablespoons stock, 1 truffle, 1 tablespoon meat jelly (see page 21)

Sauté chop in butter and put on to a serving dish. To the butter left in the pan add the Madeira, stock, truffle, peeled and cut into slices, and the meat jelly. Boil for 2 seconds, then add ½ oz. butter. Pour the sauce over the chop.

If liked, the truffled chop may be served with asparagus tips, artichokes with butter, mashed potatoes, purée of chestnuts, purée of celery, or noodles.

ÉPAULE DE VEAU
SHOULDER OF VEAL

Épaule de veau farcie

STUFFED SHOULDER OF VEAL

———————— 1 shoulder of veal, salt, pepper, vegetables for the braise
For the forcemeat 1½ lb. sausage meat, 8 oz. breadcrumbs, stock, 2 eggs, salt, pepper, nutmeg, chopped parsley

Bone the shoulder and beat the flesh flat. Season with salt and pepper.

Spread the surface with a layer of forcemeat made by mixing the sausage meat, breadcrumbs lightly moistened with stock, eggs, seasoning, nutmeg and parsley.

Roll and tie the shoulder with string, and braise on a bed of vegetables in the ordinary way. Serve with a purée of vegetables and the liquor from the braise.

Épaule de veau farcie à la bourgeoise

STUFFED SHOULDER OF VEAL WITH ONIONS AND CARROTS

1 shoulder of veal, boned and stuffed (as in the previous recipe), small onions, new carrots, *bouquet garni*, stock, 2 tablespoons potato flour, water

Partially braise the meat as described above, then add some onions, carrots and *bouquet garni*. Add enough stock to come two-thirds up meat. Cover and complete the cooking over moderate heat.

Thicken the stock with the potato flour mixed smoothly with a little cold water.

FILET MIGNON DE VEAU
FILET MIGNON OF VEAL

This fillet is found under the saddle on each side of the backbone, and corresponds exactly to the fillet of beef.

Filet de veau en cocotte au jus

FILLET OF VEAL EN COCOTTE

Cook the fillet in butter. As soon as it begins to brown, add 1 tablespoon water, and repeat this operation from time to time to obtain a perfect gravy.

Serve the fillet in an earthenware dish with its gravy.

It can be garnished with truffles or mushrooms, or served with a Provençal (see page 280) or Tyrolean sauce (see page 281).

As an accompaniment any vegetables or pasta are suitable.

FOIE DE VEAU
CALF'S LIVER

Foie de veau à l'anglaise
ENGLISH STYLE CALF'S LIVER

Cut the liver into slices of about 3−4 oz. each. Season with salt and pepper and dip in flour. Sauté in butter.

Arrange on a serving dish with alternate rashers of grilled (U.S. broiled) bacon. Sprinkle the liver with the fat that runs from the bacon.

Foie de veau sauté à la bordelaise
CALF'S LIVER WITH CÈPES AND TOMATO SAUCE

Cut the liver into slices, season with salt and pepper, coat with flour and sauté in butter. Arrange in a ring on the serving dish and garnish the centre with *cèpes à la bordelaise* (see page 601).

Sprinkle the slices of liver with tomato sauce (see page 132) slightly seasoned. Serve with it mashed potatoes, sauté potatoes, maître d'hôtel butter, etc., or cover with Italian (see page 28), piquante (see page 28), huntsman (see page 26), tomato (see page 132), Provençal (see page 280) or Tyrolean sauce (see page 281).

Foie de veau sauté lyonnaise
LYONESE STYLE CALF'S LIVER

Sauté the liver and arrange in a ring on the serving dish. Place in the middle a garnish of onions thinly sliced and cooked in butter over a low heat, and a little meat jelly (see page 21) added. At the last moment, sprinkle with a little hot vinegar.

Foie de veau à la bourgeoise
CASSEROLE LIVER WITH VEGETABLES

Lard the liver with bacon fat seasoned with spice and brown it in butter. Then proceed as indicated for calf's heart (see page 303).

Brochettes de foie de veau

SKEWERED CALF'S LIVER

Cut the liver into 1-inch squares, ½ inch thick. Season with salt and pepper and sauté quickly in butter, to brown them.

Thread these squares on skewers, alternating with pieces of bacon, sliced thinly, and slices of mushrooms sautéed in butter. Sprinkle lightly with dry breadcrumbs and grill (U.S. broil).

Serve with *sauce diable* (see page 27) or *sauce piquante* (see page 28).

Pain de foie de veau

CALF'S LIVER LOAF

1 lb. calf's liver, 4 oz. breadcrumbs, 2—3 tablespoons boiled milk, 1 tablespoon chopped onion, butter, pepper, salt, nutmeg, 3 whole eggs, 3 egg yolks, ½ pint (U.S. 1¼ cups) cream

Pound the liver with the breadcrumbs moistened with milk and onion lightly fried in butter.

Rub through a sieve.

To the resultant purée, add the seasoning, eggs and cream and mix all thoroughly well together.

Put into a buttered charlotte mould, and cook gently in a bain-marie.

Turn out on to a serving dish and serve with tomato sauce (see page 132) to which some well reduced veal stock has been added.

Note If preferred, the mixture can be cooked in dariole moulds.

FRAISE DE VEAU
MESENTERY

Mesentery should be well soaked, then scalded for a few minutes and allowed to cool.

It is cooked in stock as for calf's head (see page 331).

Fraise de veau lyonnaise

MESENTERY WITH ONIONS

Having cooked the mesentery, drain and dry well. Cut it into thin slices, season, and sauté in very hot oil. Add 2 medium-sized onions, thinly sliced, sautéed and cooked in butter to each 2 lb. of mesentery.

Sauté the two ingredients together for several minutes so as to mix them well. Serve, garnished with chopped parsley and sprinkled with hot vinegar.

Fraise de veau tyrolienne

MESENTERY WITH TOMATOES

Follow the recipe for *fraise de veau lyonnaise* above, but add 12 oz. tomatoes, peeled, seeded, chopped and sautéed in oil. Season with salt and pepper, and 1 clove garlic. Sprinkle with chopped parsley before serving.

JARRETS DE VEAU
KNUCKLE (U.S. LEG) OF VEAL

Jarrets de veau paysanne

KNUCKLE OF VEAL WITH VEGETABLES

1 3−3½-lb. knuckle (U.S. leg) veal, salt, pepper, flour, butter, 18 small onions, 24 small carrots, *bouquet garni*, white stock, 24 small new potatoes, 1 lb. fresh peas

Divide the meat into pieces about 2 inches thick. Season with salt and pepper, dip in flour and brown in butter on both sides. Add the onions, carrots, *bouquet garni* and enough white stock to cover the vegetables. Cover and cook for about 30 minutes over a low heat. Add the potatoes and peas, and, if necessary, more stock to cover the vegetables.

Cover and continue simmering for a further 40−50 minutes.

Jarrets de veau ossi-buchi

OSSOBUCCO

1 3—3½-lb. knuckle (U.S. leg) veal, salt, pepper, flour, lard, 4 oz. onion, 2 lb. tomatoes, ½ bottle white wine, white stock, *bouquet garni*, chopped parsley

Cut the meat into pieces as described above. Season with salt and pepper, dip in flour and brown in lard. When it begins to colour, add the chopped onion and let this brown slightly. Add the tomatoes, peeled, seeded and chopped, and the white wine. Add sufficient white stock to come half-way up the meat, and the *bouquet garni*. Simmer for 1½ hours.

Arrange the knuckle on a serving dish, cover with the cooking liquor and sprinkle with chopped parsley.

LANGUES DE VEAU
CALF'S TONGUE

Langue de veau braisé

BRAISED CALVES' TONGUES

Calves' tongues, bacon fat, carrots, onions, salt, pepper, white wine, stock, *bouquet garni*

Put the tongues into a pan, cover with cold water and bring to boiling point. Simmer for 15 minutes, then drain. Put some pieces of bacon fat and thinly sliced carrot and onion into the pan. Add the tongues and enough white wine and stock to come about half-way up. Season lightly and cook until the liquid is completely reduced. Cover with lightly seasoned stock, add the *bouquet garni*, then cover, and simmer until the tongues are nearly tender.

Remove the tongues, skin carefully, then return to the pan. Continue cooking until liquid is reduced almost to jelly. Serve the tongues whole or cut in half lengthwise and strain the liquor over.

Spinach, chicory, sorrel, peas and any vegetable purée can accompany this dish and all the following sauces are suitable: chasseur (see page 26), Italian (see page 28), piquante (see page 28) or tomato (see page 132).

Longe de veau

LOIN OF VEAL

The loin of veal is the equivalent to the sirloin of beef: that is to say, the part that goes from the point of the haunch to the first ribs.

Loin of veal may be roasted or braised, according to choice. If the joint is to be braised, it is generally boned, leaving a piece of skin long enough to wrap around the joint when it is stuffed.

It should be remembered that when a joint is boned it loses a little of its excellence, whether roasted or braised.

All vegetables make a suitable accompaniment: cucumber, chicory, spinach, sorrel, peas, macédoine of vegetables, braised lettuce, stuffed tomatoes, etc.

MOU DE VEAU
CALF'S LIGHTS

Mou de veau en civet

CIVET OF CALF'S LIGHTS

Beat the lights to get rid of the air, cut into pieces of about 2 oz. and season with salt and pepper.

Cook as described for civet of hare (see page 540).

Mou de veau à la provençale

PROVENÇAL STYLE CALF'S LIGHTS

———————— Calf's lights, salt, pepper, flour, 2—3 tablespoons oil, 2 tablespoons chopped onion, 1 wine glass white wine, 2 lb. tomatoes, 1 clove garlic, chopped parsley

Cut the lights as explained for the civet (see page 540), and cook for 25—30 minutes in salted water. Drain, and dry them. Season with salt and pepper, and roll in flour. Heat the oil in a frying pan and add the onion. When it begins to colour, sauté lights for a few minutes. Add the white wine, tomatoes, peeled, seeded and chopped, garlic and chopped parsley.

Cook for 30 minutes over a low heat. Serve with plain boiled potatoes.

NOIX DE VEAU ET SES DÉRIVÉS:
Escalopes, Fricandeau, Grenadins, Noisettes, Paupiettes, Médaillons

TOPSIDE OF VEAL AND ITS DERIVATIVES:
Escalopes, Fricandeau, Grenadins, Noisettes, Paupiettes, Médaillons

Noix de veau braisée

BRAISED TOPSIDE OF VEAL

———————— Topside of veal, bacon fat and rind, carrots, onions, *bouquet garni*, salt, stock

Trim the meat, and put into a casserole with some pieces of bacon fat and rind, sliced carrots and onions, a little salt and the *bouquet garni*. Add ½ pint (U.S. 1¼ cups) stock and cook until the liquid is completely reduced. Add more stock to come half-way up the meat and boil for a few minutes. Cover and cook in the oven, basting the meat frequently. Towards the end of the cooking, remove the cover so that the meat browns, but continue the basting.

Serve the joint with some of the strained liquor, and serve the rest separately.

Any of the following can be used as garnish: small carrots, peas, spinach, chicory, sorrel, cucumber, braised celery, lettuce, purée of peas, chestnut purée or noodles with butter.

Noix de veau en surprise
TOPSIDE OF VEAL WITH TRUFFLES

———————— Topside of veal, sliced truffles, cream béchamel sauce (see page 23)

Braise the topside without larding it; do not overcook and let it cool for a few moments.

Cut it three-quarters the way up horizontally, to form a lid. Make a circular incision in the rest of the joint and take out the meat, leaving about ¾ inch at the bottom and sides, thus forming a kind of box.

Fill this with the meat, cut into small pieces, to which slices of truffle have been added, the whole being mixed with cream béchamel sauce. Now put the 'lid' on and arrange on a serving dish. Serve the strained liquor separately. As an accompaniment, serve asparagus tips, cucumber cooked with cream, cèpes, or morels cooked in cream, etc., depending on the season of the year.

Note This method of treating topside of veal is rather odd, and I only give it for its originality.

NOIX DE VEAU FROID
COLD TOPSIDE OF VEAL

Noix de veau à la gelée
TOPSIDE OF VEAL WITH JELLY

———————— Topside of veal, bacon fat, calf's foot, 6 tablespoons white wine, new carrots, white stock (see page 20), butter, small tartlets, asparagus tips

Lard the topside of a piece of veal with bacon fat, cut into strips. Braise (see page 313), adding to the braise a calf's foot scalded for 8 – 10 minutes in boiling water and cut up small, and the white wine. When it is cooked, put it into an earthenware dish with its strained cooking liquor; leave until the next day.

When ready to serve, dip the dish into hot water and turn veal on an oval dish large enough to be able to surround it with new carrots cooked in white stock and butter, interspersed with small tartlets garnished with very green asparagus tips.

Accompaniments Macédoine of vegetables with mayonnaise sauce, Russian salad, or small tomatoes garnished with tunny fish salad, anchovies, hard-boiled eggs, etc.

ESCALOPES DE VEAU
ESCALOPES OF VEAL

Escalopes of veal are generally cut from the fillet (U.S. round) or from the topside. They usually weigh 3 – 4 oz.

If they are to be coated with egg and breadcrumbs and fried or sautéed, they should be beaten to flatten them, but if not, they are cut from the loin, leaving part of the meat on the bone. In this case they are only lightly beaten.

Escalopes de veau à l'anglaise
ESCALOPES OF VEAL IN THE ENGLISH WAY

———————— Seasoning, flour, escalopes of veal, egg, breadcrumbs, butter, slices ham

Season and flour the escalopes, dip in beaten egg, then in freshly made breadcrumbs, and cook in clarified butter.

Arrange in a circle, alternately with slices of ham sautéed in butter.

Serve with green peas or other vegetable or with a purée of vegetables.

Escalopes de veau milanaise
MILANESE STYLE ESCALOPES OF VEAL

Follow the instructions above for *escalopes de veau à l'anglaise* but mix some grated Parmesan cheese with the breadcrumbs.

Arrange on the serving dish in a circle, and in the centre put a garnish of *macaroni dit 'à la milanaise'* (see page 675).

Escalopes de veau sautées
SAUTÉED ESCALOPES OF VEAL

Salt, pepper, 2 escalopes cut from the loin, flour, butter, 3 tablespoons stock, 2 tablespoons meat jelly (see page 21)

Season the escalopes, dip in flour and cook in butter until a golden brown on both sides, taking great care not to let the butter burn.

Arrange on a serving dish. Add the stock and meat jelly to the butter left in the pan, boil for a second and pour over the meat. If necessary, the meat jelly may be omitted.

Any of the following make a suitable accompaniment: chicory, spinach, peas, asparagus tips, green beans, mashed potatoes, sauté potatoes, creamed potatoes, chestnut purée. Serve with either *sauce chasseur* (see page 26) or *sauce tyrolese* (see page 281).

FRICANDEAU

The fricandeau is a slice of veal taken from the topside of veal and cut with the grain. It should not exceed 1½ inches in thickness.

After lightly beating the surface of the meat it should be larded with thin strips of bacon fat and braised.

All the garnishes mentioned for braised topside of veal (see page 313) are suitable for fricandeau.

Fricandeau froid
COLD FRICANDEAU

Cold fricandeau is an excellent luncheon dish. As soon as it is cooked, it should be put into a serving dish. Skim and strain the liquor left from the meat and pour over. This should set into a jelly and makes an excellent accompaniment.

Serve with green salad.

GRENADINS

Grenadins are escalopes of veal cut a little thicker than usual, and well larded with thin strips of bacon fat.

They are braised like fricandeau and glazed at the last moment.
All the garnishes used for escalopes of veal are suitable for *grenadins*.
They can be served cold like the fricandeau, above, and make an excellent
cold entrée.

NOISETTES AND MIGNONNETTES OF VEAL

Noisettes and mignonnettes of veal are small round slices taken from
the fillet. They are invariably sautéed in butter.
Any of the garnishes or accompaniments suggested for escalopes of
veal (see page 316) can be served with noisettes and mignonnettes.

PIEDS DE VEAU
CALF'S FEET

Calf's feet must first be boned, put into cold water and brought to the boil
for a few minutes. They are then cooled and either cooked in stock or
braised according to the purpose for which they are to be used.
When making calf's foot jelly, the feet must be cooked in unsalted
water with lemon juice.
Since the appearance on the market of various gelatines, calf's foot jelly
has almost completely disappeared from modern cookery. From many
points of view I think this is a mistake.

Pieds de veau Cendrillon

CALF'S FOOT WITH TRUFFLES AND SAUSAGE MEAT

————————— 2 calf's feet, 3—4 tablespoons chopped truffles, 3—4 tablespoons
sausage meat, butter, breadcrumbs

Cook the calf's feet as suggested above. Cut into small pieces and mix
with the truffles and sausage meat. Shape into small cutlets, brush with
melted butter and roll in breadcrumbs, then grill (U.S. broil) slowly.
Serve with boiled potatoes.

Pieds de veau grillés

GRILLED CALF'S FEET

Cook the calf's feet, drain, and spread lightly with mustard. Brush with melted butter, roll in breadcrumbs and grill (U.S. broil) slowly.

Serve with *sauce piquante* (see page 28) or *sauce diable* (see page 27).

Pieds de veau provençal

PROVENÇAL STYLE CALF'S FEET

———————— 2 calf's feet, flour, 6 tablespoons oil, 1 wine glass white wine, 2 lb. tomatoes, 1 small clove garlic, parsley, seasoning

Cook the calf's feet, cut into fairly wide strips, and coat with flour. Brown the pieces in oil for a few minutes. Add the wine, tomatoes, peeled, seeded and chopped, garlic, little chopped parsley and seasoning. Simmer gently for 30 – 35 minutes. Serve with boiled potatoes.

Pieds de veau tyrolienne

TYROLEAN STYLE CALF'S FEET

———————— 2 calf's feet, flour, 4 tablespoons finely chopped or sliced onion, 6 tablespoons oil, ½ wine glass vinegar, 2 lb. tomatoes, small clove garlic, parsley, seasoning

Prepare the feet as described for *pieds de veau provençal* (see page 318) and coat with flour.

Cook the onion in the oil until lightly browned. Add the calf's feet and cook for a few minutes. Add the vinegar and allow to reduce a little. Add tomatoes, peeled, seeded and chopped, garlic, parsley and seasoning and simmer gently for 30 – 35 minutes.

This may be served in the same way as *tête de veau à la financière* (see page 332).

Pieds de veau pour hors-d'oeuvre

CALF'S FEET AS HORS-D'OEUVRE

After cooking cut calf's feet into small strips and season as liked.

Calf's feet which are to be served cold should be garnished while hot, then allowed to cool.

Provençal and Tyrolean calf's feet served cold make excellent hors-d'oeuvre. The feet should be very well cooked, and a few black olives make a good addition.

POITRINE DE VEAU
BREAST OF VEAL

When breast of veal is to be served whole, it is usually boned, split, stuffed and sewn up again.

The most usual forcemeat for stuffing breast of veal is as follows:

2¼ lb. sausage meat, 7 oz. breadcrumbs moistened with stock, chopped parsley, chopped tarragon, 1−2 eggs, salt, pepper, spices. Mix all thoroughly together. Braise gently on a moderate heat.

The time for cooking a breast of veal weighing 11 lb. varies between 3−4 hours.

Braised breast of veal may be served with its cooking gravy or a chosen garnish.

All green vegetables, purées of vegetables, and all Italian pasta, such as noodles, macaroni, spaghetti, as well as rice, go well with it.

TENDRON DE VEAU
MIDDLE-CUT OF VEAL

These pieces are cut from the ends of the ribs, from the point at which the chops are usually cut, to the sternum. To qualify for the name *tendron*, these pieces must include the full width of the breast. Cut across, they are not *tendrons*. Cut in square pieces they are used to make ragoûts and sautés.

When the *tendron* is to be braised, it should be prepared like the fricandeau (see page 316), but it may be cooked in butter in a saucepan, as explained for the *quasi* and *rouelle* of veal on page 320. With a little care a perfect gravy can be obtained.

Cooked by either method, the best garnishes for *tendrons* are: small new carrots, peas cooked with lettuce, *sauce chasseur* (see page 26), *sauce tomate* (see page 132), or various Italian pastas and mashed potatoes.

QUASI ET ROUELLES DE VEAU

The *quasi* is a piece from the rump of veal, the *rouelle* a fairly thick slice across the leg.

Quasi or *rouelle* should be cooked slowly in butter, and turned from time to time. Be careful the butter does not burn, and avoid this by adding a few tablespoons of hot water as soon as the butter begins to clarify.

All the garnishes given for topside of veal (see page 313) are suitable for *quasi* and *rouelle*.

RIS DE VEAU
SWEETBREADS

Sweetbreads are considered a delicacy and may figure on any menu.

They should be white, with no trace of blood, and be soaked for some time in cold running water, or in water which is frequently changed. Sweetbreads consist of two parts, varying in shape and quality. The almost round one, called in French the *noix*, is taken from near the heart and is the more delicate. The other, rather elongated, is taken from nearer the throat. This is called the *gorge* in French. Before cooking, the sweetbreads must be blanched. To do this, put them into a fairly large pan and cover completely with cold water. Bring quickly to boiling point, then rinse again in cold water. Trim them, then put between two cloths and press under a weight.

They are usually larded with bacon fat, or wrapped in slices of bacon fat. They can also be studded with pieces of truffle, ham or tongue.

They are then braised in either white or brown stock.

Ris de veau bonne maman
SWEETBREADS WITH VEGETABLES

Cut some vegetables, including celery, into rather wide, short julienne. Arrange the prepared sweetbreads on top and moisten with good veal stock, then braise in the usual way.

Serve the sweetbreads with the vegetables and the liquor, which should be well reduced.

Note Before braising sweetbreads, prepare a good stock from veal bones and trimmings.

Ris de veau braisés à brun

BRAISED SWEETBREADS (BROWN)

— 2—3 sweetbreads, bacon fat, onion, carrot, salt, bacon rinds, ½ pint (U.S. 1¼ cups) good veal stock, *bouquet garni*

Lard the sweetbreads or wrap in bacon fat. Put the sliced vegetables into a casserole, add a little salt and a few bacon rinds. Arrange the sweetbreads on top and add the stock. Cover and cook until the stock has reduced, then add enough stock to come two-thirds up the pan, and *bouquet garni*. Cover and cook in the oven, basting frequently. Remove the lid towards the end of the cooking to glaze the sweetbreads.

Ris de veau braisés à blanc

BRAISED SWEETBREADS (WHITE)

Prepare as for the preceding recipe, but the liquid should not be reduced too much and the sweetbreads not glazed.

Sweetbreads (brown) may be garnished *à la financière* (see page 48), with olives, mushrooms, or truffles, and accompanied by noodles, macaroni, rice, any green vegetables, purées of vegetables, or chestnut purée, etc.

Sweetbreads (white) are preferably garnished *à la toulousaine* (see page 54) with creamed cocchiletti (see page 301) and julienne of truffles or noodles with butter.

Asparagus tips always make an excellent accompaniment to braised sweetbreads, whether brown or white.

Escalopes de ris de veau

ESCALOPES OF SWEETBREAD

The escalopes are cut from sweetbreads which have been blanched and pressed (see page 320), or from braised sweetbreads.

They should be seasoned, coated with flour and fried in butter.

Escalopes de ris de veau favori

ESCALOPES OF SWEETBREAD WITH MADEIRA SAUCE

——————— Sweetbreads, foie gras, salt, pepper, flour, butter, truffle, Madeira sauce,* asparagus tips
* Reduce some demi-glace sauce (see page 22) until it is fairly thick and add enough Madeira to bring it back to its normal consistency.

Blanch and press the sweetbreads and slice. Cut an equal number of slices of foie gras. Season and flour all the slices and sauté in butter.

Arrange the sweetbreads in a ring, with a slice of foie gras on top. Add a few slices of truffle to the sauce and pour over. Garnish the centre with buttered asparagus tips.

Escalopes de ris de veau grand-duc

ESCALOPES OF SWEETBREAD WITH SEMOLINA AND TRUFFLE

——————— Slices braised sweetbread, rounds semolina (see recipe for *gnocchi à la romaine* on page 672 but omit the cheese), truffle, béchamel sauce (see page 23), grated cheese, butter, asparagus tips

Follow the recipe for white braised sweetbreads (page 321). Arrange rounds of semolina on a serving dish, put a slice of sweetbread on each, and top with a slice of truffle. Cover with béchamel sauce and sprinkle with cheese. Brush with melted butter and glaze under the grill (U.S. broiler).

Garnish with buttered asparagus tips.

Escalopes ris de veau maréchal

ESCALOPES OF SWEETBREADS WITH ASPARAGUS TIPS

——————— Slices white braised sweetbreads, egg, breadcrumbs, butter, meat jelly (see page 21), asparagus tips

Coat the escalopes with egg and breadcrumbs and fry till golden brown in clarified butter. Arrange in a ring on a serving dish. Add a little butter to some melted meat jelly and pour over. Garnish the centre with buttered asparagus tips.

Serve with *sauce suprême* (see page 23) to which a little truffle has been added.

Escalopes de ris de veau Rossini

ESCALOPES OF SWEETBREAD WITH BUTTERED NOODLES

Follow the instructions for *escalopes de ris de veau favori* on page 322, omitting the asparagus tips, replacing them with buttered noodles and Parmesan cheese.

Escalopes de ris de veau florentine

ESCALOPES OF SWEETBREAD WITH RISOTTO

This is the same as the Rossini (above) save that the noodles are replaced by risotto with Parmesan cheese.

Ris de veau grillé

GRILLED (U.S. BROILED) SWEETBREADS

Blanch and press the sweetbreads (see page 320). Cut in half lengthwise, along the thicker side. Season with salt and pepper, dip in melted butter and grill (U.S. broil) gently.

Serve with slices of grilled bacon and *sauce diable* (see page 127), *sauce béchamel* (see page 23), or maître d'hôtel butter.

Green peas are a good accompaniment.

Ris de veau Monselet

SWEETBREADS WITH TRUFFLES

Braise the sweetbreads (brown; see page 320), and put them into a fireproof dish. Cover with truffles cut in thick slices and pour the braising liquor over. Cover and seal the dish with a strip of paste made of flour and water.

Put into the oven for 7–8 minutes, then serve at once with a dish of buttered macaroni and a purée of foie gras and Parmesan cheese.

Noisettes de ris de veau Mireille

NOISETTES OF SWEETBREADS WITH TRUFFLE AND ASPARAGUS
TIPS

————————— Rounds semolina (see page 671), butter, braised sweetbreads, noisettes
of veal about ½ inch thick (see page 317), truffle, béchamel sauce (see
page 23), grated cheese, buttered asparagus tips

Fry the rounds of semolina in butter, and when brown on both sides
arrange in a ring on a serving dish. Put the braised sweetbreads on top,
and then noisettes sautéed in butter. Add a few slices of carefully peeled
truffle and cover with béchamel sauce. Sprinkle with cheese, dot with
butter, and brown in the oven or under the grill (U.S. broiler). Serve
with buttered asparagus tips.

Noisettes de ris de veau à la moelle

NOISETTES OF SWEETBREADS WITH BEEF MARROW

————————— Noisettes of veal sautéed in butter, braised sweetbreads, semolina
rounds browned in butter (see page 671), grated cheese, beef marrow
sauce (see page 28), tomato sauce (see page 132)

Arrange the noisettes and sweetbreads on the rounds of semolina as
described above and put into a fireproof dish. Sprinkle with cheese and
coat with beef marrow sauce to which a little tomato sauce has been
added. Cover, and put into the oven for 4–5 minutes before serving.

Noisettes de ris de veau Victoria

NOISETTES OF SWEETBREADS WITH MUSHROOM PURÉE

————————— Semolina rounds fried in butter (see page 671), braised sweetbreads,
noisettes of veal sautéed in butter, mushroom purée, truffle, grated
cheese, butter, asparagus tips

Arrange the rounds of semolina, sweetbreads and noisettes in a ring on
a fireproof dish, as described above. Cover with mushroom purée to
which some chopped truffle has been added.

Sprinkle with cheese, dot with butter and brown in the oven or under
the grill (U.S. broiler). Garnish the centre with asparagus tips.

Noisettes de ris de veau châtelaine
NOISETTES OF SWEETBREADS WITH ARTICHOKE PURÉE

This is the same as *noisettes de ris de veau Victoria* except that the mushroom purée is replaced by a purée of artichokes.

Vol-au-vent de ris de veau financière
SWEETBREAD VOL-AU-VENT WITH QUENELLES OF MUSHROOMS

Sweetbreads, brown stock, quenelles (see page 56), mushrooms, truffles, olives, demi-glace sauce (see page 22), butter, 1 cooked vol-au-vent case

Braise the sweetbreads in brown stock and cut into slices. Put into a pan with some quenelles, cooked mushrooms, sliced truffle and olives. Add the braising liquor to some demi-glace sauce and reduce until thick enough to bind all the ingredients. Pour the sauce over and heat through. Finally add a little butter, and fill the vol-au-vent case with the mixture. Replace the top of the vol-au-vent before serving.

RIS DE VEAU FROID
COLD SWEETBREADS

Although not much in demand, cold sweetbreads do, nevertheless, make a very enjoyable dish.

Ris de veau Richelieu
BRAISED SWEETBREADS WITH VEGETABLES AND TRUFFLE

Braise sweetbreads as instructed in *ris de veau bonne mamman* (see page 320), taking care there is sufficient braising liquor to cover the sweetbreads in the saucepan. Add a julienne of truffle a few moments before the end of the cooking.

Put the sweetbreads in a serving dish and pour over the braising liquor and garnish.

Keep the dish on ice and, when the liquor begins to turn to jelly, skim off the fat. Serve surrounded by cracked ice.

Vol-au-vent toulousaine

TOULOUSE STYLE SWEETBREAD VOL-AU-VENT

Sweetbreads, white stock (see page 20), mushrooms, truffle, quenelles (see page 56), chicken livers, *sauce suprême* (see page 23), or *sauce parisienne* (see page 22), butter, 1 vol-au-vent case

Braise the sweetbreads in white stock and slice them. Put into a pan with mushrooms, sliced truffle, quenelles and chicken livers. Cover with the sauce and heat through. Finally add a little butter and pour the mixture into the vol-au-vent case. Replace the top before serving.

ROGNONS DE VEAU
CALF'S KIDNEYS

To prepare calf's kidneys for sautéing, the fat and membrane should be removed and it should not be cut too thin, otherwise it will become hard. If it is to be grilled, it should be trimmed in such a way as to leave a thin layer of fat around. It is then cut in two lengthwise and skewered to keep its shape.

Rognon sauté aux champignons

SAUTÉ OF KIDNEYS WITH MUSHROOMS

1 calf's kidney, salt, pepper, butter, 6 tablespoons white wine, 10 small mushrooms, demi-glace sauce (see page 22), lemon juice

Cut the kidney into pieces, season with salt and pepper and sauté quickly in butter.

Put the wine and mushrooms into a pan and let the wine reduce. Add a few tablespoons demi-glace sauce, and reduce further for a few seconds. Remove from the heat, add the kidney and finally $\frac{3}{4}$ oz. butter and a few drops lemon juice. Serve immediately.

Rognon sauté aux truffes

KIDNEYS SAUTÉED WITH TRUFFLES

Prepare as in the preceding recipe but replace the white wine by Madeira and the mushrooms by slices of truffles.

Rognon de veau en casserole

CALF'S KIDNEY CASSEROLE

————————— 1 calf's kidney, salt, pepper, ½ oz. butter, 3—4 tablespoons white wine, veal stock

Trim the kidney but leave a thin layer of fat around. Season, and put into a casserole with butter. Cook in a moderate oven for about 30 minutes, turning frequently. Just before serving add the wine and a little concentrated veal stock. Serve in the casserole, with mashed potatoes, chestnut purée, asparagus tips, sauté potatoes, or *pommes de terre Macaire* (see page 651).

Rognon de veau à la crème

CALF'S KIDNEY WITH CREAM

————————— 1 calf's kidney, salt, pepper, flour, butter, 1 tablespoon Madeira, 2 tablespoons meat jelly (see page 21), 5—6 tablespoons fresh cream

Trim the kidney but leave a thin layer of fat around. Cut into 5—6 slices. Season, coat with flour, then sauté quickly in butter. Remove from the pan and keep warm.

Add the Madeira to butter and sediment left in the pan and stir well. Add the melted meat jelly and cream, bring to boiling point, and boil for 2—3 seconds.

Arrange the kidney on a hot dish and pour the sauce over.

If liked, the slices of kidney can be served on croûtons fried in butter and the dish can be garnished with asparagus tips or small new potatoes.

Rognon de veau grillé

GRILLED CALF'S KIDNEY

Trim the kidney, leaving a small layer of fat around it. Cut it in half lengthwise without completely separating it. Use two small skewers to keep it open.

Season and grill (U.S. broil) it gently, basting with melted butter.

Serve with maître d'hôtel butter.

Rognon de veau Montpensier

CALF'S KIDNEY WITH MADEIRA, ASPARAGUS TIPS
AND TRUFFLE

———————— 1 calf's kidney, 2 tablespoons Madeira, 3 tablespoons meat jelly (see page 21), juice ½ lemon, 2 tablespoons butter, asparagus tips, sliced truffle

Prepare the kidney and sauté it in butter as instructed for calf's kidney with cream (see page 327). Add the Madeira to the butter and sediment left in the pan and stir well. Add the melted meat jelly, lemon juice and butter and bring to boiling point.

Note If the meat jelly is very strong it may cause the butter to oil, in which case add 1—2 tablespoons stock or water.

Arrange the kidney in a circle on a hot dish, and pour the sauce over.

Garnish the centre with asparagus tips and put a slice of truffle on each piece of kidney.

Rognon de veau à la piémontaise

CALF'S KIDNEY WITH PIEDMONT STYLE RISOTTO

Prepare and cook the kidney as described in the preceding recipe, but arrange on a *riz à la piémontaise* (see page 668), and pour over Montpensier sauce (see above).

SELLE DE VEAU
SADDLE OF VEAL

Saddle of veal as an entrée is roasted, braised or pot-roasted. It consists of the entire back of the animal.

To facilitate the cooking of the saddle, remove the kidneys, leaving a layer of fat, and cook separately, 30 minutes before the cooking of the saddle is completed.

Pare the flank on either side, so that what is left of it, when drawn under the saddle, will just cover the *filets mignons*, on which a layer of fat should be left. Finally, tie string around the joint.

If the saddle is to be braised, the braise must be kept moist, and the joint should be frequently basted.

Cooking time for a medium-sized saddle is approximately 3 hours.

The pot-roasted or roasted saddle calls for a great deal of care and must be cooked over very moderate heat or in a moderate oven, and frequently basted.

Great care must be taken not to let the cooking fat burn and, as a precaution against this, add a few tablespoons water to keep the butter or the fat at a normal temperature.

Whatever the method of cooking, a very good gravy should be served. Any fresh vegetables or purées of vegetables make a good accompaniment for saddle of veal.

Selle de veau Metternich

SADDLE OF VEAL WITH PAPRIKA AND TRUFFLE

——————— Saddle of veal, béchamel sauce (see page 23), paprika, truffle, melted butter

Braise the saddle. When it is ready, trace a line within half an inch of its extreme edge on either side and at both ends, pressing the point of a knife into the flesh.

Proceed in the same way on either side of the chine, and carefully remove the fillets from the joint.

Slice the fillets, keeping the knife at a slant.

In the double cavity left by the removal of the fillets, put a few table-spoons béchamel sauce to which a little paprika has been added, then replace the fillets on the joint, putting between each slice a dessertspoon of the sauce already used, and 2 truffle slices.

Finally, cover the saddle with more béchamel sauce, sprinkle lightly with melted butter and glaze rapidly in the oven.

With the help of a large square spatula, place it on the serving dish.

Skim and reduce the braising liquor, and serve separately with a pilaf of rice (see page 669).

Selle de veau Orloff

SADDLE OF VEAL WITH SOUBISE AND MORNAY SAUCE

Saddle of veal, soubise sauce (see page 35), truffle, Mornay sauce (see page 34), grated cheese, butter

Braise the saddle and proceed as for *selle de veau Metternich* (see page 329). When re-forming the fillets, put a dessertspoon soubise sauce and 2 slices of truffle on each slice.

Cover the saddle with Mornay sauce to which a quarter of the amount of soubise purée has been added, sprinkle lightly with cheese, brush with melted butter, and glaze quickly in the oven.

Skim and reduce the cooking liquor and serve separately.

Note The saddle may be accompanied by a garnish of asparagus tips, cucumbers with cream or mushrooms with cream.

Selle de veau à la Talleyrand

SADDLE OF VEAL STUDDED WITH TRUFFLE

Saddle of veal, truffle, bacon slices, demi-glace sauce (see page 22), tomato sauce (see page 132), sliced truffles, butter, grated Parmesan cheese, cooked macaroni, foie gras purée

Stud the fillets of the saddle with large pieces of truffle placed symmetrically. Tie pieces of bacon over it, braise, and take off the bacon at the last moment, to glaze it. Place the saddle on a serving dish. Skin, reduce and strain the cooking liquor and pour a little round the dish.

Add a little demi-glace and tomato sauce to the rest of the cooking liquor and reduce well, then use to coat some slices of truffle.

Mix some butter and grated Parmesan cheese with the macaroni, sprinkle a little more cheese on top and then cover with the foie gras purée. Serve this with the saddle, in a separate dish.

Selle de veau Visconti

SADDLE OF VEAL WITH MACARONI AND TRUFFLE

Proceed in the same way as for the *selle de veau à la Talleyrand* (see above).

Braise it and put on the serving dish with some of the reduced cooking liquid.

Serve the rest separately.

Serve with a dish of macaroni to which some cream, grated Parmesan cheese and julienne of truffle has been added.

SELLE DE VEAU FROID

COLD SADDLE OF VEAL

Cold saddle of veal makes a magnificent joint for the side table, as every possible garnish for a cold joint is suitable: garnished artichoke bottoms, macédoine of vegetables with mayonnaise sauce, *bouquetière*, tomatoes stuffed in various ways, stuffed aubergines, etc.

Decorate the saddle with thin shapes of aspic jelly. The cooking liquid should also be served, free from grease, and allowed to become jelly.

TÊTE DE VEAU

CALF'S HEAD

1 calf's head, 1 tablespoon flour, ¼ oz. salt, juice 1 lemon, 1 onion, 1 clove, *bouquet garni*

Select a very white calf's head and cut it into pieces 2½—3 inches square. Put into a saucepan and cover with cold water, bring to the boil.

Strain and put the pieces of meat into very cold water and allow to cool thoroughly.

Put the flour, salt and lemon juice into a pan with 1¾ pints (U.S. 4¼ cups) cold water. Bring to boiling point, stirring; add the onion stuck with the clove, *bouquet garni*, and pieces of head.

Make sure the air does not come in contact with the pieces of head while they are cooking, as they will turn black. To prevent this, cover closely with a cloth. Then cook gently until the pieces of head are tender.

Tête de veau à l'anglaise

ENGLISH STYLE CALF'S HEAD

The head is usually served whole, or cut in half, without boning it. But this system is not always practical.

It is served with a piece of boiled bacon and parsley sauce.

Note Tête de veau à l'anglaise may be served cut in pieces and, in that case, the brains and tongue should accompany it.

Tête de veau financière

CALF'S HEAD WITH FINANCIÈRE GARNISH

———————— 1 calf's head, white stock, quenelles of veal (see page 57), mushroom heads, sliced truffles, olives, cock's combs and kidneys, demi-glace sauce (see page 22), Madeira

Cut the head in pieces 2½–3 inches square and cook in white stock. Arrange in a dish and cover with a *financière* garnish composed of quenelles of veal, mushroom heads, slices of truffle, olives, cock's combs and kidneys, all coated with a demi-glace sauce, to which a little Madeira has been added.

Tête de veau Godard

CALF'S HEAD WITH GARNISH

Calf's head *à la Godard* was one of the more important 'removes' in the *cuisine ancienne*. It was always served whole, surrounded by large truffled quenelles, mushroom heads, truffles, lamb and calf's sweetbreads, cock's combs and kidneys, the whole being coated in a demiglace sauce with Madeira.

In the cuisine of today the head is cut into squares, as for the *financière*, in the recipe above.

Tête de veau en tortue

CALF'S HEAD WITH CALF'S BRAINS

Cook the head in white stock and cut it into pieces 1½ inches square.

Serve in a deep dish, garnished with quenelles, mushrooms, stuffed olives, gherkins cut in the shape of cloves of garlic, sliced calf's brains and truffle.

The garnish should then be covered with a demi-glace sauce with tomato (see page 22), to which has also been added a little Madeira, few leaves of basil, sage and marjoram, few peppercorns and a pinch of cayenne pepper.

In addition, one may serve small fried eggs, hard-boiled eggs, croûtons fried in butter, or crayfish cooked in *court-bouillon* (see page 164).

Tête de veau à la vinaigrette ou à l'huile

CALF'S HEAD VINAIGRETTE OR WITH OIL

Cook the head in white stock and serve with sliced tongue, brains and sprigs of parsley.

Arrange some chopped capers, chopped onion and chopped parsley in separate piles on an hors-d'oeuvre dish. Serve this separately with vinaigrette sauce (see page 42) from which the onion has been omitted.

Tétine de veau

CALF'S UDDER

Calf's udder is especially used in Jewish cooking, where it takes the place of bacon fat.

Calf's udder cooked in stock and allowed to cool is used to advantage in forcemeat for galantines.

PRÉPARATIONS DIVERSES DU VEAU

VARIOUS WAYS TO PRESENT VEAL

Blanquette de veau à l'ancienne

BLANQUETTE OF VEAL

1½ lb. veal, water, 2 small carrots, onion stuck with 1 clove, *bouquet garni*, 6 oz. butter, 3 tablespoons flour, mushrooms and onions cooked in white stock (optional), 3 egg yolks, few drops lemon juice, grated nutmeg

The meat for a blanquette of veal is cut from the breast, shoulder and spare ribs.

Cut the meat into 1½ – 2-oz. pieces and put into a saucepan with enough cold salted water to cover. Use ¾ oz. salt to 2 pints (U.S. 5 cups) water.

Bring gently to the boil, stirring and skimming carefully.

Add the carrots, onion and *bouquet garni*.

Cover the saucepan and cook gently for 1½ hours. Melt 3 oz. of the butter, add the flour; cook for a few seconds without browning. Gradually add the cooking liquor from the veal, stir till boiling and simmer for 12 – 15 minutes, skimming frequently.

Put the pieces of veal into a dish and if liked add a garnish of mushrooms and small onions cooked in white stock. Keep hot.

Thicken the sauce with the egg yolks and the rest of the butter, the lemon juice and a little grated nutmeg. Strain through a fine sieve and pour over the veal. Pilaf of rice, noodles or spaghetti all go very well with blanquette of veal.

Fricassée de veau

FRICASSÉE OF VEAL

3 tablespoons butter, 1½ lb. veal, 1 onion, salt and pepper, 3 tablespoons flour, water,* *bouquet garni*, 3 egg yolks, 3 tablespoons cream, nutmeg, lemon juice

* In this, and the preceding recipe, the veal may be cooked in white stock (see page 20) instead of water. This will improve the flavour of the sauce in each case.

Melt the butter, add the veal, cut into small pieces, sliced onion, salt and pepper.

Cover and sauté very slowly for 12 – 15 minutes.

Add the flour, mix well, then just cover the meat with hot water. Bring to boiling point, stirring. Add the *bouquet garni*, cover and simmer for 1½ hours.

When the meat is cooked, arrange in a deep serving dish.

Remove the *bouquet garni* and thicken the sauce with the egg yolks and cream.

Add grated nutmeg and lemon juice and check the seasoning. Strain through a fine sieve and pour over the meat.

Garnish with mushrooms and small onions as for the blanquette (see page 334).

Matelote de veau

VEAL WITH ONIONS AND MUSHROOMS

1½ lb. veal, 3 tablespoons butter, 2 onions, red wine, veal stock, salt, pepper, *bouquet garni*, 1 clove garlic, 20 small glazed onions, 20 small cooked mushrooms, 4 oz. butter, 3 tablespoons flour, 1 liqueur glass brandy

Cut the veal into small pieces. Melt the butter, add the veal and chopped onions and brown lightly. Just cover with wine and veal stock, using ⅔ wine and ⅓ stock.

Add seasoning, *bouquet garni* and crushed garlic. Cover and simmer gently for about 1½ hours.

Remove the meat to a serving dish, add the glazed onions and mushrooms.

Strain the cooking liquor and reduce it by one-third. Mix the butter and flour together and add a little at a time to the liquor until it is of the required consistency. Bring to boiling point, add the brandy, then pour over the meat.

Boiled or mashed potatoes, or buttered noodles, are all very good accompaniments.

Pain de veau

VEAL LOAF

Veal loaf is a real family dish, prepared with cold roast or braised meat.

8 oz. breadcrumbs, boiled milk, 1½ lb. cooked minced veal, 3 eggs, salt, pepper, nutmeg

Moisten the breadcrumbs with some boiling milk and add to the meat. Add the beaten eggs, seasoning and grated nutmeg. Mix all well together. Put into a buttered mould and poach in a bain-marie.

Serve with tomato sauce (see page 132).

Note The breadcrumbs may be replaced with mashed potatoes.

Paupiettes de veau

PAUPIETTES OF VEAL

Paupiettes are cut from topside (U.S. rump or round) of veal, in slices of about 4—5 inches long by 2 inches wide

Flatten, trim and cover them on one side with forcemeat. Roll into the shape of a cork, cover with a slice of fat bacon, and keep in shape by tying with cotton. Braise on a bed of finely sliced carrots and onions, as for sweetbreads, or cook gently in butter, adding a tablespoon water from time to time to give them a nice golden colour and prevent them getting too dark.

FOR THE FORCEMEAT

1½ oz. breadcrumbs, little cream or milk, 6 oz. sausage meat, 1 egg, salt, pepper, grated nutmeg, chopped parsley

Moisten the breadcrumbs with a little cream or milk and then mix all ingredients well together.

Paupiettes may also be stuffed with a veal panada forcemeat (see page 54).

Any of the following garnishes go well with paupiettes: peas, spinach, chicory, chestnut purée, purée of peas, noodles with butter, tomato sauce (see page 132), *tomates sautées à la provençal* (see page 660) or *sauce chasseur* (see page 26).

SAUTÉS DE VEAU
SAUTÉ VEAL

Meat for sauté veal is cut from the breast, shoulder or spare ribs.

Sauté de veau aux champignons
SAUTÉ VEAL WITH MUSHROOMS

3 tablespoons oil, butter, 1¼ lb. veal, salt, pepper, 1 wine glass white wine, 1 pint (U.S. 2½ cups) brown stock, ¾ pint (U.S. 1⅞ cups), demi-glace sauce (see page 22), *bouquet garni*, 8 oz. mushrooms

Heat the oil and 1 oz. butter, add the meat, cut into pieces, and brown lightly. Add salt and pepper, wine, brown stock, demi-glace sauce and *bouquet garni*.

Cover, and cook gently for 1½ hours.

In another pan, sauté the mushrooms in butter.

When the meat is cooked, put it with the mushrooms. Reduce the liquor in which the meat was cooked to two-thirds its original quantity, then strain over the meat and mushrooms. Simmer for 12—15 minutes, then pour into a serving dish.

Sauté de veau à la ménagère
SAUTÉ VEAL WITH WINE AND TOMATOES

1¼ lb. veal, salt, pepper, flour, 3 tablespoons oil, 2 tablespoons butter, 2 onions, 1 wine glass white wine, 2 lb. tomatoes, 1 clove garlic

Cut the veal into pieces, season and coat with flour. Heat the oil and butter, add the meat and chopped onions and sauté until browned. Add the wine, tomatoes, peeled, seeded and chopped, and garlic. Check the seasoning. Cover and simmer for 1½ hours. If the sauce becomes too thick, add a little hot water from time to time.

Serve with boiled potatoes, with aubergines cut into rounds and fried or sautéed in oil, or with strips of grilled (U.S. broiled) red peppers.

Sauté de veau aux nouilles à la ménagère
SAUTÉ VEAL WITH BUTTERED NOODLES

————— 1½ lb. veal, salt, pepper, flour, 3 tablespoons oil, 2 tablespoons butter, 1 onion, 1 wine glass white wine, ½ pint (U.S. 1¼ cups) tomato purée, *bouquet garni*, 1 clove garlic, 1 pint (U.S. 2½ cups) stock or water

Cut the veal into pieces, season and coat with flour. Melt the oil and butter, add meat and chopped onion. Sauté until browned. Add the wine, tomato purée, *bouquet garni*, garlic and stock. Cover and simmer for 1½ hours.

Serve with buttered noodles, or sprinkled with cheese.

Sauté de veau printanier
SAUTÉ VEAL WITH SPRING VEGETABLES

————— 1½ lb. veal, salt, pepper, flour, butter, 1 pint (U.S. 2½ cups) white stock, *bouquet garni*, 12 small new onions, 18 small new carrots, 18 small new potatoes, 1 lb. fresh garden peas

Cut the meat into pieces, season, dip in flour and brown lightly in butter. Add the stock, and *bouquet garni*. Cover and cook gently for 25–30 minutes.

Add the onions, carrots, potatoes and peas, and continue to cook slowly in a covered pan for a further 30 minutes.

Sauté de veau paysanne
SAUTÉ VEAL WITH ONIONS AND CARROTS

————— 1½ lb. veal, salt, pepper, flour, 4 oz. chopped bacon fat, 3 medium-sized sliced onions, 12 oz. thinly sliced carrots, *bouquet garni*, white stock (see page 20)

Cut up the veal, season and dip in flour. Heat the bacon fat, and brown the meat in it. Remove the meat, put vegetables in the pan with the remaining fat and mix well. Add the *bouquet garni* and ½ pint (U.S. 1¼ cups) water. Replace the meat on the bed of vegetables. Cover and cook until the water has evaporated. Then add enough white stock or hot water to just cover the meat. Cover and cook slowly about 1 hour or until meat is tender. Serve with potato purée.

LE MOUTON
ET L'AGNEAU DE PRÉ-SALÉ
MUTTON AND LAMB

From the culinary point of view the products of the ovine species are divided into three categories:

Mutton — sheep that has reached full development.

Lamb — young sheep, weaned but not fully developed, and all the more prized because it is young.

Baby — one that has not yet been weaned and has not grazed. In France, the Pauillac lamb is the most perfect example of this.

Ordinary lamb, or *pré-salé* (young sheep fattened in the meadows bordering the sea), is very like mutton, although its flesh is much finer and more tender. It is cooked in the same way as mutton. All that is necessary is to adjust the time of cooking to the quality.

There are special methods of cooking baby lamb, the flesh of which is much whiter and of a different texture.

Editor's note Although popular in France, baby lamb is very seldom obtainable in England or America.

Pas-rond ou baron et double d'agneau

BARON AND DOUBLE OF LAMB

Baron of lamb consists of the saddle and the two legs, that is to say the whole lower back of the animal; this makes one of the finest and best intermediate courses of a meal.

The double consists of the two legs, not separated.

They are both usually cut from the *pré-salé* lamb and are always roasted.

If these joints are roasted, the sediment left in the pan should be deglazed with a little ordinary stock or hot water. It should not have all its fat removed, as a completely de-greased gravy loses much of its flavour and becomes an ordinary broth.

For joints roasted on a spit, it is enough to watch the cooking and the drops of fat and blood which fall into the dripping pan, which should contain a little water. After cooking, strain the contents of the dripping pan into a saucepan, add a few tablespoons ordinary stock and partially remove the fat.

Carré de mouton

LOIN OF MUTTON

Loin of mutton, which is to be served whole, is first shortened as though it is about to be cut, then the skin and the bones of the chine should be removed, also the meat at the end of the rib-bones, as is done for cutlets.

The exposed meat is then wrapped in slices of bacon or flattened kidney fat, held in place with string.

All the garnishes given for barons and doubles are suitable for the loin.

Mouton et agneau froids

COLD MUTTON AND LAMB

Cold mutton and lamb make excellent dishes which may be accompanied by various salads or garnishes.

In England these meats are often served with mint sauce, consisting of chopped mint, castor sugar and vinegar (see page 44).

Cervelles

BRAINS

All the recipes described for calf's brains and marrow (see page 261) can be applied to sheep's brains.

Côtelettes

CUTLETS

Mutton cutlets are sometimes sautéed, but grilling (U.S. broiling) is the best method of cooking them.

If they are to be breadcrumbed before being grilled, they should be seasoned, dipped in melted butter, then covered with either dried or fresh breadcrumbs.

This method of crumbing before grilling (U.S. broiling) has the advantage of keeping in the juices which run from the meat during the cooking process.

If the cutlets are to be sautéed, they should be coated with flour, then dipped in egg, coated with fresh breadcrumbs and cooked in clarified butter.

Note Dried and fresh breadcrumbs must always be freshly made.

Generally speaking, whichever method is used any of the following accompaniments may be served: potatoes, cooked in any way, green vegetables, various purées, macaroni, noodles or other pasta and one of the following sauces: onion (see page 35), tomato (see page 132), piquante (see page 28), reform (see page 39).

Côtelettes Champvallon

BAKED CUTLETS

———————— 12 cutlets (U.S. rib chops), salt, pepper, butter, 3 small white onions, white stock (see page 20), *bouquet garni*, 1 clove garlic, 1 lb. potatoes

Trim the cutlets, season, and brown lightly on both sides in butter. Remove to a fireproof dish. Sauté the sliced onions for a few minutes in the remaining butter, but do not allow to brown. Put with the cutlets, and add enough white stock almost to cover. Add the *bouquet garni* and crushed garlic. Cover, and cook in a moderate oven for 20 minutes.

Add the sliced potatoes, sprinkle with salt and pepper then return to the oven and continue the cooking, basting frequently, until potatoes are tender.

Côtelettes Maintenon

CUTLETS WITH TRUFFLES

———————— Cutlets (U.S. rib chops), butter, fried croûtons, meat jelly (see page 21) or foie gras purée, mushrooms, truffle, cooked breast of chicken, *sauce parisienne* (see page 22), breadcrumbs

Trim cutlets and sauté in butter.

Arrange some fried croûtons in the bottom of a fireproof serving dish, cover with a little meat jelly or foie gras purée, and put the cutlets on top. Cut some mushrooms, truffle and a little breast of chicken into julienne and bind with a little Parisian sauce.

Put a spoonful of this mixture on to each cutlet, smooth the surface and sprinkle lightly with dried breadcrumbs. Dot with butter and brown under the grill (U.S. broiler).

Serve with *sauce chateaubriand* (see page 147). These cutlets may be served with buttered peas or asparagus tips.

Côtelettes Montglas

CUTLETS WITH DEMI-GLACE SAUCE

These are prepared in the same way as cutlets with truffles (page 341) except that the *sauce parisienne* is replaced by a concentrated demi-glace sauce (see page 22) and tongue is added to the garnish.

Serve with demi-glace sauce, well reduced, to which a little butter and Madeira have been added.

Côtelettes à la parisienne

PARISIAN STYLE CUTLETS

Grill the cutlets and set them up in the shape of a turban. In the centre put a garnish of potatoes scooped out with a round vegetable scoop, cooked in butter and brushed with meat jelly (see page 21).

Serve with *petits pois à la française* (see page 642).

Côtelettes de mouton à la provençale (ancienne mode)

PROVENÇAL STYLE MUTTON CUTLETS (OLD METHOD)

Cutlets (U.S. rib chops), oil, croûtons, puréed onion sauce (see page 35), butter, truffle, meat jelly (see page 21)

Trim cutlets and sauté in oil. Arrange some croûtons, fried in oil, in the bottom of a fireproof dish. Coat each cutlet with onion sauce and sprinkle with a little melted butter. Reheat in the oven for a few minutes, then put a slice of truffle on each cutlet and cover it with a little buttered meat jelly.

If liked, serve with grilled mushrooms or *pommes de terre Macaire* (see page 651).

Côtelettes réforme

CUTLETS WITH MINCED HAM

Cutlets (U.S. rib chops), flour, egg, breadcrumbs, minced lean ham, butter

Flatten cutlets slightly, coat with flour, then with egg and breadcrumbs, to which one-third minced ham has been added.

Cook the cutlets in clarified butter and arrange in a ring on a serving dish.

Serve with the special reform sauce (see page 39).

Côtelettes de mouton anglaises

MUTTON CHOP

A mutton chop is a cutlet cut from the loin of mutton and should be about $1-1\frac{1}{2}$ inches thick. After trimming and rolling the flap towards the middle of the chop, fix in place with a small skewer.

This chop is always grilled (U.S. broiled) and usually eaten just as it comes from the grill (U.S. broiler). It may be accompanied by potatoes, peas, beans, etc.

Épaule boulangère

SHOULDER OF MUTTON WITH POTATOES AND ONIONS

Shoulder of lamb, salt, pepper, lard or dripping, potatoes, 3 – 4 onions, parsley, few tablespoons stock

Trim meat, season with salt and pepper and put into an oven dish. Add some lard or good dripping and place in the oven. After 20 minutes, surround with potatoes cut in pieces, and thinly sliced onions which have been cooked 10 – 12 minutes in butter but not over browned. Baste potatoes and onions and continue the cooking, basting frequently.

Before serving, sprinkle some chopped parsley over the vegetables. Add the stock to the liquor in the pan to make a good gravy.

Note Never bone the shoulder when it is to be roasted either in the oven or on a spit.

Carving at the table may appear to be a little difficult, but this is only a question of practice, and the flavour of the meat is so much better when cooked on the bone!

Gigot à l'anglaise

BOILED LEG OF MUTTON

——————— Leg of mutton, water, 1 lb. carrots, 2 onions, 2 cloves, *bouquet garni* of 2 sprigs parsley, 1 bay leaf and 2 sprigs thyme, 1 clove garlic

Trim the meat and cut off the end of the bone. Put into a pan and cover with water. Add ¼ oz. salt to 2 pints (U.S. 5 cups) water. Add carrots, cut into small oval shapes, onions each stuck with a clove, *bouquet garni* and garlic. Cover and simmer gently, allowing 20 minutes for each 1 lb. of meat and 20 minutes over. Put on to a serving dish and surround with carrots and onions. Serve with caper sauce (see page 31).

Note A purée of turnips, celery or potatoes can accompany this joint.

The stock can be used with barley, rice, or various vegetables to make an excellent soup.

Gigot braisé

BRAISED LEG OF MUTTON

Proceed as instructed for braised shoulder of mutton (see page 343).

The same garnishes are suitable, but an excellent one consists of haricot beans cooked with a piece of lean bacon and moistened with some of the cooking liquor.

Gigot boulangère

LEG OF MUTTON WITH POTATOES AND ONIONS

The procedure is exactly the same as for shoulder of mutton (see page 343).

Gigot de mouton rôti avec sauce menthe

ROAST LEG OF MUTTON WITH MINT SAUCE

This accompaniment is little used in France. In England it is an absolute 'must'. Any roast joint of mutton or lamb, whether hot or cold, is always served with mint sauce (see page 44).

In France, roast leg of mutton is usually accompanied by fresh or dried vegetables, by various purées of vegetables, or an endive salad, to which has been added croûtons lightly rubbed with garlic.

Langues de mouton
SHEEP'S TONGUES

━━━━━━━━ 12 sheep's tongues, carrots, onions, *bouquet garni*, stock

Soak tongues in cold water for some hours. Put into a pan with slightly salted water, cover and simmer for 30 minutes. Then drain and, when cooled a little, remove the skin. Put tongues into a sauté pan on a bed of sliced carrots and onions. Add *bouquet garni* and enough stock to cover. Cover and simmer until tongues are tender. Remove to a serving dish and keep hot. Reduce the liquor, remove fat, and pour over the tongues.

Serve with mashed potatoes, creamed chicory or spinach and with one of the following sauces: Tyrolean (see page 28), piquante (see page 28), Italian (see page 281), tomato (see page 132), onion (see page 35).

Pieds de mouton
SHEEP'S TROTTERS

To prepare the trotters, the little tufts of hair between the cleavage in the hoof must be removed. The trotters are then boned, blanched, and cooked in white stock.

The most usual way of serving sheep's trotters is without doubt with poulette sauce.

━━━━━━━━ Butter, 2 tablespoons flour, 1 pint (U.S. 2½ cups) boiling water, salt, freshly ground black pepper, 20 mushrooms, 3 egg yolks, squeeze lemon juice, 6−8 cooked trotters

Melt 1 oz. butter, add flour and mix well. Remove from heat and gradually add the boiling water. Return to heat, and boil for a few minutes, stirring constantly. Add salt and pepper.

To make the poulette sauce Add a little of the liquor in which the mushrooms were cooked to the egg yolks and mix, then use to thicken the sauce. Then add 3−4 oz. butter very slowly, stirring in just a very small piece at one time. Finally, add the lemon juice.

Put trotters into a casserole with the cooked mushrooms and pour sauce over. Heat through carefully before serving.

Note If preferred, the poulette sauce can be replaced by *sauce parisienne* (see page 22).

Pieds de mouton en crépinette

SHEEP'S TROTTERS SAUSAGES

—————— Sheep's trotters, onions, carrots, *bouquet garni*, water, sausage meat, truffle, sausage skins, butter, breadcrumbs

Cook the sheep's trotters until nearly tender. Drain and put into a braising pan on a bed of sliced onions and carrots. Add *bouquet garni* and cover with water. Continue the cooking over gentle heat.

Thinly slice the meat and mix with an equal quantity of sausage meat and a few thin slices of truffle. Mix well and then fill sausage cases with mixture, slightly flattening them.

Sprinkle with melted butter, dip in breadcrumbs and grill (U.S. broil) gently.

Or, when well mixed, form into cutlet shapes. Brush with melted butter and coat with dried breadcrumbs, then grill (U.S. broil) gently.

Serve with mashed potatoes and *sauce périgueux* (see page 28).

Poitrine de mouton

BREAST OF MUTTON

Breast of mutton is generally used for navarins and ragoûts. It may also be grilled (U.S. broiled), accompanied either by piquante (see page 28), or devil (see page 27) sauce, mashed potatoes, purée of peas, etc.

Poitrine grillé

GRILLED BREAST OF MUTTON

Cook the breast in stock or braise it. Leave to cook, then remove the bones and cut meat into oblong or heart-shaped pieces.

Brush with melted butter, coat with dried breadcrumbs and grill (U.S. broil).

Serve with any of the accompaniments mentioned above.

Rognons

KIDNEYS

Sheep's kidneys may be prepared in various ways, but they are always best sautéed or grilled (U.S. broiléd).

Rognons sautés aux champignons

SHEEP'S KIDNEYS SAUTÉED WITH MUSHROOMS

4 sheep's kidneys, salt, pepper, butter, 3—4 tablespoons white wine, 12 mushrooms, ½ pint (U.S. 1¼ cups) demi-glace sauce (see page 22), squeeze lemon juice

Skin the kidneys, cut in half or into slices, season, and sauté quickly in butter. Remove and keep hot. Add the white wine to the butter left in the pan and stir well.

Add mushrooms and sauce, stir till boiling, then reduce a few minutes. Remove from heat, add kidney, and 1 oz. butter a little at a time. Finally add the lemon juice and serve at once.

Note Alternatively, the white wine can be replaced by Madeira, and the mushrooms by slices of truffle.

Rognons brochette

SHEEP'S KIDNEYS ON A SKEWER

Sheep's kidneys, salt, pepper, butter, maître d'hôtel butter, breadcrumbs (optional)

Skin the kidneys, and cut through the centre lengthwise without completely separating the two halves. Pass a skewer through, so that they keep open. Season with salt and pepper, brush with melted butter and grill (U.S. broil).

Serve with maître d'hôtel butter the size of a walnut on each kidney.

Note Sometimes the kidneys are breadcrumbed before being grilled (U.S. broiled). Although it is optional, I am in favour of this method, provided the breadcrumbs are thick enough to retain the small drops of meat juice which fall from the kidney during the cooking process.

Turban de rognons à la piémontaise

KIDNEYS WITH RICE

Riz à la piémontaise (see page 668), 3—4 kidneys, salt, pepper, butter, white Piedmontese truffles, tomato sauce (see page 132), demi-glace sauce (see page 22)

Press the risotto into a buttered savarin or ring mould. Prepare the kidneys, cut in half, season and sauté quickly in butter.

Turn risotto out of mould, arrange the kidneys on it alternately with slices of truffle.

Add a little tomato sauce to a well reduced demi-glace sauce and pour over the kidneys.

Rognons sautés Turbigo

SAUTÉ KIDNEYS WITH MUSHROOMS AND CHIPOLATA SAUSAGES

3—4 kidneys, salt, pepper, butter, cooked mushrooms, grilled (U.S. broiled) chipolata sausages, 3—4 tablespoons white wine, about ½ pint (U.S. 1¼ cups) demi-glace sauce with tomato (see page 22), chopped parsley, squeeze lemon juice

Skin the kidneys, cut in half lengthwise, season and sauté in butter. Put in a ring in a deep serving dish, and arrange mushrooms and sausages in the centre.

Add the white wine to the butter left in the pan and stir well. Add the sauce and stir till boiling. Add a little butter, parsley and the lemon juice.

Selle

SADDLE OF MUTTON

Saddle of mutton is usually served roasted, rarely braised. However, a good saddle of mutton, braised with proper care, receives approval from real gourmets.

Garnish *boulangère* (see page 46) is suitable to serve with saddle of mutton and any of the following: braised lettuce, lettuce stuffed with rice, carrots, turnips, stuffed tomatoes, peas, green beans, mashed potatoes, etc.

Filets et filets mignons

FILLETS AND FILETS MIGNONS

Fillet is the name given to the half-saddle, split lengthwise. This cut, after boning, is rolled and tied, then braised or roasted like shoulder or leg and served with similar garnishes.

The *filets mignons* of mutton or lamb (U.S. tenderloin) are small pieces of lean meat found under the saddle. They are either grilled or sautéed, and are accompanied by the same garnishes as suggested for cutlets and tournedos.

NOISETTES

Noisettes of mutton, and especially those of lamb, may be classed among the finest entrées.

They are cut either from the fillet or from the ribs; in the latter case only the first 5 ribs are used. These are called *côtes de noix*.

Noisettes are usually sautéed, rarely grilled. All the recipes for tournedos may be applied to them.

Noisettes d'agneau sautées au beurre

NOISETTES OF LAMB SAUTÉED IN BUTTER

————— 6 noisettes of lamb, salt, butter, 5—6 tablespoons meat jelly (see page 21)

Sprinkle noisettes lightly with salt and sauté in 1 oz. butter, turning occasionally so that they cook evenly. Above all, be careful the butter stays light brown and does not burn or get too dark.

Arrange noisettes on a serving dish. Add melted meat jelly to fat left in the pan and stir well. Boil for a few seconds, shaking the pan well. Remove from heat and add a few pieces of butter gradually. If the butter separates from the meat jelly and becomes oily, bind with 2 tablespoons hot water, shaking the pan well. Pour sauce over noisettes.

The following are suitable garnishes: asparagus tips, peas, truffle, foie gras and *pommes de terre parisienne* (see page 654).

Cassoulet

HARICOT BEAN STEW

Editor's note This recipe is somewhat complicated, but *Ma Cuisine* would not be complete without this traditional dish which originated in Languedoc. Below is M. Escoffier's version. The leg of lamb should be braising while the haricot beans are cooking.

———————— 2 lb. haricot beans, 8 oz. bacon rind, 12 oz. bacon fat, 1 small garlic sausage, 1 onion, 2 cloves, 2 sprigs parsley, 2 cloves garlic, water, salt, pepper, 1 leg lamb, 1—2 tablespoons tomato purée, dried breadcrumbs

Soak the beans for 5—6 hours. Put bacon rind into a dish with the bacon fat, cover with boiling water and leave for 10 minutes, then drain and leave to cool.

When beans are ready, put into a pan with the bacon rind, bacon fat, garlic sausage, onion stuck with cloves, parsley and garlic. Cover with warm water, season carefully, having regard to the salty bacon fat. Cover and cook over very gentle heat.

Meanwhile braise the leg of lamb in another pan. About 20 minutes before serving, remove lamb from the braise and keep hot with a little of its cooking liquor. Put remaining liquor into a large pan, skim, and add tomato purée.

Drain the beans, remove the sausage, bacon fat and rind, onion and sprigs of parsley. Put the bacon fat with the meat and put the beans in with the liquor left from the braise. If the liquor is too thick, add some of the water in which the beans were cooked. Simmer for 15—20 minutes.

To serve Cut the bacon rind into 2-inch squares and line the bottom and sides of a large, deep serving dish.

Put the beans and sliced sausage in the bottom. Cut the leg of lamb into slices and arrange on top. Moisten with a little of the cooking liquor and cover with dried breadcrumbs.

Put into a hot oven for 5—6 minutes to brown the crumbs, then serve at once.

If liked, 1—2 preserved goose thighs can be added to the cassoulet.

Editor's note Traditionally there is a special dish for serving this cassoulet called a *cassole d'isse.*

Note The preparation of a cassoulet, varies slightly according to the custom in various districts. Instead of using braised leg of lamb, it can be cut into pieces, mixed with some pieces of breast of mutton and cooked as for a ragoût.

The bean and bacon fat would then be added after they had been cooked.

The dish is then finished off with breadcrumbs and browned as described above.

Daube à l'avignonnaise

MUTTON COOKED IN RED WINE

This dish is prepared in exactly the same way as *daube à la provençal* (see page 296), except that pieces of beef are replaced by pieces of mutton cut from the leg.

The accompaniments of the one suit the other, but the most delicious accompaniment is a dish of small white Cavaillon haricot beans cooked with a piece of streaky bacon and a small garlic sausage.

Hachis de mouton

MUTTON HASH

1 lb. lean roast mutton, 1 oz. butter, 2 tablespoons very finely chopped onion, salt, pepper, nutmeg, 3—4 tablespoons demi-glace sauce with tomato (see page 22), parsley

Cube meat very small. Heat the butter, add the onion, and when it begins to brown add the meat. Season with salt, pepper and nutmeg and heat through thoroughly, stirring from time to time. Finally add the sauce. Pour into a serving dish and sprinkle with chopped parsley.

Instead of adding demi-glace sauce, some mashed potato or *pommes de terre Macaire* (see page 651) sautéed in butter, can be substituted.

Fried or poached eggs are sometimes served with hashed mutton, in which case serve with demi-glace sauce with tomato (see page 22), to which a pinch of chopped tarragon has been added.

Hachis ménagère

MUTTON HASH WITH POTATOES

Make the hash and thicken with mashed potatoes. Turn it into a fireproof dish, sprinkle with dried breadcrumbs mixed with grated cheese, brush with melted butter and brown under the grill (U.S. broiler).

Hachis à la provençale

MUTTON HASH PROVENÇAL STYLE

1 lb. cooked meat, meat jelly (see page 21), 10 tomatoes, 2—3 tablespoons oil, salt and pepper, pinch chopped parsley, breadcrumbs, cheese

Prepare the meat for the hash and thicken with meat jelly.

Select tomatoes of medium size, and cut a slice from the stem end. Squeeze gently to extract the seeds and all moisture. Heat the oil, put in the tomatoes, with the cut sides downwards. Cook very slowly for 8 — 10 minutes. Then, turn them over, season with salt and pepper and the parsley and arrange on a fireproof dish, cut side uppermost. Fill with hash and sprinkle with dried breadcrumbs and grated cheese. Sprinkle with a little of the oil left from cooking the tomatoes and brown under the grill (U.S. broiler) before serving.

Hachis à la turque

TURKISH STYLE MUTTON HASH

4 oz. rice, 1 lb. cooked mutton, tomato sauce (see page 132), 2 aubergines, oil, breadcrumbs, parsley

Cook rice as for pilaf (see page 669). Mince the meat and prepare the hash as described above but use tomato sauce instead of demi-glace. Mix rice with the meat mixture.

Cut aubergines in half lengthwise, score the flesh and fry aubergines lightly in the oil. Remove the flesh, chop finely and add to the meat.

Arrange aubergine cases on a serving dish. Fill with meat mixture and sprinkle with breadcrumbs. Add a few drops of oil and put into a moderate oven for 10−12 minutes.
Sprinkle with parsley before serving.

Le hachis de mouton de grand'mère

GRANDMOTHER'S MUTTON HASH

10 good-sized potatoes baked in their jackets, butter, salt, pepper, 1 lb. mutton hash (see page 351), dried breadcrumbs, grated cheese

Cut a slice from the top of the potatoes, scoop out centres and mix with some butter and seasoning, then half fill the cases. Top with the hash. Sprinkle with mixture of breadcrumbs and cheese, dot with butter and brown in the oven.

Haricot de mouton à l'ancienne

HARICOT OF MUTTON THE OLD-FASHIONED WAY

4 oz. bacon fat, 2 lb. breast or shoulder of mutton, flour, lard, 15 small onions, 1¼ pints (U.S. 3⅛ cups) hot water, salt, pepper, *bouquet garni*, 1 clove garlic, 2−3 tablespoons tomato purée, 1 lb. cooked haricot beans

Cut the bacon fat into large cubes and blanch. Cut meat into pieces as for a ragoût (see page 356) and coat with flour.

Heat a little lard, add bacon fat and onions, sauté until browned. Remove to a plate and brown the meat in remaining fat. Pour off excess fat, add the hot water, seasoning, *bouquet garni* and garlic. Bring to boiling point, stirring well, then cover and simmer for 45 minutes.

Remove meat to a casserole and add the bacon fat and onions. Add the tomato purée to the liquor left in the pan and pour over the meat. Cover and finish the cooking in a moderate oven.

Just before serving, add the cooked haricot beans and simmer for 2−3 minutes.

IRISH STEW

2½—3 lb. boned breast or shoulder of mutton, 2 lb. potatoes, 4 Spanish onions, *bouquet garni*, seasonings, about 1½ pints (U.S. 3¾ cups) water

Cut meat as for a ragoût (see page 356), slice potatoes and onions thinly. Arrange in layers in a good-sized casserole. Add *bouquet garni* and seasonings and the water (the meat and vegetables should be barely covered). Cover tightly and cook in a slow oven for 1½ hours.

Serve in the casserole.

MOUSSAKA

Moussaka can be prepared in several ways and this is the simplest.

Mutton hash (see page 351), demi-glace sauce with tomato (see page 22), 6 aubergines, seasoning, flour, oil, chopped parsley, tomatoes (optional)

Prepare a mutton hash, and bind with a demi-glace sauce with tomato.

Peel the aubergines, cut them into fairly thick slices, season, coat with flour and fry in oil.

Arrange the aubergines in a shallow fireproof dish, putting the hash in layers alternating with the aubergine slices. Place the dish in a pan of hot water and put into a moderate oven for 15—20 minutes. Before serving sprinkle with parsley.

If liked, the moussaka can be garnished with tomatoes. Cut in half, remove the seeds, season with salt and pepper and fry lightly in oil. Arrange in a ring on the moussaka.

Navarin ou ragoût de mouton
NAVARIN OR RAGOÛT OF MUTTON

3 lb. mutton, cut from the shoulder or breast, clarified butter, salt, freshly ground pepper, pinch sugar, 2 tablespoons flour, 1½ pints (U.S. 3¾ cups) water, 4—5 tablespoons tomato purée (optional), parsley, 1 bay leaf, 1 large clove garlic, 15 fairly small onions, 1 lb. potatoes

Cut meat into fairly large pieces and brown quickly in a little clarified fat. Add salt, pepper and sugar. Pour off any excess fat, add flour and cook for a few moments, then add the water, tomato purée, parsley, bay leaf and crushed garlic. Bring to boiling point, stirring, then simmer gently for about 1 hour.

Remove meat to a casserole, add the onions browned in butter, and potatoes cut into the shape and size of pigeons' eggs.

Strain the liquor in which meat was cooked and pour over contents of the casserole. Cover very tightly and continue cooking in a moderate oven for about 30—40 minutes.

Remove from heat, let stand for 5—6 minutes, then remove as much of the surface fat as possible before serving.

Navarin printanier
NAVARIN OF MUTTON WITH CARROTS AND TURNIPS

Ingredients as given in the preceding recipe, but with only 8 oz. small potatoes and in addition carrots and turnips, sufficient to give 20 rounds of each, cut about the same size as the potatoes, and 8 oz. peas

Prepare exactly as described for navarin of mutton (see page 354), but baste the vegetables well with the liquor during the last part of the cooking.

Pilaw de mouton à la turque
TURKISH PILAF OF MUTTON

1 leg or shoulder of mutton, 2½ pints (U.S. 6¼ cups) water, 8 oz. fat from the sheep's tail or 3—4 tablespoons butter or oil, 4—5 tablespoons chopped onion, salt, pepper, *bouquet garni* of 2 sprigs parsley, 1 bay leaf and 2 sprigs thyme, 2 cloves garlic, 2 small red peppers, 5—6 tablespoons tomato purée, 12 oz. Carolina rice, pinch saffron

Bone meat, and cut into pieces about the size of a pigeon's egg (there should be about 3 lb. meat). Put bones and trimmings into a pan, add the water and boil well to make stock.

If fat from sheep's tail is used, chop finely and melt it, otherwise melt the butter or oil. Add the meat and onion and cook for 15—20 minutes. Add seasoning, *bouquet garni*, crushed garlic and seeded and chopped red peppers.

Add stock and tomato purée (the meat should be just covered by the stock). Cover and simmer very gently for 1¼ hours. Add well washed rice and saffron and continue to simmer a further 25 minutes.

Ragoût de mouton au riz à la française

MUTTON RAGOÛT WITH RICE

About 3 lb. mutton, cut from the shoulder and breast, lard or dripping, 4 tablespoons chopped onion, salt, pepper, 2½ pints (U.S. 6¼ cups) water, *bouquet garni*, 2—3 tablespoons tomato purée (optional), 12 oz. Carolina rice

Cut meat into fairly large pieces and brown lightly in fat. Add the onion and season with salt and pepper. When meat is sufficiently brown, add the water, *bouquet garni* and tomato pureé. Cover and cook for 1½ hours. Add carefully washed rice and continue cooking for 25 minutes. Remove from the heat, allow to stand for a few moments, then skim before serving.

Preparation of this kind of ragoût or pilaf varies with different Oriental peoples. Some add aubergines, vegetable marrows and sweet red peppers cut into strips; others, ladies' fingers or okra, and small carrots. These ingredients are cooked with pieces of meat.

Peas and flageolets, cooked separately, may also be added.

Cervelles d'agneau

LAMB'S BRAINS

Although all the recipes for calf's brains apply to lamb's brains, here is a new recipe for lamb's brains:

Cervelles d'agneau marquise

LAMB'S BRAINS MARQUISE

6 fresh brains, *court-bouillon*, lemon juice, flour, butter, cream, béchamel sauce (see page 23), 6 hard-boiled eggs, 3 medium-sized truffles, chopped parsley

Soak the brains, remove membrane and poach in *court-bouillon* to which a little lemon juice has been added. Drain and dry them, coat with flour and brown in clarified butter.

Add a little cream to 1 pint (U.S. 2½ cups) béchamel sauce, then 4 sliced hard-boiled eggs and the sliced truffles. Heat all together.

Put some of the sauce into the serving dish and arrange the brains on top. Cover with remaining sauce.

Garnish with sieved yolk of 2 hard-boiled eggs and a little chopped parsley.

CARRÉ D'AGNEAU
LOIN OF LAMB

Loin of baby lamb is preferably pot-roasted or roasted. All the garnishes for large joints of lamb are suitable.

Carré d'agneau bonne femme
LOIN OF LAMB WITH ONIONS AND POTATOES

Loin of lamb, salt, pepper, butter, 10 small onions, 2 oz. bacon fat, 2 medium-sized potatoes, 3—4 tablespoons well reduced stock

Shorten and trim the loin, season, and cook in butter for 5—6 minutes to seal the outside. Add onions, browned in butter.

Cube bacon fat, blanch and brown in butter, then add to the meat. Add potatoes, cubed or cut into olive shapes.

Brush with melted butter and cook in a moderate oven. To make gravy, add the stock to the liquor in the pan.

Carré d'agneau boulangère
LOIN OF LAMB BOULANGÈRE

Brown the loin in butter as in the previous recipe. Surround with thinly sliced onions cooked in butter without browning, and thinly sliced potatoes, taking into account the size of the joint when deciding upon the amount of vegetables. Cook in a moderate oven, basting from time to time.

Just before serving, add a few tablespoons well reduced stock.

Carré d'agneau grillé

GRILLED (U.S. BROILED) LOIN OF LAMB

Shorten and trim the loin, season, brush with melted butter and grill (U.S. broil) gently. When nearly ready, sprinkle with breadcrumbs and continue cooking until golden brown.

Serve with any garnish you choose.

Carré d'agneau Mireille

LOIN OF LAMB WITH POTATOES AND ARTICHOKES

▬▬▬▬▬▬▬▬ Loin of baby lamb, butter, potatoes, artichoke bottoms, 3 – 4 tablespoons well reduced stock

Brown loin in butter as above, then remove from baking tin. Line the bottom of the tin with a layer of potatoes, cut first into cork shapes, then sliced thinly, and ⅓ quantity of thinly sliced artichoke bottoms. Replace the meat, brush with butter and cook in a moderate oven. Add the stock to the liquid in the pan, for the gravy.

Carré d'agneau mistral

LOIN OF LAMB WITH POTATOES, ARTICHOKES AND TRUFFLES

Proceed exactly as for *carré d'agneau Mireille*, but instead of adding stock to the meat juices, add some slices of fresh truffles, gently heated in rather thick veal gravy. A few tablespoons boiling fresh cream may also be added.

The truffle season is when the Provençal lamb is at its best.

CÔTELETTES D'AGNEAU
LAMB CUTLETS

Baby lamb cutlets are generally sautéed in butter, either as they are, or dipped in flour, beaten egg and breadcrumbs (it is usual to serve two lamb cutlets per person).

Suitable garnishes are: asparagus tips with butter, or with cream, fresh peas, thinly sliced artichoke bottoms sprinkled with meat jelly (see page 21), any kind of potatoes, mushroom purée with cream, chestnut purée, chicory, spinach, morels with cream, etc.

Côtelettes d'agneau en crépinettes

LAMB CUTLETS IN CRÉPINETTES

——————— Baby lamb cutlets, butter, sausage skin (optional), sausage meat, chopped truffle

Quickly sauté the cutlets in butter. Wrap each one in a triangle of sausage skin, between 2 thin layers of very thin sausage meat, to which the truffle is added. Sprinkle with melted butter and grill (U.S. broil) gently.

Serve at the same time mashed potatoes and *sauce périgueux* (see page 28).

If the sausage skin is omitted, cook as follows:

Sauté cutlets quickly in butter. Add a little chopped truffle to some sausage meat, and press a thin layer on both sides of the cutlets. Brush with butter and grill (U.S. broil) gently.

Serve with mashed potato and *sauce périgueux* (see page 28).

Côtelettes d'agneau maréchal

LAMB CUTLETS IN EGG AND BREADCRUMBS

——————— Baby lamb cutlets, egg, breadcrumbs, butter, truffles, meat jelly (see page 21), asparagus tips

Dip cutlets in beaten egg and freshly made breadcrumbs, and cook in clarified butter, turning them so that they are evenly cooked and a nice golden colour.

Arrange in a ring with a slice of truffle on each and pour over a meat jelly to which a little butter has been added.

Put buttered asparagus tips in the centre of the dish.

Côtelettes d'agneau Sarah Bernhardt

LAMB CUTLETS WITH FOIE GRAS PURÉE

12 small lamb cutlets, butter, foie gras purée, meat jelly (see page 21), sauce parisienne (see page 22), flour, egg, breadcrumbs

Cook cutlets quickly in butter. Cover on both sides with a little foie gras purée to which a little meat jelly and just a suspicion of Parisian sauce has been added. Dip in flour, coat with egg and breadcrumbs and fry in clarified butter.

To accompany this dish, add some thinly sliced, freshly cooked artichoke bottoms and some thin slices of truffle, to the Parisian sauce.

Côtelettes d'agneau Tosca

LAMB CUTLETS WITH FOIE GRAS PURÉE AND HAM

Prepare the cutlets as in the preceding recipe but add a few tablespoons of cooked lean ham, chopped very finely, to the purée of foie gras. Coat with flour and egg and breadcrumbs and fry in clarified butter.

Arrange cutlets in a ring, and cover with a little meat jelly (see page 21), to which a little butter and a squeeze of lemon juice has been added. In the centre, put some buttered asparagus tips and a small amount of truffle cut into julienne.

Côtelettes d'agneau à la Talleyrand-Périgord

LAMB CUTLETS WITH BRAISED SWEETBREAD

Prepare cutlets as instructed for *côtelettes d'agneau Tosca* (see page 360), coat with breadcrumbs and cook in butter. Put a small slice of braised sweetbread on each one and cover with a few tablespoons of meat jelly (see page 21) to which a little butter has been added.

Serve with a garnish of truffles coated with a demi-glace sauce (see page 22), to which the cooking liquor of the sweetbreads has been added.

As an accompaniment serve a dish of buttered peas.

AGNEAU DE LAIT
BABY LAMB

BABY LAMB

The joints of baby lamb are the same as those for sheep, namely:
The baron: two legs and the saddle
The double: two legs together
The quarter: a leg to which is attached half the saddle.

Large joints of lamb should be pot-roasted or roasted and the best accompaniment is their cooking liquor.

Peas, cooked as desired, asparagus tips, artichoke bottoms, mushrooms, potatoes cooked in various ways, broad beans, flageolets, tomatoes, aubergines, vegetable marrows, braised lettuces, vegetable purées or chestnut purée, are all suitable to serve with these joints.

ÉPAULES D'AGNEAU DE LAIT
SHOULDER OF BABY LAMB

Editor's note Baby lamb, so popular in France, is seldom obtainable in Great Britain and America.

These recipes, especially the following one, may be quite impracticable for the British or American housewife, but *Ma Cuisine* as written by M. Escoffier would be quite incomplete without them and they are therefore included for your interest.

Usually shoulders of baby lamb are not boned. They are treated like *carré d'agneau boulangère* (see page 357), and grilled (U.S. broiled). This is, however, a way of cooking shoulder of lamb which does require them to be boned.

Épaule d'agneau en canetons

SHOULDER OF LAMB AS 'DUCKLING'

—————— You will need for 6 persons:
2 shoulders baby lamb, seasoning, veal, pork, 2 egg yolks, spices,
2—3 tablespoons breadcrumbs, onion, carrot, bacon rinds, *bouquet
garni*, 6 tablespoons white wine, stock, 1 hard-boiled egg, demi-glace
sauce (see page 22)

Cut off part of the front of the feet, leaving a small piece of bone which
will form the beak of the 'duckling'. Bone the shoulders, keeping the
piece of bone to which the beak is adhering, and which will form the
neck of the 'duckling'. Scallop the end of the shoulder-blade, which will
be adapted after cooking to give the illusion of a duckling's tail. Season
the meat.

Prepare a forcemeat with the veal, pork, egg yolks, salt, pepper,
spices, and breadcrumbs (see page 56), and mix all thoroughly together.
Sew this inside the shoulders and truss with the bone uppermost, so
that the meat takes the shape of a duckling. Arrange the shoulders in
a braising pan on a bed of thinly sliced onions, carrots, few bacon
rinds, the scalloped shoulder-blades and a *bouquet garni*.

Add the white wine, reduce this slightly and then add enough stock
to come half-way up.

Put the braising pan into a moderate oven and cook, basting the
shoulders frequently.

Just before serving, untruss the shoulders, cut them slightly underneath
to give the necessary balance. Imitate eyes with the whites of hard-boiled
egg, fix the tail and serve on an oval dish. Skim the cooking liquor,
add a few tablespoons much reduced demi-glace sauce and strain over
the meat.

GIGOT D'AGNEAU DE LAIT
LEG OF BABY LAMB

Leg of baby lamb is either roasted or pot-roasted in butter. All the
garnishes or sauces given for barons, doubles, quarters or loins of lamb
are applicable to the leg. Besides these there are the following recipes.

Gigot d'agneau à la normande
LEG OF LAMB NORMANDY STYLE

1 leg baby lamb, butter, 3—4 tablespoons Calvados (apple jack), 5—6 tablespoons veal stock, 2 tablespoons meat jelly (see page 21), 6 tablespoons *crème d'ysigny*, breadcrumbs fried in butter

Choose as fat a leg of lamb as possible, season, and cook in butter over low heat, basting frequently, and being careful the butter does not brown. Remove the meat from the pan and put into a casserole. Pour off three-quarters butter in which the meat was cooked. Add Calvados and stock to the remaining butter and mix well. Bring to boiling point, boil for 1 minute, then add the meat jelly and *crème d'ysigny*, and pour over the meat. Put into a fairly hot oven for 5—6 minutes, basting frequently, then cover with the breadcrumbs.

Serve in the casserole.

Mashed, sauté or *pommes de terre Byron* (see page 645) asparagus tips, peas, flageolets or fried cèpes or mushrooms are suitable accompaniments.

It may also be served with thinly sliced apples sautéed in butter.

Gigot d'agneau des cigaliers
LEG OF LAMB OF THE LITERARY SOCIETY OF THE 'CIGALIERS'

1 leg baby lamb, butter, 4—5 truffles, salt, freshly ground pepper, Armagnac brandy, garlic, 3 tablespoons white wine, 5—6 tablespoons veal stock

Cook the lamb in butter, basting frequently and being careful the butter does not burn.

Slice the truffles, season and sprinkle with a few drops Armagnac. Rub round the serving dish with garlic, put in the truffle and keep hot. When the meat is cooked, remove from the pan and keep hot.

Pour off two-thirds butter from the pan, add the wine, stir well, then reduce by half.

Add the stock and bring to boiling point. Cut the meat into fairly thick slices and arrange in the serving dish interspersing with the slices of truffle. Pour the sauce over, cover and reheat for 5—6 minutes.

Serve with a chestnut purée (see page 637), or with noodles.

Note The garlic may be omitted.

Épigrammes d'agneau

EPIGRAMS OF LAMB

─────────── You will need for 6 persons: 1 breast of lamb, 6 lamb cutlets, little béchamel sauce (see page 23), egg, breadcrumbs, butter, 3−4 tablespoons veal stock, meat jelly (see page 21), squeeze lemon juice

Braise the lamb or cook in stock. Bone, press between two plates and leave to get cold. Then cut into 6 pieces as nearly as possible the size and shape of the cutlets. Cover lightly with béchamel sauce, dip in egg and breadcrumbs and brown on both sides in clarified butter. Meanwhile sauté the cutlets. Arrange the epigrams on a serving dish alternately with the cutlets. Garnish with asparagus tips, peas, broad beans, macédoine of vegetables, etc. To make the sauce add the veal stock to the butter left in the pan, and mix well. Add the meat jelly and stir till boiling. Add a little butter in small pieces and a squeeze of lemon juice. Serve this sauce separately.

PIEDS ET LANGUE D'AGNEAU
LAMB'S TROTTERS AND TONGUES

Lamb's trotters and tongues are prepared and cooked in the same way as sheep's trotters and tongue (see pages 345−6 and 282−3).

RIS D'AGNEAU
LAMB'S SWEETBREADS

Soak the sweetbreads in cold running water for about 1 hour, then cover with cold water and bring to boiling point. Drain, dry and leave to cool. They are then cooked in butter, or braised like calf's sweetbreads (see pages 320−326), or cooked *à la poulette* (see page 265).

Ris d'agneau en pilaw

LAMB'S SWEETBREADS IN PILAF

Prepare the sweetbreads as above and cook in butter.

Have ready some rice, cooked as for pilaf (see page 669), and mix with the sweetbread in the proportion of two-thirds rice and one-third sweetbread. Serve with either tomato (see page 132), curry (see page 32), or paprika sauce (see page 32).

Ris d'agneau poulette

LAMB'S SWEETBREADS WITH ONIONS AND MUSHROOMS

8 oz. lamb's sweetbreads, butter, salt, pepper, 1 tablespoon flour, ½ wine glass white wine, white stock, 6 small onions, 1 small *bouquet garni*, 2 egg yolks, 2—3 tablespoons cream, few cooked mushrooms, squeeze lemon juice

Prepare the sweetbreads as above. Melt 1 oz. butter, add sweetbreads and sauté for a few seconds. Add seasoning and flour, cook gently for 2 minutes. Remove from heat, stir in the wine and enough white stock just to cover. (If stock is not available use hot water.)

Return to heat and stir till boiling. Add onions and *bouquet garni*. Cover and cook gently for 25 minutes.

Remove sweetbreads and onion from the sauce and keep warm.

Remove the *bouquet garni* from the sauce and thicken with egg yolks and cream (instead of using cream, yolks could be mixed with a little of the sauce before adding to the rest).

Return sweetbreads and onions to the sauce, add mushrooms. Reheat, and finish the sauce with a few pieces of butter and the lemon juice.

Vol-au-vent de ris d'agneau

LAMB'S SWEETBREADS VOL-AU-VENT

You will need for 6—8 persons:
1 lb. lamb's sweetbreads, butter, *sauce parisienne* (see page 22), 15 cooked mushrooms, 4 oz. truffle, 3—4 tablespoons Madeira, 1 vol-au-vent case

Prepare sweetbreads (see page 364), then sauté gently in butter. Add a little butter to the *sauce parisienne* (or if preferred use a cream béchamel sauce (see page 23)). Stir in the sweetbreads, cut into pieces, mushrooms, sliced truffles and Madeira.

Heat all together and pour into the vol-au-vent case.

Timbale de ris d'agneau à la Radziwill

TIMBALE OF LAMB'S SWEETBREADS

1 lb. lamb's sweetbreads, onions, carrots, white wine, veal stock, *bouquet garni*, 36 medium-sized crayfish, *court-bouillon*, crayfish butter (see page 114), 4 oz. macaroni, 4 oz. grated Parmesan cheese, truffles, butter, ¾ pint (U.S. 1⅞ cups) demi-glace sauce (see page 22)

Prepare the sweetbreads, then put on to a bed of thinly sliced onions and carrots, with 1 wine glass white wine and enough veal stock to cover. Add *bouquet garni* and braise in a moderate oven for 20−25 minutes.

Cook the crayfish in *court-bouillon* with white wine. Remove the shells, and use to make the crayfish butter.

Cook the macaroni in boiling salted water for 10 minutes, drain, return to the pan, cover with boiling stock, and continue cooking until macaroni is just tender. Strain, to make sure there is no excess liquid, then add the crayfish butter and cheese.

When sweetbreads are cooked, put into a pan with the peeled and sliced truffles, crayfish and a little butter and keep hot.

Add the liquor in which the sweetbreads were cooked to the demi-glace sauce. Reduce it a little, then pour over the sweetbreads.

To serve Put two-thirds macaroni in a dish. Put sweetbreads on top with some of the sauce and the garnish. Cover with remaining macaroni, sprinkle lightly with a little grated cheese and finish with the rest of the sauce, crayfish and truffle.

SELLE D'AGNEAU
SADDLE OF LAMB

Saddle of baby lamb, when it is real Pauillac lamb, will always find a place on the most select menus.

The best way of cooking it is to roast on a spit or pot-roast it in butter.

The best accompaniments for saddle of lamb are: asparagus tips, fresh peas, either plain boiled or cooked *à la française* (see page 642), new potatoes and carrots, young broad beans, purée of flageolets, chestnut purée (see page 637), *nouilles à l'alsacienne* (see page 677).

All these vegetables are usually served separately, save in the following recipes.

Selle d'agneau duchesse

SADDLE OF LAMB WITH ARTICHOKES AND MUSHROOMS

1 saddle of baby lamb, seasoning, butter, 6 artichoke bottoms, lemon juice, 1 tablespoon flour, white stock, 2—3 tablespoons demi-glace sauce (see page 22), truffle, tongue, cooked mushrooms, béchamel sauce (see page 23), grated cheese, 6 cooked tartlet cases, asparagus tips, 3—4 tablespoons white wine, 6 tablespoons brown veal stock, meat jelly (see page 21)

Trim the saddle, season, and cook slowly in butter, taking care the butter does not burn.

Cook the artichoke bottoms for 15 minutes in 1¾ pints (U.S. 4¼ cups) salted water to which some lemon juice and the flour has been added. Drain and put into a well buttered pan, add enough white stock to cover the artichokes. Cover the pan and finish the cooking slowly. Remove the artichokes and add the demi-glace to the liquor in which they were cooked.

Chop some truffles, tongue and mushrooms, mix together and bind with a little béchamel sauce.

Grill (U.S. broil) artichoke bottoms with mixture, sprinkle with cheese, brush with melted butter and glaze in the oven.

Fill the tartlet cases with buttered asparagus tips.

When the saddle is cooked, remove from the pan and keep hot.

Drain off two-thirds butter left in pan. Add wine and stock, stir well and bring to the boil. Add the liquor in which the artichokes were cooked, bring to boiling point again and then strain.

Place the saddle on a serving dish, arrange the artichoke bottoms and asparagus tartlets alternately round the edge, put a slice of truffle on each artichoke and cover with a thin layer of meat jelly to which a little butter has been added.

Pour a little of the sauce round the dish and serve the rest separately with a dish of *pommes de terre parisienne* (see page 654).

Selle d'agneau à la génoise
SADDLE OF LAMB GENOESE STYLE
1 saddle baby lamb, butter, 4—5 tablespoons white wine, 4—5 tablespoons brown veal stock, 8 small tomatoes, 4 tablespoons oil, seasoning, *riz à la piémontaise* (see page 668), grated Parmesan cheese

Trim the saddle and cook in butter, then remove and keep hot.
Pour off two-thirds butter, left in the pan. Add the wine and veal stock, stir well and bring to boiling point. Keep hot.

Cut a slice from the stalk ends of the tomatoes, squeeze gently to extract the juice and the seeds. Place cut side down into a frying pan in which the oil has been heated. Cook slowly for 10 minutes, then turn over, season and finish the cooking. Mix some Parmesan cheese with the rice and fill the tomato cases with it. Put the saddle on to a serving dish, arrange the tomatoes round. Pour a little of the sauce round the dish and serve the rest separately. Serve with plainly boiled peas.

Selle d'agneau Judic
SADDLE OF LAMB WITH BRAISED LETTUCE STUFFED WITH RICE
1 saddle baby lamb, 5—6 tablespoons white wine, 6 tablespoons light veal stock, braised lettuce stuffed with rice (see page 633), truffled foie gras, lamb's sweetbreads sautéed in butter, beef marrow sauce (see page 28)

Cook the saddle as in the previous recipe and keep it hot. Pour off two-thirds butter from pan, add wine, reduce a little, then add stock, bring to boiling point and boil a few minutes.

Put the saddle on to an oval serving dish and garnish with the lettuce, foie gras and sweetbreads. Pour a little of the gravy round the dish, and add the rest to the sauce. Coat the lettuce with some of this sauce and serve the rest separately.

Serve with *petits pois à la française* (see page 642).

Selle d'agneau Orloff
SADDLE OF LAMB WITH SOUBISE SAUCE
1 saddle baby lamb, butter, cream, soubise sauce (see page 35), truffle, grated Parmesan cheese, 4—5 tablespoons white wine, stock, 3 tablespoons meat jelly (see page 21)

Cook the saddle in butter and prepare as described for *selle de veau Metternich* (see page 329).

Cut the fillets into ½-inch slices.

Add a little cream to the soubise sauce and put into the cavity of the saddle, then replace the slices of meat interspersing each one with a slice of truffle and a spoonful of sauce. The saddle is now restored to its original shape.

Arrange slices of truffle down each side and coat lightly with sauce, sprinkle with cheese, brush with butter and glaze in the oven.

Pour off the excess butter from the pan in which the saddle was cooked, add the white wine, mix well and bring to boiling point. Add the stock, meat jelly and a little butter. Bring to boiling point again and serve separately.

Buttered asparagus tips, or small patties filled with asparagus tips, may be served as an accompaniment.

Selle d'agneau de lait Édouard VII

SADDLE OF BABY LAMB WITH TRUFFLED FOIE GRAS

————— 1 saddle baby lamb, salt, pepper, spice, truffled foie gras, Madeira, stock, 2 lb. shin of veal, braised, 1 calf's foot

Bone the saddle completely from the underside, leaving the skin intact, and season lightly.

Season the foie gras and marinate for some hours in Madeira. Tie in muslin and poach for 18 minutes in good stock. Leave to cool in the liquor.

When cold, remove the foie gras, place it on the centre of the saddle and re-form into its original shape. Tie with string and cook slowly in butter.

While the saddle is cooking, make some stock with the braised veal and calf's foot.

Add 1 pint (U.S. 2½ cups) of this stock to the liquor left in the pan in which the saddle was cooked. Boil for 2 minutes.

When the saddle is cooked, remove the string and place it in an oval casserole. Pour the stock over, leave to settle for a few minutes then remove the fat which will have formed on top.

Serve in the casserole.

Noisettes d'agneau ou plutôt mignonnettes d'agneau

NOISETTES OF LAMB OR MIGNONNETTES OF LAMB

———————— Salt, pepper, noisettes of baby lamb,* flour, butter, croûtons fried
in butter, 3—4 tablespoons white wine, 3—4 tablespoons veal stock,
3—4 tablespoons meat jelly (see page 21)
* Noisettes of baby lamb are preferably cut from the first ribs of
the loin allowing 2 pieces for each person.

Season the noisettes, dip in flour and sauté in butter. Arrange in a
serving dish on croûtons of the same size. Add the wine to the butter
left in the pan, mix well and bring to boiling point. Add stock meat
jelly and a little butter. Bring to boiling point again and pour over the
noisettes.

Serve with asparagus tips or plainly boiled peas.

PRÉPARATIONS DIVERSES
DE L'AGNEAU

VARIOUS DISHES MADE
WITH LAMB

Blanquette d'agneau de lait

BLANQUETTE OF BABY LAMB

———————— 1 shoulder and 2 breasts baby lamb, 1 oz. butter, salt, pepper, 2 tablespoons flour, 3 tablespoons white wine, stock or water, *bouquet garni*,
15 small onions, cooked mushrooms, 2—3 egg yolks

Cut the meat into pieces of about 2—3 oz.

Heat the butter in a pan, put in the meat, season and leave for a few
minutes for the meat to absorb the butter. Add the flour and cook
for 2 minutes. Add the wine and enough stock or water to cover the
meat. Add *bouquet garni* and onions, cover and cook over a low heat.
When the meat is cooked, put it into a serving dish with the onions
and mushrooms – which are optional. Remove the *bouquet garni* from
the stock and thicken with the egg yolks beaten with a little water or
mushroom liquor. Add a little butter and strain the sauce over the meat.

Nouilles à l'alsacienne (see page 677) or rice are suitable accompaniments.

For curry, pilaf and other stews made with baby lamb, it is advisable
to treat the meat like sautéed chicken; that is, it should be cooked in
butter before the sauce is added, and the meat, owing to its delicacy,
should not boil in the sauce.

Currie d'agneau

LAMB CURRY

1 shoulder of lamb, salt, pepper, 1 oz. butter, 2 tablespoons finely
chopped onion, 1 dessertspoon curry powder, 1 tablespoon flour,
½ pint (U.S. 1¼ cups) stock, 6 tablespoons cream

Cut meat into cubes the size of a walnut, season with salt and pepper.
Heat the butter in a pan and sauté meat slowly.

Fry the onion in butter until it begins to brown, then add the curry
powder and flour and cook for a few minutes. Add the stock, stir till
boiling and boil for 8 – 10 minutes. Strain over the meat, and lastly
add the cream.

Serve with *riz à l'indienne* (see page 668).

Pilaw d'agneau

PILAF OF LAMB

1 shoulder of lamb, butter, 2 tablespoons finely chopped onion, 8 oz.
Carolina rice, ¾ pint (U.S. 1⅞ cups) consommé

Cut meat as described above for the curry and cook slowly in butter.

Brown the onion in butter, add the rice, washed quickly in warm
water and well drained. Stir well until rice is impregnated with the
butter. Add the consommé, cover and cook for 18 minutes. Mix the
meat with the rice and serve with tomato sauce (see page 132).

Sauté d'agneau aux petits pois

SAUTÉ OF LAMB WITH PEAS

Cut a shoulder of lamb into pieces the size of a small egg, season with
salt and pepper and cook in butter.

Cook 1 lb. *petits pois à la française* (see page 642), and mix with the
pieces of lamb just before serving.

Sauté d'agneau chasseur
SAUTÉ OF LAMB WITH WINE

1 shoulder of lamb, salt, pepper, butter, oil, 6—8 oz. mushrooms, 2 shallots, 1 small glass brandy, ¼ glass white wine, 3 tablespoons tomato sauce (see page 132), 5—6 tablespoons demi-glace sauce (see page 22), pinch chopped parsley

Cut meat into pieces the size of a small egg, season, and cook gently in butter and olive oil. When cooked, remove from the pan and add the mushrooms, peeled and finely sliced. Cook for a few moments, then add the shallots, sliced finely, brandy, white wine, tomato sauce and the demi-glace sauce. Reduce a little, then add the parsley. Put the pieces of lamb back into the saucepan with the sauce.

Serve with *tomates sautées à la provençal* (see page 660), buttered flageolets, Tyrolean sauce (see page 281).

LE PORC FRAIS
FRESH PORK

Pork entrées are always roasted, the loin and the fillet being the joints most generally used. Accompaniments may consist of vegetables, either fresh or dried, sauerkraut, red cabbage, Brussels sprouts, various purées or various Italian pasta, such as noodles, macaroni or polenta; *Sauce diquante* (see page 28) and tomato sauce (see page 32) are also suitable to serve.

In addition roast pork is often served with apple marmalade or with an apple sauce.

For sauce 3—4 medium-sized apples, 2—3 tablespoons butter, sugar to taste, ¼ pint (U.S. ⅝ cup) water

Peel, quarter and slice the apples thinly, and sauté for a few minutes in the butter. Add sugar to taste and the water. Cover and cook slowly.

Carré de porc rôti
ROAST LOIN OF PORK

When meat is cooked, sprinkle with salt and put on to a serving dish.

Pour off two-thirds fat. Add about ½ pint (U.S. 1¼ cups) stock or hot water, mix well and boil until the quantity is reduced by half. Pour a little over the joint and serve the rest separately.

Serve with spinach, chicory, mashed potatoes or a purée of peas, etc.

Carré de porc à la boulangère

LOIN OF PORK WITH VEGETABLES

Roast the loin in a fireproof dish. Half-way through the cooking, surround it with 4 – 5 white onions, finely sliced, and about 2 lb. potatoes cut into fairly thick slices. Continue the cooking, basting the meat and vegetables frequently.

When cooked, remove from the oven, add 5 – 6 tablespoons good gravy and sprinkle the vegetables with chopped parsley.

Serve in the dish in which it was cooked.

Carré de porc aux haricots blancs

LOIN OF PORK WITH WHITE HARICOT BEANS

Roast the loin in a fireproof dish. When nearly done surround with 1 – 1½ lb. cooked and well drained white haricot beans. Finish the cooking slowly, basting the beans with the gravy in the dish.

Serve in the dish in which it was cooked.

Carré de porc froid

COLD LOIN OF PORK

Roast pork served cold is an excellent dish for luncheon. It can be accompanied by: potato salad, red cabbage salad cut in julienne, with finely sliced apples, green salad or vegetable salad.

In addition, apple marmalade to which a little dry mustard has been added, horseradish sauce with cream (see page 44) or *sauce piquante* (see page 28) all go well with cold pork.

Cervelles de porc

PIG'S BRAINS

These are prepared and can be cooked in the same way as ox brains, calf's brains and lamb's brains.

Côtes de porc

PORK CHOPS

Pork chops may be grilled (U.S. broiled) or sautéed.

If they are to be grilled (U.S. broiled), they should be dipped in melted butter and then in breadcrumbs.

If they are to be sautéed, coat them first with flour, then dip in beaten egg and dried breadcrumbs.

The accompaniments suggested for roast loin of pork (see page 372) are also suitable for pork chops.

Épaule de porc

SHOULDER OF PORK

Boned shoulder, salted, rolled and smoked, is cooked like ham.

Salted shoulder of pork is used as an ingredient for *potée*, which is a kind of soup consisting of salt pork and vegetables. Cabbage soup is an example.

Fresh shoulder of pork is roasted like loin (see page 372) and served with the same accompaniments.

Filet de porc

FILLET OF PORK

Fillet of pork (U.S. pork tenderloin) is the part that goes from the ham to the first ribs and is treated like loin.

Foie de porc

PIG'S LIVER

Pig's liver is generally used in forcemeat. It may, however, be prepared like calf's liver (see pages 308 – 309).

Zampino

STUFFED PIG'S LEG

This is a speciality of Italian pork butchery.

It is cooked like ham (see below), but must be pricked all over with a trussing needle, then wrapped in muslin and tied with string.

Served hot, it is accompanied by a Madeira or a tomato sauce (see page 132) or a garnish of sauerkraut, braised cabbage, French beans, purée of peas or mashed potatoes.

Zampino is often served cold, especially as an hors-d'oeuvre, in which case it is cut as thinly as possible.

JAMBON
HAM

TO COOK A HAM

Soak ham in cold water for at least 6 hours.

Scrape and cover with fresh cold water. Bring to boiling point, then simmer over a low heat.

The time for cooking varies according to the quality and weight of the ham, but allow approximately 18 – 20 minutes to the pound.

The sweeter hams of Prague and Spain should only need 15 minutes per 1 lb.

If the ham is to be eaten cold, it should be left to cool in the cooking liquor.

Braisage du jambon

BRAISED HAM

If the ham is to be served cold, remove it from the water 30 minutes before the cooking time is complete. Remove the skin and trim ham. Then put into a braising pan just large enough to hold it, and add ½ pint (U.S. 1¼ cups) Madeira, sherry, port, Marsala or Chablis – according to taste. Cover closely and continue cooking very slowly for a further 30 minutes so that the ham is impregnated with the wine. It is then glazed before serving.

Remove any fat from the braising liquor, strain and add it to a light demi-glace sauce (see page 22) and serve as an accompaniment.

Glaçage du jambon

GLAZING THE HAM

The best method is to sprinkle the ham with icing sugar. When evenly covered, put the ham into a hot oven. The sugar caramelises at once, coating the ham with a golden layer which is very appetising in appearance and delicious to taste.

Braised and glazed ham is usually accompanied by one of the following: spinach, chicory, lettuce, peas, macédoine of vegetables, broad beans, braised cabbage, sauerkraut, purée of peas, noodles with butter, risotto, etc.

Note Demi-glace sauce (see page 22) added to the braising wine is an essential accompaniment.

Jambon à la choucroute

HAM WITH SAUERKRAUT

Cook the ham (see page 375). Remove the skin and trim ham. Add a little white wine to some demi-glace sauce (see page 22). Put a little on the serving dish and arrange the ham on top. Serve the rest of the sauce separately. Serve with sauerkraut and boiled potatoes.

Jambon aux épinards

HAM WITH SPINACH

Braise the ham in Madeira. The spinach should be served separately and may be served as leaf or purée.

Add the liquor from the braise to some demi-glace sauce (see page 22) and serve with the ham.

Jambon aux fèves de marais

HAM WITH BROAD BEANS

Braise the ham, glaze it and put on to a serving dish. Remove the skins from some cooked broad beans, add a little butter and sprinkle with chopped savory or parsley.

Serve the beans separately and also the slightly thickened liquor from the braise.

Jambon aux laitues

HAM WITH LETTUCE

Braise the ham in Madeira and glaze it. Add the braising liquor to a demi-glace sauce (see page 22) and pour some of it on the ham. Serve the rest separately.

As an accompaniment, serve braised lettuce (see page 632), or the lettuce may be stuffed with chicken and rice forcemeat (see page 156).

Jambon aux nouilles fraîches

HAM WITH FRESH NOODLES

Braise the ham in Marsala and glaze it. Reduce the braising liquor, add to a demi-glace sauce (see page 22) and pour a little of it on the ham. Serve the rest separately.

As an accompaniment, serve a dish of buttered noodles to which some cream and a small quantity of truffle cut into julienne has been added.

Jambon aux nouilles à la Rossini

HAM AND TOMATOES WITH NOODLES

Braise the ham in Marsala, glaze it and put on to a serving dish.

Reduce the braising liquor and add it to a demi-glace sauce (see page 22) with 2−3 tablespoons tomato sauce (see page 132). Pour a little over the ham and serve the rest separately.

For the accompaniment Noodles, butter, purée of foie gras, veal gravy (see page 21), Parmesan cheese, truffle, demi-glace sauce

Cook the noodles in consommé, drain and add some puréed foie gras, a little veal gravy and grated cheese. Put into a serving dish and cover with thin slices of truffle warmed in butter. Then coat all with demi-glace sauce.

Jambon de Prague en croûte

PRAGUE HAM IN PASTRY

Poach the ham in water until it is about two-thirds cooked. Drain and leave to cool a little, then remove the skin and glaze ham.

Prepare some pastry, sufficient to enclose the ham completely. Roll out and place ham on the pastry, glazed side downwards. Moisten the edges of the pastry, then draw them together, enclosing the ham.

Put on to a baking tray, sealed side downwards. Make a slit in the top of the pastry to allow the steam to escape. Bake in a moderate oven until the pastry is cooked and well browned.

Remove from the oven, widen the hole in the top if necessary and pour in a large wine glass of Madeira.

Then put on to a serving dish.

Serve with demi-glace sauce (see page 22), to which some butter and Madeira has been added.

To serve the ham Remove an oblong piece of the crust the full length of the ham and then carve the ham in thin slices.

Any of the accompaniments previously mentioned are suitable to serve with this dish.

Jambon de Prague truffé

TRUFFLED PRAGUE HAM

———————— Ham, pastry, truffles, salt, freshly ground pepper, demi-glace sauce (see page 22), Madeira

Prepare the ham as described in the previous recipe, but before putting it on to the pastry slice ham thinly and intersperse each with a slice of raw truffle seasoned with salt and pepper. Continue as before and cook until the pastry is well browned.

Remove from the oven and pour in 6 tablespoons demi-glace sauce to which some Madeira has been added. Close the hole through which the sauce was poured with a 'stopper' of pastry. Serve with the rest of the sauce.

Buttered asparagus tips, chestnut purée, soubise purée or a purée of celery can be served as an accompaniment.

MOUSSES ET MOUSSELINES CHAUDES DE JAMBON
HOT MOUSSES AND MOUSSELINES OF HAM

Farce pour mousse de jambon chaude

FORCEMEAT FOR HOT HAM MOUSSE

These are prepared from a ham forcemeat. The mousse is generally poached in a mould sufficient for 6−8 persons, while the mousseline is moulded in a spoon to the shape of an egg, like a large quenelle.

For the forcemeat

1 lb. lean ham, ½ teaspoon salt, pinch white pepper, 2 egg whites, 1 pint (U.S. 2½ cups) fresh cream

Pound the ham and seasoning in a mortar. Add the egg whites gradually then rub through a fine sieve. Put the resultant purée into a bowl and place on ice for 30−40 minutes. Then add the cream, very slowly at first, then more quickly, in the way described for mayonnaise (see page 40).

If necessary add a few drops of colouring or some sweet red paprika to give the forcemeat a good pink colour.

If paprika is used, heat 1 tablespoon butter in a small pan, add 1 tablespoon paprika and warm for a few seconds, stirring all the time. Add 6 tablespoons cream and boil for 1 minute. Then strain through muslin and allow to cool before use.

TO COOK THE MOUSSE

Butter a charlotte mould liberally and fill with the forcemeat.

Put into a bain-marie, cover, and poach very carefully, taking care the water does not boil. Allow about 30−35 minutes or until mousse rises in the tin and feels firm to the touch.

Remove from bain-marie and leave for a few minutes to settle, then turn upside down on to a serving dish and leave for 1 minute before removing the mould. The mousse may be garnished with vegetables or with a *financière* garnish (see page 48).

Serve with a good brown sauce to which some Madeira, Marsala or port wine has been added.

Mousselines de jambon Alexandra

MOUSSELINES OF HAM WITH TRUFFLES

———————— Mousselines (see page 379), truffles, béchamel sauce (see page 23), grated cheese, butter, asparagus tips

Mousselines are moulded in a spoon which gives them the shape of eggs.

Put them into a buttered sauté pan and cover with slightly salted boiling water. Cover pan and keep the temperature just below boiling point, taking care not to let the water boil.

Poach for 15—18 minutes, then drain on a cloth.

Arrange in a ring on a buttered serving dish, and place a slice of truffle on each mousseline. Cover with béchamel sauce, sprinkle with cheese, brush with melted butter and glaze quickly in the oven.

Garnish the centre of the dish with some buttered asparagus tips.

Mousselines de jambon à la florentine

HAM MOUSSELINES WITH SPINACH

———————— Spinach, butter, salt, pepper, mousselines, béchamel sauce (see page 23), cheese

Blanch some spinach, drain and chop coarsely, and sauté briskly in a little butter. Season with salt and pepper and spread over the bottom of a serving dish.

Poach some mousselines as above and arrange on the spinach. Cover with béchamel sauce. Sprinkle with grated cheese, brush with melted butter and glaze quickly in the oven.

Mousselines de jambon aux petits pois

HAM MOUSSELINES WITH PEAS

Proceed as instructed for *mousselines de jambon Alexandra* (above) but replace the asparagus with buttered peas.

Soufflé de jambon
HAM SOUFFLÉ

You will need for 6 persons:
8 oz. lean ham, béchamel sauce (see page 23), pinch red pepper, pinch freshly ground pepper, 3 egg yolks, 4 egg whites

Pound the ham in a mortar with 2 tablespoons béchamel sauce and the peppers, then rub through a fine sieve.

Add a further 6 tablespoons béchamel sauce and the egg yolks and fold in the stiffly beaten egg whites. Put the mixture into a buttered soufflé dish and bake in the ordinary way for 20–25 minutes in a moderate oven.

Note A little thinly sliced truffle and some grated Parmesan cheese may be added.

Soufflé de jambon Alexandra
HAM SOUFFLÉ WITH CHEESE AND TRUFFLES

Prepare a soufflé mixture as above with Parmesan cheese and truffle added. Put into a buttered soufflé dish, with alternate layers of buttered asparagus tips.

Smooth the surface into the shape of a dome and cook in a moderate oven for about 20–25 minutes.

Soufflé de jambon périgourdine
HAM SOUFFLÉ PÉRIGOURDINE

The same as for the *soufflé de jambon Alexandra* above, omitting the asparagus tips.

Soufflé de jambon royale
HAM SOUFFLÉ WITH FOIE GRAS AND TRUFFLES

Prepare and cook a *soufflé de jambon périgourdine* as above.

As an accompaniment, serve some slices of foie gras sautéed in butter and some slices of truffle, coated with demi-glace sauce (see page 22), to which a little Madeira has been added.

Jambon froid

COLD HAM

The ham should be cooked and left to cool (see page 375). When it is cold, remove the skin, trim the ham, and remove some of the fat.

Cover with aspic jelly, coating with extra jelly as it sets, until the ham is covered with a fairly thick and even layer.

Put on to a serving dish and surround with aspic jelly, allow to set and cut into fancy shapes.

Mousse froide de jambon

COLD HAM MOUSSE

———————— You will need for 6—7 persons:
12 oz. lean cooked ham, 6 tablespoons white sauce, salt, pepper, aspic jelly, ½ pint (U.S. 1¼ cups) fresh thick cream, sliced truffles

Fix a band of stiff white paper around the outside of a soufflé dish, extending about ¾ inch above the rim.

Pound the ham in a mortar with the sauce, then rub through a fine sieve. Season carefully with salt and pepper. Stir on ice for a few minutes, then add very gradually 6 tablespoons melted aspic jelly. Finally add the slightly whipped cream.

Pour the mixture into the prepared dish and leave until set. Arrange a few slices of truffle on top of the mousse and cover with a thin layer of half-melted aspic. Keep on ice until required.

Remove the band of paper carefully, using a hot knife.

Mousse de jambon à l'alsacienne

HAM MOUSSE WITH FOIE GRAS

———————— Mousse, foie gras, aspic jelly (see page 16)

Prepare a mousse as described above and half fill a deep square dish. Smooth the surface and keep the dish on ice. When the mousse is set, arrange shells of foie gras on top, scooped out of a pâté de foie gras with a spoon dipped in hot water.

Cover these shells with half-melted aspic jelly and leave to set.

Serve in the dish, surrounded by crushed ice.

Mousse de jambon au blanc de volaille

HAM MOUSSE WITH CHICKEN'S BREASTS

Ham mousse, breast of chicken, white stock (see page 120), white chaudfroid sauce (see page 31)

Half fill a deep, square dish with ham mousse and keep on ice.

Cut some slices from the breast of chicken poached in white stock. When quite cold, cover with white chaudfroid sauce and arrange on top.

Alternatively, omit the sauce and put a slice of truffle on each piece of chicken and coat with aspic jelly.

PRÉPARATIONS DIVERSES DU PORC
VARIOUS PORK DISHES

Langue de porc

PIG'S TONGUE

Pig's tongue may be treated like calf's tongue (see page 311).

Oreilles de porc au naturel

PIG'S EARS

After being well singed and cleaned, put the ears into a pan with 2 pints (U.S. 5 cups) cold water, ¼ oz. salt, 1−2 sliced carrots, 1 onion stuck with 1 clove and a *bouquet garni*. Bring to boiling point and simmer gently.

Pig's ears may also be cut in half lengthwise and cooked with sauerkraut, cabbage, lentils or haricot beans.

Pieds de porc

PIG'S TROTTERS

Pig's trotters are cooked like pig's ears and can then be coated with breadcrumbs and grilled (U.S. broiled) or truffled.

Pieds de porc panés

BREADCRUMBED PIG'S TROTTERS

Cook the trotters and cut in half lengthwise.
Brush with melted lard or butter, dip in breadcrumbs and grill (U.S. broil) very slowly.
Serve with boiled potatoes.

Pieds de porc truffés

TRUFFLED PIG'S TROTTERS

—————— 2 pig's trotters, 12 oz. pork forcemeat, truffles, sausage skin or pig's caul, butter

Cook trotters as instructed (see page 383). Bone completely and allow to cool. Cut the flesh into large cubes and mix with the forcemeat and 6 oz. chopped truffles.

Divide into pieces of 3–4 oz. and shape into small sausages pointed at one end. Add 3 slices of truffle for each piece and cover with sausage skin or pig's caul.

Brush with melted butter and grill (U.S. broil) slowly, so they are evenly cooked through.

Arrange in a ring on a hot dish and serve with *sauce périgueux* (see page 28).

Truffled pig's trotters are also served with mashed potatoes.

Queues de porc

PIG'S TAILS

These are cooked like pig's trotters (see page 383), then brushed with lard, dipped in breadcrumbs and gently grilled (U.S. broiled).
Serve with mashed potatoes or *sauce piquante* (see page 28).

Rognons de porc

PIG'S KIDNEYS

These may be prepared according to the recipes given for calf's kidneys (see pages 326–328).

Tête de porc
PIG'S HEAD

Pig's head is generally used for cold dishes, especially brawn or 'pork cheese'. It can also be served hot, in which case it is cooked as described for pig's ears (see page 383).

Andouilles et andouillettes
SAUSAGES AND SMALL SAUSAGES MADE OF CHITTERLINGS

Small chitterling sausages are sold ready-made. They only need to be pricked, brushed with lard or butter, and grilled (U.S. broiled) slowly. Serve with mashed potatoes.

Boudins
BLACK AND WHITE PUDDINGS

Although black and white puddings (U.S. blood sausage and sausage) are usually sold ready-prepared, it may be useful to know how to make them.

Boudins blancs ordinaires
ORDINARY WHITE PUDDINGS

8 oz. lean pork, 12 oz. fresh bacon fat, 4 oz. fresh foie gras, 2 eggs, 2 oz. chopped onion, butter, 6 tablespoons cream, 1 small teaspoon salt, pinch white pepper, pinch grated nutmeg, sausage skins

Chop pork and bacon fat and pound in a mortar with foie gras. Rub through a sieve. Add eggs, onion, sautéed in butter without browning, cream and seasonings. Mix all well together.

Put mixture into sausage skins, taking care not to pack them too tightly. Tie in required lengths and put on a stand in a steamer, or fish kettle, three-quarters full of boiling water. Poach for about 12 minutes, keeping water below boiling point. Remove puddings and leave to cool.

To serve Prick the puddings lightly, wrap each one in buttered paper and grill (U.S. broil) gently.

Serve with creamed or mashed potato.

Boudins blancs de volaille

WHITE CHICKEN PUDDINGS

——————— 1 lb. fillets of raw chicken, 12 oz. fat bacon, 4 oz. chopped onion, butter, pinch thyme, ¼ bay leaf, 1 small teaspoon salt, pinch pepper, pinch nutmeg, 4 egg whites, sausage skins

Cut chicken and bacon into small pieces and pound each separately in a mortar. Then put them together and pound again, ensuring they are thoroughly mixed.

Sauté the onion lightly in a little butter with the thyme and bay leaf, taking care the onion does not brown.

Add to meat mixture with salt, pepper and nutmeg. Then add egg whites very gradually, pounding vigorously with the pestle. Rub through a fine sieve, then put mixture into sausage skins and proceed as described above.

Boudin noir

BLACK PUDDING

——————— 1 lb. pig's kidney fat, ¾ pint (U.S. 1⅞ cups) pig's blood, 8 oz. chopped onions, lard, 1 small teaspoon salt, generous pinch pepper, pinch mixed spice, 6 tablespoons cream, sausage skins

Cut fat into large cubes and partially melt. Sauté onions in lard until tender but not browned, then mix all ingredients well together.

Pack into sausage skins, fairly loosely to prevent them bursting. Tie into length required.

Put on a stand in a steamer or fish kettle three-quarters full of boiling water. Simmer very gently for 20 minutes.

If puddings rise to the surface they should be pricked with a pin, as this indicates that air bubbles are present and puddings may burst.

When puddings are cooked, remove the tray from the water and leave puddings to cool. When required for use, prick and grill (U.S. broil) gently as described for white puddings (see page 385). Serve with mashed potatoes.

Black puddings can also be accompanied by apple marmalade or apple sauce (see pages 39).

Crépinettes

SMALL FLAT SAUSAGES

2¼ lb. sausagemeat, 1 tablespoon chopped parsley, 1 liqueur glass brandy, sausage skins, butter
For truffled crépinettes, add 4 oz. chopped truffles

Mix all ingredients well together. Divide into pieces of about 3 – 4 oz. and put into sausage skins, pressing into oblong shapes.
    Brush with melted butter and grill (U.S. broil) slowly or fry in butter.
Serve with apple purée or a purée of peas.

Pâté de porc à l'anglaise

ENGLISH STYLE PORK PÂTÉ

Thin slices uncooked ham, salt, pepper, 2 oz. mushrooms, 2 small shallots, chopped parsley, pinch sage, 1 lb. sliced fresh pork, 1 lb. potatoes, 1 large onion, ½ pint (U.S. 1¼ cups) water, short pastry or flaky pastry, beaten egg

Line a pâté dish or a pie dish with ham. Add salt and pepper, mushrooms and shallots finely chopped, parsley and sage to the pork and fill up the dish with alternate layers of meat and flavourings, and sliced potato and onion.
    Add the water. Cover with a thin piece of pastry or trimmings of flaky pastry could be used. Seal edges well, brush with beaten egg, score top and cook in a moderate oven about 2 hours.

Petit salé

PICKLED PORK

Pickled pork is cooked for a long time in unsalted water.
    It can be cooked with cabbage, but in this case the pickled pork must be blanched and left in boiling water for 15 minutes to remove the taste of brine.

Poitrine de porc

BELLY OF PORK

Cook 2 – 2½ lb. shoulder or belly (U.S. bacon piece) of salt pork with carrot, onion and 6 parsnips.

Arrange vegetables around the pork and serve a pease pudding separately.

Saucisses de Francfort et de Strasbourg

FRANKFURT AND STRASBURG SAUSAGES

Poach the sausages in boiling water for 10 minutes. Longer cooking will only spoil the flavour.

Serve with grated horseradish and mashed potatoes. Sauerkraut is often served with these sausages.

Saucisses au vin blanc

SAUSAGES WITH WHITE WINE

12 small sausages, butter, 6 tablespoons white wine, ½ pint (U.S. 1¼ cups) demi-glace sauce (see page 22), fried croûtons

Cook sausages in butter. Remove from pan and keep hot.

Add the wine to the butter left in the pan, stir well then reduce. Add the sauce and finally 1 oz. butter.

Arrange sausages on croûtons and pour sauce over.

If preferred, omit the butter from the sauce, add 2 tablespoons meat jelly (see page 21) and finally thicken with 2 egg yolks and 2 tablespoons fresh cream.

Any of the following are suitable accompaniment: mashed potatoes, chestnut purée, purée of peas, pilaf of rice (see page 669), or risotto (see page 668).

COCHON DE LAIT
SUCKING PIG

A sucking pig is always cooked whole, roasted in the oven or on a spit.
The cooking time varies according to the size of the pig, but generally it is about 1½−2 hours. If the pig is stuffed, an extra 15 minutes should be allowed for every 1 lb. of stuffing.

When the sucking pig is cooked, the skin should be crisp and golden brown, and to achieve this it is advisable to baste frequently with oil. Serve with a rather thick gravy.

Farce pour cochon de lait

STUFFING FOR SUCKING PIG

Prepare a forcemeat *au gratin* (see page 58) with a pig's liver.

Add an equal quantity of sausage meat, 8 oz. breadcrumbs moistened with milk and drained, 2 eggs, 6 tablespoons brandy, and a large pinch herbs. Mix all well together. Fill a sucking pig with the stuffing, sew up the belly and roast in the oven or on a spit.

Farce à l'anglaise pour cochon de lait

ENGLISH STUFFING FOR SUCKING PIG

2−2½ lb. large white onions, 1 lb. breadcrumbs, milk, 1 lb. beef kidney fat, chopped finely, 1 teaspoon salt, pinch pepper, pinch nutmeg, 3 oz. sage, scalded and chopped, 2 eggs

Bake onions in their skins. Leave to cool, then peel and chop finely. Add breadcrumbs, moistened with milk and then well drained, with all other ingredients. Mix all well together.

Cochon de lait farci et rôti à l'anglaise

ENGLISH STYLE ROAST STUFFED SUCKING PIG

Fill a sucking pig with the forcemeat given above and sew up the skin of the belly. Brush all over with oil, and roast in the oven or on a spit.

Serve with mashed potatoes and apple sauce to which some currants have been added. These should be carefully washed and left in hot water for a few minutes to swell before adding to the sauce.

Cochon de lait Saint-Fortunat

STUFFED SUCKING PIG

6 oz. barley, liver from the sucking pig, butter, 2 tablespoons chopped fresh herbs, 8 oz. chopped, cooked chipolata sausages, 3—4 dozen braised chestnuts, salt, few tablespoons brandy, oil, brown veal stock

Cook the barley as for pilaf (see page 669). Cut liver into medium-sized cubes and sauté in butter.

Mix the liver, herbs, sausages and chestnuts with the cooked barley and mix all well together.

Sprinkle the inside of the sucking pig with salt and moisten with a few tablespoons brandy. Put in the stuffing and sew it up.

Put the pig into a roasting tin, brush with oil and baste frequently with oil during the cooking to make it crisp and golden.

When cooked, remove to a serving dish. Add some stock to the liquor left in the pan, stir well and boil for a few minutes.

Serve this gravy separately, and either a redcurrant sauce with horseradish, or a rather tart apple sauce.

Volailles

POULTRY

In the general sense, the term 'poultry' is applied to turkeys, geese, ducks and pigeons, as well as to chickens; but from the culinary point of view, 'poultry' generally refers to chicken only.

Spring chickens weighing from about $1\frac{1}{2}-3\frac{1}{2}$ lb. can be roasted, grilled (U.S. broiled) or sautéed.

Large chickens and capons weighing from about $3\frac{1}{2}-5\frac{1}{2}$ lb. are usually roasted, sautéed or boiled.

Poussins are very young chickens and are generally grilled (U.S. broiled) or served *en cocotte*.

Suprême of chicken, which is used in so many dishes, consists of the breast and wing cut from a spring chicken.

Cock's combs or crests and the liver and kidneys from chicken are used in a number of dishes and also in garnishes.

One of the best ways of cooking a chicken is to stuff it with rice and poach in white stock, which is used later to make a *sauce suprême*. Sometimes truffles are added to the sauce.

Cucumbers, artichoke bottoms, mushrooms or cèpes, or carrots are all suitable accompaniments and the cook has plenty of scope to use her imagination in preparing these for special occasions.

Several of the following recipes may be considered too advanced and perhaps expensive for the amateur cook, but all who are really interested in French *cuisine* should know of them, and will doubtless find them of interest.

Poularde Albuféra

CHICKEN STUFFED WITH RICE

———————— 1 chicken, 4 oz. rice, prepared as described below, fat bacon slices, white veal stock, 2—3 tablespoons meat jelly (see page 21), 2—3 table-spoons cream, 1 pint (U.S. 2½ cups) *sauce parisienne* (see page 22), cooked mushrooms, cock's combs and kidneys, truffle

Stuff chicken with rice and truss with legs turned back.

Cover breast with bacon slices and secure with string. Put into a pan, cover with stock and cook gently over low heat for about 1 hour or more, according to size of chicken. When tender, remove from pan, untruss and put on to a serving dish.

Add meat jelly and cream to sauce and pour over chicken.

Garnish with mushrooms, cock's combs, kidneys and sliced truffle.

Note The cream in the sauce may be replaced with 1—2 oz. butter.

TO PREPARE RICE FOR STUFFING A CHICKEN WEIGHING 3½—4½ LB.

———————— 2 oz. butter, 1 tablespoon finely chopped onion ,4 oz. Carolina rice, ½ pint (U.S. 1¼ cups) white stock, 2 oz. truffles, 2 oz. foie gras, ½ pint (U.S. 1¼ cups), *sauce parisienne* (see page 22).

Melt butter, add onion and cook for a few minutes without browning. Add rice and stir for 1—2 minutes until the rice is thoroughly impregnated with the butter.

Add stock, cover, and cook for 18 minutes.

Remove from the heat and add the cubed truffles and foie gras and the sauce.

Poularde à l'andalouse

ANDALUSIAN STYLE CHICKEN

———————— 1 3½—4-lb. chicken, fat bacon slices, butter, 6 tablespoons white wine, ½ pint (U.S. 1¼ cups) demi-glace sauce with tomato (see page 22), 3 red peppers, 3 aubergines, rice pilaf (see page 669), Spanish sausages

Wrap chicken breast in fat bacon slices, and cook slowly in butter, using a heavy pan with a tightly fitting lid.

When cooked, remove and keep hot. Add wine to butter left in the pan, stir well and bring to boiling point, then add sauce.

Put a little on to the serving dish, put the chicken on top, and surround with peppers and aubergines tossed in butter and stuffed with the rice pilaf, and the sausages.

Editor's note Spanish sausages can be bought in some delicatessen shops as red sausages or Chorizos. If not available use chipolatas.

Poularde bouillie à l'anglaise

ENGLISH STYLE BOILED CHICKEN

1 lb. streaky bacon, 1 chicken, boiling water, salt, *bouquet garni* of 2 sprigs parsley, 1 bay leaf, 2 sprigs thyme

Blanch bacon in boiling water for 10 minutes. Put chicken into a pan and barely cover with boiling water. Add salt, in the proportion of ¼ oz. per 2 pints (U.S. 5 cups) water, *bouquet garni* and bacon.

Simmer about 1 hour, or longer according to the size of the chicken. When tender, remove to a serving dish and arrange slices of the bacon around.

Serve with parsley sauce (see page 39) and some of the cooking liquor.

ANOTHER METHOD

1 chicken, *bouquet garni*, 4 oz. carrots, 4 oz. turnips, 2 sticks celery, few slices cooked tongue

Cook chicken as described in the preceding recipe with *bouquet garni* and vegetables diced large.

Arrange the vegetables around the chicken together with slices of tongue.

Serve with boiled potatoes, peas and béchamel sauce (see page 23).

Poularde Argentina

CHICKEN WITH MACARONI AND CHEESE

1 chicken, white stock, 4 oz. macaroni, butter, cheese, béchamel sauce (see page 23), slices truffle, 16 cooked tartlet cases, foie gras, asparagus tips

Prepare the chicken as described for *poularde Albuféra* (see page 392) but not stuffed, and poach in white stock.

Meanwhile, cut macaroni into short lengths and cook in boiling salted water. Drain well and add a little butter, 1 − 2 tablespoons grated cheese, 2 tablespoons béchamel sauce and a few thin truffle slices.

When the chicken is cooked, remove breast and keep hot in a little of the cooking liquor.

Spread the macaroni on the carcase in its place, smoothing the surface so that chicken retains its original shape.

Cover with béchamel sauce, sprinkle with grated cheese and dot with butter. Put into a hot oven for a few minutes to glaze.

Remove to a serving dish.

Line the tartlet cases with a little foie gras, then in half of them put some buttered asparagus tips, and in the rest put thinly sliced breast of chicken. Cover with béchamel sauce and put a thin slice of truffle on each.

Arrange tartlets alternately around the chicken.

Poularde à l'aurore

CHICKEN STUFFED WITH RICE WITH SAUCE SUPRÊME

Stuff a chicken with rice, as described for *poularde Albuféra* (see page 392), and cook in the same way.

Serve with a *sauce suprême* (see page 25) to which a little paprika has been added or with a velouté sauce (see page 29) to which a little tomato purée has been added.

Some cèpes or mushrooms, cooked in cream or fried in butter, may be served with the chicken.

Farce à gratin pour une poularde

GRATIN FORCEMEAT FOR CHICKEN

———————— 2 oz. butter, 2 oz. chopped fat bacon, 3 oz. lean veal, 3 oz. fresh pork, 3 oz. foie gras, chicken liver, 1 shallot, salt, pepper, 2–3 tablespoons brandy, 3 tablespoons white wine, 4–5 tablespoons meat jelly (see page 21), 1 truffle

Heat butter and bacon fat in a sauté pan. Add the diced veal and pork and brown over fairly brisk heat. Add the foie gras, liver and a finely chopped shallot. Season and cook for a few minutes.

Remove meat from the pan.

Add brandy and wine to the butter left in the pan, stir well, add meat jelly and bring to boiling point, stirring. Return meat to pan, add chopped truffle, and stir well together for a few minutes, so that the meat is well impregnated with the cooking liquor.

Put meat into a mortar, pound well, then rub through a sieve.

Note This forcemeat can be replaced by sausage meat to which a little finely chopped truffle and quarter its volume fried breadcrumbs have been added.

Poularde alsacienne

ALSATIAN STYLE CHICKEN

———————— 1 chicken, gratin forcemeat (see page 58), 1 slice fat bacon, butter, 1 liqueur glass brandy, 3 tablespoons white wine, ¼ pint (U.S. 1¼ cups) fresh cream, 3–4 tablespoons meat jelly (see page 21), 4 oz. truffled foie gras

Stuff chicken with forcemeat, cover breast with bacon and cook gently in butter, being careful that the butter does not become too brown. A strong pan with a tightly fitting lid is essential.

When chicken is ready, untruss and put on to a serving dish. Drain off excess fat, add brandy and wine and stir well, then allow to reduce a little.

Add cream and meat jelly and boil for 1 minute. Add sieved foie gras and mix in well.

Pour a little of the sauce over the chicken and serve the rest separately.

Poularde au céleri

CHICKEN WITH CELERY

1 chicken, 1 slice fat bacon, few bacon rinds, 2 sliced carrots, 1 sliced onion, *bouquet garni*, ½ oz. butter, 6 tablespoons white wine, seasoning, veal stock, 6—8 heads braised celery (see page 600), ½ pints (U.S. 1¼ cups) demi-glace sauce (see page 22)

Truss the chicken with its legs folded back, and cover breast with bacon. Secure with string. Put rinds, carrots, onion and *bouquet garni* into a saucepan. Lay the chicken on top, add melted butter, wine and seasoning. Cover and cook slowly until wine has reduced a little.

Then add enough veal stock to come about half-way up the chicken. Cover and cook gently for 1 hour or more according to the size of the chicken.

Baste occasionally while cooking. When the chicken is done, remove to a serving dish, untruss and arrange the celery round the dish.

Add the sauce to the cooking liquor and reduce quickly to the right consistency. Remove excess fat, then strain some of the sauce over the chicken and celery and serve the rest separately.

Poularde chanteclair

CHICKEN STUFFED WITH RICE WITH ARTICHOKES

1 chicken stuffed with rice as for *poularde Albuféra* (see page 392), 6—8 globe artichokes, squeeze lemon, 2—3 tablespoons flour, veal stock, buttered asparagus tips, ½ pint (U.S. 1¼ cups) *sauce parisienne* (see page 28), 4—5 tablespoons meat jelly (see page 21), 1½ oz. butter

Prepare, stuff and cook the chicken as described.

Meanwhile remove outside leaves from the artichokes and thin top and bottom of remainder. Cook in boiling salted water to which lemon juice and flour have been added. When three-quarter cooked, drain and put into cold water. Remove artichokes and put into a well buttered dish. Barely cover with veal stock, then cover the pan and continue the cooking until vegetable is tender and stock almost entirely reduced.

Remove artichokes to the serving dish with chicken and garnish with buttered asparagus tips.

Add sauce and meat jelly to remaining liquor, mix well and finally add butter.

Pour a little of this sauce over the chicken and serve the rest separately.

Poularde châtelaine

CHICKEN CASSEROLE WITH BRANDY AND WHITE WINE

Salt, pepper, 1 chicken, 1 slice fat bacon, carrots, onions, butter, 8—10 artichokes, white stock (see page 20), foie gras, tongue, truffle, béchamel sauce (see page 23), grated cheese, chestnuts cooked in consommé, asparagus tips, 1 liqueur glass brandy, 6 tablespoons white wine, good brown veal stock

Season chicken carefully. Truss with legs folded back and tie a piece of bacon fat over the breast. Put into a casserole on a bed of thinly sliced carrots and onions, pour a little melted butter over and cook in a moderate oven, basting frequently.

Meanwhile prepare and cook artichokes as described in the previous recipe and finish the cooking with butter and white stock. Chop a little foie gras, tongue and truffle and bind with a little béchamel sauce. Stuff artichokes with this mixture, sprinkle with grated cheese, dot with butter and glaze in the oven.

When chicken is cooked, remove from the oven, untruss and put on to a serving dish. Surround with the artichokes and chestnuts, and put a teaspoon of buttered asparagus tips in the centre of each artichoke. Add brandy and wine to the liquor remaining in the casserole. Reduce by half, then add the veal stock. Boil for 2 minutes, then strain. Pour a little over the chicken and serve the rest separately.

Poularde demi-deuil

POACHED CHICKEN WITH TRUFFLES

Slip a few slices of truffle, either raw or cooked, between the skin and the breast of a chicken, cover with a slice of bacon fat and poach gently in white stock, as instructed for *poularde Albuféra* (see page 392).

When chicken is cooked, strain cooking liquor through a piece of muslin, remove grease, reduce to quarter its volume and add it to a *sauce suprême* (see page 23) to which some slices of truffle have been added.

Pour a little of the sauce over the chicken.

Note This dish may be served with rice pilaf (see page 669) to which 3—4 tablespoons sieved truffled foie gras have been added.

Poularde Derby

STUFFED CHICKEN WITH FOIE GRAS

———— ½ oz. butter, 3 oz. Carolina rice, ½ pint (U.S. 1¼ cups) boiling stock, truffles, 2 oz foie gras, meat jelly (see page 21), 1 4½-lb. chicken, 1 slice fat bacon, 8 slices foie gras sautéed in butter, 8 croûtons, 6 tablespoons Madeira, ½ pint (U.S. 1¼ cups) brown meat stock, 1 teaspoon arrowroot, 1 tablespoon cold stock

TO MAKE THE STUFFING

Heat butter, add rice and cook for a few minutes. Add stock, cover and cook for 18 minutes. Remove from heat, add 2 oz. chopped truffle, foie gras and 2 tablespoons meat jelly.

Season chicken, stuff it, and truss with legs folded back. Cover breast with bacon, and secure with string. Brush well with butter and cook about 1 hour in a moderate oven, basting frequently and being very careful not to burn the butter.

When chicken is cooked, put on to a serving dish, untruss it, and surround with slices of foie gras arranged on croûtons. Some truffles, peeled and cooked in Madeira, and meat jelly can also be used as garnish.

Add Madeira and stock to the butter left in the pan, stir till boiling and boil for 1 minute. Mix arrowroot smoothly with the cold stock. Add to liquid, bring to boiling point and boil for 5 – 6 minutes. Remove any excess fat. Strain a little of the sauce on to the dish and serve the rest separately.

Poularde Diva

STUFFED CHICKEN WITH PAPRIKA SAUCE

Stuff a chicken exactly as described in the previous recipe, truss with legs folded back and put a slice of bacon fat over the breast. Cook gently in white veal stock for about 1 hour.

While the chicken is cooking, prepare a velouté of paprika (see page 29) and just before serving add 4 – 5 tablespoons fresh cream.

When chicken is cooked, put on to a serving dish and untruss it. Coat lightly with sauce and serve the rest separately.

Cèpes à la crème (see page 602) make a good accompaniment.

Poularde à l'écossaise

SCOTCH STYLE CHICKEN

8 oz. pearl barley, consommé, butter, 4 oz. sausage meat, chicken liver, salt, pepper, nutmeg, 1 4−4½-lb. chicken, 1 slice fat bacon, white stock, 3 tablespoons chopped carrot, 2 tablespoons chopped celery, 1 tablespoon chopped onion, ½ pint (U.S. 1¼ cups) velouté sauce (see page 22), 6 tablespoons cream, 4 oz. French beans, cooked and cut in pieces

TO MAKE THE STUFFING

Cook pearl barley in consommé and, when ready, drain carefully.

Heat 3 oz. butter until it begins to brown. Add barley, sausage meat and chopped chicken liver. Fry for 5−6 minutes, then season carefully.

Season inside of chicken, stuff it, truss, and cover breast with bacon.

Cook gently in white stock for about 1 hour or more according to size of chicken.

Meanwhile, heat a little butter, add vegetables, sauté for a few minutes, then add 3−4 tablespoons white stock and cook gently.

When vegetables are tender, add sauce and some of the liquor in which the chicken was cooked.

Finally, add cream and beans.

Coat chicken lightly with a little sauce and serve the rest separately.

Poularde Édouard VII

STUFFED CHICKEN WITH CURRY SAUCE

Stuff and cook a chicken as for *poularde Derby* (see page 398).

Make 1 pint (U.S. 2½ cups) *sauce suprême* (see page 23), add 1 teaspoon curry powder and 2 oz. canned sweet red pepper diced small.

Put chicken on a serving dish and pour the sauce over.

Serve with creamed cucumber.

Poularde à l'espagnole

SPANISH STYLE CHICKEN

8 oz. rice, 3 oz. sweet red pepper, 1 chicken, fat bacon slices, 10 tomatoes, salt, pepper, 3—4 tablespoons oil, chopped parsley, 4 oz. streaky bacon, paprika, bacon for garnish, fried onion rings, 3—4 tablespoons good stock

Cook the rice as for pilaf (see page 669), add the red pepper, diced small, and stuff the chicken. Truss, cover breast with slices of bacon fat, then pot-roast.

Cut a slice from the stalk end of each tomato, squeeze gently to extract the moisture and seeds. Season inside with salt and pepper.

Heat the oil, put in the tomatoes cut side downwards, and fry gently for 7—8 minutes. Turn over and cook a further 5—6 minutes. Drain and sprinkle with parsley.

Grill (U.S. broil) the streaky bacon and sprinkle with paprika.

Put chicken on to a serving dish and garnish with tomatoes, bacon, and onion rings.

Add the stock to the liquor left in the pan, and serve separately.

Rounds of fried aubergine may also be added to the garnish.

Poularde à l'estragon

CHICKEN WITH TARRAGON

Truss a chicken with its legs turned back, and put it into a saucepan with just enough brown veal stock to cover. And a bouquet of tarragon, cover the saucepan and cook for 50—55 minutes over a low heat.

When cooked, put chicken on to a serving dish and sprinkle with 3—4 tablespoons cooking liquor.

Scald some tarragon leaves in boiling water, cool a little, then use to garnish the breast.

Reduce cooking liquor by half, add 2 tablespoons chopped tarragon leaves and serve separately.

Poularde favorite

STUFFED CHICKEN WITH COCK'S COMBS,
KIDNEYS AND TRUFFLE

Stuff a chicken as instructed for *poularde Derby* (see page 398) and poach in white veal stock.

Dish up the chicken and garnish with cock's combs and kidneys, and slices of truffle.

Coat with *sauce suprême* (see page 23) made with the stock in which the chicken was cooked.

Poularde financière

BRAISED CHICKEN WITH MADEIRA

Braise a chicken in brown stock.

Dish up and surround with a garnish of cock's combs and kidneys, mushrooms, slices of truffle and chicken quenelles (see page 56).

Make 1 pint (U.S. 2½ cups) demi-glace sauce (see page 22), add 3–4 tablespoons Madeira and some of the stock in which chicken was cooked.

Pour some of the sauce over chicken and garnish, and serve the rest separately.

Poularde Godard

BRAISED CHICKEN WITH CHICKEN QUENELLES AND TRUFFLE

Braise a chicken in brown stock as for *poularde financière*, above, and serve with the same garnish, but in this case add a little truffle to the quenelles and some small pieces of braised calf's sweetbread to the rest of the garnish.

An extra garnish of crayfish can be used for both *poularde Godard* and *poularde financière*.

Poularde grand-hôtel

CHICKEN WITH MADEIRA, WHITE WINE AND BRANDY

1 chicken, salt, pepper, butter, 6 oz. truffles, 1 tablespoon Madeira, 2 tablespoons meat jelly (see page 21), 3—4 tablespoons white wine, 2—3 tablespoons brandy, 5—6 tablespoons well reduced brown veal stock

Joint the chicken, season, and sauté in butter until tender. (The sauté pan should be covered while chicken is cooking.)

Peel and thickly slice truffle, and season. Put into a pan with ½ oz. butter, Madeira and meat jelly. Cover and keep hot at the side of the stove.

When chicken is cooked, remove to a fireproof serving dish and arrange truffles on top. Add wine and brandy to butter left in the sauté pan, stir well, then add stock and stir till boiling. Cover very lightly and put into a moderate oven for 5—6 minutes before serving. This brings out the full aroma of the truffle.

Serve with a risotto to which some grated Parmesan cheese has been added, or with buttered noodles and cheese.

Poularde au gros sel

CHICKEN WITH ROCK SALT

1 chicken, 1 slice bacon fat, 10 small carrots, 10 small onions, 6 leeks, white stock

Truss chicken with its legs folded back. Cover breast with bacon fat and put into a pan with carrots, onions and white part of the leeks. Add enough white stock to cover. Cover and simmer for about 1 hour or until the chicken is tender.

Put on to a serving dish and surround with the carrots, onions and leeks in separate heaps. Serve some of the cooking liquor in a sauce-boat and hand a small dish of rock salt. Some rice may be cooked in the stock and served with the chicken.

Poularde aux huîtres

CHICKEN WITH OYSTERS

1 chicken, 1 slice bacon fat, white stock, 36 oysters, 1 pint (U.S. 2½ cups) *sauce suprême* (see page 23)

Truss chicken with legs folded back. Cover breast with bacon fat and put into a pan. Cover with stock and cook over a low heat for about 1 hour or until chicken is tender.

Beard the oysters, remove from shells and poach very carefully in their own juice, taking care it does not boil.

When the chicken is cooked, remove to a serving dish. Make suprême sauce using the stock in which the chicken was cooked.

Add oysters to sauce and pour over the chicken.

Poularde impératrice
CHICKEN WITH LAMB'S SWEETBREADS AND BRAINS

———— 1 chicken, 1 slice fat bacon, white stock, 2–3 lamb's sweetbreads, 3 lamb's brains, consommé, 1½ pints (U.S. 3¾ cups) *sauce suprême* (see page 23)

Prepare and cook chicken as in preceding recipe. Braise sweetbreads in stock (see page 321) and poach lamb's brains in consommé.

When chicken is cooked, put on to a serving dish and arrange sweetbreads and brains around it. Make the sauce, using some of the stock in which chicken was cooked.

Coat chicken and garnish with some of the sauce and serve the rest separately. A dish of rice may be served with it.

Poularde à l'indienne
CHICKEN WITH INDIAN STYLE RICE

Prepare and cook the chicken as for *poularde aux huîtres* (see above).

Coat with a *sauce suprême* (see page 23) to which a little curry powder has been added.

Serve with *riz à l'indienne* (see page 668).

Poularde sauce ivoire
CHICKEN WITH IVORY SAUCE

Prepare and cook a chicken, as for *poularde aux huîtres* (see above).
When ready, put on to a serving dish and coat with ivory sauce.

For the sauce Make 1 pint (U. S. 2½ cups) *sauce suprême* (see page 23) and add 3–4 tablespoons pale meat jelly (see page 21).

Serve with rice, cooked in chicken stock, and a dish of cucumber dressed with butter.

Poularde maréchale

CHICKEN STUFFED WITH TONGUE, TRUFFLE AND PÂTÉ
DE FOIE GRAS

3 oz. cooked tongue, 3 oz. truffle, 3 oz. pâté de foie gras, 2 oz. bread-crumbs fried in butter, 3 tablespoons meat jelly (see page 21), 1 chicken, 1 slice fat bacon, white stock, 1 pint (U.S. 2½ cups) *sauce suprême* (see page 23), tartlet cases, asparagus tips, cock's combs, truffle, mushrooms

Cut the tongue, truffle and foie gras into small pieces, add bread-crumbs and mix all together with meat jelly.

Stuff the chicken with this mixture, truss it, and cover breast with bacon fat.

Cook gently in stock for about 1 hour, or until tender.

Untruss, put on to a serving dish, and coat lightly with the sauce.

Fill some small tartlet cases with asparagus tips and arrange round the chicken.

As a garnish, serve separately some cock's combs, slices of truffle and mushrooms, all coated with a little of the sauce.

Poularde Isabelle de France

CHICKEN WITH FOIE GRAS, TRUFFLES AND CHAMPAGNE

4 oz. rice, white stock, 2 oz. grated Parmesan cheese, 2 oz. pâté de foie gras, 2 oz. truffles, 1 chicken, 1½ pints (U.S. 3¾ cups) *sauce suprême* (see page 23), tartlet cases, truffles, Champagne

Cook rice in stock and add cheese, mashed foie gras, and truffles, peeled and sliced.

Stuff chicken with rice mixture, then truss, and cook in stock for about 1 hour or until tender. Put chicken on to a serving dish and keep hot.

Make the sauce, using some of the stock in which the chicken was cooked, and pour some of it over the chicken.

Garnish with small tartlet cases filled with truffles cooked in Champagne, and serve the rest of the sauce separately.

Poularde Louise d'Orléans

STUFFED CHICKEN IN PASTRY

1 chicken, salt, pepper, 1 whole (about 5-oz.) pâté de foie gras, truffle, spice, 6 tablespoons Madeira, 1 slice bacon fat, veal stock, butter, pastry dough, egg or milk

Remove breast bone from chicken and season the inside.

Stud pâté with pieces of truffle, add a little spice and the Madeira.

Wrap it in a slice of bacon fat and then in muslin and poach gently in stock for about 15 – 20 minutes.

Leave to cool, then remove the muslin and bacon and put the pâté into the chicken.

Truss it, and cook in butter over very low heat for about 1 hour, basting frequently.

Untruss, and cover completely with slices of truffle. Then wrap in bacon fat or in a sausage skin.

Roll out some pastry, put chicken in the centre and fold over, so that chicken is completely encased.

Make a slit in the top to allow steam to escape and put into a baking tin.

Brush over with egg or milk and put into a moderate oven for about 30 minutes — just long enough to cook the pastry.

Serve hot or cold.

Poularde Monte-Carlo

STUFFED BAKED CHICKEN

Stuff a chicken with rice as for *poularde Derby* (see page 398) and cook in the same way.

When the chicken is ready, put it on to a serving dish and coat with *sauce suprême* (see page 23).

Prepare some tartlet cases, and fill one-third with crayfish, one-third with truffles, cut in small olive shapes, and the rest with cock's kidneys sautéed in butter.

Coat each tartlet with sauce and arrange round the chicken.

Poularde ménagère

BOILED CHICKEN WITH VEGETABLES

1 chicken, 12 small carrots, 12 small onions, 1 stick celery, 1 bay leaf, 2 sprigs parsley, white stock

Truss chicken with its legs folded back and put into a pan with the thinly sliced vegetables, bay leaf and parsley. Add enough stock just to cover. Bring to boiling point, then cover and simmer for about 1 hour or until chicken is tender.

When ready to serve, put chicken on to a dish and garnish with some of the vegetables.

A good soup can be made by putting some thin slices of bread into a tureen, adding some of the vegetables and pouring some of the chicken stock over.

3 oz. well washed rice may be cooked in the stock with the vegetables

Poularde Adelina Patti

POACHED CHICKEN STUFFED WITH RICE

Stuff the chicken with rice, prepared as instructed for *poularde Derby* (see page 398), and poach in white veal and chicken stock.

Make 1½ pints (U.S. 3¾ cups) *sauce suprême* (see page 23) and add a little paprika.

When chicken is cooked, put on to a serving dish and coat with some of the sauce.

Arrange some buttered asparagus tips, and truffle cut into julienne, on freshly cooked artichoke bottoms, and use for garnish.

Serve remaining sauce separately.

Poularde ou chapon fin aux perles du Périgord

CHICKEN OR CAPON WITH TRUFFLES

Salt, pepper, 8 oz. truffles, 1 chicken or capon, strips fat bacon, 3–4 slices very thinly cut veal, bacon rinds, onions, carrots, *bouquet garni*, 1 tablespoon brandy, 1 tablespoon white wine, 1 pint (U.S. 2½ cups) brown veal stock

Season truffles and use to stuff chicken. Truss it, and cover with bacon and veal. Secure with string.

Put some bacon rinds and a little fat bacon into a pan with thinly sliced onions and carrots.

Put the chicken on top. Add *bouquet garni* and pour brandy and wine over. Add stock. Cover and braise for about 1 hour or more until chicken is tender, basting frequently. Serve with the liquor from the braise.

Poularde piémontaise

PIEDMONT STYLE CHICKEN

8 oz. rice, 3 oz. white truffles, 1 chicken, 1 slice fat bacon, butter, 8 oz. cèpes or mushrooms, garlic, salt, pepper, chopped parsley, 6 tablespoons white wine, ¼ pint (U.S. ⅝ cup) good brown gravy

Cook rice as for risotto (see page 668), add sliced truffles and use to stuff the chicken. Cover breast with a slice of fat bacon, and cook chicken very gently in butter. Brown cèpes in butter, add a suspicion of garlic, salt and pepper. Sprinkle with parsley.

Put chicken into a serving dish encircled by cèpes.

Pour off any excess fat from the pan in which the chicken was cooked. Add wine and stir well. Add gravy, stir till boiling then reduce to half its quantity.

Serve separately.

Poularde régence

POACHED CHICKEN WITH TRUFFLES AND FOIE GRAS PURÉE

Truss a chicken with its legs turned back, cover the breast with bacon fat and poach in white veal and chicken stock.

Place the chicken on a serving dish, garnish with 10 quenelles of mousseline forcemeat of chicken (see page 56), decorated with truffles, 10 mushrooms, 10 small truffles and 10 patties filled with a purée of foie gras.

Poularde Récamier

POACHED CHICKEN WITH MACARONI AND CHEESE SAUCE

1 chicken, white stock, butter, peeled truffles, 12 cock's combs, 1 tablespoon Madeira, ¾ pint (U.S. 1⅞ cups) suprême (see page 23) or white sauce, 4 oz. macaroni, 1 pint (U.S. 2½ cups) béchamel sauce (see page 23), grated Parmesan cheese, foie gras, patties, asparagus tips

Poach the chicken in stock.

When cooked, cool a little, then remove both sides of the breast, and slice them.

Put into a pan with ½ oz. butter, 2 tablespoons sliced truffles, cock's combs and Madeira. Heat together, then add the sauce. Cover and keep hot.

Cook macaroni in boiling salted water, drain and add 3 – 4 tablespoons béchamel sauce, 2 – 3 tablespoons cheese, 1 – 2 chopped truffles and a little foie gras.

Remove as much of the carcase of the chicken as possible. Stuff with macaroni mixture and reshape as nearly as possible to its original form.

Put into a baking dish, coat with béchamel sauce and sprinkle with grated cheese.

Pour a little melted butter over and put into a moderate oven for a few minutes until golden brown.

Put on to a serving dish and surround with small patties filled with asparagus tips.

Serve the slices of chicken, etc., separately.

Poularde au riz

CHICKEN WITH RICE

Poach a chicken in white stock.

Wash 8 oz. rice, and cook for 20 minutes in 1 pint (U.S. 2½ cups) chicken stock.

When chicken is ready, put on to a serving dish with 2 – 3 tablespoons stock, and serve the rice separately.

Serve with *sauce suprême* (see page 23).

Poularde Rossini

CHICKEN STUFFED WITH FOIE GRAS AND TRUFFLES

Salt, pepper, 1 chicken, 4 oz. cooked foie gras, 4 oz. truffles, 1 slice fat bacon, butter, ½ pint (U.S. 1¼ cups) brown veal stock

Season inside of chicken and stuff with foie gras and chopped truffles. Truss it, cover the breast with bacon and cook gently in butter, basting frequently and taking care butter does not get too dark.

Remove chicken when cooked and keep hot. Pour off excess butter from pan, add stock and stir well. Bring to boiling point and reduce slightly.

Put a little sauce on a serving dish and place the chicken on top.

Serve remaining sauce separately.

Serve with a dish of buttered noodles, grated cheese and mashed pâté de foie gras.

Poularde soufflé

CHICKEN SOUFFLÉ

1 chicken, butter, 3 oz. truffles, salt, pepper, 1 lb. chicken mousseline stuffing (see page 56), 4 oz. truffled foie gras purée, ½ pint (U.S. 1¼ cups) white stock, 1 pint (U.S. 2½ cups) white sauce (see page 22)

Poach the chicken, cool a little, then remove breast and slice it. Put into a pan with ½ oz. butter. Add truffles, peeled and sliced, and season carefully. Keep hot.

Remove as much of the carcase of the chicken as possible.

Mix stuffing with foie gras purée and use to stuff chicken. Smooth the surface and reshape chicken as far as possible into its original form. Decorate with thinly sliced truffle.

Put the stock in a pan, stand chicken in this, and cover tightly. Bring to boiling point, then simmer very gently. The steam should be sufficient to cook the stuffing.

When chicken is ready, put on to a serving dish and coat with sauce, reserving 4−5 tablespoons.

Put chicken breast and truffles into a separate serving dish. Add a little butter to remaining sauce and pour over.

Poularde Souvarow

POT-ROASTED STUFFED CHICKEN

————— 1 chicken, 8 oz. cooked foie gras, 4 medium-sized truffles, salt, pepper, 1 slice fat bacon, butter, 6 tablespoons Madeira, 6 tablespoons reduced veal and chicken stock, pastry dough

Stuff chicken with foie gras, cut into fairly large pieces, and truffles, peeled and lightly seasoned. Truss chicken, cover breast with bacon fat and cook carefully in butter for about 45 minutes. Remove from pan, untruss and put into a fireproof dish. Pour off any excess butter, add the Madeira and stir well. Bring to the boil and add stock. Pour over chicken. Put the lid on the dish and seal round the edge with a strip of dough. Put into a moderate oven for about 20 minutes to finish cooking. Serve in the dish.

Poularde Stanley

CASSEROLE OF STUFFED CHICKEN

————— 3 oz. rice, 1½ pint (U.S. 3¾ cups) white stock, 2 oz. mushrooms, 2 oz. truffles cut into julienne, 1 chicken, 1 slice fat bacon, 1 lb. onions, 1 tablespoon curry powder, ¾ pint (U.S. 1⅞ cups) béchamel sauce (see page 23), 6 tablespoons cream

Cook rice in ½ pint (U.S. 1¼ cups) stock, add mushrooms and truffles and use to stuff the chicken. Truss it, and cover breast with bacon fat.

Slice onions thinly, put into boiling water for a few minutes then drain and mix with curry powder. Put onions into a casserole with the chicken and remaining stock. Cover and cook in a moderate oven about 1 hour. When chicken is cooked, untruss and put on to a serving dish. Pass contents of casserole through a fine sieve and mix the resultant purée with the sauce. Add the cream and boil fairly quickly, until the sauce is reduced to a thick creamy consistency. Then pour over the chicken.

Poularde à la Talleyrand

POT-ROASTED CHICKEN WITH MACARONI AND CHEESE

————— 1 chicken, butter, 4 oz. macaroni, stock, 1—2 tablespoons grated Parmesan cheese, 3—4 tablespoons béchamel sauce (see page 23), 4 oz. pâté de foie gras, truffles, 8 oz. mousseline forcemeat (see page 56), ½ pint (U.S. 1¼ cups) white stock, ½ pint (U.S. 1¼ cups) demi-glace sauce (see page 22)

Cook chicken in butter, cool a little, then remove the breast. Cut into fairly large pieces.

Break macaroni into very short lengths and cook in stock. Drain well and add cheese, béchamel sauce, pâté and 2 oz. truffles cut into small pieces. Mix all well together and keep hot.

Remove as much of the carcase as possible and stuff with the macaroni mixture. Cover with the forcemeat, reshaping the chicken into its original form. Decorate with a ring of truffle slices.

Put white stock into a pan, stand chicken in this and cover tightly. Bring to boiling point, then simmer very gently. The steam should be sufficient to cook the forcemeat.

When chicken is ready add a little truffle cut into julienne to the demi-glace sauce and put a little on the serving dish. Place chicken on top and serve remaining sauce separately.

Poularde Tosca
POACHED STUFFED CHICKEN WITH WHITE SAUCE

1 chicken, white stock, ½ oz. butter, 1 pint (U.S. 2½ cups) white sauce (see page 22), 1 oz. truffles cut into julienne, 2—3 sticks celery cooked in white stock and cut into small pieces

Stuff chicken as for *poularde Derby* (see page 398) and poach in white stock.

Add butter gradually to the sauce, then truffles and celery.

Put chicken on to a serving dish, coat lightly with sauce and serve the rest separately.

Poularde toulousaine
TOULOUSE STYLE CHICKEN

1 chicken, white stock, 12 small pieces braised calf's sweetbread, 12 cock's combs and kidneys, 12 small chicken quenelles, 12 mushrooms, 12 thinly sliced truffles, 12 small patties filled with duck's foie gras purée, butter, 1 pint (U.S. 2½ cups) white sauce (see page 22)

Poach chicken in stock and put on to an oval serving dish.

Arrange all the garnish round the chicken.

Add a little butter to the sauce. Pour a little over the chicken and the garnish and serve the rest separately.

Poularde à la valenciennes

VALENCIAN STYLE CHICKEN

1 chicken, butter, 6—8 Spanish sausages, sweet paprika, 6—8 grilled bacon rashers, 3—4 stuffed aubergines (see page 596), 6—8 stuffed tomatoes (see pages 658—659), 1 pint (U.S. 2½ cups) demi-glace sauce with tomato (see page 22), 2—3 oz. ham, pilaf of rice (see page 669)

Cook chicken in butter and put on to an oval serving dish.

Roll sausages in paprika and grill (U.S. broil). Arrange around chicken with rest of the garnish.

Coat chicken with a little sauce and serve the rest separately.

Add a little chopped ham to the pilaf of rice and serve in a separate dish.

Poularde Véronique

POACHED CHICKEN WITH CREAM BÉCHAMEL SAUCE

1 chicken, white stock, 3—4 tablespoons cream, 1¼ pints (U.S. 3⅛ cups) béchamel sauce (see page 23), slices braised calf's sweet-breads, small lamb's brains poached in consommé, small soft-boiled eggs, 2—3 sliced truffles

Poach the chicken in stock then put on to an oval serving dish. Add cream to the sauce and use some to coat chicken lightly. Arrange garnish round chicken. Add truffles to the rest of the sauce and serve separately.

Poularde Victoria

STUFFED POT-ROASTED CHICKEN WITH POTATOES

1 chicken stuffed and cooked as for *poularde Souvarow* (see page 410), potatoes, butter, meat jelly (see page 21), ¼ pint (U.S. ⅝ cup) brown veal stock

While chicken is cooking, cut potatoes into small dice, cook gently in butter and coat with meat jelly.

When chicken is ready, put on to a serving dish and arrange potatoes around.

Drain off any surplus butter from the pan in which the chicken was cooked, pour in the stock, stir well and bring to boiling point. Boil for a few minutes, then strain and serve separately.

Poularde à la Washington

CHICKEN STUFFED WITH SAUSAGE MEAT AND CORN

8 oz. sausage meat, 3—4 tablespoons sweet corn, pinch mixed herbs, butter, 1 chicken

Mix sausage meat with sweet corn and herbs and brown lightly in butter. Stuff chicken with this mixture, then truss, and braise it.

When ready to serve, pour a little of the liquor from the braise over the chicken and serve the rest separately.

Serve with a dish of creamed sweet corn.

SÉRIE DE FILETS OU SUPRÊMES DE VOLAILLE
RECIPES USING THE BREAST OR SUPRÉME OF CHICKEN

The breast of chicken is referred to as suprême or fillet, and it is generally taken from a spring chicken.

The simplest method of cooking the fillet is to season it lightly with salt, coat with flour, then sauté in butter. Only a few minutes cooking is required. When done, remove it from the pan, and add remaining butter to a little white stock and 1 tablespoon meat jelly (see page 21), in the proportion of 1 tablespoon jelly to each fillet. Stir well and bring to boiling point.

This should produce a fairly thick sauce with a good nutty flavour. If the butter separates from the jelly, add another 1 or 2 tablespoons white stock and shake pan well.

When the small wing bone is left attached to the fillet, it is referred to as a chicken cutlet.

After seasoning and coating with flour the cutlets are coated with egg and breadcrumbs, then cooked in butter.

If cutlets are to be grilled (U.S. broiled), egg should be omitted, and the cutlets dipped in melted butter before being coated with breadcrumbs.

Suprêmes de volaille Adelina Patti

BREAST OF CHICKEN WITH GNOCCHI

—————— You will need for 6 persons:
6 chicken breasts, salt, grated cheese, 6 cakes semolina (see *Gnocchi à la romaine*, page 672), flour, butter, white stock, 6 tablespoons meat jelly (see page 21), truffle

Cut breasts from 3 chickens, season them and cook as on page 413.

Add 2 oz. grated cheese to the gnocchi mixture, and when cold cut into pieces as nearly as possible the size of the fillets. Coat with flour and fry in butter until golden brown on both sides.

Put on to a serving dish and arrange 1 fillet of chicken on each.

Add a little stock to the pan in which the fillets were cooked, stir well, then add the meat jelly and thinly sliced truffle, allowing 3 – 4 slices for each fillet.

Heat for a few seconds then pour over the fillets.

Serve with creamed artichokes (see page 591).

Suprêmes de volaille chasseur

BREAST OF CHICKEN WITH DEMI-GLACE SAUCE

—————— You will need for 6 persons:
6 chicken breasts, croûtons or cakes of semolina, 8 oz. mushrooms very thinly sliced, 2 shallots finely minced, 4 tablespoons brandy, 6 tablespoons white wine, 3 tablespoons tomato purée, ½ pint (U.S. 1¼ cups) demi-glace sauce (see page 22), 2 tablespoons meat jelly (see page 21), pinch chopped parsley

Cook fillets as on page 413, and arrange on croûtons or semolina cakes as described above.

Add mushrooms and shallots to the pan in which fillets were cooked and sauté for a few minutes. Add brandy and wine, and allow to reduce a little.

Add tomato purée, sauce, meat jelly and parsley. Boil all together for a few minutes, then pour over the fillets.

Serve with potatoes and pilaf of rice (see page 669) or *riz à l'indienne* (see page 668).

Suprêmes de poulet la Vallière

CHICKEN BREASTS WITH TRUFFLES

Prepare as *suprêmes de volaille chasseur* (see page 414), but add a julienne
of truffles and a pinch chopped tarragon to the mushrooms.
A small pinch of cayenne will improve both dishes.

Suprêmes de volaille favorite

BREAST OF CHICKEN WITH FOIE GRAS AND MADEIRA

You will need for 6 persons:
6 chicken breasts, butter, croûtons or semolina cakes, 6 small slices
foie gras sautéed in butter, white stock, 3 tablespoons Madeira,
6 tablespoons meat jelly (see page 21), truffle

Cook fillets in butter as described in the preceding recipes and arrange on
croûtons or semolina cakes. Put a slice of foie gras on each.
   Add a little stock to the butter left in the pan in which fillets were
cooked, and mix well. Add Madeira and meat jelly, and boil for a few
minutes. Add some thin slices of truffle, allowing 3—4 for each fillet.
Boil for a further 2 minutes, then add 1 oz. butter and pour over the
chicken. Serve with buttered asparagus tips.

Suprêmes de poulet à la bordelaise

BORDEAUX STYLE CHICKEN BREASTS

You will need for 6 persons:
6 chicken breasts, 3 artichoke bottoms, 3—4 potatoes, butter, 3—4
tablespoons meat jelly (see page 21), 3—4 tablespoons white wine,
3—4 tablespoons consommé or brown veal stock

Cook fillets as described in the preceding recipes.
   Slice artichokes and potatoes very thinly and cook separately in
butter. Then mix together and bind with a little meat jelly. Press into
cutlet moulds, then turn on to serving dish and arrange cooked fillets
on top.
   Add wine to butter left in the pan on which the fillets were cooked.
Stir well and bring to boiling point. Add the stock and remaining meat
jelly. Boil for a few seconds, add butter and pour over fillets.

Suprêmes ou filets de poulet à la hongroise

HUNGARIAN STYLE CHICKEN BREASTS OR FILLETS

You will need for 6 persons:
6 chicken breasts, 1 tablespoon sweet paprika, 6 tablespoons white wine, 4 tablespoons meat jelly (see page 21), ½ pint cream (U.S. 1¼ cups)

Cook fillets as described in preceding recipes and arrange on a serving dish.

Add paprika to butter left in the pan and cook for a few seconds, stirring well. Add wine, meat jelly and cream. Bring to boiling point, and pour over the fillets.

The cream in this recipe may be replaced by the same quantity of béchamel sauce (see page 23) to which 2 − 3 tablespoons butter have been added.

Suprême ou filets de poulets à l'indienne

INDIAN STYLE CHICKEN BREASTS OR FILLETS

You will need for 6 persons:
6 chicken breasts, 1 tablespoon chopped onion, 1 dessertspoon curry powder, ½ pint (U.S. 1¼ cups) cream or béchamel sauce (see page 23), 1½ oz. butter

Cook fillets as previously described and place on a serving dish.

Add onion to butter left in the pan and sauté till lightly browned. Add curry powder and stir for a few seconds. Add cream or sauce, and strain into a small pan. Bring quickly to boiling point, then add butter, and pour over the fillets. Serve with *riz à l'indienne* (see page 668).

Suprêmes de poulet Judic

CHICKEN BREASTS WITH BRAISED LETTUCES

You will need for 6 persons:
6 chicken breasts, 3 braised lettuces (see page 632), truffle, cock's kidneys, demi-glace sauce (see page 22)

Cook fillets as in the preceding recipe and arrange 1 on each half lettuce.

Garnish with thin slices of truffle, and the kidney, and coat with a little of the sauce. Serve with pilaf of rice (see page 669) to which some peas have been added.

Suprêmes de volaille à la Maréchal
FRIED CHICKEN BREASTS WITH SAUCE

You will need for 6 persons:
Salt, pepper, 6 chicken breasts, flour, 1 egg, breadcrumbs, butter, 4—5 tablespoons brown veal stock or consommé, thin slices truffle, juice ½ lemon

Season fillets, coat with flour, then with egg and breadcrumbs and cook in butter.

Put stock into a pan and bring to boiling point. Boil for 1 minute then add truffle, allowing 3—4 slices for each fillet. Bring to boiling point again and gradually add 1—2 oz. butter, stirring well. Finally add lemon juice.

Put the fillets on to a serving dish and pour the sauce over.

Serve with buttered asparagus tips.

Another method

Season fillets, coat with flour, then dip in melted butter and coat with breadcrumbs. Grill (U.S. broil) gently.

Serve with a ragoût of thinly sliced truffles, cock's kidneys and small white mushrooms coated with a little white sauce to which 1 tablespoon Madeira and a little butter has been added.

Note Chicken cutlets, i.e. the fillet to which the wing bone is left attached, may be prepared in the same way.

Suprêmes de volaille Montpensier
CHICKEN BREASTS WITH SEMOLINA CAKES

You will need for 6 persons:
6 chicken breasts, butter, semolina cakes (see page 672), 3—4 tablespoons veal stock or consommé, 2—3 tablespoons meat jelly (see page 21), truffle

Cook fillets in butter as described previously and arrange on semolina cakes as for *poularde Adelina Patti* (see page 406). Add the stock to the butter remaining in the pan in which the chicken was cooked. Mix well and add the meat jelly and thin slices of truffle, allowing about 3—4 for each fillet. Boil for 2 minutes, then add 1 oz. butter and pour over the fillets.

Garnish with buttered asparagus tips.

Suprêmes de volaille Polignac

CHICKEN BREASTS WITH SAUCE SUPRÊME

━━━━━━━━ You will need for 6 persons:
6 chicken breasts, butter, 6 croûtons bread fried in butter, truffles, mushrooms, 1 pint (U.S. 2½ cups) *sauce suprême* (see page 23), 2—3 tablespoons white stock, 2—3 tablespoons meat jelly (see page 21)

Cook the chicken breasts in butter and arrange them on the bread croûtons.

Cut some truffles and mushrooms into julienne, add to the sauce and pour over the chicken breasts.

Add the stock to the butter left in the pan, stir well and add the meat jelly. Pour a little over the chicken and serve the rest separately.

If liked, serve with asparagus tips or green peas.

Suprêmes ou côtelettes de volaille Pojarski

CHICKEN BREASTS OR CUTLETS POJARSKI

━━━━━━━━ You will need for 6 persons:
6 chicken breasts, breadcrumbs, cream, butter, salt, pepper, nutmeg, flour, butter for cooking

Mince the chicken breasts, and for 1 lb. of chicken meat add 4 oz. breadcrumbs moistened with cream and 4 oz. butter. Mix well, and add salt, pepper and a suspicion of nutmeg.

Reshape the forcemeat into the original form of the chicken breasts, coat with flour and cook for 10—12 minutes in butter.

Garnishes are purely optional.

Suprêmes de volaille Rosemonde

CHICKEN BREASTS WITH MADEIRA AND SAUCE SUPRÊME

━━━━━━━━ You will need for 6 persons:
6 chicken breasts, butter, 6 oval-shaped croûtes puff pastry, foie gras purée, 3—4 tablespoons Madeira, 3—4 tablespoons white stock, 3—4 tablespoons meat jelly (see page 21), truffle, ½ pint (U.S. 1¼ cups) *sauce suprême* (see page 23)

Cook the chicken breasts in butter. Spread the pieces of pastry with the foie gras purée and arrange the chicken on top.

Put the Madeira into the pan in which the fillets were cooked, stir well, add the stock and meat jelly and bring to boiling point. Add some thin slices of truffle, allowing 3—4 for each fillet, and the sauce. Reheat and pour over the fillets. Serve with a mushroom purée.

Suprêmes de volaille Rossini
CHICKEN BREASTS WITH FOIE GRAS AND TRUFFLES

—————— You will need for 6 persons:
6 chicken breasts, butter, seasoning, 6 slices fresh foie gras, flour, butter, 3—4 tablespoons Madeira, 3—4 slices truffle, ½ pint (U.S. 1¼ cups) demi-glace sauce (see page 22)

Cook the chicken breasts in butter. Season the foie gras, coat with flour and sauté in butter.

Arrange the chicken breasts on a serving dish and put a slice of foie gras on each. Add the Madeira to the pan in which the chicken was cooked. Stir well, add the truffle and sauce. Bring to boiling point and pour over the chicken breasts.

Serve with buttered noodles, to which a little Parmesan cheese has been added.

Suprêmes de poulet Verdi
CHICKEN BREASTS VERDI

—————— You will need for 6 persons:
6 breasts chicken, butter, 4 oz. macaroni, Parmesan cheese, 3—4 tablespoons béchamel sauce (see page 23), cream of truffled foie gras, 3—4 tablespoons white stock, 3—4 tablespoons meat jelly (see page 21), ½ pint (U.S. 1¼ cups) cream, sliced truffles

Cook the chicken breasts in butter.

Break the macaroni into short lengths and cook in boiling salted water. Drain and add a little butter, grated Parmesan and the sauce to which a little cream of foie gras has been added.

Put the macaroni into a serving dish and arrange the chicken breasts on top.

Add the white stock to the butter remaining in the pan in which the fillets were cooked, stir well. Add the meat jelly and cream. Bring to boiling point and boil for 2 minutes, then pour over the chicken.

Warm 6 thin slices of truffle in a little meat jelly and put one on each fillet.

Blanc de volaille Vicomtesse de Fontenay

CHICKEN BREASTS WITH SEMOLINA CAKES AND WHITE SAUCE

▬▬▬▬▬ Breasts from a plump poached chicken, 6 semolina cakes, prepared as for *suprêmes de volaille Adelina Patti* (see page 414), 6 slices truffle, cream, béchamel sauce (see page 23), grated cheese, butter

Cut each breast into 3 slices. Put the cakes of semolina on to a fireproof serving dish and put a slice of chicken on each. Place a slice of truffle on each one.

Add a little cream to the sauce and pour over. Sprinkle with cheese, dot with butter and brown under the grill (U.S. broiler) or in the oven.

Garnish with buttered asparagus tips.

Blanc de volaille alsacienne

ALSATIAN STYLE CHICKEN BREASTS

▬▬▬▬▬ Breasts from a poached chicken, 6 slices foie gras sautéed in butter, truffles, *sauce suprême* (see page 23)

Cut each breast into 3 slices. Put the slices of foie gras on to a serving dish and arrange the slices of chicken on top.

Add some thinly sliced truffles to the sauce and pour over.

Serve with *nouilles à l'alsacienne* (see page 677).

Blanc de volaille Angeline

CHICKEN BREASTS WITH PAPRIKA SAUCE

▬▬▬▬▬ Breasts from a poached chicken, 6 semolina cakes (see page 672), 6 slices truffle, paprika, béchamel sauce (see page 23), Parmesan cheese, butter

Cut the breasts into 3 slices and arrange each on a cake of semolina. Put a slice of truffle on each.

Add a little paprika to the sauce and pour over. Sprinkle with grated Parmesan, dot with butter and brown under the grill (U.S. broiler) or in the oven.

Serve with pilaf of rice (see page 669) to which some green peas have been added.

Blanc de volaille aux concombres

CHICKEN BREASTS WITH CUCUMBER

Prepare as in the preceding recipe but omit the truffle and the paprika.
Serve with creamed cucumber (see page 620).

Blanc de poulet Bagration

CHICKEN BREASTS WITH PASTA AND CHEESE SAUCE

▬▬▬▬▬▬ Breasts from a poached chicken, butter, 1—2 tablespoons sliced
truffle, salt, freshly ground pepper, 8 oz. shell-shaped pasta, pinch
nutmeg, grated cheese, 1 small truffle, 3—4 tablespoons béchamel
sauce (see page 23)

Cut each breast into 2 or 3 slices. Put into a pan with ½—1 oz. butter
and the truffle. Season carefully with salt and freshly ground pepper.
Cover and keep hot.

Cook the pasta in boiling salted water, drain and return to the pan.
Add ½ oz. butter, nutmeg, and 3—4 tablespoons grated cheese. Bind with
the sauce and add the truffle, sliced thinly. Mix all well and put on to
a fireproof serving dish. Smooth the surface and arrange the chicken on
top alternately with the slices of truffle.

Cover with the sauce, sprinkle with grated cheese, dot with butter and
brown under the grill (U.S. broiler) or in the oven.

Blanc de poulet florentine

FLORENCE STYLE CHICKEN BREASTS

▬▬▬▬▬▬ Breasts from a poached chicken, butter, salt, pepper, 8 oz. spinach,
pinch nutmeg, béchamel sauce (see page 23), grated cheese

Cut the breasts into 2 or 3 slices. Put into a pan with ½ oz. butter, season
lightly and keep hot.

Cook the spinach, drain well and chop coarsely. Put into a pan with
1 oz. butter, salt, pepper and nutmeg. Heat, stirring all the time until the
moisture has been absorbed.

Put on to a fireproof serving dish and arrange the slices of chicken on
top. Cover with sauce, sprinkle with cheese and dot with butter.

Brown under the grill (U.S. broiler) or in the oven.

Blanc de poulet Mireille

CHICKEN BREAST MIREILLE

This is the same as *blanc de poulet florentine* (see page 421), except that some thin slices of truffle are added to the slices of chicken.

Season lightly, then cover the saucepan and keep warm for a few moments so that the chicken meat becomes impregnated with the aroma of truffle.

Arrange the slices of chicken and truffle alternately on the spinach, and cover with béchamel sauce (see page 23). Sprinkle with grated cheese, dot with butter and brown as before.

SÉRIE DE POULETS SAUTÉS

RECIPES FOR SAUTÉED CHICKEN

Spring chickens are best for the recipes in this section. They should be white, plump and tender. If necessary, small roasting chickens may be used.

To carve a chicken, first remove the legs. Detach the wings then remove the breast from the carcase. Finally divide the carcase in two pieces.

Poulet sauté Alice

SAUTÉED CHICKEN WITH WINE AND BRANDY

2 oz. butter, 1 tablespoon oil, 1 jointed chicken, salt, pepper, 4 oz. mushrooms, 1 shallot, 2 tablespoons brandy, 6 tablespoons white wine, 3 tablespoons meat jelly (see page 21), ½ pint (U.S. 1¼ cups) cream

Heat the butter and oil in a sauté pan just big enough to hold the pieces of chicken. Arrange the pieces of chicken in the saucepan, with the skin underneath, white meat in the middle and legs on each side, the wings on top of these and the pieces of carcase and the pinions put in last. Season with salt and pepper, cover and cook over a low heat, being careful to turn the pieces of chicken over in the butter, so that they cook evenly. The wings, being more tender than the legs, should be removed when cooked and kept warm. The legs require a few minutes longer cooking. Now add the mushrooms and shallot, both finely chopped, the brandy, white wine and meat jelly. Reduce to half its volume. Replace the wings of chicken in the saucepan, heat for a few seconds and, finally, thicken the sauce with the cream.

Serve with some *pommes de terre noisette* (see page 653).

Poulet sauté alsacienne

SAUTÉ CHICKEN ALSATIAN STYLE

━━━━━━━ 1 jointed spring chicken, ¼ pint (U.S. ⅝ cup) white Alsatian wine, 3 tablespoons meat jelly (see page 21), 3 tablespoons cream, 4 oz. truffled foie gras

Prepare the chicken and cook as in the previous recipe. Add the wine and reduce by half, then add the meat jelly and cream. Finally add the sieved foie gras. Serve with *nouilles à l'alsacienne* (see page 677).

Poulet sauté Beaulieu

SAUTÉ CHICKEN WITH ARTICHOKES AND BLACK OLIVES

━━━━━━━ 1 spring chicken, 6 tablespoons white wine, squeeze lemon juice, 3 tablespoons meat jelly (see page 21), 5—6 small artichoke bottoms, 5—6 small new potatoes, butter, 18 black olives

Cut the chicken up, cook as in the previous recipes, and keep hot.

Put the wine into the pan, stir well and bring to boiling point. Add the lemon juice and meat jelly.

Finely chop the artichoke bottoms and potatoes and cook in a little butter. Put into a serving dish and arrange the joints of chicken on top. Garnish with the olives and pour the sauce over.

Poulet sauté à la mode d'Auvergne

SAUTÉ CHICKEN AUVERGNE STYLE

━━━━━━━ 1 spring chicken, 2 tablespoons finely chopped onion, 6 tablespoons white wine, ½ pint (U.S. 1¼ cups) demi-glace sauce with tomato (see page 22), chestnuts cooked in broth, small chipolata sausages

Cut up and cook the chicken as instructed in the preceding recipes. Add the onion, and when it begins to brown add the white wine. Reduce this by half, then finally add the sauce and boil for a few minutes.

Dish up the chicken and surround it with the chestnuts and sausages.

Poulet sauté bordelaise

SAUTÉ CHICKEN WITH ARTICHOKES AND POTATOES

1 spring chicken, butter, 4—5 artichoke bottoms, 4—5 potatoes, 1 onion, 6 tablespoons white wine, 3—4 tablespoons brown veal stock, 3 tablespoons meat jelly (see page 21), fried parsley

Cut up the chicken, sauté it in butter like the preceding ones, and keep hot.

Slice the artichokes, potatoes and onion and cook each separately in a little butter.

Add the wine to the pan in which the chicken was cooked and reduce to half its quantity. Add the stock and meat jelly.

Arrange the chicken on a serving dish and pour the sauce over. Garnish with the vegetables arranged in heaps and put a little fried parsley between.

Poulet sauté bourguignonne

SAUTÉ CHICKEN BURGUNDY STYLE

4 oz. pork fat, butter, 1 spring chicken, salt and pepper, ½ pint (U.S. 1¼ cups) red Burgundy, 4 oz. mushrooms, ½ pint (U.S. 1¼ cups) demi-glace sauce (see page 22), small glazed onions

Cut the pork fat into cubes, cover with boiling water and leave for a few minutes. Then drain and dry and brown in a little butter. Remove the pieces of fat.

Prepare the chicken as described in the previous recipes and cook in the butter, adding a little seasoning.

Remove the wings when cooked and keep hot.

When the rest of the chicken is tender, add the wine and reduce to half its quantity. Add the pork fat, mushrooms, quartered and lightly browned in butter, and the sauce. Return the wings to the pan, and simmer all together for a few minutes.

Serve surrounded with glazed onions.

Poulet sauté à la bressane

SAUTÉ CHICKEN WITH COCK'S KIDNEYS

1 spring chicken, salt and pepper, flour, butter, 24 cock's kidneys, 4 oz. mushrooms, 6 tablespoons white wine, ½ pint (U.S. 1¼ cups) cream

Cut up the chicken, season with salt and pepper and coat with flour. Cook gently in butter, taking care that the butter does not turn black. When the cooking is almost complete, add the cock's kidneys and mushrooms cut in quarters and browned in butter. Add the white wine and reduce this to half, then add the cream and simmer for 8 – 10 minutes.

Poulet sauté à la paysanne catalane

SAUTÉ CHICKEN IN CATALAN COUNTRY STYLE

1 spring chicken, salt and pepper, flour, oil, 2 tablespoons chopped onion, 5 – 6 sweet red peppers, 5 – 6 tomatoes, peeled and seeded, chopped parsley, 1 small clove garlic, 6 tablespoons white wine

Cut up the chicken as usual, but divide the legs into two. Season with salt and pepper, roll them in flour and cook the pieces of chicken in oil with the onion.

Slice the peppers and fry in oil. When almost done add the tomatoes, a little chopped parsley, check seasoning and add the garlic. Simmer for 20 – 25 minutes.

If liked, some thinly sliced aubergines and courgettes floured and fried in oil can be added in addition to the peppers and tomatoes.

Put the vegetables into a serving dish and arrange the pieces of chicken on top.

Add the wine to the pan in which the chicken was cooked, reduce it for a few minutes and then pour over the chicken. Reheat before serving.

Serve with creole rice (see page 666).

Note Hare may be prepared in the same manner.

Poulet sauté aux cèpes

SAUTÉ CHICKEN WITH CÈPES OR MUSHROOMS

1 spring chicken, salt and pepper, 2 oz. butter, 1 tablespoon oil, 6 tablespoons white wine, 6 tablespoons demi-glace sauce with tomato (see page 22)

Cut up the chicken, season it with salt and pepper and sauté in the butter and oil. Add the white wine and reduce this by half. Add the sauce and boil for a few minutes. Dish up the chicken and cover with the sauce.

Serve with *cèpes à la bordelaise* (see page 601) or mushrooms.

Poulet sauté Champeaux

SAUTÉ CHICKEN CHAMPEAUX

———— 1 spring chicken, butter, glazed onions, *noisette* potatoes (see page 653), 6 tablespoons white wine, 2 tablespoons meat jelly (see page 21), 6 tablespoons veal gravy

Cut up the chicken and sauté in butter. Put on to a serving dish with the glazed onions and *noisette* potatoes and keep hot.

Add the white wine to the pan in which the chicken was cooked, stir well and bring to boiling point. Add the meat jelly and veal gravy reduced by half. Finally add 2 oz. butter and pour the sauce over the chicken.

Poulet sauté chasseur

CHICKEN SAUTÉ CHASSEUR

———— 1 spring chicken, salt and pepper, 2 oz. butter, 2 tablespoons oil, 4 oz. mushrooms, 2 finely chopped shallots, 3—4 tablespoons brandy, 6 tablespoons white wine, ¼ pint (U.S. ⅝ cup) demi-glace sauce with tomato (see page 22), pinch finely chopped parsley

Cut up the chicken, season with salt and pepper and sauté in the butter and oil. As soon as the wings are cooked, remove them and keep hot. Add the mushrooms and finely chopped shallots and cook for 2—3 minutes; add the brandy and white wine. Reduce by half and then add the sauce and the parsley. Reduce for a few seconds and replace the wings in the sauce.

Dish up the chicken and pour the sauce over.

Note Poulet sauté la Vallière is prepared in the same way as *poulet sauté chasseur*, except that a few slices of truffle cut in julienne and 1 pinch chopped tarragon are added to the mushrooms.

Both dishes may be garnished with stuffed tomatoes.

Poulet sauté au curry

CURRIED SAUTÉ OF CHICKEN

———— 1 spring chicken, salt and pepper, flour, 3 tablespoons oil, 2 tablespoons finely chopped onion, 1 small teaspoon curry powder, ½ pint (U.S. 1¼ cups) white or demi-glace sauce (see page 22), 3—4 tablespoons cream

Cut the chicken into small pieces, season with salt and pepper and coat with flour.

Heat the oil in a sauté pan, add the chicken, onion and curry powder and sauté for about 15 minutes.

Add the white sauce and continue to cook a further 15 – 20 minutes or until the chicken is tender. Finally add the cream.

Serve with *riz à l'indienne* (see page 668).

Poulet sauté à l'espagnole
CHICKEN SAUTÉ SPANISH STYLE

1 spring chicken, salt, pepper, lard, 2 tablespoons chopped onion, 8 oz. rice, 2 small red peppers, 1 pint (U.S. 2½ cups) chicken stock *For the sauce* 6 ripe tomatoes, 4 tablespoons oil, 1 small clove garlic, parsley, seasoning

Cut up the chicken, season and sauté in the lard with the onion. Add the rice and sliced peppers, and the stock. Cover the pan and cook until the chicken is tender, about 20 minutes.

To make the sauce
Peel, seed and chop the tomatoes and cook gently with the oil, chopped garlic and a little chopped parsley. Add seasoning, and serve with the chicken.

Note If liked some chipolata sausages may be cooked with the chicken.

Poulet sauté à l'estragon
CHICKEN SAUTÉ WITH TARRAGON

1 spring chicken, butter, 6 tablespoons white wine, ½ pint (U.S. 1¼ cups) demi-glace sauce with tomato (see page 22), large pinch chopped tarragon leaves

Cut up the chicken and sauté in butter. Remove the wings when they are tender and keep hot.

Add the wine to the rest of the chicken, reduce by half then add the sauce and tarragon. Cook for a few minutes, then replace the wings and cook a further few minutes.

Put the chicken on to a serving dish and pour the sauce over.

Serve with potatoes, cooked in any way preferred.

Poulet sauté florentine

CHICKEN SAUTÉ FLORENTINE STYLE

1 spring chicken, butter, oil, 6 tablespoons Madeira, ½ pint (U.S. 1¼ cups) demi-glace sauce (see page 22), brown veal stock, 3 oz. black truffles, 6 small foie gras

Cut up the chicken and sauté in the butter and oil. When it is cooked, add the Madeira, and the sauce to which a little veal stock has been added. Add the sliced truffles and cook all together for a few minutes.

Put the chicken on to a serving dish, arrange the slices of truffle on top and pour the sauce over.

Serve with a risotto (see page 668) to which some grated Parmesan cheese has been added, and arrange the slices of foie gras sautéed in butter on top.

Poulet aux fines herbes

CHICKEN WITH WINE AND PARSLEY

1 spring chicken, salt, pepper, butter, oil, 6 tablespoons white wine, 3—4 tablespoons brown veal gravy, 2 tablespoons meat jelly (see page 21), chopped parsley, juice ½ lemon

Cut up the chicken, season, and sauté in butter and oil. When the chicken is tender add the white wine and reduce it by half, then add the gravy and meat jelly.

Put the chicken on to a serving dish and sprinkle with chopped parsley. Add a little butter and the lemon juice to the remaining sauce and pour over the chicken.

Serve with potatoes or rice.

Poulet sauté hongroise

CHICKEN SAUTÉ HUNGARIAN STYLE

1 spring chicken, salt, pepper, flour, 1 oz. butter, 2 tablespoons chopped onion, ½ dessertspoon sweet paprika, 6 tablespoons white wine, 2—3 tomatoes, 3—4 tablespoons cream

Cut up the chicken, season, and coat with flour. Heat the butter, add the chicken and onion. When the onion begins to brown, add the paprika, white wine and tomatoes, peeled, seeded and chopped. Cover and cook till the chicken is tender.

Put the chicken on to a serving dish. Add the cream to the sauce, boil for a few minutes and pour over the chicken.

Serve with a pilaf of rice (see page 669).

Poulet sauté Matignon
CHICKEN SAUTÉ WITH WINE AND HERBS

1 spring chicken, salt, pepper, butter, 2 oz. carrot, 1 oz. onion, 2 oz. lean raw ham, pinch thyme, 1 bay leaf, 3—4 tablespoons brandy, 6 tablespoons white wine, 4 tablespoons meat jelly (see page 21), pinch chopped parsley, 2 oz. foie gras, 2—3 tablespoons cream

Cut up the chicken, season and sauté in butter.

Pound together the finely chopped carrot, onion and ham, add thyme and bay leaf. Put into a pan with ½ oz. butter and sauté till tender.

When the chicken is cooked, put it on to a serving dish and pour the mirepoix over it. Add the brandy and wine to the pan in which the chicken was cooked, stir well and reduce by half. Add the meat jelly and the parsley and simmer for a few minutes.

Add the foie gras, cooked and sieved, and finally add the cream.

Pour this sauce over the chicken.

Poulet sauté Marengo
CHICKEN SAUTÉ MARENGO

1 spring chicken, 2 oz. butter, oil, 6 tablespoons white wine, 12 mushrooms, 1 small clove garlic, ¼ pint (U.S. ⅝ cup) demi-glace sauce with tomato (see page 22), 4 heart-shaped croûtons fried in butter, 4 fried eggs, 4 crayfish cooked in *court-bouillon*, chopped parsley

Cut up the chicken and sauté in the butter and 1 tablespoon oil. Add the white wine, mushrooms, sautéed in a little oil, garlic and sauce. Cook all together for a few minutes.

Arrange the chicken on a serving dish and pour the sauce and mushrooms over.

Surround with the croûtons, eggs and crayfish and sprinkle all with chopped parsley.

Poulet sauté Maryland

CHICKEN MARYLAND

—————— 1 spring chicken, salt, pepper, flour, egg and breadcrumbs for coating, 3 oz. clarified butter, sweet corn fritters, potato croquettes, sliced grilled (U.S. broiled) bacon, bananas fried in butter

Cut up the chicken as in the previous recipes, season, dip in flour, then coat with egg and breadcrumbs. Heat the clarified butter and fry the legs and wings of the chicken until cooked and golden brown on both sides.

Put on to a serving dish and surround with the sweet corn fritters, potato croquettes, bacon and banana.

Serve with béchamel sauce (see page 23), to which a little grated horseradish may be added, or tomato sauce (see page 132).

Poulet sauté aux morilles

CHICKEN SAUTÉ WITH MORELS

This is prepared in the same way as *poulet sauté chasseur* (see page 426) except that the mushrooms are replaced by fresh stewed morels.

Poulet sauté à la normande

CHICKEN SAUTÉ NORMANDY STYLE

—————— 1 spring chicken, butter, 1 tablespoon finely chopped onion, 8 oz. cèpes or mushrooms sautéed in butter, 3—4 tablespoons Calvados (apple jack), ½ pint (U.S. 1¼ cups) cream, 3 tablespoons meat jelly (see page 21)

Cut up the chicken and sauté in butter. When half cooked add the onion and cèpes or mushrooms and continue the cooking, taking care that the onion does not become brown. When the chicken is tender, add the Calvados and reduce by two-thirds. Add the cream and meat jelly and boil for a few minutes.

Put the chicken on to a serving dish and pour the sauce and mushrooms over.

ANOTHER METHOD

Sauté the chicken in exactly the same way as the previous recipe, omitting the mushrooms. Serve with a compote of Reinette apples, prepared as follows:

Peel 3−4 apples, slice thinly and put in a saucepan with ½ oz. fresh butter, 4−5 tablespoons water, 1 pinch sugar, 1 small pinch powdered cinnamon, a few drops lemon juice. Cover the saucepan and cook for 12−15 minutes.

Editor's note In France, Reinette apples are considered the best variety of dessert apples.

Poulet sauté Otero

CHICKEN SAUTÉ WITH PORT WINE

Cut up the chicken, season with salt and pepper and cook it in exactly the same way as instructed for *poulet sauté la Vallière* (see page 426), except that the white wine is replaced by port wine and the sauce is finished with 2 oz. butter which should be added off the heat.

Dish up the chicken, cover it with the sauce and surround with pigeons' eggs, poached and served on round croûtons fried in butter.

Poulet sauté piémontaise

CHICKEN SAUTÉ PIEDMONTESE STYLE

1 spring chicken, salt, pepper, 2 oz. butter, 1 tablespoon oil, 12 oz. potatoes, cut into small cubes and browned in butter, 6 tablespoons white wine, 3−4 tablespoons veal gravy, 1 tablespoon meat jelly (see page 21), chopped parsley

Cut up the chicken, season and sauté gently in the butter and oil. When nearly cooked, add the potatoes and continue cooking a further 5−6 minutes.

Put the chicken on to a serving dish and arrange the potatoes round in small heaps.

Add the wine, gravy and meat jelly to the pan, stir till boiling and boil for 3−4 minutes, then pour over the chicken and sprinkle with chopped parsley.

Poulet sauté portugaise

CHICKEN SAUTÉ PORTUGUESE STYLE

This is prepared as for *poulet sauté chasseur* (see page 426) and garnished with stuffed tomatoes.
Serve with *riz à la créole* (see page 666).

Poulet sauté à la paysanne provençale

CHICKEN SAUTÉ IN PROVENÇAL COUNTRY STYLE

1 spring chicken, salt, pepper, flour, oil, 1 tablespoon finely chopped onion, 6 tablespoons white wine, 4—5 tomatoes, 1 small clove garlic, pinch chopped parsley, 24 black olives

Cut up the chicken and season with salt and pepper, then coat with flour and sauté in oil for a few moments. Add the onion, and as soon as it begins to brown add the white wine and reduce it by half. Add the tomatoes, peeled, seeded and chopped, garlic and the parsley. Continue to simmer for 15 — 18 minutes and finally add the olives.
Dish up the chicken and serve with either mashed or baked potatoes.

Poulet sauté Rosita

CHICKEN SAUTÉ IN BUTTER AND WINE

1 spring chicken, salt, pepper, 2 oz. butter, 1 tablespoon oil, 6 tablespoons white wine, ½ pint (U.S. 1¼ cups) demi-glace sauce with tomato (see page 22)
Garnish 3 red peppers, oil, garlic, salt, pepper, chopped parsley

Cut up the ehicken, season and sauté in the butter and oil. Add the white wine and reduce by two-thirds, then add the sauce.
Put the chicken on to a serving dish and pour the sauce over.

To prepare the garnish Peel the peppers, cut them in half and remove the seeds. Cook gently in oil with a suspicion of garlic. Season with salt and pepper. Arrange on the dish with the chicken and sprinkle with chopped parsley.

Poulet sauté Stanley

CHICKEN SAUTÉ WITH CURRY SAUCE

1 spring chicken, salt, pepper, 8 oz. onions, few cooked mushrooms, few slices truffle, 6 tablespoons béchamel sauce (see page 23), 6 tablespoons cream, 1 small teaspoon curry powder, ½ oz. butter

Cut up the chicken and season with salt and pepper. Slice the onions and put them into boiling salted water for 3 minutes. Drain and put into a buttered sauté pan. Arrange the pieces of chicken on top. Cover and cook gently for 25 – 30 minutes.

When the chicken is cooked, remove it to a serving dish and add the mushrooms and truffle.

Put the béchamel sauce into the pan with the onions, add the cream and curry powder. Mix well and reduce for 2 minutes, scraping the bottom of the pan well.

Strain through a piece of muslin, then return to the pan, reheat quickly and finally add the butter. Pour the sauce over the chicken.

If liked, serve with *riz à la créole* (see page 666).

Poulet sauté aux truffes

CHICKEN SAUTÉ WITH TRUFFLES

1 spring chicken, salt, pepper, butter, 4 oz. raw truffles, 3 tablespoons Madeira, 5 – 6 tablespoons demi-glace sauce (see page 22)

Cut up the chicken, season and sauté in butter. When cooked add the sliced truffles, cover and leave for a few minutes for the chicken to absorb the flavour of the truffle. Add the Madeira and sauce and reduce for 1 minute.

Put the chicken on a serving dish, arrange the truffles on top and pour the sauce over.

Serve with buttered noodles or potatoes.

Poulet sauté Vanderbilt

CHICKEN SAUTÉ VANDERBILT

▬▬▬▬▬▬ 1 spring chicken, salt, pepper, butter, 2—3 potatoes, thinly sliced, 2—3 artichokes, thinly sliced, 3 tablespoons white wine, 4 tablespoons brown veal gravy, 2 truffles, 6 tablespoons cream

Remove the legs and wings from the chicken, divide the carcase in half and bone the chicken legs. Season the pieces of chicken and sauté in butter.

Butter the bottom of a casserole, cover with the slices of potato and artichoke, season lightly and cook over low heat.

When the chicken is cooked, arrange the legs and wings on the potatoes and artichokes.

Add the white wine to the butter and remaining chicken in the pan, reduce by half, then add the gravy. Boil for 2 minutes and then remove the carcase and wing tips. Add the sliced truffle, boil for a minute and finally add the cream.

Pour over the chicken.

SÉRIE DES POULETS DE GRAIN EN CASSEROLE, EN COCOTTE, POÊLÉS ET GRILLÉS

SPRING CHICKENS IN CASSEROLE, IN COCOTTE, POT-ROASTED AND GRILLED (U.S. broiled)

Poulet casserole

CHICKEN CASSEROLE

▬▬▬▬▬▬ 1 spring chicken, salt, pepper, 1 piece fat bacon, butter, few tablespoons brown veal gravy

Season the chicken inside with salt and pepper, truss it and cover the breast with a piece of fat bacon. Cook it in butter, preferably in a casserole just large enough to take the chicken, basting it frequently.

Just before serving. untruss the chicken, put it back into the casserole
and sprinkle with the brown veal gravy.
The chicken is served, as it is, in the casserole.
Note Do not remove the fat from the cooking liquor.

Poulet cocotte bonne femme

CHICKEN IN COCOTTE BONNE FEMME

Salt, pepper, 1 spring chicken, 4 oz. sausage meat, chopped chicken
liver, 1 tablespoon breadcrumbs, pinch chopped parsley, 1 piece
fat bacon, butter, 8—10 small onions, 12 small cubes streaky bacon,
8 oz. potatoes, cut into cubes, few tablespoons fairly thick brown
veal gravy

Season the inside of the chicken. Mix the sausage meat with the chopped
liver of the chicken, breadcrumbs and parsley, and stuff the chicken
with it.

Truss the chicken and cover the breast with a strip of fat bacon.

Heat some butter in a casserole, add the chicken and the onions and
bacon. Cover and cook over a low heat, turning the chicken frequently.
Half-way through the cooking, add the potatoes and baste them well with
the butter.

Cover and continue to cook gently until the chicken is tender.

Just before serving, untruss the chicken and sprinkle it with the brown
veal gravy.

Poulet de grain cévenol

SPRING CHICKEN CÉVENNES STYLE

Prepare the chicken and stuff as in the preceding recipe, cook it in
butter in a casserole with 10 small onions. When the chicken is cooked
untruss it and put it back into the casserole.

Add 3 tablespoons white wine, reduce to half, then add ¼ pint (U.S.
⅝ cup) demi-glace sauce (see page 22) and 12 chestnuts cooked in consommé.

Serve in the casserole.

Poulet au riz de tante Catherine

CHICKEN WITH RICE AS AUNT CATHERINE MADE IT

1 spring chicken, 4 oz. sausage meat, liver from the chicken, 1 tablespoon breadcrumbs, piece fat bacon, 6 small carrots, 6 small onions, *bouquet garni* of 2 sprigs parsley, ¼ bay leaf and 1 sprig thyme, ¼ pint (U.S. ⅝ cup) water, 1¼ pints (U.S. 3⅛ cups) chicken stock, 8 oz. rice

Prepare, stuff and truss the chicken as described for *poulet cocotte bonne femme* (see page 435).

Put it into a saucepan with the carrots, onions and *bouquet garni*. Add the water, cover and put over low heat. When nearly all the water has evaporated add the stock. Cover and cook over moderate heat for about 20 minutes. Add the well washed rice and continue the cooking a further 20−25 minutes.

Remove from the heat, untruss the chicken and put on to a serving dish. Remove the *bouquet garni*, and arrange the rice round the chicken.

Poulet de printemps aux petits pois à la paysanne

SPRING CHICKEN WITH PEAS, COUNTRY STYLE

1 spring chicken, salt, pepper, piece fat bacon, 6 small onions, 6 small carrots, 6 new potatoes, water, 2 sprigs parsley, 8 oz. freshly shelled peas, 1 small lettuce.

Prepare and season inside the chicken, truss it and cover the breast with the fat bacon. Put it into a pan with the onions, carrots, potatoes. Add ¼ pint (U.S. ⅝ cup) water, put over low heat and cook until the liquid is reduced by half. Add the parsley, peas, and lettuce. Add just enough boiling water to barely cover the vegetables, add a little salt and cook over gentle heat about 35 minutes.

Untruss the chicken, put on to a dish and surround with the vegetables.

Poulet Graziella

CHICKEN WITH BRAISED STUFFED LETTUCE

Salt, pepper, 1 spring chicken, 1 piece fat bacon, 4 oz. onions, 4 oz. carrots, *bouquet garni*, butter, ¼ pint (U.S. ⅝ cup) veal stock, braised lettuce stuffed with rice (see page 633), 6 tablespoons demi-glace sauce (see page 22)

Season the chicken, truss it and cover the breast with the fat bacon. Slice the onions and carrots and put in a casserole with the *bouquet garni* and a few pats of butter. Put the chicken on top, cover and put in a moderate oven for 10 minutes. Add the stock, cover the casserole again and continue the cooking, basting from time to time.

When the chicken is cooked, about 35–40 minutes, untruss it, and put on to a serving dish. Garnish with the braised stuffed lettuce.

Add the demi-glace sauce to the liquor left in the casserole, reduce rapidly by one-third then rub through a sieve. Reheat the resultant purée and pour it over the chicken.

Poulet grand'mère

STUFFED CHICKEN CASSEROLE

1 spring chicken, 1 oz. streaky bacon, 10 small onions, 8 oz. potatoes *For the stuffing* ½ oz. butter, 1 tablespoon finely chopped onion, 3 oz. sausage meat, liver from chicken, pinch chopped parsley, 2 tablespoons breadcrumbs, salt, mixed spice

To make the stuffing Heat the butter in a pan, add the onion and cook till lightly browned. Add the sausage meat, chopped chicken's liver and all the other ingredients.

Stuff the chicken, truss it, and put into a casserole with the bacon cut into small cubes and the onions. Cover and cook in a moderate oven. When the chicken and onions have begun to brown add the potatoes cut into small cubes and continue the cooking.

Serve in the casserole.

Poulet grillé diable

GRILLED (U.S. BROILED) CHICKEN WITH DIABLE SAUCE

Truss the chicken as for an entrée, split it through the back and flatten it slightly. Season with salt and pepper, sprinkle with melted butter and partly cook it in the oven. Dab with mustard, sprinkle with breadcrumbs, and then with melted butter and finish the cooking under the grill (U.S. broiler).

Serve on a very hot dish, with devil sauce (see page 27).

Poulet grillé américaine

GRILLED (U.S. BROILED) CHICKEN AMERICAN STYLE

Grill (U.S. broil) the chicken without mustard. Surround it with tomatoes, mushrooms and slices of grilled bacon. Serve with devil sauce (see page 27), or a horseradish cream.

Poulet de grain à l'orientale

SPRING CHICKEN IN THE ORIENTAL STYLE

Prepare the chicken and cook it on a bed of vegetables as indicated for *poulet Graziella* (see page 436).

Add ¼ pint (U.S. ⅝ cup) tomato sauce (see page 132) to the ingredients left in the pan. Rub through a sieve, then heat the resultant purée and pour it over the chicken.

Serve with a rice pilaf (see page 669).

Poulet Tartarin

STUFFED CHICKEN CASSEROLE WITH WINE

4 oz. sausage meat, 1 tablespoon chopped truffle, pinch mixed herbs, salt, 1 spring chicken, piece fat bacon, butter, 3 tablespoons white wine, ¼ pint (U.S. ⅝ cup), tomato sauce (see page 132), 1 tablespoon anchovy butter

Mix the sausage meat, truffle, herbs and a little salt and use to stuff the chicken. Truss it, cover the breast with the fat bacon and cook in butter in a casserole.

When the chicken is tender, untruss it and return to the casserole.

Add the wine, and heat until it is reduced by half. Add the tomato sauce, boil for a few minutes and finally add the anchovy butter.

Serve in the casserole accompanied by a dish of cèpes or mushrooms, sautéed in oil with a little garlic and chopped parsley, and garnished with sieved yolk of hard-boiled egg. Alternatively, serve the chicken with a dish of ravioli.

Poulet vauclusienne

CHICKEN CASSEROLE WITH TOMATOES,
AUBERGINES AND OLIVES

Salt, pepper, 1 spring chicken, 3 oz. streaky bacon, chopped, 2 tablespoons oil, 2 tablespoons finely chopped onion, 1 wine glass white wine, 5—6 tomatoes, peeled, seeded and chopped, pinch chopped parsley, 1 clove garlic, 24 black olives, 2 medium-sized aubergines, flour, oil

Season the inside of the chicken, truss it and put into a casserole with the chopped bacon and oil. Put over low heat, and when the chicken begins to brown add the onion, wine, tomatoes, parsley, garlic and a little salt and pepper. Cover, and simmer gently until the chicken is tender. Add the olives.

Cut the aubergines into thin slices, dip in flour and fry lightly in oil. Put into the casserole and serve at once.

Poulet vivandière

STUFFED CHICKEN WITH CALVADOS AND APPLES

1 spring chicken, white puddings (see page 385), 1 strip fat bacon, butter, 3—4 tablespoons Calvados (apple jack), 6 tablespoons boiling cream, 2—3 Reinette apples, 3—4 tablespoons water, pinch sugar, small pinch powdered cinnamon

Stuff the chicken with the freshly cooked white puddings, cover the breast with the fat bacon and cook in butter.

When the chicken is cooked, untruss it and replace it in the saucepan. Add the Calvados and the boiling cream.

Finely slice 2 or 3 Reinette apples and put them in a saucepan with 1 tablespoon butter, the water, sugar and cinnamon. Cover the saucepan and simmer gently.

Dish up the chicken and cover it with the sauce.
Serve the apples separately.

SÉRIE DES POUSSINS
RECIPES FOR POUSSINS

Poussins à l'alsacienne

POUSSINS ALSATIAN STYLE

————— 2 poussins, salt, freshly ground pepper, 1 tablespoon cooked foie gras, liver from the poussins, sautéed in butter, 2 pieces fat bacon, butter, 3 tablespoons Alsatian wine, ¼ pint (U.S. ⅝ cup) demi-glace sauce (see page 22), 3 oz. truffles, 8 oz. fresh noodles, 4—5 small slices foie gras, sautéed in butter

Season the poussins inside with salt and pepper. Mix the foie gras and chopped liver together and use to stuff the poussins. Wrap in thin slices of fat bacon and cook in butter. When ready, untruss and keep hot. Add the wine to the pan in which they were cooked and reduce by half. Add the sauce and sliced truffles.

Cook the noodles in boiling salted water, drain well, add 3 oz. butter and season with salt and freshly ground pepper.

Put into a serving dish, and arrange the slices of foie gras on top.

Pour a little of the sauce over, and pour the rest over the poussins.

Poussins à la bohémienne

POUSSINS GIPSY STYLE

————— 2 poussins, 3—4 tablespoons breadcrumbs, livers from poussins, pinch herbs, paprika, butter, 2 tablespoons chopped onion, 6 table-spoons white wine, 6 tablespoons cream, 3—4 tablespoons foie gras

Stuff the poussins with the breadcrumbs, chopped livers, herbs and ¼ level teaspoon paprika all mixed together. Truss them and cook in butter with the onion.

When partly cooked, sprinkle with a little paprika; and when tender, untruss and put into a casserole.

Add the wine to the butter left in the pan, reduce a little, then add the cream and finally the sieved foie gras.
Serve with roast potatoes.

Poussins Cendrillon

POUSSINS WITH TRUFFLED SAUSAGE MEAT

Choose poussins as small as possible. Cut in two from the back, flatten them slightly and bone them, only keeping the ends of the wings fastened to the meat and the leg; cook them in butter over gentle heat and season with salt and pepper.

Place between 2 layers of truffled sausage meat and wrap in sausage skin. Brush with butter and grill (U.S. broil) gently for 12−15 minutes. Serve with *sauce périgueux* (see page 28).

Poussins châtelaine

POUSSINS WITH VEGETABLES

2 poussins, salt, pepper, 2 oz. streaky bacon, 1 oz. butter, 6 small onions, 6 new carrots, 6 new potatoes, 1 lettuce, 8 oz. green peas, boiling water, 1 level tablespoon flour

Prepare the poussins, season them inside with salt and pepper, replace the liver and truss them.

Cut the bacon into small cubes and put them in boiling water for a few minutes. Drain and put them into a saucepan with ½ oz. butter. Put the saucepan over moderate heat, and as soon as the bacon begins to brown put in the poussins with the onions, carrots, potatoes, shredded lettuce and peas.

Add enough boiling water to cover the poussins and the vegetables. Add a little salt, then cover the saucepan and cook for about 30 minutes.

Untruss the poussins and put them into a fairly deep serving dish. Thicken the sauce with the remaining butter mixed with the flour. Boil for a few seconds and pour over the poussins.

Poussins hermitage

POUSSINS WITH POTATO BALLS

Bone the poussins as instructed for the *poussins Cendrillon* (see page 441) and flatten them slightly. Season with salt and pepper, dip them in flour, beaten egg and freshly prepared breadcrumbs, and cook them in clarified butter.

Cut out some small potato balls with a ball cutter and cook them in butter to which 1 tablespoon melted meat glaze has been added.

When the poussins are cooked, put them on to a serving dish and arrange the potato balls round. Coat the poussins with *sauce chasseur* (see page 26) to which a few slices of truffle have been added.

Serve with green peas.

Poussins moscovite

POUSSINS STUFFED WITH SEMOLINA AND BACON

━━━━━ 1 pint (U.S. 2½ cups) milk, large pinch salt, 8 oz. semolina, butter, 2 oz. streaky bacon, cut into very small cubes, 2 poussins, 6 table-spoons cream

Boil the milk with the salt, sprinkle in the semolina, stir, and simmer for 15—18 minutes. Remove from the heat and add 1 tablespoon butter and cubes of bacon.

Stuff the poussins with this mixture, truss them and cook in butter.

When they are ready, pour the cream over and let it boil for a few seconds.

Remove the poussins, untruss them, put on to a serving dish and pour the cream over.

Serve with green peas, asparagus tips or buttered new potatoes.

Poussins à la piémontaise

PIEDMONT STYLE POUSSINS

━━━━━ 4 tablespoons chopped ham, 3—4 white truffles, livers from the poussins sautéed in butter, 2 poussins, butter, 2 oz. streaky bacon, risotto, Parmesan cheese, salt, pepper, veal gravy, 2—3 tablespoons tomato sauce (see page 132)

Mix the ham, half the truffles, finely chopped, and the chopped livers together and use to stuff the poussins. Truss, and cook in 2 oz. butter and finely chopped streaky bacon.

Prepare the risotto, add some grated Parmesan cheese and put it into a serving dish.

When the poussins are ready, untruss and arrange on the risotto. Cover with the remaining truffle, cut into slices, and season lightly with salt and pepper.

Put the veal gravy into the pan in which the poussins were cooked, reduce a little, then add the tomato sauce and a few pats of butter.

Pour this sauce over the poussins.

Poussins à la polonaise

POLISH STYLE POUSSINS

2 poussins, 4 tablespoons gratin forcemeat (see page 58), butter, breadcrumbs fried in butter, 3—4 tablespoons fairly thick gravy, 4 tablespoons cream, squeeze lemon juice

Stuff each poussin with the forcemeat. Truss them and cook in butter over a moderate heat. Put them on to a serving dish and cover with the breadcrumbs. Add the gravy to the butter remaining in the pan, stir till boiling, then add the cream and lemon juice.

Poussins Souvarow

POUSSINS STUFFED WITH FOIE GRAS AND TRUFFLES

2 oz. cooked foie gras, 4 truffles, 2 poussins, butter, salt, pepper, 3—4 tablespoons chicken stock, 3—4 tablespoons thick veal gravy, 2—3 tablespoons Madeira, pastry dough

Mix the foie gras with 2 truffles, cut into cubes and use to stuff the poussins. Partly cook them in butter. Untruss and put into a casserole just large enough to take them. Put the other 2 truffles with the poussin and add a little salt and pepper.

Add the stock, gravy and Madeira to the butter left in the pan. Stir till boiling and boil for 2 minutes. Pour over the poussins.

Cover with the lid of the casserole and then seal it with a strip of dough.

Continue the cooking in a moderate oven for about 15—18 minutes. Serve in the casserole.

Poussins valentinois

POUSSINS WITH FOIE GRAS AND TRUFFLE

▅▅▅▅▅▅▅ 2 poussins, seasoning, butter, foie gras purée, 6 slices truffle, flour, 6 tablespoons white wine, 3—4 tablespoons veal gravy, 3—4 tablespoons meat jelly (see page 21), butter

Bone the poussins, leaving a small piece of bone adhering to the wings, flatten them a little, season and put them into very hot butter for 1 minute to seal the flesh. Place them on a dish and cover the inside with a layer of foie gras purée. Put the slices of truffle in a row on one of the poussins, and cover all this with the second poussin. Sew up the edges, sprinkle with flour and cook gently in butter, turning them over from time to time so that they may be evenly cooked on both sides. Remove the thread and put the poussins on to a serving dish.

Add the white wine to the butter left in the pan, stir well and bring to boiling point. Add the gravy and meat jelly, reheat and add a few pats of butter. Pour over the poussins.

Serve with buttered asparagus tips and *pommes de terre Macaire* (see page 651).

Poussins Véronique

POUSSINS WITH GRAPES

▅▅▅▅▅▅ 2 poussins, butter, 24 muscat grapes, peeled and seeded, 6 tablespoons white wine, 2 tablespoons meat jelly (see page 21), 6 tablespoons cream

Cook the poussins in butter, then put into a casserole with the grapes.

Put the white wine into the pan with the remaining butter and reduce by two-thirds. Add the meat jelly and cream. Boil for a few seconds and pour over the poussins.

Poussins à la viennoises

VIENNESE STYLE POUSSINS

Cut the poussins in half lengthwise and flatten them. Season, dip each half into flour, then coat with beaten egg and breadcrumbs and cook them in clarified butter, or fry in deep fat.

Serve garnished with fried parsley and lemon quarters.

The following sauces are suitable to serve with this dish: tomato (see page 132), tartare (see page 42), ravigote (see page 42) or horseradish (see page 44).

PRÉPARATIONS DIVERSES DE LA VOLAILLE
RECIPES USING GIBLETS AND PINIONS (Wings)

Abatis de volaille
GIBLETS

Giblets are usually added to pot-au-feu although they can be used in excellent ragoûts.

Abatis à la bourguignonne
BURGUNDY STYLE GIBLETS

8 oz. fat pork, 2 oz. butter, 2 lb. chicken giblets, 3 tablespoons flour, 1 pint (U.S. 2½ cups) red wine, 1¾ pints (U.S. 4¼ cups) water, salt, pepper, 24 small onions, *bouquet garni* of 2 sprigs parsley, 1 bay leaf and 2 sprigs thyme, 1 clove garlic

Cut the pork into cubes. Put it into boiling water for a few minutes and then drain.

Heat the butter in a fairly large pan. Brown the pork in it, then remove and keep hot.

Put the livers aside, chop the rest of the giblets and brown in the butter. (The livers should not be added until about 10 minutes before the end of the cooking.) Add the flour, cook for a few minutes, then add the wine and water. Add a little salt and pepper, onions browned lightly in butter, *bouquet garni* and garlic. Cover and simmer very gently. Add the chicken livers and pork fat 10 minutes before the end of the cooking.

Note Mushrooms may be added if liked and the red wine can be replaced by white wine.

Potatoes and any other vegetable may be served as an accompaniment.

Ailerons

PINIONS (WINGS)

Pinions are prepared like giblets with vegetables, pilaf, etc., and make excellent luncheon dishes.

They are simmered gently in butter, and pinions from turkey may be stuffed with sausage meat.

Ailerons au beurre à la purée de marrons

PINIONS IN BUTTER WITH CHESTNUT PURÉE

4 oz. butter, 12 pinions*, salt, pepper, flour, water
*Pinions from large roasting chickens or turkey are best for this recipe.

Melt the butter in a wide, thick-bottomed pan, large enough to take the pinions side by side.

Season the pinions lightly, coat with flour, and arrange in the pan. Cover and cook very gently. As the butter begins to clarify, add 1 tablespoon water and continue the cooking, adding further tablespoons of water from time to time as the butter becomes clear. This produces a slightly brown and excellent sauce.

When the pinions are cooked, arrange on a serving dish and pour the cooking liquor over.

Serve with chestnut purée (see page 637).

Pinions may also be cooked on a bed of vegetables with a *bouquet garni* as given for braised calf's sweetbreads (see page 321) or, if preferred, with mashed potatoes, chicory, spinach or a purée of peas.

Ailerons farcis

STUFFED PINIONS

Bone the pinions, stuff them with fine sausage meat to which a few tablespoons chopped truffle have been added, and braise them on a bed of vegetables.

The same garnishes as for the preceding dish are suitable.

Ailerons farcis et grillés

STUFFED AND GRILLED (U.S. BROILED) PINIONS

After braising, let them cool, brush with butter and coat with freshly prepared breadcrumbs. Grill (U.S. broil) gently.

Serve with devil sauce (see page 27), mashed potatoes, and chestnut purée.

BALLOTTINES ET JAMBONNEAUX DE VOLAILLE

BALLOTTINES OF POULTRY

A ballottine of poultry is a joint which is boned, stuffed and rolled into the shape of a bundle.

It is a good method of using up the thighs, when the breast has been used for another purpose.

They are boned and stuffed with sausage meat, galantine forcemeat (see page 58), etc. The skin, which must be left fairly long, is sewn up again to give the thighs the required shape.

Ballottines are always braised and served with their cooking liquor. Peas, spinach, chicory, carrots or mushrooms are suitable accompaniments, and sometimes a *sauce suprême* (see page 23) with the addition of truffles.

Ballottines may also be served cold, when the cooking liquor should set in a jelly.

BOUDINS ET QUENELLES DE VOLAILLE

PUDDINGS AND QUENELLES OF POULTRY

Boudins de volaille à la Richelieu

POULTRY PUDDINGS RICHELIEU

———————— Cream chicken forcemeat (see page 56), 1 dessertspoon salpicon of chicken truffles and mushrooms bound with white sauce (see page 22), flour, egg, breadcrumbs, clarified butter

Half fill some buttered oval or oblong moulds with the forcemeat. Add the salpicon, then fill up with the forcemeat and smooth the surface.

Put the mould into a sauté pan, and cover with boiling water. Simmer very gently, cool a little, then turn out on to a cloth and drain well.

Coat with flour, then with beaten egg and breadcrumbs and brown lightly in a little clarified butter.

Serve with a *sauce périgueux* (see page 28) or with a truffled *sauce suprême* (see page 23).

Note The salpicon of chicken may be replaced with salpicon of partridge or other game, in which case the boudins should be accompanied with a chestnut purée (see page 637).

Pascalines de poulet

PASCALINES OF CHICKEN

———————— Grated cheese, 1 lb. cream chicken forcemeat (see page 56), 1 lb. choux pastry (see page 70) made with milk and without sugar, béchamel sauce (see page 23), slices of truffle, butter

Add 4 – 5 tablespoons grated cheese and forcemeat to the choux pastry and mix thoroughly well together. Shape into ovals (like half hard-boiled egg) and arrange in a buttered sauté pan.

Cover with nearly boiling salted water and poach gently about 10 minutes.

Coat a serving dish with a thin layer of béchamel sauce, and arrange the drained pascalines on it. Put a few slices of truffle on top, and then cover with more béchamel sauce.

Sprinkle with grated cheese, brush lightly with butter and brown in the oven or under the grill (U.S. broiler).

Note If liked, a little chopped truffle, chicken, ham or tongue may be added as a variation.

Quenelles de volaille

QUENELLES OF POULTRY

For fine quenelles, mousseline forcemeat (see page 56) should always be used. The quenelles are moulded, according to the use to which they are to be put, either in a tablespoon, a dessertspoon or a teaspoon.

When they are to be used for soup, it is more practical to use a forcing bag with a nozzle.

Mousseline quenelles should be covered and poached with a great deal of care in nearly boiling water. Keep just under boiling point, as the slightest boiling destroys the delicacy of the quenelle.

Poach for 10 – 12 minutes.

Quenelles à la panade à la crème ou au beurre

PANADA QUENELLES WITH CREAM OR BUTTER

These quenelles (see page 56) are usually used as garnishes.

Divide the forcemeat into pieces weighing 2½ – 3 oz. Mould the quenelles into an oval shape, poach them for 8 – 10 minutes in salted hot water and drain them.

Chopped ham, tongue or truffles may be added to the mixture, according to the dishes they are to accompany.

They can also be served as an entrée, either with thinly sliced chicken, crayfish, truffle or mushrooms and should be coated with béchamel sauce (see page 23) or *sauce suprême* (see page 23).

Blanquette de volaille à la bourgeoise

BLANQUETTE OF CHICKEN WITH VEGETABLES AND HERBS

1 tender chicken, butter, 3 tablespoons flour, hot water, salt, pepper, 20 small onions, 1 clove, bouquet of 2 sprigs parsley, 1 bay leaf and 2 sprigs thyme, mushrooms, 2 egg yolks, 2 tablespoons cream or sauce

Cut up the chicken as for sautéing, put into a pan and cover with cold water and bring to boiling point. Remove the chicken, refresh in cold water and dry. Melt 1½ oz. butter in a pan, add the flour and cook for a few minutes. Add the chicken, mix well with the flour and butter, then just cover with hot water. Bring slowly to boiling point, add a little salt and pepper, onions — 1 stuck with the clove — and the *bouquet garni*.

Cover and simmer for about 1 hour. Add a few mushrooms sautéed first in butter and cook for a few minutes longer. Put the pieces of chicken into a serving dish with the onions and mushrooms. Remove the *bouquet garni* from the pan, and add the egg yolks mixed with the cream. Finally add a few pats of butter. Pour the sauce over the chicken without allowing it to boil.

Serve with pilaf of rice (see page 669) or with buttered noodles.

Capilotade de volaille

CHICKEN CAPILOTADE

Capilotade is made with the left-overs of roast, boiled or braised chicken cut up into pieces — mixed with Italian sauce (see page 28) and simmered for 15 − 20 minutes. Sprinkle lightly with chopped parsley before serving.

Coquilles de volaille

COQUILLES OF CHICKEN

Coquilles are usually made with left-over poultry, preferably boiled or steamed.

Coquilles de volaille Mornay

COQUILLES OF CHICKEN MORNAY

Line the bottom of the coquilles (shells) with béchamel sauce (see page 23) and fill them with thin slices of chicken heated in butter, cover with more béchamel sauce. Sprinkle the surface with freshly grated cheese, brush with melted butter and brown lightly in the oven or under the grill (U.S. broiler).

Note If desired, thin slices of truffle and mushrooms may be mixed with the chicken.

Crépinettes de volaille
CHICKEN CRÉPINETTES

1 lb. chicken meat, 4 oz. lean pork, 12 oz. fresh pork, fat, 4 oz. foie gras, 3 oz. truffle, salt, pinch nutmeg, 1 tablespoon brandy, sausage skin, butter, breadcrumbs

Chop the chicken and pork and mix with the sieved foie gras and a little of the chopped truffle, reserving a few slices. Add salt, nutmeg and brandy.

Divide into pieces of about $2\frac{1}{2}$ – 3 oz. and shape into flat ovals. Place a thin slice of truffle on each and wrap in sausage skin. Brush with melted butter and coat with breadcrumbs. Grill (U.S. broil) gently or fry in butter.

Serve with *sauce périgueux* (see page 28) or *sauce suprême* with truffles (see page 23) and mashed potatoes.

CRÊTES ET ROGNONS DE COQ
COCK'S CRESTS AND KIDNEYS

Cock's crests or combs must have the skin which covers them removed and be soaked in cold water before being cooked in a very light white stock. The essential point in their preparation is that they should retain their whiteness.

Kidneys are only washed in cold water for a short time, if possible in running water, and are only added to the crests in the stock a few minutes before the latter are cooked.

The chief use of crests and kidneys is for garnishes. They do, however, become the principal ingredients of the following dishes.

Crêtes de coq à l'aurore

COCK'S CRESTS WITH COCK'S KIDNEYS AND SAUCE SUPRÊME

———————— You will need for 6 persons:
18 cock's crests, white stock, 2 truffles, 12 cock's kidneys, 3 tablespoons Madeira, ½ oz. butter, 2 tablespoons light meat jelly (see page 21), *sauce suprême* (see page 23), paprika

Cook the crests in white stock, drain, and put into a pan with the sliced truffles, kidneys browned in butter, Madeira, butter and meat jelly.

Cover and boil for 1 minute.

Put into a serving dish and coat with *sauce suprême* to which a little paprika has been added.

Serve with a rice pilaf (see page 669).

Crêtes et rognons Souvarow

CRESTS AND KIDNEYS SUVAROFF

———————— 12 large cock's crests, white stock, carrots, onions, *bouquet garni*, bacon trimmings, 2 large truffles, 3 tablespoons Madeira, 2 tablespoons meat jelly (see page 21), ⅓ pint (U.S. 1¼ cups) demi-glace sauce (see page 22), 18 fresh kidneys, flour, butter, salt, pepper

Cook the crests for 20 minutes in white stock.

Drain, and braise on a bed of carrots, onions, *bouquet garni* and a few bacon trimmings.

Remove the crests and put into a pan with the sliced truffles, Madeira and meat jelly.

Add the sauce to the cooking liquor left in the pan in which the crests were cooked. Boil for a few minutes and strain over the crests.

Wash and drain the kidneys, roll in flour and sauté in butter. Season with salt and pepper and put with the crests.

Heat all together and add 1 tablespoon butter.

Serve with *riz à la piémontaise* (see page 668) with 2−3 tablespoons foie gras purée and grated Parmesan cheese.

Brochettes de rognons de coq

BROILED COCK'S KIDNEYS

You will need for 4 persons:
24 large fresh cock's kidneys, flour, salt, pepper, butter, thin strips bacon, breadcrumbs

Wash the kidneys in cold water, dry in a cloth, then flour lightly, season with salt and pepper and cook for a few minutes in butter.

Cut the bacon into thin strips, just large enough to wrap round the kidneys.

Thread the kidneys, wrapped in bacon, on skewers (about 6 to each skewer), brush with melted butter, dip in fine breadcrumbs and grill (U.S. broil) slowly.

Serve with creamed potatoes and béarnaise (see page 30), piquante (see page 28) or devil sauce (see page 27) according to taste.

Important Kidneys should not be left in cold water for more than a few minutes.

Rognons de coq Otero

COCK'S KIDNEYS, ARTICHOKES AND RED PEPPERS

You will need for 4 persons:
20 fresh cock's kidneys, flour, butter, salt, pepper, 3 tablespoons Madeira, 3 tablespoons meat jelly, ½ pint (U.S. 1¼ cups) cream, truffles, 4 artichoke bottoms, pilaf of rice (see page 669), 2 large red peppers

Wash the kidneys in cold water, drain and dry in a cloth. Coat with flour and sauté in butter, season with salt and pepper and remove to a plate.

Add the Madeira to the butter remaining in the pan in which the kidneys were cooked and stir well. Add the meat jelly and cream and boil for a few minutes.

Put the kidneys back into the sauce and add a thin julienne of truffles.

Put the freshly cooked artichokes on to a serving dish and pour the kidneys and sauce over.

Serve with a pilaf of rice and the red peppers, peeled, grilled (U.S. broiled) and cut into julienne.

Note Be sure the kidneys are not left in water for any length of time.

Rognons de coq farcis pour entrée froide, garnitures, etc.

COCK'S KIDNEYS STUFFED FOR COLD ENTRÉES, GARNISHES, ETC.

——————— Kidneys, white stock, truffled foie gras purée, white chaudfroid sauce (see page 31)

Choose very fresh, large kidneys of equal size, poach them in the stock, let them cool and dry in a cloth. Cut lengthwise, without separating them, trim slightly and stuff them with truffled foie gras purée. Coat them with a white chaudfroid sauce, put them on an enamelled tray and place this on ice, long enough to set the sauce.

They can then be used as a garnish on a mousse of ham, tomato, chicken with paprika, woodcock, etc.

The procedure is as follows:

Choose a square dish, deep for preference; or, if not available, a glass bowl. Surround the dish with crushed ice and spread a light layer of aspic jelly on the bottom. Cover the jelly with about ½ inch of the mousse mixture. As soon as this has set, arrange the kidneys on it in two rows. Leave between the kidneys a space of ½ inch which should be garnished with green asparagus tips.

Cover the dish with half-set aspic jelly, and serve on another dish of crushed ice.

Note For a mousse of woodcock or of Aylesbury duckling, the asparagus tips should be replaced by a fine julienne of chicken's breast, truffle, mushrooms and tongue.

CROQUETTES, PALETS ET CROMESQUIS DE VOLAILLE
CHICKEN CROQUETTES, ROUNDS AND KROMESKYS

Croquettes de volaille

CHICKEN CROQUETTES

——————— 1 lb. cold cooked chicken, 4 oz. mushrooms, ½ pint (U.S. 1¼ cups) *sauce parisienne* (see page 22), beaten egg, salt and pepper, bread-crumbs, deep fat for frying, fried parsley

Cut the chicken meat, truffles and mushrooms into very small cubes. Put into a pan with the sauce, and stir over a quick heat until the mixture has reduced and is fairly thick.

Turn out on to a dish and leave to cool.

Flour a pastry board, divide the mixture into equal parts and roll into cork shapes. Dip in egg, seasoned with salt and pepper, and then roll in breadcrumbs.

Fry in deep fat for about 10 minutes, and serve garnished with fried parsley.

Périgueux (see page 28), tomato (see page 132) or curry sauce (see page 32) make a suitable accompaniment.

Palets de volaille

CHICKEN ROUNDS

Prepare a mixture exactly like the preceding one, adding a few table-spoons tongue and ham, cut very fine.

When the mixture has cooled, divide it into equal parts of about 2−2½ oz. each, put them on to a lightly floured pastry board, roll first into the shape of a ball and then flatten into small round cakes. Dip each round in beaten egg, and then roll in breadcrumbs. Fry in clarified butter until brown on both sides.

Arrange in a ring on a serving dish and cover lightly with 2−3 table-spoons buttered meat jelly (see page 21) and a squeeze of lemon juice.

If liked, one-third quantity of meat can be replaced by cooked rice.

Cromesquis

KROMESKY

Prepare the kromesky mixture in exactly the same way as for croquettes (see page 545). Divide it into equal parts of about 2 oz. then shape into oblongs on a pastry board sprinkled with flour and wrap them in sausage skins.

Coat with batter and fry in hot oil. Drain well and serve garnished with fried parsley.

Tomato sauce (see page 132) is a good accompaniment.

ÉMINCÉS DE VOLAILLE
LEFT-OVER CHICKEN

Émincé de volaille à la ménagère

CHICKEN WITH MUSHROOMS AND WHITE SAUCE

Arrange on a dish a ring of boiled potatoes lightly browned in butter. Fill the space in the middle with left-over chicken and freshly cooked mushrooms, both cut into slices, and bound with béchamel sauce (see page 23).

Sprinkle with grated cheese mixed with dried breadcrumbs. Dot with butter and brown in the oven.

Note In case the chicken is a little dry, a few hard-boiled eggs, finely chopped, may be added.

Émincé de volaille à la bonne femme

CHICKEN WITH HAM AND WHITE SAUCE

Finely chop some left-over chicken, add $\frac{1}{4}$ its volume of chopped ham and an equal quantity of rice cooked in butter.

Mix all together, put into a serving dish and coat with béchamel sauce (see page 23). Sprinkle with grated cheese, dot with butter and brown in the oven.

Émincé de volaille au curry

CURRIED CHICKEN

Put some sliced chicken into a pan with 1 tablespoon butter, and 1 tablespoon chicken stock. Cover and heat gently until the chicken is warmed through.

Add some *sauce curry à la crème* (see page 32) and serve with *riz à l'indienne* (see page 668).

Émincé de volaille Maintenon

CHICKEN WITH TRUFFLES AND MADEIRA

Cut the wings of a poached chicken into thin slices. Put them into a saucepan with 1 tablespoon butter, 4 oz. peeled and sliced truffles and 2 tablespoons Madeira. Cover the saucepan, and put over a low heat until the chicken is heated through. Bind with *sauce parisienne* (see page 22).

Serve in a ring of *riz au gras à la française* (see page 667).

Blanc de poularde marquise

CHICKEN WITH GNOCCHI AND SAUCE PARISIENNE

You will need for 8 persons:
2 medium-sized pullets, strips fat bacon, white veal stock, butter, 2 tablespoons Madeira, truffles, salt, pepper, ½ pint (U.S. 1¼ cups) *sauce parisienne* (see page 22), gnocchi (see page 671), pâté de foie gras, flour.

Choose pullets of medium size and clean them carefully. Truss them as for an entrée, wrap in strips of fat bacon, and poach them in the stock. As soon as the pullets are cooked, take them out and untruss them; cut off the breast and remove the skin.

Divide each breast into 2 thick slices and place them in a saucepan with 1 tablespoon butter, 2 tablespoons of the cooking liquor, Madeira and 8 oz. truffles cut in slices and seasoned sparingly.

Cover the saucepan, heat for a few moments and add the sauce, together with the rest of the liquor in which the pullets were cooked, reduced to quarter its volume.

Have ready some gnocchi to which has been added quarter its volume of pâté de foie gras cut into small cubes. Cool on a tray.

Cut out some thick slices with an oval-shaped cutter as nearly as possible the same size as the pieces of chicken. Dip them in flour and brown on both sides in butter.

Place the gnocchi on a serving dish, place a piece of chicken on each and on this a slice of truffle and the sauce.

Serve with some buttered asparagus tips.

Médaillon blanc de poularde duchesse
MEDALLIONS OF CHICKEN WITH ARTICHOKES

———— 2 medium-sized pullets, 12 cooked artichoke bottoms, cooked foie gras, truffle, béchamel sauce (see page 23), grated cheese, butter

Prepare and cook the pullets as described in the preceding recipe, and cut each breast into 3 medallions, i.e. thick round or oval slices.

Put the artichoke bottoms on to a serving dish and arrange a medallion of chicken on each one.

Chop the trimmings from the chicken breasts and mix with a little chopped foie gras and truffle. Bind with the sauce and arrange over the chicken.

Sprinkle with grated cheese, dot with butter and glaze in the oven or under the grill (U.S. broiler).

Serve with peas or asparagus tips.

SÉRIE DE FOIES DE VOLAILLE
RECIPES USING CHICKEN LIVERS

Foies de volaille chasseur
CHICKEN LIVERS WITH MUSHROOMS AND WHITE SAUCE

———— 10 chicken livers, salt, pepper, flour, butter, oil, 5—6 mushrooms, 1 shallot, 1 tablespoon brandy, 3 tablespoons white wine, 3 tablespoons tomato sauce (see page 132), $\frac{1}{2}$ pint (U.S. $1\frac{1}{4}$ cups) demi-glace sauce (see page 22), pinch parsley, pinch tarragon, juice $\frac{1}{2}$ lemon.

Remove the gall bladders from the livers, season, roll in flour and sauté in butter and oil mixed. Remove to a plate.

Put the sliced mushrooms into the pan, sauté for a few seconds then add the chopped shallot, brandy and wine. Reduce by two-thirds. Add the tomato sauce and the well reduced demi-glace sauce.

Put the livers back into the sauce, add the parsley and tarragon, and finally a few dabs of butter and the lemon juice, shaking the pan well so that the butter combines fully with the sauce.

Serve with rice pilaf (see page 669).

Foies de volaille en pilaw

CHICKEN LIVER PILAF

Sauté the chicken livers in butter, season with salt and pepper and mix with an equal quantity of rice cooked for pilaf (see page 669). The quantity of rice may be increased if necessary.

Serve with tomato sauce (see page 132).

Note If liked, slices of aubergines, fried or sautéed in butter, may be added.

Brochettes de foie de volaille

BROILED CHICKEN LIVERS

Chicken livers, salt, pepper, butter, chopped parsley, mushrooms, streaky bacon, dry breadcrumbs

Trim the livers, season and sauté them for 1 minute in very hot butter. Remove from the pan, put on to a plate and sprinkle with parsley.

Thread on to skewers, interspersing them with cooked or raw mushrooms cut to the same size, and small pieces of very thinly cut streaky bacon. Brush with butter and sprinkle with breadcrumbs. Grill (U.S. broil) gently.

Serve with piquante (see page 28) or devil (see page 27) sauce.

Mashed potatoes make a good accompaniment to broiled chicken livers.

Foies de volaille sautés à la provençale

CHICKEN LIVERS SAUTÉED IN THE PROVENÇAL STYLE

12 chicken livers, salt, pepper, flour, butter, oil
For the sauce 5—6 ripe tomatoes, 2 tablespoons oil, salt, pepper, 1 clove garlic, pinch parsley

Peel, seed and chop the tomatoes and put into a pan with the oil, seasoning, chopped garlic and parsley. Cover, and simmer for 18—20 minutes.

Trim the livers, season, roll in flour and sauté in half butter and half oil.

Add to the sauce, and serve with rice pilaf (see page 669).

Fricassée de poulet ménagère

FRICASSÉE OF CHICKEN

1 3-lb. chicken, 1 oz. butter, 6 tablespoons white wine, 2 pints (U.S.
5 cups) boiling water, 20 small onions, bouquet of 2 sprigs parsley,
1 bay leaf and 1 sprig thyme, 1 teaspoon salt, pinch pepper, 2 tablespoons flour, 2—3 tablespoons cold water, 15 small mushrooms,
sautéed in butter, 3 egg yolks, 3 tablespoons cream or white sauce
(see page 22), pinch chopped parsley

Prepare the chicken and cut up as for sautéing. Put the pieces into a pan
with 1 tablespoon butter and the wine and cook until the wine has
almost evaporated. Add the water and the onions — which should
have been previously boiled for a few minutes, *bouquet garni*, salt and
pepper. Boil for 6—8 minutes, then stir in the flour mixed smoothly
with the cold water. Half cover the pan, and cook over moderate heat
for 20—25 minutes. Add the mushrooms. When the chicken is tender,
remove the *bouquet garni*, and add the egg yolks mixed with the cream,
rest of the butter, and parsley.

Buttered noodles, rice pilaf (see page 669) or boiled potatoes are
a suitable accompaniment.

Note The liquid should not be allowed to boil after the eggs and
cream have been added.

Fricassée of chicken can also be prepared with a garnish of truffles,
morels or crayfish. In this case, cook the chicken in just enough veal
stock to cover it. When it is ready, remove to a fairly deep serving dish
and keep hot. Reduce the cooking liquor by two-thirds; add ½ pint (U.S.
1¼ cups) velouté sauce (see page 22). Reduce again until the sauce is
thick enough to coat the back of a spoon.

Add the egg yolks mixed with cream.

Heat the truffles or other garnish chosen in a pan with a little butter.
Add the sauce, strained through a fine sieve, and then pour it over the
chicken.

Fritot de volaille

CHICKEN FRITTERS

Take a boiled chicken and divide it into 5 parts — 2 legs, 2 wings and
the breast. Cut each leg into 3 pieces, and the wings and breast into

2 pieces each. Put them in a deep dish and sprinkle lightly with oil, lemon juice and chopped parsley.

When ready to serve, dip the pieces of chicken into a light batter and fry in deep fat.

Drain well and garnish with fried parsley.

Serve with tomato sauce (see page 132).

Mazagran de volaille

MAZAGRAN OF CHICKEN

Line an oval dish with a border of duchesse potatoes as described in the recipe for *crème turbot gratin* (see page 229).

Fill the centre with sliced chicken, truffle and mushrooms bound together with *sauce suprême* (see page 23).

Brush the potato with beaten egg and brown in the oven. Then sprinkle the chicken with breadcrumbs browned in butter and arrange some grilled (U.S. broiled) or fried chipolata sausages round the base of the mazagran.

Editor's Note In France, mazagran has a double meaning. It is applied to a dish lined with duchesse potatoes and also to cold or hot coffee if served in a glass.

MOUSSES ET MOUSSELINES DE VOLAILLE

MOUSSES AND MOUSSELINES OF POULTRY

Both mousses and mousselines are made from a base of cream mousseline forcemeat (see page 56), the only difference being that a mousse is usually made in a mould sufficient for 4−8 persons, while mousselines are made in the shape of quenelles (see page 55) and 1 or 2 are served to each person.

Mousselines de volaille Alexandra

CHICKEN MOUSSELINES ALEXANDRA

Shape the mousselines with a tablespoon and place them, as they are made, in a buttered sauté pan.

Cover them with slightly salted boiling water, pouring the water carefully through a conical strainer so as not to spoil the shape of the mousselines.

Cover the pan, and keep it at the side of the stove with the water just below boiling point, for 12−15 minutes.

Drain, and arrange in a ring on the serving dish. Place a thin slice of white chicken meat on each one and top with a slice of truffle. Coat with béchamel sauce (see page 23).

Sprinkle with grated cheese, dot with butter, and glaze quickly under the grill (U.S. broiler).

Garnish the centre with buttered asparagus tips.

Mousselines de volaille à la florentine

FLORENCE STYLE CHICKEN MOUSSELINES

Mould and poach the mousselines in the same way as in the preceding recipe. Lay them on a bed of blanched spinach, coarsely chopped, cooked in butter and seasoned with salt and pepper. Coat with béchamel sauce (see page 23), sprinkle with freshly grated cheese, dot with butter and glaze quickly under the grill (U.S. broiler).

Mousselines de volaille à l'indienne

INDIAN STYLE CHICKEN MOUSSELINES

Mould, poach, drain and arrange the mousselines in a ring on a round dish.

Coat them with *sauce curry à la crème* (see page 32) and serve *riz à l'indienne* on a separate dish (see page 668).

Mousselines de volaille au paprika

CHICKEN MOUSSELINES WITH PAPRIKA

The same method as for *mousselines de volaille à l'indienne* (see page 462), except that the curry sauce is replaced by paprika sauce (see page 29).
Serve with pilaf of rice (see page 669).

Mousseline de volaille Patti

CHICKEN MOUSSELINE WITH CRAYFISH AND SUPRÊME SAUCE

Mould and poach the mousselines as in the previous recipes, and arrange them in a ring on a serving dish.
Mix a little crayfish butter (see page 114) and some crayfish with a little *sauce suprême* (see page 23) and place in the centre.
Coat the mousselines with more sauce and put a slice of truffle on each one.

Note If preferred the mousselines may be served on croûtons fried in butter or on small rounds of semolina browned in butter (see page 67).

Sylphides de volaille

CHICKEN SYLPHIDES

Mould and poach the mousselines as usual. Cover them with béchamel sauce (see page 23) to which has been added a fine julienne of truffles. Put a little of the sauce in the bottom of some barquettes, and put a mousseline in each one.
Arrange a slice of white chicken meat on each mousseline and cover with a thin layer of the sauce. Cover this with a Parmesan soufflé mixture forced through a forcing bag with a plain nozzle. Put the sylphides in a hot oven for 4–5 minutes, to cook the soufflé, and serve at once.

Note Barquettes are oval-shaped tartlet cases.

Ursulines de Nancy

NANCY URSULINES

Mould and poach the mousselines as described previously.

Thin down a little purée of foie gras with a little meat jelly (see page 21) and put a spoonful into some barquettes.

Arrange a mousseline in each one and top with a thin slice of truffle. Coat with meat jelly to which a little butter has been added.

Put them on to a serving dish in a ring with some buttered asparagus tips in the centre.

Note Ursulines may be served as small entrées or used as a garnish for other dishes.

Pâte de poulet à l'anglaise

ENGLISH CHICKEN PIE

1 young tender chicken, salt, pepper, 3 shallots, 1 medium-sized onion, 2 oz. mushrooms, pinch chopped parsley, few thin slices veal, 4 oz. streaky bacon, 4 hard-boiled eggs, chicken stock, flaky pastry, beaten egg

Cut up the chicken as described on page 422 for sautéing and season with salt and pepper.

Chop the shallots, onion and mushrooms finely and mix with the chicken. Add the parsley.

Line the bottom and sides of a pie dish with the veal. Put in the chicken, placing the legs at the bottom.

Add the bacon cut into thin strips and the eggs cut in halves. Add enough chicken stock to come about three-quarters of the way up the dish.

Cover with flaky pastry and brush with beaten egg. Make a small hole in the centre and bake for 1–1½ hours in a moderate oven.

When the pie is cooked, pour a little extra stock through the hole in the top.

Note The flaky pastry may be replaced by plain pastry, and the eggs may be omitted. This very simple way of making pies is, on the whole, to be recommended to all good housewives.

TIMBALES

When making a timbale, it is usual to cook an empty pie-crust of the size required and to fill it, at the last minute, with the ingredient decided upon, in the same way as one would fill a vol-au-vent case.

To make this crust, line the mould chosen with pastry, and fill it with dried haricot beans, rice or crusts of bread. Put on the pastry lid, and cook it in a moderate oven. When the crust is cooked, take it out of the oven, let it cool for a little while, then remove the lid and take out the beans which may be used again for the same purpose.

Here is another method, which, though it gives an excellent result, is not used so much today.

Butter the mould and line it with pastry. Arrange some thin slices of bacon in the bottom and round the sides and fill up the mould with chopped pork and beef. Add seasoning and a little spice. Put on the pastry lid, brush with beaten egg and cook in a moderate oven.

Then remove the lid carefully, take out all the contents and replace with the chosen filling.

Note The meat can then be used for making various hot or cold dishes.

Timbale Bontoux

——————— 1 timbale case

Filling 1 Macaroni, butter, Parmesan cheese, 3—4 tablespoons well reduced demi-glace sauce with tomato (see page 22)

Cook the macaroni until it is only just tender then add a little butter, grated Parmesan and the sauce.

——————— *Filling 2* Cooked cock's crests (combs) and kidneys, truffle, truffled quenelles of chicken, demi-glace sauce with tomato (see page 22)

Mix the chopped crests, kidneys and truffle. Add the quenelles and bind all with the sauce.

Fill up the timbale case with alternate layers of the fillings.

Timbale Maréchal Foch

TIMBALE FILLED WITH CHICKEN AND VEAL

1 good-sized chicken or capon, salt, 3 oz. pork fat, 8 oz. truffle, pepper, spice, strips fat bacon, few bacon rinds, 1 large onion, 2 medium-sized carrots, 8 oz. shin of veal, *bouquet garni,* 1½ pints (U.S. 3¾ cups) white stock, 8 oz. macaroni, butter, 6 oz. pâté de foie gras, grated Parmesan cheese, 2 tablespoons Madeira, tomato sauce (see page 132), demi-glace sauce (see page 22), 1 timbale case.

Prepare the chicken, and sprinkle a little salt inside. Pound the pork fat with 2 oz. of the truffle, season with salt, pepper and spice and use to stuff the chicken. Truss with the legs folded back and wrap some strips of bacon over the breast. Put the blanched bacon rinds, sliced onion and carrots, chopped veal and *bouquet garni,* into a pan. Put in the chicken and add ½ pint (U.S. 1¼ cups) stock. Cover and put over a low heat until the liquid is completely reduced. Add another ½ pint (U.S. 1¼ cups) stock and reduce by two-thirds, then add the remaining stock. Continue the cooking for 1 – 1¼ hours until the chicken is tender.

Meanwhile, cook the macaroni in boiling salted water. Drain, and return to the pan with 3 – 4 tablespoons of the stock taken from the pan in which the chicken is cooking. Simmer 4 – 5 minutes, then add a few pats of butter, mashed pâté de foie gras and about 2 oz. grated Parmesan. Mix all well together. When the chicken is cooked untruss it, remove the breast and cut it into fairly thick slices. Put them into a small pan with the remaining truffle, sliced thinly, pinch of salt and freshly ground pepper and the Madeira.

Cut the chicken legs from the carcase, remove the drumsticks, and mince the meat from the thighs. Add this to the macaroni.

Measure the quantity of stock left in the pan in which the chicken was cooked, and add one-third its quantity of tomato sauce and the same amount of demi-glace sauce. Reduce for a few minutes and strain over the chicken and truffle. Boil for a few seconds.

Be sure all the various constituents are hot.

Put two-thirds macaroni mixture into timbale case, sprinkle with the Parmesan and arrange the slices of chicken and some of its sauce on top. Sprinkle with more cheese, add the rest of the macaroni, sprinkle again with cheese and finally add the remaining sauce and truffles.

Put on the lid, and heat in the oven for a few minutes to allow the flavour of the truffles to develop.

Note A supplementary garnish of cock's crests and kidneys may be added.

Timbale châtelaine

TIMBALE GRILLED WITH SWEETBREADS AND VEGETABLES

———————— 2 calf's sweetbreads, vegetables, about ½ pint (U.S. 1¼ cups) demi-glace sauce (see page 22), cock's crests and kidneys, truffles, 2—3 tablespoons Madeira, 8 oz. cooked macaroni, grated cheese, 1 timbale case, made in a mould rather wider than its height

Braise the sweetbreads on a bed of vegetables, then remove and keep hot. Mix the sauce with the remaining liquor in the pan, boil for a few minutes then strain.

Put the cooked cock's crests, kidneys and slices of truffle into a pan and add the Madeira, cover, boil for a few seconds and add to the sauce. Put the macaroni into the timbale case, sprinkle with grated cheese and add 2—3 tablespoons of the sauce. Arrange the sweetbreads on top in a ring and pour the sauce and garnish in the centre.

Put the lid on the timbale and heat for a few minutes in the oven.

Note A timbale is usually much appreciated and every care should be given to its preparation. With a little imagination, many varieties can be made.

VOL-AU-VENT

Vol-au-vent financière

CHICKEN QUENELLES AND CALF'S SWEETBREADS VOL-AU-VENT

Prepare a filling composed of: chicken quenelles, mushrooms, slices truffle, cock's crests and kidneys and calf's or lamb's sweetbreads, mixed with a rich demi-glace sauce (see page 22) to which some Madeira has been added. Complete the sauce at the last moment with a few dabs of butter. Pour into a hot vol-au-vent case.

If liked, the vol-au-vent can be garnished with crayfish cooked in *court-bouillon*.

Vol-au-vent toulousaine

TOULOUSE STYLE VOL-AU-VENT

The filling for this vol-au-vent is composed of: white meat of chicken thinly sliced, mushrooms, chicken quenelles, slices of truffle, cock's crests and kidneys, lamb's sweetbreads and slices of calf's sweetbreads, all mixed with a *sauce suprême* (see page 23) and thickened with egg yolks.

PILAW DE VOLAILLE
CHICKEN PILAF

Pilaf is the national rice dish of the East, and there are many ways of preparing it.

Generally speaking, the rice should be cooked with the meats chosen, but in certain cases chicken or any other meat may be cooked separately, the rice added afterwards.

It is generally accompanied by tomato or some other fairly thick sauce.

Pilaw de poulet à la grecque

GREEK CHICKEN PILAF

2 small chickens, salt, pepper, butter, 2 tablespoons oil, 1 tablespoon finely chopped onion, 8 oz. rice, 1 pint (U.S. 2½ cups) stock, 1 small red pepper, 1 bay leaf, 4 oz. sultanas

Cut the chicken into small pieces, season and cook gently in 1 oz. butter and the oil.

Meanwhile, heat a little more butter in a pan, add the onion and cook till lightly browned. Add the rice and stir well into the butter. Add the stock, chopped red pepper, bay leaf and sultanas. Cover and simmer for 18 minutes.

Add the cooked chicken to the rice and serve with tomato sauce (see page 132).
If liked this can be served in a timbale.

Pilaw de volaille à la turque

TURKISH CHICKEN PILAF

1 medium-sized or 2 small chickens, salt, pepper, 1 oz. butter, 2 tablespoons oil, 2 tablespoons finely chopped onion, 8 oz. rice, 3 tomatoes, 1 bay leaf, 2 oz. currants, 2 oz. sultanas (optional), ¼ pint (U.S. 1¼ cups) stock, pinch saffron

Cut up the chicken as for sautéing (see page 422), season and cook gently for about 10 minutes in the butter and oil.

Add the onion and when it begins to brown add the rice and mix it in well. Add the tomatoes, peeled, seeded and chopped, and bay leaf (the currants and sultanas may be added at this stage). Add the stock and saffron.

Cover and cook for about 20 minutes, when the chicken should be tender and the rice dry.

Serve with tomato sauce (see page 132).

Variation Sliced aubergines, fried in oil or red or green peppers, grilled (U.S. broiled) and cut into strips may be added.

Pilaw de volaille cuite

COOKED CHICKEN PILAF

For this pilaf left-over chicken can be used. Cut the meat into small cubes or slices and put into a saucepan with ½–1 oz. butter. Heat very slowly.

Prepare the rice as instructed for *pilaw de poulet à la grecque* (see page 468), omitting the sultanas. When the rice is cooked mix it with the chicken.

Serve with either tomato sauce (see page 132), paprika sauce (see page 29), curry sauce (see page 132), or a reduced veal gravy.

Soufflés de volaille

CHICKEN SOUFFLÉS

Chicken soufflés are made with either raw or cooked chicken.

With cooked chicken 12 oz. — 1 lb. cooked chicken meat (preferably poached), 5—6 tablespoons cold béchamel sauce (see page 23), 2 oz. butter, 5 egg yolks, seasoning, 6 egg whites

Pound the chicken, add the sauce and rub all through a fine sieve. Heat the purée slightly, add the butter, egg yolks and seasoning. Finally add the stiffly beaten egg whites.

Pour into a buttered soufflé dish and cook in a moderate oven or in a bain-marie.

The time for cooking a soufflé varies according to its size, but is generally about 20 minutes.

With raw chicken 1 lb. mousseline forcemeat of chicken (see page 56), 3—4 tablespoons béchamel sauce (see page 23), 3 egg yolks, 4 egg whites

Mix the mousseline forcemeat, sauce and egg yolks together and add the stiffly beaten egg whites. Cook as above, but in a bain-marie for preference. Serve alone or with either of the following sauces: suprême (see page 23), paprika (see page 29), or Nantua.

Editor's note Nantua sauce is prepared from a well reduced cream béchamel (see page 23) with the addition of 2 tablespoons cream, 3 oz. crayfish butter, and 1 tablespoon cooked crayfish.

Soufflé de volaille à la périgourdine

CHICKEN SOUFFLÉ PÉRIGOURDINE

This is made with raw or cooked chicken as above, with the addition of some chopped truffles.

DIVERSES PRÉPARATIONS FROIDES DE LA VOLAILLE

VARIOUS COLD PREPARATIONS OF POULTRY

Poularde en gelée au champagne

CHICKEN IN JELLY WITH CHAMPAGNE

1 chicken, salt, pepper, 1 tablespoon brandy, about 12 oz. foie gras, spice, truffles, few slices fat bacon, veal stock, 1 medium-sized onion, 2 carrots, 3 oz. pork fat, 6 oz. shin of veal, parsley, thyme, 1 bay leaf, 4 oz. butter, ½ bottle dry Champagne, 2 tablespoons calf's foot jelly

Bone the breast of the chicken, sprinkle a little salt and pepper inside and add the brandy. Trim the foie gras, season with salt, pepper and spice. Stud with pieces of truffle which have also been seasoned with salt, pepper and spice. Wrap some slices of bacon round the foie gras, then tie in muslin and poach for 15 minutes in veal stock. Leave to cool in the liquor and when quite cold remove the muslin and put the foie gras into the chicken. Truss the chicken with its legs folded back, cover the breast with a piece of pork fat and put into a pan with ½ pint (U.S. 1¼ cups) stock. Cover, and cook until the liquid is reduced by two-thirds.

Prepare a mirepoix with the vegetables, pork fat and veal, chopping all the ingredients into small pieces. Put into a pan with the butter and cook till lightly browned, then put the mirepoix with the chicken. Add the Champagne and cook until the liquid is reduced by half. Add the liquor in which the foie gras was cooked and the calf's foot jelly. Continue the cooking over a low heat for about 1 hour. Remove the pan from the heat, and leave the chicken to cool a little in the liquor. Then take it out, untruss it, and put it into a deep serving dish. Strain the cooking liquor over and leave overnight. Before serving, remove any fat from the top of the jelly with a spoon dipped in hot water.

Note If liked, chicken with Champagne can be served on a bed of rice, in which case it should be surrounded with artichoke bottoms garnished with either asparagus tips, Russian salad, crayfish or, when obtainable, plover's eggs. The jelly would then be served on a separate dish surrounded with broken ice.

Poularde rose de mai
POACHED CHICKEN WITH TOMATO MOUSSE

1 chicken, white stock, tomato mousse (see page 660), white chaudfroid sauce (see page 31) truffle, hard-boiled egg, aspic jelly (see page 116), 6 small barquettes, cooked rice

Poach the chicken in white stock and when quite cold remove the breast and the breast bone. Arrange the tomato mousse on the chicken, keeping as far as possible to the original shape, then cover completely with the chaudfroid sauce.

Decorate with slices of truffle and hard-boiled egg. Cut each side of the breast into 3 slices. Coat with chaudfroid sauce and put a slice of truffle covered with aspic on each. Keep on ice. Fill the barquettes with tomato mousse and leave to set.

Serve the chicken on a thin bed of rice and surround it with the barquettes. Place 1 slice of chicken on each and decorate with little heaps of chopped aspic.

Serve extra aspic separately.

Poularde Rose-Marie
POACHED CHICKEN WITH HAM MOUSSE

1 chicken, white stock, white chaudfroid sauce (see page 31), ham mousse (see page 379), paprika, aspic jelly (see page 116), 6—8 barquettes, cooked rice, truffle

Poach the chicken in white stock and when quite cold remove the breast. Cut each side into 3—4 slices and coat with chaudfroid sauce. Leave to set.

Trim the carcase, leaving the pinions, and reshape with the ham mousse. Leave to get quite set, then coat with chaudfroid sauce to which a little paprika has been added. Decorate as liked and cover with aspic jelly.

Fill the barquettes with ham mousse.

Serve the chicken on a thin bed of rice, arrange the barquettes round and place a slice of chicken on each. Top with a thin slice of truffle.

If liked, the barquettes may be alternated with aspic jelly set in small dariole moulds or, better still, with jellies made with shin of beef, calf's feet, chicken and beef.

The last two recipes may be adapted to any cold poultry with various mousses.

Blanc de volaille Rachel

CHICKEN BREASTS WITH CHICKEN MOUSSE

1 chicken, stock, aspic jelly (see page 116), asparagus tips, truffle, foie gras (optional)

Poach the chicken in stock and leave to get cold. Remove the breast and cut into fairly thin slices.

Make a mousse (see page 56 for general instructions) with the meat from the chicken's legs. Put a layer of aspic into a serving dish and when it has set spread the mousse on top. Leave to set. Arrange the slices of chicken on the mousse and intersperse with small heaps of asparagus tips.

Put a slice of truffle on each piece of chicken and coat the whole with aspic.

A little foie gras may be added to the mousse.

Serve with a salad composed of asparagus tips and a julienne of truffle and artichoke bottoms.

Aspic de volaille toulousaine

CHICKEN IN ASPIC TOULOUSE STYLE

1 chicken, white stock, white chaudfroid sauce (see page 31), clear aspic jelly (see page 116), foie gras scooped into 6–8 shells, truffles, cock's kidneys, asparagus tips

Poach the chicken in white stock and when quite cold remove the breast. Cut each piece into 3–4 slices and coat with chaudfroid sauce. Refrigerate until required.

Mask a ring mould with clear aspic, surround with ice and arrange the slices of chicken in the mould interspersed with the 'shells' of foie gras, slices of truffle and, if obtainable, cock's kidneys previously poached in butter and stock. Fill up the mould with jelly and leave to set. Unmould, and arrange a salad of asparagus tips and a julienne of truffle in the centre or, if preferred, serve the salad separately.

Chicken in aspic Hungarian style is prepared as above, except that a little paprika should be added to the chaudfroid sauce.

Note Lobster, prawns (U.S. shrimps), crayfish and game of all kinds may be served in aspic.

Chaudfroid de volaille
CHAUDFROID OF CHICKEN

Poach the chicken and let it cool in its cooking liquor. Cut it into even-sized pieces, and remove the skin. Coat these pieces with chaudfroid sauce (see page 31) made, as far as possible, with the cooking liquor of the chicken and arrange them on a dish. Decorate each piece with a slice of truffle, glaze with aspic jelly and leave to set. Trim the edges before serving.

Note Formerly, chaudfroid of chicken was always served on a bed of rice or bread and placed in the centre of a jelly border alternating with pieces of cock's crests and mushrooms also coated with chaudfroid sauce.

It was also served on moulds of stearine, but I prefer the arrangement I created at the Savoy Hotel in 1894, which is as follows:

Put a layer of chopped jelly at the bottom of a deep square dish; place on this the breasts of chicken cut into slices and coat with chaudfroid sauce. Garnish with cock's crests and kidneys and slices of truffle, and cover entirely with more jelly. Allow this to set.

To serve, put the dish on a block of ice or surround it with crushed ice.

This procedure has several advantages — less gelatine is used in the preparation of the jelly, the delicacy of the jelly is preserved, the service is facilitated and it is more agreeable to the eye.

Suprêmes de volaille Jeanette
BREAST OF CHICKEN JEANETTE

——————— Breast from a cold poached chicken, white chaudfroid sauce (see page 31), tarragon leaves, aspic jelly (see page 116), truffles

Cut each half of the breast into 3−4 slices and coat with white chaudfroid sauce and decorate with blanched tarragon leaves.

Line the bottom of a square dish with a light layer of very clear aspic jelly. When set, arrange some slices of truffle on it and place the slices of chicken on top. Cover with a thin layer of half-set aspic jelly.

Serve surrounded with crushed ice.

I have given the name of 'Jeanette' to this exquisite preparation in memory of the good ship *La Jeanette* which in 1881 went on a voyage of exploration to the North Pole and was caught in the ice. A single survivor returned from that unfortunate expedition.

Blanc de volaille Vicomtesse de Fontenay

BREAST OF CHICKEN WITH FOIE GRAS AND ASPARAGUS TIPS

Breast from a cold poached chicken, chaudfroid sauce (see page 31), paprika, truffle, chicken jelly,* foie gras, asparagus tips
*The jelly used in this recipe should be made from shin of veal, calf's feet and chicken.

Cut each half of the breast into 4 slices and cover with chaudfroid sauce to which a little paprika has been added. Put a slice of truffle on each piece of chicken. Set a ½-inch layer of chicken jelly in the bottom of a serving dish. Place on it slices of foie gras as nearly as possible the size of the slices of chicken. Put a chicken slice on each piece of foie gras. Arrange asparagus tips in the spaces between the slices and cover with more half-set jelly. Keep the dish on ice during the preparation and serve surrounded with crushed ice.

Note The ice is important as it is the freshness and quality of the jelly which helps to make this such an agreeable summer dish.

Mayonnaise de volaille

CHICKEN MAYONNAISE

Lettuce, salt, few drops vinegar, slices cold cooked chicken, mayonnaise sauce (see page 140), capers, pitted olives, anchovy fillets, hard-boiled egg

Shred some of the outer leaves of the lettuce and put into a salad bowl, piling it up in the centre. Sprinkle with salt and the vinegar. Remove any skin from the slices of chicken and arrange on the lettuce. Cover with mayonnaise, smooth the top and garnish with the capers, olives, fillets of anchovy, quarters of egg and small pieces of lettuce hearts.

Salade de volaille

CHICKEN SALAD

Chicken salad is made in exactly the same way as chicken mayonnaise, except that the mayonnaise sauce is replaced by an ordinary salad dressing added first before serving. However, a sauce boat of mayonnaise should always be served at the same time.

DINDONNEAU
TURKEY

Turkey is usually cooked and served whole, but an old bird can be cut into pieces and cooked as for *daube à la provençale* (see page 296). The same garnishes would be suitable for the daube of turkey.

Turkey may be roasted, braised or pot-roasted and, generally speaking, cooked in much the same way as chicken.

Dindonneau chipolata
TURKEY WITH CHIPOLATA SAUSAGES

1 lb. veal, 1 lb. fresh pork, 5 oz. breadcrumbs, water, salt, pepper, spice, 1 turkey, slices fat pork, onions, carrots, fat bacon, butter, 1 bay leaf, 1 sprig parsley, 1 sprig thyme, 2—3 tablespoons white wine, 24 small glazed onions, 24 chestnuts, cooked in consommé, 5 oz. bacon fat, 24 small carrots, cooked in consommé and glazed, 12 chipolata sausages, ¾ pint (U.S. 1⅞ cups) demi-glace sauce (see page 22)

Chop the veal and pork. Soak the breadcrumbs for a few minutes in water, then squeeze thoroughly and mix with the meat. Add salt, pepper and spice and use to stuff the turkey.

Truss it and cover the breast with slices of fat pork. Chop the onions, carrots and bacon and brown in butter. Add the bay leaf, parsley and thyme.

Put the turkey on to this mirepoix and pot-roast it, sprinkling from time to time with the white wine.

When the turkey is cooked, untruss and put on to a serving dish. Garnish with the glazed onions, chestnuts, bacon fat, cubed, blanched and browned in butter, glazed carrots and fried chipolata sausages.

Add the sauce to the pan in which the turkey was cooked. Boil for a few minutes, then strain. Remove any excess fat and pour a little of the sauce over the garnish. Serve the rest separately.

Dindonneau farci aux marrons
TURKEY STUFFED WITH CHESTNUTS

2 lb. chestnuts, white stock, 1½ lb. sausage meat, seasoning, 1 truffle (optional), 1 6-lb. turkey

Slit the chestnuts and put them into a moderate oven for about 10 minutes, then remove the outer and inner skins and cook them in white stock.

Drain and dry them and mix with the sausage meat. Add seasoning and, if liked, a chopped truffle.

Remove the breast bone from the turkey and fill with the stuffing. Truss, and roast in a moderate oven basting frequently.

Remove any excess fat from the liquor left in the roasting tin, and serve with the turkey.

DINDONNEAU FROID
COLD TURKEY

To be eaten cold, it is best that the turkey should be pot-roasted. Its vegetable cooking liquor may be added to the jelly which accompanies it.

The various recipes for whole chickens are equally suitable for turkeys.

Dindonneau en daube

TURKEY EN DAUBE

1 turkey, salt, pepper, spice, 2—3 tablespoons brandy, 2—3 tablespoons oil, 2 medium-sized onions, 2 shallots, 2 medium-sized carrots, 1 pint (U.S. 2½ cups) white wine, *bouquet garni* of 2 sprigs parsley, 2 sprigs thyme and 1 bay leaf, 1 clove garlic, crushed, few strips orange peel, piece bacon rind, 1 small piece pork fat, butter, ¾ pint (U.S. 1⅞ cups), brown veal stock

Cut the turkey into pieces weighing about 3—4 oz. each. Put into a bowl with a little salt, pepper and spice. Add the brandy, oil, chopped vegetables, wine, *bouquet garni*, garlic and orange peel. Leave to marinate for 2—3 hours.

Blanch the bacon rind and cut into pieces. Cut up the pork and brown in butter.

Put alternate layers of turkey, bacon rind and pork fat into a large casserole, tucking the *bouquet garni* into the centre. Add the marinade and the stock. Cover very closely and cook in a moderate oven for 2—2½ hours. Remove the *bouquet garni* and leave the turkey to get cold in the liquid.

OIE
GOOSE

The principal merit of goose is that it produces the best and most perfect foie gras.

It can, however, be prepared in various ways and as far as possible a young goose should be chosen.

Oie à l'alsacienne

ALSATIAN STYLE GOOSE

Stuff the goose with sausage meat and roast or pot-roast it.

Dish it up and surround it with braised sauerkraut and ham with which some sliced fat bacon has been cooked.

Oie à l'anglaise

ENGLISH STYLE GOOSE

1—1½ lb. onions, 1—1½ lb. breadcrumbs, stock, salt, pepper, pinch nutmeg, ½ oz. chopped fresh or dried sage, 1 goose

Cook the onions in the oven without removing the skin. Leave to cool, then skin and chop them. Add the breadcrumbs, moistened with a little stock, seasoning, nutmeg and sage.

Stuff the goose with this mixture, truss it and roast in the oven.

Serve with slightly sweetened apple sauce.

Oie à la bordelaise

BORDEAUX STYLE GOOSE

12 oz. sausage meat, 8 oz. breadcrumbs, browned in butter, salt, pepper, spice, 1 clove garlic, crushed, 1 goose

Mix the sausage meat, breadcrumbs and seasonings together and use to stuff the goose. Truss it and roast in the oven.

Serve the gravy separately.

Cèpes à la bordelaise (see page 601) make a suitable accompaniment.

Oie chipolata

GOOSE WITH CHIPOLATA SAUSAGES

This is prepared like *dindonneau chipolata* (see page 476).

Oie en confit

GOOSE CONSERVE

Select very fat geese. Each bird should be able to supply about 4 oz. fat. Wash and clean them carefully, and cut each into 6 pieces (the thighs, breast divided in two and the two pieces of carcase). Rub pieces with rock salt mixed with a pinch spice. Put into deep dishes, cover with salt and let them pickle for 24 hours. The following day, put all the fat which has collected into a pan and allow it to melt slowly. Wash and dry the pieces of goose, and cook them for about 2 hours in the fat. Then put the pieces into pots, previously rinsed in boiling water and cover with the cooking fat. When quite set, pour on lard to a depth of ½ inch. Leave to solidify, then tie down with greaseproof paper.

Oie aux marrons

GOOSE WITH CHESTNUTS

Follow the instructions for *dindonneau farci aux marrons* (see page 476).

Oie braisée aux navets

BRAISED GOOSE WITH TURNIPS

Follow instructions for *caneton braisé aux navets* (see page 480).

Oie en daube

GOOSE IN DAUBE

Follow the instructions for *dindonneau en daube* (see page 477), but reduce the cooking time a little.

CANARDS ET CANETONS
DUCKS AND DUCKLINGS

In French cuisine, there are three kinds of ducks: Rouen, Nantes and various kinds of wild duck. The last-named are mostly used for roasts and salmis.

In England, the Aylesbury duckling is best for size and flavour.

The Rouen duck can be roasted or used as an entrée, the characteristic of its preparation being that it should be underdone, or rare, which it seldom is when braised.

The Rouen duck is not bled like other birds, but has its neck broken.

The Nantes duck, which is less plump than the Rouen variety, is usually braised, pot-roasted or roasted.

Caneton aux nouilles à l'alsacienne
DUCKLING WITH NOODLES IN THE ALSATIAN STYLE

Choose a nice fat bird, clean it carefully and fill the inside with a gratin forcemeat carefully prepared with the liver of the duckling and foie gras. Truss and pot-roast it on a bed of vegetables.

Serve sprinkled with the cooking liquor to which some brown veal stock has been added.

Serve with *nouilles à l'alsacienne* (see page 677).

Caneton braisé aux navets
BRAISED DUCKLING WITH TURNIPS

1 duckling, butter, 3 tablespoons white wine, ½ pint (U.S. 1¼ cups) demi-glace sauce (see page 22), ½ pint (U.S. 1¼ cups) veal stock, *bouquet garni*, 1 lb. turnips, generous pinch sugar, 20 small onions, browned in butter

Brown the duckling in butter, drain off the surplus butter and add the wine. Put over low heat until the wine has reduced completely. Add the sauce, stock and *bouquet garni* and continue the cooking over low heat. Cut the turnips into elongated olive shapes and brown them in the butter which was used to brown the duckling. Sprinkle with the sugar and continue to sauté for a few minutes. When the duckling is partly cooked, remove it to a casserole, surround it with the turnips and onions, pour the sauce over it, cover and finish the cooking in the oven.

Caneton aux petits pois à la ménagère
DUCKLING WITH ONIONS AND GREEN PEAS

8 oz. fat pork, 2 oz. butter, 15 small onions, 1 duckling, 1 tablespoon flour, 1 pint (U.S. 2½ cups) water, ½ teaspoon salt, pinch pepper, 1½ lb. peas, *bouquet garni*

Cut the pork into large cubes and put into boiling water for a few minutes. Drain and dry.

Heat the butter in a pan, add the onions and pieces of pork and brown lightly. Remove from the pan, put the duckling into the remaining butter and brown on all sides. Remove to a plate.

Put the flour into the pan, stir well till it begins to brown then add the water and stir till boiling. Add seasoning and replace the duckling. Add the onions, pork fat, peas and *bouquet garni*. Cover the pan and cook slowly. Remove the *bouquet garni* before serving and arrange the onions and peas round the duckling.

If the sauce is too thick, add a little hot water.

ANOTHER METHOD

1 duckling, onions, carrots, few bacon rinds, *bouquet garni*, ½ pint (U.S. 1¼ cups) white wine, ½ pint (U.S. 1¼ cups) demi-glace sauce (see page 22), 1 lb. peas, few small onions, pork fat

Braise or pot-roast the duckling on the bed of vegetables with bacon rinds and *bouquet garni*.

When cooked, remove from pan. Add the wine and allow it to reduce a little, then add the sauce. Bring to boiling point and boil for 2 minutes. Pass through a fine strainer, leave to stand for a few minutes, then skim, and return to the pan. Put the duckling back into the pan and add the peas cooked *à la française* (see page 642) with small onions and pieces of pork fat. Simmer all together for a few minutes.

Put the duckling on to a serving dish and cover with the peas.

Caneton à la choucroute

DUCKLING AND SAUERKRAUT

Stuff the duckling according to recipe on page 481, recipe, cook it in the
same way and replace the noodles by sauerkraut braised with fat pork.
Serve the duckling with the sauerkraut and strips of fat pork round it.

Caneton aux olives

DUCKLING WITH OLIVES

Braise the duckling as in recipe on page 481, but before adding the
demi-glace sauce reduce it a little.
A few moments before serving, add 8 oz. pitted olives which have
been put into boiling water for a few minutes.
Dish up the duckling and surround with the olives and the sauce.

Suprêmes de caneton

BREAST OF DUCKLING

The breast of duckling can be removed in the same way as chicken and
may be treated in the same manner.
However, from experience I find a better result is obtained when the
breast is removed after the duckling has been cooked.

Suprêmes de caneton à la Rossini

BREAST OF DUCKLING WITH TRUFFLES

1 duckling, onion, carrot, *bouquet garni*, 3–4 tablespoons brandy,
6 tablespoons white wine, ½ pint (U.S. 1¼ cups) demi-glace sauce
(see page 22), 6 oz. truffles, salt, freshly ground pepper, 4 slices
foie gras, flour, butter, 4 croûtons bread fried in butter

Pot-roast the duckling on a bed of finely chopped onion and carrot
and a *bouquet garni*. When cooked, remove from the pan and keep hot.

Add the brandy and wine to the liquor left in the pan and reduce by two-thirds. Add the sauce, boil for a few minutes then strain into a small pan. Leave for a few minutes to settle, then skim it. Add the sliced truffles and season with salt and pepper. Keep hot, season the slices of foie gras, coat with flour and sauté in butter.

Remove the breast from the duckling and cut each half into 2 slices.

Place them on the croûtons and arrange a slice of foie gras on top. Pour the hot sauce over.

Serve with *macaroni à l'italienne* (see page 674).

Suprêmes de caneton à la piémontaise

PIEDMONT STYLE BREAST OF DUCKLING

Prepare the breast exactly the same as for *suprêmes de caneton à la Rossini* (see page 482), replacing the noodles by *riz à la piémontaise* (see page 668).

Note When dealing with duckling and poultry in general the secret of success is to use young birds.

Caneton rouennais

ROUEN DUCKLING

Unless it is to be served cold, Rouen duckling should be roasted or pot-roasted and served underdone (rare).

4 oz. fresh pork fat, 1 oz. butter, 8 oz. duckling's livers, salt, pepper, spice, 1 tablespoon chopped onion, pinch parsley, 1 Rouen duckling

Chop the pork fat and put it into a pan with the butter. Be sure the gall bladder has been removed carefully from the livers. Season them with salt, pepper and spice and add the onion and parsley.

Heat up the fat, put in the livers and sauté for 2–3 seconds, just long enough to seal them. Cool a little, pound and then rub through a sieve.

Stuff the duckling with this mixture, truss it and roast or pot-roast.

Caneton aux cerises

DUCKLING WITH CHERRIES

1 duckling, ½ pint (U.S. 1¼ cups) demi-glace sauce (see page 22), 1 lb. cherries,* 2 tablespoons castor sugar, pinch powdered cinnamon, 6 tablespoons port wine, juice and rind 1 orange, 4 tablespoons redcurrant jelly

* Canned cherries may be used for this sauce so that it can be made all the year round. Only use half the syrup from the can, put it with the port wine, cinnamon, grated rind and juice of the orange, reduce and complete the sauce as above.

Pot-roast the duckling, and when it is cooked, untruss, put on to a serving dish and keep hot. Add the sauce to the liquor left in the pan, cook until it has reduced well, then strain over the duckling.

Pit the cherries and put into a pan with the sugar and cinnamon. Cover and simmer for 5 minutes. Cool a little, then remove the cherries. Add the wine, grated orange rind and orange juice to the cherry juice and reduce it by half. Add the redcurrant jelly, stir until it has melted and then put the cherries back into the sauce.

Serve this sauce separately.

Caneton à l'orange

DUCKLING WITH ORANGE

The duckling for this dish may be roasted, pot-roasted or braised.

When roasted, it is served with a rather thick gravy made with brown veal stock and the liquor from the roasting pan, with the addition of the juice of 1 orange and a thin julienne of blanched orange rind.

Serve peeled quarters of orange separately.

When pot-roasted or braised, add ½ pint (U.S. 1¼ cups) demi-glace sauce (see page 22) to the pan in which the duckling was cooked.

Reduce it and then add some brown veal stock. Strain and add the juice of 1 orange, the rind of the orange and the rind of ¼ lemon both blanched and cut into thin julienne.

Pour a little of the sauce over the duckling and serve the rest separately.

Serve with peeled quarters of orange.

Caneton rouennais en dodine au Chambertin

ROUEN DUCKLING WITH CHAMBERTIN AND BRANDY

1 duckling, ½ pint (U.S. 1¼ cups) brown veal stock, ½ pint (U.S. 1¼ cups) Chambertin, ¼ pint (U.S. ⅝ cup) brandy, 2 shallots, pinch coarse pepper, pinch nutmeg, ½ bay leaf, 1 oz. butter, 3 tablespoons Rouennaise forcemeat (see page 483), few small mushrooms

Roast the duckling, keeping it a little underdone. Remove the breast and put it on to a plate skin side downwards (to prevent any juices running out). Partially cover the plate.

Remove the legs and the parson's nose, and pound the rest of the carcase. Add the veal stock, cover and cook over moderate heat for 15—20 minutes, then press as much as possible through a sieve.

Put the wine and brandy into a pan, add the chopped shallots, pepper, nutmeg and bay leaf and reduce quickly by two-thirds.

Add the sieved sauce, bring to boiling point and boil for a few minutes. Finally add the butter and forcemeat.

To serve Cut each piece of breast into 3—4 slices and arrange in a hot serving dish. Sprinkle with salt and freshly ground pepper. Garnish with a few small mushrooms browned in butter and cover with the sauce.

Serve with freshly cooked noodles sprinkled with brown butter.

Note If liked, the slices of duckling can be covered with slices of foie gras sautéed in butter and topped with a slice of truffle.

Variation In place of the Rouen forcemeat, the sauce may be thickened with sieved foie gras to which a little meat jelly (see page 21) has been added, and the butter may be replaced by 3—4 tablespoons cream.

Caneton en salmis à la rouennaise

ROUEN STYLE SALMIS OF DUCKLING

Follow the recipe for *caneton rouennais en dodine au Chambertin*, above.

Cut a large square of bread about ⅓ inch thick. Make a depression in the centre and fry in clarified butter.

Put some Rouennaise forcemeat (see page 483) in the centre and place the duckling on top.

Garnish with small croûtons fried in butter and cover the duckling with a thin coating of Rouennaise sauce (see page 486).

Note The legs, which are not used in this recipe, can always be grilled (U.S. broiled) and served separately.

Caneton rouennais en chemise
ROUEN DUCKLING EN CHEMISE

Clean the duck carefully and remove the parson's nose. Stuff with Rouen forcemeat (see page 483) and truss it in the usual way. Wrap the duckling in muslin, tie it with string as a galantine and poach it gently for about 40 minutes, in a rather thick brown stock.

When ready to serve remove the muslin in which the duckling has been poached and replace it by a small fringed napkin giving the illusion of a chemise. Garnish with quarters of peeled oranges and serve with Rouennaise sauce.

Editor's note Rouennaise sauce is a bordelaise sauce (see page 25) made with red wine to which is added some sieved raw duck's livers. Use 2 livers for ½ pint (U.S. 1¼ cups) sauce.

After adding the liver reheat the sauce very gently for a few minutes.

Caneton rouennais à la presse
PRESSED ROUEN DUCKLING

Roast the duckling for 20 minutes. Take off the legs, which are not used in this recipe.

Cut the breast into thin strips and place them side by side on a warm dish. Season with salt and freshly ground pepper.

Chop up the carcase and put it into the special press used for this purpose, sprinkling it with a glass of red wine, either Bordeaux or Burgundy, which has been reduced to half its volume.

Add a few drops of brandy to the sauce that comes out and pour it on the strips of duckling.

Place the dish on a hot plate and heat it well before serving.

Editor's note This recipe has been included for the benefit of those who have a duck press.

Caneton soufflé rouennais
ROUEN STYLE DUCKLING SOUFFLÉ

1 duckling, 8 oz. fillet of beef, 3 oz. foie gras or chicken's liver, 1 egg white, salmis sauce (see page 487)

Roast or pot-roast the duckling, keeping it underdone.

Remove the breast, and put on one side.

Remove the breast bone from the duckling.

Prepare a mousseline forcemeat (see page 56), using the liver from the duckling, fillet of beef, foie gras and egg white. Fill the carcase with this forcemeat, retaining as nearly as possible the original shape of the duckling.

Tie a piece of buttered paper around, so that it keeps its shape, and poach for 20 minutes.

The best way to do this is to put a brick or an upturned tin into the bottom of a braising pan.

Add boiling water to come two-thirds up. Put the duckling on a dish which can easily be removed after cooking and place it on the brick.

Cover the pan and poach gently, keeping the water just below boiling point.

When ready to serve, coat the duckling lightly with the salmis sauce.

Slice the breast which has been kept on one side, add a few slices of truffle and coat with the rest of the sauce.

Serve this separately.

SALMIS SAUCE

2 medium-sized carrots, 2 medium-sized onions, 2 sticks celery, butter, 1 tablespoon chopped lean ham, 1 sprig thyme, ½ bay leaf, crushed, 2 tablespoons Madeira, trimmings and chopped carcase from a duckling or chicken, 1 pint (U.S. 2½ cups) white wine, ½ pint (U.S. 1¼ cups) demi-glace sauce (see page 22), ½ pint (U.S. 1¼ cups) game stock

Cut up the vegetables and brown in 2 oz. butter with the ham, thyme and bay leaf.

Add the Madeira, trimmings and carcase and cook all together for a few minutes.

Add the wine and reduce to two-thirds the quantity.

Add the sauce and simmer gently for 45 minutes. Strain, pressing as much through as possible. Return to the pan, add the stock and leave at the side of the stove for about 1 hour. Bring to the boil and correct the consistency. Pass through a tammy cloth, reheat and finally add a little butter.

Caneton à la cuiller

BRAISED DUCKLING WITH CARROTS AND ONIONS

———————— Carrots, onions, veal stock made from knuckle of veal, 1 duckling, ½ pint (U.S. 1¼ cups) demi-glace sauce (see page 22), 3 tablespoons Rouennaise forcemeat (see page 483), foie gras, port wine jelly

Slice the carrots and onions thinly and put into a pan with the veal stock. Put in the duckling and braise it until it is well cooked. Leave to cool a little, then remove the bread carefully and bone the legs.

Add the demi-glace sauce to the cooking liquor, and reduce until there is about ¾ pint (U.S. 1⅞ cups) sauce left.

Add the forcemeat, and pass through a fine sieve.

Put a layer of sauce in the bottom of a casserole, arrange the flesh from the legs on top and cover with a little more sauce.

Add some slices of foie gras and then the sliced breast. Cover with the rest of the sauce.

Finally fill up the dish with port wine jelly. Keep on ice for 24 hours before serving.

Terrine de caneton à la gelée

TERRINE OF DUCK WITH JELLY

———————— 1 duckling, salt, pepper, 4 tablespoons brandy, Rouennaise forcemeat (see page 483), 1 strip pork fat, aspic jelly (see page 116)

Remove the breast bone from the duckling, season inside with salt and pepper and sprinkle with 1 tablespoon brandy. Remove the legs and discard the parson's nose.

Fill the duckling with the forcemeat and put it into a pan just large enough to hold it. Pour the remainder of the brandy over and sprinkle very lightly with salt. Put a strip of bacon fat over and put, uncovered, in a bain-marie.

Cook in a moderate oven for about 40 minutes.

Remove when cooked and fill the dish with rather thick hot aspic jelly.

Leave overnight to get quite set.

Before serving, skim off any fat that may have risen to the surfa

Timbale de caneton à la toulousaine

TIMBALE OF DUCKLING TOULOUSE STYLE

2 ducklings, salmis sauce (see page 487), 1½ pints (U.S. 3¾ cups) aspic jelly (see page 116), flaky pastry, strips pork fat, sausage meat, 1 beaten egg, Rouennaise forcemeat (see page 483), foie gras, truffle, port wine jelly

Roast the ducklings, keeping them underdone. Cool and remove the breasts.

Prepare a salmis sauce with the legs and carcase, and when it is ready add an equal quantity of aspic jelly.

Cut the breasts into slices (3−4 from each side). Coat with the sauce when it begins to thicken.

Line a pâté or raised pie mould with flaky pastry (the mould should be wide in proportion to its height). Put some strips of pork fat in the bottom and fill up with sausage meat, piling it into a dome shape. Cover with another strip of pork fat, and then with the pastry lid. Seal the edges, make a hole in the top and glaze with beaten egg. Decorate with leaves of pastry. Bake in a moderate oven.

When quite cold, remove the lid completely, using a sharp knife, and take out the contents of the pastry case. (This sausage meat can be used in another dish.)

Mix 3−4 tablespoons Rouennaise forcemeat with the same quantity of the salmis sauce and put a fairly thick layer in the bottom of the pastry case.

Arrange some of the slices of duckling in a ring on top, alternating with slices of foie gras and truffle. Cover with another layer of salmis sauce and continue to fill up the case with slices of duckling, foie gras and truffle.

Finally fill up with port wine jelly.

Replace the pastry lid and refrigerate until required.

Aiguillettes de caneton aux cerises

AIGUILLETTES OF DUCKLING WITH CHERRIES

Prepare and arrange the strips of duckling on a mousse, exactly as in Rouen style duckling soufflé on page 486. Place round the strips a row of cherries cooked with 1 tablespoon sugar, grated rind 1 orange and 2 tablespoons Bordeaux wine.

Cover it all with port wine jelly.

Leave until jelly sets and serve the dish surrounded by crushed ice.

Foie gras

PRÉPARATIONS CHAUDES DE FOIE GRAS

HOT FOIE GRAS

Whole foie gras served hot is not always appreciated. However, here are a few recipes.

There are three ways of cooking foie gras: poaching, braising or in a pâté.

Foie gras poché

POACHED FOIE GRAS

1 firm fresh foie gras, about 1½ lb. truffles, salt, pepper, spice, 3 tablespoons brandy,.3 tablespoons Madeira, strips pork fat

Trim the foie gras and remove any sinews.

Cut the truffles into quarters, season with salt, pepper and spice and stud the foie gras. Pour the brandy and Madeira over the foie gras and season it lightly. Cover with strips of pork fat, and tie up in muslin like a galantine.

Poach over a very low heat for 20−25 minutes.

Serve, with *garniture financière* (see page 48) or with Madeira sauce with truffles, noodles, ravioli or macaroni.

Foie gras braisé

BRAISED FOIE GRAS

———————— Foie gras, truffles, salt, pepper, spice, strips pork fat, onion, carrot, 2 oz. streaky bacon, butter, *bouquet garni* of 2 sprigs parsley, 1 small bay leaf and 2 sprigs thyme, 6 tablespoons white wine, ½—¾ pint (U.S. 1⅝ cups) brown veal stock, 1 dessertspoon potato flour or little demi-glace sauce (see page 22)

Stud the foie gras with truffles as described on page 491. Season, wrap it in strips of pork fat, and secure them with string.

Cut up the onion, carrot and streaky bacon and brown in butter. Add the *bouquet garni* to the mirepoix. Pour off any excess butter. Put the foie gras on to the vegetables, add the white wine, cover, and reduce by two-thirds. Add the stock, cover the pan again and cook slowly for 25—30 minutes. Before serving, the cooking liquor may be thickened with potato flour or with the demi-glace sauce.

Foie gras en pâté

FOIE GRAS IN PASTRY

———————— Foie gras, truffle, salt, pepper, spice, 3—4 tablespoons brandy, 3—4 tablespoons Madeira, pastry, strips pork fat, beaten egg

Trim and stud the foie gras as in the previous recipes, and season with salt, pepper and spice.

Put it into a basin and pour the brandy and Madeira on top. Leave to soak for 2 hours. Roll out the pastry and cut into 2 oval shapes one larger than the other.

Wrap the foie gras in strips of pork fat and place it on the smaller piece. Damp the edges and cover with the second piece of pastry. Press the edges well together, then neaten them and make a hole in the top of the pastry to allow the steam to escape.

Glaze with beaten egg and cook in a moderate oven for 30—35 minutes.

Foie gras chaud à l'alsacienne

HOT FOIE GRAS ALSATIAN STYLE

———————— Foie gras, braised as in the previous recipe, truffles, 3—4 tablespoons demi-glace sauce (see page 22), 1 tablespoon Madeira

Remove the foie gras when cooked, take off the strips of pork fat and put it into a serving dish.

Cover with a few slices of truffle and sprinkle with a little of the cooking liquor from which the fat has been removed.

Add the Madeira to the sauce and pour over.

Serve with *nouilles à l'alsacienne* (see page 677).

Escalopes de foie gras

FRIED SLICED FOIE GRAS

Cut slices, each about 3 oz., from a firm fresh foie gras. Season with salt and pepper, coat with flour and sauté in butter.

Alternatively, after coating with flour, coat with egg and breadcrumbs and cook as before. Any of the following make suitable accompaniments: asparagus tips, green peas, noodles (see page 677) or cooked as for *macaroni à l'italienne* (see page 674), *topinambours à la parisienne* (see page 661), *cèpes à la crème* (see page 602) or mashed potatoes.

Escalopes de foie gras favorite

SLICES OF FOIE GRAS WITH DEMI-GLACE SAUCE

Season the slices of foie gras, coat with flour and fry on both sides in butter.

Arrange on croûtons of bread, fried in butter. Put a few slices of truffle on top and coat with demi-glace sauce (see page 22).

Serve garnished with buttered asparagus tips.

Escalopes de foie gras Rossini

SLICES OF FOIE GRAS ROSSINI

These are prepared in the same way as for *escalopes de foie gras favorite*, except that the asparagus tips are replaced by *macaroni à l'italienne* (see page 674).

Escalopes de foie gras Richelieu

SLICES OF FOIE GRAS WITH TRUFFLE

———————— Slices foie gras, egg and breadcrumbs, butter, truffle, 2—3 tablespoons meat jelly (see page 21), 2—3 tablespoons stock, juice 1 lemon

Coat the slices of foie gras with egg and breadcrumbs and fry in clarified butter until golden brown on both sides. Put on to a serving dish and place 2 slices of truffle on each one.

Heat the meat jelly and stock together, until the jelly has melted, then add 3 oz. butter a little at a time, and stir well. Finally add the lemon juice.

Note If the butter and meat jelly begin to separate add 1 tablespoon hot water.

Pour the sauce over the foie gras and serve with mushroom purée (see page 606) or chestnut purée (see page 637).

Mignonnettes de foie gras

MIGNONNETTES OF FOIE GRAS

———————— 6 oz. cooked foie gras, 2 oz. chicken forcemeat (see page 56), flour egg, breadcrumbs, butter

Mash the foie gras with a fork. Add the forcemeat and mix well.

Shape the mixture into small round cakes.

Coat with flour then with egg and breadcrumbs and cook gently in clarified butter.

Arrange in a ring on a serving dish and garnish as liked with asparagus tips, peas, mushroom purée (see page 606), etc. If liked the mignonnettes may be served on rounds of fried semolina, see recipe for gnocchi (see page 671).

Serve with Richelieu sauce (see above).

Note A variety of small entrées can be prepared from the last few recipes simply by changing the garnish.

PRÉPARATIONS FROIDES DU FOIE GRAS
COLD FOIE GRAS

Parfaits, pâtés et terrines de foie gras
PARFAITS, PÂTÉS AND TERRINES OF FOIE GRAS

However much care and attention one gives to the preparation of these dishes, it is often difficult to get results as good as those obtained by well-known manufacturers and it is nearly always advisable to buy from them.

Parfait de foie gras
PARFAIT OF FOIE GRAS

Parfaits of foie gras lend themselves to many culinary preparations. In principle, they are served in a terrine, coated in rich jelly.

A SIMPLE METHOD OF PREPARING A PARFAIT

2 very firm livers, truffles, salt, pepper, spice, 6 tablespoons brandy, 6 tablespoons Madeira, strips pork fat, veal stock, Champagne or port wine jelly

Remove the gall bladders carefully from the livers, trim and remove the membranes. Stud with truffles cut into quarters and put into a basin. Season with salt, pepper and spice and pour over the brandy and Madeira. Cover, and leave to soak for 5–6 hours.

Wrap in strips of pork fat, then tie up in muslin as for a galantine.

Poach gently in veal stock for 20 minutes, then leave to cool in the liquor.

Remove the muslin and strips of fat, and pack the livers side by side in a suitable dish just large enough to take them.

Cover with the jelly.

Aspic de foie gras
FOIE GRAS IN ASPIC

Mask a fancy or plain tube mould with aspic jelly (see page 116) and decorate it with hard-boiled egg white and truffles. Fill it with neatly shaped pieces of *parfait de foie gras* (see previous recipe) slightly overlapping, and alternate them with jelly and slices of truffle.

The pieces of foie gras may be replaced by shells of foie gras scooped out with a tablespoon dipped in hot water. Keep the mould surrounded with crushed ice. When ready to serve, unmould the aspic on to a dish.

The parfait in aspic may also be served whole, in which case it is set in an oval mould lined with jelly decorated with slices of truffle.

Serve on a 'cushion' with truffles cooked in Madeira, alternating them with aspic set in small dariole moulds.

Mousse de foie gras
FOIE GRAS MOUSSE

————————— Aspic jelly (see page 116), truffle, 8 oz. butter, pinch salt, 6—8 tablespoons thick cream, about 1 lb. parfait of foie gras (see page 495)

Mask a charlotte mould with aspic and decorate it with a few slices of truffle.

Rub the parfait of foie gras through a sieve and add the softened butter and salt. Whisk until it is frothy and then add the half-whipped cream. Pour into the mould, and keep refrigerated until required.

The mousse may also be prepared by substituting chicken jelly for the butter, but this involves a certain risk, as the mousse begins to melt as soon as it is unmoulded, which does not happen when it is made with butter.

The butter mousse can also be used as a filling for tartlets, barquettes, small brioches, etc., but in these cases omit the cream.

Foie gras au paprika doux (mode hongroise)
FOIE GRAS WITH PAPRIKA (HUNGARIAN STYLE)

————————— 1 fresh foie gras, salt, 1—2 large onions, 1 tablespoon paprika

Trim the foie gras, season with salt, and put it into a suitably sized casserole.

Slice the onions thinly and arrange round the foie gras. Sprinkle with the paprika and cook in a moderate oven for 30 – 35 minutes, by which time the onion should be a good brown colour.

Remove from the oven and leave to get cold. This dish is usually made the day before it is required and is served with mashed potatoes.

Note When using paprika and curry powder it is always advisable to test its strength as both contain varying amounts of cayenne pepper.

Editor's note M. Escoffier records that this recipe was given to him by Mme Katurko, the celebrated Hungarian dancer.

TERRINES

Terrines are only pies without pastry, and apart from the details of preparation which distinguish them, all the recipes given for pies may be used for terrines.

Preparation of a terrine An earthenware dish is generally used and the inside is first lined with strips of pork fat, then filled with successive layers of forcemeat, fillets of the main ingredient, pork fat and truffles.

For poultry and game birds, the filling may be enclosed in the skin of the bird, as described in the recipes for galantines, pheasant and partridge pies, etc.

When the terrine is filled, and completed with a strip of pork fat and a bay leaf, it is covered with a lid.

To cook the terrine Put it in a roasting pan, pour a little hot water round it, and renew the water from time to time if necessary. Cook in a moderate oven.

The time required for cooking varies, as for pies, according to the size of the terrine and the nature of the ingredients.

Examination of the fat which rises to the surface during cooking can, in the absence of definite indications of the state of the cooking, furnish useful information. Thus, so long as the fat appears to be cloudy, this means that the ingredients in the terrine are still exuding gravy which mixes with the fat and clouds it. But if it appears to be clear, the assumption is that the dish is ready.

When the terrine is removed from the oven leave it for a few minutes, then take off the lid, cover with a board or a plate and put a weight on top. This, however, should not be too heavy.

Pâté et terrine de foie gras

PÂTÉ AND TERRINE OF FOIE GRAS

Editor's note This is an expensive and rather specialised recipe but may be of interest to some readers.

> 1 fresh foie gras, truffles, salt, pepper, spice, 3—4 tablespoons brandy, 3—4 tablespoons Madeira, strips pork fat, veal stock made with knuckle of veal and calf's feet (see page 20), aspic jelly (see page 116), flavoured with Moselle, Champagne or port wine

Clean the foie gras and remove the gall bladder. Stud it with truffles and put it into a bowl. Add salt, pepper, spice, brandy and Madeira. Cover and leave to marinate for a few hours.

Wrap the foie gras in strips of pork fat and then in muslin and tie up both ends with string. Poach for about 20 minutes in the veal stock, then remove the pan from the heat and leave the foie gras in the stock for about 30 minutes. Then remove, and leave to get quite cold. Take out of the muslin, remove the pork fat and put the foie gras into a terrine.

Cover with the jelly and leave to set.

Gibier à plume

GAME BIRDS

Among the number of edible birds, I will only mention those which are in common use.

Various pheasants, grey and red-legged partridge, rock partridge, American partridge, pigeons, hazel-grouse, wood grouse, prairie fowl, the true grouse, sand grouse, bustard

Various wild duck: teal, pintail, shoveller

Woodcock, snipe, small snipe

Plover, lapwing, wader, rail, water hen, scoter

Quail, landrail, Virginia quail

Ortolans

Pheasant and woodcock need to be hung, as this makes them tender and gives them a special taste. When they are too fresh they are dry and tasteless, but when they are hung they become tender and full of flavour. Other types of game birds are usually cooked without being hung.

Formerly, pheasants and partridge were larded before roasting. Nowadays this practice has been abandoned as it spoils the delicacy of the flesh. A strip of pork fat wrapped round the bird is much more efficacious than larding to protect it against the heat of the oven.

The flesh of the pheasant is always a little dry and it is advisable to put a little grated pork fat on a small piece of butter inside before cooking.

Many of the recipes given for chicken and other poultry may be applied to pheasant. It may be cooked *en cocotte* with butter or cream (see page 435) or *parmentier* roasted in the oven or on a spit, or pot-roasted.

Editor's note In many countries song birds, wild birds and some game birds are protected by law. We have included recipes for thrushes, larks, etc., for their interest value.

PIGEONNEAUX
YOUNG PIGEONS (SQUABS)

In principle, only young but fully grown pigeons should be used. An old pigeon can only be used in a stew or in forcemeat.

Pigeonneaux à la bordelaise

BORDEAUX STYLE PIGEONS

2 pigeons, seasoning, butter, 2 artichoke bottoms, 2 potatoes, fried onion rings, fried parsley, 3 tablespoons white wine, ¾ pint (U.S. 1⅞ cups) meat jelly (see page 21), ½—¾ pint (U.S. 1¼—1⅞ cups) meat stock, lemon juice

Divide the pigeons in two, flatten each half a little, season and sauté in butter.

Slice the artichoke bottoms and cut the potatoes into strips. Sauté both in butter, and put with the pigeons.

Put on to a serving dish with little heaps of artichoke bottoms and potatoes interspersed with the onion rings and parsley.

Add the white wine to the pan in which the pigeons were cooked. Reduce to half, then add the meat jelly and stock.

Boil for 2 minutes.

Remove from the heat, add a little butter and lemon juice and pour over the pigeons.

Pigeonneaux chasseur

PIGEONS CHASSEUR

See *poulet sauté chasseur* on page 426, and proceed in the same way.

Pigeonneaux crapaudine

PIGEONS WITH DEVIL SAUCE

Divide the pigeons in two horizontally, from the tip of the breast to the wings. Open them, flatten slightly, season with salt and pepper and dip in melted butter and breadcrumbs. Grill (U.S. broil) them gently and serve on a very hot dish.

Serve with devil sauce (see page 27).

Pigeonneaux financière

POT-ROAST PIGEONS

Pot-roast the birds, and serve them in a deep entrée dish. Surround with the following garnish: mushrooms, slices of truffle, chicken quenelles, cock's crests and kidneys and pitted olives — all coated in a demi-glace sauce (see page 22) with Madeira

Pigeonneaux Gauthier au beurre d'écrevisse

PIGEONS WITH CRAYFISH BUTTER

Divide the pigeons in two, put them into a small sauté pan and almost cover with melted butter, slightly acidulated with a few drops of lemon juice. Poach them over a low heat.

When cooked, place the half-pigeons in a ring on a serving dish and cover them with a velouté sauce thickened with egg yolks (see page 22) and to which a little crayfish butter has been added.

If liked, some slices of truffle and cèpes browned in butter may be added.

Serve with *nouilles à l'alsacienne* (see page 677).

The word 'Gauthier' does not mean a special kind of pigeon. It was formerly used to describe 'innocent' pigeons, that is to say young ones taken from the nest and hardly grown.

Pigeonneaux aux petits pois à la ménagère
PIGEONS WITH ONIONS AND PEAS

▄▄▄▄▄▄▄▄▄▄ 4 oz. streaky bacon, butter, 12 small onions, 2 pigeons, 1 lb. peas, parsley, ¾ pint (U.S. 1⅞ cups) boiling water, ¼ teaspoon salt, pinch pepper, carrots (optional), new potatoes (optional)

Cut the bacon into cubes, blanch it, and put into a pan with some butter. Add the onions and sauté both until brown. Remove from the pan, put in the pigeons and brown them lightly. Return the bacon and the onions to the pan and add the other ingredients. Cover, and cook gently over a low heat.

If liked, a few small carrots and new potatoes may be added with the peas.

ANOTHER METHOD

▄▄▄▄▄▄▄▄▄▄ 2 pigeons, 2 pieces fat pork, butter, 1 tablespoon white stock, ½ pint (U.S. 1¼ cups) demi-glace sauce (see page 22), *petits pois à la française* (see page 642)

Cover the pigeons with the pork and cook in butter. Remove from the pan and untruss them.

Add the white stock to the butter left in the pan, stir well and bring to boiling point. Add the sauce and bring again to boiling point. Boil for a few minutes, then put the pigeons back into the sauce and add the peas. Heat through and serve.

Pigeonneaux à la polonaise
POLISH STYLE PIGEONS

▄▄▄▄▄▄▄▄▄▄ 2 pigeon's livers, 3—4 chicken's livers, salt, pepper, pinch spice, 1 dessertspoon chopped onion, ½ shallot, pinch parsley, butter, 1 tablespoon grated pork fat, 2 pigeons, strip fat bacon, breadcrumbs fried in butter, 3—4 tablespoons veal stock or gravy

Chop the livers, add seasoning, spice, finely chopped onion and shallot and parsley. Heat ¼ oz. butter and the pork fat in a frying pan, put in the livers and sauté for a few seconds, just to seal the livers. Cool and rub through a sieve. Stuff the pigeons with this mixture, truss and cover with a strip of fat bacon. Cook in butter, then put on to a serving dish and cover with fried breadcrumbs. Add the veal stock to the butter left in the pan. Boil for 1 minute, then strain and serve separately.

Pigeonneaux sautés aux tomates à la provençale
PIGEONS SAUTÉ PROVENÇAL STYLE

Divide the pigeons in two lengthwise, season with salt and pepper, and proceed as instructed for *poulet sauté à la paysanne provençale* (see page 432).

Cotelettes de pigeonneaux Yvette
FRIED PIGEON CUTLETS

Cut the pigeons in two and bone them, leaving the pinions and the ends of the drumsticks. Flatten them slightly, season with salt and pepper, flour them, dip in beaten egg and breadcrumbs and cook in clarified butter.

Serve with some artichoke bottoms and finely chopped truffles, and covered with cream béchamel sauce (see page 23).

Suprêmes de pigeonneaux Rossini
PIGEON'S BREASTS WITH TRUFFLES

2 pigeons, fat bacon, butter, 6 oz. truffles, salt, freshly ground pepper, demi-glace sauce (see page 22)

Cover the pigeon's breasts with fat bacon and cook in butter. Untruss them and remove the breasts. Put them into a pan with the sliced truffles, salt, pepper and ½ oz. butter. Heat all together for a few minutes, then put on to a serving dish and coat with the sauce.

Pâté de pigeonneaux à l'anglaise
PIGEON PIE

slices bacon, 1 shallot, 2 pigeons, salt, pepper, chopped parsley, 2 hard-boiled eggs, gravy, puff pastry (see page 681), beaten egg

Line the bottom and sides of a pie dish with the slices of bacon sprinkled with chopped shallot. Cut each pigeon into 4 pieces and put into the dish. Sprinkle with salt, pepper and chopped parsley and add the hard-boiled eggs cut in halves. Half fill the dish with gravy and cover with the pastry. Neaten the edges and brush with beaten egg. Make a hole in the top to allow the steam to escape and cook for 1 – 1¼ hours in a moderate oven.

Timbale de pigeonneaux La Fayette

PIGEON TIMBALE

> 36 crayfish, mirepoix of vegetables, white wine, butter, 6 oz. truffles, salt, pepper, 6 pigeons, pork fat, 8 oz. macaroni, 4 oz. grated Parmesan cheese, pinch nutmeg, béchamel sauce (see page 23), 1 cooked timbale case, wide in proportion to its height (see page 465)

Cook the crayfish in the mirepoix with white wine, remove the shells and use them to make some crayfish butter.

Put the crayfish into a small pan with 1 oz. butter and 2 tablespoons of the liquor in which they were cooked. Add the sliced truffles, salt and freshly ground pepper. Keep hot.

Wrap the pigeons in strips of pork fat and cook in butter. Remove the breasts, take off the skin, and keep the breasts hot in a little of the butter left from cooking them and the meat jelly.

Cook the macaroni in boiling salted water till only just tender, drain and add 3 oz. butter, the cheese and nutmeg.

Mix the crayfish butter with the béchamel sauce. Add some of the sauce to the macaroni and some to the crayfish and truffles. Put the macaroni in the timbale, then the crayfish and truffle. Put the pigeons' breasts on top and cover with the remaining sauce. Decorate with slices of truffle.

Vol-au-vent de pigeonneaux

PIGEON VOL-AU-VENT

The vol-au-vent may be filled with *pigeonneaux financière* (see page 501), in which case the pigeons are divided into 4.

They may also be filled with the breasts of the pigeons, crayfish tails and slices of truffle, coated with creamed béchamel sauce (see page 23) to which some crayfish butter (see page 114) has been added.

Pigeons en compote

PIGEON STEW

This recipe has been devised principally to deal with somewhat older birds, in which case pigeons are braised in stock on a bed of vegetables.

Garnish Small glazed onions, mushrooms, streaky bacon cut in cubes, blanched and browned in butter

Dish up the pigeons. Add ¼ pint (U.S. ⅝ cup) demi-glace sauce (see page 22) to the cooking liquor, boil for a few minutes, strain through a conical sieve and pour à little over the garnish. Boil for a further 2 – 3 minutes and pour over the pigeons.

Note A very large number of recipes could be given in which pigeons, squabs, and wood pigeons may be used. Many of the recipes for chickens and partridges can be applied to these birds.

PIGEONNEAUX FROIDS

COLD PIGEONS (SQUABS)

Pigeonneaux en terrine à la gélee

TERRINE OF PIGEON IN JELLY

2 oz. pork fat, 1 oz. butter, 3 oz. chicken's livers, 1 dessertspoon chopped onion, chopped parsley, 2 pigeons, salt, pepper, spice, 1 tablespoon brandy, strip bacon fat, brown jellied veal stock, prepared in advance, water

Heat the pork fat and butter in a pan, add the livers, onion and parsley. Sauté for a few minutes to seal the livers then remove, cool a little and rub through a sieve.

Remove the breast bone and the legs from the pigeons. Season the inside and fill with the forcemeat.

Put into a casserole just large enough to take them, pour the brandy over, and wrap in the bacon fat. Cover and cook in the oven in a bain-marie for about 35 minutes.

Remove from the oven, cover with the jellied meat stock and leave to cool.

Just before serving, brush the top of the jelly with a little warm water.

Note The chicken liver forcemeat may be replaced with truffled foie gras and the pigeons braised as in the preceding recipe.

FAISAN
PHEASANT

Faisan à la bohémienne

BOHEMIAN STYLE PHEASANT

1 plump, tender pheasant, salt, 8 oz. foie gras, paprika, goose fat or butter, 1 strip pork fat, 1 onion, 8 oz. rice, 3 tablespoons white wine, 6 tablespoons cream, 2—3 tablespoons meat jelly (see page 21)

Clean the pheasant carefully and retain its liver.

Sprinkle a little salt inside.

Cut the foie gras into pieces the size of a walnut. Add the liver from the pheasant, cut up in the same way, season with salt and paprika and sauté for 3 minutes in goose fat or butter. Stuff the pheasant with this mixture. Truss it and cover the breast with the pork fat.

Put into a casserole with some goose fat or butter. Add the thinly sliced onion and cook for 35—40 minutes according to the size of the bird. Cook the rice as for pilaf (see page 669).

When the pheasant is cooked, remove to a serving dish, untruss and keep it hot. Pour a little of the liquor from the casserole over the rice. To the rest, add 1 dessertspoon paprika and the wine. Stir well and reduce by two-thirds. Add the cream and boil for a few seconds. Add the meat jelly if available, strain.

Pour a little of the sauce over the pheasant and serve the rest separately.

Serve the rice in a separate dish, and if liked this can be replaced by potatoes, cut into small cubes and cooked in butter with 1 tablespoon chopped onion.

Faisan casserole

PHEASANT CASSEROLE

1 pheasant, salt, 1 tablespoon grated pork fat, 1 strip pork fat, butter, 1 tablespoon brandy, 3 tablespoons fairly thick gravy

Choose a young pheasant and clean it thoroughly. Sprinkle the inside with a little salt and add the grated pork fat. Truss it and wrap it in a strip of pork fat.

Put it into a casserole with some butter, and cook in a moderate oven, or over low heat, for about 35 minutes until the pheasant is tender. Remove from the casserole, untruss, then return to the casserole and pour over the brandy and the gravy.

Faisan poêlé à la choucroute
POT-ROAST PHEASANT WITH SAUERKRAUT

1 pheasant, butter, 2 carrots, 1 onion, 2 sprigs parsley, 2 sprigs thyme, 1 bay leaf, few bacon rinds, 1 tablespoon brandy, $\frac{1}{2}$ pint (U.S. 1$\frac{1}{4}$ cups) demi-glace sauce (see page 22), sauerkraut, white wine, pork fat, streaky bacon

Prepare and truss the pheasant as in the previous recipe. Butter a braising pan, just large enough to take the pheasant, add the thinly sliced carrots and onion, parsley, thyme, bay leaf and bacon rinds.

Put in the pheasant and cook in a moderate oven, basting frequently.

When cooked, pour the brandy over the pheasant. Remove, untruss and keep the pheasant hot. Add the sauce to the liquor left in the pan, stir well and boil for a few minutes.

Strain, leave to settle for a minute or two, then skim. While the pheasant is cooking, braise the sauerkraut in white wine with a piece of pork fat. Cut the streaky bacon into pieces and brown in butter.

Drain the sauerkraut well and put on to a serving dish. Arrange the pheasant on top and surround with the pieces of bacon. Serve the sauce separately. Boiled potatoes may accompany this dish.

Faisan poêlé au celeri
POT-ROAST PHEASANT WITH CELERY

Prepare and cook the pheasant as in the previous recipe but replace the sauerkraut with braised celery dressed with a little of the sauce and serve separately.

Place the pheasant on a serving dish and pour 3−4 tablespoons of the liquor left in the pan over it.

Faisan en cocotte
PHEASANT EN COCOTTE

Follow the recipe for pheasant casserole (see page 506) and add a garnish of small glazed onions, mushrooms and slices of truffle.

Faisan à la crème
CREAMED PHEASANT

———————— 1 pheasant, butter, 1 onion, 3—4 tablespoons white wine, ½ pint (U.S. 1¼ cups) cream, 3 tablespoons meat jelly (see page 21), juice ½ lemon

Prepare and truss the pheasant and cook in butter with the onion cut into quarters. When cooked, sprinkle with the wine. Remove the pheasant, untruss and keep hot.

Add the cream and meat jelly to the liquor left in the pan. Boil for 4—5 minutes, then add the lemon juice. Put the pheasant into a deep serving dish and strain the sauce over it.

Faisan grillé à la diable
GRILLED (U.S. BROILED) PHEASANT WITH DEVIL SAUCE

For this dish very young pheasants, as tender as possible, must be chosen.

Follow the recipe for *poulet grillé diable* (see page 437) and serve with rashers of streaky bacon.

Faisan à la Sainte-Alliance
PHEASANT STUFFED WITH WOODCOCK FORCEMEAT

———————— 2 woodcock, beef marrow, fresh pork fat, salt, freshly ground pepper, pinch herbs, about 5 oz. truffles, 1 plump tender pheasant, 1 piece bread large enough to take the pheasant, butter, 4 fillets anchovy, 1 Seville orange

Bone the woodcocks and put the livers on one side. Poach some beef marrow (quarter quantity of the woodcock flesh) and leave it to cool. Then chop the woodcock flesh and the beef marrow and mix with the same quantity of chopped pork fat. Add seasoning and the herbs and truffles cut into quarters and seasoned. Stuff the pheasant with this mixture, truss it and keep it in a cool place for 24 hours (this is done to allow the flavour of the truffles to permeate the pheasant). Then roast on a spit, or if this is not possible put the pheasant in a roasting tin on a fairly high grid and roast carefully.

Fry the large bread croûton in butter.

Pound the livers from the woodcock with the same amount of grated pork fat, anchovy fillets, 1 oz. butter and another 1 oz. truffle. Mix thoroughly well together and spread on the prepared croûton. When the pheasant is three-quarters cooked arrange the croûton under it so that it will catch the juices coming from the bird, then continue the cooking.

Serve the pheasant on the croûton and surround it with slices of bitter orange.

Serve the gravy separately.

Salmis de faisan

SALMIS OF PHEASANT

1 young pheasant, 1 piece fat bacon, truffle, 1–2 tablespoons meat jelly (see page 21), 1½ oz. butter, 1 dessertspoon brandy, ½ pint (U.S. 1¼ cups) white wine, 2 shallots, pinch coarse ground pepper, ½ pint (U.S. 1¼ cups) demi-glace sauce (see page 22)

Clean the pheasant and put the liver on one side. Truss and put a piece of fat bacon over the breast, then roast until about three-quarters cooked.

Cut off the wings and remove the pinions, divide each wing into 2 slices. Remove the legs and cut into 2 pieces.

Skin the pieces of pheasant, trim them and keep hot in a sauté pan with a few slices of truffle, the meat jelly, ½ oz. butter and the brandy.

Pound the carcase with the trimmings and the liver and put all into a pan with the wine, chopped shallots and pepper. Reduce to about one-third the quantity, add the sauce and the liquor left in the roasting tin. Simmer for 15 minutes, then strain, pressing as much as possible through the strainer.

Return to the pan, reduce again for a few minutes and then strain once more. Reheat, add the remaining butter a little at a time.

Put the pieces of pheasant into a serving dish and pour the sauce over.

Note About 12 mushrooms may be added with the truffle and some mousseline quenelles made with pheasant meat and moulded in a tablespoon (see page 56).

If quenelles are served, it may only be necessary to use the wings of the pheasant, and the legs can be used in another dish.

If preferred, the white wine may be replaced by red wine.

Salmis may be served hot or cold.

Faisan à la mode de Monseigneur

PHEASANT WITH BRANDY, TRUFFLES AND FOIE GRAS

————————— 1 plump, tender pheasant, salt, freshly ground pepper, 1 tablespoon brandy, 3 oz. grated pork fat, 4—5 truffles, 6 oz. foie gras, pinch spice, 1 piece fat bacon, butter, 3—4 tablespoons brown veal stock, flour, 6 tablespoons Madeira

Clean the pheasant carefully and retain the liver. Season inside and sprinkle with brandy.

Mix well together the pork fat, 1 chopped truffle, liver from the pheasant and about 4 oz. foie gras. Season, add the spice and pound all well. Stuff the pheasant with this mixture, truss it, cover the breast with a piece of fat bacon and cook in a casserole.

Slice the rest of the truffles and put into a pan with 1 oz. butter, salt, pepper and the stock. Keep hot, but do not let it boil.

Cut the remaining foie gras into 6 slices, season, coat with flour and just before they are required, sauté in butter.

Remove the pheasant from the casserole, untruss and take off the wings. Cut each into 2 slices, remove the legs, put the drumsticks aside and cut the thighs in half.

To serve Put the wings and thighs into a hot terrine or casserole, alternating them with the slices of foie gras. Cover with the forcemeat from the pheasant and then add the truffles drained from the liquor in which they were keeping hot. Add the Madeira to the pan in which the pheasant was cooked, add the liquor from the truffles and boil for a few seconds.

Pour over the pheasant in the casserole. Cover, and heat for about 5 minutes to allow the truffles to develop its aroma, then serve at once.

Faisan sauté

SAUTÉ OF PHEASANT

Sauté of pheasant is not very often served, except when cooking old birds in a daube. Pheasant meat, being always a little dry, does not take kindly to being sautéed. But if you wish to do this, choose very young pheasants and sauté them in plenty of butter.

Suprêmes de faisan

BREAST OF PHEASANT

The best way of serving the breast of pheasant is to stuff the inside of a young pheasant with 1 tablespoon grated pork fat, seasoned with salt and pepper. Truss the pheasant, lard it and cook it in a casserole. As soon as it is cooked, take off both sides of the breast, remove the skin and serve as for breast of chicken.

Suitable accompaniments are truffles, mushrooms, chestnut, celery or onion purée, or *sauce chasseur* (see page 26), *à la Vallière* (see page 415) or *au paprika rose* (see page 32).

Côtelettes de faisan à l'anglaise

ENGLISH STYLE PHEASANT CUTLETS

Take the wings from a young and tender pheasant, leaving a small piece of pinion. Season with salt and pepper, coat with flour and then with beaten egg and freshly prepared breadcrumbs. Cook in clarified butter.

Put on to a serving dish and, if liked, sprinkle with 2−3 tablespoons light meat jelly (see page 21) melted with a little butter and a little chopped tarragon added.

Serve with slices of grilled bacon, peas or asparagus tips.

FAISAN FROID
COLD PHEASANT

Chaudfroid de faisan

CHAUDFROID OF PHEASANT

Prepare as for chaudfroid of chicken (see page 474) but replace the white sauce with a brown chaudfroid, using, as far as possible, the cooking liquor of the pheasant.

Mousses de faisan

PHEASANT MOUSSES

1 young hen pheasant, salt, strips bacon or pork fat, carrots, onions, *bouquet garni*, 3—4 tablespoons brandy, 6 tablespoons Madeira, ½ pint (U.S. 1¼ cups) brown veal stock, 8 oz. foie gras, 3 oz. butter, ½ pint (U.S. 1¼ cups) thick cream, aspic jelly (see page 116)

Clean the pheasant and retain the liver. Sprinkle inside with salt, then truss, lard and pot-roast on a bed of thinly sliced carrots and onions and a *bouquet garni*. When the pheasant is cooked, remove from the pan and leave to get quite cold, then bone it completely.

Pound the carcase with the trimming and liver, and put all back into the pan with the brandy, Madeira and stock. Cover and simmer for about 20 minutes. Strain through a fine sieve into a small clean pan and reduce until it is syrupy.

Pound the pheasant meat, rub through a sieve and put the resultant purée into a bowl. Add the syrupy liquor, sieved foie gras and softened butter. Beat until it is frothy, then add the half-whipped cream.

Pour into a charlotte mould masked with aspic jelly or into small masked baba moulds and keep on ice until required.

ANOTHER METHOD OF SERVING THE MOUSSE

Coat some slices of pheasant breast with brown chaudfroid sauce (see page 26) and arrange on top of the mousse. Put a slice of truffle on each slice and cover the whole with aspic.

Alternatively the slices of chicken can be replaced with poached eggs.

PINTADE

GUINEA-FOWL

Nearly all the recipes for pheasant may be used for guinea-fowl.

During the close season for shooting, a young truffled guinea-fowl may appear with dignity on the best of tables.

PERDREAUX GRIS ET PERDREAUX ROUGE

GREY AND RED-LEGGED PARTRIDGES

Grey partridges are usually preferred to the red-legged variety. They may be pot-roasted on a bed of vegetables or roasted on a spit, but only young birds should be cooked in this way. Older ones may by used for forcemeat and in the preparation of fumet (see page 547).

Nearly all the recipes given for pheasant, hot or cold, can be applied to partridge.

Perdreaux bourguignon

BURGUNDY STYLE PARTRIDGE

1 partridge, 1 tablespoon chopped streaky bacon, 1 tablespoon fried breadcrumbs, strip pork fat for larding, onions, carrots, *bouquet garni*, 6—8 small glazed onions, 6—8 mushrooms, butter, 1 tablespoon brandy, 3 tablespoons red wine, ½ pint (U.S. 1¼ cups) demi-glace sauce (see page 22)

Stuff the partridge with its liver, finely chopped and mixed with the bacon and breadcrumbs. Truss, and wrap in the pork fat. Chop the onions and carrots, put into a pan with the *bouquet garni*. Put in the partridge and pot-roast it.

When it is cooked, remove from the pan, untruss and put on to a serving dish with the glazed onions and mushrooms sautéed in butter. Keep hot.

Add the brandy and wine to the pan in which the partridge was cooked. Reduce to one-third its volume, then add the sauce. Boil for a few minutes, then strain over the partridge and its garnish.

Note If demi-glace sauce is not available, add an equal amount of good stock, thickened with 1—2 teaspoons flour.

Perdreaux aux choux

PARTRIDGES WITH CABBAGE

1 medium-sized cabbage, 1 piece pork fat, 1 small Paris sausage, 1—2 carrots, strips bacon or pork fat for larding, 1 older partridge, 1¾ pints (U.S. 4¼ cups) stock, 2 young partridges

Prepare the cabbage, cut into quarters and blanch for a few minutes in plenty of fast-boiling water. Drain and press out as much of the water as possible. Cut up the pork fat, and blanch in the same way.

Put the cabbage, pork fat, sliced sausage and sliced carrots into a pan. Truss and lard the older partridge and put with the cabbage. Add the stock, cover and cook gently.

Remove the pieces of pork fat and sausage when they are cooked and keep hot.

Have the 2 young partridges trussed and larded, and allow 20 minutes for them to cook on a spit or in the oven.

When ready put three-quarters cabbage, well drained, on a serving dish, and surround with the carrots, sausage and pieces of pork fat. Divide each partridge in two, arrange on the bed of vegetables and cover with the rest of the cabbage. Reheat in the oven for a few minutes before serving.

Note The older partridge, having served to flavour the cabbage, can be used in various ways such as for croquettes or in a ragoût — but it might well be tender enough to serve on another occasion as it is.

Perdreaux en casserole

PARTRIDGE CASSEROLE

Exactly the same method as for pheasant casserole (see page 506).

Perdreaux à la diable

PARTRIDGES WITH DEVIL SAUCE

Choose quite young partridges and follow the recipe for grilled (U.S. broiled) chicken diable.

Serve with grilled (U.S. broiled) bacon and devil sauce (see page 27).

Perdreaux à la crème
PARTRIDGE IN CREAM

Follow the recipe for *faisan à la crème* (see page 508).

Crépinettes de perdreau
PARTRIDGE CRÉPINETTES

Follow the recipe for *crépinettes de volaille* (see page 454) but the partridge crépinettes should be smaller than those of chicken.

Serve with chestnut purée (see page 637).

Les perdreaux de grand'mère
PARTRIDGE CASSEROLE WITH WINE AND BRANDY

2 young partridges, 1 dessertspoon freshly grated pork fat, truffles, salt, pepper, pieces pork or bacon fat for larding, butter, 3—4 tablespoons white wine, 3—4 tablespoons brandy, well reduced brown veal stock

Chop the livers from the partridges and mix with the pork fat, a little chopped truffle and seasoning. Stuff the birds with this mixture, truss and lard them and cook in butter.

When they are ready, divide each one in half, put them into a hot casserole just large enough to take them. Cover them with sliced truffles and sprinkle with a little salt and freshly ground pepper. Cover and keep hot.

Add the wine and brandy to the pan in which the partridges were cooked. Reduce by two-thirds, then add the well reduced veal stock.

Pour this over the partridges. Cover with a piece of aluminium foil or greaseproof paper and put on the lid, so that the casserole is tightly sealed. Put it into the oven for a few minutes with the door ajar and allow time for the flavour of the truffles to be absorbed.

Serve with chestnut purée (see page 637) or with a celery salad.

Mousse et mousseline de perdreau
MOUSSE AND MOUSSELINE OF PARTRIDGE

Follow the recipe for mousse and mousseline of chicken (see page 461) or mousse of hare (see page 544).

Soufflé de perdreau aux truffes
TRUFFLED PARTRIDGE SOUFFLÉ

> 1 young partridge, salt, pieces pork or bacon fat for larding, butter, 3 tablespoons béchamel sauce (see page 23), pepper, grated nutmeg, 3 egg yolks, 1 truffle, 3—4 tablespoons Madeira, 1 tablespoon meat jelly (see page 21), 4 egg whites, 4 tablespoons demi-glace sauce (see page 22)

Clean the partridge, leaving the liver inside. Sprinkle inside with salt, then truss, lard, and cook in butter. Cool, then bone the partridge, and pound the meat with the sauce.

Rub through a sieve, season carefully, add nutmeg and egg yolks.

Cut the truffle into slices, and put into a small pan with a little seasoning, the Madeira and meat jelly. Cover and bring to boiling point, then add the truffle slices to the partridge mixture. Finally add the stiffly beaten egg whites. Pour into a soufflé dish and cook in a moderate oven.

Add the demi-glace sauce to the liquor in which the truffles were heated, together with the fumet from the pan in which the partridge was cooked. Boil for a few seconds and lastly add ½ oz. butter.

Serve this sauce separately.

Soufflé de perdreau Vicomtesse de Fontenay
PARTRIDGE SOUFFLÉ WITH CREAM

Prepare a truffled soufflé as in the previous recipe, but reduce the sauce considerably and then add 6 tablespoons cream. Bring to boiling point again, boil for a few minutes and strain before serving.

Suprêmes de perdreau Vicomtesse de Fontenay
BREAST OF PARTRIDGE WITH WHITE WINE AND CREAM

> You will need for 6 persons:
> 3 young partridges, salt, pepper, pork fat, truffle, butter, ½ pint (U.S. 1¼ cups) white wine, peppercorns, ½ pint (U.S. 1¼ cups) demi-glace sauce (see page 22), 4 tablespoons foie gras, 3—4 tablespoons cream

Clean the partridges carefully, season inside and insert a piece of grated pork fat — the size of a walnut — and a few truffle trimmings. Truss, wrap in strips of pork fat and cook in butter.

When they are cooked, leave to cool, then remove the breasts and put into a small pan with ½ oz. butter and some slices of truffle.

Pound the legs and the carcase.

Put the wine and a few crushed peppercorns into the pan in which the partridges were cooked. Reduce it by half then add the pounded carcase and legs and the demi-glace sauce. Bring to boiling point and boil for a few minutes. Strain into a small pan, reheat, and add the sieved foie gras and cream.

Put the breast of the partridge and the truffle on to a serving dish and pour the sauce over.

Serve with *nouilles à l'alsacienne* (see page 677).

Suprêmes de perdreau Rossini
PARTRIDGE BREASTS WITH FOIE GRAS AND MARSALA

Follow the instructions for the previous recipe, but replace the white wine with Marsala.

In addition, season, flour, and sauté in butter 6 slices of foie gras, and place one on each breast of partridge before adding the truffles and the sauce.

Serve with buttered noodles to which a little grated Parmesan cheese has been added.

PERDREAUX FROIDS
COLD PARTRIDGES

All the recipes for cold pheasant are applicable to partridges.

CAILLES
QUAILS

Quails should be chosen very plump. Thin ones are only usable when boned and stuffed with a fine truffled forcemeat. Quails should not be refrigerated too long or they lose their flavour and may become rancid. The same applies to ortolans.

Cailles Brillat-Savarin

QUAILS WITH WINE AND BRANDY

You will need for 6 persons:
6 plump quails (preferably those which have been shot), salt, pepper, brandy, pieces pork or bacon fat for larding, mirepoix of onion, carrot, 1 sprig parsley, 1 sprig thyme and bay leaf, streaky bacon, 5 oz. veal from knuckle, truffle, 6 slices foie gras, butter, 6 tablespoons white wine, 6 tablespoons Frontignan wine (Muscatel), ½ pint (U.S. 1¼ cups) brown veal stock

lean the quails, removing the intestines and gizzard, season inside and add a few drops brandy.

Truss, lard and pot-roast on the bed of vegetables, with the bacon and veal cut into small cubes. Add also a few trimmings of truffle. They should take about 10 minutes to cook.

Then untruss, remove the larding fat and put the quails into a casserole. Cover with sliced truffles, season, and add the slices of foie gras sautéed in butter. Cover and keep hot.

Add 2 small glasses brandy and the wine to mirepoix, reduce by two-thirds, then add the veal stock. Reduce again by one-third then strain over the ingredients in casserole. Keep tightly covered until required for use.

Serve with a risotto, to which butter and grated Parmesan cheese has been added.

Cailles aux raisins

QUAILS WITH GRAPES

Allow 1 quail and 10 grapes per person, butter, 3—4 tablespoons white wine, grape juice, 1 dessertspoon very reduced veal stock

Cook the quails in butter and put them on to a serving dish with the grapes, peeled and seeded.

Put the wine, juice from a few grapes and the stock into the pan in which the quails were cooked. Boil for a few minutes and pour over the quails.

Cailles en caisse

QUAILS IN PAPER CASES

You will need for 4 persons:
4 quails, 4 chicken's livers, gratin forcemeat (see page 58), truffle, 4 strips pork fat, butter, 4 tablespoons *duxelles, 4 tablespoons fumet, 4 tablespoons demi-glace sauce (see page 22)

Bone the quails, and use their livers and chicken's livers to make the gratin forcemeat, add also a little chopped truffle. Stuff the quails with the forcemeat, wrap round a thin strip of pork fat and put into a buttered sauté pan.

Press them well together, so that they do not lose their shape during the cooking. Sprinkle with melted butter and cook for 10 minutes in a hot oven.

Put 1 tablespoon of the duxelle mixture into each of the 4 oval paper cases, previously brushed with oil. Put 1 quail into each case.

Add the fumet, made from the bones of the quail, to the demi-glace sauce and pour 1 tablespoon over each quail.

Heat for a few minutes in the oven with the door ajar and place a slice of truffle on each quail just before serving.

DUXELLES

1 teaspoon chopped onion, 1 tablespoon oil and butter mixed, 4 tablespoons mushroom stalks and trimmings, salt, pepper, nutmeg, pinch chopped parsley

Fry the onion in the oil and butter. Chop the mushroom stalks and press in a cloth to remove as much moisture as possible. Add to the onion, and stir over a fairly brisk heat, until the mixture is dry. Add the seasoning and flavouring and use as required.

Cailles en casserole

QUAIL CASSEROLE

Cover the quails with vine leaves and a strip of pork fat. Cook them in butter in a pan in which they can be served.

Add a dish of old Armagnac brandy and 1 small teaspoon good brown veal gravy for each quail.

Cailles aux cerises

QUAILS WITH CHERRIES

You will need for 4 persons:
4 quails, butter, 6 tablespoons port wine, finely grated rind 1 orange, pinch powdered cinnamon, 1 can cherries, 2—3 tablespoons brown veal stock, 2 dessertspoons redcurrant jelly

Truss the quails and cook in butter. Put the wine, orange rind, cinnamon and 3—4 tablespoons cherry juice into a pan and reduce to quarter of the quantity. Add the stock and reduce again by half. Add the jelly and when it has melted allow it to boil for a few minutes. Sieve to remove orange rind and add cherries. Boil for 2 minutes, then pour over quails.

Note As the cherry season is so short, it is better to use canned cherries which are available all the year round.

Cailles Figaro

QUAILS WITH TRUFFLES

You will need for 4 persons:
Truffle, salt, pepper, few drops brandy, 4 quails, 4 sausage skins,* 2 tablespoons veal stock or meat jelly (see page 21)

Season 4 pieces of truffle with salt and pepper and sprinkle with the brandy. Put 1 piece into each quail, and put the quail in a sausage skin with 1 dessertspoon of the veal stock reduced to a jelly, or meat jelly can be used. Tie up, leaving a space of about ¾ inch at each end so the skin does not burst.

Poach the quails in veal stock for about 15 minutes. Drain and serve in the sausage skin on a table napkin. In this way all the aroma of the quail is preserved until the last minute. Serve with thinly sliced truffle heated in a little Madeira.

Editor's note If sausage skin is not available, the quail could be tied in pig's caul, but it is best to remove it before serving.

Cailles Judic

QUAILS WITH COCK'S KIDNEYS AND TRUFFLES

You will need for 6 persons:
6 quails, onion, carrot, *bouquet garni*, 3 lettuces, 3 tablespoons white wine, ½ pint (U.S. 1¼ cups) demi-glace sauce (see page 22), cock's kidneys, truffles

Pot-roast the quails on a bed of onion, carrot and the *bouquet garni*. Braise the lettuces (see page 632) and arrange on a serving dish with the quails on top. Add the wine to the pan in which the quails were cooked and reduce completely. Then add the sauce, and reduce for a further few minutes.

Put a few cock's kidneys and slices of truffle into a pan, strain the sauce over, boil for a few seconds, then pour over the quails.

Serve with rice, cooked according to taste.

Cailles à la normande ou cailles à la crème

QUAILS NORMANDY STYLE

You will need for 6 persons:
6 quails, salt, pepper, butter, 3—4 tablespoons Calvados (apple jack), 3 tablespoons meat jelly (see page 21), ½ pint (U.S. 1¼ cups) cream

Season the quails with salt and pepper and cook in butter in a casserole. Pour the Calvados over and add the meat jelly and cream. Boil for a few seconds, then serve just as they are in the casserole.

Serve with rather tart apples, thinly sliced and cooked in butter.

Cailles à la piémontaise

PIEDMONT STYLE QUAILS

You will need for 6 persons:
6 quails, butter, 3—5 tablespoons veal stock, 4—5 tablespoons Asti, white truffles, salt, freshly ground pepper

Cook the quails in butter in a casserole for 10 minutes, then remove and keep hot.

Reduce the veal stock until it is fairly thick, then put it into the casserole with the Asti, stir well and bring to boiling point. Return the quails to the casserole with some thin slices of truffle seasoned with salt and freshly ground pepper. Cover and keep at the side of the stove for 5—6 minutes, but do not allow to boil.

Serve in the casserole, accompanied by a risotto to which some butter and grated Parmesan cheese have been added.

Cailles en pilaw

PILAF OF QUAILS

————————— You will need for 6 persons:
6 quails, salt, pepper, butter, 8 oz. rice

Clean the quails, season inside and truss with the legs drawn back. Cook in butter for 8 – 10 minutes. Cook the rice for 18 minutes as instructed for pilaf (see page 669).

Mix the rice with the quails and keep at the side of the stove for a few minutes.

Serve with a fairly thick veal gravy.

Cailles orientales

ORIENTAL QUAILS

Prepare as in the previous recipe for pilaf of quails, but add a pinch of saffron and 1 – 2 pimentos to the quails while they are cooking.

Mignonnettes de caille Rachel

MIGNONNETTES OF QUAIL

————————— You will need for 6 persons:
6 plump quails, butter, salt, 6 oz. foie gras, 2 oz. chicken's livers, flour, breadcrumbs, about 4 oz. flaky pastry

Cut the birds in half, then bone them, keeping the ends of the feet attached. Put each half into very hot butter for a few seconds to seal the flesh. Drain and sprinkle lightly with salt and leave to cool.

Mash the foie gras with a fork and add the chopped chicken's liver. Mix well and spread over the inside of each half quail.

Dip them in flour, then in melted butter and coat with breadcrumbs.

Fry in butter until nicely golden on both sides. Arrange each half quail on a square of flaky pastry and serve with Chateaubriand sauce and buttered asparagus.

CHATEAUBRIAND SAUCE

———————— 1 oz. shallots, 1 sprig thyme, ½ bay leaf, 1 oz. mushroom trimmings, ¼ pint (U.S. ⅝ cup) white wine, ½ pint (U.S. 1¼ cups) veal stock, 4 oz. maître d'hôtel butter

Put the shallots, thyme, bay leaf, mushroom trimmings and wine into a pan and reduce almost entirely. Add the stock and reduce again until there is about ¼ pint (U.S. ⅝ cup) liquid altogether. Strain through muslin and add the maître d'hôtel butter.

When serving this sauce with mignonnettes of quails, add a few drops of truffle essence.

Cailles Richelieu

QUAILS WITH BRANDY AND TRUFFLE

———————— You will need for 6 persons: 6 plump quails, salt, brandy, truffle, carrot, onion, celery, butter, good veal stock

Clean the quails, removing the intestines and the gizzards. Sprinkle inside with a little salt and a dash of brandy. Put a piece of truffle in each quail and truss.

Cut the vegetables into julienne and cook in a little butter. Arrange the quails on top, putting them close together. Season with a little salt. Add some veal stock, which should have been reduced until it is gelatinous and amber in colour. Cover the pan, bring to boiling point and cook for 10 minutes.

Remove the quails to a serving dish. Remove excess fat from the cooking liquor and pour it over the quails.

Serve with pilaf of rice (see page 669).

Cailles à la turque

TURKISH STYLE QUAILS

Follow the recipe for pilaf of quails (see page 522) but add some aubergines, cubed or sliced thinly and sautéed in butter, to the rice.

Serve with tomato sauce (see page 132).

Cailles Souvarow

QUAILS STUFFED WITH FOIE GRAS

You will need for 6 persons:
6 plump quails, salt, brandy, foie gras, 6 strips bacon fat, 6 truffles, freshly ground pepper, butter, 6 tablespoons well reduced veal stock or 4—5 tablespoons meat jelly (see page 21), 4—5 tablespoons Madeira

Clean the quails, removing the intestines and the gizzards. Sprinkle inside with salt and a dash of brandy and stuff with the foie gras.

Fold back the legs, but do not truss the quails. Wrap each one in a strip of bacon fat and put closely together in a casserole with the truffles. Season with salt and freshly ground pepper. Dab a little butter on top and add the stock or meat jelly and the Madeira.

Cover the dish very tightly and cook in a moderate oven for about 20 minutes.

CAILLES FROIDES
COLD QUAILS

Chaudfroid de cailles

CHAUDFROID OF QUAILS

Quails, salt, pepper, cooked foie gras, truffle, game gratin forcemeat (see page 58), veal stock, brown chaudfroid sauce (see page 26), hard-boiled egg, aspic jelly (see page 116)

Bone the quails, and season with salt and pepper. Put a small piece of foie gras and strip of truffle into the forcemeat and use to stuff the quails. Re-form into their natural shape, wrap in a piece of muslin and poach in rather thick veal stock for 18 minutes. Leave to cool in the stock. When quite cold, remove the quails and dry gently with a cloth.

Coat with the sauce, decorate the breast of each with chopped truffle and the white of the hard-boiled egg.

Cover with aspic jelly and refrigerate until required for use.

Note The quails may be served in small individual china dishes or paper cases.

Cailles Richelieu

QUAILS RICHELIEU

Prepare and cook as instructed for hot *cailles Richelieu* (see page 523). Arrange them in a serving dish and pour over the vegetables and the cooking liquor. There should be sufficient to just cover the quails.

Leave to get quite cold, then, just before serving, remove the small amount of fat that has risen to the surface.

RÂLE DE GENÊTS OU ROI DES CAILLES
LANDRAILS

The landrail is a very fine game bird, which gourmets often consider should only be roasted. But, from experience, the landrail cooked in butter in a casserole loses none of its qualities.

A dash of brandy and a few tablespoons white wine should be added to the butter left in the casserole, and with each landrail serve a croûton of bread fried in butter and spread with truffled foie gras.

GRIVES
THRUSHES

Grives à la bonne femme

THRUSHES WITH BRANDY

4 thrushes, butter, 4 oz. bacon fat, brandy, 4 tablespoons croûtons fried in butter

Remove the gizzards and cook the birds in butter with the finely chopped bacon fat.

When they are cooked, sprinkle with a few drops of brandy and serve with the croûtons.

Note Cèpes or mushrooms browned in butter and seasoned with salt, pepper, pinch garlic and chopped parsley may be mixed with the thrushes.

Grives farcies

STUFFED THRUSHES

———————— 4 thrushes, salt, pepper, 2 tablespoons gratin forcemeat (see page 58), truffled foie gras, 8 small pieces truffle, 4 strips pork fat, butter, 4 croûtons, large enough to take 1 bird and fried in butter

Bone the birds and season with salt and pepper. Stuff each bird with 1 dessertspoon forcemeat, 2 small pieces truffled foie gras and 2 small pieces truffle.

Reshape, and wrap each bird in a strip of pork fat. Arrange close together in a buttered sauté pan, dab with butter and cook for 10 minutes.

Serve each on a croûton, slightly hollowed out, and garnish with gratin forcemeat or foie gras.

Suitable accompaniments are: ragoût of truffles and mushrooms (see page 606), or cock's kidneys browned in butter, with sliced truffles.

Grives des Ardennes à la liégeoise

THRUSHES WITH JUNIPER BERRIES

———————— Butter, thrushes, 2 juniper berries per bird, rounds bread about 1 inch in diameter, fried in butter

Heat some butter in a casserole, put in the birds and cook on top of the stove, uncovered. When they are nearly cooked sprinkle with the chopped juniper berries and add the croûtons.

Serve very hot.

Grives en salmis (à la façon du chasseur)

SALMIS OF THRUSHES

———————— 6 thrushes, salt, pepper, 6 strips pork fat, 6 slices toast, 2 shallots, 1 clove garlic, 6 tablespoons red or white wine, *bouquet garni* of 1 sprig parsley, 1 sprig thyme and 1 bay leaf, bread croûtons

If possible, the birds for this salmis should be cooked on a spit, alternatively they can be cooked under a grill (U.S. broiler) and should be turned during the cooking.

Remove the gizzards, season and wrap each bird in a strip of pork fat. Arrange on the spit or on the grill (U.S. broiler) with the pieces of toast in the pan underneath, so that drops of fat or gravy from the birds are absorbed by the toast.

Chop the shallots and put into a pan with the garlic, wine and *bouquet garni*. Reduce to half and then add a few small croûtons, enough to absorb the wine and give a thin purée.

Serve the birds on the pieces of toast, remove the *bouquet garni* and pour the purée over.

Serve with *cèpes à la bordelaise* (see page 601) or *à la provençale* (see page 602).

Risotto aux grives à la piémontaise

PIEDMONT STYLE THRUSH RISOTTO

Thrushes, *riz à la piémontaise* (see page 668), black or white truffles, demi-glace with tomato (see page 22)

Prepare and cook the birds as instructed for the stuffed thrushes (see page 526). Serve them on the rice and cover with thinly sliced white or black truffles. Coat with the sauce.

Timbale de grives à la napolitaine

TIMBALE OF THRUSHES WITH MACARONI AND CHEESE

Thrushes, *macaroni napolitaine* (see page 676)

Prepare and cook the birds as instructed for stuffed thrushes (see page 526).

The macaroni may be put into a separate serving dish or in a pastry case.

Garnish the birds with truffles or mushrooms and coat all with demi-glace with tomato (see page 22).

MERLES DE CORSE
CORSICAN BLACKBIRDS

Corsican blackbirds have a well merited reputation. All the recipes for thrushes may be applied to them.

GRIVES FROIDES
COLD THRUSHES

Grives à la strasbourgeoise

CHAUDFROID OF THRUSHES

4—6 thrushes, butter, white Alsatian wine, demi-glace sauce made with knuckle of veal (see page 22), aspic jelly (see page 116), 4—6 rounds foie gras, truffle

Prepare and cook the birds as instructed for stuffed thrushes (see page 526) and leave them to get cold.

Fry the bones from the birds in butter, add some wine and demi-glace sauce and reduce until the mixture is thick enough to coat the birds.

Mask the bottom of a serving dish with aspic and when it has set arrange the foie gras on it.

Coat the birds with the thickened sauce and arrange one on each round of foie gras. Put a slice of truffle on each and coat with aspic.

ALOUETTES OU MAUVIETTES
LARKS

All the recipes given for thrushes may be applied to larks.

Alouettes du père Philippe

LARKS IN POTATOES

12 larks, allowing 2—3 per person, foie gras, truffle, gratin forcemeat (see page 58), butter, 12 roast potatoes, 4 tablespoons meat jelly (see page 21), juice ½ lemon

Bone the larks, insert a small piece of foie gras and a small piece of truffle into the forcemeat and use to stuff the birds. Cook in butter.

Cut a slice from the top of each roast potato. Remove the pulp, brown it in butter and then replace in the potato case.

Place a lark in each one. Heat the meat jelly, add the butter very gradually and finally the lemon juice. Pour over the birds.

Note If the sauce begins to curdle while adding the butter, add 1—2 tablespoons hot water.

Alouettes à la piémontaise

LARKS WITH POLENTA

8—12 oz. maize flour, 2 pints (U.S. 5 cups) boiling salted water, 3—4 tablespoons butter, 3—4 tablespoons grated Parmesan cheese, 12 larks, 6 tablespoons white wine, 6 tablespoons tomato sauce (see page 132)

Sprinkle the maize flour into the water, stirring all the time. Cook for 20—25 minutes, stirring frequently.

Add the butter and 3 tablespoons grated cheese. Prepare the birds and cook them in butter, then put into a charlotte mould and fill up with the polenta. Keep hot.

Add the wine to the pan in which the birds were cooked and reduce by half. Add the sauce and reduce again for a few minutes. Turn out the mould, sprinkle with the rest of the cheese and pour the sauce over.

Mauviettes ou alouettes froides

COLD LARKS

The recipes for cold larks are the same as those for cold thrushes.

ORTOLANS
ORTOLANS OR GAME BUNTING

The ortolan has no real gastronomic value unless it is roasted and eaten as soon as cooked.

Ortolans froids

COLD ORTOLANS

The best way of preparing ortolans to serve cold is to cook them on a spit wrapped in vine leaves and to serve them on a small cushion of freshly cooked flaky pastry, cooled and covered with foie gras.

Serve with aspic jelly (see page 116).

BECS-FIGUES
BLACK CAPS

These are small birds much appreciated in Provence. All the recipes for larks and ortolans may be applied to them.

BÉGUINETTES
GARDEN WARBLERS

Small birds from the North of France, which are very popular in Belgium. They are cooked according to the recipes for larks.

BÉCASSES, BÉCASSINES, BÉCASSEAUX
WOODCOCK, SNIPE, YOUNG WOODCOCK

Bécasse

WOODCOCK

For the woodcock to retain all its delicate flavour, it should be plump and slightly high.

Bécassine

SNIPE

This small bird of the woodcock species should, for preference, be eaten fresh. In its normal state it should, after being plucked, look like a white ball of fat.

Bécasseau

YOUNG WOODCOCK

These birds are smaller than the snipe, and are treated in the same way.

They may be cooked in many different ways, but the one most appreciated by gourmets is on a spit or in a saucepan in butter, and served on a croûton saturated with their juice and covered with their mashed intestines and livers.

However, a salmis of woodcock, to which a few fresh truffles are added, is well worth the praise of the lover of good things.

With the raw flesh of the woodcock, exquisite mousses and mousselines can be made and, with its cooked flesh, delicious soufflés.

Bécasses en salmis

SALMIS OF WOODCOCK

3 woodcock, 3 strips pork fat, butter, salt, freshly ground pepper, truffles, 3 tablespoons meat jelly (see page 21), ½ pint (U.S. 1¼ cups) red or white Burgundy, 2 shallots, peppercorns, 3 tablespoons brandy, ½ pint (U.S. 1¼ cups) demi-glace sauce (see page 22), pinch nutmeg, 3—4 tablespoons thick espagnole sauce (see page 21), 6 small slices bread

Clean the woodcock and remove the gizzards. Truss, and wrap each in a strip of pork fat. Coat in butter, allowing about 15—18 minutes.

Remove the legs, cutting off the feet, and the complete breasts and wings, making 12 pieces in all.

Arrange these in a sauté pan with 2 tablespoons butter and season lightly. Cover with slices of truffle and add the meat jelly. Keep warm. Pound the carcases, skin and trimmings from the birds, but retain the livers and intestines.

Put the wine into a pan with the chopped shallots and a few crushed peppercorns and reduce to half the volume. Add the pounded carcases and 2 tablespoons brandy. Cover and boil for 10 minutes, then add the demi-glace sauce and boil for another 10 minutes.

Strain through a fine sieve, pressing as much through as possible. Reheat, add 2 tablespoons butter and pour over the pieces of woodcock. Reheat all, without allowing the sauce to boil. Chop the livers and intestines and cook in butter for a few minutes. Season and add the nutmeg and the remaining brandy. Finally add the espagnole sauce.

Fry the slices of bread in butter and spread with this mixture. Serve with the salmis.

Bécasse à la mode du Docteur Féraud de Grasse
WOODCOCK — A RECIPE FROM DOCTOR FÉRAUD OF GRASSE

Prepare a salmis as instructed on page 531, and just before serving add a slice of foie gras sautéed in butter.

The late eminent doctor, who merited the title of Prince of Gastronomy, said this dish should always be accompanied by an excellent Burgundy, either a Clos de Vougeot or a Chambertin.

Bécasse en salmis à la châtelaine
SALMIS OF WOODCOCK À LA CHÂTELAINE

Prepare a salmis as instructed for salmis of woodcock (see page 531) but at the last moment add 6 tablespoons very fresh cream to the sauce.

Mousse et mousselines de bécasse
MOUSSE AND MOUSSELINES OF WOODCOCK

See mousses and mousselines of pheasant, partridge, etc. (pages 512, 515).

Soufflé de bécasse
SOUFFLÉ OF WOODCOCK

See partridge soufflé (page 516).

Note In general, all the hot and cold recipes for partridges are applicable to woodcock.

BÉCASSES FROIDES
COLD WOODCOCK

Roast the woodcocks on a spit or cook them in a sauté pan leaving the flesh pink. Leave to get cold. Serve accompanied by a good aspic jelly (see page 116).

Salmis de bécasse en gelée

SALMIS OF WOODCOCK IN JELLY

Prepare the salmis as instructed in salmis of woodcock (see page 531).
Put the pieces on to a serving dish, reshaped into half woodcocks.
Cover them with the truffles and the sauce. When the salmis is quite
cold, cover it with aspic as instructed for *suprêmes de volaille Jeannette*
(see page 474) and keep refrigerated until required.

Suprêmes de bécasse à l'alsacienne

BREAST OF WOODCOCK IN ASPIC

Prepare a salmis of woodcock (see page 531). Put the legs aside for
other uses, coat the breasts with the sauce and keep in the refrigerator
until required.

Put a thin layer of aspic jelly (see page 116) in the bottom of the
serving dish. When it has set, arrange some slices of foie gras on it,
close together. Put the breasts of woodcock on the foie gras and decorate
each with 2 slices truffle. Coat with aspic and refrigerate until required.

Note I must repeat that the demi-glace sauce used to make the sauce for
a salmis should, when possible, be made with knuckle of veal, so that it
is sufficiently gelatinous to set.

LE GRAND ET LE PETIT COQ DE BRUYÈRE

THE WOOD-GROUSE AND THE GREAT WOOD-GROUSE

These two birds, common enough in England and in the northern
countries, are found only rarely in France.

They are usually roasted on a spit or in the oven and are eaten hot
or cold and may also be used for salmis.

OTHER GAME BIRDS

Gelinotte

HAZEL-GROUSE

The hazel-grouse of the French mountains is considered a bird of high gastronomic value. All the recipes given for partridges are suitable for hazel-grouse, which has unfortunately become very rare in France. The hazel-grouse which come from Russia have a rather too pronounced taste of the pine buds on which they feed, a taste which gourmets do not appreciate.

Tétras

GROUSE

The true grouse is found only in Scotland and in England. It is the Englishman's favourite game bird.

Grouse is generally roasted in the oven or on a spit. Served hot, it is accompanied by bread sauce, chip potatoes, breadcrumbs fried in butter, and game gravy.

Served cold, it is accompanied by aspic jelly (see page 116).

Colin

AMERICAN PARTRIDGE

This bird, the use of which has become fairly common, comes to us from California. Unfortunately it is always frozen.

In size, it comes midway between the quail and the partridge. There is little variety in the methods of cooking but recipes for quail and partridges may be applied to it.

American partridges are usually roasted or cooked in butter in a sauté pan.

Francolin ou perdrix d'asie

FRANCOLIN OR ASIAN PARTRIDGE

This is treated in the same way as the grey partridge.

Canepetière ou petite outarde à collier

THE LITTLE BUSTARD AND THE GREAT BUSTARD

These birds come principally from Tunisia or Algeria and are sometimes found in France. They are generally roasted or used in salmis.

Guignard

DOTTEREL

This is a bird about the size of a blackbird. All the recipes for thrush or plover apply to it. It makes an excellent pâté.

GIBIERS D'EAU
WATER FOWL

Wild duck, teal, pintail, shoveller, golden plover, lapwing, various waders, water hen, rail, marsh quail, etc.

Canard sauvage

WILD DUCK

This is the largest and the most appreciated of this group of birds.

It can be roasted with Seville or sweet oranges, used for salmis, or cooked as most of the recipes given for Rouen duckling (see page 483).

Teal is a smaller edition of the wild duck, and is prepared in the same way.

Pilet ou canard à longue queue

PINTAIL

This is smaller than the wild duck. Certain gourmets consider it to be the best of the water fowl. It is cooked in the same way as wild duck.

Souchet ou rouge de rivière

SHOVELLER

This is prepared in the same way as the pintail.

Pluvier doré et vanneau

GOLDEN PLOVER AND LAPWING

Although these birds are much the same in appearance, the flesh of the plover is much more delicate than that of the lapwing. The flesh of the lapwing has a more pronounced fishy taste. They are both roasted or cooked in a sauté pan.

With the golden plover some excellent hot and cold entrées may be made.

The various recipes for partridge and woodcock are well suited to the golden plover.

The various waders, water hens, rails, marsh quails, etc., are only served roasted.

Gibiers

GAME

LE CHEVREUIL
VENISON

The chief joints of venison are loin, saddle and legs. The smaller ones are neck or scrag, shoulder, breast, and the top of the loin which is generally cut into small pieces and prepared like *boeuf à la bourguignonne* (see page 285) or used as in the recipe for *daube à la provençale* (see page 296). The loin is divided into cutlets, noisettes are cut from the saddle and the haunch is usually roasted or pot-roasted.

Côtes de chevreuil aux cerises

CUTLETS OF VENISON WITH CHERRIES

Sauté the cutlets quickly in oil or butter. Arrange them in a ring, alternating with croûtons cut into heart shapes and fried in butter. Coat with poivrade (see page 29) or venison sauce.*

Serve with cherry sauce.

Noisettes of venison are cooked and served in the same way as the cutlets.

Venison sauce Add 2 tablespoons melted redcurrant jelly and 5 tablespoons cream to 1 pint (U.S. 2½ cups) poivrade sauce (see page 29). Be sure to remove the poivrade sauce from the heat before adding the jelly and cream.

Sauce aux cerises

CHERRY SAUCE

8 oz. canned cherries, 3 tablespoons port wine, pinch cinnamon 1 clove, juice 1 orange, 1 dessertspoon grated orange rind, 4—5 tablespoons redcurrant jelly

Drain the cherries from the syrup.

Put 3—4 tablespoons of the syrup into a pan with the port wine, cinnamon, clove, orange juice and orange rind. Boil until reduced by half. Add the redcurrant jelly and when it has melted add the cherries.

Note The cherry sauce may be replaced with a chestnut purée, mashed potatoes, apple sauce, celery purée, sliced bananas sautéed in butter, creamed cèpes, etc.

Selle de chevreuil

SADDLE OF VENISON

Trim the saddle carefully and lard it. It may be marinated for some hours, if liked, simply by sprinkling a few tablespoons oil and the same amount of brandy and white wine over it and adding a thinly sliced onion and a few sprigs parsley.

The saddle is then roasted or pot-roasted.

Small pears, cooked in red wine with a little sugar, cinnamon and grated lemon rind, make a good accompaniment to pot-roasted saddle of venison.

Also, chestnut purée, celery purée, apple sauce, banana rings sautéed in butter or mashed potatoes may be served.

Selle de chevreuil à la crème

CREAMED SADDLE OF VENISON

Saddle of venison, strips bacon or pork fat for larding, 2 tablespoons oil, 1 onion, 1 carrot, 2 sprigs parsley, 1 bay leaf, 1 tablespoon vinegar, 6 tablespoons white wine, few peppercorns, butter, ½ pint (U.S. 1¼ cups) cream, 2 tablespoons meat jelly (see page 21)

Trim the saddle and lard it. Mix the oil, thinly sliced onion and carrot, parsley, bay leaf, vinegar, wine and peppercorns. Pour over the saddle and marinate for several hours.

Then place it in a roasting tin, put some butter on top and arrange the onion and carrot round.

Roast in a moderate oven.

When the saddle is cooked, remove to a serving dish and keep hot.

Put the wine from the marinade into the roasting tin, stir well, then boil until almost completely reduced. Add the cream and meat jelly and boil for a few moments, then strain and serve with the saddle.

Chestnut purée (see page 637) makes a suitable accompaniment.

Selle de chevreuil avec diverses sauces

SADDLE OF VENISON WITH DIFFERENT SAUCES

Roast saddle of venison may be accompanied by the following sauces: venison (see page 537), poivrade (see page 29), chasseur (see page 26), or with a special horseradish sauce.

This is particularly appreciated as an accompaniment to the saddle of venison when the garnish includes apple sauce or bananas cooked in butter.

This special horseradish sauce is composed of melted redcurrant jelly with the addition of grated horseradish, in the proportion of 3 tablespoons redcurrant jelly to 1 tablespoon horseradish.

Redcurrant jelly should always accompany dishes prepared with venison.

SANGLIER
WILD BOAR

Once a boar has lost its youth, it is not, alas, of much use for culinary purposes. The best way to use it is in a daube, either in red or white wine, or *à la mode provençale* (see page 296), and it should be served with a chestnut purée (see page 637).

The young boar is, on the contrary, much appreciated. Its noisettes, cutlets and quarters can be prepared like those of venison, and the same accompaniments that have been suggested for venison may be served with the piglet.

The daube of wild boar may be completed with prunes cooked in wine with a little sugar and the grated rind of an orange.

LIÈVRE ET LEVRAUT
HARE AND LEVERET

Except for terrines, pâtés or forcemeat, old hares are not of much use. Whichever way it is cooked a hare should not be more than 1 year old and should weigh not more than 6½ lb. Its age may be estimated by the fragility of its ears.

Civet de lièvre

CIVET OF HARE

1 young hare, vinegar, 3—4 tablespoons brandy, 3—4 tablespoons oil, salt, freshly ground pepper, 3 onions, 8 oz. streaky bacon, butter, 2 tablespoons flour, red wine, *bouquet garni* of 2 sprigs parsley, 2 sprigs thyme and 1 bay leaf, 1 clove garlic, 25 small glazed onions, 25 mushrooms, browned in butter

Skin the hare and, while cleaning, collect the blood. Add a little vinegar to prevent it from clotting. Reserve this blood and the liver, from which the gall, and any part which may have been contaminated by it, has been removed.

Cut the hare into pieces and put them into a bowl with the brandy, the oil, salt, pepper and 1 sliced onion. Leave to marinate for some hours.

Cut the bacon into pieces and put into boiling water for a few minutes, then drain, dry, and brown in butter.

Remove from the pan, add the remaining 2 onions cut into quarters and brown. Add the flour and cook until it begins to brown. Add the pieces of hare, drained from the marinade, and stir for a few minutes over low heat. Add enough red wine to just cover and the *bouquet garni*. Cover and simmer gently.

Mix the blood of the hare with 3—4 tablespoons of the liquor in which the hare is cooking.

Cut the liver into slices and sauté lightly in butter. Just before the hare is ready to serve, add the blood and the liver.

Put the pieces of hare into a casserole, add the browned bacon, glazed onions and mushrooms and strain the sauce over.

Serve with heart-shaped croûtons fried in butter.

Civet de lièvre de la mère Jean

CIVET OF HARE WITH CÈPES

Prepare the civet as in the previous recipe, but omit the mushrooms. When it is cooked, put the pieces of hare into a casserole. Heat up the sauce, add 6 tablespoons cream and pour it over the hare.

Serve with *cèpes à la provençale.*

Sauté the cèpes in oil, and season with salt, freshly ground pepper, suspicion of garlic and a little chopped parsley. Add one-third quantity of small croûtons browned in oil.

Civet de lièvre à la lyonnaise

CIVET OF HARE LYONESE STYLE

Prepare the civet as in the previous recipes, omitting the mushrooms from the garnish and replacing them with chestnuts cooked in consommé.

In certain districts, stoned prunes are added to the civet.

Côtelettes de lièvre

HARE CUTLETS

The preparation of these cutlets may be carried out in three ways:

1 Croquette mixture bound with brown stock, in which cooked hare meat is the main ingredient. The method is exactly the same as that for ordinary croquettes.

2 By the Pojarski method (see page 542).

3 With hare forcemeat, made according to the recipe for *farce à la panade et au beurre* (see page 56).

The last two are made in small buttered cutlet moulds and covered with chopped roast hare fillet bound with a very well reduced demi-glace sauce (see page 22). The cutlets are poached in the moulds in salted water, and they will become detached from the moulds while they are cooking. They are then coated with egg and breadcrumbs and browned in clarified butter.

Côtelettes à la Pojarski

HARE CUTLETS POJARSKI

Take the flesh of the two thighs of a leveret and remove the sinews. Chop, add quarter its weight of butter and the same amount of white breadcrumbs moistened with cream.

Divide this mixture into pieces of about 2 oz. and shape into cutlets. Cook in clarified butter and serve with a cream sauce.

Garnish as liked.

Cuisses de lièvre

HARE'S THIGHS

These are used in various ways:

1 In the preparation of civets
2 With the sinews removed and larded, they may be roasted
3 Chopped, and used in Pojarski cutlets
4 For various forcemeats

Filets de lièvre

FILLETS OF HARE

———— Fillets of hare, pork fat, butter, salt, 3—4 tablespoons white wine, ½ pint (U.S. 1¼ cups) poivrade sauce (see page 29), 3—4 tablespoons cream

Cut the fillets from the whole length of the hare.

Remove the sinew, and stud with small pieces of pork fat. Divide into 2—3 pieces according to the size of the fillet.

Put into a small pan with a little butter, sprinkle with salt and cook quickly until slightly pink, but be careful the butter does not burn.

Put straight on to a serving dish or if preferred dish on fried croûtons.

Put the wine into the pan in which the fillets were cooked, stir well and add the poivrade sauce reduced a little; bring to boiling point, then strain and add the cream.

Pour over the fillets.

If preferred, the poivrade sauce may be replaced by chasseur sauce (see page 26), bordelaise sauce (see page 25), or redcurrant with horseradish (see page 44).

Chestnut purée (see page 637) makes a good accompaniment.

Filets de levraut chasseur

FILLETS OF LEVERET WITH BRANDY AND WINE

Fillets of hare, salt, freshly ground pepper, oil, butter, 6 oz. mushrooms, 2 shallots, 3 tablespoons brandy, 3 tablespoons white wine, $\frac{1}{4}$ pint (U.S. $\frac{5}{8}$ cup) demi-glace sauce (see page 22), 2 tablespoons tomato sauce (see page 132), 2—3 tablespoons meat jelly (see page 21), chopped parsley

Cut the fillets into small noisettes, season and sauté quickly in the oil and butter. Remove and keep hot.

Add the sliced mushrooms to the remaining fat, sauté for a few minutes, then add the chopped shallots, brandy and wine.

Reduce, then add the demi-glace sauce, tomato sauce, meat jelly and a little chopped parsley.

Bring to boiling point and boil for a few seconds, then put the noisettes back into the sauce and reheat before serving.

Filets de levraut La Vallière

FILLETS OF LEVERET LA VALLIÈRE

Follow the previous recipe, but add a few slices of truffle cut into julienne and a few chopped leaves of tarragon.

Filets de levraut Mornay

FILLETS OF LEVERET MORNAY

2 fillets of leveret, salt, pepper, butter, croûtons, 6 tablespoons Madeira, ¼ pint (U.S. ⅝ cup) demi-glace sauce (see page 22), 2—3 tablespoons meat jelly (see page 21), 4 oz. truffle

Trim the fillets and cut across into small noisettes about ⅓ inch thick. Season and sauté quickly in butter. Cut the croûtons into rounds the same size as the noisettes and allow 1 for each noisette. Brown in butter, and keep hot with the noisettes. Add the Madeira to the pan in which the noisettes were cooked and stir well. Add the sauce and meat jelly and boil for a few seconds. Add the sliced truffle, remove from heat, add 3 oz. butter, a little at a time. Return the noisettes and croûtons to the sauce and mix all well together. Serve at once, with chestnut purée (see page 637).

The butter may be replaced with 6 tablespoons cream.

Mousse et mousseline de lièvre

MOUSSE AND MOUSSELINE OF HARE

The method and ingredients for the forcemeat for mousseline of hare are the same as for other mousselines (page 56), using the hare meat as the principal ingredient.

Mousse of hare is moulded and cooked like chicken mousse and is accompanied by a sauce of game fumet.

Mousselines are moulded in a tablespoon or in little buttered dariole moulds, and are poached like chicken mousselines; these too are accompanied by a game fumet sauce.

Serve with a purée of chestnuts, celery or lentils.

Soufflé de lièvre

HARE SOUFFLÉ

2 thighs of hare, salt, freshly ground pepper, butter, 4—5 tablespoons demi-glace sauce (see page 22), 4 egg yolks, pinch grated nutmeg, little truffle essence, 5—6 egg whites

Remove the sinews from the hare, cut into pieces the size of a walnut, season and sauté in butter. Pound in a mortar, then rub through a sieve.

Mix the sauce, which should be fairly thick, egg yolks, nutmeg and truffle essence with the hare purée and finally fold in the stiffly beaten egg white.

Bake in a moderate oven and serve with a *sauce périgueux* (see page 28).

Râble de lièvre

SADDLE OF HARE

The saddle includes the whole of the hare's back, from the beginning of the neck down to the tail, but it is usually taken from the three first ribs.

The sinews having been carefully removed, the saddle is larded or simply wrapped in strips of pork fat; it is then roasted.

Saddle of hare, like saddle of venison, may be slightly marinated, and the same sauces and garnishes are suitable.

LAPEREAUX DE GARENNE
WILD RABBIT

Wild rabbit is cooked in the same way as civet of hare (see page 540).

Gibelotte of rabbit is a civet, to which potatoes, cut in quarters, are added.

Rabbit is also prepared *en blanquette* and can be used in a fricassée in the same way as chicken (see page 460).

Recipes for fillets of leveret apply equally well to wild rabbit.

Lapereau sauté chasseur

SAUTÉ WILD RABBIT

Follow the recipe for fillets of leveret (see page 543).

Lapereau sauté La Vallière

SAUTÉ OF WILD RABBIT LA VALLIÈRE

Follow the recipe for *levraut chasseur* (see page 543) but add 1 truffle cut into julienne and a few chopped leaves of tarragon to the sauce. Generally speaking, nearly all the recipes for sautéing chicken may be applied to wild rabbit.

The following make excellent luncheon dishes and are economical:

Sauté of rabbit with tomatoes, accompanied by a dish of rice or boiled potatoes.

Pilaf of rabbit, adding sautéed rabbit to rice. For pilaf of rice see page 669.

Rabbit sauté *à l'italienne*, when is with mushrooms, curry, paprika and cream.

Although wild rabbit is considered a very 'everyday' dish, excellent entrées may be made with its fillets, such as fillets Rossini following the recipe for *suprêmes de volaille Rossini* (see page 419), and served with chestnut purée or asparagus tips. It can also be used in a mousse or mousseline.

Galantines, Pâtés, Terrines

GALANTINES, PIES, TERRINES

Pâtés pour pâtés moulés

PASTRY FOR MOULDED PIES

Paste or pastry for moulded pies can be made with butter or lard.

With butter 1 lb. sifted flour, 4 oz. softened butter, 1 egg, ¼ oz. salt, approximately ¼ pint (U.S. ⅝ cup) cold water

With lard 1 lb. sifted flour, 4 oz. lard, softened almost to melting point, 1 egg, ¼ oz. salt, approximately ¼ pint (U.S. ⅝ cup) tepid water

With experience, the paste can be made straight on the board or table.

Alternatively, put the flour into a bowl and make a well in the middle.

Add the fat, egg and salt and mix all together adding the water gradually and kneading well with the hands until a smooth dough is formed, free from cracks.

Wrap in a cloth and keep in a cold place till required.

This paste should be prepared about 24 hours in advance.

Fumets pour pâtés et terrines

FUMETS FOR PIES AND TERRINES

Fumets are obtained with the bones and trimmings of poultry and game with the addition of some meat jelly made from knuckle of veal, calf's feet and pieces of bacon rind (see page 21).

Farces

FORCEMEAT

The different forcemeats for galantines, pâtés and terrines have been
given in the section for forcemeats (see pages 55 — 59)

GALANTINES

———————— 1 chicken or game bird,* salt, pepper, brandy, 4 oz. pork fat, 2 oz.
lean ham, 2 oz. tongue, 3 oz. truffles, 8 oz. lean veal, 8 oz. lean pork,
1 lb. fresh pork fat, 3 eggs, salt, 3 tablespoons pistachio nuts, 2 tablespoons chopped onion (optional), strips pork fat, knuckle of veal,
1 calf's foot, *bouquet garni*, carrots, onions, aspic jelly (see page 116)
*It does not matter if the poultry or game for the galantine is a little
tough.

Bone and skin the bird, keeping the skin as far as possible in one piece.

Remove the white meat, cut into strips and season.

Put it into a basin with 3 — 4 teaspoons brandy, pork fat, ham and
tongue, all cut into strips and the truffles cut into quarters.

Remove the remaining flesh from the carcase, chop, and put into
a mortar with the chopped veal, pork, seasoning, and pork fat. Pound
thoroughly adding the eggs 1 at a time, then ⅔ pint (U.S. approx. 1 cup)
brandy and chopped peeled nuts.

Rub through a sieve and add 2 tablespoons chopped truffle.

Spread out the skin of the bird on the table, and put on a layer of the
forcemeat. On this place a layer of the white meat, etc., which was put
on one side.

Repeat in layers till all ingredients are used up, finishing with a layer
of forcemeat.

Draw the edges of the skin together and sew up. Wrap some strips
of pork fat round the galantine, roll in a cloth and secure at both ends
and twice round the middle with string.

Weigh the galantine in order to calculate the time for cooking.
Allow 30 minutes for each 1¼ lb.

Have previously prepared some white stock made with a knuckle of veal, calf's foot, *bouquet garni*, carcase and trimmings of the bird and 2 pints (U.S. 5 cups) water. Cook the galantine in the stock, simmering for the calculated time.

When the galantine is cooked, remove from the pan, drain and remove the cloth and skin. Tie up in a clean cloth, put between two plates with a weight on top and leave overnight to get quite cold.

Do not use too heavy a weight or the liquid will escape and the galantine will be dry and tasteless.

The following day, remove the cloth and coat with aspic jelly.

PÂTÉS DE POISSONS

FISH PIES

Pâté d'anguille

EEL PIE

Eels, butter, mushrooms, shallots, parsley, fish forcemeat (see page 214), paste (see page 547), beaten egg

Choose medium-sized eels caught in running water. Remove the skins, fillet them and cut the fillets into strips about 2½ inches long. Sauté for a few seconds in butter with chopped mushrooms, shallots and parsley. Allow this to cool.

Line a buttered oblong mould with paste and fill this with alternate layers of fish forcemeat and the strips of eel.

Cover with a lid of paste, wetting the edges to make it stick. Decorate the top of the crust with pieces of paste cut into fancy shapes, starting from the edges and meeting in the centre. Make a hole in the centre for the escape of steam during the cooking.

Glaze the pie with beaten egg and cook it in a moderate oven, allowing 30 minutes for every 1¾ lb.

Farce de poisson

FISH FORCEMEAT

———————— 1 lb. pike meat, 6 oz. *panade à la frangipane* (see page 55), 8 oz. butter, 2 egg whites, ¼ oz. salt, pinch pepper, cayenne pepper and grated nutmeg

Prepare as *farce à la panade et au beurre* (see page 56).

Pâté de saumon

SALMON PIE

———————— 1½ lb. salmon, tail end, salt, pepper, paste (see page 547), 3 oz. truffle, 1 lb. pike forcemeat (see page 214), beaten egg, jellied fish stock

Cut the salmon into 4 fillets and remove the skin. Season with salt and pepper. Line a buttered oblong mould with paste.

Add a little chopped truffle to the forcemeat, and put a layer on the bottom and round the sides of the paste.

Put in 2 fillets of salmon, cover with another layer of forcemeat, add some thin slices of truffle and cover again with a thin layer of forcemeat. Put the remaining 2 fillets on top and cover with the remaining forcemeat. Cover with a lid of the paste and decorate as for the eel pie (see page 549). Glaze with beaten egg and cook as in the previous recipe.

When the pie is cold, pour a little jellied fish stock through the hole in the top.

PÂTÉS DE VIANDE
MEAT PIES

Pâté de veau et jambon

VEAL AND HAM PIE

———————— 1 lb. fillet veal, 8 oz. ham, 6 oz. fresh pork fat, salt, pepper, brandy, paste (see page 547), strips fat bacon, veal and pork forcemeat (see page 58), 1 bay leaf, 1 oval slice pork fat, jellied stock

Cut the veal, ham and pork fat into strips. Season and sprinkle with brandy.

Line a fluted oval pie mould with paste, put a few strips of fat bacon in the bottom and put a layer of forcemeat in the bottom and round the sides.

Fill up the mould with alternate layers of fat, ham, veal and fat and lastly cover with a layer of forcemeat.

Put the bay leaf in the centre and cover with an oval slice of pork fat.

Cover with strips or a lid of paste.

Decorate and cook as in the previous recipes. When the pie is cold, pour some jellied stock through the hole in the top.

Pâté de veau et jambon (ancienne méthode)

VEAL AND HAM PIE (AN OLD METHOD)

1 lb. fillet veal, 8 oz. lean ham, 8 oz. pork fat, salt, freshly ground pepper, grated nutmeg, butter, 6 oz. truffles (optional), 3—4 tablespoons brandy, 6 tablespoons Madeira, paste (see page 547), slices pork fat, jellied stock

Cut the veal, ham and pork fat into wide strips. Season and sauté in butter for 8—10 minutes.

Add the quartered truffles, brandy and Madeira and continue to sauté for a few minutes longer.

Line a pie mould with paste, put slices of pork fat in the bottom and round the sides and fill up with the meat, alternating with the truffles. Cover with a lid of paste and cook in a moderate oven as for the previous pies.

Just before the pie is quite cold add some good jellied stock through the hole in the top.

Chicken and game pies may be made in the same way, simply replacing the veal with the chosen ingredient.

Terrines may also be prepared in the same way.

PÂTÉS DE VOLAILLE
POULTRY PIES

Pâté de poulet
CHICKEN PIE

2 medium-sized chickens, chicken forcemeat (see page 56), 3—4 oz. truffles (optional), paste (see page 547), strips pork fat, tongue, 1 bay leaf, egg, jellied chicken stock

Bone the chickens and remove the breasts.

Prepare the forcemeat with the meat from the legs, adding a little chopped truffle if liked.

Line a round or oval pie mould with paste. Put some strips of pork fat round the sides and fill with alternate layers of forcemeat, seasoned slices of chicken breast, slices of tongue and slices of truffle if obtainable. Put a bay leaf in the centre and cover with a paste lid. Decorate with leaves cut from the paste, glaze with egg and bake in a moderate oven.

Before it is quite cold add some jellied chicken stock through the hole in the centre.

Pâté de caneton
DUCK PIE

8 oz. lean veal, 8 oz. lean pork, 1 lb. fresh pork fat, 3 eggs, brandy, 3 tablespoons pistachio nuts, 8 oz. gratin forcemeat (see page 58), 8 oz. poached and truffled foie gras, 1 duck, truffle, salt, pepper, spice, paste (see page 547), strips pork fat, egg for glazing, jellied stock made with duck fumet (see page 547)

Make a forcemeat with the veal, pork, pork fat, eggs, ¼ pint (U.S. ⅝ cup) brandy and pistachio nuts as for chicken galantine (see page 548).

Add the gratin forcemeat and the foie gras cut into large strips.

Bone the duck, and discard the 'parson's nose'. Leave the legs attached to the skin, remove the breast and cut it into slices. Season with salt, pepper, spice and a dash of brandy.

Spread out the skin and fill it as described for the chicken galantine (see page 548) with alternate layers of forcemeat and slices of duck. Re-form as far as possible into the original shape.

Line an oval pie mould with the paste, and put some strips of pork fat in the bottom and round the sides. Put in the duck and cover with a lid of paste. Decorate with leaves of paste, glaze with beaten egg and bake in a moderate oven.

Before it is quite cold, pour some jellied stock through the hole in the top of the pie.

Pâté de pigeon

PIGEON PIE

Bone the pigeons and stuff them with chicken galantine forcemeat (see page 548), mixed with a few tablespoons cooked ham, truffles and foie gras cut in cubes.

Re-form into their original shape and proceed as for duck pie (see page 552).

Pâté de pintade

GUINEA FOWL PIE

Proceed as for duck pie (see page 552).

PÂTÉS DE GIBIER
GAME PIES

Pâté d'alouettes

LARK PIE

———— Larks, gratin forcemeat (see page 58), foie gras, pork fat, paste (see page 547), sausage meat

Bone the larks. Stuff with forcemeat and put a small cube of foie gras in each. Wrap each bird in a slice of pork fat.

Butter a small raised pie mould, and line with paste. Mix some sausage meat with one-third its volume of forcemeat and spread over bottom and sides of the paste. Put in the birds, cover with a layer of forcemeat and then with a strip of pork fat. Cover with a paste lid and proceed as for chicken pie (see page 552).

Pâté de bécasses

WOODCOCK PIE

Woodcocks, salt, pepper, spice, few drops brandy, gratin forcemeat (see page 58), poached truffled foie gras, paste (see page 547), pork fat, jellied stock made with fumet from bones and trimmings (see page 547)

Bone the birds, spread out as flat as possible, and season with salt, pepper, spice and brandy. Cover with a layer of forcemeat and a little foie gras. Re-form as far as possible into their original shape.

Line an oval pie mould with paste and put some thin slices of pork fat in the bottom and round the sides.

Put in the birds, cover with a thin layer of forcemeat and then with a strip of pork fat. Cover with a paste lid and proceed as for chicken pie (see page 552).

Before it is quite cold fill up with the jellied stock.

Pâté de faisan

PHEASANT PIE

1 pheasant, 5 oz. fillet veal, 5 oz. lean pork, 10 oz. fresh pork fat, 5 oz. gratin forcemeat (see page 58), brandy, 6 small slices poached truffled foie gras, truffle, salt, spice, paste (see page 547), strips pork fat

Bone the pheasant and remove the breasts. Cut each into 3 slices. Using the flesh from the legs, liver from the pheasant, veal, pork and pork fat, make a forcemeat as described for chicken galantine (see page 548).

Add the gratin forcemeat and 2 tablespoons brandy.

Spread out the skin of the pheasant and cover it with a fairly thick layer of forcemeat.

Arrange the slices of breast, foie gras and slices of truffle alternately on top and season with salt, spice and a few drops of brandy. Re-form the pheasant into its original shape.

Line a pie mould with paste and put strips of pork fat in the bottom and round the sides. Put in the pheasant. Cover with a paste lid and proceed as for chicken pie (see page 552).

Pâté de grives

THRUSH PIE

Proceed exactly as instructed for lark pie (see page 553).

Pâté de bécassines, de pluviers, vanneaux, chevaliers

SNIPE, PLOVER, LAPWING AND WADER PIE

The same method for all these as for lark pie (see page 553).

Pâté de lièvre

HARE PIE

1 hare, strips fresh pork fat, lean ham, truffles, salt, pepper, spice, 3—4 tablespoons brandy, 6 tablespoons Madeira, 8 oz. lean pork, 8 oz. fresh pork fat, powdered thyme, 7 oz. gratin forcemeat (see page 58), paste (see page 547), bay leaf, jellied stock made with hare fumet (see page 547)

Bone the saddle and the legs. Remove all the tendons from the meat and put it into a bowl with about the same quantity of strips of pork fat and ham and a little truffle.

Add salt, pepper and spice, brandy and the Madeira and leave to marinate for several hours.

Prepare a forcemeat with the rest of the meat from the hare, liver, pork and pork fat. Season well with salt, pepper, spice and powdered thyme.

Rub all through a sieve and add the gratin forcemeat.

Line a buttered oval fluted mould with paste. Cover the bottom and sides with strips of pork fat and fill up with alternate layers of forcemeat and the marinated ingredients, finishing with a layer of forcemeat. Finally add a strip of pork fat and 1 bay leaf.

Cover with a paste lid and bake in a moderate oven.

When nearly cold pour in some jellied stock.

Pâté de perdreaux

PARTRIDGE PIE

See woodcock pie and proceed in the same way (see page 554).

Rôtis et garnitures pour les rôtis
ROASTS AND GARNISHES FOR ROASTS

RÔTIS
ROASTS

There are two ways of roasting — on the spit or in the oven.

Roasting on a spit is generally better than roasting in the oven but the spit is not always available and the oven has to be used. This way of .oasting meat requires a good deal of care, particularly for poultry.

Generally speaking, poultry and game should be larded or wrapped in pork fat. This is not only to protect the breast of poultry and game against the too rapid action of the heat, but also to prevent them being dried up while the legs are being cooked, as the legs take much longer to cook than the breast. The strips of pork fat should cover the whole of the breast of poultry and game, and should be kept in place by tying round with string.

Certain joints of meat have a much better flavour when care has been taken to cover them with slices of beef fat or of fresh veal fat.

In France they have a very bad habit of boning joints and removing all the fat; this is a great mistake, as by this means the meat loses half its flavour and is hopelessly dried up.

The fact that fat is absolutely necessary for the nourishment of the meat while it is being cooked is often lost sight of, as it gives the meat a much fuller flavour.

I must admit that the English pay much more attention to that important point than the French, and they are quite right.

Never add any liquid at all during the cooking of meat, either in the oven dish or in the dripping pan. Whether the roast is cooked on the spit or in the oven it must always be basted with its own cooking liquor from time to time.

LE JUS DES RÔTIS
THE GRAVY OF ROASTS

This is a very important consideration, which is often neglected.

Correct gravy is made by adding water or other liquid to the pan in which the roast was cooked, the essential ingredient being the juices which drop from the joint during the cooking process. But, to get the best results, it is important that neither the cooking dish nor the gravy should be burned; the gravy should be simply 'caramelised' at the bottom of the dish.

An important point is that, for joints roasted in the oven, the oven dish should be chosen to fit the joint to be cooked, as this lessens the danger of the gravy burning.

In private houses, deglazing alone will, at a pinch, be sufficient to make the gravy to accompany the joint; but in restaurants and hotels, this is supplemented by preparing in advance a stock taken from the bones and trimmings of the same kind as the joint for which it is intended, or from the bones and meat of veal, which give a neutral stock.

Deglazing the cooking dish When the joint is taken from the spit or the oven, pour into the oven dish or the dripping pan the quantity of liquid necessary to make the gravy, taking into account the fact that it is to be reduced. Reduce by one-third; strain through a fine sieve or muslin and, if necessary, remove any excess fat.

It is a mistake to remove all the fat or to clarify it. Treated thus the gravy is clearer, and perhaps nicer to look at, but it will have lost half its flavour, for it must not be forgotten that the fat gives the gravy its real flavour.

Serving the joint should be simple. Put it on to a hot dish, and pour a little of the gravy round. For poultry, watercress is usually served with the birds, but this must be added only at the last moment.

The gravy is always served separately.

Game birds are served on cushions of bread, fried in butter and covered with a special gratin forcemeat (see page 58).

When lemons are served with a roast, they should be served separately. It is quite wrong to decorate the edges of a dish with lemons, gherkins, etc. The beauty of the edges of the dish is that it should be quite clean and spotless.

Game birds are served in England with four accompaniments: gravy, bread sauce, fried breadcrumbs and chip potatoes.

Note In northern countries, roasts are always accompanied by a rather tart apple sauce, or by a compote of cherries, prunes, apricots, etc.

Sauces et appareils pour rôtis à l'anglaise
SAUCES AND GARNISHES FOR ENGLISH ROASTS
VARIOUS SAUCES

Apple sauce, bread sauce, fried breadcrumbs, horseradish sauce, cranberry sauce

Note Cranberry sauce is a special accompaniment to turkeys, wild duck and roast pork.

For other English sauces, see hot English sauces (see pages 37–40).

Farce à la crème (pour dindes, canards et oies)
FORCEMEAT WITH CREAM (FOR TURKEYS, DUCK AND GEESE)

———————— 4 large white onions, butter, pinch chopped sage, 8 oz. breadcrumbs, milk, 4 oz. veal fat, salt, pepper

Cook the onions in the oven without peeling them. When they are cooked, peel, chop finely, add a little butter and sage.

Soak the breadcrumbs in milk, then squeeze very dry. Chop the veal fat and mix all ingredients together. Add seasoning.

Note This quantity is sufficient for a medium-sized turkey or goose. For a duck reduce by one-third.

Farce (pour le veau et le porc)
STUFFING (FOR VEAL AND PORK)

———————— Chopped beef fat, breadcrumbs, salt, pepper, chopped parsley, grated nutmeg, eggs

Mix equal quantities of beef fat and breadcrumbs. Add seasoning, little chopped parsley and nutmeg. Bind with beaten egg.

Yorkshire pouding (pour les rôtis de boeuf)
YORKSHIRE PUDDING (FOR ROAST BEEF)

8 oz. flour, 1 pint (U.S. 2½ cups) milk, 2 eggs, salt, pepper, nutmeg

Mix the flour smoothly with the milk and eggs. Add seasoning and nutmeg.

Pour into a pan containing hot fat from the beef and cook in a moderate oven.

If the beef is being cooked on a spit, put the batter under it, so that it may be impregnated with the gravy which drops from the meat.

Cut into squares and serve on a separate dish.

RÔTIS DE BOEUF
ROAST BEEF

Côte de boeuf
ROAST BEEF

Ribs of beef are cooked without being boned. The bones are merely shortened.

If they are roasted in the oven, place them in a rather deep pan proportionate in size to the joint. Cook at moderate heat, so that the cooking liquor does not burn; baste frequently.

Average time of cooking 15 minutes for every 1 lb. and 15 minutes over.

If it is being cooked on the spit, the cooking time is the same.

Contre-filet rôti
ROAST SIRLOIN

If the sirloin is roasted without being boned, the projecting bones of the vertebrae should be broken at their base, but not detached, and the yellow ligament should be severed at several points.

If the joint is boned, it should be covered with beef kidney fat sliced and flattened. If no kidney fat is available, tie some pork fat on it, but this is not nearly as good as the kidney fat.

Average time for cooking in the oven 15 minutes for every 1 lb. and 15 minutes over.

Filet de boeuf

FILLET OF BEEF

Remove any gristle or sinew from the meat and stud with pork fat or wrap in strips of pork or beef fat and secure with string.

Roast in a fairly hot oven or on a spit allowing about 15 minutes to 1 lb. and 15 minutes over.

RÔTIS DE VEAU
ROAST VEAL

Carré

LOIN AND BEST END NECK (U.S. LOIN AND RIBS)

Brush the meat with melted butter and put into a roasting pan with some chopped veal kidney fat. Baste frequently and allow 30 minutes per 1 lb.

ANOTHER METHOD

Loin of veal can also be cooked in butter in a covered pan.

Care must be taken to see the butter does not burn or the gravy will be spoiled.

Choose a pan which just fits the joint. Heat some butter in it, put in the joint, cover and cook in a moderate oven, basting frequently. Allow 30 minutes per 1 lb.

As the butter begins to colour add 2 tablespoons hot water, and repeat this process throughout the cooking.

When the veal is cooked put on to a serving dish.

Add ½ pint (U.S. 1¼ cups) boiling water to the butter left in the pan. Boil for 5–6 minutes. Season before serving.

Longe et épaule de veau à l'anglaise
LOIN AND SHOULDER OF VEAL IN THE ENGLISH STYLE

This joint is stuffed with veal stuffing (see page 559).

It is accompanied by bacon or boiled ham.

Note For fillet of veal, proceed exactly as instructed for loin of veal, but watch the cooking carefully.

The secret of this way of cooking veal is not to let the butter burn.

RÔTIS DE MOUTON ET D'AGNEAU
ROAST MUTTON AND LAMB

Gigot
LEG OF MUTTON

Average time of cooking 30 minutes per 1 lb.

Épaules
SHOULDER OF MUTTON

Shoulder of mutton may be boned, seasoned, rolled and tied with string.

Note The time for cooking lamb joints is approximately the same as for mutton joints, but remember that both should always be well cooked.

RÔTIS DE PORC
ROAST PORK

Rôtis de porc à l'anglaise
ROAST PORK IN THE ENGLISH WAY

Leg, loin and fillet (U.S. tenderloin) of young animals are generally roasted. The skin is left on the joint and it is heavily scored horizontally. Pork should always be well cooked. Allow 35 minutes per 1 lb.

Sage and onion stuffing, apple sauce or cranberry sauce are suitable accompaniments.

RÔTIS DE VOLAILLES
ROAST POULTRY

Poularde

CHICKEN

Truss the chicken, season it inside and out, wrap it in a strip of pork fat and roast it in a moderate oven or preferably on a spit.

The average time of cooking for a 3-lb. chicken is 1 hour.

Gauge the state of cooking by letting a few drops of gravy from the inside of the chicken fall on a plate. It should be quite colourless. Pour a little of the cooking liquor over it and serve with the rest of the gravy and some watercress.

Poularde rôti à l'anglaise

ROAST CHICKEN IN THE ENGLISH WAY

Roast the chicken as in the previous recipe. Put it on a dish, surround it with rolls of grilled bacon and sausages and serve bread sauce with it.

Poularde truffé

TRUFFLED CHICKEN

1 chicken, salt, pepper, fresh pork fat, 12 oz. truffles, pinch nutmeg, 3 tablespoons brandy, strips fat for larding

Choose a good plump chicken, clean, and leave the skin of the neck as long as possible. Sprinkle with salt and pepper.

Pound 1 lb. pork fat and rub through a sieve. Cut the truffles into quarters, put into a pan with salt, pepper, nutmeg, 2−3 tablespoons pork fat and the brandy. Heat for a few moments then mix with the sieved pork fat and use to stuff the chicken.

Put a few slices of truffle under the skin of the breast.

Leave in a cold place overnight.

Truss and lard the chicken, wrap in buttered greaseproof paper and roast in a moderate oven about 1½ hours.

Poulet reine

SPRING CHICKEN

Clean carefully and sprinkle inside and out with salt. Truss, lard, and roast on the spit or in the oven.

Time of cooking 40 minutes

POUSSIN

Time of cooking 12—15 minutes

Dindonneau rôti

ROAST TURKEY

Proceed exactly as for roast chicken (see page 563).

Note Before trussing the turkey, it is necessary to clear its legs of tendons, which can be done by making 2 incisions on the inside of the legs, above and below the articulation joining the foot to the drumstick. Take these tendons one by one, roll them round a larding needle and, by turning it gently, the tendons roll round it and are thus easily pulled out.

Dindonneau rôti à l'anglaise

ROAST TURKEY IN THE ENGLISH WAY

Stuff the turkey with sage and onion stuffing or chestnut stuffing (see below), roast it gently and serve it surrounded with sausages and slices of grilled bacon.

SAGE AND ONION STUFFING

4 large onions, butter, 8—9 leaves or 1 tablespoon dried sage, salt, pepper, 8 oz. breadcrumbs, soaked in milk and pressed well

Bake the onions in the oven without skinning them. Then skin, chop and sauté lightly in butter. Add sage, finely chopped if leaves are used, seasoning and breadcrumbs and mix all well together.

CHESTNUT STUFFING

——————— 1 lb. chestnuts, milk or stock, 2 oz. chopped ham or bacon, 3 oz. bread-crumbs, 2 teaspoons chopped parsley, 1 oz. butter, little grated lemon rind, salt, pepper, pinch sugar, 1 egg

Slit the thick end of the chestnuts and put into the oven for a few minutes with a little water. Then remove the outer and inner skin and put the nuts in a pan just covered with milk or stock. Cook till tender, then rub through a sieve. Add all the other ingredients and bind with the beaten egg.

Dindonneau truffé

TRUFFLED TURKEY

Proceed in exactly the same way as for truffled chicken (see page 563) but increase the amount of forcemeat.

Truss and lard the bird, wrap it in greaseproof paper, and roast it on a spit or in the oven.

If the bird is roasted in the oven, it should be put into an uncovered pan.

Time of cooking

1 5–8-lb. turkey, 20 minutes per lb.
1 9–10-lb. turkey, 15 minutes per lb.
Over 14-lb. turkey, 12 minutes per lb.
Very large turkeys are not generally cooked on a spit in the average household, but for a turkey of medium size, allow approximately the same time as for roasting.

Serve with liquor from the pan, with excess fat removed, and a thin *sauce périgueux* (see page 28).

Pigeonneaux

YOUNG PIGEONS (SQUAB)

Choose fledgling pigeons. Clean and empty them, leaving the liver inside, and sprinkle inside and out with salt. Truss, lard, and cook in butter or roast them on a spit.

Time for cooking About 20 minutes.

Pintade

GUINEA FOWL

Roast guinea fowl is delicious, but only if it is very young.

Clean it carefully and sprinkle inside and out with salt. Truss and lard it. Roast on a spit, or in the oven with butter, basting frequently.

All the recipes given for pheasant may be applied to guinea fowl.

Time for cooking About 45 minutes.

Caneton nantais

NANTES DUCKLING

Time for cooking a 2–3-*lb. bird* About 45 minutes.

Caneton rouennais

ROUEN DUCKLING

Whether in the oven or on the spit, the Rouen duckling must be cooked by a brisk fire.

For a bird weighing 2–3 lb. when drawn, about 45 minutes cooking time must be allowed.

Caneton d'Aylesbury à l'anglaise

AYLESBURY DUCKLING COOKED IN THE ENGLISH WAY

Aylesbury duckling is the equivalent of the French Nantes duckling and is generally stuffed with sage and onion (see page 564).

Its usual accompaniment is apple sauce, but melted redcurrant jelly or cranberry sauce may be served with it.

Oie rôtie à l'anglaise

ROAST GOOSE IN THE ENGLISH WAY

The goose must be stuffed with sage forcemeat (see page 564). It is served with the accompaniments given above for *caneton à l'anglaise*. It is generally served at Michaelmas.

RÔTIS DE VENAISON
ROAST VENISON

Chevreuil

VENISON OR ROEBUCK

The legs and saddle are generally roasted. These joints are not marinated and the legs are usually studded with pork fat and the saddle is more often wrapped in pork fat.

Average time for cooking in the oven 10 minutes per 1 lb.

Venaison à l'anglaise

VENISON IN THE ENGLISH STYLE

In England venison is supplied by the stag or the fallow deer. The most highly esteemed joint is the haunch, which consists of one leg with half the saddle attached.

Venison should be well hung but not marinated. To preserve it and to keep it dry while it is hanging, it should be rubbed with a mixture of flour and pepper. To roast it, rub off the flour and wrap it in a flour and water paste, then wrap in greaseproof paper and tie with string. The cooking time is 4 hours.

Before serving, remove the paper and the pastry, dredge the joint with salt and flour, brush with melted butter and brown in the oven.

Roast venison should be accompanied by redcurrant jelly.

Lièvre

HARE

The only part of the hare used for roasting is the saddle, which includes the part beginning at the root of the neck and ending at the tail.

All the tendons should be removed and it should be larded or wrapped in strips of pork fat and roasted in the oven for about 20 minutes.

The ordinary accompaniment to the saddle of hare is a thin poivrade sauce (see page 29).

In Great Britain and in northern countries redcurrant jelly and tart apple sauce are served with saddle of hare, and even prunes and pears in red wine.

Marcassin

YOUNG WILD BOAR

The joints preferred are the ribs and the saddle, which are cooked like roast pork.

Roast of young wild boar should be served with a rather thick gravy or with a thin poivrade sauce (see page 29).

RÔTIS DE GIBIERS À POIL ET À PLUMES
ROAST GROUND AND FEATHERED GAME

Bécasse

WOODCOCK

Woodcock should be hung for several days with its plumage on. It should not be plucked until it is ready to eat. It is not drawn; only the gizzard is removed.

Truss it, piercing the legs with the beak, having removed the eyes, and wrap in pork fat.

Time for cooking in a hot oven About 20 minutes.

Serve on a cushion of bread fried in butter and deglaze the cooking liquor with brandy and 2 tablespoons stock which should be served separately.

Bécassine

SNIPE

The recipe for woodcock (see above) applies to snipe, except that the croûton for the snipe, after being fried in butter, is covered with a light layer of gratin forcemeat for game (see page 58).

Cooking time 15 – 20 minutes.

Cailles
QUAILS

These must be chosen white and plump. Wrap them first in a buttered vine leaf and cover this with a thin strip of pork fat.

Roast them in a fairly hot oven for about 25 minutes.

Serve them on small croûtons of bread, fried in butter and covered with gratin forcemeat for game (see page 58). They may be surrounded by bunches of watercress and slices of lemon. Separately serve their gravy which should naturally be very thick.

Canards sauvages
WILD DUCKS

Wild duck is not larded and is cooked in a quick oven so as to be underdone. It may be served surrounded by watercress and slices of lemon.

Cooking time 20 minutes.

Canard sauvage rôti à l'anglaise
WILD DUCK COOKED IN THE ENGLISH WAY

Roast the duck as instructed above and serve with apple or cranberry sauce handed separately.

Canard sauvage à la bigarade
WILD DUCK WITH BIGARADE SAUCE

Roast in the same way as in the previous recipe. Garnish with orange slices and serve a thin bigarade sauce separately (see page 24).

Sarcelle
TEAL

Teal is treated like wild duck.

Cooking time About 20 minutes.

Note The cooking time is always variable as it depends on the fatness of the birds.

Coq de bruyère, gelinotte, grouse

WOOD GROUSE, HAZEL-GROUSE AND GROUSE

The wood grouse is not generally very popular. However, if chosen young the flesh has a flavour which appeals to many gourmets.

Hazel-grouse should be used very fresh. Truss, lard and allow about 20 minutes cooking time in a hot oven.

Grouse should also be used very fresh. The time of cooking, which varies according to the size of the bird, is about 25 minutes.

Note These birds should be kept underdone. Only the breast is usually eaten.

According to the custom in England, they are accompanied by bread sauce, fried breadcrumbs and chip potatoes.

Faisan

PHEASANT

Pheasant for roasting should be wrapped in pork fat and not studded with lard. An excellent method, which brings out the flavour, is to stuff it with 3 oz. pork fat pounded with a few truffles, or simply with pork fat by itself, and season with salt and pepper. As the flesh of the pheasant is inclined to be dry, the fat penetrates inside and improves the flavour. This procedure applies equally well to partridges.

Average time for cooking 40 – 45 minutes according to size.

Serve with the cooking liquor, with the excess fat removed.

Faisan truffé

TRUFFLED PHEASANT

For truffling the pheasant, see truffled chicken (page 563).

———————— *For the stuffing* 12 oz. fresh pork fat, 6 oz. truffles, 1 – 2 tablespoons brandy

Prepare as for the truffled chicken and wrap the pheasant in strips of pork fat. Cook in a moderate oven about 45 minutes. Serve with a thin *sauce périgueux* (see page 28).

Grives

THRUSHES

Remove the thrushes' gizzards. Put 1 juniper berry into each and roast in a hot oven for 15 minutes. Serve on croûtons fried in butter. Serve the deglazed cooking liquor separately.

Mauviettes

LARKS

Wrap each one in a thin strip of pork fat; spit them three at a time and cook them in butter in a flat saucepan for 7 or 8 minutes.

Serve them on croûtons fried in butter, and with the deglazed gravy separately. Optionally, the larks may be surrounded by bunches of watercress.

Merles de Corse

CORSICAN BLACKBIRDS

These are treated in exactly the same way as thrushes.

Ortolans

Wrap each ortolan in a vine leaf, place in an oven dish containing salted water and seal them in a hot oven for 4 – 5 minutes.

The small quantity of water at the bottom of the oven dish gives off steam which prevents the fat of the ortolans from melting, and consequently no pork fat or butter or stock is necessary.

ANOTHER WAY OF COOKING ORTOLANS

Poach them in a very thick consommé. Serve with a little of the cooking liquor.

Ortolans au jus d'ananas 'fantaisie'

ORTOLANS WITH PINEAPPLE JUICE

For 10 ortolans, heat 1 oz. fresh butter in a small casserole. Roll the ortolans in this butter, salt them lightly and then put them into a very hot oven for 5 minutes.

Take them out of the oven and sprinkle with pineapple juice. Cover the casserole and leave for a few minutes to absorb the pineapple flavour, then serve immediately.

Perdreau rôti

ROAST PARTRIDGE

Season the partridge inside and out with salt, wrap it in a buttered vine leaf and a very thin strip of pork fat.

Cook in a moderately hot oven or on a spit for 25 minutes.

Serve on a croûton fried in butter and covered with a gratin forcemeat (see page 58). Garnish with watercress and serve with a thick rich gravy.

Perdreau truffé

TRUFFLED PARTRIDGE

3 oz. fresh pork fat, 3 oz. truffles, salt, pepper, dash brandy, partridge, slice pork fat

Pound and sieve the pork fat, add the truffles cut into quarters, seasoning and brandy.

Stuff the partridge, truss and wrap in a thin slice of pork fat.

Cook on a spit if possible or roast for 35 minutes.

Pluviers et vanneaux

PLOVERS AND LAPWINGS

Draw these birds completely, and wrap in strips of pork fat. Cook on a spit or in a sauté pan, and keep underdone.

Serve as soon as they are ready, accompanied with a thick gravy.

Time for cooking 15—20 minutes.

Salades

SALADS

SALADES SIMPLES ET COMPOSÉES

SIMPLE AND COMPOUND SALADS

Simple salads consist of raw green salad plants and often accompany hot roasts. Compound salads usually consist of a variety of vegetables and are usually served as accompaniments to entrées or to cold roasts.

Assaisonnement des salades

SALAD DRESSINGS

1 Oil and vinegar – can be used with all salads in the proportion of 3 parts oil to 1 part vinegar with the addition of salt and freshly ground pepper.

2 Cream – particularly suits lettuce salads, to which various fruits may be added: oranges, bananas, grapefruit, etc.

The proportions are: 3 parts thin cream to 1 part vinegar, or, preferably, 1 part lemon juice, salt and pepper.

3 Egg – made with hard-boiled egg yolks, pounded or sieved, and put into the salad bowl with mustard, oil, vinegar, salt and pepper. To a salad made in this way add a finely chopped white of hard-boiled egg.

4 Pork fat – seasoning with pork fat is specially used with dandelion salad, corn salad and with red and green cabbage. Here, oil is replaced by pork fat cut into small strips and browned in a frying pan. The hot fat and strips of pork are poured over the salad in a warm salad bowl, previously seasoned with salt and pepper.

Heat a few tablespoons vinegar in the frying pan and pour over the salad. Mix it all very well. Cover the salad with a plate and leave for a few moments before serving.

5 Mustard and cream – is suitable for beetroot, celeriac and green salads with beetroot added.

1 small dessertspoon mustard mixed with ½ pint (U.S. 1¼ cups) thin cream, juice 1 lemon, salt and pepper.

6 Horseradish with cream – is prepared in the same way as mustard and cream, with the mustard replaced by grated horseradish. If desired, lightly whipped cream may be used.

Note Raw onion and garlic should be used in moderation in salads as many people dislike them.

SALADES SIMPLES — SALADES VERTES

SIMPLE SALADS — GREEN SALADS

Lettuce, chicory, endive, celery, corn salad, dandelion leaves, purslane, watercress, rampion, salsify leaves, etc.

Salade de betteraves

BEETROOT SALAD

Beetroot is an auxiliary ingredient of simple and compound salads. If possible, it should be cooked in the oven rather then boiled in water.

It is then cut into thin slices or in julienne and is seasoned with oil or with mustard.

BEETROOT FOR HORS-D'OEUVRE OR TO ACCOMPANY COLD MEATS

———————— Sliced cooked beetroot, grated horseradish, red wine, peppercorns, 1 bay leaf

Put the beetroot into a dish with one-third its quantity of grated horse-radish. With a few peppercorns and bay leaf boil enough red wine to cover it. Pour over the beetroot and horseradish and leave to marinate for 24 hours.

Salade de céleri

CELERY SALAD

Cut the celery stalks in pieces and leave in cold water for some hours to make them curl. Season according to taste.

Salade de céleri-rave

CELERIAC SALAD

Cut the celeriac into fine julienne. Season with a light mayonnaise (see page 40) with plenty of mustard.

Salade de chou-fleur

CAULIFLOWER SALAD

Cook the cauliflower carefully, keeping it firm. Drain and divide into small flowerets. Add oil and vinegar dressing and sprinkle with chopped chervil.

Salade de chou rouge

RED CABBAGE SALAD

Choose a young, tender red cabbage. Remove the hard core and the stems of the leaves. Cut the leaves into fine julienne. Add oil and vinegar dressing some hours before required.

Red cabbage may also be marinated as instructed for beetroot (see page 574).

Salade de concombres

CUCUMBER SALAD

Peel the cucumber, slice it thinly and sprinkle with salt.

Leave to stand for a little while, then strain off the water. Add oil and vinegar dressing and sprinkle with chopped chervil.

Salades de légumes secs, haricots, lentilles
DRIED VEGETABLE SALADS, HARICOT BEANS AND LENTILS

Cook the beans or lentils, drain well and add oil and vinegar dressing (see page 573) while the beans are still warm.

Sprinkle with chopped parsley and serve with finely chopped onion, rinsed in cold water and squeezed tightly in a cloth.

Salade de haricots verts
FRENCH BEAN SALAD

Cook the beans in salted water, rinse in cold water, then dry in a cloth.

Rub the bottom of a salad bowl with garlic and add salt, freshly ground pepper, a little vinegar and 3 times the amount of olive oil. Mix all well together and put in the beans. Thinly sliced tomatoes and fillets of anchovy are sometimes added to this salad.

In Provence they sometimes make a salad of French beans, potatoes and vegetable marrow, all cooked in salted water, drained and seasoned as above.

Salade de pommes de terre
POTATO SALAD

Cook the potatoes in salted water, cut them into the shape of corks and slice them thinly while they are still warm. Season with oil, vinegar and chopped herbs. According to the quality of the potatoes, a little boiling stock is sometimes added to the seasoning.

Salade de pommes de terre à la parisienne
PARISIAN STYLE POTATO SALAD

Select potatoes that do not crumble. Cook in salted water. Drain, then slice thinly while still hot, and marinate in dry white wine, allowing ½ pint (U.S. 1¼ cups) wine to 2 lb. potatoes. Just before serving, dress with oil, vinegar, chopped parsley, chervil and tarragon. Mix gently to avoid breaking the roundels of potato.

Note When the potatoes are to be mixed with other vegetables, they should be cut into small cubes and cooked in salted water. Watch them carefully so that they are not over-cooked and drain as soon as they are ready.

Salade de tomates
TOMATO SALAD

Choose firm tomatoes, peel, cut into thin slices and arrange on an hors d'oeuvre dish. Dress with oil, vinegar, salt, freshly ground pepper, chopped tarragon and parsley. Surround tomatoes with thin rings of onions.

SALADES COMPOSÉES
COMPOUND SALADS

Salade Alice
ALICE SALAD

Medium-sized red dessert apples, lemon juice, apple balls, cut with a very small vegetable ball cutter, redcurrants, almonds or walnuts, salt, cream, lettuce

Cut a slice from the stalk end of the apple and remove as much of the fruit as possible. Rub the inside of the apple case with lemon juice to prevent it discolouring. Mix the apple balls, redcurrants and chopped nuts. Sprinkle with salt and lemon juice and bind with the cream. Fill the apple cases, replace the lids and serve on hearts of lettuce cut into halves or quarters.

Salade américaine
AMERICAN SALAD

Tomatoes, pineapple, orange, banana, cos lettuce, mayonnaise (see page 40)

Peel, seed and slice the tomatoes, cut the pineapple in small slices, peel and divide the orange into sections and slice the banana thinly.

Cut the lettuce in half and arrange the fruits alternately on it.

Serve with a thin mayonnaise sauce or with cream to which orange and lemon juice, salt and a pinch sugar have been added.

Salade andalouse

TOMATO AND SWEET RED PEPPER SALAD

————— Rice, tomatoes, sweet red pepper, oil and vinegar dressing (see page 573), parsley, onion and garlic (optional)

Cook some rice for 18 minutes in boiling salted water and drain well.

Add equal quantities of tomatoes, peeled and quartered, and red pepper, peeled and cut into strips.

Add the dressing and a little chopped parsley. If onion and garlic are used, the onion should be chopped finely and the garlic crushed.

Note The red peppers may be grilled (U.S. broiled) for a few minutes to loosen the skins.

Salade du bon viveur

CRAYFISH AND ARTICHOKE SALAD

————— Crayfish, truffle, cooked artichoke bottoms, oil and wine vinegar dressing (see page 573), sieved hard-boiled egg yolk

Mix equal parts of crayfish, thinly sliced truffle and artichoke bottoms.

Make the dressing, season it rather highly and pour over the ingredients.

Salade Carmen

GRILLED SWEET RED PEPPER AND CHICKEN SALAD

————— Rice, sweet red peppers, grilled (U.S. broiled) for a few minutes to loosen the skin, white meat of chicken, cooked green peas, mustard, chopped tarragon, oil and vinegar dressing (see page 573)

Cook the rice in boiling salted water for 18 minutes and drain well.

Add an equal quantity of red peppers, peeled and cut into strips, chicken meat, cut into cubes, and peas.

Add a little mustard and tarragon to the dressing and pour over.

Salade Théodora

ARTICHOKE, MUSHROOM AND CRAYFISH SALAD

————— Cooked artichoke bottoms, mushrooms, asparagus tips, cooked but firm, crayfish, mayonnaise sauce (see page 40), oil, vinegar, seasoning, truffle, hard-boiled egg

Slice artichoke bottoms and mushrooms thinly and mix with the asparagus and crayfish in equal parts.

Coat with mayonnaise sauce to which a little extra oil, vinegar and seasoning has been added and garnish with truffle and hard-boiled egg.

Salade demi-deuil

ASPARAGUS AND TRUFFLE SALAD

———————— Asparagus tips, truffles, oil and wine vinegar dressing (see page 573), chopped parsley, mustard

Mix the asparagus tips and finely sliced truffles together in equal parts.

Make the dressing, add a little chopped parsley and a little mustard to taste, and pour over the asparagus and truffle.

Salade Gabrielle d'Estrées

BREAST OF CHICKEN AND ASPARAGUS TIPS SALAD

———————— Breast of cooked chicken, truffle, asparagus tips, mustard, cayenne pepper, thin mayonnaise sauce (see page 40), cooked cucumber (optional)

Cut the chicken and truffle into julienne and mix with the asparagus tips.

Add a little mustard and a pinch cayenne pepper to some thin mayonnaise sauce and pour over.

A little cucumber cooked and cut into strips can be added to taste.

Salade favorite

CRAYFISH, TRUFFLE AND ASPARAGUS TIPS SALAD

———————— Crayfish, finely chopped white Piedmont truffles, asparagus tips
Dressing Olive oil, lemon juice, salt, pepper, chopped celery, chopped tarragon

Mix the ingredients together in equal quantities. Make the dressing (see page 573) with the oil, lemon juice and seasoning, using the lemon juice in place of vinegar. Add a little chopped celery and tarragon and pour over.

Salade japonaise

JAPANESE SALAD

———————— Potatoes, Chablis, mussels, truffle, mayonnaise sauce (see page 40), oil, vinegar, freshly ground pepper

Cook the potatoes, drain and, while still warm, slice thinly and marinate in a little Chablis. Add half the amount poached mussels (see page 250) and the same quantity of sliced truffle.

Coat with mayonnaise to which a little extra oil, vinegar and pepper have been added.

Salade Isabelle

TRUFFLE, CELERY, MUSHROOM AND ARTICHOKE SALAD

———————— Truffle, celery, mushrooms, cooked potatoes, cooked artichoke bottoms, oil and vinegar dressing (see page 573), chopped chervil

Slice equal quantities of all the ingredients except the chervil and arrange in heaps on the serving dish.

Pour the dressing over and sprinkle with the chervil.

Salade japonaise aux fruits

JAPANESE FRUIT SALAD

———————— Pineapple, oranges, tomatoes, lemon juice, pinch salt, orange juice, lettuce hearts, pinch sugar, fresh cream

Prepare all the fruits and cut them into cubes. Sprinkle the pineapple with a little lemon juice. Add a pinch salt to the tomatoes and squeeze a little orange juice over the oranges.

Arrange equal amounts of pineapple and orange on the lettuce hearts.

Add a little lemon juice, a pinch salt and a pinch sugar to the cream and put a spoonful on each serving. Decorate with pieces of tomato and serve the rest of the cream separately.

Salade Jockey-Club

ASPARAGUS TIPS, TRUFFLE AND CHICKEN SALAD

———————— Asparagus tips, truffles, breast of cooked chicken, oil and vinegar dressing (see page 573), mayonnaise sauce (see page 40)

Mix equal parts of asparagus tips, truffles and chicken cut into julienne.

Prepare an oil and vinegar dressing. Add a little mayonnaise sauce to it and pour over the salad.

Salade de légumes

VEGETABLE SALAD

———————— Carrots, turnips, potatoes, French beans, peas, asparagus tips, sprigs cauliflower, oil and vinegar dressing (see page 573), chopped parsley, chopped chervil

Cut equal quantities of carrots, turnips and potatoes into small balls with a vegetable ball cutter, or into dice.

Prepare the same quantity of French beans, fresh peas, asparagus tips, cut into small pieces, and sprigs of cauliflower.

Arrange in separate heaps on the serving dish. Pour the dressing over and sprinkle with the parsley and the chervil.

Salades de nonnes

RICE AND CHICKEN SALAD

———————— Rice, cooked white chicken meat, oil and vinegar dressing (see page 573), mustard, grated truffle

Cook the rice in boiling salted water for 18 minutes. Drain and dry, and add one-third the quantity of white chicken meat cut into julienne

Add the dressing to which a little mustard has been added and sprinkle with grated truffle.

Salade d'oranges
(pour canards rôtis, canards sauvages, sarcelles, etc.)

ORANGE SALAD
(FOR ROAST DUCK, WILD DUCK, TEAL, ETC.)

Peel some oranges, removing all the white pith. Cut across in half, remove the pips, then slice thinly.

Put into a serving dish and add a dash of kirsch.

Salade orientale

ORIENTAL SALAD

8 oz. tomatoes, 4 oz. green pepper, 4 oz. red pepper, 4 oz. cooked ladies' fingers (okra), oil and vinegar dressing (see page 573), anchovy essence, 8 oz. rice, cooked in boiling salted water

Peel, seed and quarter the tomatoes, peel the peppers and cut them into strips, cut the okra into strips and put all together into a bowl. Add some oil and vinegar dressing to which a little anchovy essence has been added, and finally add the rice. Mix all well together.

Salade Otero

APPLE AND PRAWN (U.S. SHRIMP) SALAD

8 medium-sized red dessert apples, ¾ pint (U.S. 1⅞ cups) shelled prawns (U.S. shrimps), 4 oz. truffles, 2 oz. red pepper, 2 oz. grated horseradish, pinch salt, freshly ground pepper, juice 1 lemon, thick cream

Cut a slice from the stalk end of each apple and prepare as for *salade Alice* (see page 577).

Take 2 oz. of the apple and chop finely. Add the prawns (U.S. shrimps), truffles cut into julienne, peeled and chopped pepper, horseradish, salt, pepper and lemon juice. Bind with half-whipped cream and pile into the apple case.

Replace the lids.

Salade Rachel

TRUFFLE, POTATO AND CELERY SALAD

Truffle, potatoes, celery, asparagus tips, oil and vinegar dressing (see page 573), 1—2 tablespoons thin mayonnaise (see page 40)

Mix equal quantities of truffle, potato and celery, all cut into julienne, and the same quantity of asparagus tips.

Add a little dressing and then thin mayonnaise.

Salade régence

REGENCY SALAD

Truffle, cock's kidneys, butter, cooked asparagus tips, oil, wine vinegar or lemon juice, salt, freshly ground pepper, celery

Cut the truffle into very fine strips, brown the kidneys in butter and mix equal quantities of each with the same amount of asparagus.

Make a dressing with oil, vinegar or lemon juice and seasoning and add a little chopped celery.

Salade russe

RUSSIAN SALAD

———————— Carrots, turnips, potatoes, French beans, peas, truffles, mushrooms, tongue, lean ham, white meat of chicken, lobster meat, capers, gherkins, sausages, fillets of anchovy, mayonnaise sauce (see page 40)
To decorate Asparagus tips, hard-boiled egg, etc.

Take equal parts of all the ingredients and cut them into cubes. Bind with mayonnaise sauce and decorate to taste with asparagus tips, sliced hard-boiled egg, etc.

Salade Tosca

TOSCA SALAD

———————— Cooked breast of chicken, white truffles, celery, oil, vinegar, salt, freshly ground pepper, mustard, anchovy essence, grated Parmesan cheese, sieved hard-boiled egg yolk, chopped parsley, chopped tarragon

Cut the chicken, truffles and celery into small pieces and mix together.

Pour over a dressing made with the oil, vinegar, seasonings and a little anchovy essence.

Sprinkle with grated cheese, egg yolk, the parsley and tarragon.

Salade aux truffes

TRUFFLE SALAD

———————— Truffles, sieved hard-boiled egg yolk, lemon juice, oil, salt, freshly ground pepper

Cut the truffles into very thin slices.

Mix the egg yolk smoothly with a little lemon juice and oil. Add seasoning and pour over the truffle.

Salade aux truffes blanches

WHITE TRUFFLE SALAD

This is prepared in the same way as the previous salad, replacing the black truffles with the white.

Salade Victoria

LOBSTER, CUCUMBER AND RICE SALAD

—————— Lobster or spiny lobster, cucumber, cooked rice, oil and vinegar dressing (see page 573), curry powder, asparagus tips and diced truffles to taste

Mix equal parts of lobster meat, diced cucumber and rice.

Add the dressing to which a little curry powder should be added in the proportion of $\frac{1}{2}$ teaspoon to $\frac{1}{4}$ pint (U.S. $\frac{5}{8}$ cup) dressing.

Asparagus tips and diced truffles can be added to the salad to taste.

Salade Waldorf

APPLE AND CELERY SALAD

—————— Chopped apples, chopped celery or celeriac, chopped walnuts, thin mayonnaise sauce (see page 40)

Mix equal parts of apple and celery and add some walnuts. Bind with the mayonnaise.

Salade Véronique

FRUIT SALAD WITH CREAM

—————— Grapes, pineapple, 2 oranges, walnuts, cream, juice 1 lemon, pinch salt, pinch sugar, lettuce hearts (optional)

Skin and pip the grapes, cut the pineapple into cubes, peel and cut up 1 orange. Mix the fruit together and add small pieces of walnuts.

Mix the cream with the juice of the second orange and lemon juice, add the salt and the sugar. Bind the fruit lightly with some of the cream.

This salad can be served in orange skins or on lettuce hearts.

Serve the rest of the cream sauce separately.

Véronique salad is especially good served with cold duck.

Légumes
VEGETABLES

———————————

Blanchissage
BLANCHING

The term blanching is applied to two processes which have different ends
in view.

In the first case, for peas, French beans, cauliflower, Brussels sprouts
and green vegetables generally, blanching is really the method of cooking.
The vegetables are put into plenty of salted water and this preserves their
green colour.

The proportion of salt required is 1 level teaspoon to 1 pint (U.S. 2½
cups) water.

Vegetables cooked in this way should be served at once and not allowed
to get cold. If vegetables have to be prepared in advance they should not
be left soaking in cold water or they will lose some of their flavour.

Secondly, vegetables such as cabbage, celery, chicory, etc., are blanched
to remove some of the natural bitterness or strong flavour.

New vegetables such as carrots, turnips and onions are not blanched.

Cuisson des légumes à l'anglaise
VEGETABLES IN THE ENGLISH WAY

Cook in boiling salted water, drain, season as required, and put into a hot
vegetable dish with a knob of butter.

Cuisson des légumes secs
COOKING DRIED VEGETABLES

The soaking of dried vegetables is quite wrong. If they are this year's and of good quality, it will be sufficient to put them into cold water, and bring very slowly to the boil. Then skim, and continue to cook slowly with the lid on the pan. White haricot beans must not be salted until shortly before the end of the cooking.

If the vegetables are old or of an inferior quality, they may be soaked for about 2 hours, which will give them time to swell.

If they are soaked for too long, they will start to ferment, and this will spoil the vegetables and their flavour will be lost.

Braisage des légumes
BRAISING OF VEGETABLES

———————— Onions, carrots, strips pork fat, white stock

Slice the onions and carrots and put into a well greased pan with strips of pork fat.

Blanch the vegetable which is to be braised, drain, cool and trim and then put into the pan on the bed of vegetables. Cover and allow to sweat for a few minutes.

Add enough stock to just cover the vegetables, then cover and continue the cooking in a moderate oven.

When the vegetable is cooked, drain well and serve.

Artichoke bottoms, celery and cardoons are usually accompanied by a demi-glace sauce (see page 22) to which a little butter and lemon juice have been added.

Liaison des légumes à la crème
COMBINING VEGETABLES WITH CREAM

When the vegetables are cooked, drain well, add seasoning and a little boiling cream. When it is all absorbed add a little butter.

Crèmes et purées de légumes

CREAMS AND PURÉES OF VEGETABLES

To make a purée of dried or root vegetables, cook and drain, then rub through a sieve. Repeat and add a little butter or cream.

For fresh vegetables, French beans, cauliflower, Brussels sprouts, etc., add one-third of their volume of creamed potatoes.

Artichauts à la barigoule

ARTICHOKES BARIGOULE

4 large globe artichokes, salt, pepper, $\frac{1}{2}$ oz. butter, 1 tablespoon oil, 4 oz. fresh pork fat, 2 shallots, 8 oz. mushrooms, 1 tablespoon chopped parsley, pinch grated nutmeg, onions, carrots, *bouquet garni*, 6 table-spoons white wine, brown stock, 6—7 tablespoons demi-glace sauce (see page 22)

Trim the stalk of the artichokes and cut off the tips of the leaves. Blanch and remove the choke.

Season inside with salt and pepper.

Heat the butter, oil and about 3 oz. of the pork fat in a pan. Add the finely chopped shallots, chopped mushrooms, parsley, and nutmeg and check seasoning. Cook for a few minutes over brisk heat. Fill the arti-chokes with this mixture.

Cut the remaining pork fat into squares and place on top. Tie into shape, and put into a pan on a bed of chopped onions and carrots. Add the *bouquet garni* and white wine. Cover and cook until the wine is reduced by two-thirds.

Add enough stock to reach half-way up the artichokes, then cover and continue to cook slowly.

When ready to serve, remove the artichokes, untie them and remove the pieces of pork fat. Reduce the cooking liquor by two-thirds, add the demi-glace sauce and bring to boiling point.

Leave to stand for a few minutes, remove surface fat, reheat and pour over the artichokes.

Coeurs d'artichauts grand-duc

ARTICHOKE HEARTS WITH ASPARAGUS TIPS AND TRUFFLES

4—5 globe artichokes, lemon juice, 1 tablespoon flour, white stock, béchamel sauce (see page 23), asparagus tips, truffles, grated cheese, butter, meat jelly (see page 21)

Choose tender artichokes of medium size. Remove the hard leaves and cut the others horizontally across just above the heart. Trim the bottoms, sprinkle lightly with lemon juice and cook in salted water to which the juice of ½ lemon and the flour has been added. Three-quarters through the cooking, take the bottoms out, cool, remove the choke and place them in a well buttered sauté pan. Add white stock to come half-way up; cover and finish cooking.

Put a thin layer of béchamel sauce on a serving dish and arrange the artichokes in a ring.

Reduce the cooking liquor to quarter its volume and add about ¼ pint (U.S. ⅝ cup) béchamel sauce.

Fill the artichoke bottoms with a small garnish of buttered asparagus tips and truffles cut into very small cubes. Cover the artichoke hearts completely with the sauce, sprinkle with grated cheese, brush with melted butter and glaze in the oven or under the grill (U.S. broiler).

Put some buttered asparagus tips in the centre of the ring of artichokes. Heat 4—5 slices of truffle in a little butter and melted meat jelly and place one slice on each artichoke.

Artichauts frits

FRIED ARTICHOKES

4 globe artichokes, 3 oz. flour, pinch salt, pinch pepper, 3 eggs, 3 tablespoons oil, butter, fried parsley

Choose medium-sized artichokes. Remove the large leaves and trim the bottoms, leaving the small tender white leaves round them. Remove the choke and cut the bottoms into small pieces. Put into cold water to which a little vinegar has been added.

Put the flour into a bowl, add salt and pepper. Add drained artichokes and mix well with the flour. Add beaten eggs and oil and stir till smooth and all the pieces of artichokes well coated. Fry gently in butter and serve garnished with fried parsley.

Artichauts avec sauces divers

ARTICHOKES WITH DIFFERENT SAUCES

Cut the artichokes evenly all round to two-thirds their height. Trim, tie up and cook rapidly in slightly salted boiling water. Drain, put into cold water so that the choke can be removed, then return to their cooking liquor for a few moments to reheat, and serve on a folded table napkin. Serve with either a butter sauce (see page 30), hollandaise sauce (see page 33) or mousseline sauce (see page 34). If the artichokes are to be served cold, serve with a vinaigrette sauce (see page 42).

Artichauts à la provençale

ARTICHOKES IN THE PROVENÇAL WAY

Choose small artichokes. Cut off the tops of the leaves and remove the first row of hard leaves. Put them into a casserole containing fairly hot oil. Season with salt and pepper, cover, and cook in a slow oven. 1 small clove garlic and some small onions may be added to taste.

Artichauts en ragoût aux petits pois à la provençale

PROVENÇAL STYLE RAGOÛT OF ARTICHOKES WITH PEAS

6 globe artichokes, oil, few small onions, salt, pepper, 1 lb. peas, ¼ lettuce, 4—5 sprigs parsley, 3 tablespoons water, 2 oz. streaky bacon

Choose small artichokes, trim and put into a casserole with a little oil, the onions, and seasoning.

Cover and cook in a moderate oven for 10 minutes. Add the peas, lettuce, parsley, water and the bacon cut into strips. Cover and continue the cooking in a moderate oven. Serve in the casserole.

Fonds d'artichauts au gratin à la toulousaine
ARTICHOKE BOTTOMS AU GRATIN

————————— 4—5 artichokes, 6 tablespoons white wine, juice ½ lemon, white stock, about ½ pint (U.S. 1¼ cups) béchamel sauce (see page 23), foie gras, truffle, grated cheese, butter, 12—15 cock's kidneys, meat jelly (see page 21), asparagus tips

Prepare and cook the artichoke bottoms as described in the recipe for *coeurs d'artichauts grand-duc* (see page 588). Having removed the chokes, put the artichokes in a buttered sauté pan. Add white wine and lemon juice and reduce completely. Add stock to come half-way up the artichokes. Cover, and cook over low heat.

Arrange in a ring on a serving dish.

Reduce the cooking liquor until it is syrupy, then add it to the béchamel sauce.

Fill the centre of the artichokes with a little foie gras and truffle cut into cubes, and add a little of the sauce. Then cover the artichokes with the remaining sauce, sprinkle with cheese, brush with melted butter and glaze under the grill (U.S. broiler) or in the oven.

Brown the cock's kidneys in butter, coat with melted meat jelly and place 3 on each artichoke.

Garnish the centre of the dish with buttered asparagus tips.

Artichokes prepared in this way, and with a variety of garnish, may also be used as garnishes for light entrées.

Note The cock's kidneys may be replaced with slices of braised calf's sweetbreads with a slice of truffle placed on each slice, and coated lightly with a little melted meat jelly to which a nut of butter has been added.

Fonds d'artichaut à l'italienne
ARTICHOKE BOTTOMS IN THE ITALIAN WAY

————————— 4—5 globe artichokes, 6 tablespoons white wine, dash lemon juice, ½ pint (U.S. 1¼ cups) brown veal stock, about ¾ pint (U.S. 1⅝ cups), Italian sauce (see page 28), pinch chopped parsley, butter

Prepare and cook the artichokes as instructed for *coeurs d'artichauts grand-duc* (see page 588).

Remove the chokes and put the bottoms into a well greased sauté pan, add the wine and the lemon juice. Reduce, and add the stock, then complete the cooking.

Put the artichokes on to a serving dish. Add the Italian sauce to the cooking liquor with the parsley. Reduce to the consistency required, add a little butter and pour over the artichoke bottoms.

Quartiers d'artichauts à l'italienne
ARTICHOKE QUARTERS IN THE ITALIAN WAY

4—5 globe artichokes, lemon, onions, carrots, 6 tablespoons white wine, brown stock, about ¾ pint (U.S. 1⅞ cups) Italian sauce (see page 28), 1 oz. butter

Choose medium-sized artichokes, trim and cut each into 4 pieces. Remove the chokes, rub each piece of artichoke with a cut lemon to prevent it discolouring and throw into cold water as each piece is prepared. Then put into boiling water, cook for 8—10 minutes, and drain.

Put some finely chopped onions and carrots into a sauté pan. Put the artichoke quarters on top, add the wine. Reduce, then add enough brown stock to come half-way up the artichokes. Cover and cook over moderate heat. Put on to a serving dish and keep hot.

Strain the cooking liquor, remove excess fat, and reduce a little. Add the Italian sauce, bring to boiling point and boil for a few seconds. Add the butter and pour over the artichokes.

Artichauts à la crème
CREAMED ARTICHOKES

6 globe artichokes, hot water, 1 tablespoon flour, butter, pinch salt, pinch sugar, juice ¼ lemon, ½ pint (U.S. 1¼ cups) béchamel sauce (see page 23), 2—3 tablespoons cream

Choose medium-sized artichokes and prepare as described for *coeurs d'artichauts grand-duc* (see page 588). Divide into quarters and then cut each quarter in half. Cook for 10 minutes in boiling salted water to which the flour has been added. Drain, put into a pan and just cover with hot water. Add ½ oz. butter, salt, sugar, and lemon juice. Cover and cook over low heat. When cooked, drain and keep hot.

Reduce the cooking liquor completely, then add the béchamel sauce to which the cream has been added. Bring to boiling point, add the artichokes and finally a few dabs butter.

Artichauts périgourdine
CREAMED ARTICHOKES WITH TRUFFLES

Follow the previous recipe for creamed artichokes but add some truffles, cut into strips and seasoned with salt and freshly ground pepper.

Note Creamed artichokes and *artichauts périgourdine* can be served au gratin in small cocottes. Butter the dishes, fill with the mixture, sprinkle with grated cheese and brush with a little melted butter. Then brown under the grill (U.S. broiler) or in the oven.

Artichauts sautés
SAUTÉED ARTICHOKES

Choose very tender artichokes. Remove the leaves and chokes, trim the bottoms and slice thinly. Season with salt and pepper and sauté in butter. Sprinkle with herbs before serving.

They can also be sautéed in oil and a little garlic may be added to taste.

Asperges
ASPARAGUS

Asparagus should be as fresh as possible, carefully scraped, washed in running water, tied in bundles and cooked in plenty of boiling salted water.

Asparagus is generally served on an asparagus dish, or on a table napkin.

Sauces suitable for hot asparagus are: butter (see page 30), hollandaise (see page 33) or mousseline (see page 34). Melted butter, and melted butter with chopped hard-boiled egg, can also be served with asparagus.

Cold asparagus is served with oil and vinegar, mayonnaise (see page 40) or mayonnaise with whipped cream.

Asperges à la milanaise
ASPARAGUS IN THE MILANESE MANNER

Asparagus, grated Parmesan cheese, brown butter

Cook the asparagus and drain well. Put on to a serving dish and sprinkle the tips with grated cheese. Pour some brown butter liberally over the cheese and brown under the grill (U.S. broiler).

Asperges Mornay

ASPARAGUS MORNAY

———————— Asparagus, béchamel sauce (see page 23), grated Parmesan cheese melted butter

Cook the asparagus and drain well. Arrange in rows on a serving dish and coat the tips with a little béchamel sauce. Sprinkle with cheese, brush with melted butter and brown under the grill (U.S. broiler).

Asperges polonaises

ASPARAGUS IN THE POLISH MANNER

———————— Asparagus, hard-boiled egg yolks, chopped parsley, fine breadcrumbs' butter, brown butter

Cook and drain the asparagus and arrange in rows on a serving dish. Sprinkle the tips with sieved egg yolk and parsley mixed together.

Add some freshly made breadcrumbs and butter to the browned butter and cover the tips with the mixture.

Pointes d'asperges au beurre

ASPARAGUS TIPS IN BUTTER

Asparagus tips are generally used as garnish but they may also be served as a vegetable.

Cut off the tips 2 inches from the end and tie in bundles. Cut the rest of the tender part into small pieces. Wash and cook quickly in boiling salted water. This helps to keep them green.

When they are cooked, drain well, and sauté for a few seconds to get rid of the superfluous moisture.

Remove from the heat, add some butter and put into a serving dish with the tips in little bundles on top.

Asparagus tips may also be served in patties or tartlets.

Pointes d'asperges à la crème

ASPARAGUS TIPS WITH CREAM

Prepare the asparagus and cook in salted water as in the previous recipe. Dress them with fresh boiling cream.

Tartelettes de pointes d'asperges petit-duc

TARTLETS OF ASPARAGUS TIPS

——————— Asparagus tips, butter or cream, cooked tartlet cases, béchamel sauce
(see page 23), grated cheese, truffle, meat jelly (see page 21)

Prepare and cook the asparagus tips in boiling salted water. Drain well
and add a little butter or cream. Arrange in tartlet cases and cover
completely with a thin coating of béchamel sauce. Sprinkle with grated
cheese, brush with melted butter and brown under the grill (U.S. broiler)
or in the oven.

Arrange the tartlets on a serving dish. Heat some thin slices of truffle
in meat jelly and butter and place 1 slice on each tartlet.

Note These tartlets are sometimes used as garnish to various joints of
meat and poultry.

Elegant little entrées can be made by putting a small slice of breast of
chicken, or lamb or braised calf's sweetbread on top of the tartlet,
in place of the truffle, then covering with a little meat jelly to which
some butter has been added.

Aubergines à la bordelaise

AUBERGINES SAUTÉED WITH SHALLOTS AND PARSLEY

——————— Aubergines, salt, pepper, flour, oil, shallots, garlic to taste, breadcrumbs, chopped parsley

Peel and cut the aubergines in slices, season lightly and coat with flour.
Sauté in hot oil until brown, then add a little chopped shallot, crushed
garlic to taste and a few breadcrumbs. Cook all together for a few minutes
and serve sprinkled with parsley.

Aubergines à l'égyptienne

AUBERGINES EGYPTIAN STYLE

——————— You will need for 4 persons:
6 aubergines, oil, 2 tablespoons chopped onion, salt, pepper, chopped
parsley, 3 tablespoons breadcrumbs, 3 tablespoons tomato sauce (see
page 132), garlic to taste, 3—4 tomatoes

Cut 4 aubergines in half lengthwise, trim the edge and slit the centre to facilitate the cooking. Sauté in oil, then drain well.

Remove the pulp and chop. Put the empty skins in a buttered fireproof dish.

Peel the other 2 aubergines, cut into slices and fry in oil. Drain, chop and mix with the pulp taken from the other 4.

Heat a little oil, brown the onion, then add the pulp from all the aubergines, seasoning, parsley, 2 tablespoons breadcrumbs, tomato sauce and garlic to taste. Mix all well, and use to fill the aubergine skins. Sprinkle with the rest of the breadcrumbs, brush with oil, and cook in a moderate oven for 20 minutes.

Cut the tomatoes into slices and sauté for a few minutes in oil. Season and put 2−3 slices on each aubergine.

Sprinkle with parsley before serving.

Aubergines frites

FRIED AUBERGINES

Peel the aubergines and cut into thin slices. Sprinkle with salt, coat with flour and fry in hot oil.

Serve immediately, as the aubergines should be eaten while crisp.

Note They may also be dipped in flour, beaten egg and breadcrumbs and fried, or dipped in batter as for fried artichokes.

AUBERGINES AU GRATIN

6 aubergines, ½ oz. butter, 1 tablespoon oil, 2 small shallots, 8 oz. mushrooms, 6 tablespoons breadcrumbs, 3 tablespoons tomato sauce (see page 132), salt, pepper, chopped parsley

Prepare and cook the aubergines as described for *aubergines à l'égyptienne* (see above). Remove the pulp and chop it. Heat the butter and oil, add the chopped shallots and chopped mushrooms and cook for a few minutes. Add the pulp from the aubergines, 3 tablespoons breadcrumbs, tomato sauce, seasoning and a little chopped parsley. Mix all well and use to fill the aubergine skins.

Sprinkle with the remaining breadcrumbs, brush with oil and brown in the oven. Sprinkle with chopped parsley before serving.

Aubergines à la napolitaine
AUBERGINES IN THE NEAPOLITAN MANNER

——————— Aubergines, salt, flour, oil, grated Parmesan cheese, fairly thick tomato sauce (see page 132)

Choose aubergines of medium size, peel, and cut into 6 pieces lengthwise. Sprinkle lightly with salt, coat with flour, fry in oil, and drain well.

Cover the bottom of a casserole with grated cheese. Add a light coating of tomato sauce. Cover with half the quantity of aubergines, then repeat the layers and finish with a layer of cheese. Keep hot for a few minutes before serving, to give the cheese time to get incorporated with the sauce.

Aubergines à l'orientale
AUBERGINES ORIENTAL STYLE

——————— 8 small aubergines, salt, flour, oil, 2 tablespoons chopped onion, 3—4 tablespoons thick tomato sauce (see page 132), pepper, squeeze garlic juice, chopped parsley, 3 tablespoons breadcrumbs

Peel the aubergines and cut 6 of them in slices lengthwise. Cut the pulp of the other 2 into cubes and fry.

Sprinkle the slices of aubergine lightly with salt, coat with flour and fry in oil. Drain well.

Brown the onion in a little oil, add the fried aubergine pulp and the tomato sauce. Season with salt and pepper, add the garlic juice and a little chopped parsley. Simmer for a few minutes, then add the breadcrumbs.

Spread a little of this forcemeat between the slices of aubergine and re-form into their original shape.

Put them side by side into a casserole just large enough to take them, pour over a little oil and cook for 20—25 minutes in a moderate oven.

Serve hot or cold in the dish in which they were cooked.

Aubergines farcies à la provençale
STUFFED AUBERGINES PROVENÇAL STYLE

Prepare the aubergines and fry as for *aubergines à l'égyptienne* (see page 594), drain them, remove the pulp, chop and mix with a forcemeat prepared exactly as instructed for *aubergines à l'orientale* (see page 596), with the addition of a small teaspoon anchovy essence.

Stuff the aubergines, sprinkle with dry breadcrumbs mixed with grated cheese; brush lightly with oil and put in the oven. Sprinkle with parsley before serving.

ANOTHER METHOD

Peel the aubergines, cut in halves lengthwise and cook in salted water. Dry in a cloth and remove the pulp, leaving ⅓ inch thickness behind. Put the aubergine halves in an oiled casserole; fill with the same preparation as in the first recipe and cover the surface with a thin layer of bread dipped in water and well pressed to extract all the moisture. Pour a little oil over and cook in a moderate oven for 30—35 minutes.

Note In Turkey and Serbia the forcemeat is mixed with some rice pilaf (see page 669) and minced cooked mutton.

Aubergines à la ménagère provençale et niçoise

AUBERGINES WITH TOMATOES AND CHEESE

▬▬▬▬▬▬ 4—5 aubergines, salt, oil, 1 clove garlic, 6—8 ripe tomatoes, pepper, chopped parsley, grated cheese

Choose medium-sized aubergines, peel, cut into fairly large slices and sprinkle lightly with salt.

Cook in a small quantity of oil — it should hardly cover the aubergines.

When they are cooked, drain and put on one side. Chop the garlic and put into the remaining oil. Add the tomatoes, peeled, seeded and chopped. Add seasoning and a little chopped parsley and simmer 15—20 minutes.

Put the tomato into a casserole, arrange the aubergines on top and sprinkle liberally with grated cheese.

Put into a moderate oven for 7—8 minutes and serve at once.

Note Poached or fried eggs may be put on top of the tomatoes or the dish can be accompanied with rice, cooked for 18 minutes in boiling salted water or with rice pilaf (see page 669).

Cardons

CARDOONS

Remove the hard stems and those that are wilted, and cut the cardoons into pieces of 2—2½ inches in length. Peel, and throw them immediately into cold water acidulated with lemon juice, to prevent them from blackening. Prepare the heart of the cardoon in the same way, after removing the fibrous parts, and cook it in salted water acidulated with lemon juice, into which a few tablespoons flour have been put. Add about 12 oz. chopped veal or beef fat which will form a layer on top and prevent the cardoons discolouring.

Cardons au jus

CARDOONS WITH GRAVY

Cook the cardoons, put them into a vegetable dish, and cover them with a good veal gravy, very reduced and slightly thickened with arrowroot.

Cardons à la milanaise

MILANESE STYLE CARDOONS

Proceed as instructed for *asperges à la milanaise* (see page 592).

Cardons à la moelle

CARDOONS WITH BEEF MARROW

Cook the cardoons and drain them thoroughly.

Put the stems into a dish. Cut the heart into slices and arrange on top with slices of poached beef marrow.

Coat with *sauce moelle* (see page 28).

Cardons au parmesan

CARDOONS WITH PARMESAN CHEESE

———————   Cardoons, demi-glace sauce with tomato (see page 22), grated Parmesan cheese

Cook the cardoons and drain well. Put in layers in a casserole, adding a little sauce and grated cheese to each layer. Cover with more sauce, sprinkle with cheese and glaze quickly under the grill (U.S. broiler) or in the oven.

Other suitable sauces are *bordelaise* (see page 25), *béchamel* (see page 23) or *italienne* (see page 28).

They can also be prepared *à la Mornay* (see page 593).

If a plain demi-glace sauce is used a little butter should be added at the last moment.

Carottes glacées pour garnitures
GLAZED CARROTS FOR GARNISHES

Peel the carrots, leave whole, or cut into halves or quarters according to their size, then trim. If the carrots are old, blanch them in salted water for 10 minutes and drain well.

Put the carrots into a pan with just sufficient water to cover, add pinch salt, 1 oz. sugar and 2 oz. butter to each 1 pint (U.S. 2½ cups) water.

Cook over low heat until the liquid is syrupy, then leave the carrots to sauté for a few minutes longer so that they are well glazed.

Carottes à la crème
CREAMED CARROTS

Prepare the carrots as in the previous recipe and, when the moisture is reduced to the state of syrup, cover them with boiling cream. Boil for a few minutes and put into a vegetable dish.

Note The cream may be replaced, if necessary, by butter or béchamel sauce (see pages 30, 23), reduced and with cream added.

Carottes à la Vichy
CARROTS VICHY

Slice the carrots thinly and, if they are old, blanch them for 10 – 12 minutes and drain.

Put them into a pan with just enough water to cover. Add 2 – 3 oz. butter, pinch salt and 1 oz. sugar to every 1 pint (U.S. 2½ cups) water.

Cook as for glazed carrots and sprinkle with chopped parsley before serving.

Carottes au riz gratinées
CARROTS WITH RICE, AU GRATIN

———————— *Carottes à la Vichy* (see page 599), rice, stock, 3–4 tablespoons grated cheese, freshly made breadcrumbs, butter

Mix cooked carrots with two-thirds quantity of rice cooked for 15 minutes in stock. Add grated cheese and put into a shallow casserole. Sprinkle with breadcrumbs and cheese mixed together, add a little melted butter and put into a moderate oven for about 12 minutes.

Céleri en branches et céleri-rave
CELERY AND CELERIAC

Celery for braising should be white and tender.

Cut in lengths of 3–3½ inches. Remove the green stalks and trim the roots, wash carefully, blanch for 12–15 minutes and cool.

Braise on a bed of thinly sliced carrots and onions moistened with stock.

When it is cooked, divide each stick in half, and serve in a vegetable dish.

All the recipes given for cardoons are applicable to stick celery.

Purée de céleri
CELERY PURÉE

Slice the celery thinly and cook in slightly salted water. Drain and heat it on the stove until all the moisture has evaporated.

Rub through a sieve. Put the resultant purée into a saucepan and add quarter or one-third of its volume very creamy mashed potatoes. Just before serving, add a few dabs of butter.

Serve in a vegetable dish.

Céleri à l'italienne
CELERIAC WITH ITALIAN SAUCE

Peel the celeriac, and divide it, according to its size, into 2–4 pieces. Cut these into slices ½ inch thick, trim and partly cook in slightly salted water, drain, and put into a well buttered sauté pan. Cover and finish cooking. When ready, add enough Italian sauce (see page 28) to cover. Boil for a few minutes and serve sprinkled with chopped parsley.

Céleri-rave au jus

CELERIAC WITH GRAVY

Prepare the celeriac as in the previous recipe. Finish cooking in butter and add some good, slightly thickened veal gravy, or a demi-glace sauce (see page 22) to which, at the last moment, a few dabs of butter have been added. Serve in a vegetable dish.

Céleri-rave à la niçoise

CELERIAC NIÇOISE

————— Celeriac, butter, tomato sauce (see page 132), grated cheese, butter

Prepare and partly cook the celeriac as instructed for *à l'italienne* (see page 600).

Fry the pieces in butter. Put a layer of thick tomato sauce into a casserole. Arrange the celeriac on top, sprinkle with cheese and add some melted butter. Put into a moderate oven for 5—6 minutes and serve.

CÈPES

Cèpes should not be washed — only wiped. However, for safety, they can be rinsed in plenty of cold water, and dried thoroughly in a cloth.

Editor's note Cèpes belong to the mushroom family but they have a different texture and flavour. They are available in England, canned in brine. Only two of the following recipes require fresh cèpes.

Cèpes à la bordelaise

BORDEAUX STYLE CÈPES

————— 1 lb. fresh cèpes, salt, pepper, oil, 1 teaspoon chopped shallot, 1 tablespoon breadcrumbs, squeeze lemon juice, chopped parsley

Wipe the cèpes, trim the heads and chop the stalks. Add a little seasoning. Heat some oil in a sauté pan, and cook the cèpes until they begin to brown, then add the shallot and breadcrumbs. Sauté all together for a few minutes. Put into a serving dish, add the lemon juice and sprinkle with parsley or, if preferred, add 2 tablespoons melted meat jelly (see page 21).

Cèpes à la crème
CREAMED CÈPES

———————— Canned cèpes, butter, onion, cream, 3—4 tablespoons béchamel sauce
(see page 23)

Rinse the cèpes and dry, then cut into slices and sauté in butter without allowing them to brown.

Brown a little onion in butter, add to the cèpes and cover with boiling cream. Reduce for a few moments and then add the béchamel sauce.

Cèpes à la crème au paprika
CREAMED CÈPES WITH PAPRIKA

———————— Fresh cèpes, $\frac{1}{2}$ oz. butter, 1—2 teaspoons sweet paprika, 2 tablespoons cream

Prepare the cèpes as in the previous recipe. Warm the butter and mix in the paprika, then add the cream, and mix all into the sauce.

Note Be careful of the quality of the paprika: it should be bright red and above all very sweet. Do not confuse it with cayenne pepper.

Cèpes au fromage
CÈPES WITH CHEESE

———————— Canned cèpes, salt, pepper, flour, oil, butter, grated cheese, demi-glace
sauce with tomato (see page 22)

Rinse and dry the cèpes and cut into not too thin slices. Season, coat with flour and sauté in oil or butter. Put into small cocottes, sprinkle with cheese and cover with the sauce. Add a little melted butter and put into a moderate oven for a few minutes.

Note Tomato sauce without demi-glace (see page 132) can be used.

Cèpes à la provençale
CÈPES PROVENÇAL STYLE

Proceed as instructed for *cèpes à la bordelaise* (see page 601) adding 1 crushed clove garlic.

Serve in a vegetable dish and complete with a little lemon juice and chopped parsley.

Champignons

MUSHROOMS

Under this simple name are included only the cultivated mushroom and the British field mushroom. The British are very fond of their field mushrooms grilled and served on buttered toast.

The French cultivated mushroom does not lend itself well to being grilled (U.S. broiled).

There are, however, several different kinds of mushroom which grow quite naturally in the woods in France and which, when sprinkled with olive oil, seasoned with salt and pepper and 1 pinch dried breadcrumbs and grilled (U.S. broiled), are much appreciated.

Champignons à la crème

CREAMED MUSHROOMS

Proceed as instructed for *cèpes à la crème* (see page 602). Cultivated mushrooms and the British variety both lend themselves to this method of preparation.

Croûtes aux champignons

MUSHROOM CROÛTES

1 lb. small mushrooms, butter, juice ¼ lemon, salt, pepper, ¾ pint (U.S. 1⅞ cups) velouté sauce (see page 22), 2—3 egg yolks, 2—3 table-spoons cream or milk, 6 slices bread

Carefully wash the mushrooms, put into a pan with a generous ½ oz. butter, lemon juice and seasoning. Cover and fry for a few minutes over brisk heat.

Add the velouté sauce and boil for 4—5 minutes. Remove from the heat and add the egg yolks and cream beaten together. Finally add 2 oz. butter. Keep hot at the side of the stove.

Cut 6 pieces of bread about ½ inch thick and 2½—3 inches square. Remove a piece about ¼ inch thick from the centre to form a kind of case. Fry in butter and arrange on a serving dish. Fill the hollows with the mushrooms.

Note The velouté sauce may be replaced by a béchamel sauce (see page 23) to which some butter has been added.

Champignons grillés

GRILLED MUSHROOMS

Choose medium-sized field mushrooms. Wash carefully, remove the stalks, season with salt and pepper and sprinkle with oil. Grill (U.S. broil) gently. Garnish the hollow side of the mushrooms with a small teaspoon maître d'hôtel butter.

Champignons farcis

STUFFED MUSHROOMS

1 lb. mushrooms, salt, pepper, oil, 2 tablespoons grated pork fat, 3 shallots, demi-glace sauce with tomato (see page 22), chopped parsley, breadcrumbs

Select medium-sized mushrooms, remove the stalks, wash carefully and dry.

Put them into a gratin dish, season with salt and pepper, sprinkle lightly with oil and place in a moderate oven for 5 minutes.

Chop the mushroom stalks with a few more well washed mushrooms. Twist in a cloth to remove as much moisture as possible.

Heat the pork fat and oil in a pan, add the chopped mushrooms, finely chopped shallots and seasoning. Cook over brisk heat until all the moisture has evaporated, then add the well reduced sauce, little parsley and 1 tablespoon breadcrumbs. Mix all well together and put a spoonful into the hollow of each mushroom. Sprinkle with breadcrumbs, brush over with oil and brown in the oven.

Champignons sautés aux fines herbes

SAUTÉED MUSHROOMS WITH PARSLEY

Mushrooms, salt, pepper, butter or oil, chopped parsley, garlic to taste

Wash and dry the mushrooms, chop finely and season with salt and pepper.

Heat some butter or oil in a pan, and sauté the mushrooms over brisk heat. Sprinkle with chopped parsley before serving.

If garlic is used, rub it over the bottom of the pan before heating the butter.

Flan grillé aux champignons

LATTICED MUSHROOM FLAN

——————— Pastry (see page 682), mushrooms, butter, 1 tablespoon finely chopped onion, salt, pepper, fairly thick béchamel sauce (see page 23), cream, egg for glazing

Line a buttered flan dish with the pastry. Thinly slice the mushrooms and sauté in butter with the onion. Season and add some béchamel sauce to which a little cream has been added. Cool a little, then pour into the pastry case. Damp the edge of the pastry and lattice with thin strips of pastry. Brush over with beaten egg and bake in a fairly hot oven.

Tartelettes grillées aux champignons

LATTICED MUSHROOM TARTLETS

Proceed exactly as for latticed mushroom flan, using tartlet cases of convenient size.

Note Excellent entrées can be made by omitting the pastry lattice and placing a slice of braised calf's sweetbread, breast of chicken, or foie gras on top of the mushroom filling, or alternatively a few cock's kidneys browned in butter, or chopped lamb's kidney.

In each case a little buttered meat jelly (see page 21) should be poured over the top.

Champignons tournés ou cannelés pour garnitures

TURNED OR GROOVED MUSHROOMS FOR GARNISHING

——————— *For 1 lb. mushrooms* 5 tablespoons water, pinch salt, 1 oz. butter, juice ½ lemon

Take fresh and firm mushrooms, wash quickly in plenty of water and dry them in a cloth.

Cut the stalks off flush with the heads. Turn or groove the mushrooms with the point of a small knife and as they are done throw them into the liquor (above) and cook for 3—4 minutes.

Purée de champignons
MUSHROOM PURÉE

———————— 1 lb. mushrooms, 4 oz. butter, 6 tablespoons cream, ¾ pint (U.S.
⅜ cup) béchamel sauce (see page 23), salt, pepper, pinch nutmeg

Wash and dry the mushrooms, peel quickly and rub through a wire
sieve. Put the resultant purée into a sauté pan with half the butter and
stir over brisk heat until the moisture has evaporated. Add the boiling
cream and sauce. Season carefully and add the nutmeg. Reduce if
necessary and finally add the rest of the butter.

Purée de champignons truffés
PURÉE OF TRUFFLED MUSHROOMS

Prepare the purée as instructed above and add 2 heaped tablespoons
finely sliced truffles.

Morilles
MORELS

This spring mushroom is the one preferred by gourmets.

There are two similar kinds of morels, the pale one and the brown,
and there is a third kind of a reddish colour, rather different from the
other two but very delicate in flavour.

In spite of the opinion of certain connoisseurs, who consider that to
wash morels detracts from their flavour, it is necessary to wash them
in plenty of water, because of the impurities and the sand which they
may contain.

HOW TO COOK MORELS

If they are very small, they are left whole; if they are large, they must
be halved or quartered. After thoroughly washing and draining, put
them into a saucepan with 1 oz. butter, the juice 1 lemon, pinch salt

and pinch pepper for every 1 lb. morels. Cover the pan, cook for 2 minutes, then leave at the side of the stove for a few minutes before serving.

Croûtes aux morilles

MOREL CROÛTES

Cook and serve as for mushroom croûtes (see page 603), being careful to allow the moisture to evaporate before adding the sauce.

Morilles à la crème

CREAMED MORELS

These are prepared like creamed cèpes and mushrooms (see page 602).

Morilles à la poulette

MORELS WITH VELOUTÉ SAUCE

1 lb. morels, ½ pint (U.S. 1¼ cups) velouté sauce (see page 22), 3 egg yolks, 3 tablespoons water or stock, butter, chopped parsley

Cook the morels as instructed on page 606. Strain, and reduce the cooking liquor. Add the sauce, and boil for a few minutes, then add the morels.

Mix the egg yolks with the water or stock. Stir into the morels and reheat without boiling. Finally add a little butter and chopped parsley.

Morilles sautées

SAUTÉ MORELS

Wash the morels thoroughly in plenty of water. Take them out with both hands so that any impurities will remain at the bottom of the water. Dry in a cloth and cut into halves or quarters, according to size.

Sauté in butter in a frying pan over brisk heat and season with salt and freshly ground pepper. Add a small clove garlic to taste.

Serve sprinkled with chopped parsley.

Vol-au-vent de morilles à la châtelaine

MOREL VOL-AU-VENT

———— Creamed morels (see page 607), truffles, 1 vol-au-vent case, soft-boi'ed eggs, cream sauce (see page 38)

Prepare the morels with plenty of sauce and add one-third quantity of sliced truffles.

Pour into the vol-au-vent case and put small soft-boiled eggs on top, allowing 1 for each person. Cover lightly with cream sauce.

Mousserons, oronges et girolles

MOUSSERONS, ORONGES AND SKIRRET

One may apply the different recipes for morels to these edible mushrooms, but the best way to prepare them is to wash them thoroughly and dry in a cloth, then sauté them briskly in butter or oil. Season with salt, pepper and a clove garlic if liked, or 1 shallot chopped finely.

Sprinkle with parsley before serving.

Brionne ou chayotte

CUSTARD MARROW

This excellent vegetable is not very widespread. It is in season from November until the end of February.

It is cooked like cucumber or vegetable marrow and the recipes for *quartiers d'artichauts à l'italienne* and *artichauts à la crème* (see page 591) can also be applied to custard marrow.

Chicorée

CHICORY

There are three kinds of chicory:
Curly chicory, called endive in Great Britain
Endive, called chicory in Great Britain
Escarole, which is usually eaten in salad

Chicorée à la crème

CREAMED ENDIVE (U.S. CHICORY)

6 endives (U.S. chicory), butter, salt, pepper, nutmeg, 6 tablespoons cream, 3–4 tablespoons béchamel sauce (see page 23)

Wash the endives (U.S. chicory) in plenty of water and cook for 15 minutes in slightly salted boiling water. Drain, press well to remove as much water as possible and chop.

Heat 4 oz. butter in a sauté pan, add the endive and seasoning. Stir over brisk heat until the moisture has evaporated. Add the boiling cream and bring again to boiling point.

Add the sauce and finally a few dabs butter.

ANOTHER METHOD

6 endives (U.S. chicory), salt, pepper, nutmeg, 6 tablespoons stock, strips pork fat, 6 tablespoons cream, ¼ pint (U.S. ⅝ cup) béchamel sauce (see page 23), butter

After careful washing, cook the endives (U.S. chicory) for 10 minutes in fast boiling slightly salted water. Drain, and press well to remove as much water as possible, then chop. Add seasoning and stock.

Line a casserole with thin strips of pork fat. Put in the endive (U.S. chicory) and cover with another strip of fat. Put on the lid and cook in a slow oven for 45–50 minutes.

Remove from the oven, take out the strips of fat and add the cream and sauce. Reheat and finally add a few dabs butter.

Pain de chicorée à la crème

CREAMED ENDIVE (U.S. CHICORY) LOAF

6 endives (U.S. chicory) cooked as in the previous recipe (1st method), 3–4 eggs, cream sauce (see page 38), 2–3 tablespoons meat jelly (see page 21)

To the cooked endives (U.S. chicory) add the cream and béchamel sauce and the beaten eggs. Put the mixture into a buttered charlotte mould and poach in a bain-marie.

When it is ready, leave to settle for a few minutes before unmoulding. Then cover with a cream sauce to which a little meat jelly has been added.

Purée de chicorée

ENDIVE (U.S. CHICORY) PURÉE

Follow either of the methods for creamed endive (U.S. chicory) (see page 609).

Sieve the endive (U.S. chicory) and add one-third quantity of creamy potato.

Reheat before serving.

Soufflé de chicorée

ENDIVE (U.S. CHICORY) SOUFFLÉ

8 oz. endives (U.S. chicory) cooked as for creamed endive (see page 610), 3 egg yolks, grated cheese, 3–4 egg whites

Sieve the cooked endive (U.S. chicory).

Add the egg yolks and 3 good tablespoons grated cheese. Add stiffly beaten egg whites and put into a buttered soufflé dish.

Sprinkle with grated cheese and cook in a moderate oven.

Endives belge

CHICORY (U.S. ENDIVE)

1½ lb. chicory (U.S. endive), ½ pint (U.S. 1¼ cups) water, 3 tablespoons butter, pinch salt, juice ½ lemon

Wash and drain the chicory (U.S. endive) and put into a pan with the water, butter, salt and lemon juice. Cover, bring quickly to boiling point and simmer for 30–35 minutes.

Endives à la crème

CREAMED CHICORY (U.S. ENDIVE)

When the chicory (U.S. endive) is cooked, put it into a hot vegetable dish and cover with fairly thick béchamel sauce (see page 23), to which some cream and a little butter has been added.

Endives au jus

CHICORY (U.S. ENDIVE) WITH GRAVY

When the chicory (U.S. endive) is cooked drain it well and cover with brown veal stock. Simmer for 8—10 minutes.

Endives à la meunière

CHICORY (U.S. ENDIVE) À LA MEUNIÈRE

When the chicory (U. S. endive) is cooked, coat it with flour and brown lightly in butter.

ANOTHER METHOD

Wash and drain and put the chicory (U.S. endive) into a well buttered sauté pan. Sprinkle lightly with salt, cover, and cook over a gentle heat.

When ready the butter should be clarified and slightly browned; the outside leaves of chicory (U.S. endive) should also be slightly coloured.

Endives Mornay

CHICORY MORNAY

When the chicory (U.S. endive) is cooked, drain well and coat with flour, then brown in butter.

Put a little Mornay sauce (see page 34) into a serving dish. Arrange the chicory (U.S. endive) on top and cover with more sauce.

Brush with melted butter; glaze under the grill (U.S. broiler) or in oven.

Endives à la moelle

CHICORY (U.S. ENDIVE) WITH BEEF MARROW

Chicory (U.S. endive), slices beef marrow poached in consommé or stock, demi-glace sauce with tomato (see page 22), butter

Cook the chicory as in the previous recipe. When it has been browned, put on to a serving dish and arrange the slices of beef marrow on top. Coat with the sauce to which a little butter has been added.

Endives à la napolitaine

CHICORY (U.S. ENDIVE) WITH CHEESE AND TOMATO SAUCE

———————— Chicory (U.S. endive), grated cheese, fairly thick tomato sauce (see page 132), butter

Cook the chicory in the ordinary way, drain and put it into a fireproof serving dish. Sprinkle with cheese, coat with the tomato sauce and sprinkle more cheese on top. Brush with melted butter and put into a moderate oven for 5–6 minutes.

Choux

CABBAGE

Under this heading I am including:

White cabbage, which is used for making sauerkraut

Red cabbage, which serves as a vegetable and for hors-d'oeuvre

White-heart or Savoy cabbage, which is best for braising and for plain boiling

Scotch kale and spring cabbage, which are usually served plainly boiled

Cauliflower and broccoli, of which the flower is usually cooked, but the leaves and stalks (if sufficiently tender) are often plainly boiled

Brussels sprouts

Kohlrabi and swede, the roots of which may be prepared like turnips, and the leaves boiled, if they are young and tender

Choucroute

WHITE CABBAGE WITH WINE

———————— About 6 lb. white cabbage, salt, pepper, 1½ lb. pork fat, small knuckle ham, 2 legs smoked goose, if possible, 2 onions, 2 cloves, *bouquet garni*, 2 oz. juniper berries, 1 bottle white Alsatian wine, white stock, poached Strasbourg sausage

Put the cabbage into a large tall saucepan, season lightly. Add the blanched pork fat, ham, goose legs, onions stuck with cloves, *bouquet garni* and juniper berries tied in muslin. Add the wine, and enough stock to cover the cabbage. Put on the lid and simmer for 2½ – 3 hours.

After 1 hour, remove the piece of pork fat and put on one side.

When ready to serve, remove the *bouquet garni*, onions and juniper berries. Drain the cabbage and put on to a serving dish. Surround with the pork fat cut into slices, thin slices of ham, poached Strasbourg sausage and goose legs.

SAUERKRAUT

Use firm white cabbages, remove the outer leaves and cut cabbages in half. Remove the centre stalk, then wash and drain thoroughly. Shred, using a fairly coarse vegetable grater.

Put the shredded cabbage into a large earthenware or wooden tub, sprinkling each layer with coarse salt. When full, cover with a lid and press down with a heavy weight. Leave for 6 weeks, when fermentation should be complete and the sauerkraut ready for use.

Note Sauerkraut can be obtained from most delicatessens ready for use or bought in cans.

Chou rouge à la flamande

RED CABBAGE IN THE FLEMISH WAY

1 red cabbage, salt, pepper, nutmeg, vinegar, 6 tablespoons red wine, 3–4 russet apples, 1 tablespoon brown or granulated sugar

Cut the cabbage into quarters. Take off the outer leaves and the stalk and cut the quarters into fine julienne. Season, sprinkle with vinegar and put the julienne into a well buttered casserole. Add the wine, cover, and cook in a slow oven.

When the cabbage is three-quarter cooked, add the apples cut into 4 – 8 pieces, according to size, and the sugar. Cooking should take place very slowly, with no liquor other than the vinegar and wine.

Note In Limoges peeled and chopped raw chestnuts are cooked with the cabbage.

Chou rouge mariné pour hors d'oeuvre

MARINATED RED CABBAGE FOR HORS-D'OEUVRE

———————— 1 red cabbage, salt, 2—3 cloves garlic, 1 bay leaf, few peppercorns, ½ pint (U.S. 1¼ cups) vinegar, ½ pint (U.S. 1¼ cups) red wine

Cut the cabbage into julienne as in the preceding recipe, put it in a bowl, sprinkle with fine salt and leave for 5 – 6 hours, moving it about frequently. Drain, and put into a saucepan with the garlic, bay leaf, and peppercorns. Cover with vinegar and red wine, which has been boiled and cooled, and leave to marinate for 24 hours.

Note This marinated cabbage is an excellent accompaniment to boiled beef.

Chou à l'anglaise

BOILED CABBAGE

Divide the cabbage into quarters, remove the stalk and the outside leaves and cook in plenty of boiling salted water. Drain, and press well to remove as much moisture as possible.

Chop or cut into squares.

Cabbage prepared thus serves usually as an accompaniment to joints of beef, mutton, etc.

Chou braisé

BRAISED CABBAGE

———————— 1 cabbage, pork fat, salt, pepper, nutmeg, 1 carrot, 1 onion stuck with 1 clove, *bouquet garni*, stock

Divide the cabbage into 4 pieces and remove the stalk and the outer leaves. Wash it carefully, blanch in boiling water, and drain.

Line a casserole with a few thin slices of pork fat. Put in the pieces of cabbage, season and add the carrot cut into quarters, onion and *bouquet garni*.

Add just enough stock to cover.

Put a few more strips of pork fat on top, cover, and cook in a slow oven for 1½−2 hours.

Braised cabbage is generally used as a garnish.

Chou a la façon des petits restaurants

CABBAGE AS COOKED IN SMALL RESTAURANTS

—————— 1 2½−3-lb. cabbage, 1 oz. butter, 8 oz. pork fat, 2 tablespoons finely chopped onion, salt, pepper

Cook the cabbage in boiling salted water, drain, press out as much moisture as possible and chop. Heat the butter in a pan, add the pork fat, cut into small cubes, and the onion. Cook until the onion begins to brown, then add the cabbage. Season, and cook for 15−20 minutes, stirring occasionally.

Chou farci

STUFFED CABBAGE

—————— 1 cabbage, salt, pepper, 1 clove garlic, 1 onion, 8 oz. streaky bacon, 1 tablespoon chopped parsley, 6 oz. blanched rice, 2 eggs, 3 tablespoons grated cheese, pot-au-feu (see page 61) made with mutton

Remove the hard outside leaves of the cabbage and pull off the next four rows. Wash and blanch these leaves, drain and arrange on a piece of muslin, to form a bed for the filling.

Blanch the remaining inside leaves, press well to extract the moisture and chop finely. Add seasoning, chopped garlic, finely chopped onion, bacon, cut into small pieces, parsley, rice, beaten eggs and the cheese. Mix all these ingredients very well together and put into the centre of the cabbage leaves. Draw up the edges of the muslin so that the shape of the cabbage is re-formed.

Tie securely and put into a pot-au-feu where it should cook at the same time as the meat.

To serve Put the cabbage on to a serving dish and remove the muslin carefully. Serve the rest of the pot-au-feu as described on page 61.

Note Some sausage meat may be added to the stuffing, and instead of cooking cabbage in a pot-au-feu it may be cooked in ordinary stock.

Chou farci pour garnitures
STUFFED CABBAGE AS A GARNISH

1 medium-sized cabbage, 1 onion, butter, 8 oz. pork fat, 8 oz. sausage meat, salt, pepper, rice pilaf (see page 669), 1 carrot, 1 onion, strips pork fat

Remove and discard the outer leaves of the cabbage. Remove the rest of the leaves, wash, and cook in plenty of salted water. Select as many of the larger leaves as required to make 12 little cabbages; if not large enough use two together.

Finely chop the rest of the cabbage. Chop the carrot and onion and brown lightly in butter. Add the pork fat cut into cubes, and the sausage meat. Cook for a few minutes, then add the chopped cabbage and cook for 8 – 10 minutes, stirring occasionally. Season and add an equal amount of rice pilaf. Mix all well together. Put 2 – 3 spoonfuls of this stuffing on the cabbage leaves and shape up into balls. Butter a sauté pan or casserole, and put some finely chopped carrot and onion in the bottom. Put in the little cabbages and cover with strips of pork fat. Add enough stock to moisten. Cover and cook in a moderate oven for 30 – 35 minutes.

As an alternative, a little truffled purée of foie gras can be mixed with the rice.

Choux frisés, choux de printemps, choux de mai, feuilles de brocolis, de choux raves et de choux-navets
CURLY CABBAGE, SPRING CABBAGE, BROCCOLI LEAVES, KOHL-RABI AND TURNIP TOPS

These various types of cabbage are either plainly boiled, or cooked in butter like Brussels sprouts.

Choux-fleurs et brocolis
CAULIFLOWER AND BROCCOLI

Cauliflower and broccoli are cooked in the same way.

Broccoli is especially good when served in a salad with olive oil.

Chou-fleur à l'anglaise
CAULIFLOWER IN THE ENGLISH WAY

In England cauliflower is often cooked whole with some of the tender green leaves left round the flower. It should be allowed to soak for a short while in salted water to rid it of any insects embedded in the flower.

A better method is to divide the cauliflower into flowerets, and any tender leaves can be cooked with them.

Cook the flowerets in boiling salted water for 7−8 minutes. Drain off the water, and cover with fresh boiling water. Add a little salt, ½ oz. butter and continue the cooking.

Serve with melted butter, hollandaise sauce (see page 33) or cream sauce (see page 38).

Note. The water in which the cauliflower was finally cooked can be used for a vegetable soup.

Fritots de chou-fleur
CAULIFLOWER FRITTERS

———— Cauliflower flowerets, salt, pepper, chopped parsley, oil, lemon juice, batter, fat, fried parsley, tomato sauce (see page 132)

Drain the flowerets well after cooking. Season and sprinkle with chopped parsley, then marinate for 20 minutes in oil and lemon juice. Coat with batter, fry in hot fat and serve with fried parsley and tomato sauce.

Chou-fleur au gratin
CAULIFLOWER AU GRATIN

———— Cooked cauliflower flowerets, butter, salt, pepper, béchamel sauce (see page 23), grated cheese, fine dry breadcrumbs

After draining the flowerets, sauté them for a few minutes in butter until the moisture evaporates.

Season and put a layer of béchamel sauce into a fireproof serving dish. Arrange the cauliflower flowerets on top as nearly as possible in the original shape. Cover with sauce, and sprinkle with grated cheese and breadcrumbs mixed together. Brush with melted butter and brown in the oven or under the grill (U.S. broiler).

Chou-fleur milanaise

CAULIFLOWER MILANESE

—————— Cooked cauliflower flowerets, butter, grated cheese

Sauté the well drained flowerets in butter. Sprinkle the bottom of a buttered fireproof dish with cheese. Put in the cauliflower and sprinkle with more cheese. Leave for a few minutes in a warm place and just before serving pour a little browned butter over the cauliflower.

Chou-fleur polonaise

POLISH STYLE CAULIFLOWER

—————— Cauliflower flowerets, 4 oz. butter, 2—3 hard-boiled egg yolks, chopped parsley, 2 tablespoons breadcrumbs

Cook the cauliflower as in recipe on page 617 and sauté the flowerets for a few minutes in butter. Put into a serving dish and sprinkle the top with a mixture of sieved hard-boiled egg yolk and parsley. Heat the butter until it begins to brown, add the breadcrumbs, and when they are brown, pour all over the cauliflower.

Purée de chou-fleur

CAULIFLOWER PURÉE

Cook the cauliflower in flowerets. Drain well and sauté for a few moments in butter. Rub through a sieve, then put the resultant purée into a pan and add quarter its volume of fairly stiff creamed potatoes.
    Reheat before serving.

Choux de Bruxelles à l'anglaise

ENGLISH STYLE BRUSSELS SPROUTS

—————— 1 lb. Brussels sprouts, salt, freshly ground pepper, 3 oz. butter

Trim and wash the sprouts carefully and cook in boiling salted water. Drain well and put into a serving dish. Season with salt and pepper and pour over the melted butter.

Choux de Bruxelles au beurre

BRUSSELS SPROUTS WITH BUTTER

——————— 1 lb. Brussels sprouts, 5 oz. butter, salt, pepper

Cook the sprouts as in the previous recipe, drain well, and return to the pan with the butter and seasoning. Sauté for a few minutes until the sprouts are well impregnated with the butter.

Choux de Bruxelles sautés

BRUSSELS SPROUTS SAUTÉ

Cook the sprouts in boiling, salted water, drain well and put them in a saucepan containing hot butter. Sauté until they are lightly browned, then put into a vegetable dish and sprinkle with chopped parsley.

Brussels sprouts may also be cooked in the same way as cauliflower au gratin (see page 617), cauliflower Milanese (see page 618) or Polish style cauliflower (see page 618).

Purée de choux de Bruxelles à la flamande

BRUSSELS SPROUTS PURÉE WITH CREAMED POTATOES

——————— Brussels sprouts, butter, creamed potatoes

Cook the sprouts in boiling, salted water, drain well, then toss in butter for 5—6 minutes.

Rub through a sieve and add one-third quantity of creamed potatoes. Reheat and add a few dabs of butter just before serving.

Chou-marin

SEA-KALE

Sea-kale is an excellent vegetable much appreciated in England. It is trimmed, tied in bundles of 4—6 pieces and cooked in boiling salted water.

Sea-kale is served on a table napkin like asparagus or on a special dish.

All the sauces served with asparagus are suitable for sea-kale.

Chou de mai

SPRING CABBAGE

Spring cabbage, which is a great favourite in Belgium, is cooked like ordinary cabbage (see page 614).

Note As far as possible, cauliflower, broccoli, Brussel ssprouts, cabbage, sea-kale, etc., should always be served hot.

Concombres à la crème

CREAMED CUCUMBERS

Cucumbers, butter, cream, few tablespoons béchamel sauce (see page 23)

Peel the cucumbers and cut into oval or oblong shapes. **Blanch them** for some minutes and strain.

Then stew in butter until all the moisture has evaporated, at which point the cucumbers should be cooked. Add a little boiling cream, boil for 2 minutes and finally add the béchamel sauce.

As a variation, sweet paprika or a mild curry powder may be added to the sauce.

Concombres farcis

STUFFED CUCUMBERS

Cucumbers, butter, salt, pepper, creamed chicken forcemeat (see page 56)

Peel the cucumbers, cut into pieces 1 – 1½ inches thick, remove the seeds, blanch and drain.

Arrange the pieces side by side in a well buttered sauté pan, season lightly and cook till tender. Remove from the heat and fill the hollows with the forcemeat. Cover the pan and poach for 15 minutes in a very slow oven or on the side of the stove.

Cucumbers prepared in this way are used as a garnish to accompany braised chicken, veal or lamb and for delicate entrées such as the following:

Sprinkle the pieces of cucumber, prepared and cooked as above, with some good meat jelly (see page 21). Arrange them in a ring on a round serving dish and put a slice of calf's sweetbread or breast of chicken on each and top with a slice of truffle. Add a little *sauce suprême* (see page 23) to the cooking liquor from the cucumber and pour over the pieces of cucumber. Alternatively, this entrée can be served with buttered asparagus tips or truffles coated with *sauce parisienne* (see page 22).

Or the pieces of cucumber can be coated with Mornay sauce (see page 34), lightly browned and accompanied by buttered asparagus tips.

ANOTHER METHOD OF STUFFING CUCUMBERS — 1

—————— Cucumbers, truffle, mushroom, tongue, *panade à la frangipane* (see page 55), strips pork fat, onion, carrots, veal stock, demi-glace sauce (see page 22)

Peel the cucumbers and cut in half lengthwise. Remove the seeds with a small spoon, then blanch and drain at once.

Mix a little finely chopped truffle, mushroom and tongue with the forcemeat and stuff the cucumbers right to the edges. Put the two halves together, wrap in strips of pork fat and then in muslin. Secure with fine string and braise on a bed of chopped onions and carrots with a little veal stock.

When the cucumbers are cooked, put them on to a serving dish and unwrap carefully so that they do not come apart, then cut into 1½ – 2-inch lengths.

Add some demi-glace sauce to the cooking liquor, reduce to a coating consistency and strain over the cucumbers.

ANOTHER METHOD OF STUFFING CUCUMBERS — 2

Follow the recipe as above, and when the cucumbers are arranged in the dish in sections, sprinkle with grated cheese.

To the demi-glace sauce (see page 22) add half its volume of tomato sauce (see page 132). Reduce to a coating consistency and pour over the cucumbers.

Sprinkle liberally with grated cheese, dot with butter and put into a moderate oven for 4 – 5 minutes.

Alternatively, cover the cucumbers with *sauce moelle* (see page 28) or Italian sauce (see page 28) to which the reduced cooking liquor of the cucumbers should be added. Or they may be coated with *sauce suprême* (see page 23) with truffles, or béchamel sauce (see page 23) with cream, then sprinkled with cheese, dotted with butter and glazed in the oven or under the grill (U.S. broiler).

COURGETTES

With few exceptions, all the recipes for aubergines are applicable to courgettes.

They may be served plain boiled or accompanied by melted butter, cream sauce (see page 38) or hollandaise sauce (see page 33), or they may be sautéed in butter for a few minutes and cooked *à la Mornay* (see page 593).

Tian de courgettes à la provençale

TIAN OF COURGETTES PROVENÇAL

The name *tian* is given to a round dish, which is very popular in Provence; it is about 2 inches in height and of various sizes.

> 1 lb. courgettes, salt, pepper, pinch nutmeg, oil, pinch garlic, 4 oz. rice, ½ pint (U.S. 1¼ cups) water, grated cheese, chopped parsley, 1 slice bread

Peel and thinly slice the courgettes, season with salt, pepper and nutmeg and cook gently in oil with the garlic. Cook the rice in the boiling water for 18 minutes. Mix the courgettes and rice together, add 2 – 3 tablespoons grated cheese and a little chopped parsley. Put into the *tian*.

Dip a slice of bread into water, press well to extract the moisture and spread over the top. Sprinkle with grated cheese, brush with oil and brown in a moderate oven.

ANOTHER METHOD

> 1 lb. tomatoes, 2–3 tablespoons chopped onion, oil, salt, pepper, chopped parsley, 1 small clove garlic, 6 tablespoons white wine, 1 lb. courgettes, prepared and cooked in oil as above, grated cheese

Peel, seed and chop the tomatoes.

Fry the onion in a little oil, until it begins to brown, add the tomatoes, salt, pepper, parsley, garlic and wine. Cook over low heat for 20 minutes.

Put the courgette into the *tian* and sprinkle with grated cheese. Cover with the tomatoes and put into a moderate oven for 5 – 6 minutes.

Serve with boiled rice.

Note In place of the *tian*, a soufflé dish or gratin dish could be used.

Épinards

SPINACH

As far as possible, spinach should not be cooked until the last moment. But it is far more important that it should be fresh and young.

Wash the spinach thoroughly in several waters. Put into a pan with only the water adhering to the leaves. If the spinach is rather coarse, put it into a very small quantity of boiling water with a little salt. When cooked, drain and press well to extract as much water as possible.

Chop or rub through a sieve.

Reheat with salt and pepper, put into a serving dish and add a nut of butter.

Épinards à la crème

CREAMED SPINACH

1 lb. cooked spinach, 2 oz. butter, cream, pinch salt, pinch pepper, pinch nutmeg, pinch sugar

Chop or sieve the spinach and put into a pan with the butter. Stir over brisk heat until all the moisture has evaporated. Add ¼ pint (U.S. ⅝ cup) cream and the salt, pepper, nutmeg and sugar. Put into a serving dish and add 2−3 tablespoons boiling cream.

Épinards au gratin

SPINACH AU GRATIN

1 lb. cooked spinach, butter, salt, pepper, nutmeg, grated cheese, butter, béchamel sauce (see page 23), breadcrumbs, 4 oz. chopped lean ham (optional)

Chop the spinach and dry off with butter as described in the previous recipe. Add seasoning, 3 tablespoons grated cheese and 3 oz. butter.

Put into a gratin dish and coat with sauce. Sprinkle with grated cheese and breadcrumbs mixed together. Dot with butter and brown in the oven.

Chopped lean ham can be added to the spinach.

Subrics d'épinards

SPINACH SUBRICS

———————— Cooked spinach, butter, pancake batter (see page 704), oil or clarified butter

Chop spinach and dry off in butter as described on page 623. Mix with an equal quantity of fairly stiff batter. Heat some oil or clarified butter in a pan, and fry the mixture in spoonfuls, leaving room between each so that the subrics do not touch each other. Allow 1 minute for the underside, then turn and brown the other side.

Note The oil or butter should be very hot.

Crêpes aux épinards

SPINACH PANCAKES

The same mixture as for subrics, but made slightly thinner; excellent pancakes may be made, proceeding as for ordinary pancakes.

Note Subrics and pancakes make excellent garnishes for beef and veal entrées.

Soufflé aux épinards

SPINACH SOUFFLÉ

Prepare as instructed for endive (U.S. chicory) soufflé (see page 610) and cook in the same way.

Souffle d'épinards aux anchois

SPINACH SOUFFLÉ WITH ANCHOVIES

Prepare as for endive (U.S. chicory) soufflé (see page 610), but add a few chopped fillets of anchovy.

Soufflé d'épinards au jambon

SPINACH AND HAM SOUFFLÉ

Proceed as for the anchovy soufflé, replacing the anchovies by lean ham cut into very small cubes.

Soufflé d'épinards aux truffes

TRUFFLED SPINACH SOUFFLÉ

Proceed as for the soufflés on page 624, replacing the anchovies or the ham with thinly sliced truffles.

Note These varieties of spinach soufflé may be served as vegetables, if needed, or as accompaniments to certain roast or braised meat joints.

Fenouil tubéreux

FLORENCE FENNEL

This vegetable is little used in France. This is a mistake, as it is excellent. It is cooked in salted water and then prepared like cardoons and celery (see pages 498, 600, 601).

Feuilles de vigne farcis ou dolmas (cuisine turque)

STUFFED VINE LEAVES OR DOLMAS (TURKISH STYLE)

———————— Mutton, chopped mutton fat, preferably from the tail of the sheep, chopped onion, parsley, cooked rice, salt, pepper, paprika, vine or cabbage leaves, mutton broth, egg yolks, lemon juice

Chop the mutton finely or put through a mincer, add a little mutton fat, onion, parsley, rice, seasoning and a little paprika and mix all well together.

Blanch and dry the leaves. Divide the forcemeat into pieces the size of a walnut and wrap in the leaves, making a round shape.

Put close together in a shallow pan, and cover with mutton broth. Put a plate on top to keep them in position. Bring to boiling point, then simmer gently.

Arrange in a pyramid on a serving dish. Reduce the cooking liquor by about two-thirds then thicken with egg yolks mixed with a little of the liquor. Add lemon juice to taste and pour over the dolmas.

Dolmas are really only small stuffed cabbages, but in Turkey they play a large part in the national cuisine. They are prepared in various ways, with leaves of vine, mallow, fig or cabbage.

Fèves

BROAD BEANS (U.S. SHELL BEANS)

When the beans are large and in full season, remove the inner skin and cook in boiling salted water to which 3–4 sprigs of savory, tied together, have been added.

When the beans are tender, drain and put into a serving dish. Chop the leaves of savory and sprinkle on top.

Fèves à l'anglaise

ENGLISH STYLE BROAD BEANS (U.S. SHELL BEANS)

Choose very tender beans and only remove the black part on top of the head. Cook in boiling salted water, drain and add some butter before serving.

If the beans are older, skin them as described above.

Fèves à la crème

CREAMED BROAD BEANS (U.S. SHELL BEANS)

———— Broad beans (U.S. shell beans), butter, cream, salt, sugar, nutmeg

Cook the beans in boiling salted water, drain, add a little butter and some cream. Reheat till boiling, then add salt, sugar and nutmeg to taste.

Fèves béchamel

BROAD BEANS (U.S. SHELL BEANS) WITH BÉCHAMEL SAUCE

Cook as in the preceding recipe, but replace the cream with béchamel sauce (see page 23).

Purée de fèves

BROAD BEAN (U.S. SHELL BEAN) PURÉE

———— Broad beans (U.S. shell beans), few tablespoons boiling cream, butter

Cook the beans in boiling salted water, drain well and rub through a sieve. Return the purée to the pan and add cream and some butter.

Note When the beans are very young, right at the beginning of the season, they can be cooked in their pods and served like peas with butter or like *laitues à la ménagère* (see page 631).

Fèves à la provençale

PROVENÇAL STYLE BROAD BEANS (U.S. SHELL BEANS)

2 lb. broad beans (U.S. shell beans), 6 oz. streaky bacon, 3 tablespoons oil, 2 tablespoons chopped onion, 2 lettuces, salt, pepper, nutmeg, water, little flour (optional)

If the broad beans (U.S. shell beans) are large and fully matured, remove the skin; if they are young and tender this is not necessary.

Cut up the bacon and put it into a pan with the oil and onion. Sauté for a few minutes, but do not allow the onion to brown. Add the hearts of the lettuce, cut into pieces, and the beans and cook together for a few minutes, stirring. Add seasoning and enough hot water to cover.

Cover the pan and cook gently until the beans are tender. If necessary, thicken the liquor with a little flour.

Gombos

OKRA OR LADIES' FINGERS

This vegetable is not very popular in France, but, on the other hand, Americans and Orientals are very fond of it.

There are two varieties of this vegetable — the long and the round okra. They are both cooked the same way.

Gombos à la crème

CREAMED OKRA

Cut away both ends of the okra and cook in boiling salted water. Drain throoughly and sauté for a few minutes in butter.

Put into a serving dish and coat with béchamel sauce (see page 23) to which a little cream has been added.

Gombos à l'orientale

EASTERN STYLE OKRA

——————— 1 lb. okra, 2 tablespoons oil, 2 tablespoons chopped onion, 4—5
tomatoes, 1 small clove garlic, chopped parsley, salt, pepper, 1 dessertspoon curry powder (optional)

Blanch the okra in salted water and drain well. Heat the oil, add the onion
and cook till lightly browned. Add the tomatoes, peeled, seeded and
chopped, garlic, little chopped parsley, and seasoning. Add the okra and
curry powder if used. Cover and simmer for 25 — 30 minutes.

Serve with *riz à l'indienne* (see page 668).

Jets de houblon

HOP SHOOTS

The edible part is separated from the fibrous by breaking off the ends
of the shoots like asparagus. After washing them in several waters they
are cooked in salted water with the addition of the juice of 1 small lemon
for every 1¾ pints (U.S. 4¼ cups) water.

Hop shoots are served with butter, cream, or *sauce parisienne* (see
page 22).

When served as a vegetable, they are usually accompanied by poached
eggs.

Haricots blancs secs

DRIED WHITE HARICOT BEANS

——————— 2 pints (U.S. 5 cups) haricot beans, water, 1 onion stuck with 2 cloves,
2 medium-sized carrots, 1 clove garlic (optional), salt

Put the beans into a pan and cover with warm water. Bring to boiling
point, remove from the heat and leave for 1 minute. Then drain, and
cover with fresh warm water. Add the onion, carrots and garlic to taste.
Cover and cook very slowly.

Note Add salt when the beans are nearly cooked.

Haricots blancs à l'américaine

AMERICAN STYLE WHITE HARICOT BEANS

Cook the beans as in the preceding recipe, but add a piece of bacon with the other ingredients.

When the beans are cooked, drain and put into a serving dish with the bacon cut into small pieces and coat with tomato sauce (see page 132).

Haricots blancs au beurre

WHITE HARICOT BEANS IN BUTTER

Cook the beans as in the previous recipes and drain well. Add salt and freshly ground pepper and 3 – 4 oz. butter.

Haricots blancs à la bretonne

BRETON STYLE WHITE HARICOT BEANS

2 pints (U.S. 5 cups) haricot beans, salt, pepper, butter, 2 tablespoons finely chopped onion, lightly browned in butter, tomato sauce (see page 132), chopped parsley

Cover and drain the beans and season well. Mix some butter and the onion with some thick tomato sauce. Pour over the beans and sprinkle with chopped parsley.

Haricots blancs à la crème

WHITE HARICOT BEANS WITH CREAM

1 pint (U.S. 2½ cups) haricot beans, ½ pint (U.S. 1¼ cups) boiling cream, salt, pepper

Cook and drain the beans. Return to the pan, add the cream and a little seasoning. Allow to boil for a few minutes before serving.

Haricots blancs à la lyonnaise

LYONESE STYLE WHITE HARICOT BEANS

These are haricot beans with butter, to which finely chopped onions, lightly browned in butter, have been added. Sprinkle with chopped parsley.

Haricots blancs au gratin à la ménagère

WHITE HARICOT BEANS AU GRATIN

Cook the beans and drain well. Put into a casserole and add a little rather fatty mutton stock. Sprinkle with breadcrumbs and brown in the oven.

Purée de haricots blancs

WHITE HARICOT BEAN PURÉE

———— 1½ lb. haricot beans, 3 oz. butter, 6 tablespoons boiling cream or milk

Cook and drain the beans, then rub through a sieve. Return the purée to a pan and add the butter and cream.

Haricots flageolets

GREEN HARICOT BEANS

These beans are mostly used fresh, but canned or dried flageolets may be used out of season.

They are cooked in the same way as white haricot beans.

They make a very smooth purée and are sometimes used to improve a purée of French beans.

Haricots rouge

RED HARICOT BEANS

Red haricot beans are cooked in the same way as white haricot beans.

———— To 2 pints (U.S. 5 cups) water, add ⅓ pint (U.S. 1¼ cups) red wine, 6 oz. pork fat, 1 *bouquet garni*

When the beans are cooked, drain, remove the pork fat, cut it into cubes and brown it in butter. Put the beans into a serving dish, add a little melted butter and the pork fat.

Haricots verts fins

FRENCH BEANS

Choose fresh young beans. Cook in plenty of salted water, keeping them firm, but not too firm.

Drain, return to the pan and add for every 1 lb. beans about 2 oz. butter cut into small pieces.

Season with salt and pepper and sauté for a few minutes before serving.

Note Do not put any parsley with French beans.

Haricots panachés

MIXED BEANS

This is composed of equal parts of French beans and flageolets, dressed with butter.

Sometimes the beans are lightly browned in the butter.

Haricots verts à la provençale

PROVENÇAL STYLE FRENCH BEANS

———————— 1 lb. French beans, oil, salt, pepper, 2 tablespoons chopped onion, 4—5 tomatoes, 1 small clove garlic, chopped parsley

Cook the beans, drain, sauté for a few minutes in a little oil and season.

Lightly brown the onions in oil, add tomatoes, peeled, seeded and chopped, seasoning, garlic and a little chopped parsley. Cook gently for 15—20 minutes, then mix with the beans.

Many people, for some unknown reason, dislike cooking in olive oil. If they were to taste French beans cooked *à la provençale*, I am sure that they would change their minds.

Laitues à la ménagère

LETTUCES WITH ONIONS

———————— 6 lettuces, 6 small onions, salt, 1—2 lumps sugar, 3 tablespoons water, 2—3 sprigs parsley

It is essential that the lettuces should be chosen fresh and not too large. Take off the outer, coarse leaves.

Cut each lettuce in half and wash in plenty of cold water. Shake well to remove excess water and put into a buttered sauté pan with the onions, seasoning, sugar, water and parsley.

Cover, and cook over gentle heat.

Laitues à la crème

CREAMED LETTUCES

Cook the lettuces as in the previous recipe but omit the onions.

Just before serving, add ¼ pint (U.S. ⅝ cup) cream and simmer for a few minutes.

Laitues braisés au jus

BRAISED LETTUCES

Lettuces, onions, carrots, few bacon rinds, *bouquet garni*, salt, pepper, strips pork fat, brown veal stock, heart-shaped croûtons, butter, 2—3 tablespoons demi-glace sauce (see page 22) or potato flour

Blanch the lettuces, and press to remove as much water as possible. Cut each in half.

Put the finely chopped vegetables, bacon rinds and *bouquet garni* into a buttered sauté pan. Arrange the lettuces on top, season, and cover with thin strips of pork fat. Add enough stock to cover. Put the lid on the pan and cook in a moderate oven.

When ready, fold each lettuce half over on to itself and arrange in a ring on a serving dish. Fry the croûtons in butter and arrange between the pieces of lettuce.

Add the demi-glace sauce to the cooking liquor, or thicken it with a little potato flour. Strain, and pour over the lettuce.

For lettuces with beef marrow, add some slices of beef marrow poached in consommé.

For lettuces with Parmesan cheese, add a few tablespoons tomato sauce to the cooking liquor, rub through a sieve and reheat.

Arrange the lettuces on a serving dish, sprinkle with grated Parmesan cheese and coat with the sauce. Keep hot for a few minutes before serving, to allow time for the cheese to mix with the sauce.

Laitues farcis

STUFFED LETTUCES

Lettuces, chicken forcemeat (see page 56), chopped ham, truffle, 3—4 tablespoons demi-glace sauce (see page 22), fried croûtons

Blanch the lettuces, cut in half lengthwise and braise as in the preceding recipe.

On each half, place 1 tablespoon forcemeat with a little chopped ham and truffle. Fold each half lettuce over on to itself and put into a buttered dish. Sprinkle with a little of the cooking liquor. Cover and put into a slow oven for 4 – 5 minutes, just long enough to poach the forcemeat.

Add demi-glace sauce to the rest of the cooking liquor and reheat.

Arrange the lettuce on croûtons and strain the sauce over.

Laitues braisés à la piémontaise

BRAISED LETTUCE WITH RISOTTO AND TOMATO SAUCE

Lettuces, risotto (see page 668), tomato sauce (see page 132), grated Parmesan cheese

Blanch and braise the lettuces as in the last two recipes. Put 1 tablespoon of risotto on each half lettuce and fold over so that the rice is enclosed. Arrange on a buttered dish, sprinkle with a little of the cooking liquor and keep hot.

Add a few tablespoons tomato sauce to the rest of the cooking liquor and finish as described for lettuces and then add Parmesan cheese.

Laitues farcis au riz à la toulousaine

LETTUCES STUFFED WITH RICE AND TRUFFLED FOIE GRAS

Lettuces, rice pilaf (see page 669), truffled foie gras, demi-glace sauce see page 22)

Prepare and cook the lettuces as in the preceding recipe, but omit the risotto and replace with rice pilaf to which a little mashed truffled foie gras has been added. Arrange the lettuces in a dish, add a few tablespoons demi-glace sauce to the braising liquor, reheat and pour over the lettuce.

Note Braised or stuffed lettuces make excellent garnishes for joints of meat and poultry, and for entrées generally.

Cuisson de lentilles

TO COOK LENTILS

1 lb. lentils, water, 1 carrot, 1 onion stuck with 2 cloves, 1 clove garlic, 1 small *bouquet garni*, salt

Wash the lentils, put into a pan and cover with warm water. Add the vegetables, garlic, *bouquet garni* and salt. Cover, and simmer at the side of the stove until the lentils are cooked.

Note The smaller variety of lentils are best, and they should never be allowed to soak for any length of time before cooking.

Lentilles au beurre

BUTTERED LENTILS

1 lb. lentils, 3 oz. butter, pinch chopped parsley

Cook the lentils as in the preceding recipe, drain and add the butter.
Sprinkle with parsley before serving.

Purée de lentilles

LENTIL PURÉE

Proceed in the same way as for haricot bean purée (see page 630).

Lentilles à la ménagère

LENTILS WITH ONION

1 lb. lentils, 2 tablespoons chopped onion, butter or oil, 1 tablespoon flour, salt, pepper, nutmeg, dash vinegar, chopped parsley

Cook the lentils as described previously, drain but retain a little of the cooking liquor with them. Brown the onion in butter or oil, add the flour and cook till browned. Add to the lentils, with seasoning and nutmeg. Bring to boiling point and simmer for a few minutes. Add vinegar and sprinkle with parsley before serving.

Mais

MAIZE (SWEET CORN)

Maize should be chosen fresh, tender and milky.

Strip back the husks, or leaves, without removing them. Remove the silky tassel, then replace the husks. Cook in boiling, slightly salted water. Turn back the husks to expose the cob and serve on a table napkin, with butter.

If corn is to be served off the cob, it should be dressed with butter like peas.

Corn can also be cooked in the oven on a grid or grilled (U.S. broiled). In this case, the leaves should be removed.

Cook until the grains have swollen and have taken a golden brown colour. They can then be removed or served on the cob.

If you cannot get fresh corn, excellent canned or frozen corn is available.

Croquettes de maïs

CORN CROQUETTES

1 can creamed corn, béchamel sauce (see page 23), egg yolks, flour, egg and breadcrumbs, deep fat for frying

Put the contents of the can into a saucepan and reduce over a low heat until most of the liquid has dried off. Add enough sauce to give a creamy consistency, then thicken with egg yolks. Turn out on to a wetted plate and leave to get cold and firm.

Form into balls on a floured board and flatten slightly. Coat with flour, then with egg and breadcrumbs. Fry in deep fat or in clarified butter in a frying pan, turning once so that both sides are browned.

Soufflé de maïs

CORN SOUFFLÉ

1 can creamed corn, béchamel sauce (see page 23), 3—4 egg yolks, 5 egg whites, 3—4 tablespoons grated cheese (optional), 1 level teaspoon paprika (optional)

Prepare the croquette mixture as in the previous recipe, thickening it with the egg yolks.

Fold in the stiffly beaten egg whites and pour into a buttered soufflé dish. Cook in a moderate oven.

Grated cheese and paprika can be added to taste.

Marrons

CHESTNUTS

Slit the shells and put the chestnuts into the oven for 7—8 minutes in a dish containing a little water. This is to enable them to be peeled easily.

Marrons étuvés

STEWED CHESTNUTS

As soon as the chestnuts are peeled, put them into a pan with a stick of celery. Just cover with stock or consommé and simmer till the chestnuts are tender.

Marrons braisés et glacés

BRAISED AND GLAZED CHESTNUTS

—————————— Chestnuts, brown veal stock, butter

Choose large chestnuts and peel them carefully. Put them in one layer in the bottom of a sauté pan. Add enough stock to cover and cook slowly, keeping the nuts whole. (It is not advisable to shake the pan whilst the nuts are cooking.)

When the nuts are nearly cooked, add some butter (about 3 oz. for 24 chestnuts).

Reduce the liquor to quarter its volume, when it should have the consistency of jelly.

Roll the nuts carefully around in this jelly. Prepared in this way, the chestnuts are generally used as a garnish.

Chestnuts may also be boiled or grilled (U.S. broiled).

To boil

Cook in salted water with a sprig of fennel, then drain, wrap in a cloth and leave to dry in the oven for 10 minutes.

To grill (U.S. broil)

Slit the skin, and put into a special chestnut pan, i.e. holed frying pan, or on a charcoal grill.

When the chestnuts are cooked, wrap in a cloth for about 10 minutes.

Purée de marrons

CHESTNUT PURÉE

———— Chestnuts, stock or consommé, pinch sugar, pinch salt, butter

Peel the chestnuts, removing the inner skin, and cook in stock or consommé, using just enough to cover the chestnuts.

When they are cooked, the liquor should be considerably reduced. Rub all through a sieve, return the purée to the pan, add sugar and salt if required. Add butter to thicken.

Navets

TURNIPS

Either as a vegetable or as a garnish, turnips are prepared like carrots. They may be served glazed, creamed, etc.

They may also be served stuffed, according to the following recipes.

Navets farcis

STUFFED TURNIPS

———— Turnips, cooked minced mutton or duck, butter, sugar, 3—4 tablespoons stock or consommé, demi-glace sauce (see page 22)

Choose young, medium-sized turnips of a good shape. Cut a thin slice from the underside so that they will stand up, and cook in boiling salted water.

When they are three-quarter cooked, drain, and using a vegetable scoop or a small spoon, remove some of the pulp, making a small round case. Mash or chop the pulp removed and mix with the minced meat. Fill the turnip cases with this mixture. Heat some butter in a sauté pan, add a little sugar and put in the turnips. Complete the cooking in the butter, basting frequently.

Arrange the turnips on a serving dish. Add stock or consommé to the butter left in the pan and mix well. Add some demi-glace sauce, bring to the boil and boil for a few minutes, then pour over the turnips.

Navets farcis à la semoule
TURNIPS STUFFED WITH SEMOLINA

———————— Semolina, consommé or stock, butter, grated cheese, turnips, demi-glace sauce (see page 22)

Cook some semolina in consommé or stock, and add some butter and grated cheese.

Prepare the turnips as in the previous recipe and fill with this stuffing, then finish cooking in butter as before, and arrange on a serving dish. Add 3—4 tablespoons stock to the butter left in the pan and mix well. Add some demi-glace sauce and reduce for 2 minutes, then pour over the turnips.

ANOTHER METHOD

Put the turnips, stuffed with semolina as above, on to a serving dish and sprinkle with grated cheese. Coat with demi-glace sauce and tomato (see page 22) and sprinkle more cheese on top.

Keep hot for a few minutes before serving, so that the cheese mixes well with the sauce.

Navets farcis châtelaine
TURNIPS STUFFED WITH SWEETBREADS

———————— Braised calf's sweetbreads, truffle, cooked ham, béchamel sauce (see page 23), turnips, prepared for stuffing as in previous recipes, butter, grated cheese

Chop some sweetbreads, truffle and ham and bind all together with a little béchamel sauce. Fill the turnips with this mixture. Arrange the turnips in a pan with some butter, cover and cook over gentle heat until the butter begins to brown, then remove from the heat.

Put the turnips on to a serving dish, coat with béchamel sauce, sprinkle with grated cheese and dot with butter.

Brown in the oven.

Purée de navets
TURNIP PURÉE

———————— 1 lb. turnips, 1 tablespoon butter, pinch salt, 1 dessertspoon sugar, water, creamed potatoes

Slice the turnips thinly. Blanch them for a few minutes in boiling water, then drain and put into a saucepan with the butter, salt, sugar and just enough water to cover. Put on the lid and cook over a low heat. Rub through a sieve, return the purée to the pan and add one-third its quantity creamed potatoes.

Pousses ou feuilles de navets

TURNIP TOPS

Young turnip tops are much appreciated in Great Britain as a luncheon vegetable.

They are cooked in the same way as green cabbage (see page 614).

Oignons farcis

STUFFED ONIONS

6—8 onions, butter, sugar, 3—4 tablespoons duxelles,* little cooked chicken, veal or mutton, 2—3 tablespoons stock, ½ pint (U.S. 1¼ cups) demi-glace sauce (see page 22)

Choose onions slightly over medium size and cut a slice off the top. Blanch them quickly and drain. Put some butter into a sauté pan, add the onions cut side uppermost and sprinkle with a little sugar. Cover and cook over low heat. When ready, they should be a light brown colour.

Remove the centre of the onion with a small spoon, leaving a shell of about ⅛ inch.

Mix the duxelles with the finely chopped or minced meat and use to stuff the onions. Put them back into the sauté pan and leave at the side of the stove for about 10 minutes, then arrange on a serving dish.

Add the stock to the butter left in the pan and mix well. Add the sauce, reduce for a few minutes and pour over the onions.

*For the duxelles
1 dessertspoon butter, 1 dessertspoon oil, 1 teaspoon finely chopped onion, 4 tablespoons mushroom stalks or trimmings, salt, pepper, pinch nutmeg, chopped parsley

Heat the butter and oil and fry the onion lightly. Add the chopped mushroom trimmings, washed and pressed in a cloth to remove the moisture. Stir over brisk heat until all the moisture has evaporated, season, and add the nutmeg and a little chopped parsley.

All the recipes for turnips can be applied to onions.

Oignons glacés

GLAZED ONIONS

1 lb. small onions, white stock, 3—4 oz. butter, 1 dessertspoon sugar

Choose onions of equal size and peel them. Put into a pan with enough stock to almost cover. Add the butter, cover and cook till tender.

When the onions are cooked, the liquor should be reduced to a jelly consistency.

If browned onions are required, put them into a large pan and add enough butter to cover them. Add the sugar and cook very gently. With a little care, light brown, evenly coloured onions should result.

Oseille

SORREL

4 lb. fresh sorrel, 6 oz. butter, 2 oz. flour, 1½ pints (U.S. 3¾ cups) consommé, salt, pepper, pinch sugar, 4—5 egg yolks, 3—4 tablespoons cream, brown veal stock

Shred the sorrel, wash in several waters and cook gently in a small quantity of water. Drain thoroughly.

Melt 3 oz. butter, add the flour and cook for a few minutes. Add the consommé, stir till boiling and boil for 3 minutes. Add seasoning and sugar. Add the sorrel, cover and cook over low heat for 35—40 minutes. Rub through a sieve and return the purée to the pan. Bring to boiling point.

Mix the egg yolks and cream together, add a little of the sorrel, then add to the sorrel in the pan. Reheat without boiling and finally add the rest of the butter. Put into a serving dish and sprinkle with a little good brown veal stock.

Oxalis

OCA

This is a sprightly plant of very elegant appearance, originating in Mexico. Its leaves resemble those of clover and in the summer the plant has a quantity of pink flowers. Its flavour is more pleasant than that of sorrel and it may replace sorrel with advantage. It is easily reproduced by means of the tubers which grow in large quantities on its roots.

Patates douces
SWEET POTATOES

This vegetable originated in India, and there are several varieties of it. It is found in Asia, Africa and Great Britain, and is used a great deal in Spain. The Virginia sweet potato is considered the best and is also more widely used, since it feeds part of the population of Africa.

The flavour resembles that of chestnuts, and the same recipes apply to it.

At the Spanish Court, I have eaten very small glazed potatoes, prepared by M. Marechal, the Court chef. They are cooked in the ashes of a wood fire and, after peeling them, one sprinkles them with orange juice and a little sugar.

Sweet potatoes lend themselves to many ways of cooking, each with more flavour than the last.

This valuable tuber is little known in France; it can, however, be cultivated in some districts. It is not damaged by either hail or frost, which are a constant danger to ordinary potatoes.

Petits pois
PEAS

However they are to be prepared, peas should be chosen very green and are best when picked and shelled at the last moment.

This vegetable can easily be spoiled by careless cooking.

Petits pois à l'anglaise
ENGLISH STYLE PEAS

Cook quickly in boiling salted water and drain well. Put into a serving dish and add some butter.

The English always add a sprig of fresh mint to the peas while they are cooking, and leave a few of the mint leaves on the peas.

Petits pois bonne femme

PEAS WITH ONIONS

2 lb. peas, butter, 12 small onions, 4 oz. pork fat, 1 lettuce, few sprigs parsley, pinch salt, 1 lump sugar, water, 1 tablespoon flour

Shell the peas, melt the butter in a pan and add the onions and pork fat cut into cubes and blanched. Sauté until the onions are lightly browned. Add the peas, chopped lettuce, parsley, salt and the sugar. Add just enough hot water to cover. Put a lid on the pan and cook till the peas are tender. Mix the flour smoothly with a little cold water, add to the peas and stir till boiling.

Petits pois à la flamande

FLEMISH STYLE PEAS

8 oz. carrots, 1 oz. butter, pinch salt, pinch sugar, water, 1 lb. freshly shelled peas

Scrape or peel the carrots and put into a pan with $\frac{1}{2}$ oz. butter, salt and sugar. Add enough hot water to cover. When half cooked, add the peas and continue to cook both vegetables together. Add the rest of the butter before serving.

Petits pois à la française

PEAS COOKED THE FRENCH WAY

2 lb. peas, 1 lettuce heart, 2 sprigs parsley, 12 small onions, 6 oz. butter, salt, 2 lumps sugar, 6 tablespoons water

Put the peas, lettuce and parsley tied together, onions, half the butter, salt and sugar into a large pan. Add the water, cover the pan tightly and cook over moderate heat. Just before serving, remove the lettuce and parsley. Put the peas into a serving dish, add the rest of the butter, cut the lettuce into quarters and place on top of the peas.

Petits pois aux laitues

PEAS WITH LETTUCE

6 lettuces, 2 lb. peas, 1 sprig parsley, 2 lumps sugar, pinch salt, 12 small onions, 3 oz. butter, 3—4 tablespoons water

Remove the coarse outer leaves of the lettuces and cut each in half. Wash in plenty of water and put the lettuces into a pan large enough to take them without squeezing. Add the peas, parsley, sugar, salt, onions, butter and the water. Cover and cook over moderate heat.

Put the peas into a serving dish, fold over the lettuces and arrange in a ring on top of the peas.

Purée de pois frais

FRESH PEA PURÉE

—————— 2 lb. peas, 4 oz. butter, pinch sugar

Cook the peas in boiling salted water, drain and rub through a sieve. Return the purée to the pan, add butter and sugar and reheat.

This purée may also be prepared with peas cooked *à la française* (see page 642). The purée is not so green, but it has more flavour.

Petits pois princesse ou mange-tout

PEAS PRINCESSE

Cut the complete pods into 2–3 pieces each and cook them according to the recipes for other peas.

Piments

PEPPERS

Peppers used in the kitchen are of several kinds. Some, like chillis and cayenne pepper, are very strong and are only used as seasoning.

Large, sweet, green, red or yellow peppers are used either in hors-d'oeuvre, as a garnish, or, combined with tomatoes, onions, vinegar, olive oil and sugar, as a relish which admirably accompanies cold meat and curries.

Spaniards, Portuguese, Indians and all Orientals eat a great many peppers, both the strong and the sweet kind.

To remove the skin, hold the pepper on a fork over a gas flame. This will loosen it and it can then be removed easily. Open up one side and extract the seeds.

Piments doux farcis

STUFFED SWEET PEPPERS

────────── Red peppers, risotto (see page 668) or rice pilaf (see page 669), butter, demi-glace sauce with tomato (see page 22)

Choose medium-sized peppers, skin and remove the seeds. Fill with risotto, or, if preferred, with rice pilaf to which a little tomato and some minced cooked mutton has been added.

Arrange the peppers in a fireproof dish and add some butter. Cover and cook in a moderate oven for 15−20 minutes.

Put on to a serving dish and coat with the sauce.

The recipe for stuffed onions (see page 639) can be applied to peppers.

Note As a special dish, a boned quail stuffed with foie gras can be put in with the risotto, and the peppers coated with demi-glace sauce.

Piments pour viandes froides

PEPPER PICKLE

────────── 1 lb. Spanish onions, ½ pint (U.S. 1¼ cups) oil, 2½ lb. sweet peppers, 2 lb. tomatoes, 1 clove garlic, 1 level teaspoon ground ginger, 1 lb. sugar, 8 oz. sultanas, 1 level teaspoon allspice, 1¾ pints (U.S. 4¼ cups) wine vinegar

Peel and chop the onions and brown lightly in the oil. Peel and seed the peppers, cut into strips and put with the onions. Stew gently for 15−20 minutes. Add tomatoes, peeled, seeded and chopped, crushed garlic and all other ingredients. Cover and cook very slowly for 2½ hours.

Note This should not be made in an iron saucepan.

Pommes de terre Anna

POTATOES ANNA

────────── Potatoes, butter, salt

Choose small potatoes or cut larger ones into cork shapes and slice thinly. Wash and dry in a cloth.

Put some butter into a casserole or sauté pan and arrange the potatoes in layers, overlapping each other and reversing the overlapping with each layer. Sprinkle each layer lightly with salt and dabs of butter. Cover and cook in a hot oven for 30 minutes. Pour off the excess butter before serving.

Pommes de terre Byron

POTATOES WITH CREAM AND CHEESE

12 large potatoes, butter, salt, pepper, cream, grated Parmesan cheese

Cook the potatoes in the oven, and when tender remove the pulp. Heat some butter in a frying pan, add the potato pulp and seasoning and fry for a few minutes.

Put a flan ring on to a fireproof serving dish, fill with the potato pulp and press down well, then remove the ring. Pour some cream over the potato, sprinkle with cheese and brown in the oven or under the grill (U.S. broiler).

Pommes de terre château

CHÂTEAU POTATOES

Cut the potatoes into the shape of large olives and cook gently in clarified butter until tender and golden brown.

Pommes de terre à la crème

CREAMED POTATOES

Potatoes, butter, cream

Peel some large potatoes and cut out balls with a vegetable scoop. Cook in boiling salted water, drain and return to the pan.

For each 8 oz. potato balls, add $\frac{1}{2}$ oz. butter, 6 tablespoons boiling cream and a pinch salt. Boil for a few moments before serving.

Croquettes de pommes de terre

POTATO CROQUETTES

2 lb. potatoes, 3 oz. butter, salt, pepper, nutmeg, 1 whole egg, 1 egg yolk, flour, egg and breadcrumbs for coating, deep fat for frying

Peel and quarter the potatoes and cook quickly in a little boiling salted water. Drain, dry for a few minutes at the side of the stove, then rub through a sieve. Return the purée to the pan, add butter, seasoning and nutmeg and stir over gentle heat for a few minutes to dry off. Remove from the heat, add the beaten egg and egg yolk. Mould into cork shapes, coat with flour and then with egg and breadcrumbs.

Fry in deep fat for 5—6 minutes, or, if preferred, mould into flat cakes, coat with flour and egg and breadcrumbs and fry in butter in a frying pan.

Pommes dauphine

CROQUETTE POTATOES WITH CHOU PASTE

Croquette mixture as in previous recipe, 8 oz. chou paste (without sugar) (see page 687), egg

Combine the croquette mixture and chou paste well together. Shape into brioche and arrange on a buttered dish. Brush with egg and cook in a moderate oven.

Pommes duchesse au Chester

DUCHESS POTATOES WITH CHESHIRE CHEESE

Cheshire cheese, potato croquette mixture as in previous recipe, 1 egg

Add 3 oz. grated cheese to the croquette mixture and mould into small biscuit shapes. Put on to a buttered baking tray and brush with beaten egg. Put a thin slice of cheese on each and put into a moderate oven for 7—8 minutes.

Pommes de terre fondantes

FONDANT POTATOES

There are many ways of making fondant potatoes. I will give only two which seem to me to be the most interesting.

———— 12 potatoes, water, salt, butter

Choose floury potatoes, peel and cut into ordinary egg shapes. Put side by side into a sauté pan, completely covering the bottom of the pan. Add hot water to come half-way up the pan, the salt and 4 oz. butter; cover and put into a moderate oven. When the cooking water is completely evaporated, the butter will clarify and brown the potatoes. When the potatoes are cooked, flatten them slightly with a fork, taking care not to break them, add a few dabs butter and keep them covered for a few moments to give them time to absorb the butter.

ANOTHER METHOD

Choose floury potatoes, peel and cook in salted water, but do not over-cook them. Drain off the water completely and leave at the side of the stove for a few moments to dry off. Mash with a fork, and add some melted butter very slowly. Season lightly and mould into egg shapes with a buttered tablespoon. Put on to a baking tray, brush with melted butter and brown in the oven.

Pommes de terre en allumettes

MATCH POTATOES

Peel and square off the potatoes at the ends and at the sides, then cut into small sticks like matches, and fry in hot deep fat. They should be eaten dry and crisp

Potatoes cut into long ribbons with a special tool — *pommes chatouillard* — or with a knife, are also cooked in deep fat.

Pommes de terre chip

CHIP POTATOES

These are potatoes cut into very thin slices.

Put them into very cold water for 10 minutes, then drain, dry in a cloth and fry in deep fat until they are very crisp.

In England, no roast game is ever served without chip potatoes.

Pommes de terre collerette

COLLERETTE POTATOES

Cut the potatoes into cork shapes and groove them with a special knife.

Fry in deep fat, like chip potatoes.

Pommes de terre en liards

POTATOES EN LIARDS

These are collerette potatoes without being grooved.

Pommes de terre paille

STRAW POTATOES

Cut the potatoes in long, thin julienne, put into cold water for a few moments, drain, and dry well in a cloth. Fry in hot deep fat and after a few minutes remove the frying basket and drain. Just before serving, put them again into the hot fat to make them very crisp. Drain well and sprinkle lightly with salt.

Pommes de terre Pont-neuf

DEEP FRIED POTATOES

Square off the potatoes at the sides and cut them into slices of equal thickness — about ¼ inch. Plunge them into deep fat and fry until the outside is crisp.

This is the genuine kind of fried potatoes.

Pommes de terre soufflées

SOUFFLÉ POTATOES

Square off the sides of the potatoes and cut them into slices of equal thickness — about ¼ inch. Wash them in cold water, drain and dry and put them into deep fat which is not too hot.

When the potatoes are in the fat, raise the heat which has been lowered by the immersion of the potatoes. Keep at the same temperature until they are cooked, when they will rise to the surface of the frying fat.

Remove the frying basket, reheat the fat, and when very hot put the basket back for a few minutes. The sudden contact with the very hot fat will cause the potatoes to swell. Drain well and sprinkle lightly with salt before serving.

Nids pour le dressage des pommes de terre frites

POTATO NESTS

Cut the potatoes as for straw potatoes (see page 648). Put them in a special frying basket called a 'nest mould', placing the straws one on top of the other, being careful to cut off the parts that overlap the edges of the mould. Shut the mould and fry until golden brown. Remove from the fat and unmould.

Pommes de terre gratinées

POTATOES AU GRATIN

This dish is made in several ways.

————————— *Method 1* Potato purée, grated cheese, breadcrumbs, butter

Butter a gratin dish, put in the potato purée and smooth the top. Sprinkle with cheese and breadcrumbs mixed together, brush with melted butter and brown in the oven.

————————— *Method 2* Potatoes, butter, grated cheese, cream, boiling milk, salt, pinch nutmeg, breadcrumbs

Cook some large potatoes in salted water, drain and cut into fairly thick slices. Put into buttered egg dishes or ramekins, mash lightly with a fork, add a little melted butter and sprinkle with cheese. Add a little cream to the boiling milk and add enough to moisten the potatoes. Season lightly with salt and nutmeg. Sprinkle with cheese and breadcrumbs mixed together, brush with melted butter and brown in the oven.

Gratin de pommes de terre dauphinoise

POTATOES AU GRATIN DAUPHINOISE

2 lb. potatoes, salt, freshly ground black pepper, pinch nutmeg, 1 egg, 1¼ pints (U.S. 3⅛ cups) boiled milk, grated Gruyère cheese, garlic, butter

Peel and slice the potatoes thinly. Put into a bowl with salt, pepper, nutmeg, beaten egg, milk and about 4 oz. grated cheese. Mix all well together.

Rub a casserole round with garlic, butter well and put in the potato mixture. Sprinkle liberally with grated cheese and add a few dabs butter. Cook in a moderate oven for 35 – 40 minutes.

Pommes de terre au lard

POTATOES WITH PORK

8 oz. pork fat, butter, 12 – 15 small onions, 1 tablespoon flour, 1¼ pints (U.S. 3⅛ cups) white stock, 2 lb. large potatoes, pinch pepper, *bouquet garni* of 1 sprig parsley, 1 sprig thyme and 1 bay leaf, chopped parsley

Cut the pork fat into cubes, blanch it, and brown in butter with the onions. Remove on to a plate. Add the flour to the remaining butter and cook for a few minutes. Add the stock, potatoes, cut into quarters – pork, onions, pepper and the *bouquet garni*. Cover and cook gently. Sprinkle with chopped parsley before serving.

Note Water may be used instead of stock, but extra salt will be required.

Pommes de terre Lorette

LORETTE POTATOES

Ingredients as for *pommes dauphine* (see page 646), 6 oz. grated cheese, flour

Add the cheese to the potato and chou paste mixture. Shape into pieces the size of an egg, coat with flour and fry in deep fat for 6 – 8 minutes.

Pommes de terre lyonnaise

LYONESE POTATOES

2 lb. potatoes, butter, 8 oz. onions, salt, pepper, chopped parsley

Peel and boil the potatoes, drain, and cut into slices, then sauté in butter.

Peel and thinly slice the onions and sauté in butter till cooked and golden brown. Add the potatoes, season, and cook both ingredients together for 2−3 minutes, mixing them well together.

Sprinkle with chopped parsley before serving.

Pommes de terre Macaire

POTATOES MACAIRE

Bake some large potatoes in the oven. As soon as they are cooked, cut a slice from the top and remove the pulp. Put it into a frying pan with a little butter and seasoning, and cook till brown, then put back into the potato case.

Pommes de terre Maire (spécialité du restaurant Maire)

POTATOES MAIRE (SPECIALITY OF THE RESTAURANT MAIRE)

1 lb. new potatoes, milk, salt, pepper, nutmeg, 8 oz. butter

Cook the potatoes in salted water, then peel and cut into slices. Put them into a fairly shallow pan and add enough milk to cover and season. Put the pan over fairly brisk heat and cook until the milk is reduced by two-thirds, taking care to stir round the bottom of the pan with a metal spoon. When the milk has reduced sufficiently, remove from the heat and add the butter a little at a time.

Pommes de terre à la maître d'hôtel

MAÎTRE D'HÔTEL POTATOES

Potatoes, white stock, salt, pepper, butter, chopped parsley

Peel some medium-sized potatoes and cook in salted water. Drain and cut into slices. Put into a pan and just cover with boiling stock. Add seasoning and cook until the stock has reduced completely. Add a generous quantity of butter and sprinkle with chopped parsley before serving.

Pommes de terre Mireille

SAUTÉED POTATOES WITH ARTICHOKES

1 lb. large potatoes, 8 oz. artichoke bottoms, butter, 3 oz. truffles, 3 tablespoons melted meat jelly (see page 21), chopped parsley

Cut the potatoes and artichokes into very thin slices. Heat some butter in a sauté pan, add the potatoes and artichokes and cook over brisk heat for about 10 minutes.

Put into a serving dish and mix in the sliced truffles. Melt ½ oz. butter in the meat jelly and pour over. Sprinkle with parsley.

Pommes de terre ménagère

FRIED MASHED POTATOES WITH CHIVES

2 lb. large potatoes, salt, pepper, 3 tablespoons chopped chives, 3—4 tablespoons boiling milk, flour, butter, oil or lard for frying

Cook the potatoes in salted water, then drain thoroughly and mash with a fork. Add seasoning, chives, boiling milk and mix thoroughly. Shape into small balls the size of an egg, then flatten slightly into small cakes. Coat with flour and fry on both sides.

Note 1 beaten egg may be added with the milk.

Pommes de terre Mireille à la crème

CREAMED POTATOES WITH ARTICHOKES

1 lb. large potatoes, 8 oz. artichoke bottoms, 3 oz. truffles, boiling cream, grated cheese

Prepare and cook the potatoes and artichokes as above.

Add the truffles and mix all well. Put into egg dishes or ramekin cases, and cover with boiling cream. Sprinkle generously with grated cheese and put into the oven for 4—5 minutes before serving.

Pommes de terre Mirette

POTATOES WITH TRUFFLES AND CHEESE

1 lb. potatoes, butter, 3 tablespoons chopped truffles, 4 tablespoons meat jelly (see page 21), pinch finely chopped tarragon, 2 tablespoons tomato sauce (see page 132), 1 oz. butter, grated cheese

Cut the potatoes into cubes about 1 – 1½ inches long and blanch in boiling water for 2 minutes. Drain, and cook in butter until they are tender. Add the truffles, meat jelly, tarragon, sauce and butter and mix all well together.

Put into egg dishes or ramekins, sprinkle with cheese and brush with melted butter.

Put into the oven for a few minutes before serving.

Pommes de terre Nana

POTATOES NANA

Dariole moulds are generally used for preparing potatoes Nana.

Butter them well and fill with thinly sliced potatoes. Season with salt and pepper between the layers, and cook for about 20 minutes in a hot oven.

When ready to serve, unmould and coat with château sauce (melted meat jelly (see page 21) with butter and lemon juice).

Pommes de terre Ninon

POTATOES WITH TRUFFLED FOIE GRAS

6 large potatoes, butter, truffled foie gras, 3 egg yolks, 6 tablespoons cream, seasoning, château sauce (see previous recipe)

Bake the potatoes in the oven. When cooked, remove the pulp and fry it gently in butter. Remove from heat, add about one-third its volume of truffled foie gras. Mix egg yolks and cream together and add to the potato mixture. Add seasoning and mix all well. Put into buttered dariole moulds and cook in a hot oven for 5 minutes.

Unmould and coat with château sauce.

Pommes de terre noisette

NOISETTE POTATOES

Take out pieces of potato the size of walnuts, with a vegetable scoop. Cook them gently in butter and season with salt. These potatoes should be soft and golden brown.

Pommes de terre parisienne

PARISIAN POTATOES

These are noisette potatoes, prepared as in the previous recipe, but when cooked, rolled in melted meat jelly (see page 21).

Pommes de terre persillées

POTATOES WITH PARSLEY

Boil the potatoes in salted water, then drain and add some melted butter and chopped parsley.

As a variation, fried breadcrumbs may be added.

Pommes de terre Rosine

POTATOES ROSINE

2 lb. potatoes, prepared as for croquettes (see page 646), sultanas, flour, egg and breadcrumbs, butter

Prepare the croquette mixture and add quarter amount sultanas. Divide into pieces the size of an egg and shape into flat cakes. Coat with flour, then egg and breadcrumbs, and fry in butter until brown on both sides.

Pommes de terre à la savoyarde

SAVOYARD POTATOES

Proceed as for the potatoes au gratin dauphinoise (see page 650), replacing the milk by consommé.

Pommes de terre Voisin

POTATOES VOISIN

These are prepared exactly like potatoes Anna (see page 644), except that between each layer of potatoes a thin layer of grated cheese is sprinkled. They are cooked in the same way.

Purée de pommes de terre
POTATO PURÉE

2 lb. large potatoes, 4 oz. butter, boiling milk

Peel the potatoes, cut into quarters and cook in salted water until they are just tender. Drain and dry off at the side of the stove for a few minutes. Rub through a sieve, then add butter and enough boiling milk to give the required consistency. Reheat before serving.

Note The potatoes for a purée should not be overcooked.

Quenelles de pommes de terre
POTATO QUENELLES

Potato croquette mixture (see page 646), chou pastry without sugar (see page 687), butter, grated cheese, breadcrumbs fried in butter (optional)

Prepare the croquette mixture and add quarter amount ordinary chou pastry. Shape into quenelles with a tablespoon and poach in salted water. Butter a fireproof serving dish and sprinkle it with cheese. Drain the quenelles and arrange on the dish, sprinkle with cheese, brush with melted butter and brown lightly in the oven.

Before serving, pour over a little brown butter, or sprinkle with breadcrumbs fried in butter.

As a variation, coat the quenelles with demi-glace sauce and tomato (see page 22), then sprinkle with cheese and brown in the oven.

Soufflé de pommes de terre
POTATO SOUFFLÉ

Potato purée, eggs

Prepare the purée (see above), keeping it rather firm. To about 1 lb. of the purée, add 4 egg yolks and beat in well, then add the stiffly beaten egg whites.

Put into a buttered soufflé dish and cook in a moderate oven.

Salsifis

SALSIFY

There are two kinds of salsify — white and black. The same recipes apply to both kinds. Whichever method of cooking is used, salsify must be carefully scraped and washed, and then cooked in lightly salted water to which has been added 1 dessertspoon flour for every 2 pints (U.S. 5 cups) water.

Salsifis à la crème

CREAMED SALSIFY

———————— Salsify, butter, béchamel sauce (see page 23), few tablespoons cream

Cook the salsify, drain and cut into sticks 1½−2 inches long. Sauté in butter for a few minutes, then cover with béchamel sauce. Bring to the boil for a few moments and complete the sauce with the cream.

Salsifis frits

FRIED SALSIFY

———————— Salsify, salt, pepper, squeeze lemon juice, few drops oil, pinch parsley, frying batter, deep fat for frying, fried parsley

Cook the salsify, drain and put on to a dish. Add seasoning, lemon juice, oil and parsley. Marinate for 20−25 minutes, turning from time to time. Then drain, coat with batter and fry in deep fat.

Drain and serve garnished with fried parsley.

The salsify can be coated with batter and fried without first marinating it.

Salsifis au gratin

SALSIFY AU GRATIN

———————— Salsify, béchamel sauce (see page 23), grated Gruyère cheese, grated Parmesan cheese, pinch nutmeg, breadcrumbs, butter

Cook the salsify and mix with some sauce as described in the recipe for creamed salsify (see page 656). Add a little grated Gruyère and Parmesan cheese and the nutmeg.

Arrange on a fireproof serving dish. Sprinkle with grated cheese and breadcrumbs mixed together, brush with melted butter and brown under the grill (U.S. broiler).

Salsifis à la poulette

SALSIFY WITH WHITE SAUCE

———————— Salsify, butter, salt, pepper, white sauce (see page 22), egg yolks, lemon juice, chopped parsley

Cook the salsify and cut into $2\frac{1}{2}$ – 3-inch lengths. Add a little butter and sauté for a few minutes. Season, add some white sauce. Bring to boiling point and boil for a few minutes. Just before serving, thicken with egg yolks, using 2 – 3 to each 1 pint (U.S. $2\frac{1}{2}$ cups) sauce. Finally add a little butter, lemon juice and parsley.

Salsifis sautés

SAUTÉED SALSIFY

Cook the salsify and cut into small sticks. Toss in butter until brown. Season, and serve sprinkled with chopped parsley.

Tomates à farcir

TOMATOES FOR STUFFING

As far as possible, choose firm tomatoes of medium size. If they are too large, it will be necessary to cut them in half. If they are of medium size or small a piece is cut off horizontally, at the stem end.

Press gently, to extract the seeds. Season the inside with salt and pepper, place on an oiled tray and partly cook them in the oven. Then stuff the tomatoes in various ways as desired.

Tomates farcies au gratin à la française

STUFFED TOMATOES AU GRATIN

6 tomatoes, 6 tablespoons duxelles (see page 639), demi-glace sauce with tomato (see page 22), 2 tablespoons white wine, breadcrumbs, oil, chopped parsley

Prepare the tomatoes for stuffing.

Put the duxelles into a small pan with 3 tablespoons sauce and the wine. Reduce for a few minutes, then add enough fresh breadcrumbs to stiffen.

Fill the tomatoes with the mixture, sprinkle with dry breadcrumbs and brush lightly with oil. Cook in a moderate oven. Arrange on a serving dish, pour some demi-glace sauce with tomato round and sprinkle with parsley.

Tomates farcies aux oeufs brouillés au fromage

TOMATOES STUFFED WITH SCRAMBLED EGGS AND CHEESE

Tomatoes, grated cheese, scrambled egg, butter

Prepare the tomatoes for stuffing and cook completely. Add a little cheese to the scrambled egg and fill the tomato cases. Sprinkle more cheese on top and brush lightly with melted butter. Brown very quickly under a hot grill (U.S. broiler).

Note The scrambled eggs with cheese may be replaced by scrambled eggs with ham and mushrooms, in which case the eggs should be covered with 1 tablespoon château sauce (see page 653) with a little tomato sauce added.

Tomates farcies à la piémontaise

PIEDMONT STYLE STUFFED TOMATOES

Tomatoes, risotto (see page 668), grated cheese, butter, fairly thick demi-glace sauce (see page 22)

Prepare the tomatoes for stuffing and cook them completely. Place them on a serving dish and fill with creamy risotto. Sprinkle the surface with grated cheese and brush with melted butter. Put into the oven for a few minutes and serve coated lightly with the demi-glace sauce.

Tomates farcies à la provençale
PROVENÇAL STYLE STUFFED TOMATOES

6—8 tomatoes, salt, pepper, oil, 2 tablespoons finely chopped onion, 4 tomatoes, peeled, seeded and chopped, pinch chopped parsley, 1 small clove garlic, 4 tablespoons breadcrumbs, stock, 2 fillets anchovies, breadcrumbs, grated cheese (optional)

Prepare the tomatoes for stuffing, season inside and place cut side downwards into a pan containing a little hot oil. When half cooked, turn over, cook for another minute, then arrange in a fireproof serving dish.

Brown the onion lightly in a little oil, add the chopped tomato, pinch salt, parsley and crushed garlic. Cook for 15 minutes.

Add the breadcrumbs moistened with a little stock, finely chopped anchovy fillets and, if necessary, a little more stock.

Fill the tomato cases, sprinkle with breadcrumbs or with a mixture of cheese and breadcrumbs, pour over a little oil from the pan in which the tomatoes were cooked, and put into a slow oven for about 10 minutes.

Serve hot or cold.

Tomates farcies à la semoule
TOMATOES STUFFED WITH SEMOLINA

6—8 tomatoes, 5 oz. semolina, 1 pint (U.S. 2½ cups) boiling stock, salt, pepper, nutmeg, 2 egg yolks, 1 tablespoon butter, grated cheese, breadcrumbs

Prepare and cook the tomatoes as in the previous recipe. Sprinkle the semolina into the boiling stock, season carefully and cook over low heat for 15—20 minutes.

Remove from the heat, and bind with egg yolk and butter. Add 3 tablespoons grated cheese. Stuff the tomatoes, sprinkle with a little cheese and breadcrumbs mixed together, brush with melted butter and cook in a slow oven for 5—6 minutes.

Note A few tablespoons chopped ham may be added to the semolina.

In addition to the above recipes, tomatoes may be stuffed with minced lamb, veal, chicken or sausage meat. Sprinkle with grated cheese and breadcrumbs, brush with melted butter and brown in the oven.

Tomates frites

FRIED TOMATOES

Choose medium-sized firm tomatoes, dip them into boiling water for a second and peel them. Cut into slices about ⅛ inch thick, and take out the seeds. Season with salt and pepper, dip each slice into a light batter and then into very hot deep fat. Drain and serve.

Mousse de tomates

TOMATO MOUSSE

——————— 1 tablespoon chopped onion, butter, 6 tablespoons white wine, 12 oz. ripe tomatoes, salt, pepper, cayenne pepper, 1 sprig parsley, 4 tablespoons chicken velouté sauce (see page 22), 6 tablespoons calf's foot jelly, 7–8 tablespoons thick cream

Fry the onion for 1 minute in butter, add the wine and reduce by half. Add tomatoes, coarsely chopped, seasoning and parsley. Cover, and cook over low heat for 25–30 minutes. Add sauce and calf's foot jelly. Boil for a few minutes, then strain through muslin or a tammy cloth. Check the seasoning and add the half-whipped cream. Pour into a serving dish and refrigerate until required.

Tomates sautées à la provençale

PROVENÇAL STYLE SAUTÉ TOMATOES

——————— Tomatoes, salt, pepper, oil, chopped parsley, 1 clove garlic, breadcrumbs

Cut the tomatoes in half, remove the seeds and add seasoning. Heat a little oil in a sauté pan, add the tomatoes, cut side down, and cook for a few minutes. Turn them over, sprinkle with chopped parsley, crushed garlic and breadcrumbs and put into a moderate oven for 5–6 minutes to finish the cooking.

Soufflé de tomates

TOMATO SOUFFLÉ

——————— 8 oz. thick tomato purée, 3 oz. grated Parmesan cheese, 2 tablespoons béchamel sauce (see page 23), 2 tablespoons meat jelly (see page 21), 3 egg yolks, 5 egg whites

To the tomato purée add the cheese, béchamel sauce, meat jelly and egg yolks. Fold in the stiffly beaten egg whites. Pour into a buttered soufflé dish and bake in a moderate oven.

Note As a variation, add a few thin slices of truffle, seasoned with salt and freshly ground pepper. A ragoût of sliced truffles and cock's combs browned in butter and mixed with a little Madeira sauce may be served with the soufflé.

For Madeira sauce Add a little Madeira to a well reduced demi-glace sauce (see page 22).

Topinambours au beurre

JERUSALEM ARTICHOKES WITH BUTTER

Peel and cut the artichokes into the shape of large olives and cook gently in butter.

Topinambours à la parisienne

PARISIAN STYLE JERUSALEM ARTICHOKES

Cook the artichokes in butter. When they are ready, add some boiling cream and boil for a few minutes before serving.

Topinambours à la Mornay

JERUSALEM ARTICHOKES MORNAY

Cook the artichokes in butter. Arrange on a gratin dish and coat with béchamel sauce (see page 23). Sprinkle with grated cheese, dab with butter and brown in the oven or under the grill (U.S. broiler).

Purée de topinambours

JERUSALEM ARTICHOKE PURÉE

— Artichokes, butter, mashed potatoes, seasoning

Peel and thinly slice the artichokes and cook in butter. Rub through a sieve or put through a tammy cloth. Add quarter volume of creamy mashed potato, a little butter and seasoning. Return to the pan and reheat.

Crosnes du Japon

CHINESE ARTICHOKES

However they are to be cooked, the artichokes must be very fresh.

The best way of peeling them is to rub them in a stout cloth with some coarse salt. Then put into cold water and remove the last traces of peel, blanch and dry them.

The recipes for Jerusalem artichokes may be applied to them (see pages 661).

After blanching and draining, cook in butter and roll in a few tablespoons meat jelly (see page 21). Sprinkle with chopped parsley before serving.

Editor's note Chinese artichokes are somewhat rare in Great Britain but are like Jerusalem artichokes in flavour.

Crosnes à la crème

CHINESE ARTICHOKES WITH CREAM

———— Chinese artichokes, butter, cream, pinch salt, pinch grated nutmeg

Cook the artichokes in salted water, drain well and sauté in butter for a few moments; add a little boiling cream, salt and grated nutmeg and let simmer for a few minutes.

If liked, 2−3 tablespoons thin béchamel sauce (see page 23) may be added with the cream.

Put into a serving dish and coat with either *sauce suprême* (see page 23), *sauce parisienne* (see page 22) or béchamel sauce (see page 23).

They may also be cooked in the same way as *cèpes bordelaise* (see page 601) or *cèpes provençal* (see page 602).

Purée de crosnes

CHINESE ARTICHOKE PURÉE

Proceed as instructed for artichoke purée (see page 661).

Truffes

TRUFFLES

Editor's note The following recipes aré included with the knowledge that they all require fresh truffles, which are difficult to obtain in Great Britain and America. This book, however, would not be complete without them and they will, undoubtedly, be of much interest to the student of French cuisine.

Truffes sous le cendre

TRUFFLES COOKED UNDER CHARCOAL CINDERS

Choose some nice fresh truffles, clean them carefully, but do not peel them. Salt them sparingly and add a dash of brandy.

First wrap each truffle in a thin slice of pork fat, then in two pieces of greaseproof paper, moistening the outer one with water. Lay them on a bed of hot charcoal cinders and cover with another layer of cinders. On top of this place a sheet of iron containing more cinders, so that a regular heat may be sustained.

Allow 30−45 minutes, according to the size of the truffles.

Remove the outer piece of greaseproof paper and serve on a folded napkin with butter.

Truffes au champagne

TRUFFLES IN CHAMPAGNE

Truffles, Champagne, veal stock, salt, freshly ground pepper

Select good-sized truffles and peel them carefully. Put into a pan and just cover with equal quantities of Champagne and veal stock. Add a little salt (the amount will depend on the strength of seasoning in the stock) and pepper. Cover, and boil for 5 minutes, then draw to the side of the stove and leave for 10 minutes.

Put into a serving dish, reduce the cooking liquor by two-thirds, strain over the truffles. Serve at once.

Truffes à la crème
CREAMED TRUFFLES

8 oz. truffles, 1 oz. butter, 2—3 tablespoons Madeira, 2 tablespoons meat jelly (see page 21), salt, freshly ground pepper, cream, béchamel sauce (see page 23)

Peel the truffles and cut into fairly thick slices. Put into a pan with ½ oz. butter, Madeira and meat jelly. Add a little seasoning, cover and boil for 2 seconds. Remove from the heat. Add a little cream to the béchamel sauce and pour over the truffles. Bring to boiling point again and finally add the remaining butter.

Truffes à la serviette
TRUFFLES WITH MADEIRA

Truffles, Madeira, veal stock, salt, freshly ground pepper

Follow the recipe for truffles in Champagne (see page 663), but replace the Champagne by Madeira.

Timbale de truffes
TIMBALE OF TRUFFLES

Ordinary pastry (see page 547), slices pork fat, truffles, salt, pepper, 2—3 tablespoons meat jelly (see page 21), 6 tablespoons Madeira, egg for glazing

Line a buttered timbale mould or charlotte tin with pastry. Arrange some slices of pork fat on the bottom and round the sides. Fill with the peeled truffles and add a little seasoning. Put the meat jelly and Madeira together in a pan and bring to boiling point. Pour over the truffles.

Cover with another slice of pork fat. Cover with a pastry lid. Brush over with beaten egg and cook for 40—50 minutes in a hot oven.

When cooked, unmould and serve on a table napkin.

Pâtes alimentaires
FARINACEOUS DISHES

Le riz

RICE

Rice is the best, the most nutritive and unquestionably the most widespread foodstuff in the world.

Note It is always as well to wash rice before cooking it.

Riz pour hors-d'oeuvre et salades

RICE FOR HORS-D'OEUVRE AND SALADS

Wash 8 oz. rice and cook for 18 minutes in 3 pints (U.S. 7½ cups) fast-boiling water to which 1 teaspoon salt has been added. Pour the rice on to a sieve, cool a little, then pour hot water over and drain again.

The wise housewife will keep the water in which the rice has been cooked, as it can be used for a vegetable soup. This water contains part of the rice starch, which is highly nutritive.

Riz à l'anglaise

RICE COOKED IN THE ENGLISH WAY

Cook the rice in salted water, as indicated for Indian rice (see page 668), drain, and dry on a sieve. Put it into a vegetable dish and add some melted butter.

One-third of its volume of boiled peas may be added to this.

One may serve this rice as a vegetable to accompany meat.

Riz au beurre

BUTTERED RICE

——————— You will need for 4—5 persons: 8 oz. rice, 3 oz. butter, ¼ teaspoon salt, 1 pint (U.S. 2½ cups) hot water

Put the rice into a saucepan of convenient size with half the butter, salt and water. Cover and cook for 18 minutes over a brisk heat. At this point the rice should be cooked and should have absorbed all the liquid. Take the saucepan from the fire and with a fork mix the rest of the butter with the rice.

Rice prepared in this way may be eaten as a vegetable and served with fish, poultry, meat, etc.

Riz à la créole

CREOLE RICE

——————— 8 oz. rice, 1 pint (U.S. 2½ cups) water, 1 level teaspoon salt, 2 oz. lard

Put the rice into a pan with the hot water, salt and 1 oz. lard. Cover and cook for 18 minutes over fairly brisk heat. At this point the rice should be cooked and should have absorbed all the liquid. Add the rest of the lard, mixing it in well with a fork.

Cubans generally serve this rice at all meals, and particularly with fried eggs.

ANOTHER METHOD

——————— 2 oz. lard, 1 finely chopped onion, 1—2 small sweet peppers, 3—4 tomatoes, 8 oz. rice, 1 pint (U.S. 2½ cups) boiling stock, pinch saffron (optional)

Heat the lard, add the onion and cook till lightly browned. Add the thinly sliced peppers and tomatoes, peeled, seeded and chopped. Cook for a few minutes, add the rice and stock. Cover and cook for 20 minutes. Add the saffron if used.

Riz au curry

CURRIED RICE

———————— 1 tablespoon chopped onion, butter, 2 teaspoons mild curry powder, 8 oz. rice, 1 pint (U.S. 2½ cups) boiling stock

Brown the onion lightly in 2 oz. butter. Add curry powder and rice and stir for a few minutes with a wooden spoon until the rice is hot. Add the stock, cover and cook for 18 minutes. Remove from the heat and add a few dabs of butter.

Note Fish stock can be used if more applicable.

Riz à la fermière

RICE WITH CABBAGE AND BACON

———————— ½ cabbage, 2 oz. lard, 1 large onion, 8 oz. streaky bacon, 1 lb. rice, 2¼ pints (U.S. 6¼ cups), boiling water, ½ teaspoon salt, pinch pepper, grated cheese

Cut the cabbage into julienne and cook for 12 minutes in boiling salted water. Drain well.

Heat the lard in a large pan, add chopped onion and bacon, cubed and blanched. Cook until onion begins to brown, then add cabbage and continue cooking for 10 – 12 minutes. Add rice, water and seasoning. Cover and cook for 25 minutes.

Remove from the heat and stir in 3 – 4 tablespoons grated cheese.

Riz au gras à la française

RICE WITH NUTMEG

———————— 8 oz. rice, 1 oz. butter, salt, pepper, nutmeg, 1 pint (U.S. 2½ cups) boiling stock

Cook the rice in 2 pints (U.S. 5 cups) salted boiling water for 2 minutes, drain well. Heat the butter in a pan, add rice, seasoning and pinch nutmeg. Sauté for 2 minutes, add stock, cover and cook for 18 – 20 minutes.

If the rice is to accompany boiled chicken, use the stock for cooking the rice.

Riz à la milanaise

RICE COOKED IN THE MILANESE WAY

—————— 8 oz. rice, 3 oz. butter, 1 tablespoon finely chopped onion, salt, pepper, 1 pint (U.S. 2½ cups) boiling consommé or veal stock, 3—4 tablespoons grated Parmesan cheese

Cook the rice for 18 minutes as for pilaf (see page 669). Remove from the heat, add the remaining 2 oz. butter in little pieces and finally add the cheese.

Riz à l'indienne

INDIAN RICE

Cook 8 oz. rice in 2½ pints (U.S. 6¼ cups) boiling water with 1 teaspoon salt for 18 minutes. Drain on a sieve and dry off for a few minutes in the oven before serving.

Use as an accompaniment to curried eggs, fish, lamb or poultry.

Note Indian rice may be steamed instead of boiled.

Riz à la piémontaise

RICE COOKED IN THE PIEDMONT WAY (RISOTTO)

—————— 4 oz. butter, 1 tablespoon finely chopped onion, 8 oz. rice*, salt, pepper, 1 pint (U.S. 2½ cups) boiling consommé, grated Parmesan cheese
*Piedmont rice is best for this dish, but if not obtainable use Carolina.

Heat half the butter in a pan, add the onion, and when it begins to brown mix in the rice and stir with a wooden spoon for 1 minute and add seasoning. Add one-third of consommé, continue to stir, and, when liquid is absorbed, add another one-third of consommé. When absorbed, add the rest. Continue cooking and continue to stir the rice. By this process a creamy rice is obtained to which finally the rest of the butter and cheese is added.

Note If preferred, the risotto can be cooked by adding the consommé all at once, in which case the pan should be covered and the rice cooked without stirring. Butter and grated cheese is then added as before.
Also a little chopped ham and sliced white Piedmont truffles may be

added. Rice is a popular basis or accompaniment for ragoûts, chicken sauté, game, etc.
Italians prefer the rice rather undercooked, generally 15—16 minutes is allowed.

Riz pilaw

RICE PILAF

—————— 1 tablespoon finely chopped onion, 2 oz. butter, 8 oz. rice, salt, pepper, 1 pint (U.S. 2½ cups) boiling consommé or veal stock

Brown the onion in 1 oz. butter. Add rice and seasoning and cook for 1 minute, stirring well so that the rice is fully impregnated with the butter. Add the consommé, cover and cook for 18 minutes. Remove from the heat and add the rest of the butter.
Rice pilaf is a good accompaniment to many egg, fish, meat, poultry and vegetable dishes.

Riz à la portugaise

PORTUGUESE STYLE RICE

—————— 3 tablespoons oil, 1 tablespoon chopped onion, 8 oz. rice, 2 sweet peppers, grilled (U.S. broiled) and skinned, 2 tomatoes, salt, pepper, pinch saffron, 1 pint (U.S. 2½ cups) boiling stock

Heat the oil, add the onion and sauté until it begins to brown. Add rice, chopped sweet peppers, tomatoes, peeled, seeded and chopped, seasoning, saffron and stock.
Cover, and cook for 18 minutes.
Sausages are usually served with rice cooked in this way.

Riz au paprika

RICE WITH PAPRIKA

Proceed exactly as for curried rice (see page 667), simply replacing the curry powder with paprika. Add ordinary stock or fish stock, as required.
Both curried rice and rice with paprika can be served as accompaniments to dishes of fish, poultry or meat.

Riz à la turque

RICE IN THE TURKISH WAY

This is rice pilaf (see page 669) to which is added sautéed tomatoes, aubergines, baby marrows, ladies' fingers, etc.

Turks and Oriental people in general use mutton fat for cooking these dishes.

Riz préparé pour farcir les volailles

RICE FOR STUFFING POULTRY

For poached chicken with *sauce suprême* (see page 23)

————— *Riz au gras à la française* (see page 667), truffles, ham, mushrooms cooked in butter, foie gras, cut into pieces

To the required amount of rice for stuffing add some truffles, ham and mushrooms cut into julienne, and a little foie gras.

For pot-roasted chicken.

————— *riz pilaw* (see page 669), truffles, foie gras, 2—3 tablespoons meat jelly (see page 21), cock's kidneys browned in butter, butter

To the required amount of rice, add some chopped truffles and foie gras, meat jelly, few cock's kidneys and a little butter.

Eau de riz

RICE WATER

————— 5 oz. rice, 2½ pints (U.S. 6¼ cups) water, 4 oz. sugar, lemon or orange slices

Boil the rice in the water for 20—25 minutes. Strain the water off into a jug, add the sugar and a few lemon or orange slices. Keep in a cool place.

This is a nourishing drink which is very pleasant during the hot weather. It may be mixed with soda water if liked.

The rice may be used in a vegetable soup, or browned in butter, or added to cooked fish, prawns (U.S. shrimps), lobster, tunny fish, various vegetables, etc., to make small salads for hors-d'oeuvre.

Fondues au parmesan (mode belge)

PARMESAN FONDUE (BELGIAN METHOD)

————————— 2½ oz. butter, 2¼ oz. flour, 1 pint (U.S. 2½ cups) milk, salt, pepper, nutmeg, 5 egg yolks, 3 oz. grated Parmesan cheese, flour, egg and breadcrumbs for coating, fried parsley, pinch cayenne pepper (optional)

Prepare a white roux with the butter and flour. Add the milk gradually and stir till boiling. Season and cook uncovered, over low heat for 25 minutes.

Remove the skin which will have formed on top and add the egg yolks and cheese.

Turn out on to a flat buttered dish, spread a little butter on top and leave to cool.

Turn out on to a floured board and cut into rounds with a 1 – 1½-inch round cutter.

Coat with flour, then with egg and breadcrumbs and fry in deep fat.

Serve on a table napkin with fried parsley.

These fondues are generally served as an hors-d'oeuvre or savoury. A pinch of cayenne pepper may be added to taste.

GNOCCHI AU GRATIN

————————— 1 pint (U.S. 2½ cups) milk, pinch salt, pinch nutmeg, 4 oz. butter, 8 oz. flour, 6 eggs, 5 oz. grated Parmesan cheese, béchamel sauce (see page 23), melted butter

Put the milk, salt, nutmeg and butter into a pan and bring to boiling point.

Remove from the heat and add the sifted flour. Mix well, return to the heat and cook over fairly brisk heat until the mixture leaves the sides of the pan cleanly. Remove from the heat and add eggs one at a time, beating each in thoroughly before the next is added. Add 4 oz. grated cheese.

Drop pieces the size of a walnut into boiling salted water, and cook until they rise to the surface.

Put a little béchamel sauce into the bottom of a gratin dish. Arrange the drained gnocchi in the dish and coat with the sauce. Sprinkle with the remaining cheese and brush with melted butter. Brown in the oven o r under the grill (U.S. broiler).

Gnocchi à la romaine

ROMAN GNOCCHI

1¾ pints (U.S. 4¼ cups) milk, 8 oz. semolina, salt, pepper, nutmeg, 2 egg yolks, grated Gruyère cheese, grated Parmesan cheese

Boil the milk, sprinkle in the semolina, season and cook over low heat for 20 minutes. Remove from the heat and stir in the egg yolks.

Turn on to a damp dish and spread out about ¼ inch thick.

When quite cold, cut into rounds with a 2-inch cutter. Put the rounds into a buttered dish, sprinkle with a little Gruyère and Parmesan cheese mixed together and brown quickly in the oven or under the grill (U.S. broiler).

Note 3—4 oz. grated Parmesan cheese may be added to the semolina with the egg yolks.

Gnocchi de pommes de terre

POTATO GNOCCHI

2 lb. potatoes, 4 oz. butter, 2 whole eggs, 2 egg yolks, 5 oz. flour, salt, pepper, nutmeg, grated cheese, butter

Boil the potatoes, drain well, and rub through a sieve. Add the butter, eggs, flour and seasonings.

Divide into pieces the size of a pigeon's egg, roll into balls and then flatten slightly with a fork. Poach in boiling salted water and drain on a cloth.

Butter a gratin dish and arrange the gnocchi in layers, sprinkling cheese between each layer. Brush with melted butter and brown in the oven.

The gnocchi can also be floured and fried in butter till brown on both sides. Put on to a serving dish and sprinkle with grated cheese. Add a little more butter to that left in the pan, heat until lightly browned, then pour over the gnocchi.

Note Gnocchi can be shaped with a tablespoon and cooked as directed for quenelles (see page 56).

Noques au parmesan

NOQUES WITH PARMESAN CHEESE

8 oz. butter, 2 whole eggs, 2 egg yolks, salt, pepper, nutmeg, 5 oz. flour, 1 egg white, grated Parmesan cheese, browned butter

Put the butter into a warm bowl and beat for a few minutes. Gradually add the lightly beaten eggs and egg yolks. Season, add the flour and stiffly beaten egg white. Drop a dessertspoon of mixture at a time into boiling water and poach for a few minutes, then drain on a cloth.

Put into a serving dish, sprinkle liberally with grated cheese and pour over a little browned butter.

POLENTA

Polenta is an exclusively Piedmontese preparation made from maize flour. To get the best results, the maize should be ground the day before it is used.

The people of Piedmont are very fond of this dish and use it for many purposes. A special pan and spatula is generally reserved for polenta.

TO COOK POLENTA

1 lb. maize flour, 3½ pints (U.S. 8¾ cups) water, 1 teaspoon salt, grated cheese, melted butter

Sprinkle the maize flour slowly into the salted water and cook for 20 minutes, stirring all the time. Pour on to a board or buttered dish and spread evenly. Mark into pieces, sprinkle with grated cheese and melted butter. When cold, the polenta can be cut into slices and grilled (U.S. broiled) and served in place of bread.

It can also be cut into fancy shapes, coated with flour and browned in butter or oil.

Polenta is sometimes served as an accompaniment to small birds cooked in butter.

Put pieces of polenta, sprinkled with cheese and melted butter into a buttered charlotte mould lined with thin slices of white truffle. Cook in a moderate oven, then unmould and surround with the small birds.

Add 6 tablespoons white wine and some rather thick gravy to the butter left in the pan in which the birds were cooked. Boil up and pour over the polenta and the birds. Sprinkle with grated Parmesan cheese and serve with a demi-glace with tomato sauce (see page 22).

LASAGNE

This is a kind of pasta cut in ribbons and slightly crimped. Lasagne may be prepared like macaroni and noodles.

MACARONI

Macaroni is cooked in boiling water, salted at the rate of ¼ oz. salt to 2 pints (U.S. 5 cups) water. The time of cooking depends upon the quality of the flour used to make the macaroni.

Neapolitan macaroni requires 14 minutes boiling time. A glass of cold water is then added to arrest the cooking, and it is immediately drained. Macaroni, and similar pasta, must never be allowed to cool, and should only be cooked just before it is required. Macaroni reheated is very unsatisfactory.

MACARONI AU GRATIN

8 oz. macaroni, 1 oz. butter, 3 oz. grated Gruyère cheese, 3 oz. grated Parmesan cheese, salt, pepper, nutmeg, 2 tablespoons béchamel sauce (see page 23), breadcrumbs

Cook the macaroni in salted water and drain thoroughly. Add butter, 2 oz. grated Gruyère and 2 oz. grated Parmesan cheese, seasoning and sauce. Mix all well together. Put into a buttered gratin dish, sprinkle with the rest of the cheese mixed with some breadcrumbs, and brown in the oven.

Macaroni à l'italienne

ITALIAN MACARONI

1 lb. macaroni, salt, pepper, nutmeg, 2 oz. grated Gruyère cheese, 2 oz. grated Parmesan cheese, 2 oz. butter

Cook the macaroni in boiling salted water and drain thoroughly. Season, add the cheese and the butter, a little at a time. Mix all well together before serving.

Macaroni au jus

MACARONI WITH GRAVY

8 oz. macaroni, 2—3 tablespoons good beef stock, 1 oz. butter, 1½ oz. grated Parmesan cheese, 1½ oz. grated Gruyère cheese, pinch freshly ground pepper

Cook the macaroni in 2 pints (U.S. 5 cups) salted water for 12 minutes. Drain thoroughly.

Add the stock and continue to cook until the macaroni has absorbed the stock.

Add butter, cheese and pepper. Mix all well together and serve with a demi-glace sauce (see page 22).

This may have a garnish of truffles, mushrooms, cock's combs and kidneys or calf's sweetbread mixed with a thick demi-glace sauce.

2—3 tablespoons mashed truffled foie gras may also be added to the garnish.

Macaroni dit à la milanaise

MILANESE STYLE MACARONI

1 lb. macaroni, salt, pepper, nutmeg, 2 oz. grated Gruyère cheese, 2 oz. grated Parmesan cheese, 2 oz. butter
Garnish Ham, tongue, mushrooms, truffles, demi-glace sauce with tomato (see page 22)

Cook and finish the macaroni as described for *macaroni à l'italienne* (see page 674).

Cut all the ingredients for the garnish into julienne and mix with the sauce.

Macaroni Nantua

MACARONI NANTUA

Prepare 8 oz. creamed macaroni with truffles (see below) and complete it with 2 oz. crayfish butter (see page 114) and 24 crayfish tails. Put some thin slices of truffle on the macaroni.

Macaroni napolitaine

NAPLES STYLE MACARONI

———————— Braised beef, red or white wine, tomatoes, macaroni, grated Parmesan cheese

Braise the beef in red or white wine and include some tomatoes. The meat must be cooked for a long time, until it is almost reduced to a purée, then rub all through a sieve.

Cook the macaroni in boiling salted water, until just tender, then drain. Sprinkle the bottom of a deep dish with grated cheese, cover with a layer of the meat purée, then a layer of macaroni and continue in layers until the ingredients are used up.

Macaroni aux truffes

MACARONI WITH TRUFFLES

———————— 8 oz. macaroni, 2 oz. butter, 2 oz. grated Parmesan cheese, 2 oz. grated Gruyère cheese, salt, pepper, nutmeg, cream, 6—8 tablespoons béchamel sauce (see page 23), 3 oz. truffles

Cook the macaroni in salted water and drain thoroughly. Add the butter, cheese and seasoning. Add a little cream to the sauce, and add to the macaroni with the thinly sliced truffles. Serve in a dish or in a vol-au-vent case.

If preferred, this dish can be finished as for *macaroni au gratin* (see page 674).

CANNELONI

This is a kind of pasta which can be bought in the form of a tube 4 inches long and about 1¼ inches in diameter.

Canneloni farcis

STUFFED CANNELONI

Canneloni, chicken forcemeat, foie gras, game, meat or *farce à gratin* (see page 58), grated cheese, demi-glace sauce with tomato (see page 22), butter

Cook the canneloni like macaroni and drain well. Split lengthwise and fill with the chosen forcemeat, then re-shape.

Place side by side in a fireproof serving dish, sprinkle with cheese and coat with the sauce. Sprinkle more cheese on top, dot with butter, and put into a very moderate oven for a few minutes, so that the cheese mixes well with the sauce. Serve at once.

Note Canneloni can be made by very thinly rolling out some noodle pasta (see below). Cut into pieces about 4 inches long and 2½ inches wide, and cook in salted water.

Nouilles

NOODLES

These are usually bought ready to cook. But if possible, it is better to make the paste oneself and have it fresh.

1 lb. flour, ½ oz. salt, 4 whole eggs, 5 egg yolks

Sift the flour and salt, add the beaten eggs and yolks and enough water to make a firm paste. Roll and fold twice, and cool for 1 hour before using.

Cook the noodles in salted water like macaroni. All the recipes given for macaroni are applicable.

For *nouilles à l'alsacienne* it is usual to serve them on crisp noodles, made by sautéing the raw noodles in butter.

Ravioli

PREPARATION OF RAVIOLI

There are several ways of making ravioli. Formerly the ravioli pastry was rolled out very thinly into a large square.

About 1–1½ inches from the edge of the square of pastry, place a teaspoon of the stuffing, and continue doing so down the pastry, leaving about ¾ inch between. Brush round the stuffing with a wet brush and cover with a second layer of pastry. Press the spaces between the ravioli with the finger to seal them, then with the aid of a roulette divide up the ravioli. They should be about 1¼ inches across. If you have no roulette, divide them with a knife. Continue until all the stuffing is used.

COOKING RAVIOLI

Put the ravioli into a saucepan of lightly salted boiling water and cook for 10–12 minutes. Take them out of the water with a skimmer and place on a napkin folded in four, to dry thoroughly. Sprinkle the serving dish with grated cheese and 2–3 tablespoons of the daube gravy. Arrange the ravioli in layers, alternating each layer with grated cheese and gravy.

Cover and keep hot for some minutes, to give the cheese and gravy time to mix well.

Note A few tablespoons tomato sauce may be added to the daube gravy.

I have given the old Provençal recipe for ravioli, but, for the stuffing, the beef may be replaced by braised veal, chicken with foie gras added, or with left-over meats.

In this case, instead of the gravy from the daube, fairly thick demi-glace sauce with tomato (see page 22) may be used.

Note Ravioli is considered an excellent family dish but gourmets do not despise it.

Ravioli may well replace macaroni in the preparation of timbales, either of fish, calf's sweetbreads, chicken or game, and it may serve as accompaniment to various poultry dishes, braised or sautéed.

When demi-glace sauce is not available, the following makes an excellent substitute:

———— 2 oz. butter, 2 tablespoons chopped streaky bacon, 2 tablespoons chopped onion, 2 tablespoons chopped carrot, 6 tablespoons white wine, 12 oz. tomato, salt, pepper, parsley, 1 bay leaf, 1 small clove garlic

Melt the butter in a pan, add the bacon, onion and carrot and sauté until lightly browned. Add the wine, chopped tomatoes, seasoning and herbs. Cover and simmer for 30 – 35 minutes, then strain through a fine sieve.

Ravioli à la provençale

PROVENÇAL STYLE RAVIOLI

To prepare this dish in the old Provençal style, it is necessary to prepare a daube of beef the day before.

The meat will serve as a foundation for the forcemeat and the gravy will cover the ravioli.

PROVENÇAL STYLE DAUBE OF BEEF

———— 2 lb. chuck steak or silverside, 2 large onions, 2 carrots, salt, pepper, spice, *bouquet garni* of 1 bay leaf, 1 sprig parsley and 1 sprig thyme, 2 cloves garlic, 1 bottle red wine, 2 – 3 tablespoons vinegar, 2 oz. pork fat, 4 tablespoons oil, 1 strip orange peel, ½ pint (U.S. 1¼ cups) hot water

Cut the beef into pieces of about 3 – 4 oz. and put them into a bowl with 1 onion cut into quarters, sliced carrots, salt, pepper, spice, *bouquet garni* and the garlic. Add the wine and vinegar and leave to marinate for 4 – 5 hours. Chop the pork fat, and put into a pan with the oil and 1 chopped onion. Brown lightly, add the meat drained from the marinade and cook for 12 – 15 minutes, stirring occasionally. Add the marinade, liquid and vegetables, *bouquet garni* and strip of orange peel. Cover and cook until the liquid has reduced by half. Add the hot water, cover and simmer for about 5 hours.

Cool a little, remove the meat and put to one side.
Strain the liquor, and leave to get cold.

Farce à ravioli

RAVIOLI STUFFING

──────── Beef from the daube, spinach, ½ brain, butter, salt, pepper, 2 egg yolks, 2—3 tablespoons grated Parmesan cheese, 2—3 tablespoons liquor from the daube

Pound meat well. Add one-third its quantity of spinach, blanched in salted water, chopped and browned in butter, the ½ brain sautéed in butter, seasoning, egg yolks, cheese and liquor from the daube, from which the fat should not have been removed.

Check the seasoning and strain through a tammy cloth or sieve.

Pâte à ravioli

RAVIOLI PASTE

──────── 1 lb. flour, pinch salt, 2 tablespoons oil, ¼—½ pint (U.S. ⅝—1¼ cups) warm water

Sieve the flour and salt on to a table and spread into a ring. Put the oil and ¼ pint (U.S. ⅝ cup) warm water into the centre and gradually work the flour into it, adding extra water as required to make a firm but pliable paste. Avoid too much kneading. Roll the paste into a ball and leave to rest for 30—40 minutes.

Entremets

SWEETS

PÂTES ET COMPOSITIONS DIVERSES

VARIOUS PASTES AND PASTRY

Feuilletage

PUFF PASTRY

1 lb. flour, ¼ oz. salt, ½ pint (U.S. 1¼ cups) water, 1 lb. butter

Sift the flour and salt into a bowl and mix to a paste with the water. Avoid kneading too much and leave for 20 minutes.

Roll into a square of about 8 inches and of even thickness. Put the slightly softened butter in the centre, fold the edges of the paste in towards the centre, enclosing the butter completely.

Leave to rest for 10 minutes, then roll into an oblong. Fold in 3 and roll again.

Repeat four times, leaving the pastry to rest for 10 minutes after the second and fourth rollings.

The rolling distributes the butter evenly throughout the paste, and ensures even rising. After the sixth rolling, leave again to rest before use.

MAKING PUFF PASTRY

To get a perfect puff pastry, the two ingredients which constitute it (the dough and the butter) must be of exactly the same consistency.

The butter must always be 'worked' or softened before adding to the paste. This is done by putting the butter in the middle of a tea towel lightly sprinkled with flour. The edges of the cloth are now drawn together so that the butter is completely enveloped and can then be softened with the palm of the hand. During the preparation, the pastry should be kept cool, but it must never be placed directly on ice. To ensure that the butter is evenly distributed, the rolling must be done evenly and without hurrying.

Pâte à foncer ordinaire

ORDINARY LINING PASTE

——————— 1 lb. flour, ¼ oz. salt, 8 oz. butter, ⅜ pint (U.S. approx. 1 cup) water

Sift the flour and salt on to a board and arrange in a ring. Put the softened butter and water in the centre and gradually work in the flour. Knead well, shape into a ball and wrap in a cloth. Keep cool until required.

Note Kneading is done by working the paste beneath the palm of the hand, pushing it away from the worker. The object is to obtain a perfectly smooth blending of all the ingredients.

Pâte à foncer fine (pour tartes aux fruits et flans speciaux)

FINE LINING PASTRY (FOR FRUIT TARTS AND SPECIAL FLANS)

——————— 1 lb. flour, ¼ oz. salt, 2 oz. castor sugar, 2 egg yolks, 10 oz. softened butter, ¼ pint (U.S. ⅝ cup) water

Sift the flour and salt on to a board and arrange in a ring. Put the other ingredients in the centre and mix well. Work in flour gradually; knead twice. Form into a ball, roll in a cloth and keep cool until required.

Rognures ou demi-feuilletage

PUFF PASTE TRIMMINGS OR HALF PUFF PASTE

The puff paste trimmings can be used as cases for tartlets and barquettes and for croûtons, etc.

They should be collected into a ball and kept until wanted in a cool place. They should, however, be used within 48 hours.

Pâte à galette ordinaire
ORDINARY BISCUIT PASTE
▬▬▬▬▬▬ 1 lb. flour, ¼ oz. salt, ½ oz. sugar, 9½ oz. butter, ¼ pint (U.S. ⅝ cup) water

Make a paste as in the previous recipe but do not knead. Let it rest in a cool place for 1 hour.

Roll out three times, leaving an interval of 8−10 minutes between each. After rolling the last time, let the pastry rest for some minutes before using.

Pâte sèche sucrée pour différents usages
SWEET SHORT PASTRY FOR VARIOUS USES
▬▬▬▬▬▬ 1 lb. sifted flour, 7 oz. butter, 5 oz. sugar, 3 eggs, ½ tablespoon orange flower water

Make a paste in the usual manner, knead it twice, and keep it cool until required.

Pâte à petits gâteaux
PASTRY FOR SMALL TEA BISCUITS
▬▬▬▬▬▬ 1 lb. sifted flour, 10 oz. butter, 10 oz. castor sugar, 1 whole egg, 4 egg yolks, 1 tablespoon orange flower water

Mix ingredients as usual, roll out the pastry twice, put it in a cloth in a bowl and leave in a cool place for 1 hour.

Roll out about ⅛ inch thick and cut into shapes with a pastry cutter. Put the biscuits on a tray and glaze with egg yolks. Decorate with split almonds, crystallised half cherries, angelica, crystallised orange peel, etc. Cook in a hot oven. When the biscuits are cooked, brush over with gum arabic.

Note Gumming is a process for making the surface of cakes and biscuits glossy. The gum arabic is applied with a small brush.

Editor's note A syrup made with milk and sugar may be used instead of gum arabic.

Galette de plomb

SMALL GALETTES

▬▬▬▬▬▬ 1 lb. flour, ¼ oz. salt, 12 oz. butter, ½ oz. castor sugar, 1 whole egg, 2 egg yolks, ¼ pint (U.S. ⅝ cup) milk

Make the paste as described in the previous recipes. Roll into a ball and leave in a cool place for 2 hours.

Roll out the paste about ½ inch thick and cut into rounds of the size required.

Put on to a wetted baking tray, decorate the edge and glaze with beaten egg. Score the top of the galettes with the point of a knife and cook in a fairly hot oven.

Pâte à dumplings et à poudings (cuisine anglaise)

DUMPLING AND PUDDING DOUGH (ENGLISH RECIPE)

▬▬▬▬▬▬ 1 lb. flour, ¼ oz. salt, 1 lb. dry beef suet, about ¼ pint (U.S. ⅝ cup) water, 2 oz. sugar*
*Only if the paste is to be used for fruit puddings.

Sift the flour and salt into a basin. Remove any skin from the suet and chop finely. Mix with the flour and add enough water to make a fairly firm dough. Do not knead. Keep in a cool place until required for use.

Pâte à brioche ordinaire

ORDINARY BRIOCHE DOUGH

▬▬▬▬▬▬ 1 lb. sifted flour, ½ oz. dry yeast, water, 6 eggs, ¼ oz. salt, 1 oz. sugar, 8 oz. butter

Put 4 oz. flour into a basin. Make a well in the middle, add the yeast and a little warm water and mix well. Add a little more water to make a fairly soft dough which forms the leaven. Roll into a ball, make a double incision in the form of a cross, cover and leave in a warm place until it doubles its size.

Put the rest of the flour in a bowl, make a well in the centre, add 2 tablespoons water or milk and 4 eggs. Mix well and knead the dough thoroughly. Add the other 2 eggs, one at a time, continuing the kneading. Work in the salt and sugar dissolved in a little warm water, then the softened butter. Mix all very well together.

When the 'leaven' has doubled its size, work it into the dough, kneading and mixing well. Cover the bowl and keep in a temperate place for 10–12 hours.

After 5–6 hours, remove the dough to a floured board, beat it with the hand to arrest the fermentation, then put it back into the bowl, cover and leave for a further 5–6 hours.

Note By increasing the amount of butter used, a much finer brioche is obtained; it may be increased to 1 lb., but 14 oz. is better. The amounts of the other ingredients remain the same.

The more butter used in the brioche, the less kneading it requires.

This paste is used for various timbales of fruit, in which case the dough is placed in a charlotte mould to ferment and cook.

Pâte à brioche mousseline

MOUSSELINE BRIOCHE DOUGH

———————— 2 oz. softened butter, 1 lb. brioche dough as in the previous recipe

Mix the butter well into the dough.

Butter a mould or charlotte tin and put in the dough, being careful the mould is not more than two-thirds full.

Put aside in a warm place until the dough has risen to the top of the mould. Brush with melted butter, and cook in a moderate oven.

Pâte à brioche commune

COMMON BRIOCHE DOUGH

———————— 1 lb. sifted flour, ¼ oz. dry, fresh yeast, 6 tablespoons warm milk, 4 eggs, ¼ oz. salt, 7 oz. butter

Make a leaven with 4 oz. flour, the yeast and the milk.

Knead the dough like that of the ordinary brioche (see page 684) and proceed in exactly the same way.

Note This dough should be kept fairly stiff, as it is rolled out with a rolling pin.

If it is specially prepared for *coulibiac*, the ingredients remain the same, but the sugar is omitted.

Editor's note Coulibiac is a hot fish pie.

Pâte à beignets viennoise

BATTER FOR VIENNA FRITTERS

———— 1 lb. sifted flour, 7 oz. butter, 6 eggs, ⅝ oz. yeast, ¼ oz. salt, 1 oz. sugar, 6 tablespoons warm water

Proceed in exactly the same way as for ordinary brioche dough (see page 684).

Pâte à Savarin

SAVARIN DOUGH

———— 1 lb. flour, ⅝ oz. yeast, 6 tablespoons warm milk, 8 eggs, 12 oz. butter, ¼ oz. salt, 1 oz. sugar

Sift the flour into a wooden bowl. Make a hole in the centre, add the yeast and the milk. Add the eggs and mix the dough with the hands for a few minutes. Scrape off the pieces that adhere to the sides of the bowl and mix with the rest of the dough. Dot the surface with the softened butter divided into small pieces. Cover and keep in a fairly warm place until it doubles in size.

Add the salt, knead the dough with the hands to incorporate the butter and beat it vigorously until it is firm enough to be lifted in one piece.

Add the sugar and knead for some moments until the sugar is well mixed.

Note Savarin moulds should not be more than one-third full, as the dough will rise considerably.

Pâte à baba

BABA BATTER

———— 1 lb. sifted flour, 10 oz. butter, 7 eggs, ⅝ oz. yeast, ¼ oz. salt, ½ oz. sugar, 6 tablespoons warm milk, 1½ oz. sultanas, 1¼ oz. currants

Proceed in the same way as for Savarin dough (see previous recipe), adding the fruit at the end, with the sugar. As in the case of the savarins, the moulds must not be filled more than one-third full.

Pâte à Mazarine

MAZARIN BATTER

Take the required amount of ordinary brioche dough (see page 684) and add the same quantity of baba batter (see page 686), a little at a time. Mould in plain Genoese cake tins.

Pâte à chou ordinaire

ORDINARY CHOU PASTE

1 pint (U.S. 5 cups) water, 8 oz. butter, 2 level teaspoons salt, ¾ oz. sugar, 12 oz. sifted flour, 8 eggs, few drops orange flower water

Put the water, butter, salt and sugar into a pan and bring to boiling point. Remove from the heat, add the flour and mix well. Return to the heat, and cook fairly quickly until the paste leaves the sides of the pan. Remove from the heat and beat in the eggs, two at a time, being careful that the egg is well mixed in before adding any more. Finally, add the orange flower water.

Pâte à beignets soufflés

PASTE FOR SOUFFLÉ FRITTERS

Generous ¾ pint (U.S. 2⅛ cups) water, 3½ oz. butter, 1½ level teaspoons salt, ¼ oz. sugar, 12 oz. sifted flour, 6−7 eggs, according to size

Put the water, butter, salt and sugar into a pan and bring to boiling point. Remove from the heat, add the flour and mix well. Return to the heat and cook until the paste leaves the sides of the pan. Remove from the heat and add the eggs, two at a time, mixing well between each addition.

This paste can be used for gnocchi or *pommes dauphine* (see pages 671, 646), etc., in which case the sugar is omitted.

Pâte à ramequins et à gougère

RAMEKIN OR GOUGÈRE BATTER

The preparation of this paste is the same as that of ordinary chou paste (see page 687), observing the following modifications:

1 Replace the water by the same quantity of milk and omit the sugar and the orange flower water.

2 When the eggs are incorporated in the paste, complete with 5 oz. freshly grated or chopped Gruyère cheese.

Pâte à génoise ordinaire

ORDINARY GENOESE BATTER

———————— 8 oz. sugar, 8 eggs, 6 oz. sifted flour, 3½ oz. melted butter, flavouring of 1 dessertspoon vanilla sugar *or* grated orange or lemon rind *or* 1½ tablespoons liqueur

Put the sugar and eggs together in a copper bowl and beat over hot water until the mixture is pale in colour and thick enough to leave a trail.

Remove from the heat, and continue to beat until the mixture is cold. Add the sifted flour, fold in lightly, then add the butter slowly, and flavouring.

Put into buttered tins or moulds as required and bake in a moderate oven.

Pâte à biscuit à la cuiller

SPONGE FINGERS BATTER

———————— 8 oz. castor sugar, 8 eggs, 1 dessertspoon orange flower water, 6 oz. sifted flour, sugar and water for sprinkling

Put the sugar and egg yolks together in a bowl and beat until the mixture becomes pale in colour and is thick enough to leave a trail. Add the orange flower water and fold in the flour gradually. Lastly, fold in the stiffly beaten egg whites.

Put the mixture into a forcing bag with a plain ½-inch pipe. Pipe in fingers on to a tray lined with greaseproof paper. Sprinkle with sugar and add a few drops water.

Cook in a moderate oven.

Pâte à biscuit manqué

MANQUÉ BATTER

———————— 8 oz. castor sugar, 9 egg yolks, 1½ tablespoons rum, 7 oz. sifted flour, 8 well beaten egg whites, 5 oz. butter

Beat the sugar and egg yolks together until the mixture becomes pale and thick. Add rum and fold in flour. Beat the egg whites stiffly and fold into the mixture. Lastly add melted butter. Pour into buttered and floured moulds and bake in a moderate oven.

Pâte à biscuit punch

PUNCH BISCUIT PASTE

———————— 8 oz. castor sugar, 6 egg yolks, 1 large whole egg, ½ dessertspoon orange sugar, ½ dessertspoon lemon sugar, 3 dessertspoons rum, 6 oz. sifted flour, 4 egg whites, 5 oz. butter

Beat the sugar, egg yolks and the 1 whole egg until the mixture is light and frothy. Add the flavourings, and fold in the flour. Add the stiffly beaten egg whites and finally the melted butter.

Put into buttered tins or flan cases and bake in a moderate oven.

Pâte sablée

SUGARED PASTE

———————— 1 lb. sifted flour, 10 oz. butter, 4 oz. vanilla, sugar, pinch salt, 3 egg yolks, 6–7 tablespoons milk.

Mix as usual and roll out twice. Make it into a ball and let it rest for 1 hour.

Pâte à biscuit de Savoie

SWISS SPONGE CAKE OR BISCUIT BATTER

——————— 8 oz. castor sugar, 7 egg yolks, 1 dessertspoon vanilla sugar, 5 oz. flour mixed with 5 oz. potato flour, 7 egg whites stiffly beaten, icing sugar

Beat the sugar and egg yolks together until the mixture is thick enough to leave a trail. Add the vanilla sugar, and fold in the flour and potato flour sifted together. Fold in the stiffly beaten egg whites. Butter some moulds, sprinkle with icing sugar or potato flour and two-thirds fill with the mixture.

Cook in a moderate oven.

Pâte à frire

FRYING BATTER

——————— 8 oz. flour, ⅔ pint (U.S. approx. 1 cup) warm water, pinch salt, 2 tablespoons oil, 2 egg whites

Sift the flour into a bowl, make a well in the centre and add the water, salt and oil. Beat till smooth. Leave to stand for 1 hour, and just before using, add the stiffly beaten egg whites.

If the batter is intended for sweet dishes, add 1 tablespoon sugar and brandy to taste.

Pâte à ravioli

RAVIOLI PASTA

Ravioli pasta is simply a mixture of flour and warm salted water, to which is added 3−4 tablespoons oil per 1 lb. flour.

This pasta sould be kept rather soft.

One can also make ravioli with noodle paste, or with ordinary puff paste.

Ravioli aux fruits

RAVIOLI WITH FRUIT

——————— Puff pastry (see page 681), jam, redcurrant jelly, blanched chopped and browned almonds

Roll the pastry thinly, and using whichever kind of jam is chosen, make up as for ravioli (see page 678). Cook in slightly salted boiling water for 12−15 minutes. Drain well. Brush with melted redcurrant jelly and roll in the almonds.

Ravioli aux pommes

RAVIOLI WITH APPLES

3−4 dessert apples, 5 tablespoons water, 4 tablespoons castor sugar, ¼ oz. butter, 2 tablespoons apricot jam, puff pastry (see page 681), apricot sauce (see page 739), kirsch, macaroons

Peel and slice the apples, put into a pan with the water, sugar and butter, cover and cook for 10−12 minutes, or until tender. Add the jam and mix well.

Roll the pastry thinly, and, using the apple filling, make up as for ravioli (see page 678).

Cook in slightly salted boiling water for 12−15 minutes. Drain well. Brush with apricot sauce to which a little kirsch has been added and roll in crushed macaroons.

CROÛTES DIVERSES
VARIOUS CROÛTES

Croûtes de bouchées

PUFF PASTRY SHELLS

Roll out the puff pastry 6 times (see page 681), leaving the pastry about ¼ inch thick. Cut into rounds with a 3-inch fluted pastry cutter. Put upside down on to a moistened baking tray and glaze with beaten egg yolk. Using a 1½-inch plain cutter dipped in hot water, make a circular incision in the centre of each round.

Bake in a hot oven. Remove the centre piece which will form the lid, and carefully remove any soft paste from the inside, leaving a hollow case.

These shells are really small vol-au-vent cases. Smaller shells for garnishes can be made using smaller cutters.

Croûte à flan, cuite à blanc

FLAN CASES, COOKED BLIND

For an 8-inch case, use 8 oz. lining paste (see page 682). Roll into a round about 9 – 10 inches in diameter. Butter the flan case and stand it on a baking tray. Lift the paste with both hands and place in the case, pressing it against the sides so that it fits snugly. Run the rolling-pin across the top, and the trimmings thus obtained can be used for the top of the case if required. Prick the bottom of the paste and line it with buttered paper. Fill with rice, split peas or crusts of bread and cook in a moderate oven about 25 minutes. Remove the paper and the filling, glaze the edge of the flan case and return to the oven for a few minutes to dry off.

Croûtes de tartelettes

TARTLET CASES

These cases, which are very widely used, are made in plain or fluted tartlet tins of various sizes, as required. They are made of fine lining paste or puff pastry trimmings (see page 682).

Roll out the paste to about ⅛ inch thick and, with a fluted pastry cutter, cut the size required. Butter the tins and line with the rounds of paste. Prick the bottom, line with greaseproof paper and fill with split peas. Cook for 10 – 12 minutes in a moderate oven. Take out the paper and the split peas, glaze the edges of the pastry and return to the oven for a few minutes to dry off.

Croûte de grande timbale

RAISED PIE

Butter a charlotte mould. If liked, decorate the sides with noodle paste (see page 677) cut into fancy shapes and lightly moistened, but this is optional. Roll out some lining paste (see page 682) into a round about 8 inches in diameter and sprinkle it with flour. Fold in half, then draw the edges carefully towards the centre, forming a kind of skull cup and keeping the paste free of creases. Flatten it to an even thickness and put into the mould, pressing it well into the bottom and sides so that it takes the shape of the mould.

Line the mould with greaseproof paper and fill right to the top with split peas, using enough to make a domed top. Put a piece of greaseproof paper on top and then cover with a thin layer of paste. Press the edges well together so that the mould is sealed and crimp with the thumb and finger. Lightly moisten the top of the mould and decorate with leaves cut from the paste.

Cut three rounds of paste of different sizes with a fluted cutter. Remove a piece from the centre of each with a small plain cutter, and put the rings, one on top of the other, on top of the mould.

Make a hole in the centre of the pie to allow steam to escape. Glaze with beaten egg and cook in a moderate oven.

When the pie is cooked, carefully remove the cover and take out the peas and the paper. Glaze the inside of the pie and return to the oven for a few minutes to dry off.

Note For all pies which are to be filled with a fatty mixture, I am of the opinion that the split peas should be replaced by raw minced meat.

The inside of the case should be lined with thin strips of pork fat, and then filled up with equal parts of rather fat pork and beef and seasoned with salt, pepper and spice.

Using this method, the paste becomes impregnated with the meat fat and is very pleasant to eat, which is not the case when peas, etc., have been used. The pie is finished and cooked in the usual way, then the filling is removed and can be used up in various ways.

For this kind of pie, it is wise to choose a fairly wide mould in proportion to its height, as it makes the serving easier.

Timbale de riz de veau aux nouilles
TIMBALE OF CALF'S SWEETBREADS AND NOODLES
——————— Noodles, butter, grated cheese, timbale case, cooked as above, braised calf's sweetbreads, foie gras
Garnish Cock's combs, cock's kidneys, truffle, demi-glace sauce (see page 22), Madeira

Cook the noodles in boiling salted water, drain and add some butter and grated cheese. Half fill the timbale case with the noodles. Add some slices of sweetbread alternating with slices of foie gras.

Garnish with cock's combs and kidneys and slices of truffle.

Mix some of the cooking liquor from the noodles and a little Madeira with the demi-glace sauce and pour over the garnish.

Croûte de vol-au-vent
VOL-AU-VENT CASE
——————— Puff pastry (see page 681), beaten egg for glazing

Having rolled the pastry six times, roll out to a thickness of ¾ inch. Use a plain cutter the size and shape required, dip it into hot water and cut the pastry cleanly.

If a cutter of the right size is not available, use a plate or saucepan lid, etc., as a stencil, and cut round with a sharp knife.

Put the pastry upside down on a moistened baking tray and glaze the top with beaten egg.

Make an incision with a round or oval cutter dipped in hot water, about 1¼ inches from the edge — this will form the lid. Make a criss-cross pattern on this piece and bake in a hot oven.

When the vol-au-vent is cooked, remove the lid carefully and take out any soft paste from inside.

CRÈMES DIVERSES, MERINGUES, PÂTE
VARIOUS CREAMS, MERINGUES, PASTES

Crème à l'anglaise
CUSTARD CREAM
——————— 1 lb. sugar, 16 egg yolks, 1¾ pints (U.S. 4¼ cups) boiled milk, vanilla pod,* orange or lemon peel or 3 tablespoons liqueur

*If a vanilla pod, orange or lemon peel is used for flavouring, infuse it in the milk while it is heating. If liqueur is used, add to the custard when cold.

Put the sugar and egg yolks together in a pan and beat until the sugar has dissolved and the mixture is thick and creamy. Add the milk and cook over gentle heat until the mixture is thick enough to coat the back of the spoon. Avoid letting the custard boil or it will curdle.

If it is required hot, strain into a bain-marie and keep over very low heat, to avoid the eggs being overcooked. If required cold, strain into a bowl and stir while cooling.

Note 1 level dessertspoon arrowroot, mixed with 2 tablespoons cold milk may be added to the sugar and egg yolks. This will prevent curdling should the custard boil.

Crème au beurre

BUTTER CREAM

Prepare a custard cream (see page 694) and flavour with vanilla. Take 1 pint of this cream, stir until it is scarcely warm and incorporate 1 lb. softened butter, adding very small quantities at a time.

Crème au beurre aux marrons

BUTTER CREAM WITH CHESTNUTS

1 lb. trimmings or broken marrons glacés, 4 oz. butter, ¼ pint (U.S. ⅝ cup) syrup, kirsch or rum

Crush the marrons glacés and beat with the butter. Add the syrup and flavour with kirsch or rum.

Crème au beurre au sirop

BUTTER CREAM WITH SYRUP

12 oz. sugar, ½ pint (U.S. 1¼ cup) water, flavouring*, 12 egg yolks, 1 lb. butter

*It is best to use flavouring essence for this butter cream, but if vanilla pod, orange or lemon rind is preferred, it should be infused with the syrup. If liqueur is used, add it when the cream is only just warm.

Dissolve the sugar in the water and heat to 218° F. or 28° measured on a saccharometer. Beat the egg yolks lightly and add the syrup slowly, stirring all the time. Put over a gentle heat and stir until the mixture is thick enough to coat the back of the spoon. Strain through muslin and incorporate the butter, adding a very little at a time.

Crème fouettée, dite 'crème Chantilly'
CHANTILLY CREAM

─────── 1½ pints (U.S. 3¾ cups) fresh thick cream, 3 oz. castor sugar, 1 oz. vanilla sugar

Keep the cream refrigerated for 5 – 6 hours before use, but it should not be too thick. Beat until the volume is doubled, but avoid overbeating or the cream will 'butter'. Add the sugar and refrigerate until required for use.

Crème frangipane
FRANGIPANI PASTRY CREAM

─────── 2½ pints (U.S. 6¼ cups) milk, ½ vanilla pod, 8 oz. sugar, 8 oz. flour, 4 whole eggs, 8 egg yolks, pinch salt, 1 oz. crushed macaroons, butter

Boil the milk with the vanilla pod. Put the sugar, flour, whole eggs, egg yolks and salt into pan, mix all together, stirring with a wooden spoon. Add the milk a little at a time, and bring to the boil, stirring. Boil for 2 minutes and pour into a bowl.

Add 3 oz. butter and crushed macaroons and pour a little more melted butter on the top.

Crème pâtissière
PASTRY CREAM

─────── 1 lb. castor sugar, 12 egg yolks, 4½ oz. flour, 1¾ pints (U.S. 4¼ cups) milk, vanilla pod infused in the milk

Put the sugar, egg yolks and flour together in a pan and add the milk very slowly. Cook like the frangipani pastry cream (see above) and 'put into a bowl.

Crème Saint-Honoré
SAINT-HONORÉ CREAM

This is the pastry cream as in the previous recipe with the addition of 15 well beaten egg whites added after the cream has boiled.

In hot weather, it is advisable to add ½ oz. gelatine to the quantity of mixture given in the recipe, and also to omit the egg whites and add some Chantilly cream (see page 696) when the pastry cream is almost cold.

Crème renversée
FLAVOURED EGG CUSTARD

━━━━━━━ ½ vanilla pod, orange or lemon peel, 1¾ pints (U.S. 4¼ cups) boiling milk, 7 oz. lump sugar, 4 whole eggs, 8 egg yolks

Infuse the vanilla or lemon or orange peel in the milk whilst it is heating and add the sugar. Put the whole eggs and egg yolks in a bowl, beat for a few minutes, then add the boiling milk, gradually, whisking all the time. Strain through muslin, and carefully remove the froth which will have formed on the surface. Pour into moulds and poach in a bain-marie. Turn out when cold and serve with custard cream (see page 694) or zabaglione (see page 738).

Meringue ordinaire
SIMPLE MERINGUE

━━━━━━━ 10–12 egg whites, 1 lb. castor sugar

Beat the egg whites stiffly, add the sugar slowly, mixing it in very lightly and keeping the egg white as frothy as possible. Cook at a very low temperature; in fact, the cooking of meringues is more a drying process.

Meringue italienne montée en génoise
ITALIAN MERINGUE

━━━━━━━ 1 lb. castor sugar, 8–10 egg whites

Put the sugar and egg whites in a copper bowl and beat over a pan of warm water until the mixture sticks to the whisk.

If the meringue is not to be used at once, keep in a cold place covered with paper.

Meringue italienne au sucre cuit

ITALIAN MERINGUE WITH BOILED SUGAR

━━━━━━━━━ 1 lb. sugar, 8–10 egg whites

Boil the syrup (see below) to the large ball stage – 246° F. or 40° on saccharometer.

Beat the egg whites stiffly. Pour the syrup in a steady stream on to the egg whites, beating all the time until the syrup is absorbed.

Cuisson du sucre

SUGAR BOILING

Beginning with a syrup, sugar passes through six distinct stages before it eventually caramelises. These are small and large thread, small and large ball, small and large crack.

Put the quantity of sugar required into a strong pan. Add 1 tablespoon glucose to each 1 lb. sugar and just enough water to enssure the melting of the sugar. Bring to boiling point and skim carefully. Any impurities left in the sugar might cause it to granulate.

When it begins to boil, i.e. when bubbles appear close together, it is an indication that the water has evaporated and at this stage the sugar begins to cook. From this point the sides of the pan must be brushed with a little cold water to prevent the sugar crystallising on to them.

The degrees of cooking follow quickly and may be ascertained as follows:

Small thread Wet the finger and thumb, dip quickly into the sugar, then separate them and small brittle threads should appear.

Large thread After a little longer boiling, repeat the test and the threads should be longer and less brittle.

Small ball When tested as above, the sugar should form a soft ball.

Large ball At this stage the sugar will form a harder ball.

Small crack When the wet finger is dipped in the sugar, the film of sugar will break when dipped in cold water and sticks to the teeth when bitten.

Large crack This stage is reached when the film of sugar breaks clean, like glass.

If the sugar is not removed from the heat at this stage, it will caramelise.

Editor's note In many of the following recipes, M. Escoffier indicates the required degree of boiling by giving the reading on a saccharometer. As this instrument is not in general use in the household, I have given the equivalent temperature in degrees Fahrenheit.

SPUN SUGAR

8 oz. lump sugar, ¼ pint (U.S. ⅝ cup) water, pinch cream of tartar, 1 teaspoon glucose

Put all ingredients together into a strong pan. Heat slowly until sugar has dissolved, then boil to 310° F. Whilst boiling brush down any sugar splashes on the side of the pan with a pastry brush dipped in cold water. This prevents the formation of sugar crystals.

When the syrup reaches 310° F., remove the pan at once from the heat, and stand the base of the pan in cold water for a few minutes to prevent the temperature of the syrup rising any higher.

Brush a rolling-pin with oil and put a clean sheet of paper on the floor. Dip a fork into the syrup and shake quickly backwards and forwards over the rolling-pin, held over the paper. Hold the fork high over the rolling-pin so that the threads of sugar are as long as possible.

Pâte d'amande au miel

ALMOND PASTE WITH HONEY

1 lb. blanched crushed almonds, 1 lb. castor sugar, 3½ oz. honey, 3 tablespoons vanilla sugar

Mix ingredients together and pound thoroughly in a mortar.

Pâte d'amande à l'abricots

ALMOND PASTE WITH APRICOTS

Follow the preceding recipe but replace the honey with apricot paste flavoured with kirsch.

Pâte d'amande fondante

ALMOND PASTE FONDANT

8 oz. blanched almonds, 1 tablespoon vanilla sugar or 1 tablespoon liqueur, 1 lb. sugar boiled to 290° F. (see page 698)

Crush the almonds and put them into a mortar with the flavouring. Gradually add the syrup and pound vigorously with the pestle.

Pâte de pistache fondant

PISTACHIO PASTE FONDANT

8 oz. blanched pistachio nuts, 2 oz. blanched almonds, 2 tablespoons vanilla sugar, 8 oz. sugar boiled to 275° F. (see page 698), 3 tablespoons icing sugar

Crush the pistachios and almonds and put into a mortar with vanilla sugar. Add the syrup slowly and pound all well together. Turn out on to a marble slab and work in the icing sugar.

ENTREMETS CHAUDS
HOT SWEETS

Beignets

FRITTERS

FRYING BATTER FOR FRUIT AND FLOWER FRITTERS

8 oz. flour, pinch salt, 2 tablespoons melted butter, $\frac{1}{4}$ pint (U.S. $\frac{5}{8}$ cup) beer, $\frac{1}{4}$ pint (U.S. $1\frac{1}{4}$ cups) warm water, 1 tablespoon brandy, 2 egg whites

Sift the flour and salt into a bowl, add butter, beer and water and mix all well. Add brandy and, lastly, stiffly beaten egg whites.

FRYING BATTER FOR FRUIT FRITTERS GLAZED IN THE OVEN

1 lb. flour, $\frac{1}{4}$ pint (U.S. $\frac{5}{8}$ cup) beer, little warm water, 2 tablespoons melted butter, pinch salt, pinch sugar, 1 egg

Mix the flour smoothly with the beer and a little water, but avoid stirring too much.

Leave in a warm place to ferment, then, just before use, add the other ingredients.

Beignets d'abricots

APRICOT FRITTERS

—————— Apricots, sugar, kirsch, brandy or rum, frying batter (see page 700)

Choose fresh fruit, cut in half, sprinkle with sugar and soak for 1 hour in kirsch, brandy or rum.

Dip in batter, and fry in deep fat.

Drain well, sprinkle with sugar and glaze in the oven.

Beignets de fraises

STRAWBERRY FRITTERS

Select large, firm strawberries, sugar them well, sprinkle with kirsch and leave to soak for 30 minutes.

Just before serving, dip in frying batter and fry in deep fat. Drain well and sprinkle with castor sugar.

Beignets en fleurs d'acacia

ACACIA BLOSSOM FRITTERS

Select fresh acacia blossoms, cut off the stalks, put into a bowl, sprinkle with sugar and brandy and soak for 30 minutes.

Just before serving, dip in batter and fry in deep fat, drain, and sprinkle with sugar.

Note Elderflower, marrow blossom and vine-tendril fritters are treated in the same way.

Beignets de crème

CREAM FRITTERS

Prepare a frangipani pastry cream (see page 696). Place it on a buttered tray, in an even layer of ½ inch, and leave to cool.

Cut into pieces with a knife or pastry cutter. Coat with batter (see page 704) or with egg and breadcrumbs and fry in deep fat.

If coated with batter, sprinkle with icing sugar and glaze in the oven.

If coated with egg and breadcrumbs, just sprinkle with sugar.

Beignets viennois chauds ou beignets à la dauphine

VIENNA FRITTERS OR DAUPHINE FRITTERS

Follow the recipe for *beignets viennoise ou krapfen* (see page 716), but when the fritters are cooked, sprinkle with sugar and serve hot.

Beignets soufflés

SOUFFLÉ FRITTERS

Prepare an ordinary chou paste (see page 687) and flavour to taste. Put pieces the size of a small walnut into moderately hot fat. Increase the heat slightly and cook till the fritters are well risen.

Drain thoroughly, sprinkle with sugar, and serve hot.

Beignets favoris

MACAROON FRITTERS

———— Macaroons, apricot jam, syrup, liqueur or rum, frying batter (see page 700), deep fat for frying, sugar

Use soft macaroons and carefully hollow out the centre. Sandwich two together with apricot jam and dip into syrup flavoured with liqueur or rum. Coat with batter and fry in deep fat. Drain well, sprinkle with sugar and serve hot.

Note Apricot jam may be replaced by any other kind and the liqueur may be kirsch, maraschino, Curaçao, etc. The jam may also be replaced by frangipani cream (see page 696) to which a little chopped crystallised fruit soaked in kirsch has been added.

Instead of coating the macaroons in batter and frying in deep fat, they can be coated with flour, then with egg and breadcrumbs and fried in butter.

Many other variations can be made and the fritters may be accompanied by a sauce flavoured with rum or liqueur.

Charlotte de pommes

APPLE CHARLOTTE

Bread, butter, 2½—3 lb. cooking apples, 3 tablespoons castor sugar, juice 1 lemon, 2—3 tablespoons water, 3 tablespoons apricot jam, apricot sauce (see page 739), 1½—2 pints (U.S. 3¾—5 cups) water

Well butter a charlotte mould. Cut out some heart-shaped croûtons of bread, about ¼ inch thick.

Dip in melted butter and arrange them in a circle in the bottom of the mould, allowing them to overlap slightly.

Cut some oblong pieces of bread of the same thickness and the same height as the mould, dip in melted butter and line the sides of the mould. These pieces should also overlap.

Peel and slice the apples thinly, put into a pan with ½ oz. butter, sugar, lemon juice and water and cook until reduced to a thick pulp. Stir in the jam.

Fill the mould with the apple mixture, taking care that it is well filled as the apple mixture will shrink a little during the cooking. Cover with another piece of bread dipped in melted butter.

Bake in a moderate oven 30—35 minutes.

When cooked, leave in the mould for a few minutes before turning out.

Serve with apricot sauce.

Note Apple charlotte is sometimes served cold, in which case it should be decorated with Chantilly cream (see page 696) and served with apricot sauce (see page 739) flavoured with rum.

COMPOSITIONS POUR CRÊPES ET PANNEQUETS

PANCAKE MIXTURES

Composition pour crêpes ordinaires

ORDINARY PANCAKE BATTER

Method 1 8 oz. sifted flour, 3 eggs, 1 pint (U.S. 2½ cups) milk or water, 2 tablespoons brandy, 1 tablespoon orange flower water (optional), pinch salt, 2 tablespoons melted butter

Mix the flour smoothly with the eggs and enough milk to make a fairly fluid batter. Add brandy, orange flower water and salt. Leave to stand for 1 hour.

Heat some butter in a small pan, pour in 1 tablespoon batter and cook quickly on one side, toss, and brown the other.

Serve very hot.

Method 2 8 oz. sifted flour, 3 oz. castor sugar, pinch salt, 6 eggs, ½ pint (U.S. approx. ⅓ cup) milk, 1 dessertspoon vanilla or orange sugar, 3 dessertspoons brandy, kirsch or rum, 1 tablespoon melted butter

Mix the flour, sugar and salt. Gradually add eggs and milk and beat well. Add other ingredients.

Method 3 8 oz. sifted flour, 2 oz. sugar, pinch salt, 3 eggs, ⅛ pint (U.S. ⅜ cup) cream, 3 dessertspoons brandy, 3 dessertspoons melted butter, generous ¾ pint (U.S. approx. 2⅛ cups) milk, 3 dessertspoons almond syrup, 2 oz. macaroons, crushed finely

Mix the flour, sugar and salt. Add eggs, stir lightly, then add cream, brandy, butter and milk. Strain through a fine strainer, then add syrup and macaroons.

Method 4 8 oz. flour, 2 oz. sugar, pinch salt, 3 eggs, 2 egg yolks, 1⅛ pints (U.S. approx. 2¾ cups) milk, 3 egg whites

Mix flour, sugar and salt. Add whole eggs, egg yolks and milk. Beat well, add flavouring to taste and strain through a fine sieve.
Finally, fold in stiffly beaten egg whites.

Crêpes Suzette

The pancakes are cooked in the ordinary way and then finished at the table with the following sauce:

3 oz. butter, 3 oz. castor sugar, 3 tablespoons Curaçao, juice 1 tangerine, sugar for sprinkling

Cream the butter, add the sugar and beat in well, add Curaçao and tangerine juice.
Put the cooked pancakes in a pan over a spirit stove. Sprinkle with sugar, pour the sauce over and serve very hot.

Pannequets aux confitures

JAM PANCAKES

Small thin pancakes (see page 704), jam, icing sugar

Spread the pancakes with jam and roll up. Trim the two ends and cut the pancakes in half. Arrange in a serving dish, sprinkle with icing sugar and glaze under the grill (U.S. broiler) or criss-cross with a hot iron.

Pannequets à la crème

CREAM PANCAKES

Small thin pancakes (see page 704), frangipani cream (see page 696), crushed macaroons, icing sugar

Spread the pancakes with the cream and sprinkle with macaroons. Roll up and finish as in the preceding recipe for jam pancakes.

CROQUETTES

Croquettes de marrons

CHESTNUT CROQUETTES

————— Marrons glacés, macaroons, kirsch or rum, flour, egg, breadcrumbs, butter

Use trimmings or broken marrons glacés, mash with a fork and add about one-third the quantity of macaroons, soaked in kirsch or rum and crushed finely.

Divide the mixture in pieces the size of a small egg. Roll into balls and then flatten into small cakes. Coat with flour, egg and breadcrumbs and, just before serving, brown on both sides in clarified butter.

Serve with apricot sauce flavoured with kirsch, and Chantilly cream (see page 696).

Croquettes de riz

RICE CROQUETTES

Prepare a mixture as indicated in rice for sweets (see page 718). Divide it into pieces the size of an egg and shape like pears or apricots. Coat with egg and breadcrumbs and fry in deep fat. Drain on a cloth and sprinkle with sugar.

Serve with apricot sauce (see page 739) or a zabaglione (see page 738).

Croquettes de semoule

SEMOLINA CROQUETTES

————— 1½ pints (U.S. 3¾ cups) milk, 4 oz. sugar, butter, pinch salt, 8 oz. semolina, 3 eggs, flour, egg and breadcrumbs, sugar for sprinkling

Bring the milk to boiling point with the sugar, 2 oz. butter and salt. Sprinkle in the semolina and cook over gentle heat for 25 minutes. Add the beaten eggs and a few dabs of butter and cook for a few minutes without boiling.

Spread out about ½ inch in thickness on to a buttered dish and leave to get cold.

Cut into rounds, squares or oblongs, coat with flour, then with egg and breadcrumbs and fry in clarified butter till brown on both sides. Drain, sprinkle with sugar and serve with apricot sauce (see page 739), flavoured to taste or with custard cream (see page 694).

Note Chopped crystallised fruits, or currants and sultanas soaked in kirsch or rum may be added to the semolina mixture.

CROÛTES AUX FRUITS
FRUIT CROÛTES

Fruit croûtes, once considered as good sweets, are somewhat neglected today, and are replaced by iced sweets, which have come into favour lately. It would, however, be a great mistake to abandon them completely.

Croûte aux fruits

FRUIT CROÛTES

1 stale unsoaked savarin, sugar, peaches, apricots, pears, apples, pineapple, crystallised cherries, angelica, apricot sauce (see page 739), kirsch

Cut the savarin into slices, allowing 2 for each person. Arrange on a tray, sprinkle with sugar and put into a moderate oven to brown.

Cut some peaches and apricots in halves, quarter the pears and cut the apple into eighths. Cook very carefully in a little syrup.

Arrange the slices of savarin in a serving dish in a circle alternately with thin slices of pineapple, cut to the same size.

Arrange the remaining fruit on top and decorate with cherries and angelica.

Cover with apricot sauce flavoured with kirsch.

Croûte à la lyonnaise
CROÛTE LYONESE

━━━━━━━ 1 stale mousseline brioche cooked in a charlotte mould (see page 685), castor sugar, 1 lb. trimmings or broken marrons glacés, apricot jam, 4 tablespoons kirsch, maraschino or rum, 5—6 tablespoons cream, cherry sauce (see page 739)

Cut the brioche into slices about ½ inch thick and arrange on a baking tray. Sprinkle liberally with sugar and put into a moderate oven until the sugar begins to caramelise.

Rub the marrons glacés through a sieve. Put the resultant purée into a bowl, add one-third the quantity of jam, the liqueur and cream.

When the slices of brioche are cold, spread with the mixture and arrange on a serving dish in a ring. Cover with cherry sauce and serve with Chantilly cream (see page 696) flavoured with vanilla.

Croûte au madère
MADEIRA CROÛTE

━━━━━━━ Currants, sultanas, crystallised fruit, slices mousseline brioche prepared and glazed ás in the previous recipe, apricot syrup, Madeira

Pour a little hot water over the currants and sultanas and leave them for a few minutes to swell, then drain well.

Chop the crystallised fruit and mix with the currants and sultanas.

Arrange the slices of brioche on a serving dish in a ring. Put the fruit in the centre and pour over the apricot syrup flavoured with Madeira.

Note The slices of brioche can be spread with apricot jam.

Croûtes aux pommes à la bonne femme
APPLE CROÛTES WITH APRICOT SAUCE

━━━━━━━ 12 slices ½-inch-thick bread, butter, castor sugar, apple purée prepared as for apple charlotte (see page 703)

Remove the crusts from slices of bread and cut into pieces 2 × 2½ inches. Brown in clarified butter, sprinkle with sugar and brown in the oven.

Prepare the apple purée and cover each piece of bread with the apple to a depth of about ½ inch. Smooth the surface, sprinkle liberally with sugar and make a criss-cross pattern on top with a red-hot iron.

Serve with apricot sauce (see page 739) flavoured to taste.

Croûte à la normande

NORMANDY STYLE APPLE CROÛTES

— Bread slices prepared and glazed as in the previous recipe, apple purée prepared as for apple charlotte (see page 703), apricot jam, apricot syrup, rum

Cover the croûtes with a layer of thick apple purée to which one-third the amount of apricot jam has been added.

Arrange on a serving dish in a ring and fill the centre with apple purée.

Cover with apricot syrup flavoured with rum and serve with Chantilly cream (see page 696).

Croûte aux abricots à la valentinoise

APRICOT CROÛTES WITH FRANGIPANI CREAM

— Apricots, syrup flavoured with vanilla, almonds, castor sugar, frangipani cream (see page 696), croûtes prepared as in previous recipes, apricot jam, maraschino, kirsch

Peel the apricots and cook very lightly in a thin syrup flavoured with vanilla. Remove from the heat.

Blanch and pound a few almonds with sugar, add to some frangipani and spread over the croûtes. Arrange on a serving dish, remove the kernels from the apricots and put them on top of the croûtes.

Add a little apricot jam to the syrup in which the apricots were cooked. Flavour with a little maraschino and kirsch and pour over the apricots. Sprinkle with shredded almonds, browned and lightly caramelised.

Note Canned apricots may be used for this sweet and any other fruit can be used in the same way. It is usual to serve Chantilly cream (see page 696) with croûtes.

OMELETTES
OMELETS

Sweet omelets come under four different headings:
  Liqueur omelets
  Jam omelets
  Soufflé omelets
  Surprise omelets

Omelette aux confitures à l'abricot
APRICOT JAM OMELET

————— 6 eggs, salt, sugar, butter, 2 tablespoons apricot jam

Beat the eggs, add a little salt and sugar and cook in the ordinary way. Just before folding, add the warmed apricot jam.

Put on to a hot serving dish, sprinkle liberally with sugar and criss-cross the top with a red-hot iron.

Note Mirabelle, strawberry, and redcurrant omelets are prepared in the same way.

Omelette au rhum
RUM OMELET

Season the eggs with a little salt, add a little sugar and cook as an ordinary omelet.

Put on to a hot dish and sprinkle with sugar. Sprinkle with warm rum and set light to it as the omelet is served.

Note Kirsch and brandy omelets are prepared in the same way.

Omelette soufflée
SOUFFLÉ OMELET

————— 8 oz. castor sugar, 6 eggs, icing sugar, flavouring to taste

Beat the castor sugar and egg yolks together until the mixture becomes pale and thick enough to leave a trail.

Add the flavouring.

Beat the egg whites stiffly and fold into the mixture. Butter an oval fireproof dish, sprinkle it with icing sugar and put in the omelet mixture, shaping it into a mound (some of the mixture can be put into a forcing bag and used to decorate the top of the omelet).

Smooth the surface with the blade of a knife and cook in a moderate oven.

Two minutes before removing it from the oven, sprinkle thickly with icing sugar. The sugar will melt and caramelise the top.

Note Flavouring of vanilla, lemon, orange, rum or liqueur may be used. If a liqueur flavour is preferred, a few macaroons or biscuits should be soaked in the liqueur chosen, and then put into the omelet.

The same applies to soufflés.

Omelette en surprise
SURPRISE OMELET

Genoese pastry (see page 688), ice cream, ordinary or Italian meringue (see page 697).

Cook some Genoese pastry and, when cold, cut a slab about ¾ inch in thickness and as long as required. Put it on to a fireproof serving dish and place the ice cream in the centre. Cover with a ½-inch layer of firm meringue, using a forcing bag to give a decorative appearance. Put at once into a very hot oven, so that the meringue will brown quickly and the ice cream will not melt.

Omelette en surprise Montmorency
SURPRISE OMELET MONTMORENCY

Follow the previous recipe but use vanilla and kirsch ice cream (see page 780).

Serve with Jubilee cherries (see page 729).

Omelettes diverses en surprise
VARIOUS SURPRISE OMELETS

Following the procedure indicated on page 711 one can vary surprise omelets indefinitely by using different flavoured ice cream.

The outside always looks the same. The name indicates the composition of the inside.

POUDINGS
PUDDINGS

The variety of hot puddings is infinite, and it would be impossible to give them all.

Pouding aux amandes
ALMOND PUDDING

4 oz. butter, 4 oz. castor sugar, 4 oz. flour, ½ pint (U.S. 1¼ cups) almond milk,* 5 eggs, split browned almonds

Editor's note No recipe is given for almond milk, which consists of almonds, sugar and water all pounded well together. A few drops of almond essence added to ½ pint (U.S. 1¼ cups) milk will give the necessary flavour to this pudding.

Cream the butter, and sugar and flour and beat well together. Add the milk gradually. Put the mixture into a pan and cook until it becomes smooth and dry and leaves the side of the pan (as for chou paste). Remove from the heat, beat in the egg yolks, then fold in the stiffly beaten egg whites.

Put into a well buttered mould, sprinkle with almonds and poach in a bain-marie or cook in a steamer. Serve with zabaglione (see page 738).

Pouding aux amandes à l'anglaise
ENGLISH ALMOND PUDDING

4 oz. butter, 5 oz. castor sugar, 8 oz. almonds, pinch salt, 1 dessertspoon orange flower water, 2 whole eggs, 2 egg yolks, 6 tablespoons cream

Cream the butter and sugar. Add finely chopped almonds and all the other ingredients and mix well.

Pour into a buttered pie dish and cook in a moderate oven, standing the dish in a pan of water.

Pouding de biscuits

BISCUIT PUDDING

8 oz. ladies' finger or boudoir biscuits, 1 oz. candied peel, 1 pint (U.S. 2¼ cups) boiling milk, 5 oz. sugar, 2 oz. crystallised fruit, 2 oz. sultanas, kirsch, 5 egg yolks, 3 oz. melted butter, 3 egg whites, biscuit (U.S. cookie) crumbs

Crush the biscuits and peel into a pan with the milk and sugar. Stir over the heat for a few minutes then add the chopped fruit and sultanas soaked in kirsch, egg yolk and butter. Mix all well, remove from the heat and add the stiffly beaten egg whites.

Butter some plain moulds and sprinkle with finely crushed biscuit crumbs. Fill with the mixture and poach in a bain-marie or cook in a steamer.

Serve with apricot or chocolate sauce (see pages 739, 738).

Note The mixture may be put into a soufflé mould and baked in a moderate oven, but in this case increase the egg whites to 5.

Pouding diplomate

DIPLOMAT PUDDING

Lady's finger biscuits or boudoir biscuits, rum or Madeira, crystallised fruit, currants, *crème renversée* (see page 697)

Fill a buttered mould with the biscuits soaked in rum or Madeira, alternating with chopped crystallised fruit and currants, soaked in the same liquid.

Finish by very slowly filling the mould with *crème renversée*. Poach in a bain-marie or cook in a steamer.

POUDINGS DE FRUIT
À L'ANGLAISE

ENGLISH FRUIT PUDDINGS

Pouding de pommes

APPLE PUDDING

———— 1 lb. sifted flour, ¼ oz. salt, 2 oz. sugar, 8 oz. finely chopped suet, about ½ pint (U.S. 1¼ cups) water, apples, sugar, grated lemon rind, pinch powdered cinnamon

Mix the flour, salt, sugar and suet together. Add enough water to make a fairly soft dough. Avoid too much kneading and leave to rest for 1 hour in a cool place before using.

Roll out to about ¼ inch in thickness and line a pudding basin, reserving enough dough for the lid. Fill with thinly sliced apples, add sugar, lemon rind and cinnamon. Cover with a lid of the dough, pressing the edges well together. Cover with a cloth and tie securely. Put into a pan of boiling water and boil for 2 hours.

Note Other fruit may be used in the same way.

Pouding de prunes

PLUM PUDDING

———— 1 lb. beef suet, 8 oz. breadcrumbs, 8 oz. flour, 8 oz. apples, peeled and chopped, 8 oz. seeded raisins, sultanas and currants, mixed, 6 oz. mixed chopped, candied peel, 1 oz. ground ginger, 4 oz. chopped almonds, 8 oz. brown sugar, grated rind and juice ¼ orange, grated rind and juice ½ lemon, ½ oz. mixed spice, 3 eggs, ½ pint (U.S. 1¼ cups) rum or brandy, ½ pint (U.S. 1¼ cups) stout

If possible, soak the dried fruit in brandy or rum for some days in advance.

Mix all ingredients thoroughly and put into buttered pudding basins, filling right to the rim. Cover with a buttered and floured cloth and tie securely.

Boil or steam for 5 – 6 hours.

To serve Turn the pudding out on to a hot dish. Pour a little hot rum or brandy over the pudding and set alight.

The pudding is accompanied by either a zabaglione (see page 738)

made with rum or brandy butter (see below), or an English custard cream thickened with arrowroot (see page 694).

Note To make brandy butter: Beat 4 oz. sugar with 4 oz. butter to a cream, and add 3−4 tablespoons brandy.

Pouding à l'américaine
AMERICAN PUDDING

3 oz. breadcrumbs, 4 oz. brown sugar, 4 oz. flour, 5 oz. chopped beef marrow, 4 oz. chopped crystallised fruit, 1 whole egg, 3 egg yolks, pinch grated orange rind, pinch grated lemon rind, pinch powdered currants, pinch grated nutmeg, 6 tablespoons brandy or rum

Mix all ingredients well together, put into a buttered pudding basin and cook in a bain-marie or a steamer.

Serve with zabaglione (see page 738) made with rum.

Pouding à la Clermont
CLERMONT PUDDING

Follow the previous recipe for American pudding but replace the beef marrow with melted butter and add 6 oz. chopped marrons glacés and 3 tablespoons cream

Turn into a buttered pudding basin and sprinkle with potato flour. Poach in a bain-marie or cook in a steamer.

Serve with a custard cream flavoured with rum or an apricot sauce flavoured with rum (see pages 694, 739).

Pouding au pain à l'anglaise
ENGLISH BREAD AND BUTTER PUDDING

Slices bread, butter, currants, sultanas *crème renversée* (see page 697)

Remove the crust from the bread and spread with butter. Cover the fruit with tepid water and leave to swell for a few minutes, then drain well.

Arrange the buttered bread and fruit alternately in a greased pie-dish and cover with the custard mixture.

Bake in a moderate oven.

Note The slices of bread may be toasted before buttering, or they can be replaced by biscuits (U.S. cookies).

Pouding au pain à la française

FRENCH BREAD PUDDING

———— 10 oz. white bread (without crust), 1¾ pints (U.S. 4¼ cups) boiling milk, 8 oz. sugar, vanilla, 4 whole eggs, 6 egg yolks, 4 egg whites

Put the bread into a basin. Add the milk, sugar and vanilla flavouring and leave to soak for a few minutes.

Rub through a sieve, add the beaten eggs and egg yolks and then the stiffly beaten egg whites. Mix all well together.

Pour into a buttered mould or into small baba moulds and poach in a bain-marie or cook in a steamer.

Serve with either custard cream flavoured with vanilla, chocolate sauce or a fruit sauce (see pages 694, 738 – 741).

White bread may be replaced by black bread, in which case add a little chopped crystallised fruit, pinch powdered cinnamon and 4 tablespoons honey.

Serve with apricot sauce flavoured with rum (see page 739).

Note This pudding can be cooked in a pie-dish like the English bread and butter pudding in the previous recipe.

Beignets viennoise ou krapfen

KRAPFEN OR COLD FRITTERS

———— Brioche dough (see page 684), apricot or cherry jam or redcurrant jelly, syrup

Prepare the dough and roll out to about ¼ inch in thickness.

Cut into rounds with a 2½-inch plain cutter. Put half the round on to a piece of buttered paper, and put a spoonful of jam or jelly in the centre of each. Damp the edges and cover with another round of dough. Press the edges lightly to seal them.

Cover with a cloth and leave to stand for 30 minutes. Loosen the fritters from the paper and fry in deep fat until brown. Drain and dip in a thin hot syrup flavoured to taste. Remove when a little of the syrup has been absorbed and serve cold.

POUDINGS AUX PÂTES ET AU RIZ
MILK PUDDINGS

Pouding au tapioca

TAPIOCA PUDDING

1¾ pints (U.S. 4¼ cups) milk, 5 oz. sugar, pinch salt, 5 oz. butter, 6 oz. tapioca, 6 egg yolks, 4 egg whites

Put the milk into a pan with the sugar, salt and 3 oz. butter. Bring to boiling point, sprinkle in the tapioca slowly, stir well, then pour into a pie-dish and cook for 20 — 25 minutes in a slow oven.

Remove from the oven, cool a little then add egg yolks, rest of the butter and stiffly beaten egg whites.

Pour into a buttered and floured charlotte mould and poach in a bain-marie or steam carefully until the pudding is elastic to the touch.

Leave to stand for 7 — 8 minutes before turning out.

Serve with custard cream, zabaglione or a fruit sauce (see pages 738 — 741).

Note This pudding may be put into a soufflé dish and baked in a moderate oven.

Serve with custard cream or a fruit sauce as above.

Sago, semolina or vermicelli pudding can be prepared in the same way.

Pouding de tapioca, de sagou, de semoule à l'anglaise

TAPIOCA, SAGO AND SEMOLINA PUDDINGS IN THE ENGLISH WAY

Whatever the medium used, the grain is cooked in sweetened milk, flavoured to taste.

For 2 pints (U.S. 5 cups) milk 4 oz. grain, 2 oz. sugar, flavouring to taste, 4 eggs

The pudding is cooked in a buttered pie-dish in a very slow oven.

Pouding de tapioca au caramel

TAPIOCA PUDDING WITH CARAMEL

Prepare the mixture for tapioca pudding (see page 717) and pour it into a charlotte mould coated with sugar cooked to the caramel stage (see page 698). Poach in a bain-marie without boiling and serve without sauce.

Note Sago and semolina puddings may also be prepared with caramel. Candied fruits cut into small cubes may be added to these puddings.

Riz pour entremets

RICE FOR SWEETS

——————— 2 pints (U.S. 5 cups) milk, vanilla pod or pieces lemon or orange peel, 5 oz. sugar, pinch salt, 2 oz. butter, 6 oz. rice, 6 egg yolks

Heat the milk with the flavouring, sugar, salt and butter.

Wash the rice, put into 1½ pints (U.S. 3¾ cups) water and boil for 1 minute, then drain off the water. When the milk is boiling, strain on to the rice, cover and cook gently for 25—30 minutes — preferably in the oven. Do not stir the rice while it is cooking. Remove from the oven and stir in the egg yolks carefully without breaking up the rice.

Pouding de riz

RICE PUDDING

Prepare the rice as instructed in *riz pour entremets* (see above recipe). Incorporate into it 6 well beaten eggs for every 6 oz. raw rice. Put into a buttered mould sprinkled with potato flour. Cook in a bain-marie like the other puddings and serve in the same way.

Pouding de riz à l'anglaise

ENGLISH RICE PUDDING

——————— 4 oz. rice, 2 pints (U.S. 5 cups) boiling milk, sugar, 2 oz. butter, pinch salt, 3 egg yolks, 5—6 tablespoons cream

Boil the rice in 1½ pints (U.S. 3¾ cups) water for 2 minutes, then drain off the water and add the milk, 2—3 oz. sugar, butter and salt. Cover and simmer for 20—25 minutes by which time the rice should be cooked.

Add egg yolks mixed with the cream, then turn the pudding into a buttered pie-dish, sprinkle with sugar and peel and put into the oven to brown.

Serve with a chocolate or fruit sauce (see pages 738—741) or with stewed fruit.

Pouding de semoule à la crème
CREAMED SEMOLINA PUDDING

6 oz. semolina, 2 pints (U.S. 5 cups) boiling milk, flavouring, 4—5 oz. sugar, pinch salt, ½ oz. butter, 3 egg yolks, 5—6 tablespoons cream

Sprinkle the semolina into the milk, add flavouring, sugar, salt and butter. Cover and cook for 20—25 minutes over very low heat. Add egg yolks and cream mixed together and pour into a buttered pie dish. Sprinkle with sugar and brown in the oven.

Serve with a chocolate or fruit sauce (see pages 738—741) or with stewed fruit.

POUDINGS SOUFFLÉS
SOUFFLÉ PUDDINGS

For soufflé puddings, use the following recipe for Saxon pudding as a basis.

Pouding saxon
SAXON PUDDING

3 oz. butter, 3 oz. castor sugar, 3 oz. sifted flour, ½ pint (U.S. 1¼ cups) boiling milk, 5 eggs potato flour

Cream the butter, add the sugar and flour and beat well. Stir in the milk and beat till the mixture is smooth. Cook over fairly brisk heat until the mixture dries and leaves the side of the pan, like chou paste. Remove from the heat, beat in the egg yolks, then fold in the stiffly beaten egg whites.

Pour into a well buttered mould, sprinkle with potato flour and poach in a bain-marie or steam carefully.

Serve with custard cream or zabaglione flavoured to taste (see pages 694, 738).

Pouding soufflé au citron

LEMON SOUFFLÉ PUDDING

The recipe is the same as for Saxon pudding (see page 719), but it is flavoured with lemon. Serve with apricot syrup flavoured with rum or kirsch, or with custard cream or chocolate sauce (see pages 694, 738).

Note The same foundation recipe is used for orange, kirsch, Curaçao, vanilla or Bénédictine puddings.

Finely chopped almonds and a few tablespoons orgeat syrup may be added to the Saxon pudding.

Editor's note Orgeat syrup was originally made with barley and almonds. A little almond essence could be used instead.

Pouding mousseline

MOUSSELINE PUDDING

4 oz. butter, 4 oz. castor sugar, 10 egg yolks, 7 egg whites, crushed macaroons

Cream the butter and sugar, add the egg yolks, one at a time, beating the mixture well. Put into a pan and cook over very low heat until the mixture is thick enough to coat the back of the spoon. Remove from the heat and fold in the stiffly beaten egg whites.

Butter a soufflé dish and sprinkle with crushed macaroons. Pour in the mixture and cook in a bain-marie in a moderate oven.

Serve with Chantilly cream flavoured to taste, English custard cream, chocolate sauce, etc. (see pages 694, 738).

A purée of strawberries or raspberries flavoured with kirsch or Curaçao, and mixed with Chantilly cream, are flavourings most to be recommended while the fruit is in season.

Pouding roulé à l'anglaise

ROLY-POLY PUDDING

Prepare a paste with suet (see dumpling and pudding dough, page 684) and let it rest for an hour before being used.

Roll into an oblong shape about ¼ inch thick and spread with a layer of jam. Roll up into the form of a large sausage. Wrap in a buttered and floured cloth and cook in boiling water or steam for 1½ hours.

To serve Cut the roll into slices and arrange in a ring. Serve with a fruit sauce.

Note Roly-poly pudding may be prepared by replacing the suet paste with ordinary short paste (see page 683).

RISSOLES

The preparation of rissoles as sweets is the same as that for hors-d'oeuvres. The difference is that they are filled with fruit compotes or jam, variously flavoured creams or with chestnut purée, either plain or added to apricot jam and flavoured with kirsch or rum.

The pastry used can be trimmings of puff paste, or fine lining paste (see pages 681—682).

SOUFFLÉS

SIMPLE BASIC SOUFFLÉ MIXTURE

1 oz. flour, ¼ pint (U.S. ⅝ cup) milk, 1—2 oz. sugar, 1 oz. butter, 3 egg yolks, 4 egg whites

Mix the flour smoothly with a little of the milk. Put the rest of the milk on to heat with the sugar. Add the flour, stir till boiling and boil for 2 minutes. Remove from the heat, add the butter and egg yolks and beat in well.

Finally add the stiffly beaten egg whites and fold in lightly.

CREAM SOUFFLÉ FOR A LARGE QUANTITY

8 oz. sugar, 8 oz. flour, 4 whole eggs, 8 egg yolks, vanilla pod (optional), 1¾ pints (U.S. 4¼ cups) boiling milk, 4 oz. butter, 10 egg whites

Mix the sugar, flour, whole eggs and 3 egg yolks together in a pan. Infuse the vanilla pod in the milk and, when boiling, pour gradually on to the egg mixture. Cook as for frangipani cream (see page 696).

Remove from the heat, stir in the butter, the remaining 5 egg yolks and the stiffly beaten egg whites.

COOKING AND PRESENTING SOUFFLÉS

Special soufflé dishes are used for soufflés. They should be buttered and sprinkled with sugar. A baked soufflé should be cooked in a moderate oven, and 2 minutes before the end of the cooking sprinkled with sugar and returned to the oven. The sugar will caramelise and glaze the soufflé.

Soufflé aux amandes

ALMOND SOUFFLÉ

Follow the basic soufflé recipe (see page 721), add 2 oz. finely chopped browned almonds, 2 – 3 tablespoons orgeat syrup (see Editor's note, 720) or a few drops almond essence.

Pour into a soufflé dish and bake in a moderate oven as described above.

Soufflé aux avelines

HAZEL-NUT SOUFFLÉ

Prepare the basic soufflé (see page 721) adding 1½ oz. hazel-nut praline (see page 739).

Cook as usual.

Soufflé aux cerises

CHERRY SOUFFLÉ

Prepare the basic soufflé mixture (see page 721) and flavour it with vanilla. Add some very small macaroons soaked in kirsch and cook in the usual way.

Serve with a compote of cherries mixed with 2 – 3 tablespoons red-currant jelly and Chantilly cream (see page 696).

Soufflé au chocolat

CHOCOLATE SOUFFLÉ

Prepare and cook a vanilla soufflé as in previous recipe and serve with a chocolate sauce and Chantilly cream (see pages 738, 696).

Soufflé au Curaçao

CURAÇAO SOUFFLÉ

Follow the recipe for cream soufflé (see page 721), flavour it with orange and add some macaroons soaked in Curaçao.
Serve with Chantilly cream (see page 696).

Soufflé Elizabeth

CREAM SOUFFLÉ WITH MACAROONS AND PRALINE VIOLETS

This is composed of cream soufflé with vanilla flavouring (see page 721) arranged in alternate layers with pieces of macaroon soaked in kirsch and praline violets.
When the soufflé is cooked cover with spun sugar (see page 699) and serve at once.

Soufflé aux fraises

STRAWBERRY SOUFFLÉ

Add some macaroons soaked in kirsch or Curaçao to the cream soufflé mixture (see page 721) and cook in the ordinary way.
Serve with strawberries soaked in sweetened orange juice and Curaçao and coated with strawberry purée, and Chantilly cream (see page 696).

Soufflé Hilda

LEMON FLAVOURED CREAM SOUFFLÉ

Flavour the cream soufflé mixture (see page 721) with lemon. Serve with a purée of sweetened raspberries and Chantilly cream (see page 696).

Soufflé Palmyre

PALMYRA SOUFFLÉ

Prepare a vanilla flavoured cream soufflé mixture (see page 721). Put it into a soufflé dish in layers alternating with lady's finger biscuits soaked in kirsch and anisette. Cook in the usual way.

Soufflé praline

ALMOND PRALINE SOUFFLÉ

Prepare a cream soufflé with vanilla flavouring (see page 721) and add some almond praline (see page 739).

Sprinkle a few chopped browned almonds on top and cook in the usual way.

Soufflé Rothschild

CREAM SOUFFLÉ WITH CANDIED FRUIT

Make a cream soufflé mixture (see page 721) and add some chopped candied fruit soaked in kirsch.

Serve with Chantilly cream (see page 696) with the addition of a sweetened purée of strawberries, when in season, or a Chantilly cream flavoured with kirsch.

Soufflé Sarah Bernhardt

CREAM SOUFFLÉ WITH MACAROONS AND STRAWBERRIES

Make a cream soufflé (see page 721) flavoured with vanilla and put into a soufflé dish alternating with macaroons soaked in dry Curaçao. Cook as usual.

Serve with strawberries, sweetened and soaked in Curaçao, and covered with a strawberry purée, and Chantilly cream (see page 696).

SOUFFLÉS À BASE DE PURÉE
DE FRUITS
SOUFFLÉS WITH A FRUIT BASE

Soufflé aux fraises

STRAWBERRY SOUFFLÉ

1 lb. strawberries, 13—14 oz. castor sugar, 2—3 tablespoons kirsch, 8 egg whites

Remove the stalks from the strawberries and rub the fruit through a fine sieve. To the resultant puɪée add 3−4 oz. sugar and the kirsch. Beat the egg whites till stiff. Add the rest of the sugar and beat again, then fold in the strawberry purée.

Put into a soufflé dish and cook in the ordinary way.

Soufflé de pommes à la parisienne
PARISIAN STYLE APPLE SOUFFLÉ

━━━━━━━ Compote of apples (see page 770), apricot jam, 2 tablespoons rum, 6−7 egg whites, 8 oz. castor sugar

Prepare the apples as for a charlotte, adding one-third their quantity of apricot jam and the rum.

Beat the egg whites stiffly, add the sugar and beat again, then fold into the apple purée, put into a soufflé dish and cook in the ordinary way.

Serve with apricot syrup flavoured with rum and Chantilly cream (see page 696).

Note Liqueur soufflés are usually made with a cream soufflé base, but in order to preserve the aroma of liqueur it is necessary to soak some broken biscuits (U.S. cookies) or macaroons with the chosen liqueur, and add to the soufflé mixture. Rum, anisette, Curaçao, Bénédictine, Chartreuse, Lérina, Izzara, crème de caçao, etc., may be used.

Pain perdu
FRIED BRIOCHE WITH VANILLA SUGAR

━━━━━━━ Brioche (see page 684), milk, vanilla, sugar, egg, butter, vanilla sugar

Cut the brioche into ½-inch slices, dip them lightly in sweetened cold milk flavoured with vanilla, then in moderately sweetened beaten egg. Fry in hot clarified butter till brown on both sides.

Serve sprinkled with vanilla sugar.

Note The brioche may be replaced by slices of buttered toast.

TIMBALES

The cases foɪ timbales are made either of brioche dough (see page 684), lining paste (see page 682), or of short sweet pastry (see page 683),

Timbale d'Aremberg

AREMBERG TIMBALE

1 cooked brioche (see page 684), apricot compote (see page 768), pears, caramelised almonds,* apricot syrup maraschino
*To caramelise the almonds, split them and brown in the oven. Sprinkle liberally with sugar and return to a hot oven or put them under the grill (U.S. broiler) for a few minutes

When the brioche is quite cold, cut a piece from the top and reserve for the lid. Scoop out the soft paste inside the brioche leaving the case about ½ inch thick at the bottom and sides.

Spread some apricot compote over the bottom and sides, and fill up with alternate layers of pears cut into quarters and poached in syrup and apricot compote with the almonds. Arrange the timbale on a serving dish, replace the lid and coat with apricot syrup flavoured with maraschino.

Timbale de cerises et marrons à la Clermont

TIMBALE OF CHERRIES AND CHESTNUTS

Prepare a brioche as in the previous recipe, and fill with stoned cherries, halved, cooked in syrup, and marrons glacés. Coat with apricot jam flavoured with kirsch and replace the lid before serving.

Timbale de pêches à la Condé

TIMBALE OF PEACHES

Peaches, syrup lightly flavoured with vanilla, almonds, lining paste (see page 682), rice cooked in milk (see page 718), kirsch, compote of apricots (see page 768)

Peel the peaches, cut in halves and cook in the syrup.

Butter a charlotte mould and decorate it with split almonds, then line it with the paste, reserving a piece for the top. Put in a layer of rice flavoured with kirsch, arrange some peaches on top and cover with a thin layer of apricot compote. Add another layer of rice, peaches and apricot compote and finish with a layer of rice.

Put the lid of paste on top and press the edges together. Make a hole in the top to allow steam to escape. Bake in a moderate oven 30−35 minutes. When ready, unmould and serve with apricot syrup flavoured with kirsch.

ENTREMETS DE FRUITS CHAUDS
HOT FRUIT SWEETS

Abricots bourdaloue
BOURDALOUE APRICOTS

———————— Apricots, light syrup, apricot jam, frangipani cream (see page 696), crushed macaroons

Peel the apricots, split in half and cook in a light syrup. Drain off the syrup, put it into a pan with some apricot jam and reduce until it is of a coating consistency.

Put a good thick layer of frangipani cream in the bottom of a fruit dish. Arrange the apricots on top and cover with the thickened syrup. Sprinkle the crushed macaroons on top and serve with Chantilly cream (see page 696).

Pears, peaches, apples, bananas and cherries can be prepared in the same way. If cherries are used, cover them with a compote of apricots (see page 768) flavoured with either kirsch or rum.

Some chopped marrons glacés may also be added to cherries bourdaloue.

Abricots à la Condé
APRICOTS CONDÉ

———————— Rice cooked in milk (see page 718), vanilla, apricots, peeled and cooked in syrup, crystallised fruit, apricot syrup, kirsch

Flavour the rice with vanilla and press into a buttered ring mould. Unmould on to a serving dish and arrange the apricots, whole or halved, on the ring of rice. Decorate with the fruit and coat with apricot syrup flavoured with kirsch.

Peaches, pears and bananas can be served in the same way.

Abricots à la Cussy

APRICOTS WITH MACAROONS AND MERINGUE

Macaroons, kirsch, apricot jam, frangipani (see page 696), apricots poached in a light syrup, Italian meringue (see page 697)

Choose large macaroons, arrange them in a ring on a serving dish and sprinkle lightly with kirsch.

Put a small spoonful of apricot jam on each and then a spoonful of frangipani. Top with half an apricot. Cover with the meringue and decorate with piped meringue.

Dry off in a very moderate oven and serve with apricot sauce flavoured with kirsch.

Peaches may be prepared in the same way.

As a variation the frangipani may be replaced with marrons glacés prepared as follows:

Use trimmings or broken marrons glacés and rub through a sieve. Flavour with kirsch or rum and add 2−3 tablespoons cream.

If rum is used for flavouring, the apricot sauce to accompany the dish should also be flavoured with rum.

Abricots meringués

APRICOT MERINGUE

Rice cooked in milk (see page 718), apricots, halved and poached in syrup, meringue (see page 697), icing sugar

Butter a serving dish and cover with a good layer of rice, about ¾ inch thick. Arrange the apricots on top. Cover with meringue and decorate with piped meringue. Sprinkle with icing sugar and put into a moderate oven to dry off the meringue and brown it lightly.

Serve with apricot or redcurrant sauce (see pages 739, 740).

Ananas Condé

PINEAPPLE CONDÉ

Pineapple, kirsch, rice cooked in milk (see page 718), glacé cherries, angelica, syrup flavoured with kirsch

Cut some slices of pineapple in half through the middle and soak in kirsch.

Prepare a ring of rice as described for apricots Condé (see page 727), arrange the pineapple on top and decorate with cherries and angelica. Pour over a syrup flavoured with kirsch.

Bananes flambées
BANANAS FLAMBÉ

———————— Bananas, castor sugar, flour, butter, kirsch or rum

Peel the bananas and sprinkle them with sugar, coat with flour, and cook in clarified butter.

Arrange the bananas side by side on a long dish, sprinkle with sugar and warmed kirsch or rum and set it alight at the table.

As a variation, the bananas may be surrounded by jubilee cherries (see below).

Cerises jubilé
JUBILEE CHERRIES

———————— 1 lb. white heart cherries, water, 4 oz. sugar, 6 oz. redcurrant jelly, kirsch

Stone the cherries and put them into a saucepan with a little water and the sugar. Cover and cook for 6—8 minutes. Add the redcurrant jelly.

Half fill a serving dish with the cherries and cover with the syrup in which they were cooked. Add some warmed kirsch and set alight at the table.

Note Canned cherries may be used if cherries are not in season.

Flan de cerises à la danoise
DANISH CHERRY FLAN

———————— Lining paste (see page 682), fresh or canned cherries, sugar, powdered cinnamon, 2 oz. sugar, 2 oz. butter, 2 oz. ground almonds, 1 egg, redcurrant jelly, rum

Line a flan tin with the paste. Fill with cherries and sprinkle with sugar mixed with a little cinnamon.

Cream the sugar and softened butter, add the almonds and egg. Mix well and spread over the cherries. Bake in a moderate oven.

When cool, brush the surface with redcurrant jelly and glaze with rum.

Flan aux cerises meringue

CHERRY FLAN MERINGUE

———————— Lining paste (see page 682), sugar, cherries, milk, meringue (see page 697)

Line a buttered flan tin with the paste, prick the bottom, sprinkle with sugar and fill with stoned cherries. Add a little milk and bake in a moderate oven.

When the flan is cold, cover the cherries with meringue and decorate with piped meringue. Put into a slow oven to dry off and lightly brown the meringue.

ANOTHER METHOD

———————— Fresh or canned cherries, sweet short pastry (see page 683), frangipani (see page 696), redcurrant jelly, rum or kirsch

Stone the cherries and, if fresh ones are used, cook them in a light syrup.

Line a buttered flan tin with the pastry. Fill three-quarters full with frangipani, add the cherries, pressing them well into the frangipani. Bake in a moderate oven.

When cooked, cover with a thin layer of redcurrant jelly and glaze with rum or kirsch.

Nectarines ou brugnons

NECTARINES

Nectarines are prepared in the same way as peaches.

Pêches Condé

PEACHES CONDÉ

Proceed in exactly the same way as for apricots Condé (see page 727).

Pêches bourdaloue

BOURDALOUE PEACHES

Divide the peaches in half, peel them and poach in syrup lightly flavoured with vanilla. Proceed as for bourdaloue apricots (see page 727).

Pêches flambées

PEACHES FLAMBÉ

Plunge the peaches into boiling water for 2 seconds, then put them immediately into iced water. Peel them and put into a hot syrup flavoured with kirsch. Keep hot until required.

Put the peaches into a fairly shallow serving dish with a little of the syrup. Add kirsch and set it alight at the table.

Before finally adding the kirsch, a purée of raspberries, strawberries, or redcurrant juice may be added to the syrup.

Pêches impératrice

PEACHES WITH RICE AND APRICOTS

Rice cooked in milk (see page 718), kirsch, maraschino, peaches, syrup flavoured with vanilla, apricot compote (see page 768), apricot sauce flavoured with kirsch (see page 739), crushed macaroons

Flavour the rice with kirsch and maraschino and put a layer in a shallow charlotte tin or soufflé mould. Peel and halve the peaches and poach in syrup flavoured with vanilla. Arrange on top of the rice. Cover with apricot compote and then with another thin layer of rice. Cover with apricot sauce flavoured with kirsch and maraschino and sprinkle with macaroons.

Put into a very moderate oven for a few minutes, but do not let the macaroons brown.

•

Pêches meringuées

PEACH MERINGUE

Follow the recipe for apricot meringue (see page 728) but instead of rice use a flan case cooked 'blind' and put a layer of frangipani (see page 696) in the bottom. Instead of macaroons add 1 oz. crushed praline to the cream (see page 739).

Arrange the half peaches on the cream and cover with thick apricot sauce.

Cover with meringue and finish as for the apricot meringue.

Pochage des pêches

POACHED PEACHES

The best way to poach peaches is as follows: Choose just ripe peaches, dip them into boiling water for a few seconds, then into ice cold water. They are then quite easy to peel.

Place them in a bowl and cover with hot syrup, flavoured with vanilla.

If they are to be served hot, keep them hot without boiling.

If they are to be served cold, leave them to cool in the syrup.

Poires bourdaloue

PEARS BOURDALOUE

Pears bourdaloue are cooked in a light syrup and may be served whole, in halves or in quarters, according to their size.

Proceed as for *abricots bourdaloue* (see page 727).

Poires Condé

PEARS CONDÉ

Take some small pears, peel them carefully and cook them as for compote (see page 770). Serve them on a ring of rice and proceed as for apricots Condé (see page 727).

Poires impératrice

PEARS IMPÉRATRICE

Take some good-sized pears and divide them into four, peel them and cook in a light syrup, flavoured with vanilla. Proceed as indicated for *pêches impératrice* (see page 731).

Poires crassane

PEARS CRASSANE

━━━━━━━━ 1 cooked savarin (see page 686), kirsch, pears cooked in syrup flavoured
with vanilla, canned cherries, trimmings of marrons glacés, apricot
syrup flavoured with kirsch

Soak the savarin in kirsch and arrange the pears in the centre.
Decorate with cherries and chopped marrons glacés and coat with
apricot syrup flavoured with kirsch.
Serve with Chantilly cream (see page 696).

Poires Madeleine

PEARS IN A SAVARIN

━━━━━━━━ 3—4 medium-sized pears, ½ oz. butter, 3 tablespoons sugar, 6 tablespoons water, apricot jam, 1 savarin, soaked in rum, Chantilly cream
(see page 696)

Choose juicy pears such as comice or duchesse, peel and slice thinly and
cook with the butter, sugar and water as described for apple charlotte
(see page 703).
Add one-third their quantity of apricot jam and put into centre of
savarin. Pile some Chantilly cream in a peak in the centre.
Pears in a savarin may be served hot or cold.

Beignets de pommes

APPLE FRITTERS

━━━━━━━━ Russet apples, brandy or rum, castor or icing sugar, batter, deep fat
for frying

Peel and core some russet apples of medium size and cut into ½-inch
slices. Soak for 15—20 minutes in brandy or rum and sugar.
Drain for a few minutes, then dip in batter and fry in deep fat. Drain,
then sprinkle with castor or icing sugar and glaze quickly in a very hot
oven.

Pommes au beurre

BUTTERED APPLES

Colville or russet apples, butter, 3—4 tablespoons light syrup, 2—3 drops lemon juice, small croûtons of brioche,* apricot purée
*The brioche croûtons may be replaced by breadcrumb croûtons, fried in butter, sprinkled with castor sugar and browned in the oven.

Peel and core the apples and cut into 4—6 pieces. Butter a sauté pan, add the syrup and the lemon juice. Add the apples and cook carefully.

Brown the brioche croûtons in the oven, then put them on to a serving dish and arrange the pieces of apple on top. Add a little apricot purée and ½—1 oz. butter to the syrup in which the apples were cooked, and when lightly thickened pour over the apples.

Pommes bonne femme

BAKED APPLES

Core some russet apples and groove them slightly all round.

Place them on a buttered tray, fill with butter and castor sugar, put a little water in the bottom of the tray and bake slowly in a moderate oven. Serve them just as they are.

Pommes bourdaloue

APPLES BOURDALOUE

Peel and core the apples and cut into quarters. Poach in a light syrup flavoured with vanilla then follow the recipe for apricots bourdaloue (see page 727).

Pommes châtelaine

APPLES CHÂTELAINE

Peel and core the apples and cut into quarters. Poach in a light syrup flavoured with vanilla then follow the recipe for *abricots à la Cussy* (see page 728).

Pommes Condé

APPLES CONDÉ

Peel, core and quarter some large apples, and poach in vanilla flavoured syrup.

Arrange on a ring of rice cooked in milk (see page 718). Decorate with candied cherries and angelica rings, and cover them with apricot syrup flavoured with kirsch.

Pommes impératrice

APPLES IMPÉRATRICE

Follow the recipe for *pêches impératrice* (see page 731) but replace the peaches by apple quarters poached in vanilla flavoured syrup.

Pommes meringuées

APPLE MERINGUE

Proceed as indicated for apricot meringue (see page 728), replacing the apricots by apple quarters cooked in vanilla flavoured syrup.

Pommes moscovite

BAKED APPLES WITH KÜMMEL FLAVOURED APRICOT SAUCE

─────── Apples, butter, sugar, lemon juice, egg whites, apricot syrup, kümmel or anisette

Choose well shaped apples of even size and peel them two-thirds of the way up. Remove the pulp very carefully to form a case.

Poach the apple cases in a light syrup, then drain and put on one side.

Cook the pulp and some extra apples, thinly sliced with a little butter, sugar and lemon juice, as for apple charlotte (see page 703).

Add one-third quantity of stiffly beaten egg white and fill the apple cases with the mixture. Bake in a slow oven for 10–12 minutes.

Serve with apricot syrup flavoured with kümmel or anisette.

Rabotte de pommes ou douillon normand
APPLE DUMPLINGS

Prepare the apples like those for *bonne femme* (see page 734) and enclose each one in rich short pastry (see page 683). Cover each dumpling with a small circle of the same pastry. Glaze with beaten egg or sugar syrup, groove the pastry and cook in a fairly hot oven for 15–20 minutes.

Before serving sprinkle the apples with sugar.

Flan de pommes
APPLE FLAN

——————— Rich short pastry (see page 683), apple purée as for apple charlotte (see page 703), rice cooked in milk (see page 718), redcurrant jelly, crushed macaroons

Line a buttered flan tin with the pastry, and half fill with apple purée. Cover with a layer of rice about $\frac{1}{2}$ inch thick, smooth the surface and cook in a moderate oven until the pastry is done.

Remove from the oven, cover with melted redcurrant jelly and sprinkle with macaroons.

Flans de pommes divers
VARIOUS APPLE FLANS

By varying the preceding recipe, a variety of flans and tarts can be made which are usually served as luncheon sweets.

One may prepare flans filled with a layer of charlotte apples, with different fresh fruit on top, such as apricots, bananas, cherries, peaches, plums, etc. These flans may be finished in the normal way, by coating them with apricot purée or redcurrant jelly, by covering them with a layer of meringue, or by covering them with a layer of frangipani cream (see page 683), sprinkled with sugar and criss-crossed with a red-hot iron.

Using a flan case baked 'blind', other variations can be made. For example:

Put a fairly thick layer of apple charlotte (see page 703) into a baked flan case, cover with chestnut purée, smooth the surface and cover with a thin layer of apricot sauce (see page 739). Glaze with rum. Alternatively, flavour the apricot sauce with kirsch and cover with piped Chantilly cream (see page 696).

ENTREMETS ANGLAIS
ENGLISH SWEETS

MINCE PIES

1 lb. finely chopped beef suet, 1¼ lb. cold cooked fillet of beef, cut in very small cubes, 1 lb. raisins, seeded and chopped, 1 lb. currants, 1 lb. sultanas, 1 lb. chopped candied orange and lemon peel, 8 oz. raw apples, peeled, cored and chopped, juice 2 oranges, 1 oz. mixed spice. 6 tablespoons brandy, 6 tablespoons rum, 6 tablespoons Madeira

Mix all together thoroughly, put into jars, seal closely and keep for at least one month.

When required for use, line some deep buttered tartlet tins with ordinary short or puff pastry (see page 682), fill with the above mixture, cover with another round of pastry, make a hole in the top, press the edges well together, glaze and cook in a hot oven.

Editor's note Meat is not generally used in mincemeat in England, but readers in the U.S.A. will know that it is a general ingredient in American recipes for mincemeat.

Tartes de fruits à l'anglaise

ENGLISH FRUIT TARTS

These are made in pie-dishes or pie plates. Whatever fruit is used, it should be washed, peeled and seeded according to its kind, and may be left whole, sliced, or cut into quarters.

Put the fruit in the dish with brown or castor sugar. If the fruit is hard, like apples, add a little water. Soft fruit will not require additional water.

Moisten the rim of the dish and put a strip of short pastry round the edge. Moisten the pastry, then put on the pastry lid and press the edges well together. Glaze with milk or with a sugar and water syrup and cook in a moderate oven.

All English pies and tarts are made in the same way, and any fruit may be used, even when it is unripe, such as green gooseberries. Often several fruits are mixed in the same tart, as, for instance, in blackberry and apple tarts; apple and rhubarb; gooseberry and blackcurrant, etc.

Serve with cream.

SAUCES POUR ENTREMETS CHAUDS ET PRALINES
SAUCES FOR HOT SWEETS AND PRALINES

Sauce anglaise

ENGLISH SAUCE

See English custard cream (page 694).

Sauce au chocolat

CHOCOLATE SAUCE

───────── 8 oz. chocolate, ¾ pint (U.S. 1⅞ cups) water, 1 tablespoon vanilla sugar, 3 tablespoons cream, butter

Dissolve the chocolate in the water. Add sugar and cook over low heat for 20 – 25 minutes. Add cream and a piece of butter the size of a walnut.

Sabayon

ZABAGLIONE

───────── 8 oz. sugar, 6 egg yolks, ½ pint (U.S. 1¼ cups) dry white wine, 3 – 4 tablespoons rum or kirsch

Mix the sugar and egg yolks together and beat over a pan of warm water until the mixture is thick enough to leave a trail. Add the wine and continue beating till the mixture is thick and frothy. Add flavouring.

Note Madeira, sherry, Marsala, asti, Champagne, etc., can be used in place of white wine and no further flavouring should be necessary.

Pralin à la grace royale (pour gâteaux et entremets divers)

PRALINE FOR VARIOUS CAKES AND SWEETS

───────── 2 egg whites, 3 tablespoons icing sugar, chopped almonds

Stir the egg whites and sugar together until thick. Add sufficient almonds ot make a thick or thin praline as required.

Pralin pour soufflés divers, crèmes et glaces
PRALINE FOR SOUFFLÉS, CREAMS AND ICES
——————— 1 lb. castor sugar, 1 lb. dry almonds or hazel-nuts or a mixture of the nuts

Boil the sugar to the caramel stage, 350° F. (see page 698) and add the nuts.

Turn out on to an oiled marble slab and leave to cool. Pound in a mortar, then rub through a sieve. If the praline is not required for immediate use, store in an airtight tin.

Sauce aux fruits
FRUIT SAUCE

Apricots, redcurrants and mirabelles are very suitable for a sauce to serve with sweets. The fruit is cooked as for jam but made thinner. It is put through a tammy cloth or fine sieve and flavoured with Madeira, rum, kirsch or maraschino.

Editor's note Mirabelle is a small yellow plum with a strong flavour.

Sauce à l'abricot
APRICOT SAUCE
——————— Apricot jam, syrup boiled to 28° measured by a saccharometer or 218° F. (see page 698), kirsch, maraschino, rum or Madeira

Put the jam through a tammy cloth or a fine sieve and dilute to the consistency required with the syrup. Bring to boiling point and skim carefully. When the sauce coats the back of the spoon, add flavouring to taste.

Note If the sauce is required for a fruit tart add butter in the proportion of ½ oz. to ½ pint (U.S. 1¼ cups) sauce.

Sauce aux cerises
CHERRY SAUCE

Cook the cherries as for jam. Reduce the syrup, add the same quantity of redcurrant jelly and flavour with kirsch.

Sauce aux fraises

STRAWBERRY SAUCE

Choose 1 lb. ripe strawberries. Remove the stalks and wash in plenty of cold water. Take them out by hand, shaking them to see that all impurities remain in the water. Place in a bowl and pour over 1 pint (U.S. 2½ cups) hot syrup (not boiling), flavoured with vanilla. Leave to cool and strain through a tammy cloth or fine sieve.

Sauce framboises

RASPBERRY SAUCE

Proceed as for strawberry sauce, above.

Sauce groseille

REDCURRANT SAUCE

Dissolve some redcurrant jelly and flavour it with kirsch.

Sauce à l'orange

ORANGE SAUCE

Strain some marmalade through a fine tammy cloth, add one-third its volume of tammied apricot jam and flavour with Curaçao.

Sauce mirabelle

MIRABELLE SAUCE

This is prepared in the same way as apricot sauce (see page 739).

Sauce noisette

NUT SAUCE

Prepare 1 pint English cream custard (see page 694), add to this 1 tablespoon fine praline of hazel-nuts (see page 739) and a little vanilla sugar.

Sauce de fruits liés

THICKENED FRUIT SAUCE

These accompaniments to sweets, which are commonly used in the countries of northern Europe, have the advantage of being economical.

Slightly thicken a purée of sweet fruit with arrowroot and flavour at the last moment with liqueur or flavouring essence.

These are often used as a coating for flans or tartlets.

ENTREMETS FROIDS

COLD SWEETS

Cold sweets are usually accompanied by sauces of various kinds, creams, syrups and fruit purées. Strawberries, raspberries, redcurrants and apricots are generally used and are often flavoured with liqueurs. Kirsch, Curaçao, rum and maraschino are the ones mostly used.

Bavarois

BAVARIAN CREAM

This sweet is seldom used today as it has been replaced by creams and mousses. However, here is the recipe:

8 oz. sugar, 8 egg yolks, 1 vanilla pod, 1 pint (U.S. 2½ cups) milk, ½ oz. gelatine, water, 1 pint (U.S. 2½ cups) cream

Beat the sugar and egg yolks till white and creamy. Infuse the vanilla pod in the milk and, when boiling, pour on to the egg and sugar mixture. Add the gelatine, dissolved in a little water. Cook very gently until the mixture is thick enough to coat the back of the spoon, but be careful it does not boil. Strain through a fine sieve, and leave to cool, stirring occasionally.

When the mixture begins to set add the well beaten cream.

Pour into oiled moulds and leave to set.

If preferred the moulds can be coated with caramel.

When ready to serve, dip the mould quickly into hot water, dab the top dry with a cloth and turn out on to a serving dish.

Crème bavaroise au café

BAVARIAN COFFEE CREAM

Turn the cream out on to a serving dish, cover it with cream sauce (see page 694) flavoured with coffee essence and add a few tablespoons Chantilly cream (see page 696).

Crème bavaroise aux cerises

BAVARIAN CREAM WITH CHERRIES

—————— Bavarian cream, cherries, redcurrant jelly

Prepare the cream according to the basic recipe (see page 741) and turn out on to a serving dish. Have ready some cherries cooked in syrup. Add enough redcurrant jelly to thicken the syrup and, when quite cold, pour the cherries and syrup round the cream.

Crème bavaroise au chocolat

BAVARIAN CHOCOLATE CREAM

Prepare the cream according to the basic recipe (see page 741), turn out on to a serving dish and cover with chocolate sauce (see page 738).

Crème bavaroise aux fraises

BAVARIAN CREAM WITH STRAWBERRIES

Prepare the cream according to recipe on page 741. Turn it out on to a serving dish and surround with strawberries soaked in kirsch, maraschino and sugar and coat with a purée of sweetened raw strawberries.

Crème bavaroise aux framboises

BAVARIAN CREAM WITH RASPBERRIES

Follow the previous recipe but use raspberries instead of strawberries.

  If preferred, the kirsch and the maraschino may be replaced by Curaçao, rum or anisette.

Crème bavaroise aux marrons

BAVARIAN CREAM WITH CHESTNUTS

————— Bavarian cream, marrons glacés, apricot sauce (see page 739), kirsch, maraschino

Prepare the cream as in the original recipe (see page 741), but before adding the whipped cream, and when the cream is just beginning to set, fold in one-third quantity of sieved marrons glacés flavoured with kirsch.

When the cream has set, turn it out on to a serving dish, surround with marrons glacés and coat with apricot sauce flavoured with kirsch and maraschino.

If preferred, the cream mixture can be put straight into a serving dish and, when cold, piped with Chantilly cream (see page 696). The sauce is then served separately.

Crème bavaroise aux pêches

BAVARIAN CREAM WITH PEACHES

Prepare the cream as in the original recipe (see page 741). Turn out on to a serving dish and surround with quarters of peaches, poached in a light syrup and flavoured with vanilla. Cover with apricot syrup flavoured with kirsch and maraschino.

Blanc-manger

BLANCMANGE

Blancmange, like Bavarian cream, has passed out of fashion, at any rate in its original form, and has been replaced by Chantilly mousse, flavoured with almonds and iced.

Blancmange, as its name indicates, should be as white as snow, and it is a contradiction in terms to speak about a 'raspberry or a strawberry blancmange'. The best one can say is a 'blancmange accompanied by raspberries or strawberries'.

Blanc-manger moderne

MODERN BLANCMANGE

8 oz. sweet almonds, 2—3 bitter almonds, 5 oz. castor sugar, 2—3 tablespoons water, 5—6 tablespoons cream, 4 tablespoons kirsch, sweetened Chantilly cream (see page 696), spun sugar (see page 699)

Blanch the almonds and pound them as finely as possible with the sugar, water, cream and kirsch.

Rub through a fine sieve, and mix the resultant purée with 1 pint (U.S. 2½ cups) Chantilly cream.

Pour into a mould and freeze.

When ready to serve, unmould, and pile some more Chantilly cream on top, to resemble a peak in the Alps.

Arrange some spun sugar round the bottom.

Note If the almond mixture is not sieved, it must be pounded into a very fine paste.

The original blancmange was simply an almond milk jelly, flavoured with kirsch.

Blanc-manger à l'anglaise

ENGLISH BLANCMANGE

2¼ oz. cornflour, 3 oz. sugar, 1½ pints (U.S. 3¾ cups) milk, flavouring, 6 tablespoons cream

Mix the cornflour and sugar to a smooth cream with some of the cold milk. Put the rest on to heat.

Add the mixed cornflour and stir till boiling. Boil for 8—10 minutes, beating all the time.

Remove from the heat, add flavouring and cream.

Rinse out a mould with a light syrup or water, pour in the mixture and leave to set.

Turn out and serve alone or with stewed fruit or with raspberry or strawberry purée.

Note Instead of pouring the mixture into a mould, it can be served in small dishes and piped with Chantilly cream (see page 696).

CHARLOTTES

The charlotte mould can be lined, either with lady's finger biscuits, meringues or wafers.

CHARLOTTE CHANTILLY

Line the inside of a charlotte mould with lady's finger biscuits. Fill with Chantilly cream flavoured with vanilla and sweetened. Unmould on to a serving dish, and serve with a fruit sauce, either apricot, strawberry, raspberry or redcurrant, or a chocolate sauce (see pages 739 – 741, 738).

CHARLOTTE HÉLÈNE

Line a charlotte mould with meringues shaped like lady's finger biscuits. Fill with vanilla flavoured Chantilly cream (see page 696), mixed with crystallised violets.

Unmould when set, and decorate the top of the charlotte with piped Chantilly cream and crystallised violets. Serve with chocolate sauce (see page 738).

CHARLOTTE MONTMORENCY

Line a charlotte mould with lady's finger biscuits, and fill with vanilla ice. Unmould on to a serving dish. Decorate the top of the charlotte with Chantilly cream (see page 696) and serve with a compote of stoned cherries in redcurrant jelly (see page 769).

CHARLOTTE NORMANDE

Line a charlotte mould with lady's finger biscuits, and fill with a thick compote of apples prepared as for a charlotte (see page 703), with the addition of one-third its volume of Chantilly cream (see page 696).

Unmould on to a serving dish, and decorate the top with Chantilly cream.

Serve with apricot sauce, flavoured with kirsch (see page 739).

CHARLOTTE RUSSE

Line the bottom and sides of a charlotte mould with lady's finger biscuits. Fill with either Bavarian cream (see page 741) or with vanilla ice. Fresh fruit may be added, in layers, either apricots, pineapple, bananas, peaches, strawberries or raspberries, soaked in kirsch or maraschino. Otherwise add pieces of marrons glacés sprinkled with a few tablespoons rum or kirsch.

CRÈMES POCHÉES
COOKED CREAMS

Cooked creams are only a variation of English custard creams.

Cooked creams are prepared either in special little pots, small dishes, or moulds. The moulds are turned out when they are cold, and are called *crèmes renversées* (inverted creams) to distinguish them from those which are served in the containers in which they are cooked.

Caramel creams are the perfect type of *crème renversée*.

Creams which are served in the dishes in which they are cooked are lighter than the others, because they do not require so many eggs.

Crème pochée à la vanille
COOKED VANILLA CREAM

1¾ pints (U.S. 4¼ cups) milk, 6 oz. sugar, ½ vanilla pod, 4 whole eggs, 6 egg yolks

Boil the milk, add the sugar and vanilla pod and leave to stand for 20 minutes.

Whisk the eggs and egg yolks, add the milk very slowly and beat well. Strain through a fine sieve, leave to stand for a few minutes, then skim off the froth which will have formed on the surface.

Pour into buttered moulds or into specially designed pots.

Put the moulds into a bain-marie, cover, and poach very gently, keeping the water always below boiling point.

If it boils, the air contained in the cream becomes too hot, escapes, and forms air bubbles, which, when the cream is cold, form holes and spoil the appearance of the cream.

If the creams are cooked in the dishes in which they are to be served, use 1 whole egg and 8 egg yolks to the quantity of milk given in the recipe.

If the creams are to be unmoulded, leave them to stand for some minutes before turning out.

This cream may be flavoured with chocolate, coffee, vanilla, orange or almond or hazel-nut pralines (see page 738−739).

Crème pochée au caramel

CARAMEL CREAM

Line the bottom and sides of a mould with sugar cooked to the light caramel stage, and fill it with vanilla cream, as in the previous recipe.

Poach and unmould as instructed for vanilla cream.

Crème pochée Montmorency

CREAM MONTMORENCY

Prepare a caramel cream as in the previous recipe. Unmould and decorate with Chantilly cream.

Serve with a compote of cherries (see page 769) and add a little redcurrant jelly to the cherry syrup.

Crème pochée à la viennoise

VIENNESE CREAM

This is a caramel cream in which the sugar, cooked to a light caramel stage, is dissolved in the hot milk instead of being used to line the mould. It is poached and served like a caramel cream.

It may be accompanied by whipped cream flavoured with vanilla.

CRÈMES À BASE DE CRÈME FOUETTÉ

CREAMS WITH A BASIS OF WHIPPED CREAM

Biscuit Marie-Rose
MARIE-ROSE GÂTEAU
————————— Chantilly cream (see page 696), macaroons

Line the mould* with stiff white paper. Prepare 1 pint (U.S. 2¼ cups) Chantilly cream and add quarter amount of crushed macaroons. Fill the mould, seal it completely and put on ice for 1½−2 hours.

Unmould, remove the paper and pipe with more Chantilly cream.

Serve with whole strawberries, sweetened and soaked in Curaçao and mixed with a sweetened strawberry purée.

*A special Comtesse Marie mould should be used, which is square in shape.

Biscuit Chantilly aux framboises
CHANTILLY GÂTEAU WITH RASPBERRIES

This is the same as Marie-Rose gâteau above, replacing the strawberries with fresh raspberries soaked in kirsch and mixed with a purée of sweetened raspberries.

Brise d'avril
APRIL BREEZE
————————— 1 lb. strawberries, kirsch, maraschino, sugar, 1¾ pints (U.S. 4¼ cups) Chantilly cream (see page 696), pralined violets

Soak the strawberries in a mixture of kirsch, maraschino and sugar. Rub through a sieve then mix with the cream and whip lightly together. Serve in individual dishes and decorate with pralined violets.

The Chantilly cream can be replaced with Bavarian cream (see page 741) or butter cream (see page 695) and the flavouring can be kirsch, rum, coffee, chestnut purée, etc.

This kind of gâteau is easy to make and is always appreciated.

Biscuit Guillot

GUILLOT GÂTEAU

Lady's finger biscuits, kirsch, butter cream (see page 695), Chantilly cream (see page 696)

Take a Comtesse Marie mould (see Marie Rose gâteau, page 748) of medium size, cover the bottom with white paper and put a row of lady's finger biscuits lightly sprinkled with kirsch on the paper. Cover the biscuits with a layer of butter cream then add another layer of biscuits and another of cream, continuing in the same way until the mould is full. Refrigerate until set, then unmould and decorate with piped Chantilly cream.

Serve with an apricot syrup, flavoured with kirsch or maraschino, or with strawberries, cherries, etc.

GELÉES
JELLIES

The basis of jellies is gelatine and water.

The best gelatine is obtained by cooking calf's feet, but as its preparation is a little complicated it is often replaced by commercial gelatine.

Gelée de pieds de veau

CALF'S FOOT JELLY

Calf's feet, water

To each 1¾ pints (U.S. 4¼ cups) jelly add 10 oz. sugar, grated rind ½ orange and ½ lemon, juice 1 orange and 1 lemon

Soak the calf's feet well, put into a pan, cover with cold water and bring to boiling point. Drain off the water, then cover with clean cold water, allowing 3 pints (U.S. 7½ cups) for each calf's foot. Bring to boiling point, skim carefully, then cover and simmer very gently for about 7 hours.

Strain off the liquor and remove all the grease.

To test the gelatinous strength, put a little on ice and if too stiff add a little boiled water and test again.

To clarify the jelly, see the following recipe.

Gelée à base de gélatine

JELLY BASED ON GELATINE

————— 1½ oz. gelatine, 1½ pints (U.S. 3¾ cups) water, 8 oz. sugar, grated rind and juice 1 orange and 1 lemon, flavouring
To clarify 1 egg white, 4 tablespoons white wine

Dissolve the gelatine in the water, add sugar, orange and lemon rind and juice.

Beat the egg white and wine together in a good-sized pan. Add the jelly very slowly, beating vigorously all the time. Continue beating until the liquid boils. Move to the side of the stove, cover and simmer for 15 minutes. Then strain through a jelly cloth. If the jelly is not quite clear, strain again. Leave to cool before adding flavouring of liqueur, wine or fruit.

The most suitable liqueur is kirsch, maraschino, rum, Curaçao or anisette and it should be added in the proportion of 1 part liqueur to 9 parts jelly.

If Champagne, Madeira, Marsala or other wine is used add 3 parts wine to 7 parts jelly.

FOR FRUIT JELLIES

Stand the mould in a bowl of crushed ice. Arrange the fruit in layers adding jelly between each layer and leaving one layer to set, before adding the next. Keep the mould on ice until quite set and required for use.

Jellies can also be made from fruit juices such as strawberry, raspberry and cherry.

————— 12 oz. strawberries, 6 oz. raspberries, 1¼ pints (U.S. 3¼ cups) syrup, vanilla, ¼ pint (U.S. ⅝ cup) liqueur, 1½ oz. gelatine, 6 tablespoons warm water

Prepare the fruit carefully, cover with hot syrup and add a little vanilla flavouring. Cover the bowl and leave in a cool place for 2 hours. Pour through a tammy cloth allowing the syrup to drip through.

Add the chosen liqueur, and the gelatine dissolved in the warm water. Pour into glasses and leave till set.

Some fresh fruit may first be put into the glasses.

POUDINGS FROIDS
COLD PUDDINGS

Pouding diplomate

DIPLOMAT PUDDING

Lady's finger biscuits, kirsch, 1 pint (U.S. 2¼ cups) Bavarian cream (see page 741), sultanas, syrup, apricot jam, apricot syrup flavoured with kirsch or maraschino

Dip the biscuits in kirsch and arrange in a charlotte mould alternately with layers of partly set Bavarian cream. On each layer of biscuits, put a sprinkling of sultanas soaked in warm syrup, and here and there a teaspoon of apricot jam.

Refrigerate until required, then unmould and coat with the apricot syrup.

Pouding diplomate aux fruits

DIPLOMAT PUDDING WITH FRUIT

Diplomat pudding (see above), peaches, apricots, cherries or pears. syrup, apricot purée, kirsch, maraschino

Prepare the pudding as in the previous recipe. Poach the chosen fruit in syrup, then remove the fruit, and thicken the syrup with apricot purée. Flavour with kirsch and maraschino.

Unmould the pudding and arrange the fruit and syrup round it.

Pouding aux marrons

CHESTNUT PUDDING

6 oz. trimmings or broken marrons glacés, 1 pint (U.S. 2¼ cups) vanilla ice cream (see page 780), ¼ pint (U.S. ⅝ cup) sweetened whipped cream, macaroons, rum

Sieve the marrons glacés and mix with the ice cream and whipped cream.

Pack into an iced pudding mould alternately with layers of macaroons soaked in rum. Put to freeze.

When ready, unmould, and surround with marrons glacés.

Serve with apricot sauce (see page 739) flavoured with rum.

Pouding de riz Joséphine
RICE PUDDING JOSEPHINE

──────── 8 oz. rice, 1 pint (U.S. 2½ cups) boiling milk, pinch salt, 2 teaspoons butter, 1 vanilla pod, 4 oz. sugar, 3 egg yolks, 3 tablespoons cream, kirsch, maraschino, 1 lb. strawberries, Chantilly cream (see page 696)

Wash the rice, put into plenty of cold water and bring quickly to boiling point. Drain off the water, add the milk, salt, butter and vanilla pod. Bring to boiling point, cover and simmer for 12 minutes. Add sugar and simmer a further 10−12 minutes when all the milk should have been absorbed.

Remove from the heat, remove vanilla pod, add egg yolks and cream. Flavour with kirsch and maraschino and leave to cool.

Hull the strawberries, put three-qnarters to soak in sweetened kirsch and maraschino, and rub the rest through a sieve. Add the resultant purée to the strawberries being soaked.

Put the cooked rice into a serving dish, arrange the strawberries in a ring on the rice and pile some Chantilly cream in the centre.

ENTREMETS DE FRUITS FROIDS
COLD FRUIT SWEETS

Abricots Mireille
APRICOTS WITH ICE CREAM

──────── Apricots, sugar, kirsch, maraschino, vanilla ice cream (see page 780), apricot syrup, Chantilly cream (see page 696), spun sugar (see page 699), crystallised violets or jasmin

Choose some ripe apricots, peel them and remove the stones. Place them in a deep dish and sprinkle with castor sugar, cover, and leave for 1 hour, then sprinkle with kirsch and maraschino. Break the stones, peel the kernels and put them back into the apricots.

Arrange the apricots in a ring on a bed of vanilla ice cream and cover with a thin layer of apricot syrup flavoured with kirsch and maraschino. Place a pyramid of Chantilly cream in the centre of the dish, and cover with a light veil of spun sugar. Sprinkle with crystallised jasmin flowers or violets.

Abricots duchesse
APRICOTS WITH MERINGUES AND ICE CREAM
Apricots, meringues (see page 697), vanilla ice cream (see page 780), apricot syrup, kirsch, maraschino, spun sugar (see page 699), strawberries

Prepare the apricots as in the previous recipe, but if they are not quite ripe, cook them for a few minutes.

Allow 1 meringue shell for each person and fill it with ice cream. Place an apricot on top. Cover the bottom of the serving dish with a thin layer of thick apricot syrup flavoured with kirsch and maraschino. Arrange the meringue on top, enclosed in a nest of spun sugar, and top each with a fine strawberry.

Mousse à l'ananas au sirop
PINEAPPLE MOUSSE WITH SYRUP
1 ripe pineapple, sugar, 1 pint (U.S. 2½ cups) syrup (see page 698), 16 egg yolks, vanilla, 1 pint (U.S. 2½ cups) cream

Peel the pineapple and break up the pulp with a fork. Put it into a bowl, sprinkle lightly with sugar and leave covered.

Boil the syrup to 218° F. Leave to cool, then pour on to the beaten egg yolks. Flavour with vanilla and strain through a fine sieve. Add to the pineapple pulp. Heat very gently, beating all the time until the mixture is thick enough to leave a trail. Remove from the heat, and continue beating until the mixture is quite cold.

Whip the cream and fold into the pineapple mixture. Turn into an iced pudding mould or an iced gâteau mould and freeze for about 2 hours.

Mousse d'ananas à la crème
PINEAPPLE MOUSSE WITH CREAM
8 oz. sugar, 8 egg yolks, ½ pint (U.S. 1¼ cups) boiled milk, 8 oz. pineapple pulp, ½ pint (U.S. 1¼ cups), Chantilly cream (see page 696)

Prepare an English custard cream (see page 694) with the sugar, egg yolks and milk; let cool, beating all the time. Add the pineapple pulp prepared as in the previous recipe, and, when the mixture is quite cold, add the Chantilly cream.

Pour the mixture into a gâteau mould and freeze.

Ananas à la parisienne

PINEAPPLE SAVARIN

1 savarin (see page 686), kirsch, iced pineapple mousse (see page 753), strawberries, sugar, pineapple, apricot purée, maraschino, Chantilly cream (see page 696)

Sprinkle the savarin with kirsch and half fill with iced pineapple mousse. Decorate with large strawberries dipped in kirsch and sugar.

Cut some slices of pineapple in half, soak in kirsch and arrange in a ring on the savarin.

Thicken the syrup with an apricot purée flavoured with maraschino, and pour it over the pineapple.

Serve with Chantilly cream.

Bananes en salade

BANANA SALAD

Use ripe bananas, peel them and cut into slices. Put into a deep dish, sprinkle with sugar, and a few tablespoons orange juice, and leave for 15–20 minutes.

Just before serving, put them into a glass dish and sprinkle with kirsch.

Segments of orange, with all the white pith removed, may be added to the bananas.

Mousse de bananes

BANANA MOUSSE

Prepare an English custard cream as indicated for the pineapple mousse (see page 694), replacing the pineapple with 8 oz. sieved banana. Add ½ pint (U.S. 1¼ cups) Chantilly cream (see page 696) and freeze in the same way.

Note All fruit mousses may be made quite easily by adding to 8 oz. fruit purée 8 oz. castor sugar and 1 pint (U.S. 2½ cups) well beaten cream. Put into a mould and freeze.

Cerises au vin de Bordeaux ou soupe aux cerises à la française.

CHERRIES IN CLARET, OR FRENCH CHERRY SOUP

━━━━━━━ 1 lb. cherries, 8 oz. castor sugar, grated rind ½ orange, 1 small piece cinnamon stick, 5—6 tablespoons redcurrant jelly, 1½ bottles claret

Stone the cherries and put into a pan with the sugar, orange rind, cinnamon, and redcurrant jelly.

Add the claret, cover and bring to boiling point.

Simmer very gently for 10—12 minutes.

Leave to get cold, then serve in glasses with sweet biscuits (U.S. ookies) or macaroons.

Cerises Mireille

CHERRIES WITH MERINGUES

━━━━━━━ 1 lb. cherries, 6 oz. raspberries, 1 vanilla pod, 10 very small meringues (see page 697), 1 pint (U.S. 2½ cups) Chantilly cream (see page 696)

Stone the cherries, sieve the raspberries and put together in a pan with the vanilla pod. Cover and bring to boiling point, cool a little, then bring again to the boil. Draw to the side of the stove and leave for 10—12 minutes. Remove the vanilla pod and pour into a bowl and leave to cool.

Mix the meringues with the cream, put into an iced gâteau mould lined on the bottom and sides with white paper. Cover and freeze in the ordinary way.

When ready to serve, unmould, decorate with some of the cherries, pour a little of the syrup on top and serve the rest of the cherries and syrup separately.

Note Instead of meringues, small macaroons soaked in kirsch, maraschino, Curaçao or rum may be used.

The mousse may be accompanied by fresh strawberries, peaches or apricots.

The strawberries should not be cooked, simply soaked in liqueur and sugar, but the peaches and apricots may be poached in vanilla syrup.

Figues à la mode du Carlton, à Londres

FIGS AS SERVED AT THE CARLTON HOTEL IN LONDON

Peel some fresh figs, halve them lengthwise and put into a silver or glass dish and keep them on ice.

Prepare a raspberry purée, add double the quantity of Chantilly cream (see page 696) and cover the figs completely with the mixture.

Figues à la crème et liqueurs

FIGS WITH CREAM AND LIQUEURS

Peel some figs, halve them lengthwise and put them into a serving dish. Sprinkle lightly with sugar and add 2−3 tablespoons maraschino or Curaçao and keep on ice till required.

When ready to serve, cover with Chantilly cream (see page 696).

Note After being cooked in syrup or in the oven, fresh figs can be served on a bed of rice, semolina, frangipani, etc. But, in my own opinion, fresh figs cooked in the oven are the best.

To do this, take some figs with unblemished skins and place them in an earthenware dish with a few tablespoons water. Sprinkle with sugar and bake them in the oven like apples. The sugar caramelises during the cooking of the fruit and has an excellent taste, which syrup, usually too sweet, does not possess.

Figs cooked like this in the oven, served cold and accompanied by Chantilly cream, constitute a very delicate dessert.

Dried figs may be cooked like prunes in syrup, or with red wine, and are served with rice or semolina pudding.

Mousse aux fraises

STRAWBERRY MOUSSE

To each 1 pint (*U.S. 2½ cups*) *strawberry purée* 1 lb. sugar, 1¼ pints (U.S. 3⅛ cups) thick cream

Choose some ripe strawberries, preferably wild ones, and rub through a sieve. Add the sugar and stiffly whipped cream.

Apricots, bananas, raspberries, mirabelles, peaches, etc., can be used in the same way.

Fraises à la créole

STRAWBERRIES CREOLE STYLE

—————— Rice cooked in milk (see page 718), egg yolks, kirsch, maraschino, 1 lb. strawberries, sugar, pineapple, syrup

When the rice is cooked, add the egg yolks and flavour with kirsch or maraschino. Then press into a ring mould and keep on ice till required.

Hull and wash the strawberries carefully, sprinkle with sugar, kirsch and maraschino. Cover, and leave for 15–20 minutes.

Cut the pineapple into thin slices and then in halves, put into a bowl and sprinkle with kirsch.

Unmould the rice on to a serving dish. Fill the centre with the strawberries, and arrange the pieces of pineapple on the rice ring.

Cover with syrup flavoured with kirsch and maraschino and serve with Chantilly cream (see page 696).

Fraises Jeanne Granier

STRAWBERRIES WITH GRAND MARNIER AND CURAÇAO

—————— 1 lb. strawberries, sugar, Grand Marnier, orange ice (see page 784), Curaçao, syrup mousse (see below)

Hull and wash the strawberries, put them into a bowl and sprinkle with sugar and Grand Marnier. Cover and keep on ice till required.

Put a layer of ice cream in the bottom of a serving dish, and arrange the strawberries and their juice on top. Flavour the syrup mousse with Curaçao but do not freeze it. Pour over the strawberries.

Mousse au Curaçao

CURAÇAO MOUSSE

—————— ½ pint (U.S. 1¼ cups) syrup (see page 698), 8 egg yolks, 2 tablespoons Curaçao, 3 tablespoons whipped cream

Boil the syrup to 218° F. and when cool pour over the beaten egg yolks. Strain through a fine sieve, then put into a pan and whisk over very gentle heat, until the mixture is thick enough to leave a trail. Remove from the heat, and continue whisking till cold.

Just before serving add the Curaçao and cream.

Fraises Lérina

STRAWBERRIES LÉRINA

1 medium-sized ripe Cantaloup melon, 1 lb. wild strawberries, sugar, 6 tablespoons Lérina liqueur,* 2—3 tablespoons orange juice
Editor's note Lérina liqueur is no longer obtainable but Chartreuse or Izzara make an excellent substitute.

Cut a slice from the stalk end of the melon about 3 inches in diameter. Remove the seeds, and scoop out the pulp with a dessertspoon. Put the pulp into a bowl with the strawberries. Sprinkle with sugar and add the liqueur and orange juice. Leave to soak for 1 hour, then fill the melon with the fruit and replace the top.

Fraises Monte-Carlo

STRAWBERRIES WITH CURAÇAO MOUSSE

Strawberries, sugar, Curaçao, raspberries, Curaçao mousse (see page 757), meringues (see page 697), spun sugar (see page 699), Chantilly cream (see page 696), crystallised violets

Take some of the largest strawberries, put them into a bowl and sprinkle with sugar and Curaçao. Keep on ice till required.

Make a purée with the smaller strawberries and a few raspberries, add a little sugar and keep on ice.

Prepare the mousse, put it into a square Comtesse Marie mould (see page 748) and freeze. Allow 1 meringue shell per person and prepare the spun sugar.

When ready to serve, unmould the mousse on to an oval serving dish. Put the meringues into a nest of spun sugar and arrange at either end of the dish. Mix some Chantilly cream with the strawberry and raspberry purée, using about half as much cream as purée. Put a spoonful into each meringue and arrange 2—3 of the strawberries soaked in Curaçao on top. Cover with the rest of the fruit and cream purée and cover this with a light veil of spun sugar. Sprinkle with crystallised violets.

Fraises Ritz

STRAWBERRIES WITH RASPBERRIES AND CHANTILLY CREAM

1 lb. large strawberries, sugar, 4 oz. wild strawberries, 4 oz. raspberries, ½ pint (U.S. 1¼ cups) Chantilly cream (see page 696)

Put the hulled strawberries into a serving dish. Sprinkle with sugar and keep on ice till required.

Rub the wild strawberries and the raspberries through a sieve and mix the purée with the well beaten cream.

When ready to serve cover the strawberries completely with the cream.

Fraises Romanoff
STRAWBERRIES ROMANOFF

Soak some large strawberries in orange juice and Curaçao. Put them into a silver or a glass dish and cover them with Chantilly cream (see page 696).

Fraises Sarah Bernhardt
STRAWBERRIES WITH PINEAPPLE AND CURAÇAO MOUSSE

———————— Strawberries, Grand Marnier, sugar, pineapple mousse (see page 753), Curaçao mousse (see page 757)

Take some large strawberries, hull them and soak in Grand Marnier and sugar.

Have ready the pineapple mousse, unmould it and surround with the strawberries. Cover with the very cold, but not frozen, Curaçao mousse. Serve with some macaroons.

THIS IS A QUICKER VERSION OF THE RECIPE

Put some vanilla ice cream (see page 780) with thick pineapple purée into a serving dish. Arrange the strawberries on top and cover with the very cold, but not frozen, Curaçao mousse.

Fraises Tosca
STRAWBERRIES TOSCA

———————— Strawberries, orange juice, kirsch, sugar, raspberries, Chantilly cream (see page 696), macaroons

Take some large strawberries and soak them in orange juice, kirsch and sugar. Cover them with a purée of raspberries, mixed with the same amount of Chantilly cream. Sprinkle the top with crushed macaroons.

Mandarines glacées

ICED TANGERINES

—————— Tangerines, tangerine ice (see page 784)

Cut a piece about ¾ inch in diameter from each tangerine with a plain pastry cutter. Empty them and keep the skins in the refrigerator.

Add the juice from the tangerines and a few thin strips of tangerine peel to the ice and fill the tangerine skins. Replace the lids and serve on a bed of crushed ice.

Melon glacé

ICED MELON

—————— 1 melon, sugar, kirsch, maraschino, orange ice (see page 784)

Choose a good ripe melon, and cut a slice off the top about 3 inches in diameter. Remove the seeds and spoon out the pulp. Cut it into cubes and put them into a bowl. Sprinkle with sugar, kirsch and maraschino.

Sprinkle the inside of the melon with sugar. When ready to serve, mix the melon with orange ice and fill up the melon case.

Replace the lid.

ORANGES

Formerly, orange jelly flavoured with kirsch was a very popular dish, being served in the skin of the orange, which was given the form of a small basket with a handle. Nowadays, jellies are replaced by ice cream.

However, these little baskets filled with wild strawberries soaked in kirsch and sugar, and covered with orange jelly, certainly had their charm.

The jelly may be replaced by orange ice (see page 784) with 3 or 4 large strawberries, dipped for a moment in Curaçao and sugar, placed on top.

Finally, they may be covered lightly with spun sugar (see page 699).

Pêches Adrienne

PEACHES WITH STRAWBERRY ICE CREAM AND CURAÇAO MOUSSE

1 peach for each person, sugar, strawberry ice cream (see page 779), vanilla, 1 meringue shell for each person (see page 697), Curaçao mousse (see page 757), spun sugar (see page 699), crystallised rose petals

Choose ripe peaches, dip them into boiling water and then into iced water, and remove the skins.

Sprinkle with sugar and leave in a cool place till required.

Flavour the ice cream with vanilla and put it into a shallow serving dish. Press the meringue shells lightly down into the ice cream, place a peach in each one and cover with a thin layer of mousse. This should be very cold but not frozen. Cover with a veil of spun sugar and sprinkle with crystallised rose petals.

Pêches aiglon

PEACHES WITH VANILLA ICE CREAM

Peaches, syrup (see page 698), vanilla ice cream (see page 780), pralined violets, spun sugar (see page 699)

Prepare the peaches as in the previous recipe. Boil the syrup to 218° F., pour over the peaches and leave them to cool in the syrup.

When ready to serve, put a bed of vanilla ice cream on the serving dish, arrange the drained peaches on top, sprinkle with the pralined violets and cover with spun sugar.

Editor's note This dish was originally served on a block of ice carved to represent an eagle — hence its name.

Pêches à l'aurore

PEACHES WITH ZABAGLIONE AND CURAÇAO

Peaches, syrup, kirsch, iced strawberry mousse (see page 756), zabaglione (see page 738), Curaçao

Peel the peaches as in the previous recipe, cover with boiling syrup flavoured with kirsch and leave the peaches to cool in the syrup.

Drain the peaches, arrange them on the strawberry mousse and cover with zabaglione flavoured with Curaçao.

Pêches Alexandra

PEACHES WITH STRAWBERRY MOUSSE AND MARASCHINO

———— Peaches, syrup, vanilla, vanilla ice cream (see page 780), strawberry purée, maraschino, crystallised rose petals

Peel the peaches as in the previous recipes, cover with boiling syrup flavoured with vanilla and leave them to cool in the syrup.

Drain the peaches, arrange them on the ice cream and cover with strawberry purée flavoured with maraschino. Sprinkle with crystallised rose petals before serving.

Pêches cardinal

PEACHES WITH STRAWBERRY PURÉE AND KIRSCH

———— Peaches, strawberry purée, kirsch, maraschino, almonds

Prepare some ripe peaches as described in the recipe for *pêches Adrienne* (see page 761). Remove the stone by pushing it out through the stalk end with a larding needle.

Put the peaches on to a serving dish, cover with the strawberry purée flavoured with kirsch and maraschino and sprinkle with split almonds.

Pêches au Château-Lafite

PEACHES CHÂTEAU-LAFITE

———— Peaches, 1 bottle Château-Lafite wine, 8 oz. sugar, 6 tablespoons redcurrant jelly

Peel the peaches as described in the previous recipes and halve them. Put into a pan, cover with the wine and add sugar and jelly. Poach gently, then leave to cool in the liquid.

Serve with macaroons.

Pêches dame blanche

PEACHES WITH ICE CREAM AND CRYSTALLISED PINEAPPLE

———— Peaches, syrup, crystallised pineapple, vanilla ice cream (see page 780), Chantilly cream (see page 696)

Peel the peaches and cover with boiling syrup as described for *pêches aiglon* (see page 761). Leave to cool in the syrup.

Add a little crystallised pineapple to the vanilla ice cream. Put it into a serving dish, and arrange the peaches in a ring on the ice cream. Pile some Chantilly cream in the centre.

Pêches Eugénie

PEACHES WITH CHAMPAGNE ZABAGLIONE

Peaches, wild strawberries, 2—3 tablespoons kirsch and maraschino mixed together, zabaglione made with Champagne (see page 738)

Choose ripe peaches, peel and stone them and put into a serving dish with the strawberries. Sprinkle with kirsch and maraschino and keep on ice till required.

When ready to serve, cover with the cold zabaglione.

Pêches Melba

PEACH MELBA

Peaches, sugar, vanilla ice cream (see page 780), raspberry purée, sliced 'green' almonds (optional)

Peel and stone the peaches (see page 761), and sprinkle with sugar.

Put the ice cream into a serving dish or in individual dishes, arrange the peaches on top and cover with the sweetened purée.

Note Finely sliced 'green' almonds may be sprinkled on top, but dried almonds should not be used.

Pêches petit-duc

PEACHES WITH ICE AND CHANTILLY CREAM

Peaches, vanilla ice cream (see page 780), redcurrant jelly, Chantilly cream (see page 696)

Prepare the peaches as for *pêches Melba* (see above). Arrange in a ring on the ice cream and cover with redcurrant jelly. Pile some Chantilly cream in the centre.

Pêches rose-chéri

PEACHES WITH CHERRIES AND ICE CREAM

6 peaches, syrup (see page 698), 8 oz. white heart cherries, 4 oz. castor sugar, 4 oz. redcurrant jelly, vanilla ice cream (see page 780), Chantilly cream (see page 696)

Peel and stone the peaches, cover with boiling syrup, and leave to cool in the syrup.

Stone the cherries, put into a pan with the sugar and cook gently for 7−8 minutes. Add the jelly, and when it has melted turn all out into a bowl and leave to cool.

When ready to serve put the ice cream on to a serving dish and arrange the peaches and cherries on top. Add the cherry syrup to double its quantity of Chantilly cream and pour over the fruit.

Pêches Trianon

PEACHES WITH WILD STRAWBERRIES AND ICE CREAM

6 peaches, 1 lb. wild strawberries, sugar, Curaçao, vanilla ice cream (see page 780), 6 large macaroons, Chantilly cream (see page 696)

Prepare the peaches as in the previous recipe.

Put half the strawberries into a bowl, sprinkle with sugar, and add 6 tablespoons Curaçao.

Prepare a purée with the rest of the strawberries. Pour it over the strawberries and Curaçao and leave for 30 minutes.

Put a bed of ice cream into a serving dish. Dip the macaroons in Curaçao and arrange on top. Put a peach on each macaroon and cover with the strawberry mixture. Finally cover with Chantilly cream.

Poires bohémienne

PEARS WITH MARRONS GLACÉS AND RUM

Pears, vanilla flavoured syrup, vanilla ice cream (see page 780), marrons glacés, rum, apricot syrup

Choose some juicy, medium-sized pears, poach them in the syrup and leave to cool.

When ready to serve put a bed of vanilla ice cream in a glass dish, add some broken marrons glacés and sprinkle lightly with rum. Place the pears on top and cover with apricot syrup flavoured with rum.

Poires cardinal

PEARS WITH STRAWBERRY PURÉE

Pears, vanilla flavoured syrup, strawberry purée, sugar, kirsch, maraschino

Choose juicy, medium-sized pears and poach them in vanilla flavoured syrup. Leave to cool in the syrup.

Put into a serving dish and cover with sweetened strawberry purée flavoured with kirsch and maraschino.

Poires florentine

FLORENCE STYLE PEARS

Pears, vanilla flavoured syrup, 8 oz. sugar, ¼ vanilla pod, 1¾ pints (U.S. 4¼ cups) water, 10 oz. semolina, 3 egg yolks, 6 tablespoons cream, 3 tablespoons kirsch and maraschino mixed together, apricot syrup, Chantilly cream (see page 696)

Peel and quarter the pears and cook carefully in the vanilla syrup. Put the sugar and vanilla pod into a pan with the water and bring to boiling point. Sprinkle in the semolina slowly and simmer for 18−20 minutes.

Remove from the heat, add the egg yolks, cream and the kirsch and maraschino.

Rinse out a ring mould with apricot syrup, then press in the semolina mixture. Leave in the refrigerator for 1 hour.

Unmould on to a serving dish, fill the centre with the well drained pears and cover all with the apricot syrup flavoured with kirsch and maraschino.

Put a mound of Chantilly cream on the pears.

Poires Hélène
PEARS HÉLÈNE

▬▬▬▬▬▬ Pears, vanilla flavoured syrup, vanilla ice cream (see page 780), pralined violets

Poach the pears in the syrup and leave to cool. When ready to serve, arrange them on a bed of vanilla ice cream and sprinkle with pralined violets.

Serve with a hot chocolate sauce (see page 738).

Poires Mary Garden
PEARS WITH CHERRIES AND ICE CREAM

▬▬▬▬▬▬ Pears, light syrup (see page 698), compote of cherries (see page 769), raspberry flavoured redcurrant jelly, vanilla ice cream (see page 780)

Peel and poach the pears in a light syrup and leave to cool. Drain the cherries from their syrup and thicken it with the jelly.

When ready to serve, put a bed of ice cream into a serving dish, arrange the cherries on top and pour the syrup over.

Poires Melba
PEARS MELBA

▬▬▬▬▬▬ Pears, vanilla flavoured syrup, vanilla ice cream, raspberry purée

Choose juicy pears of medium size, poach them in vanilla flavoured syrup and leave to cool. Serve on a bed of vanilla ice cream and cover with raspberry purée.

Poires Richelieu
PEARS POACHED IN CLARET

▬▬▬▬▬▬ Pears, 1 bottle claret, 4 oz. sugar, pinch cinnamon, grated rind 1 orange, 3—4 tablespoons redcurrant jelly

Peel and poach the pears in the claret with sugar, cinnamon, and orange rind. When they are ready remove and put into a bowl. Add the red-currant jelly to the wine and boil for a few minutes.

Pour over the pears and leave to get cold.

Serve with Chantilly cream (see page 696) and some large macaroons.

Pommes châtelaine

APPLES AND APRICOT MOULD

———— Apples cooked as for apple charlotte (see page 703), apricot compote (see page 768), lady's finger biscuits, Chantilly cream (see page 696), praline (see page 739)

Mix the apples and apricots together in the proportion of one-thirds apricots and two-thirds apple. Leave to cool.

Line the bottom and sides of a charlotte mould with the biscuits and fill with the fruit mixture. When ready to serve, turn out and decorate with piped Chantilly cream.

Sprinkle with crushed praline.

Pommes aux raisins de Smyrne

APPLES AND SULTANAS WITH BRIOCHE

———— 6 medium-sized apples, syrup, 4 oz. sultanas, 6 tablespoons Madeira, ¼ pint (U.S. ⅝ cup) sweetened apricot purée, 12 slices brioche cut into half-moon shapes (see page 684), castor sugar

Peel and quarter the apples and poach gently in a light syrup. Leave to cool.

Plump the sultanas in 2–3 tablespoons boiling syrup. Add the Madeira, apricot purée and the syrup in which the apples were cooked. Boil for a few minutes and leave to cool.

Put the slices of brioche on a tray, sprinkle with sugar and put into a moderate oven to caramelise lightly.

When ready to serve, arrange the slices of brioche in a ring on a serving dish, put the apples on top and cover with the sultana mixture.

Serve alone, or with Chantilly cream (see page 696).

Note The sultanas may be replaced with glacé cherries.

COMPOTES

For a compote, the fruit is cooked in a light syrup and flavoured according to the fruit used. It can be cooked whole, or cut into halves or quarters and is served in a dish or in individual glasses with the syrup.

Fruit for compote should not be too ripe.

It is generally better to serve it cold, but can be served hot if preferred.

Compote d'abricots

APRICOT COMPOTE

Halve the apricots and remove the stones, dip apricots quickly into boiling water, then peel, and cook in a light syrup.

Remove the kernel from the stones, blanch and leave to soak in syrup flavoured with kirsch.

When cooked put half an almond into each half apricot and pour over the syrup in which they were cooked and in which the almonds were soaked.

Compote d'ananas

PINEAPPLE COMPOTE

Peel a fresh pineapple and cut it into slices.

Remove the hard centre and cook in syrup flavoured with vanilla.

Arrange in a circle in the serving dish and pour the syrup over.

Compote de bananes

BANANA COMPOTE

Peel the bananas and cook them for 4–5 minutes in syrup flavoured with kirsch or rum.

Serve them in individual dishes with the syrup.

Compote de cerises

CHERRY COMPOTE

Stem and stone the cherries and put into a pan with 6 oz. sugar to
2 lb. cherries. Cover and simmer for 5 – 6 minutes. Keep covered while
cooling.

Note Compote of cherries can be made with claret using 8 oz. sugar
and ½ pint (U.S. 1¼ cups) claret to 2 lb. cherries.
Serve in individual dishes with macaroons or biscuits (U.S. cookies).

Compote de fraises

STRAWBERRY COMPOTE

In order to get a good compote of strawberries, the fruit should not
be cooked too much. Choose large strawberries and remove their stalks.
Put them into a dish, cover with syrup flavoured with vanilla and half
cooled. Cover the bowl and leave to cool.

By this method the strawberries are enabled to keep their real flavour,
which disappears when the fruit has been boiled, even for a few seconds.

Compote de framboises

RASPBERRY COMPOTE

Choose some large, very fresh raspberries. Carefully remove the
stalks, place them in a bowl and cover with warm raspberry flavoured
syrup, cover, and leave to cool. Serve in individual dishes with the syrup.

Compote de mirabelles

MIRABELLE COMPOTE

Choose some real Metz mirabelles, stone them and cook for
10 – 12 minutes in syrup, flavoured with vanilla. Serve in a fruit dish
with the syrup.

Compote de nectarines brugnons

NECTARINE COMPOTE

Choose some ripe nectarines, plunge them into boiling water for 2 seconds, then into cold water. Peel and cook them whole in a vanilla flavoured syrup. Serve in a fruit dish with the syrup.

Compote de pêches

PEACH COMPOTE

Peel the peaches as for nectarines (see above) and cook them, whole or in halves, in syrup flavoured with vanilla.

Compote de poires

PEAR COMPOTE

Choose some juicy pears of medium size, peel them and cook in a light syrup flavoured with vanilla.

Certain kinds of firm-fleshed pears are more often cooked in sweetened red wine. Add the zest of a lemon and a pinch of cinnamon.

Compote de pommes

APPLE COMPOTE

Any apples may be used for compote, but cooking apples are best. If cooked whole, remove cores with a corer, peel, dip in lemon juice, put into cold water immediately. Poach in a light syrup, flavoured with vanilla. Watch carefully to see they are not overcooked.

Compote de pruneaux

COMPOTE OF PRUNES

Wash and soak the prunes, then cook slowly in half red wine and half water, adding 2−3 oz. sugar, pinch cinnamon and a strip of lemon peel to 1 lb. prunes.

Compote de reines-claude

GREENGAGE COMPOTE

Choose firm greengages, stone them and poach without boiling, in a light syrup flavoured with vanilla.
Serve in individual dishes.

Compote de rhubarbe

RHUBARB COMPOTE

Cut the rhubarb into pieces about 2−3 inches long, string if necessary and put into a shallow dish or pan. Half cover with syrup, cover and cook in a slow oven or over very moderate heat so that the rhubarb is kept whole.

ENTREMETS FROIDS DIVERS
VARIOUS COLD SWEETS

Biscuit Monte-Carlo

MONTE-CARLO GÂTEAU

Meringue (see page 697), Chantilly cream (see page 696), grated chocolate, chocolate icing (U.S. frosting), crystallised violets

Use 4−5 flan rings and put them on a slightly damp board covered with greaseproof paper.

Half fill the rings with meringue. Dry them off in a very cool oven and leave for 24 hours.

Place the discs of meringue one on top of the other, spreading each disc with Chantilly cream and sprinkling it with grated chocolate.

Cover the top disc with chocolate icing and pipe Chantilly cream round the gâteau in between the discs.

Pipe some rosettes of cream round the edge and put a crystallised violet on each rosette.

Croûte Joinville

SAVARIN WITH PINEAPPLE AND LIQUEUR

1 savarin (see page 686), syrup, kirsch, pineapple, Chantilly cream (see page 696), grated chocolate, apricot syrup, maraschino

Cut the savarin into slices and soak lightly in syrup flavoured with kirsch. Cut the pineapple into slices and soak in kirsch.

Arrange the slices of savarin and pineapple alternately in a circle on a serving dish. Fill the centre with cream and sprinkle with grated chocolate.

Flavour the apricot syrup with kirsch and maraschino and pour round.

Croûte mexicaine

BRIOCHE WITH PINEAPPLE AND ICE CREAM

1 brioche (see page 684), sugar, pineapple, apricot syrup, rum, vanilla orange or strawberry ice cream (see page 779)

Cook the brioche in a medium-sized charlotte mould the day before it is required.

Cut in half and then into half-moon shaped slices. Sprinkle with sugar and put into a moderate oven to caramelise lightly.

Arrange the slices on a serving dish in a ring, alternately with slices of pineapple. Cover with apricot syrup flavoured with rum, and pile, the ice cream in the centre.

Croûte normande à la Chantilly

BRIOCHES WITH APPLES AND CHANTILLY CREAM

1 brioche, apricot syrup, kirsch, maraschino, apples cooked as for apple charlotte (see page 703), apricot compote (see page 768), Chantilly cream (see page 696), vanilla

Prepare the slices of brioche as in the previous recipe and arrange in a ring on a serving dish. Flavour the cold syrup with kirsch and maraschino and pour over the slices of brioche.

Mix the apples and apricots together and pile into the centre. Cover with vanilla flavoured Chantilly cream, shaping it up into a peak.

Mont-Blanc aux marrons

CHESTNUT MONT BLANC

━━━━━━ Chestnuts, vanilla sugar, Chantilly cream (see page 696), vanilla

Shell and skin the chestnuts and cook gently in water or milk, with a pinch salt.

Drain and rub through a sieve.

Sprinkle with vanilla sugar, and without compressing them lift carefully with two forks and arrange in a ring on a serving dish or, if preferred, on a savarin flavoured with kirsch. Pile some vanilla flavoured Chantilly cream in the centre, piling it up to create an illusion of the snowy peaks of Mont-Blanc.

Mousse Monte-Carlo

MERINGUE AND CREAM MOULD

━━━━━━ Medium-sized meringue shells (see page 697), 1 pint (U.S. 2¼ cups) thick cream, ½ pint (U.S. 1¼ cups) syrup boiled to 220° F., syrup, grated rind 1 tangerine, Chantilly cream (see page 696), crystallised violets

Line the bottom of a charlotte mould with the meringues. Beat the cream stiffly, and add the cooled syrup in which the tangerine rind has been infused. Pour into the mould and freeze.

Unmould and cover with Chantilly cream flavoured with tangerine. Sprinkle with crystallised violets.

Mousse d'oeuf au caramel

MERINGUE WITH CUSTARD CREAM

━━━━━━ Caramelised sugar as for caramel cream (see page 698), meringue (see page 697), English custard cream flavoured with vanilla, chocolate or coffee (see page 694)

Line a charlotte mould with the caramelised sugar. Fill with the meringue and poach in a bain-marie as for the caramel cream. Leave to cool before unmoulding, then cover with custard cream, flavoured to taste.

Macédoine de fruits rafraîchis

CHILLED MACEDOINE OF FRUIT

—————————— Fresh fruit, syrup boiled to 220° F. (see page 698), kirsch, maraschino

Use any fruit in season and prepare according to its kind. Flavour the syrup with kirsch and maraschino and, when cool, pour over the fruit.

Mix very carefully so that the fruit is not broken and leave in the refrigerator for 30 minutes before serving.

Oeufs à la neige

FLOATING ISLANDS

—————————— Meringue (see page 697), milk, sugar, vanilla, egg yolks

Mould the meringue into egg shapes using a spoon and poach carefully in boiling milk, sweetened and flavoured with vanilla. Turn during the cooking so that they cook evenly. When the meringue is set, remove carefully and drain on a cloth. Use the milk in which the meringues have been cooked to make an English custard cream (seee page 694).

Arrange meringues in a serving dish and pour custard cream over.

Riz impératrice

RICE WITH CUSTARD CREAM, KIRSCH AND MARASCHINO

—————————— 8 oz. rice, 1¾ pints (U.S. 4¼ cups) boiling milk, pinch salt, ¼ vanilla pod, ½ oz. butter, 8 oz. castor sugar, kirsch, maraschino, ¼ oz. gelatine, ½ pint (U.S. 1¼ cups) thick cream, ½ pint (U.S. 1¼ cups) English custard cream (see page 694) apricot syrup

Wash the rice, put into plenty of boiling watei and boil for 2 minutes. Drain off the water, add the boiling milk, salt, vanilla and butter, and simmer for 10−12 minutes, then add the sugar.

Pour the rice into a bowl, cool a little and flavour with kirsch and maraschino. Add the dissolved gelatine and whipped cream to the custard cream and mix with the rice.

Pour into a mould and leave to set.

Unmould and cover with apricot syrup flavoured with kirsch and maraschino.

Röd-Gröd (Danish sweet)

REDCURRANT AND RASPBERRY MOULD

8 oz. redcurrants, 8 oz. raspberries, 1½ pints (U.S. 3¾ cups) water, 12 oz. sugar, 1½ oz. ground sago, 1½ oz. potato flour, ¼ pint (U.S. ⅝ cup) red wine, ¼ vanilla pod

Put the redcurrants and raspberries into a pan with the water. Heat slowly to boiling point, then rub through a fine sieve. There should be about 2¼ pints (U.S. 5⅝ cups) liquid. Return to the pan, add sugar, sago and potato flour mixed smoothly with the wine, and vanilla.

Stir till boiling, then boil for 2 minutes, stirring all the time.

Rinse some moulds with syrup or water and sprinkle with sugar. Pour in the mixture and leave overnight in a cold place.

Unmould and serve with cream.

Semoule flamri

SEMOLINA AND WINE MOULD

½ pint (U.S. 1¼ cups) white wine, ½ pint (U.S. 1¼ cups) water, 8 oz. semolina, 8 oz. castor sugar, pinch salt, 2 whole eggs, 6 egg whites, strawberry or raspberry purée, cherries for decoration

Put the wine into a pan with the same amount of water and bring to boiling point.

Sprinkle in the semolina slowly and simmer for 20 minutes. Add the sugar, salt and whole eggs.

Beat the egg whites stiffly and fold into the mixture.

Turn into a buttered mould and poach in a bain-marie or cook in a steamer.

When cold, unmould and cover with the fruit purée.

Decorate with cherries.

Suédoise de fruits

SUÉDOISE OF FRUIT

This is a jelly moulded in layers with stewed fruits. The colour and arrangement should be varied as much as possible.

If strawberries and raspberries are included they should be used raw.

Tivoli aux fraises

TIVOLI OF STRAWBERRIES

———————— Kirsch jelly, Bavarian cream (see page 741), strawberry purée, strawberries, kirsch, maraschino, Chantilly cream (see page 696), vanilla

Mask a ring mould with a thick layer of kirsch jelly. Fill with a Bavarian
cream mixture to which some strawberry purée has been added and
leave to set.

Unmould and serve with strawberries soaked in kirsch and maraschino
and Chantilly cream flavoured with vanilla.

JUNKET

———————— 1¾ pints (U.S. 4¼ cups) milk, 2 oz. sugar, flavouring, 6 drops rennet

Heat the milk to blood heat (98° F. or 36° C.). Remove from the heat,
add sugar and flavouring.

Stir in the rennet and leave to set.

Glaces et les poudings glacés

ICES AND ICE PUDDINGS

GLACES

ICES

METHOD OF FREEZING ICES

There are two stages in the making of ices:

1 The preparation of the mixture
2 The packing and moulding.

Packing consists of surrounding the mould with crushed ice, rock salt and saltpetre.

According to their type, ices are either frozen in their moulds, like ice gâteaux, ice parfaits, ice soufflés, mousses, bombes, etc., or they are moulded first and frozen afterwards in ice pails. Cream ices are made by the latter process.

Ice pails are usually worked by hand and consist of a metal freezer in a bucket containing the freezing mixture. They can also be worked mechanically.

The freezing mixture consists of 40 lb. ice, 6 lb. salt and 1 lb. saltpetre. This should be well pressed down in the bucket, and the churning should be continued until the ice cream is ready.

Editor's note The above method of freezing is now out of date, but it is included to interest the reader.

ORDINARY ICE MIXTURES

Mixtures for ices are of two kinds: those with cream and those with syrup, the latter being mainly used for fruit ices.

As the number of eggs and the amount of sugar needed vary a great deal, the recipes that follow only give approximate amounts of these ingredients.

If richer ices are required, increase the amount of sugar and the number of eggs per 1¾ pints (U.S. 4¼ cups) milk, while if lighter ices are wanted, reduce the quantities.

To give an idea of the difference that can exist in the composition of ices, they may have for 1¾ pints (U.S. 4¼ cups) milk, between 7 and 16 egg yolks, and between 7 oz. and 1 lb. sugar.

BASIC RECIPE FOR ICE CREAM

———————— 10 egg yolks, 10 oz. sugar, 1¾ pints (U.S. 4¼ cups) boiling milk

Beat the eggs and sugar over hot water until the mixture is thick enough to leave a trail.

Add the milk very slowly and stir over gentle heat until the mixture is thick enough to coat the back of the spoon. Be very careful the mixture does not boil or it will curdle.

Strain, and stir occasionally whilst cooking.

Glace aux amandes

ALMOND ICE CREAM

———————— 4 oz. sweet almonds, 5 bitter almonds, 2—3 tablespoons water, 1¾ pints (U.S. 4¼ cups) boiling milk, 10 oz. sugar, 10 egg yolks

Blanch the almonds and pound them very finely, gradually adding the water.

Add the boiling milk and leave for 20 minutes, then proceed as in the previous recipe.

Glace aux avelines

HAZEL-NUT ICE CREAM

———— 4 oz. hazel-nuts, 2—3 tablespoons cold milk, 1¾ pints (U.S. 4¼ cups) boiling milk, 10 oz. sugar, 10 egg yolks

Roast the nuts then pound finely, gradually adding the cold milk. Add the boiling milk, leave for 20 minutes, then proceed as in the previous recipe.

Glace au café

COFFEE ICE CREAM

———— 1¾ pints (U.S. 4¼ cups) boiling milk, 4 oz. freshly roasted coffee, 10 oz. sugar, 10 egg yolks

Pour the boiling milk on to the coffee, leave for 20 minutes, then strain and proceed as before.

Note The ground coffee can be replaced with a suitable quantity of coffee essence.

Glace au chocolat

CHOCOLATE ICE CREAM

———— 8 oz. chocolate, ¼ pint (U.S. ⅝ cup) water, 6 tablespoons cream, 1¼ pints (U.S. 3⅛ cups) vanilla ice cream (see page 780)

Dissolve the chocolate in the water and add the cream. Add to the partly frozen vanilla ice, mix thoroughly and continue the freezing.

Glace aux fraises à la crème fraîche

STRAWBERRY ICE WITH FRESH CREAM

———— 1 lb. strawberries, 8—12 oz. sugar, 1 pint (U.S. 2½ cups) cream

Rub the strawberries through a sieve, add the sugar and cream and freeze.

Glace aux marrons

CHESTNUT ICE CREAM

▬▬▬▬▬ 1¾ lb. chestnuts, milk, pinch salt, 1¾ pints (U.S. 4¼ cups) vanilla ice cream mixture (see below), 3—4 tablespoons Chantilly cream (see page 696)

Split the chestnuts at the thick end and put into the oven for a few minutes with a little water.

Remove the outer and inner skin and cook in milk with a pinch salt.

Drain and rub through a sieve. Add to the vanilla ice cream mixture, add the cream and freeze.

Note The chestnuts may be replaced by sieved marrons glacés.

Glace aux noix

WALNUT ICE CREAM

▬▬▬▬▬ 4 oz. peeled walnuts, 1¾ pints (U.S. 4¼ cups) boiling milk, 10 oz. sugar, 10 egg yolks

Pound the nuts finely and soak in the milk for 20 minutes, then proceed as for almond ice cream (see page 778).

Glace à la vanille

VANILLA ICE CREAM

▬▬▬▬▬ 1¾ pints (U.S. 4¼ cups) milk, ½ vanilla pod, 10 oz. sugar, 10 egg yolks

Boil the milk, add the vanilla pod and leave for 20 minutes, then proceed as described on page 778.

To increase the richness of the ice cream add ¼—½ pint (U.S. ⅝—1¼ cups) cream before freezing.

Glace pralinée

PRALINÉ ICE CREAM

──────── 4 oz. almond praline (see page 738), 1¾ pints (U.S. 4¼ cups) vanilla ice cream mixture (see page 780)

Pound and sieve the praline, add to the ice cream mixture and freeze.

Glace à la vanille et à la fraise

VANILLA AND STRAWBERRY ICE CREAM

──────── Vanilla ice cream mixture (see page 780), ¾ pints (U.S. 1⅞ cups) strawberry purée, ¼ pint (U.S. ⅝ cups) cream

Prepare the vanilla ice cream mixture and add the strawberry purée and cream. Freeze in the usual way.

Compositions pour glaces aux fruits

FRUIT WATER ICES

These are made in two ways:

1 Pulp the fruit and rub through a sieve. Mix the resulting purée with the same quantity of sugar syrup (see page 698), boiled to 220° F. and left to cool. Add the juice ½ lemon.

2 Cook the fruit to a pulp, using approximately 10 oz. sugar to 1 lb. fruit. Rub through a sieve and add enough water to register 19−20° on a saccharometer.

Composition des glaces aux liqueurs

LIQUEUR ICES

──────── 1¾ pints (U.S. 4¼ cups) syrup (see page 698), 6 tablespoons liqueur, juice ½ lemon

Prepare the syrup and boil to 218° F. When cool add the liqueur and lemon juice.

COMPOSITIONS DIVERSES POUR GLACES AUX FRUITS
FRUIT ICES

Glace à l'abricot

APRICOT ICE

———————— 1 pint (U.S. 2¼ cups) apricot purée, 1 pint (U.S. 2¼ cups) syrup (see page 698) boiled to 220° F., juice 1 lemon

Mix the purée and the syrup together. When both are quite cold, then add lemon juice.

If a saccharometer is available, the mixture should register 19−20°. Other fruits can be prepared in the same way.

Glace à l'ananas

PINEAPPLE ICE

———————— 1 pint (U.S. 2¼ cups) syrup (see page 698) boiled to 220° F., 6 table-spoons grated or pounded pineapple, kirsch, maraschino

Mix the cold syrup and pineapple together and flavour to taste with kirsch and maraschino.

The saccharometer reading should be 18−20°.

Glace aux bananes

BANANA ICE

———————— 1 pint syrup (see page 698) boiled to 220° F., 1 lb. banana pulp, juice 2 lemons, kirsch

Add the cold syrup to the banana pulp and leave for 1½ hours. Add the lemon juice and flavour with kirsch.

The saccharometer reading should be 20−22°.

Glace aux cerises

CHERRY ICE

———————— 1 pint (U.S. 2¼ cups) stoned cherries, 1 pint (U.S. 2¼ cups) syrup (see page 698), kirsch, juice ½ lemon

Crush the cherries and pound the stones. Add the syrup, flavoured with kirsch, and boiled to 220° F. Leave for 1 hour, then pass through a sieve and add the lemon juice.
The saccharometer reading should be 20–21°.

Glace au citron

LEMON ICE

Juice 4–5 lemons, thinly pared rind 3 lemons, 1 pint (U.S. 2½ cups) syrup (see page 698) boiled to 215° F.

Put the lemon juice, lemon rind and cold syrup together and leave for 2–3 hours, then strain.
The saccharometer reading should be 22°.

Glace aux fraises

STRAWBERRY ICE

1 pint (U.S. 2½ cups) strawberry purée, 1 pint (U.S. 2½ cups) syrup (see page 698) boiled to 220° F., juice 1 lemon, juice 1 orange (optional)

Mix the purée with the cold syrup and add the lemon juice.

Glace aux framboises

RASPBERRY ICE

Proceed as for strawberry ice, above.

Glace à la groseille

REDCURRANT ICE

1 pint (U.S. 2½ cups) redcurrant juice, 1 pint syrup (see page 698) boiled to 220° F.

Mix the fruit juice and cold syrup together.
The saccharometer reading should be 20°.

Glace à la mandarine
TANGERINE ICE

4—5 tangerines, 1¼ pints (U.S. 3⅛ cups) syrup (see page 698) boiled to 212° F., juice 2 oranges, juice 1 lemon

Extract the juice from the tangerines, and cover the peel with the boiling syrup. Leave to get cold, then strain and add the juice from the tangerines, orange and lemon juice.

The saccharometer reading should be 21—22°.

Glace au melon
MELON ICE

1 pint (U.S. 2½ cups) pulp from a ripe melon, 1 pint (U.S. 2½ cups) syrup (see page 698) boiled to 220° F. juice 2 oranges, juice 1 lemon

Mix the fruit pulp with the cold syrup. Add orange and lemon juice and pass through a fine sieve.

The saccharometer reading should be 22°.

Glace aux prunes mirabelles
MIRABELLE ICE

Follow the recipe for apricot ice (see page 782).

Note The flavour of such fruits as apricots, raspberries, strawberries, mirabelles, peaches, pears, and melon, when used for ices, harmonises well with Chantilly cream (see page 696) flavoured with vanilla.

Glace à l'orange
ORANGE ICE

Follow the recipe for tangerine ice (see above), replacing tangerines with oranges.

Glace aux pêches
PEACH ICE

Proceed as for apricot ice (see page 782), preferably using juicy hothouse peaches.

Glace aux poires

PEAR ICE

1 lb. pears, 1 lb. sugar, juice 1 lemon, boiled water

Choose juicy pears, peel, core and pound them with the sugar. Add lemon juice and rub all through a sieve.

Add enough boiled water to bring the saccharometer reading up to 22° F.

GLACES MOULÉES
MOULDED ICES

Glace Alhambra

ALHAMBRA ICE

Line the bottom and sides of a gâteau mould with vanilla ice cream (see page 780) and fill it with strawberry mousse (see page 756).

Freeze for 1½ hours.

Glace Carmen

CARMEN ICE

Line the bottom and sides of a fluted mould with apricot ice (see page 782) and fill the centre with raspberry flavoured Chantilly cream (see page 696).

Glace Comtesse Marie

COMTESSE MARIE ICE

Line the bottom and sides of a plain square mould with strawberry ice (see page 783) and fill with vanilla ice cream (see page 780).

When frozen, unmould and pipe with vanilla ice cream.

Glace Diane

DIANA ICE

Line the bottom and sides of a Madeleine mould with vanilla ice cream (see page 780). Fill with chestnut mousse (see page 796) flavoured with kirsch and maraschino.

Glace Francillon

FRANCILLON ICE

Line the sides and bottom of a madeleine mould with coffee ice cream (see page 779) and fill with brandy flavoured ice.

Glace Madeleine

MADELEINE ICE

———————— Crystallised pineapple, kirsch, maraschino, vanilla ice cream (see page 780), Chantilly cream (see page 696)

Cut some pineapple into cubes and soak in kirsch and maraschino, then mix with the ice cream and add one-third quantity of Chantilly cream. Put into a Madeleine mould and freeze.

Note One may vary these ices in many ways. It is just a question of taste and imagination. The choice of moulds is optional.

Petites glaces moulées

SMALL MOULDED ICES

These ices, which are served mainly at evening parties or for decorating larger ices, are made in small hinged moulds in the shape of flowers, fruits, birds, posies, etc. They may be made of any kind of frozen mixture but should be in keeping with the mould, e.g. a strawberry shaped mould should be filled with strawberry ice.

Mandarines givrées

FROSTED TANGERINES

Cut a small piece about 1 inch in diameter from the stalk end of some tangerines and remove all the pulp. Fill with tangerine ice (see page 784), and replace the lid. Damp the outside of the tangerines and put into the deep freeze.

When covered with frost, serve on a bed of crushed ice.

Mandarines glacées aux perles des alpes

ICED TANGERINES WITH CHARTREUSE LIQUEUR SWEETS

Proceed exactly as instructed for the frosted tangerines in the previous recipe but mix the tangerine ice with some small Chartreuse liqueur sweets. Cover and frost them. Serve in the same way, on a bed of crushed ice.

Meringues glacées

ICED MERINGUES

Fill some meringue shells (see page 697) with various ice cream moulded in a spoon. Serve on a table napkin.

Meringues glacées Hélène

ICED MERINGUES HÉLÈNE

Fill some meringue shells (see page 697) with vanilla ice cream (see page 780), placing on them three crystallised violets. Serve with hot chocolate sauce (see page 738).

Note The shells may also be filled with Chantilly cream (see page 696) sprinkled with grated chocolate and served with a hot chocolate sauce (see page 738).

COUPES

We will now deal with coupes which are filled with various flavoured ices, or with ice cream with Chantilly cream or fruit added.

Coupe Adelina Patti

Fill the coupes glasses to the brim with vanilla ice cream (see page 780). Place some brandy cherries rolled in castor sugar in a ring round the edge, with their stalks hanging down, so that they may be taken with a finger and thumb. Put a small rosette of Chantilly cream (see page 696) in the centre of each coupe.

Coupe d'Antigny

STRAWBERRY COUPE

Cream, strawberry ice cream (see page 779), peaches, halved and poached in vanilla flavoured syrup, spun sugar (see page 699)

Add a little cream to the strawberry ice cream and three-quarters fill the coupe glasses.

Put a half peach on top and cover with a light veil of spun sugar.

Note If the peach is large, it can be partly divided into quarters, but the shape should be retained.

Coupe bohémienne

CHESTNUT COUPE

Marrons glacés, vanilla ice cream (see page 780), thick rum flavoured apricot sauce (see page 739)

Break up some marrons glacés and mix with the ice cream. Pile into the coupe glasses and coat with the apricot sauce.

Coupe châtelaine

RASPBERRY COUPE

Raspberries, sugar, Curaçao, brandy, apricot ice (see page 782), Chantilly cream (see page 696)

Soak some raspberries in sugar, Curaçao and brandy and then arrange in the bottom of some coupe glasses. Fill with apricot ice and pipe some Chantilly cream on top.

Kirsch and maraschino may be used if preferred instead of Curaçao and brandy.

Coupe clo-clo

CHESTNUT AND STRAWBERRY COUPE

———————— Marrons glacés, maraschino, vanilla ice cream (see page 780), Chantilly cream (see page 696), strawberry purée

Break up some marrons glacés and soak them in maraschino, then mix with the ice cream.

Fill the coupe glasses to the brim with the ice cream and put a marron glacé in the centre of each.

Mix some strawberry purée with the cream and pipe round the edge.

Coupe Emma Calvé

CHERRY COUPE

———————— White heart cherries, sugar, 2—3 tablespoons redcurrant jelly, few drops Noyau liqueur, vanilla ice cream (see page 780), Chantilly cream (see page 696) flavoured with raspberry

Stone the cherries and cook them carefully in sugar. Strain off the juice, add the redcurrant jelly and the liqueur. Leave to get cold.

Half fill the coupe glasses with ice cream, arrange the cherries and the syrup on top and finish with a mound of cream.

Coupe favorite

PINEAPPLE COUPE

———————— Pineapple, kirsch, maraschino, vanilla ice cream (see page 780), small round meringues (see page 697), pineapple ice (see page 782), strawberry purée flavoured with kirsch, Chantilly cream (see page 696)

Chop some pineapple, soak it in kirsch and maraschino and put into the bottom of coupe glasses, then half fill them with vanilla ice cream.

Hollow out the meringues, fill them with pineapple ice and arrange in the centre of the ice cream. Cover with strawberry purée and pipe a ring of Chantilly cream round the meringue.

Coupe Hélène

VANILLA COUPE

Fill some coupe glasses to the brim with vanilla ice cream (see page 780) and decorate with a ring of pralined violets.

Pipe some Chantilly cream (see page 696) in the centre and sprinkle with grated chocolate.

COUPE JACQUES

Crystallised fruit, kirsch, maraschino, lemon ice (see page 783), strawberry ice (see page 783), peaches, strawberries

Cut the crystallised fruit into small pieces and soak in kirsch and maraschino, then put into the bottom of some coupe glasses. Fill up with half lemon and half strawberry ice and smooth the surface.

Cut the peaches into quarters and arrange in a ring on top, then put a large strawberry in the centre.

Coupe Madelon

VANILLA AND MACAROON COUPE

Vanilla ice cream (see page 780), macaroons, kirsch, apricots, peeled and poached in syrup, apricot sauce (see page 738), maraschino, Chantilly cream (see page 696)

Fill some coupe glasses with ice cream. Dip the macaroons in kirsch and put one in the centre of each glass. Top with half an apricot. Flavour the apricot sauce with kirsch and maraschino and pour a little over the apricot. Pipe a little Chantilly cream round the macaroon.

Coupe Marie Thérèse

BANANA COUPE

Bananas, kirsch, maraschino, strawberry ice cream (see page 779)

Slice the bananas, soak in kirsch and maraschino and arrange in small coupe glasses.
Cover with the strawberry ice cream.

Coupe Melba

VANILLA AND RASPBERRY COUPE

———————— Vanilla ice cream (see page 780), half peaches poached in vanilla flavoured syrup, almond praline (see page 738), raspberry purée, Chantilly cream (see page 696), spun sugar (see page 699)

Fill some coupe glasses three-quarter full with the ice cream.
Put a peach in the centre, rounded side downwards, and put a piece of almond praline in the cavity left by the stone.
Add a little cream to the raspberry purée and pour over the top.
Cover with a light veil of spun sugar.

Coupe Mireille

STRAWBERRY AND PEACH COUPE

———————— Strawberry ice cream (see page 779), peaches, peeled and poached in vanilla flavoured syrup, redcurrant jelly

Fill some coupe glasses two-thirds full with the ice cream. Place half a peach on top and cover it with redcurrant jelly.

Coupe Odette

BANANA AND CURAÇAO COUPE

———————— Bananas, Curaçao, orange ice (see page 784)

Slice the bananas and soak them in Curaçao, then put into small coupe glasses and fill with orange ice.

Coupe petit-duc
VANILLA AND MERINGUE COUPE

Vanilla ice cream (see page 780), small round meringues (see page 697), redcurrant jelly, Chantilly cream (see page 696)

Fill some coupe glasses with the ice cream. Hollow out the meringues, fill with redcurrant jelly and arrange in the centre of the ice cream. Cover with a rosette of Chantilly cream.

Note The meringue may be replaced with half a peach poached in vanilla flavoured syrup. Fill the cavity left by the stone with redcurrants and pipe with Chantilly cream.

Coupe Yvette
CHESTNUT AND CRYSTALLISED FRUIT COUPE

Marrons glacés, crystallised fruit, kirsch, apricots, peeled, stoned and poached in syrup flavoured with kirsch, Chantilly cream (see page 696)

Cut the marrons glacés and crystallised fruit into small pieces and soak in kirsch, then three-quarter fill some coupe glasses with the mixture. Arrange an apricot on top and pipe a ring of Chantilly cream round the apricot.

Note By using a little imagination many variations of these coupes can be prepared.

GLACES LÉGÈRES
LIGHT ICES

These ices comprise iced gâteaux, bombes, iced mousses, iced puddings and iced soufflés.

Biscuits glacés
ICED GÂTEAUX

Formerly, an iced gâteaux was prepared from an English custard cream, using 1 lb. sugar, 12 egg yolks, 1¾ pints (U.S. 4¼ cups) milk and flavouring to taste.

Today, the milk is replaced by the same quantity of whipped cream.

The mixture was cooked as described on page **694** then strained and left to cool, stirring frequently during the cooling process. The bowl was then placed on ice and beaten until the cream thickened and was then frozen.

For gâteaux, bombes, etc., the following method has been adopted:

———— 16 egg yolks, 1 pint (U.S. 2½ cups) syrup (see page 698) boiled to 220° F., 1¾ pints (U.S. 4¼ cups) whipped cream

Beat the egg yolks and gradually add the cold syrup. Strain through a fine sieve and cook in a bain-marie. Pour into a bowl and leave to get quite cold then add to the whipped cream.

ANOTHER METHOD

Beat the eggs and syrup over a pan of warm water until the mixture is thick enough to leave a trail, then remove from the heat and continue beating on ice until it is quite cold. Then add flavouring and 1¾ pints (U.S. 4¼ cups) whipped cream.

Vanilla, orange or tangerine flavouring may be used or, if a liqueur flavour is preferred, kirsch, maraschino, Curaçao or anisette are all suitable.

Moulage des petits biscuits glacées
THE MOULDING OF SMALL ICED GÂTEAUX

Gâteaux are moulded in rectangular moulds, the shape and size of bricks. They have two lids, one for the top and one for the bottom.

The mixtures in the compartments are usually of different colours and flavours from the one in the centre. Thus, for instance, one may be filled with a strawberry mixture and the other with a coffee mixture, while the centre could have a vanilla mixture. When they are frozen and turned out, these little bricks are cut vertically and one gets rectangles in which the three colours are quite distinct.

The rectangles are placed in small paper cases and may have a decoration on top. The different mixtures for bombes may be used for gâteaux. This is a matter for the individual.

Large gâteaux are moulded in square moulds, called *Comtesse Marie*. The moulds are lined with some sort of ice cream and then filled with a mousse mixture, to which is added small biscuits or macaroons, flavoured with a liqueur that harmonises with the mousse.

BOMBES

Bombes are moulded in plain circular moulds, rounded off at the top.

MOULDING OF BOMBES

First coat the bottom and sides of the mould with a thin layer of ice cream, according to the kind of bombe being prepared. The centre is then filled with the main mixture. Place a piece of white paper on top and put the lid on the mould.

The freezing will take about 2 hours.

Bombe apricotine

APRICOT BOMBE

Line the mould with apricot ice (see page 782) and fill with kirsch flavoured mousse.

Bombe Aïda

STRAWBERRY BOMBE

Line the mould with strawberry ice cream (see page 779) and fill with a mousse flavoured with kirsch and maraschino.

Bombe Alhambra

STRAWBERRY AND VANILLA BOMBE

Line the mould with vanilla ice cream (see page 780) and fill with strawberry ice cream (see page 779).

When ready to serve, unmould on to a serving dish and surround it with large strawberries soaked in kirsch and maraschino.

Bombe andalouse

APRICOT AND TANGERINE BOMBE

Line mould with apricot ice (see page 782) and fill with tangerine mousse (see page 796).

Bombe brésilienne

VANILLA AND PINEAPPLE BOMBE

Line the mould with vanilla ice cream (see page 780) and fill with pineapple mousse (see page 796).

Bombe cardinal

RASPBERRY AND VANILLA BOMBE

Line the mould with raspberry ice (see page 783) and fill with vanilla ice cream (see page 780).

Bombe diplomate

VANILLA, KIRSCH AND MARASCHINO BOMBE

Line the mould with vanilla ice cream (see page 780) and fill with a mousse flavoured with kirsch and maraschino, and to which some chopped crystallised fruit soaked in kirsch, has been added.

Bombe favorite

CHESTNUT AND APRICOT BOMBE

Line the mould with chestnut ice cream (see page 780) and fill wir apricot mousse (see page 796) flavoured with rum.

Bombe Monte-Carlo

VANILLA AND STRAWBERRY BOMBE

Line the mould with vanilla ice cream (see page 780) and fill wit strawberry mousse (see page 796). Serve with large strawberries soake in sugar and Curaçao.

Bombe Nélusko

CHOCOLATE AND VANILLA BOMBE

Line the mould with chocolate ice cream (see page 779) and fill with vanilla mousse (see page 796).

MOUSSE GLACÉE
ICED MOUSSES

Mousses are made either with English custard cream (see page 694) or with syrup. The syrup method is particularly suitable for fruit mousses.

Composition de mousse glacée aux fruits
ICED FRUIT MOUSSES

Boil a syrup (see page 698) to 220° F. Leave to cool, then add the same quantity of fruit purée and double the quantity of whipped cream.

Composition de mousse glacée à la crème
ICED CREAM MOUSSES

1 lb. castor sugar, 16 egg yolks, 1 pint (U.S. 2½ cups) milk, 1 pint cream, ½ oz. powdered gum tragacanth, flavouring

Prepare an English custard cream (see page 694) with the sugar, eggs and milk. Cool, beating frequently, then add the cream, gum tragacanth and flavouring. Beat over ice until the mixture is thick and frothy.

Line the mould with white paper, pour in the mixture and seal the mould. Freeze for 2−3 hours.

Parfait au café
COFFEE PARFAIT

8 oz. freshly ground coffee, ¼ pint (U.S. ⅝ cups) water, 16 egg yolks, 1 pint (U.S. 2½ cups) syrup (see page 698) boiled to 219° F., 1¾ pints (U.S. 4¼ cups) thick cream

Put the coffee and the water into a pan. Reduce slowly until there is about 6 tablespoons liquid.

Beat the egg yolks and gradually add the cold syrup, add the coffee and strain through a fine sieve. Beat over hot water until the mixture is thick enough to leave a trail, then remove from the heat and continue beating over ice until the mixture is quite cold. Add to the whipped cream. Pour into a mould and freeze.

Poudings glacés

ICED PUDDINGS

Iced puddings are only ice creams or mousses moulded in bombe or madeleine moulds, alternately with biscuits (U.S. cookies) or macaroons impregnated with a chosen liqueur and with crystallised fruit cut into small pieces and soaked in the same liqueur. The moulds are sealed and then frozen for about 2 hours. They are then unmoulded and served with a cream, vanilla, fruit or chocolate sauce.

Soufflés glacés

ICED SOUFFLÉS

Iced soufflés are prepared with mousse or bombe mixtures flavoured to taste, and frozen in an ordinary soufflé dish.

Tie a band of stiff white paper round the outside of the soufflé dish, standing $1-1\frac{1}{2}$ inches above the rim of the dish. When the mixture is poured in it should come above the rim. Freeze in the ice box of a refrigerator.

Remove the band of paper before serving and, according to the kind of soufflé, sprinkle with praline, crushed macaroons or grated chocolate.

SORBETS

Sorbets are half-frozen ices made with liqueur or wine and were originally served in the middle of a meal. For a sorbet with a wine base, Frontignan, Lunel, Rincio, Samos are most suitable.

———————— To $\frac{1}{2}$ pint (U.S. $2\frac{1}{2}$ cups) wine: add the juice 2 lemons and juice 1 orange and about $\frac{3}{4}$ pint (U.S. $1\frac{7}{8}$ cups) syrup boiled to 215° and left to get cold.
This should read 15° on the saccharometer.

For a sorbet with liqueur, 6 tablespoons liqueur is required to $1\frac{3}{4}$ pints (U.S. $4\frac{1}{4}$ cups) syrup, but it is not added until the sorbet is completely frozen.

Lemon, tangerine and orange sorbets are made by infusing the peel of the fruit in the syrup and then adding the juice of the fruit.

When the sorbet is sufficiently frozen, quarter its volume of Italian meringue (see page 697) or whipped cream is stirred into it and finally the chosen liqueur.

GRANITÉS

These are like sorbets, but do not include meringue or cream. They have a base of fruit juice. When made the granité has a slightly gritty texture.

MARQUISES

Marquises are made generally with pineapple, strawberries and kirsch.

When frozen, some thick Chantilly cream (see page 696) is added, flavoured with pineapple or strawberry.

Punch à la romaine
ROMAN PUNCH

1 pint (U.S. 2¼ cups) syrup (see page 698), boiled to 215° F., dry white wine or dry Champagne, juice 2 oranges, juice 3 lemons, grated rind 1 lemon, boiled water, 2 egg whites, 4 oz. sugar, 6 tablespoons rum

Prepare the syrup, leave it to get cold, then add enough wine or Champagne to give a reading of 18° on the saccharometer.

Add orange and lemon juice and lemon rind, cover and leave for 1 hour. Strain, and adjust the saccharometer reading to 18° by adding some boiled water.

Freeze and then add quarter its volume of Italian meringue (see page 697) in the proportion of 2 egg whites to 4 oz. sugar.

Just before serving, add the rum gradually.

SPOOMS

Spooms are merely sorbets made with syrup boiled to 210° F. and with double the amount of Italian meringue added (see page 697) as they are required to be very light and frothy.

Spooms usually have a basis of wine, such as Champagne, Muscatel, Frontignan and various sweet wines of Bordeaux. They are served in glasses like sorbets.

TROU NORMAND

This is a lemon granité, served in a cone in a sorbet glass, half filled with old Calvados (apple-jack).

Savories et Sandwichs
SAVOURIES AND SANDWICHES

SAVORIES
SAVOURIES

It is usual in England to finish a meal with a savoury, of which English people are very fond.

Although these dishes are not in much favour in France, I am giving here some of the more attractive ones.

Canapés écossais
HADDOCK ON TOAST

1 small smoked haddock, 1 tablespoon butter, 2 tablespoons hot milk, pinch salt, pinch cayenne pepper, 2—3 tablespoons hot cream, buttered toast

Mince the flesh of the haddock and put it into a small saucepan with the butter, milk, salt, pepper and cayenne papper. Cover, bring to boiling point and boil for 2 minutes, then remove from the heat. Stir the haddock rapidly, as for mashed potatoes, and finally add the hot cream. Serve on buttered toast.

As a variation, the haddock may be sprinkled with cheese and melted butter and browned under the grill (U.S. broiler) or topped with a slice of grilled bacon.

Anges à cheval (ou huîtres en brochette)

ANGELS ON HORSEBACK

━━━━━━━ Oysters, streaky bacon, buttered toast, breadcrumbs, cayenne pepper

Wrap each oyster in a slice of streaky bacon. Arrange on a spit, grill (U.S. broil) and put on buttered toast. Sprinkle with dried breadcrumbs mixed with a pinch cayenne pepper and serve very hot.

Canapés aux crevettes roses

PRAWNS (U.S. SHRIMPS) ON TOAST

━━━━━━━ Prawns (U.S. shrimps), ½ oz. butter, pinch freshly ground pepper, pinch salt, pinch grated nutmeg, pinch cayenne pepper, béchamel sauce (see page 23), cream, hot buttered toast, grated cheese, butter

Shell the prawns (U.S. shrimps) and put into a pan with the butter, and seasonings. Heat gently, add some béchamel sauce to which a little cream has been added and put on to the toast. Sprinkle with grated cheese, dot with butter and brown under the grill (U.S. broiler).

Note Prawns (U.S. shrimps) on toast make an excellent hot hors-d'oeuvre.

Canapés au fromage

TOASTED CHEESE

Prepare some toast and butter it. Cover with melted cheese and a slice of grilled (U.S. broiled) bacon.

Canapés de Roquefort et bacon grillé

ROQUEFORT CHEESE AND GRILLED BACON ON TOAST

━━━━━━━ 4 oz. Roquefort cheese, 1 oz. butter, pinch cayenne pepper, buttered toast, rashers streaky bacon

Pound the cheese with the butter and cayenne. Spread thickly on the toast and brown under the grill (U.S. broiler). Top with a rasher of grilled (U.S. broiled) bacon.

Canapés à la moelle

BEEF MARROW ON TOAST

Beef marrow, stock, meat jelly (see page 21), cayenne pepper, buttered toast

Cut the marrow into ½-inch slices and poach lightly in stock. Drain, dip in meat jelly to which a little cayenne has been added and serve on buttered toast.

Canapés de saumon fumé

SMOKED SALMON ON TOAST

Choose some rather well smoked salmon, cut it into very thin slices and put it on hot buttered toast.

Note It is not advisable to keep salmon too long in the refrigerator or to preserve it too long in salt.

Champignons grillés

MUSHROOMS ON TOAST

Mushrooms on toast are a great favourite in England, and are eaten frequently. Clean them carefully, season with salt and pepper, sprinkle with melted butter or olive oil and grill (U.S. broil). Serve on hot buttered toast.

ANOTHER WAY OF PREPARING MUSHROOMS ON TOAST

Choose some fresh mushrooms, slice them thinly and sauté in butter with plenty of seasoning.

Add a little béchamel sauce (see page 23) and place them on very hot buttered toast.

Sprinkle with grated cheese, brush with melted butter and glaze under the grill (U.S. broiler).

Serve at once.

Laitances à la diable
DEVILLED SOFT ROES ON TOAST

——————— Mackerel or herring soft roes, butter, salt, pepper, cayenne pepper, hot buttered toast

Poach the roes in butter, add seasoning and serve on hot buttered toast.

Crème frite au fromage
CHEESE FRITTERS

——————— 4 oz. flour, 2 oz. cream of rice or rice flour, 3 whole eggs, 2 egg yolks, 1 pint (U.S. 2½ cups) milk, salt, pepper, cayenne pepper, pinch nutmeg, 4—5 oz. Gruyère cheese, egg and breadcrumbs for coating, butter

Mix the flour, cream of rice and eggs smoothly. Add milk and seasoning and boil all together over fairly brisk heat for 5 minutes stirring all the time. Add most of the grated cheese and turn the mixture out on to a wet plate. Leave to cool, then cut into even-sized pieces. Dip in egg and then in breadcrumbs mixed with the remaining cheese, and fry in hot butter.

DIABLOTINS

Fill some puff or short pastry with a purée of foie gras, chicken, game, creamed cheese, haddock, brandade, truffled salt cod, etc., and fry in deep fat.

Sardines à la diable
DEVILLED SARDINES ON TOAST

Bone and skin some sardines, spread with mustard, sprinkle with cayenne pepper and serve on hot buttered toast.

SCOTCH WOODCOCK

Prepare some scrambled egg, arrange on fairly thick fingers of buttered toast and criss-cross with fillets of anchovy.

Tartelettes Agnès Sorel

TARTLETS WITH QUICHE FILLING

———— Short pastry (see page 682), eggs, cream, grated cheese, salt, cayenne pepper, beef marrow, meat jelly (see page 21)

Line some tartlet tins with the pastry, and fill with a quiche mixture made with the eggs, cream, cheese, seasoning and cayenne. Cook in a moderate oven, and just before serving add a slice of poached beef marrow dipped in melted meat jelly.

Tartelettes aux champignons

MUSHROOM TARTLETS

———— Button mushrooms, butter, salt, pepper, nutmeg, béchamel sauce (see page 23), cream, short pastry (see page 682)

Wash, and slice the mushrooms thinly and sauté them in butter. Add seasoning and a little béchamel sauce to which cream has been added. Line some tartlet tins with the pastry, fill with mushroom mixture and criss-cross with thin strips of pastry. Bake in a moderate oven.

Tartelettes forestière

MUSHROOM AND TRUFFLE TARTLETS

Follow the previous recipe, but add some slices of truffle to the mushrooms.

Barquettes Tosca

BARQUETTES WITH CRAYFISH FILLING

———— Boat-shaped pastry cases, see barquettes (page 110), *écrevisses à la bordelaise* (see page 236), Parmesan soufflé mixture (see page 238)

Cook the pastry cases blind, fill with the crayfish mixture and cover with the soufflé.

Put into a hot oven for a few minutes.

WELSH RAREBIT

——————   Cheshire cheese, 2—3 tablespoons pale ale, made mustard, cayenne pepper, buttered toast

Cut the cheese into small pieces and put into a pan with the ale, mustard and pepper to taste. Stir until the cheese has melted, then pour on to the hot toast.

Alternatively grate the cheese and spread a thick layer on the hot buttered toast. Add a pinch cayenne and put into the oven or under the grill (U.S. broiler) until the cheese has melted.

SANDWICHS
SANDWICHES

Sandwiches are usually made with thin slices of bread, lightly buttered and seasoned with salt and mustard. Thin slices of ham or tongue are put on one slice, which is then covered by another. But the filling of sandwiches is largely a matter of taste, and they may be made of roast beef, pressed beef, veal, chicken, pheasant, foie gras, *rillettes*, hard boiled eggs, caviare, cheese, tomatoes, etc. The shape of sandwiches is usually square or rectangular and generally about 3 inches by 1½ inches.

Sandwiches for parties are made much smaller and it is better to pound or chop the filling and mix it with the butter and seasoning before spreading on the bread.

Editor's note   Rillettes are made from cooked pork, well seasoned and pounded in a mortar. In France they are made and sold commercially.

Confitures et gelées

JAMS AND JELLIES

CONFITURES
JAM

Jam consists of fruit and sugar boiled together.

The amount of sugar used depends on the nature of the fruit and the amount of sugar contained in the fruit itself. For acid fruit, the amount of sugar should be kept about equal to that of the fruit.

If too much sugar is used, the flavour of the fruit is weakened and crystallisation will take place in time. If too little sugar is used, the jam will have to be cooked longer to reach the desired consistency and the flavour of the fruit is spoilt by protracted evaporation. Finally, if the cooking time is too short, the jam will ferment.

In making jam, therefore, the fruit itself is the guide to the amount of sugar.

CUISSON DES CONFITURES, MISE EN POTS, BOUCHAGE

THE COOKING OF JAM, POTTING, AND SEALING

The cooking time for jam, whether it be whole fruit jam or jelly, can only be decided approximately. It is a mistake to try to fix an exact time, as the cooking time depends entirely on the rate of cooking and the greater or less amount of evaporation of the natural moisture of fruit.

In principle, the quicker the cooking the better the jam, because the jam keeps its colour better.

However, without continuous watching and a great deal of care, a fruit jam should not be cooked too quickly, because of the risk of burning. On the other hand, when it is a question of jellies or the fruit juice alone, the cooking process should be as speedy as possible.

When the steam escaping from the jam is less dense and the jam is boiling steadily, it means that the evaporation is over and that the actual cooking, which takes very little time, is proceeding. From this moment, test the jam frequently. The jam sticking to the skimmer drops off fairly quickly, then after a few minutes, it begins to gather on the middle of the skimmer, and to fall off slowly in large separate drops.

This is what is called the *nappe*, and is a sure sign that the jam is ready.

As soon as this point is reached, take the jam from the heat. Let it cool for 7—8 minutes, then pour into warmed jars.

On the following day, press a round of paper soaked in glycerine on the top of each jar, touching the jam (glycerine is better than brandy).

Cover with a double piece of paper and tie securely. Keep in a cool dry place.

Confiture d'abricots

APRICOT JAM
—————— 6 lb. apricots, 4½ lb. sugar, ¾ (U.S. 1⅞ cups) water

Cut the apricots in half and remove the stones. Break the stones, remove the kernels and blanch them.

Put the sugar into a preserving pan with the water. When it has dissolved, bring to boiling point and boil for a few minutes, skimming it well. Add the apricots and cook over moderate heat, stirring very frequently until the nappe stage is reached. Stir in the almonds, and pot the jam when it has cooled a little.

Confiture de cerises

CHERRY JAM
—————— 4 lb. cherries, 3—4 lb. sugar (depending on the sweetness of the cherries), water, 1¼ pints (U.S. 3⅛ cups) redcurrant juice

Stone the cherries. Put the sugar into a preserving pan, add just enough water to moisten. When it has dissolved, bring to boiling point and boil for 5 minutes, skimming carefully. Add the cherries and redcurrant juice and cook quickly until the nappe stage is reached.

Note Be careful to remove the scum as it rises, or the jam will be cloudy. This is also a contributary cause of fermentation.

Confiture de fraises

STRAWBERRY JAM

Strawberries are more difficult to deal with. There are several means of making jam with them but here is the simplest and the quickest:

4 lb. strawberries, 3 lb. sugar, water

Hull the strawberries and if considered necessary wash them, but drain very thoroughly.

Put the sugar into a preserving pan with enough water to moisten it. Bring slowly to boiling point and boil to 230° F. Skim carefully. Add the strawberries and leave at the side of the stove for 7−8 minutes so that the liquid in the fruit dissolves out.

Remove the strawberries carefully and continue to boil the syrup for about 10 minutes or until it appears to be ready.

Put the strawberries back into the syrup for 5 minutes or until the nappe stage is reached.

Leave to cool before filling the jars so that the strawberries will be well distributed and will not rise to the top of the jars.

Confiture de prunes

PLUM OR GREENGAGE JAM

Take some Victoria plums or greengages. If one wants to preserve the green colour of the greengages, never make more than 8−9 lb. at a time, and never soak the fruit and the sugar beforehand, as this will spoil the colour.

Otherwise, proceed as for apricot jam (see page 806).

Confiture de tomates

TOMATO JAM

This jam is made in different ways: either the pulp is sieved or the tomatoes are simply sliced finely, after being peeled and seeded.

First method

Slice the tomatoes finely and rub through a sieve. Put the purée that results into the preserving pan and boil for 5−6 minutes, stirring with a wooden spatula. Now pour through a cloth stretched over an inverted stool, as for straining a jelly, and let it drain through thoroughly. When it has drained, weigh out the same amount of sugar as there is liquid and put the sugar in the preserving pan with a little water; let it dissolve and cook to the small ball stage, 230° F., carefully skimming when it comes to the boil.

A vanilla pod may be added when the sugar is put on to boil.

When the sugar has reached the stage indicated, add the tomato pulp and ¼ pint (U.S. ⅝ cup) redcurrant juice for every 1 lb. pulp. The addition of redcurrant juice is essential.

Put the preserving pan over a brisk heat and stir constantly until the nappe stage is reached.

Second method

Take some firm tomatoes, dip them for a few seconds in boiling water, then remove and put them into cold water, peel, and cut them in halves, crosswise, take the seeds out and slice finely.

Weigh the same amount of sugar as there is tomato and put it in the preserving pan with ¼ pint (U.S. ⅝ cup) water to 5½ lb. sugar; bring to the boil for a few moments and skim well.

Add the tomato juice and grated rind of 1 lemon or 1 lemon thinly sliced. Cook over brisk heat, stirring constantly and taking care that the jam does not stick to the bottom of the pan. Take the pan off when the jam reaches the nappe stage.

Third method

Peel the tomatoes, divide into quarters and seed them. Place them, in rows, in a casserole, sprinkling each row with pale brown sugar, allowing 3½ lb. sugar to 4½ lb. tomatoes. Add, if you wish, a few slice⸍

lemon. Cover the casserole and put in a very slow oven for 2½ – 3 hours, watching to see that it does not burn.

This method, called 'Housewife's choice', may be applied to other fruit.

Note Sometimes 1 pint (U.S. 2½ cups) white wine to 4½ lb. tomato is added, or the same quantity of white wine vinegar.

Confiture d'orange

MARMALADE

Take some Seville oranges with bright, thick, soft skins, free from blemishes. Prick them fairly deeply with a skewer, so that they will cook more easily, and put them into a preserving pan of boiling water. Boil for 30 minutes, then drain, leave to cool and keep under a tap of cold running water for 12 hours, or soak for 18 – 20 hours in cold water, renewing it frequently. The object of this is to soften the skins and to wash away any bitterness.

Dry the oranges, cut them up small and remove the pith and the pips. Strain through a coarse sieve and weigh the pulp.

Dissolve an equal quantity of sugar in a pan and boil for 5 minutes, skimming it thoroughly.

Now add the orange pulp and ¼ pint (U.S. ⅝ cup) apple juice per 1 lb. orange purée.

Bring to the boil. During the first part of the boiling, skim with the greatest care. During the second, stir constantly with a wooden spatula, until the marmalade reaches the nappe stage.

Note A certain quantity of orange peel cut into fine julienne and well cooked is added to the marmalade at the last moment.

ANOTHER RECIPE

Soak the oranges in running water for 24 hours. Cook them whole in water until a straw can penetrate the skin, then take them out and put them into cold water. When they are quite cold, cut into thin slices and remove the pips. Weigh the oranges and take the same amount of lump sugar and put it in the preserving pan. Add enough water to cover, and boil for 5 minutes, skimming carefully.

Add the chopped oranges and ¼ pint (U.S. ⅝ cup) apple juice for each lb. fruit. Continue boiling, stirring constantly till nappe stage is reached.

GELÉES DE FRUITS FRAIS
FRESH FRUIT JELLIES

Gelée de cassis

BLACKCURRANT JELLY

Take some ripe blackcurrants, remove their stalks and put them in a preserving pan with ½ pint (U.S. 1¼ cups) water for 4½ lb. fruit. Put this on the corner of the stove and allow the fruit to soften. During this preliminary cooking the skins of the blackcurrants burst and the juice escapes. Pour the currants through a tammy cloth placed over a bowl, and twist the cloth to extract the juice.

Measure the juice and allow 3½ lb. sugar to every 3½ pints (U.S. 8¾ cups) juice.

Put the sugar into a pan, add enough water to moisten. Bring slowly to boiling point, then boil to the small ball stage, 230° F., skimming carefully.

Add the blackcurrant juice and ¾ pint (U.S. 1⅞ cups) whitecurrant juice to 3½ pints (U.S. 8¾ cups) blackcurrant juice. (This is optional but is added to soften the colour.) Leave at the side of the stove for a few minutes to give the ingredients time to blend, then boil over fairly brisk heat until the nappe stage is reached.

Gelée de coings

QUINCE JELLY

Choose some ripe quinces, peel them, cut into slices, remove the seeds and put into cold water.

Put them in the preserving pan with 3¼ pints (U.S. 8¾ cups) water for every 2 lb. prepared fruit and cook slowly, without stirring. As soon as they are cooked, pour through a tammy placed over a bowl and let them drain through.

Put the juice back in the preserving pan with 3½ lb. lump sugar per 3¼ pints (U.S. 8¾ cups) juice. Let the sugar melt, then cook over brisk heat until it reaches the nappe stage, skimming carefully from time to time.

As soon as the jelly is cooked, strain it through muslin stretched over a bowl to clear it.

Gelée de groseilles

REDCURRANT JELLY

Take two-thirds redcurrants and one-third whitecurrants. Wash them carefully and remove the stalks. Weigh out 4 lb. sugar to 4 lb. prepared fruit.

Dissolve the sugar in a preserving pan with a little water. Cook to the small ball stage, 230° F., skimming as soon as it boils.

Put the currants in the sugar and keep on the corner of the stove for 7 — 8 minutes to blend the fruit and sugar, then cook over brisk heat until the mixture reaches the nappe stage, skimming very carefully. Pour through a tammy cloth stretched over a bowl, and then pot in the usual way.

Note 6 oz. raspberries per 4 lb. currants may be added.

Gelée de groseilles à froid

UNCOOKED REDCURRANT JELLY

Wash some redcurrants, remove the stalks, crush them and pass through a fine sieve.

Measure the juice and add 4½ lb. sugar to each 3½ pints (U.S. 8¾ cups) juice. Leave in a cool place for 2 — 3 hours, stirring frequently to facilitate the dissolving of the sugar. Pour into jars and leave uncovered for 2 — 3 days.

Cover in the usual way and leave for 2 days, exposing the jars to the sun for 2 — 3 hours each day.

Note This jelly is very delicate and should be kept in a very dry place.

Gelée d'oranges

ORANGE JELLY

———— 12 4 — 5-oz. oranges, ½ pint (U.S. 1¼ cups) apple juice, 1 lb. lump sugar, water, 1 tablespoon grated orange sugar, obtained by rubbing the orange skin with lump sugar

Squeeze the oranges and strain the juice.

Dissolve the sugar in a little water then add orange and apple juice and boil until the nappe stage is reached. Add the orange rind and pot in the usual way.

Note A thin julienne of candied orange peel may be added to the jelly.

Gelée de pommes

APPLE JELLY

Peel and quarter the apples and put into a preserving pan with 3½ pints (U.S. 8¾ cups) water for each 4 lb. apples.

Cook slowly until the apples are only just cooked then strain through muslin, but do not exert any pressure.

Measure the juice and allow 4 lb. lump sugar to 3½ pints (U.S. 8¾ cups) juice and ½ vanilla pod. Boil till it reaches the nappe stage, then strain as described for quince jelly (see page 810).

Note The apple pulp can be used for other dishes.

Les boissons de table

BEVERAGES

Of all the various drinks, such as beer, cider, perry, etc., the most popular is wine.

It is a stimulant owing to the alcohol it contains, as well as to its bouquet and other ingredients.

Wine in moderation restores energy and is a healthy drink.

Young wines, however, have rather more acidity and persons of weak digestion and elderly people should therefore avoid or slightly sweeten them.

BAVAROISE

This is a drink that used to be served at evening parties.

8 egg yolks, 8 oz. sugar, 6 tablespoons syrup flavoured with orange flower water, 1 pint (U.S. 2½ cups) freshly made tea, 1 pint (U.S. 2½ cups) boiling milk, ¼ pint (U.S. ⅝ cup) kirsch or rum

Beat the egg yolks and sugar together until the mixture is thick to leave a trail.

Add the syrup, tea and boiling milk whisking all the time so the mixture is very frothy. Finally add the kirsch or rum.

If vanilla, orange or lemon flavour is preferred the flavouring shou be added to the milk 15 minutes before it is required for use.

For chocolate flavour, dissolve some chocolate in the milk and add a little vanilla.

For coffee flavour, infuse 4 oz. freshly ground coffee in the milk or use freshly made coffee instead of milk.

A Bavaroise should be served in a special glass and be very frothy.

Bischoff

BISHOP

1 bottle Champagne, 1 sherry glass lime blossom tea, 1 orange, ½ lemon, syrup boiled to 220° F., 4 liqueur glasses brandy

Mix the Champagne, lime blossom tea and thinly sliced orange and lemon. Add enough syrup to give a reading of 18° on the saccharometer. Leave for 1 hour, then strain and freeze like a granité (see page 798).

Just before serving add the brandy.

Café glacé

ICED COFFEE

1¼ pints (U.S. 3⅛ cups) boiling water, 10 oz. freshly ground coffee, 1¼ lb. lump sugar, 1¾ pints (U.S. 4¼ cups) boiled milk, vanilla, 1 pint (U.S. 2½ cups) cream

Slowly pour the boiling water on to the coffee and strain. Add the sugar and leave it to dissolve, then cool. Add the cold boiled milk flavoured with vanilla, and the cream.

Freeze and serve in very cold cups.

Café noir glacé

ICED BLACK COFFEE

Prepare some strong coffee in the ordinary way, sweeten it sparingly and freeze.

Serve in sorbet glasses.

Orangeade

Juice 4 oranges, juice 1 lemon, 1¾ pints (U.S. 4¼ cups) water, ½ pint (U.S. 1¼ cups) syrup boiled to 218° F., zest 1 orange

Mix the orange and lemon juice with the water. Add the syrup and zest of the orange.

Strain and cool in a bucket of ice or in the refrigerator.

Limonade

LEMONADE

Proceed as for orangeade, substituting lemons for oranges.

Boissons fraîches

COOL DRINKS

Cool drinks made from cherries, redcurrants, whitecurrants and raspberries are all prepared in the same way as orangeade.

Marquise au Champagne

CHAMPAGNE AND PINEAPPLE

▬▬▬▬▬ 1 pint syrup (U.S. 2½ cups) boiled to 219° F., 1 pint pineapple juice Champagne, 3—4 tablespoons Italian meringue (see page 697)

Mix the cold syrup and pineapple juice and add enough Champagne to give a saccharometer reading of 15°. Freeze as for a sorbet (see page 797). Add the meringue and beat till frothy.

Serve in sorbet glasses.

SPRINCHADE

▬▬▬▬▬ Fruit ice (see pages 782—785), 5—6 tablespoons Italian meringue (see page 697)

Prepare a fruit ice registering 18° on the saccharometer and half freeze.
Add the meringue and beat till frothy and firm.

Serve in sorbet glasses.

Sprinchade au citron

SPRINCHADE WITH LEMON

▬▬▬▬▬ 1 pint (U.S. 2¼ cups) syrup boiled to 219° F., juice 6 lemons, soda water or Champagne, 5—6 tablespoons Italian meringue (see page 697)

Mix the syrup with the lemon juice and add enough soda water or Champagne to give a saccharometer reading of 18°.

Freeze as for a sorbet (see page 797) and add the meringue, beating until the mixture is frothy.

Serve in sorbet glasses.

Punch glacé à la romaine
ICED ROMAN PUNCH

1¾ pints (U.S. 4¼ cups) sorbet mixture (see page 797), juice 2 oranges, rum, 5—6 tablespoons Italian meringue (see page 697)

Prepare the sorbet mixture and add the orange juice and 6 tablespoons rum. Freeze and add the meringue, beating until the mixture is frothy.

Pile into sorbet glasses and add 1 tablespoon rum to each glass.

Punch marquise
MARQUISE PUNCH

1¾ pints (U.S. 4¼ cups) Sauternes, 7 oz. lump sugar, strip lemon peel, 1 clove, ½ pint (U.S. 1¼ cups) brandy, slices lemon

Put the wine into a copper pan with the sugar, lemon peel and clove. Leave until the sugar has dissolved, then heat until a fine white froth appears on the surface. Remove the lemon peel and clove and pour into a punch bowl. Add the warmed brandy and set it alight. Leave to burn itself out, then serve with a slice of lemon in each glass.

Punch chaud au thé
HOT PUNCH WITH TEA

1 orange, 1 lemon, castor sugar, water, 1 lb. lump sugar, ¼ bottle brandy, 1 pint (U.S. 2½ cups) freshly brewed tea

Peel the orange and lemon very thinly, put the peel into a bowl and sprinkle with the sugar. Leave for 15 minutes, then add ½ pint (U.S. 1¼ cups) warm water.

Put the lump sugar into a copper bowl, add a little cold water and leave till the sugar has dissolved. Add the orange and lemon juice and brandy. Warm all together, then set it alight. When the flames have died down, add the strained infusion of orange and lemon peel and lastly add the tea.

Fraises des bois ou de quatre-saison au Champagne
WILD STRAWBERRIES OR ALPINE STRAWBERRIES IN CHAMPAGNE

Wild or Alpine strawberries, sugar, orange ice (see page 784), Champagne

Choose fresh ripe strawberries, put them into a bowl surrounded by crushed ice and sprinkle with sugar. When ready to serve, arrange the strawberries in Champagne glasses, cover with orange ice and, at the last moment, pour over some Champagne.

Note Other fruits and ices can be served in the same way.

Vin chaud

MULLED WINE

———— 7 oz. lump sugar, 1 bottle red wine, strip lemon peel, 1 piece cinnamon stick, 1 blade mace, 1 clove, slices lemon

Put the sugar into a copper pan. Add the wine and leave until the sugar has dissolved.

Add the flavourings and warm gently until a fine white froth appears on the surface.

Strain and serve with a thin slice of lemon in each glass.

Vin chaud à l'orange

MULLED WINE WITH ORANGE

———— ½ pint (U.S. 1¼ cups) boiling water, 12 oz. lump sugar, thinly peeled rind 1—2 oranges, 1 bottle Burgundy or Claret, slices orange

Pour the boiling water on to the sugar. Add the orange peel and leave for 15 minutes. Strain and add the warmed wine.

Serve with a slice of orange in each glass.

Vin à la française

WINE FRENCH STYLE

———— 8 oz. lump sugar, 1 bottle claret, 2 lemons

Put the sugar into a bowl with a little water and leave till the sugar has dissolved.

Add the claret and 1 lemon cut into thin slices and the pips removed. Stir well and serve with a slice of lemon in each glass.

Note Half siphon soda water or fizzy lemonade may be added.

RATAFIAS

Ratafias, or household liqueurs, which were very popular, are no longer fashionable nowadays, which is very regrettable.

Ratafias can be made with all sorts of fruit.

Put the chosen fruit into a wide-mouthed jar and cover with colourless brandy. Cover the jar tightly and expose to the sun for 40 days.

Decant, and add ½ pint (U.S. 1¼ cups) syrup, boiled to 219° F each 1¾ pints (U.S. 4¼ cups) fruit juice. Filter and put into stopp bottles.

Ratafia de merises

WILD CHERRY RATAFIA

▬▬▬▬▬▬ 3 lb. ripe wild cherries, 7—8 pints (U.S. 8¾ — 10 pints) colourless brandy, 2 lb. sugar

Stem and stone the cherries. Pound half the stones, put them into a wide-mouthed jar and cover with brandy.

Put the cherries in another jar, cover with 7 pints (U.S. 8¾ pints) brandy, close the jar tightly and expose to the sun for 40 days.

Put the two infusions together and add the sugar. When the sugar has dissolved, filter the liquid through filter paper, then bottle.

Liqueur de fraises et framboises préparée en quelques heures

STRAWBERRY AND RASPBERRY LIQUEURS MADE IN A FEW HOURS

▬▬▬▬▬▬ 1½ lb. strawberries, 12 oz. ripe raspberries, 1 lb. lump sugar, vanilla, few coriander seeds, 1¾ pints (U.S. 4¼ cups) old Armagnac brandy

Wash the strawberries and put into a bowl with the raspberries.

Prepare a syrup with the sugar and boil it to 219° F. Add a little vanilla flavouring and the coriander seeds. Cool and pour over the fruit. Cover and leave to soak for 3—4 hours.

Put a tammy cloth over a basin and cover it with a piece of muslin. Pour the fruit and syrup through and let it drip very gently to get a clear liquid. Mix the syrup with the brandy, then bottle.

Note Infusions of this kind made with syrup and good Armagnac can be made quickly and will retain the flavour of the fruit.

Index

I

W